Journal of the

Oriental Society

(Volume 42)

Editor Franklin Edgerton, Maxl. Margolis

Alpha Editions

This edition published in 2020

ISBN : 9789354048302 (Hardback)

ISBN : 9789354048807 (Paperback)

Design and Setting By
Alpha Editions
www.alphaedis.com
email - alphaedis@gmail.com

TABLE OF CONTENTS

IV

RECURRENT AND PARALLEL PASSAGES IN THE PRINCIPAL UPANISHADS AND THE BHAGAVAD-GĪTĀ

WITH REFERENCES TO OTHER SANSKRIT TEXTS

George C. O. Haas
New York City

Intensive study of those wonderful old treasuries of Hindu theosophic lore, the Upanishads and the Bhagavad-Gītā, is requisite for any understanding of their contents, except of the most superficial kind. For adequate interpretation of their meaning one must take into account the background of Vedic ritual and of legendary lore, the origin and development of metaphysical conceptions in India, the sequence and interrelation of the various texts, and other matters of a similar nature. In intensive study of this kind it is naturally essential to make careful comparison of expressions of the same thought in various passages and to assimilate and combine, or on the other hand differentiate and contrast, the statements, according to their nature and their context; and it is to facilitate such comparison that I have prepared for publication the present collection of recurrences and parallels, which constitutes a by-product, so to speak, of certain work in this field upon which I have been engaged for a number of years.

The material here assembled falls, broadly speaking, into three categories: (1) repeated episodes and passages, long or short; (2) recurrences of the same ideas and of the same similes; (3) allusions and the like. As will be seen at a glance, this collection of repetitions and parallels differs altogether in scope and in arrangement from Col. George A. Jacob's *Concordance to the Principal Upanishads and Bhagavad-Gîtâ* (Bombay, 1891), which is invaluable for tracing a presumable quotation, studying a technical term, or investigating a special usage. The present paper, while omitting notice of the repetition of brief formulas and phrases (see a subsequent paragraph), includes similarities of thought and of imagery, which are in many cases not revealed by a concordance, as well as numerous references to other Sanskrit texts; and its sequential arrangement makes available, section by section and line by line, without the necessity of search or collation, the material gathered in relation to each Upanishad and thus renders it serviceable in connection with consecutive reading or critical examination of any portion of the text.[1]

The following texts have been included in this study:—

Bṛhad-Āraṇyaka [Bṛh.]	Īśā, or Īśāvāsya
Chāndogya [Chānd.]	Muṇḍaka [Muṇḍ.]
Taittirīya [Tait.]	Praśna
Aitareya [Ait.]	Māṇḍūkya [Māṇḍ.]
Kauṣītaki [Kauṣ.]	Śvetāśvatara [Śvet.]
Kena, or Talavakāra	Maitri, or Maitrāyaṇa
Kaṭha, or Kāṭhaka	Bhagavad-Gītā [BhG.]

The Upanishads are taken up in the order here given, which is the approximate order of their antiquity, so far as that has been ascertained (cf. Hume, *Thirteen Principal Upanishads*, London, 1921, p. xii–xiii). The Bhagavad-Gītā, which is included because of its close association for many centuries with the Upanishads, is placed last, as not being strictly a text of the same class.

It has seemed worth while to add also a number of references to the Mahānārāyaṇa Upanishad, which clearly belongs in the group of older Upanishadic texts. The numerous minor and later Upanishads, however, have not been included in the scope of this study; recurrent passages in them are for the most part merely quotations from the earlier treatises, and inclusion of references to them would have added considerably to the

---

[1] To make sure that nothing of consequence should be overlooked, I have gone thru every page of Jacob's *Concordance* after completing my own collection of material, and I have examined also the annotations in the translations of Deussen and of Hume. It is a pleasure to acknowledge the help derived from the labors of these scholars, and especially also to express my appreciation of comments and suggestions received from Professors A. V. Williams Jackson, E. Washburn Hopkins, Louis H. Gray, Franklin Edgerton, and Mr. Charles Johnston.

length of this paper without commensurate advantage. On the other hand numerous references to other Sanskrit texts, especially to the philosophic sections of the Mahābhārata, have been inserted because of their interest. I include also, for the convenience of the reader, a few stray citations of important Brāhmaṇa parallels, tho I have not made a search for others of the same kind. Quotations of Vedic mantras and the like in the Upanishads are not noted unless the passage happens to be considered in another connection.

In order to avoid needless expansion, it has been found necessary to omit notice of the repetition of brief formulas and phrases, as well as of sentences and turns of expression recurring at intervals in a series of sections, but found nowhere else. As chief among these may be mentioned the following:—

apa punarmṛtyuṃ jayati Bṛh. 1. 2. 7; etc. [see 3].
eṣa ta ātmā sarvāntaraḥ Bṛh. 3. 4. 1; etc.
ato 'nyad ārttam Bṛh. 3. 4. 2; etc.
dugdhe—annādo bhavati Chānd. 1. 3. 7; etc.
sarvam āyur eti Chānd. 2. 11. 2; etc.
etad evāmṛtaṃ dṛṣṭvā tṛpyati Chānd. 3. 6. 3; etc.
vāg eva brahmaṇaś caturthaḥ pādaḥ Chānd. 3. 18. 3; etc.
nāsyāvarapuruṣāḥ kṣīyante Chānd. 4. 11. 2; etc.
etad amṛtam abhayam etad brahma Chānd. 4. 15. 1; etc.; Maitri 2. 2.
bhavaty asya brahmavarcasaṃ kule Chānd. 5. 12. 2; etc.
annamayaṃ hi—vāg iti Chānd. 6. 5. 4; etc.
sa ya eṣo 'ṇimaitadātmyam—śvetaketo Chānd. 6. 8. 6—7; etc.
sa yo . . . brahmety upāste—bravītv iti Chānd. 7. 1. 5; etc.
sarveṣu lokeṣu kāmacāro bhavati Chānd. 7. 25. 2; etc.
saiṣā prāṇe sarvāptir Kauṣ. 3. 3, 4.
tad eva brahma—upāsate Kena 4—8.

All the occurrences of these expressions can be found, if required, in Jacob's *Concordance.*

No attempt has been made to decide whether one parallel passage is quoted from another. In many instances there is undoubtedly distinct quotation from an older and more authoritative Upanishad; in others the passages are drawn from a common source, as in the case of citations from the Vedas and related texts; some of the minor correspondences may be fortuitous, due to the similarity of subject and point of view. On quotations from and allusions to the Kaṭha Upanishad in the Śvetāśvatara consult Deussen, *Sechzig Upanishad's des Veda*, p. 289; on quotations in the Maitri, p. 312—313; for comment on special parallels see the references to Deussen in **4, 125, 210,** below. For thoro discussion of parallels between the Upanishads and the Mahābhārata see Hopkins, *Great Epic of India* (New York, 1901), p. 27—46, cf. p. 85—190; consult also the collection of references in Holtzmann, *Das Mahābhārata* (Kiel, 1895), 4. 20—26.[2]

Before concluding these introductory paragraphs I wish to call attention briefly to a specially interesting group of parallel passages—assembled in a Conspectus[3] on an adjoining page—relating to the elements of man's constitution designated by the term *nāḍī*. Despite the suggestion of the phrase *hṛdayasya nāḍyas,* we have here no reference to arteries or veins, nor on the other hand to nerves or analogous filaments of the bodily structure; the details of the description preclude any anatomical identification. These vessels are stated to be minute as a hair divided a thousandfold; they are filled with substance of various colors; they conduct the *prāṇa,* or life energy; they have a special relation to the phenomena of sleep; one of them is the means of egress from the body at death; and so on. It is evident that, in using the term *nāḍī,* the writers of the Upanishads had in mind those same vessels that are so elaborately described, in later Hindu writings on Yoga and related subjects, as channels of variously specialized vital energy in the subtle 'etheric' vehicle that co-exists as a counterpart of the gross physical body in the composite human organism. In fact, the Maitri Upanishad (at 6. 21) actually mentions the name of the principal channel, *Suṣumnā,* which is so frequently referred to in connection with the companion channels *Iḍā* and *Piṅgala* in later texts. We must therefore avoid the misleading translation 'artery' or 'vein' and choose as a rendering some word of less definite connotation, such as 'duct', or 'tube', or 'channel'.[4]

---

[2] The earliest collection of comparative material relating to the Upanishads, so far as I know, is that of Weber, *Indische Studien,* 1. 247—302; 380—456 (1850); 2. 1—111; 170—236 (1853); 9. 1—173 (1865).

[3] Each individual statement in the Conspectus has prefixt to it the serial number of the entry under which its parallels are recorded. Statements markt with the same number thus relate to the same phase of the subject and may profitably be compared with one another.

[4] Woods, in translating Yoga-sūtra 3. 31, renders the word 'tube' (*The Yoga-system of Patañjali,* Cambridge, Mass., 1914, p. 261).

SPECIAL ABBREVIATIONS AND SYMBOLS

C.	Calcutta text of the Mahābhārata.
D.	Deussen, *Sechzig Upanishad's des Veda*, Leipzig, 1897.
M	Mādhyaṃdina recension of Bṛh. [=Śat.Br.10.6.4—5; 14.4—9], ed. and tr. O. Böhtlingk, St. Petersburg, 1889.
Mahānār.	Mahānārāyaṇa Upanishad.

=	indicates 'recurs verbatim at'.
=(var.)	indicates 'recurs, but with one or more variants, at'.
≎	indicates 'substantially the same passage recurs at'.
cf.	indicates 'something of a similar nature is found at'.
[ ]	square brackets enclose descriptive words indicating the passage or subject matter referred to.
—	a dash replaces Sanskrit words omitted for brevity, the reference being to the entire passage from the first word printed to the last.
. . .	three points indicate the omission of irrelevant words.
098	heavy-face figures refer to the serial numbers of the entries in the list of recurrences and parallels.

Particular attention is called to the somewhat arbitrary use of the signs = and ≎. These do not indicate that a following reference is coextensive with the passage in question. What *is* equal or similar is the *passage* referred to, *not* necessarily the section of an Upanishad indicated by the numerical designation. Thus 'Kaṭha 4. 9a—b = Bṛh. 1. 5. 23' means (*not* that the two lines of the Kaṭha stanza constitute *all* of Bṛh. 1. 5. 23, but) that the two lines occur *in* the section of Bṛh. indicated. Where the passage *to* which reference is made is in metrical form, the citation can of course be given exactly.

CONSPECTUS OF PASSAGES RELATING TO THE 'CHANNELS OF THE HEART'

(see page 4)

Bṛh. 2. 1. 19

24 *yadā suṣupto bhavati yadā na kasyacana veda*

25 *hitā nāma nāḍyo dvāsaptatisahasrāṇi*

26 *hṛdayāt purītatam abhipratiṣṭhante*

24 *tābhiḥ pratyavasṛpya purītati śete*

Bṛh. 4. 2. 2—3

61 [Indha (Indra) and Virāj]

63 *ya eṣo 'ntar hṛdaye lohitapiṇḍo...*

64 *enayor eṣā sṛtiḥ saṃcaraṇī yaiṣā hṛdayād ūrdhvā nāḍy uccarati*

65 *yathā keśaḥ sahasradhā bhinna*

25 *evam asyaitā hitā nāma nāḍyo 'ntar hṛdaye pratiṣṭhitā bhavanty eva tābhir vā etad āsravad āsravati (tasmād eṣa praviviktāhāratara ivaiva bhavaty asmāc charīrād ātmanaḥ)*

Bṛh. 4. 3. 20

25 *tā vā asyaitā hitā nāma nāḍyo*

65 *yathā keśaḥ sahasradhā bhinnas tāvatāṇimnā tiṣṭhanti*

71 *śuklasya nīlasya piṅgalasya haritasya lohitasya pūrṇā*

Bṛh. 4. 4. 8—9

84 *aṇuḥ panthā vitataḥ purāṇo...*

249 *tena dhīrā api yanti brahmavidaḥ svargaṃ lokam ita ūrdhvaṃ vimuktāḥ*

71 *tasmiñ chuklam uta nīlam āhuḥ piṅgalaṃ haritaṃ lohitaṃ ca*

84 *eṣa panthā brahmaṇā hānuvittas*

249 *tenaiti brahmavit puṇyakṛt taijasaś ca*

Chānd. 8. 6. 1—3

25 *atha yā etā hṛdayasya nāḍyas*

71 *tāḥ piṅgalasyāṇimnas tiṣṭhanti śuklasya nīlasya pītasya lohitasyety...*

84 *tad yathā mahāpatha ātata... evam evaitā ādityasya raśmaya...*

24 *tad yatraitatsuptaḥ samastaḥ samprasannaḥ svapnaṃ na vijānāty āsu tadā nāḍīṣu sṛpto bhavati*

Chānd. 8. 6. 6 = Kaṭha 6. 16

247 *śataṃ caikā ca hṛdayasya nāḍyas* |

64 *tāsām mūrdhānam abhiniḥsṛtaikā* |

249 *tayordhvam āyann amṛtatvam eti* |

250 *viṣvaṅṅ anyā utkramaṇe bhavanti* ||

Tait. 1. 6. 1

265 *sa ya eṣo 'ntar hṛdaya ākāśaḥ tasminn ayam puruṣo manomayaḥ...*

266 *antareṇa tāluke ya eṣa stana ivāvalambate*

Kauṣ. 4. 19

25 *hitā nāma hṛdayasya nāḍyo*

26 *hṛdayāt purītatam abhipratanvanti*

65 *yathā sahasradhā keśo vipāṭitas tāvad aṇvyaḥ*

71 *piṅgalasyāṇimnā tiṣṭhante śuklasya kṛṣṇasya pītasya lohitasyeti*

24 *tāsu tadā bhavati yadā suptaḥ svapnaṃ na kaṃcana paśyaty*

Muṇḍ. 2. 2. 6

247 *arā iva rathanābhau saṃhatā yatra nāḍyaḥ*

265 *sa eṣo 'ntaś carate*

Praśna 3. 6—7

247 *atraitad ekaśataṃ nāḍīnām*

25 *tāsāṃ śataṃ śatam ekaikasyāṃ dvāsaptatir dvāsaptatiḥ pratiśākhānāḍīsahasrāṇi bhavanty*

486 *āsu vyānaś carati*

249 *athaikayordhva udānaḥ...*

Maitri 6. 21

64 *ūrdhvagā nāḍī suṣumnākhyā*

486 *prāṇasaṃcāriṇī*

266 *tālvantarvicchinnā*

249 *tayā ... ūrdhvam utkramet*

Maitri 6. 30

265 ... | *dīpavad yaḥ sthito hṛdi* |

71 *sitāsitāḥ kadrunīlāḥ* | *kapilā mṛdulohitāḥ* ||

64 *ūrdhvam ekaḥ sthitas teṣāṃ* |

249 *yo bhittvā sūryamaṇḍalam* | *brahmalokam atikramya* | *tena yānti parāṃ gatim* ||

250 *yad asyānyad raśmiśataṃ* | ... | *tena devanikāyānāṃ* | *svadhāmāni prapadyate* ||

Maitri 7. 11

61 [Indra and Virāj]

265 *samāgamas tayor eva* | *hṛdayāntargate suṣau* |

63 *tejas tallohitasyātra* | *piṇḍa evobhayos tayoḥ* ||

64 *hṛdayād āyatā tāvac* | *cakṣuṣy asmin pratiṣṭhitā* | *sāraṇī sā tayor nāḍī* | *dvayor ekā dvidhā satī* ||

LIST OF RECURRENCES AND PARALLELS

1 Bṛh. 1. 2. 3 *sa tredhā ''tmānaṃ vyakuruta* =[5] Maitri 6. 3.

2 Bṛh. 1. 2. 4 *manasā vācam mithunaṃ samabhavad* cf. *mana evāsyātmā vāg jāyā* Bṛh. 1. 4. 17.

3 Bṛh. 1. 2. 7 *apa punarmṛtyuṃ jayati* (recurs thrice) an old formula; it occurs, for example, in Tait. Br. 3. 11. 8. 6 (cf. Kauṣ. Br. 25. 1).

4 Bṛh. 1. 3. 1—21 [contest of gods and devils] ⇕ Chānd. 1. 2; Jaiminīya Up. Br. 1. 18. 5; cf. ibid. 2. 1. 1; 2. 4. 1 (Oertel, *JAOS* 15. 240—245). (According to D. p. 69, the Bṛh. version is older than that in Chānd.) On the superiority of breath see **124**.

5 Bṛh. 1. 3. 22 [*sā + ama = sāma(n)*] ⇕ Chānd. 1. 6. 1, etc.; cf. Bṛh. 6. 4. 20. See also Chānd. 5. 2. 6. (Oertel, *JAOS* 16. 235, in a note on Jaiminīya [Talavakāra] Up. Br. 1. 54. 6, assembles refs. to numerous similar passages, to which should be added Ait. Br. 3. 23.)

6 Bṛh. 1. 3. 23 [etymological explanation of *udgītha*] cf. Chānd. 1. 6. 7—8.]

7 Bṛh. 1. 4. 1 *ātmaivedam agra āsīt* ⇕ Bṛh. 1. 4. 17; Ait. 1. 1; cf. Maitri 2. 6, and see **10**.

8 Bṛh. 1. 4. 6 [food and the eater of food] cf. Maitri 6. 10.

9 Bṛh. 1. 4. 7 *sa eṣa iha praviṣṭa — viśvambharakulāye* ⇕ Kauṣ. 4. 20.

10 Bṛh. 1. 4. 10—11 *brahma [vā idam agra āsīt* = (var.) Maitri 6. 17; cf. **7**.

11 Bṛh. 1. 4. 15—16 [desires, etc.] cf. Chānd. 8. 1. 6 — 8. 2. 10. See also **457**.

12 Bṛh. 1. 4. 17 *ātmaivedam agra āsīd eka eva* see **7**.

13 Bṛh. 1. 4. 17 *mana evāsyātmā vāg jāyā* see **2**.

14 Bṛh. 1. 4. 17 *pāṅktam idaṃ sarvam — ya evaṃ veda* ⇕ Tait. 1. 7.

15 Bṛh. 1. 5. 3 *manasā hy eva paśyati— mana eva* = Maitri 6. 30.

16 Bṛh. 1. 5. 14—15 *ṣoḍaśakalas* see **501**. On the wheel analogy in 1. 5. 15 see **434, 522**.

17 Bṛh. 1. 5. 17—20 [Transmission ceremony] see **313**.

---

[5] On the special use of the signs =, ⇕, and —, see page 5.

18 Bṛh. 1. 5. 23 *yataś codeti — gacchati* [AV. 10. 18. 16a—b] = Kaṭha 4. 9a—b. *sa evādya sa u śva[s]* = Kaṭha 4. 13d.

19 Bṛh. 1. 6. 1 *nāma rūpaṃ karma* cf. MBh. 12. 233. 25 (C. 8535).

20 Bṛh. 2. 1. 1—19 [dialog of Gārgya and Ajātaśatru] ⇕ Kauṣ. 4. 1—19. Cf. Bṛh. 3. 9. 10—17.

21 Bṛh. 2. 1. 5 *pūrṇam apravarti* = Chānd. 3. 12. 9; Kauṣ. 4. 8.

22 Bṛh. 2. 1. 15 [Kṣatriya instructing Brahman] cf. Chānd. 5. 3. 5, 7; Kauṣ. 4. 19; and the implication in Chānd. 1. 8. 2.

23 Bṛh. 2. 1. 17 [ether within the heart] see **265**.

24 Bṛh. 2. 1. 19 *yadā suṣupto bhavati . . . tābhiḥ pratyavasṛpya* cf. Chānd. 8. 6. 3; Kauṣ. 4. 19.

25 Bṛh. 2. 1. 19 *hitā nāma nāḍyo* ⇕ Bṛh. 4. 3. 20; Kauṣ. 4. 19; Praśna 3. 6; cf. Yājñavalkīya Dharma-sūtras 3. 108. See **65, 70, 247**.

26 Bṛh. 2. 1. 19 *hṛdayāt purītatam abhipratiṣṭhante* ⇕ Kaus. 4. 19.

27 Bṛh. 2. 1. 20 [spider and thread analogy for creation] cf. Muṇḍ. 1. 1. 7a; Śvet. 6. 10b. (The simile recurs in a different connection in Maitri 6. 22.)

28 Bṛh. 2. 1. 20 [sparks from fire as analogy of creation] see **421**.

29 Bṛh. 2. 1. 20 *sarve prāṇāḥ — satyasya satyam* = (var.) Maitri 6. 32.

30 Bṛh. 2. 1. 20 *prāṇā vai — eṣa satyam* = Bṛh. 2. 3. 6.

31 Bṛh. 2. 2. 4 *sarvasyāttā — ya evaṃ veda* cf. Chānd. 5. 2. 1; see also Bṛh. 6. 1. 14; Chānd. 5. 18. 1.

32 Bṛh. 2. 3. 1 *dve — rūpe mūrtaṃ caivāmūrtaṃ ca* = (var.) Maitri 6. 3; *dve — rūpe* recurs also at Maitri 6. 15; cf. *mūrtir amūrtimān* Maitri 6. 14 end, and see **498**.

33 Bṛh. 2. 3. 3, 5 [formless Brahma] cf. Muṇḍ. 2. 1. 2a.

34 Bṛh. 2. 3. 3 [Person in the sun] see **149**.

35 Bṛh. 2. 3. 5 [person in the right eye] see **61** and cf. **177**.

36 Bṛh. 2. 3. 6 [lightning as descriptive of the divine Person] cf. Bṛh. 5. 7; Kena 29.

37 Bṛh. 2. 3. 6 *neti neti* see **57**.

38 Bṛh. 2. 3. 6 *prāṇā vai — eṣa satyam* = Bṛh. 2. 1. 20.

39 Bṛh. 2. 4 [dialog of Yājñavalkya and Maitreyī] ⇕ Bṛh. 4. 5.

40 Bṛh. 2. 4. 5 end [⇕ 4. 5. 6 end] *ātmano . . . vijñānenedaṃ sarvaṃ viditam* see **409**.

41 Bṛh. 2. 4. 10 [= (var.) 4. 5. 11] = (var.) Maitri 6. 32; the

part *ṛgvedo — vyākhyānāny* recurs also at Bṛh. 4. 1. 2; similar lists at Chānd. 7. 1. 2, 4; 7. 2. 1; 7. 7. 1; Maitri 6. 33; cf. also Muṇḍ. 1. 1. 5.

42 Bṛh. 2. 4. 12 [simile of the solution of salt] see **210**.

43 Bṛh. 2. 4. 12 *na pretya saṃjñā 'sti* cf. MBh. 12. 219. 2 a—b (C. 7931).

44 Bṛh. 2. 4. 14 [duality involved in cognition] = Bṛh. 4. 5. 15 ⇕ 4. 3. 31; cf. Maitri 6. 7.

45 Bṛh. 2. 5. 15 *yathā rathanābhau — samarpitā* ⇕ Chānd. 7. 15. 1; see **434**.

46 Bṛh. 2. 5. 19 *rūpaṃ — babhūva* = Kaṭha 5. 9 b; 5. 10 b.

47 Bṛh. 2. 6 [Line of Tradition, *vaṃśa*] ⇕ Bṛh. 4. 6; cf. 6. 5. The course of doctrinal transmission is traced also at Bṛh. 6. 3. 6—12; Chānd. 3. 11. 4 ⇕ 8. 15; Muṇḍ. 1. 1. 1—2; BhG. 4. 1—2. (For a discussion of the Bṛh. lists see D. p. 376—378.)

48 Bṛh. 3. 2. 13 *puṇyo vai puṇyena — pāpena* = (var.) Bṛh. 4. 4. 5.

49 Bṛh. 3. 5. 1 *putraiṣaṇāyāś ca — eṣaṇe eva bhavatas* ⇕ Bṛh. 4. 4. 22.

50 Bṛh. 3. 6 *idaṃ sarvam . . . otaṃ ca protaṃ ca* = (var.) Maitri 6. 3; cf. Bṛh. 3. 8; Muṇḍ. 2. 2. 5 b; Maitri 7. 7. On water as a primal substance see **112**.

51 Bṛh. 3. 6 [gradation of worlds] cf. Kauṣ. 1. 3.

52 Bṛh. 3. 7 *eṣa — antaryāmī* cf. Māṇḍ. 6.

53 Bṛh. 3. 8. 8—9 [characterization of the Imperishable] cf. Muṇḍ. 1. 1. 6—7 and see **412**.

54 Bṛh. 3. 9. 1—9, 18, 26 end [dialog of Yājñavalkya and Śākalya] ⇕ Jaiminīya Br. 2. 76—77 (Oertel, *JAOS* 15. 238—240).

55 Bṛh. M 3. 9. 3 [Vasus] *vāsayante* cf. Chānd. 3. 16. 1.

56 Bṛh. 3. 9. 4 [Rudras] *rodayanti* cf. Chānd. 3. 16. 3.

57 Bṛh. 3. 9. 26 *sa eṣa neti nety — na riṣyati* = Bṛh. 4. 2. 4; 4. 4. 22; 4. 5. 15; *neti neti* recurs also at Bṛh. 2. 3. 6.

58 Bṛh. 3. 9. 28, stanzas 4—5 [man cut down like a tree] cf. MBh. 12. 186. 14 (C. 6896).

59 Bṛh. 4. 1. 2 [literature-list] see **41**.

60 Bṛh. 4. 2. 2 . . . *santam indra ity — devāḥ* = Ait. 3. 14 ⇕ Śat. Br. 6. 1. 1. 2 (cf. 11). Cf. Ait. Br. 3. 33; 7. 30.

61 Bṛh. 4. 2. 2—3 [Indha (Indra) and Virāj] cf. Maitri 7. 11, stanzas 1—3, and the allusion in Tait. 6; the 'person in the right eye' is referred to also at Bṛh. 2. 3. 5; 5. 5. 2; Kauṣ. 4. 17; cf. **177.**

62 Bṛh. 4. 2. 3 [ether within the heart] see **265.**

63 Bṛh. 4. 2. 3 *ya eṣo 'ntar hṛdaye lohitapiṇḍo* ⇕ Maitri 7.11, stanza 2, c.

64 Bṛh. 4. 2. 3 *yaiṣā hṛdayād ūrdhvā nāḍy uccarati* cf. Chānd. 8. 6. 6 = Kaṭha 6. 16; Praśna 3. 7; Maitri 6. 21; 6. 30; 7. 11, stanza 3.

65 Bṛh. 4. 2. 3 *yathā keśaḥ sahasradhā bhinna[s]* = Bṛh. 4. 3. 20 ⇕ Kauṣ. 4. 19.

66 Bṛh. 4. 2. 3 *hitā nāma nāḍyo* see **25.**

67 Bṛh. 4. 2. 4 *sa eṣa neti nety* see **57.**

68 Bṛh. 4. 3. 16 *sa vā eṣa — buddhāntāyaiva* = Bṛh. 4. 3. 34.

69 Bṛh. 4. 3. 19 *yatra supto — paśyati* = Māṇḍ. 5.

70 Bṛh. 4. 3. 20 *hitā nāma nāḍyo — tiṣṭhanti* see **25, 65.**

71 Bṛh. 4. 3. 20 *śuklasya nīlasya—pūrṇā* ⇕ Bṛh. 4. 4. 9 a—b; Kauṣ. 4. 19; Maitri 6. 30.

72 Bṛh. 4. 3. 20 [dream experiences] cf. Chānd. 8. 10; Praśna 4. 5.

73 Bṛh. 4. 3. 22 [ethical distinctions superseded] cf. Kauṣ. 3. 1.

74 Bṛh. 4. 3. 31 [duality involved in cognition] see **44.**

75 Bṛh. 4. 3. 33 [gradation of blisses] ⇕ Tait. 2. 8 [⇕ Śat. Br. 14. 7. 1. 31—39 = Bṛh. M 4. 3. 31—39]. Cf. the gradation of worlds, **51.**

76 Bṛh. 4. 3. 34 recurs entire in Bṛh. 4. 3. 16.

77 Bṛh. 4. 4. 2 [unification of the functions at death] see **320.**

78 Bṛh. 4. 4. 2 *ātmā niṣkramati — mūrdhno vā* cf. Tait. 1. 6. 1; note also Ait. 3. 12 (*sīman*); see **249.**

79 Bṛh. 4. 4. 4 [analogy of the transformation of gold] cf. Maitri 3. 3.

80 Bṛh. 4. 4. 5 *puṇyaḥ puṇyena—pāpena* = (var.) Bṛh. 3. 2. 13.

81 Bṛh. 4. 4. 6 [he who desires and he who is free from desire] cf. Muṇḍ. 3. 2. 2.

82 Bṛh. 4. 4. 6 [acts determine one's reincarnate status] see **192.**

83 Bṛh. 4. 4. 7 *yadā sarve pramucyante* [stanza] = Kaṭha 6. 14.

84 Bṛh. 4. 4. 8—9 *aṇuḥ panthā . . . eṣa panthā* cf. Chānd. 8. 6. 2 and see **249.**

85 Bṛh. 4. 4. 9 *tasmiñ chuklam — lohitaṃ ca* see **71.**

86 Bṛh. 4. 4. 10 = Īśā 9. Bṛh. M 4. 4. 10 = Īśā 12.

87 Bṛh. 4. 4. 11 = (var.) Īśā 3; pāda a recurs also as Kaṭha 1. 3c.

88 Bṛh. 4. 4. 14b = (var.) Kena 13b.

89 Bṛh. 4. 4. 14c—d = Śvet. 3. 10c—d. On pāda c see also **541**.

90 Bṛh. 4. 4. 15c—d see **369**.

91 Bṛh. 4. 4. 16c *jyotiṣāṃ jyotir* cf. Muṇḍ. 2. 2. 9c.

92 Bṛh. 4. 4. 18a—c ⟡ Kena 2a—c; see **333**.

93 Bṛh. 4. 4. 19 = (var.) Kaṭha 4. 11a—b; 4. 10c—d.

94 Bṛh. 4. 4. 21 [stanza] cf. Muṇḍ. 2. 2. 5c—d.

95 Bṛh. 4. 4. 22 [ether within the heart] see **265**.

96 Bṛh. 4. 4. 22 *sarvasyeśānaḥ sarvasyādhipatiḥ* = Bṛh. 5. 6. Cf. *viśvādhipo* Śvet. 3. 4b, and see **98**.

97 Bṛh. 4. 4. 22 *na sādhunā — kanīyān* = Kauṣ. 3. 8. Cf. Maitri 2. 7.

98 Bṛh. 4. 4. 22 *eṣa sarveśvara — setur vidharaṇa* = (var). Maitri 7. 7. The phrase *eṣa sarveśvara* recurs Māṇḍ. 6. *eṣa setur vidharaṇa — asambhedāya* ⟡ Chānd. 8. 4. 1; cf. Muṇḍ. 2. 2. 5d; Śvet. 6. 19c. See **96**.

99 Bṛh. 4. 4. 22 *putraiṣaṇāyāś ca — bhavatas* ⟡ Bṛh. 3. 5. 1.

100 Bṛh. 4. 4. 22 *sa eṣa neti nety* see **57**.

101 Bṛh. 4. 4. 22 end [moral self-judgment escaped by the 'knower'] cf. Tait. 2. 9; see also Chānd. 4. 14. 3. On cessation of karma see **449**.

102 Bṛh. 4. 5 [dialog of Yājñavalkya and Maitreyī] ⟡ Bṛh. 2. 4.

103 Bṛh. 4. 5. 6 end [⟡ 2. 4. 5 end] *ātmani . . . vijñāta idaṃ sarvaṃ viditam* see **409**.

104 Bṛh. 4. 5. 11 [literature-list] see **41**.

105 Bṛh. 4. 5. 13 *prajñānaghana eva* = Māṇḍ. 5. On the reference to salt see **210**.

106 Bṛh. 4. 5. 15 [duality involved in cognition] = Bṛh. 2. 4. 14 ⟡ 4. 3. 31; cf. Maitri 6. 7.

107 Bṛh. 4. 5. 15 *sa eṣa neti nety* see **57**.

108 Bṛh. 4. 6 [Line of Tradition, *vaṃśa*] ⟡ Bṛh. 2. 6; see **47**.

109 Bṛh. 5. 1 *pūrṇam—pūrṇam evāvaśiṣyate* [stanza ⟡ AV. 10. 8. 29] ⟡ MBh. 5. 46. 10 (C. 1755).

110 Bṛh. 5. 4 *tad vai tad* cf. *etad vai tat* Kaṭha 4. 3, 5, etc.

111 Bṛh. 5. 4 *satyam brahma* cf. Chānd. 8. 3. 4.

112 Bṛh. 5. 5. 1 [creation from water] cf. Ait. 1. 1—3; Kaṭha 4. 6. On water as a primal substance cf. also Bṛh. 3. 6; Chānd. 7. 10.

113 Bṛh. 5. 5. 1 *tad etat tryakṣaraṃ satyam iti* ⇕ Chānd. 8. 3. 5.

114 Bṛh. 5. 5. 2 [person in the right eye] see **60** and cf. **177**.

115 Bṛh. 5. 6 the thought and similes recur at Chānd. 3. 14. 2—3; see **165**. On *sarvasyeśānaḥ sarvasyādhipatiḥ* see **96**.

116 Bṛh. 5. 7 [Brahma as lightning] cf. Bṛh. 2. 3. 6; Kena 29.

117 Bṛh. 5. 9 [universal fire] = Maitri 2. 6. On the digestive fire cf. Maitri 6. 17; on the bodily heat and the sound heard on stopping the ears cf. Chānd. 3. 13. 8; Maitri 6. 22.

118 Bṛh. 5. 10 [course of the soul after death] cf. in general **127, 128**.

119 Bṛh. 5. 13. 1 *uktham prāṇo — utthāpayaty* ⇕ Kauṣ. 3. 3.

120 Bṛh. 5. 14. 1—7 [Gāyatrī meter] see **159**. On *turīya* (3, 4, 6, 7) see **519**.

121 Bṛh. 5. 14. 4—5 [Sāvitrī stanza] see **130**.

122 Bṛh. 5. 15 = Īśā 15—18. The stanza *hiraṇmayena pātreṇa* etc. = (var.) Maitri 6. 35. With the 'golden vessel' cf. Muṇḍ. 2. 2. 9 a.

123 Bṛh. 6. 1. 1—5 ⇕ Chānd. 5. 1. 1—5.

124 Bṛh. 6. 1. 7—14 [rivalry of the functions and superiority of breath] ⇕ Chānd. 5. 1. 6 — 5. 2. 2; Kauṣ. 2. 14 (9); cf. also Bṛh. 1. 3. 1—19; Chānd. 1. 2. 1—9; Kauṣ. 3. 2—3; Praśna 2. 2—4; see also MBh. 14. 23. 6—22 (C. 689—708). Cf. the somewhat similar story at Ait. 3. 1—10.

125 Bṛh. 6. 2. 1—16 [*pañcāgnividyā* and the course of the soul in incarnations] ⇕ Chānd. 5. 3—10. (D. p. 137—139 has an extended discussion and tabular comparison of these parallels, incl. also Bṛh. **M** [Śat. Br. 14. 9. 1. 12—16]; see also D. p. 132—133.)

126 Bṛh. 6. 2. 2 [worlds reacht after death] cf. Bṛh. 1. 5. 16; Muṇḍ. 2. 1. 6 c—d.

127 Bṛh. 6. 2. 15 [course to the Brahma-world] ⇕ Chānd. 4. 15. 5—6; 5. 10. 1—2; cf. Muṇḍ. 1. 2. 5, 6, 11; 3. 1. 6; Praśna 1. 10; Maitri 6. 30 end; BhG. 8. 24, 26. See also Bṛh. 5. 10.

128 Bṛh. 6. 2. 16 [course to the lunar world and to rebirth]

⇕ Chānd. 5. 10. 3—6; cf. Praśna 1. 9; Muṇḍ. 1. 2. 7—10; BhG. 8. 25, 26. See also Bṛh. 5. 10.

129 Bṛh. 6. 3. 2 [oblations in incantation ceremony] ⇕ Chānd. 5. 2. 4—9; cf. Kauṣ. 2. 3 (2).

130 Bṛh. 6. 3. 6 [Sāvitrī stanza] quoted also at Śvet. 4. 18c; Maitri 6. 7; 6. 34. Cf. Bṛh. 5. 14. 4—5; Chānd. 3. 12.

131 Bṛh. 6. 3. 6—12 [Line of Tradition, *vaṃśa*] see **47**.

132 Bṛh. 6. 3. 12 [reviving of a dried stump] ⇕ Chānd. 5. 2. 3.

133 Bṛh. 6. 3. 12 [restrictions on imparting mystic knowledge] cf. Chānd. 3. 11. 5—6; Muṇḍ. 3. 2. 10—11; Śvet. 6. 22; Maitri 6. 29; BhG. 18. 67.

134 Bṛh. 6. 4. 1 *eṣāṃ vai bhūtānām — oṣadhaya* = (var.) Chānd. 1. 1. 2.

135 Bṛh. 6. 4. 3 *lomāni barhiś* = Chānd. 5. 18. 2.

136 Bṛh. 6. 4. 9 *aṅgād aṅgāt — adhijāyase* [2 lines] = Kauṣ. 2. 11 (7).

137 Bṛh. 6. 4. 12 [deprivation of an offender] cf. Kaṭha 1. 8.

138 Bṛh. 6. 4. 20 [*ama* and *sā*] see **5**.

139 Bṛh. M 6. 4. 26 *aśmā bhava* [stanza] = (var.) Kauṣ. 2. 11 (7).

140 Bṛh. 6. 5 [Line of Tradition, *vaṃśa*] see **47**.

141 Chānd. 1. 1. 1 = Chānd. 1. 4. 1.

142 Chānd. 1. 1. 2 *eṣām bhūtānām — oṣadhayo rasa* = (var.) Bṛh. 6. 4. 1.

143 Chānd. 1. 1. 8—9 [the syllable *Om*] ⇕ Tait. 1. 8. Cf. **726**, **818**.

144 Chānd. 1. 2 [contest of gods and devils] see **4**.

145 Chānd. 1. 3. 3 [explanation of *vyāna*] cf. Maitri 2. 6.

146 Chānd. 1. 4. 1 = Chānd. 1. 1. 1.

147 Chānd. 1. 5. 1 *atha khalu — eṣa praṇava* = Maitri 6. 4.

148 Chānd. 1. 6. 1 [*sā* + *ama* = *sāma(n)*] see **5**.

149 Chānd. 1. 6. 6 *atha ya eṣo — puruṣo* = Maitri 6. 1; Mahānār. 13 (Ātharv. rec. 12. 2). On the 'golden Person in the sun' see also Bṛh. 2. 3. 3; Maitri 6. 35.

150 Chānd. 1. 6. 7—8 [etymological explanation of *udgītha*] cf. Bṛh. 1. 3. 23.

151 Chānd. 1. 7. 5 *ya eṣo 'ntar akṣiṇi puruṣo dṛśyate* see **177**.

152 Chānd. 1. 8. 2 *brāhmaṇayor vadator* see **22**.

153 Chānd. 2. 21. 1 [Agni, Vāyu, Āditya] cf. the similar collocation at Chānd. 3. 15. 6; Maitri 4. 5; 6. 35; note also Chānd. 2. 24. 5, 9, 14.

154 Chānd. 2. 23. 2 (3) [Prajāpati produced *bhūr, bhuvaḥ, svar*] see **180**.

155 Chānd. 3. 1. 2 [nectar in the sun] cf. Tait. 1. 10; Maitri 6. 35.

156 Chānd. 3. 11. 1—3 [perpetual illumination in the Brahma-world] cf. Chānd. 8. 4. 1—2; Śvet. 4. 18 a; Maitri 6. 24; and see **387**.

157 Chānd. 3. 11. 4 [Line of Tradition] ⟡ Chānd. 8. 15; see **47**.

158 Chānd. 3. 11. 5—6 [restrictions on imparting mystic knowledge] see **133**.

159 Chānd. 3. 12 [Gāyatrī meter] cf. Bṛh. 5. 14. 1—7; see also BhG. 10. 35 b.

160 Chānd. 3. 12. 7 [space as Brahma] cf. Chānd. 3. 18. 1.

161 Chānd. 3. 12. 9 *pūrṇam apravarti* = Bṛh. 2. 1. 5.

162 Chānd. 3. 13. 8 [bodily heat; the sound heard on stopping the ears] see **117**.

163 Chānd. 3. 14. 1 *sarvaṃ khalv idam brahma* = (var.) Maitri 4. 6.

164 Chānd. 3. 14. 1 [purpose determines state after death] see **786**.

165 Chānd. 3. 14. 2—3 the thought and some of the words recur at Bṛh. 5. 6; cf. Maitri 7. 7 init. *manomayaḥ — ākāśātmā* = Maitri 2. 6. With *manomayaḥ prāṇaśarīro* cf. Muṇḍ. 2. 2. 7 e. On the epithet *ākāśātman* see **656**.

166 Chānd. 3. 14. 4 [all doubts cleared away] cf. Muṇḍ. 2. 2. 8 b.

167 Chānd. 3. 15. 6 [Agni, Vāyu, Āditya] see **153**.

168 Chānd. 3. 16 [analogy of man's life and the sacrifice] ⟡ Jaiminīya Up. Br. 4. 2. 1 (Oertel, *JAOS* 15. 245—246).

169 Chānd. 3. 16. 1 [Vasus] *vāsayanti* cf. Bṛh. **M** 3. 9. 3.

170 Chānd. 3. 16. 3 [Rudras] *rodayanti* cf. Bṛh. 3. 9. 4.

171 Chānd. 3. 19. 1 *ādityo brahmety* = Maitri 6. 16.

172 Chānd. 3. 19. 1 [primordial Non-being] ⟡ Chānd. 6. 2. 1; Tait. 2. 7.

173 Chānd. 3. 19. 1 [the cosmic egg] cf. Maitri 6. 36, stanza; cf. also MBh. 12. 311. 3—4 (C. 11571—2); and see Hopkins, *Great Epic*, p. 187.

174 Chānd. 4. 3. 1—7 ⟡ Jaiminīya Up. Br. 3. 1. 1—2 (Oertel, *JAOS* 15. 249—251).

175 Chānd. 4. 4. 5 [bringing of fuel as sign of pupilship] cf. Chānd. 5. 11. 7; 8. 7. 2; etc.; Kauṣ. 1. 1; 4. 19; Muṇḍ. 1. 2. 13; Praśna 1. 1.

176 Chānd. 4. 14. 3 [evil adheres not to the 'knower'] cf. Bṛh. 4. 4. 22 end; Tait. 2. 9; Īśā 2d; see also **449**. On the simile of water and lotus-leaf see **607**.

177 Chānd. 4. 15. 1 *ya eṣo 'kṣiṇi puruṣo—brahmeti* = Chānd. 8. 7. 4; cf. 1. 7. 5; see also **35, 60**. The part *eṣa ātmeti—brahmeti* = Chānd. 8. 3. 4; 8. 8. 3; 8. 10. 1; 8. 11. 1; Maitri 2. 2.

178 Chānd. 4. 15. 5—6 [course to the Brahma-world] see **127**.

179 Chānd. 4. 16 [silence of the Brahman priest at the sacrifice] ⇳ Jaiminīya Up. Br. 3. 4. 2 (Oertel, *JAOS* 15. 247—248).

180 Chānd. 4. 17. 1—3 [Prajāpati produced *bhūr, bhuvaḥ, svar*] ⇳ Chānd. 2. 23. 2 (3); cf. Maitri 6. 6.

181 Chānd. 5. 1. 1—5 ⇳ Bṛh. 6. 1. 1—5. (For discussion of this parallel see D. p. 132—133.)

182 Chānd. 5. 1. 6 — 5. 2. 2 [rivalry of the functions] see **124**.

183 Chānd. 5. 2. 1 *na ha vā evaṃvidi — bhavatīti* see **31**.

184 Chānd. 5. 2. 2 *purastāc—adbhiḥ paridadhati* ⇳ Maitri 6. 9.

185 Chānd. 5. 2. 3 [reviving of a dried stump] ⇳ Bṛh. 6. 3. 12.

186 Chānd. 5. 2. 4—9 [oblations in incantation ceremony] see **129**.

187 Chānd. 5. 2. 6 *amo nāmāsy* see **5**.

188 Chānd. 5. 3—10 [*pañcāgnividyā* and the course of the soul in incarnations] see **125**. Sections 4—10 are apparently alluded to in Muṇḍ.; see **426**.

189 Chānd. 5. 3. 5, 7 [Kṣatriya instructing Brahman] see **22**.

190 Chānd. 5. 3. 5 *yathāham eṣāṃ—nāvakṣyam* ⇳ Praśna 6. 1.

191 Chānd. 5. 10. 1—6 [course to the Brahma-world and to the lunar world] see **127, 128**. With 5. 10. 4—6 cf. Muṇḍ. 2. 1. 5b—d; see **426**.

192 Chānd. 5. 10. 7 thoughts and acts determine one's reincarnate status] cf. Bṛh. 4. 4. 6; Kauṣ. 1. 2; Kaṭha 3. 7—8; 5. 7; Praśna 3. 3 [see **481**]; 3. 7; Śvet. 5. 7, 12; Maitri 3. 2; 6. 34, stanzas 3—4. Cf. also Manusmṛti 12. 55; Yājñavalkīya Dharma-sūtras 3. 207; MBh. 14. 36. 30—31 (C. 1016—7); and see in general **236, 786**.

193 Chānd. 5. 10. 9a—b cf. MBh. 14. 51. 18 (C. 1442).
194 Chānd. 5. 11. 1—2 cf. the similar introduction Praśna 1.1.
195 Chānd. 5. 11. 7 [bringing of fuel] see **175**.
196 Chānd. 5. 18. 1 *sarveṣu lokeṣu — annam atti* see **31**.
197 Chānd. 5. 18. 2 *lomāni barhir* = Bṛh. 6. 4. 3.
198 Chānd. 5. 19—23 ['Hail!' to *prāṇa, apāna,* etc.] cf. Maitri 6. 9.
199 Chānd. 5. 24. 3 [simile of the reed laid on a fire] cf. MBh. 13. 26. 42 (C. 1800).
200 Chānd. 6. 1. 3 *yena — avijñātaṃ vijñātam* see **409**.
201 Chānd. 6. 2. 1 [primordial Non-being] ≎ Chānd. 3. 19. 1; Tait. 2. 7.
202 Chānd. 6. 2. 3—4 *bahu syām prajāyeyeti* = Tait. 2. 6. Cf. Bṛh. 1. 2. 4; 1. 4. 3.
203 Chānd. 6. 3. 1 *trīṇy eva bījāni — udbhijjam* see **298**.
204 Chānd. 6. 4. 5 cf. Muṇḍ. 1. 1. 3; see **409**.
205 Chānd. 6. 5. 1 *tasya yaḥ sthaviṣṭho dhātus* cf. Maitri 2. 6.
206 Chānd. 6. 7 [a person consists of sixteen parts] see **501**.
207 Chānd. 6. 8. 6 *tad uktam purastād* namely at 6. 4. 7—6. 5. 4.
208 Chānd. 6. 8. 6 *vāṅ manasi — devatāyām* = Chānd. 6. 15. 2; cf. Praśna 3. 9—10.
209 Chānd. 6. 9. 1 [unified condition of honey] cf. Maitri 6. 22.
210 Chānd. 6. 13 [solution of salt in water] cf. Bṛh. 2. 4. 12; Maitri 6. 35; 7. 11. (The allusion to salt in Bṛh. 4. 5. 13 is apparently a modified form of Bṛh. 2. 4. 12; see D. p. 481.)
211 Chānd. 6. 15. 1 [consciousness of a dying person] ≎ Chānd. 8. 6. 4.
212 Chānd. 6. 15. 1—2 [unification of the functions at death] see **320**.
213 Chānd. 6. 15. 2 *vāṅ manasi — devatāyām* see **208**.
214 Chānd. 7. 1. 1 *adhīhi bhagavo* cf. Tait. 3. 1.
215 Chānd. 7. 1. 2, 4 [literature-list] see **41**.
216 Chānd. 7. 1. 3 [ignorance of Ātman confest] cf. Maitri 1. 2.
217 Chānd. 7. 1. 3 *tarati śokam ātmavid* ≎ Muṇḍ. 3. 2. 9.
218 Chānd. 7. 2. 1 = (var.) Chānd. 7. 7. 1. See also **41**.
219 Chānd. 7. 9. 1 *yady api — vijñātā bhavati* = (var.) Maitri 6. 11.
220 Chānd. 7. 10 [water as a primal substance] see **112**.

221 Chānd. 7. 15. 1 *yathā vā arā nābhau samarpitā* ⇕ Bṛh. 2. 5. 15; see **434**.

222 Chānd. 7. 16—23 *vijijñāsitavya* see **638**.

223 Chānd. 7. 24. 1 *sve mahimni* see **590**.

224 Chānd. 7. 25. 1—2 cf. Muṇḍ. 2. 2. 11.

225 Chānd. 7. 25. 2 *ātmaratir ātmakrīḍa* ⇕ Muṇḍ. 3. 1. 4c.

226 Chānd. 7. 26. 2 *na paśyo* [stanza] = (var.) Maitri 7. 11, stanza 6.

227 Chānd. 7. 26. 2 [the Ātman manifold] cf. Maitri 5. 2; 6. 26 end.

228 Chānd. 7. 26. 2 [a pure nature requisite for mystic attainment] cf. Muṇḍ. 3. 1. 8c—d.

229 Chānd. 7. 26. 2 [liberation from all knots (of the heart)] see **396**.

230 Chānd. 7. 26. 2 *tamasas pāraṃ* see **787**.

231 Chānd. 8. 1. 1—5 [Brahma-city, abode] cf. Kaṭha 2.13d; Muṇḍ. 2. 2. 7c; 3. 2. 1a—b, 4d; see also **543**. On the 'ether within the heart' see **265**.

232 Chānd. 8. 1. 1 *yad anveṣṭavyaṃ yad vāva vijijñāsitavyam* see **638**.

233 Chānd. 8. 1. 5 *na vadhenāsya hanyate* = Chānd. 8. 10. 2; 8. 10. 4; cf. Kaṭha 2. 18d = BhG. 2. 20d.

234 Chānd. 8. 1. 5 *asmin kāmāḥ samāhitā* = (var.) Maitri 6. 30, 35, 38.

235 Chānd. 8. 1. 5 *eṣa ātmā — satyasaṃkalpo* = Chānd. 8. 7. 1; 8. 7. 3; (var.) Maitri 7. 7. The epithets *vijara vimṛtyu viśoka* recur also at Maitri 6. 25; 7. 5.

236 Chānd. 8. 2 [creative power of desire] cf. Muṇḍ. 3. 1. 10. Cf. in general **81**, **786**.

237 Chānd. 8. 3. 4 *eṣa samprasādo — etad brahmeti* = Maitri 2. 2. As far as *rūpeṇābhiniṣpadyate* the passage recurs also at Chānd. 8. 12. 3. See also **177**.

238 Chānd. 8. 3. 4 *etasya brahmaṇo nāma satyam* cf. Bṛh. 5. 4.

239 Chānd. 8. 3. 5 *trīṇy akṣarāṇi satīyam iti* ⇕ Bṛh. 5. 5. 1.

240 Chānd. 8. 4. 1 *sa setur vidhṛtir — asambhedāya* see **98**.

241 Chānd. 8. 4. 1—2 [endless day] see **156**.

242 Chānd. 8. 5. 3 [marvels of the Brahma-world] cf. Kauṣ. 1. 3.

243 Chānd. 8. 6. 1 *yā etā hṛdayasya nāḍyas — lohitasyeti* see **25**, **71**.

244 Chānd. 8. 6. 2 *yathā mahāpatha* cf. Bṛh. 4. 4. 8—9.

245 Chānd. 8. 6. 3 *tad yatraitatsuptaḥ — nāḍīṣu sṛpto bhavati* see **24**. *tad — svapnaṃ na vijānāty* recurs at Chānd. 8. 11. 1.

246 Chānd. 8. 6. 4 [consciousness of a dying person] ⇕ Chānd. 6. 15. 1.

247 Chānd. 8. 6. 6 *śataṃ caikā ca hṛdayasya nāḍyas* = Kaṭha 6. 16 ⇕ Praśna 3. 6; cf. Muṇḍ. 2. 2. 6; Maitri 6. 30 (*raśmi-śatam*). See also **25**, **65**.

248 Chānd. 8. 6. 6 *tāsām mūrdhānam abhiniḥsṛtaikā* see **64**.

249 Chānd. 8. 6. 6 *tayordhvam āyann amṛtatvam eti* = Kaṭha 6. 16; cf. Bṛh. 4. 4. 8—9; Praśna 3. 7; Maitri 6. 21; 6. 30; 7. 11, stanza 3.

250 Chānd. 8. 6. 6 *viṣvaṅṅ anyā utkramaṇe bhavanti* = Kaṭha 6. 16 ⇕ Maitri 6. 30.

251 Chānd. 8. 7—8 [instruction of gods and devils] cf. Maitri 7. 10.

252 Chānd. 8. 7. 1; 8. 7. 3 *eṣa ātmā — satyasaṃkalpo* see **235**.

253 Chānd. 8. 7. 3 *so 'nveṣṭavyaḥ sa vijijñāsitavyaḥ* see **638**.

254 Chānd. 8. 7. 4; 8. 8. 3; 8. 10. 1; 8. 11. 1 *eṣa ātmeti — brahmeti* see **177**.

255 Chānd. 8. 10 [dream experiences] cf. Bṛh. 4. 3. 20; Praśna 4. 5.

256 Chānd. 8. 10. 2; 8. 10. 4 *na vadhenāsya hanyate* see **233**.

257 Chānd. 8. 11. 1 *tad — svapnaṃ na vijānāty* = Chānd. 8. 6. 3; see **245**.

258 Chānd. 8. 12. 3 *eṣa samprasādo — rūpeṇābhiniṣpadyate* see **237**.

259 Chānd. 8. 12. 4 [the soul as agent in the senses] see **333**.

260 Chānd. 8. 13 *vidhūya pāpaṃ* see **449**.

261 Chānd. 8. 13 *akṛtaṃ . . . brahmalokam* cf. *akṛtaḥ* [*lokaḥ*] Muṇḍ. 1. 2. 12 b.

262 Chānd. 8. 15 [Line of Tradition] ⇕ Chānd. 3. 11. 4; see **47**.

263 Chānd. 8. 15 [conditions of attainment] see **526**.

264 Tait. 1. 1 ⇕ Tait. 1. 12.

265 Tait. 1. 6. 1 *sa ya eṣo 'ntar hṛdaya ākāśaḥ tasminn ayam puruṣo manomayaḥ* cf. Muṇḍ. 2. 2. 6; Maitri 6. 30; 7. 11, stanza 2. For the 'ether within the heart' see

Bṛh. 2.1.17; 4.2.3; 4.4.22; Chānd. 8.1.1—3; Maitri 6. 22, 27, 28.

266 Tait. 1.6.1 *antareṇa tāluke — sendrayoniḥ* cf. *tālvantarvicchinnā* Maitri 6.21.

267 Tait. 1.6.1 *yatrāsau keśānto — śīrṣakapāle* see **78**.

268 Tait. 1.7 *pāṅktam idaṃ sarvam — ya evaṃ veda* ⇕ Bṛh. 1.4.17.

269 Tait. 1.8 [the syllable *Om*] ⇕ Chānd. 1.1.8—9. Cf. **726, 818**.

270 Tait. 1.10 [nectar in the sun] cf. Chānd. 3.1.2; Maitri 6.35.

271 Tait. 1.12 ⇕ Tait. 1.1.

272 Tait. 2.2a—d *annād vai — antataḥ* = Maitri 6.11. See esp. **728**.

273 Tait. 2.2k—n *annād bhūtāni — ucyate* = Maitri 6.12. See esp. **728**.

274 Tait. 2.2—5 *annarasamaya* etc. see **649**.

275 Tait. 2.4 *yato vāco* [stanza] = (var.) Tait. 2.9.

276 Tait. 2.4 *ātmā vijñānamayaḥ* cf. Muṇḍ. 3.2.7c; also Praśna 4.9 (*vijñānātman*).

277 Tait. 2.5 *ātmā "nandamayaḥ* cf. Tait. 2.8 end; 3.10.5; Māṇḍ. 5.

278 Tait. 2.6 *bahu syām prajāyeyeti* see **202**.

279 Tait. 2.7 [primordial Non-being] ⇕ Chānd. 3.19.1; 6.2.1.

280 Tait. 2.7 *tat sukṛtam ucyate* cf. Ait. 2.3.

281 Tait. 2.8 *bhīṣā 'smād* [stanza] ⇕ Kaṭha 6.3.

282 Tait. 2.8 [gradation of blisses] see **75**.

283 Tait. 2.8 *sa yaś cāyam puruṣe — ānandamayam ātmānam upasaṃkrāmati* ⇕ Tait. 3.10.4—5. See also **277**.

284 Tait. 2.9 *yato vāco* [stanza] = (var.) Tait. 2.4.

285 Tait. 2.9 [moral self-judgment escaped by the 'knower'] see **101**.

286 Tait. 3.1 *adhīhi bhagavo brahma* (5 times) cf. Chānd. 7.1.1.

287 Tait. 3.1 [creation and reabsorption of beings] see **532**.

288 Tait. 3.10.4 [*brahmaṇaḥ parimara*] ⇕ Ait. Br. 8.28, where this incantation is described. Cf. the *daiva parimara* of Kauṣ. 2.12 (8).

289 Tait. 3.10.4—5 *sa yaś cāyam puruṣe* etc. see **283**.

290 Ait. 1. 1 *ātmā vā idam eka evāgra* see **7**.
291 Ait. 1. 2—3 [creation from water] see **112**.
292 Ait. 2. 3 *puruṣo vāva sukṛtam* cf. Tait. 2. 7 d.
293 Ait. 3. 1—10 [efforts of various bodily functions] see **124**.
294 Ait. 3. 12 *etam eva sīmānaṃ* cf. **78**.
295 Ait. 3. 14 . . . *santam indra ity — devāḥ* see **60**.
296 Ait. 4. 6 ⇕ Ait. 5. 4.
297 Ait. 5. 2 *prajñānam* . . . *dhṛtir* . . . *smṛtiḥ* cf. Maitri 6. 31.
298 Ait. 5. 3 *bījānītarāṇi — codbhijjāni* cf. Chānd. 6. 3. 1; see also Manusmṛti 1. 43—46; MBh. 12. 312. 5 (C. 11594); 14. 42. 33 (C. 1134).

299[6] Kauṣ. 1. 1 [bringing of fuel] see **175**.
300 Kauṣ. 1. 2 *yathākarma yathāvidyaṃ* cf. *yathākarma yathāśrutam* Kaṭha 5. 7 d. On the dependence of one's reincarnate status on past acts see **192**.
301 Kauṣ. 1. 3 [gradation of worlds] cf. Bṛh. 3. 6.
302 Kauṣ. 1. 3 [marvels of the Brahma-world] cf. Chānd. 8. 5. 3.
303 Kauṣ. 1. 4 [looking down on chariot-wheels] cf. Maitri 6. 28 end.
304 Kauṣ. 1. 7 (6) [series of terms: *prāṇa, vāc,* etc.] cf. Kauṣ. 2. 15 (10).
305 Kauṣ. 2. 1 *tasmai vā etasmai — dadāma ta iti* = Kauṣ. 2. 2 (1).
306 Kauṣ. 2. 8 (5) *yat te susīmaṃ hṛdayam* [stanza] recurs in altered form at Kauṣ. 2. 10 (6).
307 Kauṣ. 2. 11 (7) *aṅgād aṅgāt — adhijāyase* [2 lines] = Bṛh. 6. 4. 9.
308 Kauṣ. 2. 11 (7) *aśmā bhava* [stanza] = (var.) Bṛh. M 6. 4. 26.
309 Kauṣ. 2. 11 (7) *mā vyathiṣṭhāḥ* = BhG. 11. 34.
310 Kauṣ. 2. 12 (8) *daivaḥ parimara* cf. *brahmaṇaḥ parimara* Tait. 3. 10. 4.
311 Kauṣ. 2. 14 (9) [rivalry of the functions] see **124**.
312 Kauṣ. 2. 14 (9) *ākāśātmā* see **656**.

---

[6] Note that a translation of this Upanishad is comprised in A. Berriedale Keith's *Śāṅkhāyana Āraṇyaka*, London, 1908, p. 16—41 (Oriental Translation Fund, new series, vol. 18).

313 Kauṣ. 2. 15 (10) [Transmission ceremony] cf. Bṛh. 1. 5. 17—20. With the series of terms (*vāc*, *prāṇa*, etc.) cf. the series in Kauṣ. 1. 7 (6).

314 Kauṣ. 3. 1 [deeds of Indra] cf. Ait. Br. 7. 28; TS. 2. 5. 1.

315 Kauṣ. 3. 1 [ethical distinctions superseded] cf. Bṛh. 4. 3. 22.

316 Kauṣ. 3. 2—3 [superiority of *prāṇa*] see **124**.

317 Kauṣ. 3. 3 the latter half of this section parallels the former (tho not so clearly in the recension publisht in the Ānandāśrama Sanskrit Series, which has omissions and additions).

318 Kauṣ. 3. 3 *uktham prāṇo — utthāpayaty* ⇳ Bṛh. 5. 13. 1.

319 Kauṣ. 3. 3 [unification of the functions in sleep] ⇳ Kauṣ. 4. 20; cf. Praśna 4. 2; Māṇḍ. 5 (*ekībhūtaḥ*).

320 Kauṣ. 3. 3 [unification of the functions at death] cf. Bṛh. 4. 4. 2; Chānd. 6. 15. 1—2; see also BhG. 15. 8.

321 Kauṣ. 3. 8 [spokes fixt in the hub] see **434**.

322 Kauṣ. 3. 8 *na sādhunā — kanīyān* = Bṛh. 4. 4. 22. Cf. Maitri 2. 7.

323 Kauṣ. 4. 1—19 [dialog of Gārgya and Ajātaśatru] ⇳ Bṛh. 2. 1. 1—19. Cf. Bṛh. 3. 9. 10—17.

324 Kauṣ. 4. 19 [bringing of fuel as sign of pupilship] see **175**.

325 Kauṣ. 4. 19 [Kṣatriya instructing Brahman] see **22**.

326 Kauṣ. 4. 19 *hitā nāma hṛdayasya nāḍyo* see **25**.

327 Kauṣ. 4. 19 *hṛdayāt purītatam abhipratanvanti* see **26**.

328 Kauṣ. 4. 19 *yathā sahasradhā keśo vipāṭitas* see **65**.

329 Kauṣ. 4. 19 *piṅgalasyāṇimnā — lohitasyeti* see **71**.

330 Kauṣ. 4. 19 *tāsu tadā bhavati — paśyaty* see **24**.

331 Kauṣ. 4. 20 (19) [unification of the functions in sleep] see **319**.

332 Kauṣ. 4. 20 *sa eṣa iha praviṣṭa — viśvambharakulāye* ⇳ Bṛh. 1. 4. 7.

333 Kena 2a—c ⇳ Bṛh. 4. 4. 18a—c. Cf. Chānd. 8. 12. 4; Maitri 6. 31; see also Bṛh. 2. 4. 11; Kauṣ. 3. 4. Kena 2d = 13d.

334 Kena 3a—b [the Supreme not to be apprehended by the senses] see **394**.

335 Kena 3e—h = (var.) Īśā 10; see **404**.

336 Kena 13b = (var.) Bṛh. 4. 4. 14b. Kena 13d=2d.
337 Kena 29 [lightning as suggestive of Brahma] cf. Bṛh. 2. 3. 6; 5. 7.

338[7] Kaṭha 1.1 the same story, partly in the same words, is found in Tait. Br. 3. 11. 8.
339 Kaṭha 1. 3c = Bṛh. 4. 4. 11a = (var.) Īśā 3a.
340 Kaṭha 1. 7 cf. Vāsiṣṭha Dharma-śāstra 11. 13, where the words recur.
341 Kaṭha 1. 8 [deprivation of an offender] cf. Bṛh. 6.4.12.
342 Kaṭha 1. 12d = Kaṭha 1. 18d.
343 Kaṭha 1. 17c—d. = (var.) Śvet. 4. 11c—d.
344 Kaṭha 1. 21b—c [question declared difficult; another choice advised] cf. Maitri 1. 2.
345 Kaṭha 1. 26 [dissatisfaction with life] see **587**.
346 Kaṭha 2. 4 = (var.) Maitri 7. 9.
347 Kaṭha 2. 5 = (var.) Muṇḍ. 1. 2. 8; Maitri 7. 9.
348 Kaṭha 2. 7 cf. BhG. 2. 29.
349 Kaṭha 2. 12b *gūḍham anupraviṣṭaṃ guhāhitaṃ* cf. Kaṭha 3. 1b; 4. 6c; Muṇḍ. 2. 1. 8d; 3. 1. 7d; Maitri 2. 6; 6. 4.
350 Kaṭha 2. 13d *vivṛtaṃ sadma* see **231**.
351 Kaṭha 2. 15 ⟺ BhG. 8. 11.
352 Kaṭha 2. 16 = (var.) Maitri 6. 4.
353 Kaṭha 2. 18, 19 = (var.) BhG. 2. 20, 19. On Kaṭha 2. 18d see **757**.
354 Kaṭha 2. 20 = (var.) Śvet. 3. 20; etc. [see **544**]. On the doctrine of *prasāda* cf. also Muṇḍ. 3. 2. 3 [see **356**]; Śvet. 6. 21; and see Hopkins, *Great Epic*, p. 188.
355 Kaṭha 2. 22c—d = Kaṭha 4. 4c—d.
356 Kaṭha 2. 23 = Muṇḍ. 3. 2. 3.
357 Kaṭha 3. 1b *guhām praviṣṭau* see **349**.
358 Kaṭha 3. 1d *pañcāgnayo ye ca triṇāciketāḥ* ⟺ Manusmṛti 3. 185a; cf. MBh. 13. 90. 26c (C. 4296a).
359 Kaṭha 3. 3—5 [the soul riding in the chariot of the body] cf. Śvet. 2. 9c; Maitri 2. 3—4; 2. 6 end; 4. 4; see also MBh. 3. 2. 66 (C. 112); 3. 211. 23 (C. 13942);

---

7 On parallels between Kaṭha and MBh. see Hopkins, *Great Epic*, p. 29—32.

5.34.59 (C.1153); 5.46.5 (C.1745); 11.7.13 (C.175); 12.240.11 (C.8744); 14.51.3 (C.1426); Mārkāṇḍeya Purāṇa 1.42(43); Böhtlingk, *Ind. Sprüche,* 1118; 'Tschhakli' Up., D.p.846—847.

360 Kaṭha 3.4 [the soul called 'the enjoyer'] cf. Śvet.1.8c, 9b, 12c; and esp. Maitri 6.10.

361 Kaṭha 3.7—9 [rebirth or release according to one's thoughts and acts] see **192.**

362 Kaṭha 3.9d [RV.1.22.20a] = Maitri 6.26; also Rāmāyaṇa G.6.41.25d.

363 Kaṭha 3.10—12 = (var.) MBh.12.247.3—5 (C.8953—5). Kaṭha 3.10 ♤ BhG.3.42; cf. MBh.12.297.19c—d (C.10919a—b).

364 Kaṭha 3.15 ♤ MBh.12.240.17—18 (C.8750—1).

365 Kaṭha 4.1a *parāñci khāni vyatṛṇat* cf. *khānīmāni bhittvā* Maitri 2.6.

366 Kaṭha 4.3d = Kaṭha 5.4d.

367 Kaṭha 4.3; 4.5; etc. *etad vai tat* cf. *tad vai tat* Bṛh.5.4.

368 Kaṭha 4.4c—d = Kaṭha 2.22c—d.

369 Kaṭha 4.5c—d = Kaṭha 4.12c—d; Bṛh.4.4.15c—d. Pāda c recurs also as Kaṭha 4.13c; pāda d as Īśā 6d.

370 Kaṭha 4.6 *yaḥ pūrvaṃ tapaso jātam adbhyaḥ* see **112**. On *guhām praviśya* (pāda c) see **349.**

371 Kaṭha 4.9a—b [AV.10.18.16a—b] = Bṛh.1.5.23.

372 Kaṭha 4.10c—d, 11a—b = (var.) Bṛh.4.4.19c,d,a,b.

373 Kaṭha 4.12a—b [person of the size of a thumb] see **541.** Kaṭha 4.12a,c = 4.13a,c. Kaṭha 4.12c—d = 4.5c—d; see **369.**

374 Kaṭha 4.13b [light without smoke] see **658.**

375 Kaṭha 4.13d *sa evādya sa u śva[s]* = Bṛh.1.5.23.

376 Kaṭha 5.1a [eleven-gated citadel, the body] see **543.**

377 Kaṭha 5.2 [RV.4.40.5] recurs Mahānār.10.6 (Ātharv. rec. 9.3).

378 Kaṭha 5.3c *madhye vāmanam āsīnaṃ* see **541.**

379 Kaṭha 5.4d = Kaṭha 4.3d.

380 Kaṭha 5.6b *guhyam brahma* see **535.**

381 Kaṭha 5.7d *yathākarma yathāśrutam* cf. *yathākarma yathāvidyaṃ* Kauṣ.1.2. Regarding the dependence of one's reincarnate status on past acts see **192.**

382 Kaṭha 5.8c—f = Kaṭha 6.1c—f.
383 Kaṭha 5.9b (=10b) = Bṛh.2.5.19.
384 Kaṭha 5.9c (=10c, 11c), 12a *sarvabhūtāntarātmā* cf. Muṇḍ.2.1.4d.
385 Kaṭha 5.12 = (var.) Śvet.6.12. Kaṭha 5.12c—d = (var.) 5.13c—d.
386 Kaṭha 5.13a—b = Śvet.6.13a—b.
387 Kaṭha 5.15 = Muṇḍ.2.2.10; Śvet.6.14. Cf. Maitri 6.24; BhG.15.6, 12. Cf. *ekaḥ sūryaḥ sarvam idaṃ vibhāti* MBh.3.134.8 (C.10658).
388 Kaṭha 6.1 [eternal fig-tree with root above] see **813**. Kaṭha 6.1c—f = 5.8c—f.
389 Kaṭha 6.3 ⇕ Tait.2.8.
390 Kaṭha 6.9 = (var.) Śvet.4.20; Mahānār.1.11; MBh.5.46.6 (C.1747). See esp. also **541**.
391 Kaṭha 6.10 = Maitri 6.30. Pāda d recurs BhG.8.21.
392 Kaṭha 6.11c *apramattas* cf. Muṇḍ.2.2.4; 3.2.4b (*pramādāt*).
393 Kaṭha 6.11d *prabhavāpyayau* cf. Māṇḍ.6.
394 Kaṭha 6.12 [the Supreme not to be apprehended by the senses] cf. Kena 3a—b; Muṇḍ.3.1.8a—b.
395 Kaṭha 6.14 = Bṛh.4.4.7.
396 Kaṭha 6.15 [liberation from the knots of the heart] cf. Chānd.7.26.2; Muṇḍ.2.2.8a; 3.2.9.
397 Kaṭha 6.16 = Chānd.8.6.6 See **247—250**.
398 Kaṭha 6.17a—b [person of the size of a thumb] see **541**.

399 Īśā 2d *na karma lipyate nare* see **176**.
400 Īśā 3 see **87**.
401 Īśā 5 ⇕ BhG.13.15. Cf. Muṇḍ.2.1.2b.
402 Īśā 6 ⇕ BhG.6.29; MBh.12.240.21 (C.8754); Manusmṛti 12.91; cf. also BhG.4.35c—d; MBh.5.46.25 (C.1784) [with *kiṃ śocet* cf. Īśā 7c]; Āpastambīya Dharma-sūtras 1.23.1. For recurrences of pāda d see **369**.
403 Īśā 9 [stanza] = Bṛh.4.4.10.
404 Īśā 10 = (var.) Kena 3e—h. Īśā 10c—d = 13c—d.
405 Īśā 11 = Maitri 7.9. Cf. Īśā 14.
406 Īśā 12 = Bṛh.M 4.4.10.

407 Īśā 15—18 = Bṛh. 5. 15. Īśā 15 = (var.) Maitri 6. 35.

408 Muṇḍ. 1. 1. 1—2 [Line of Tradition] see **47.**

409 Muṇḍ. 1. 1. 3 *kasmin . . . vijñāte sarvam idaṃ vijñātam* cf. Bṛh. 2. 4. 5 end; 4. 5. 6 end; Chānd. 6. 1. 3. With the whole section cf. esp. also Chānd. 6. 4. 5.

410 Muṇḍ. 1. 1. 4 *parā caivāparā ca* see **498.**

411 Muṇḍ. 1. 1. 6—7 [characterization of the Imperishable] cf. Bṛh. 3. 8. 8—9.

412 Muṇḍ. 1. 1. 6d [the Imperishable as the source of beings] cf. Māṇḍ. 6; Śvet. 5. 5a; note also Śvet. 4. 11a; 5. 2a (*yoni*).

413 Muṇḍ. 1. 1. 7 [spider and thread analogy for creation] see **27.**

414 Muṇḍ. 1. 1. 9a = Muṇḍ. 2. 2. 7a; cf. *sarvajña* Māṇḍ. 6.

415 Muṇḍ. 1. 2. 4 [the seven flames] cf. Muṇḍ. 2. 1. 8b; Praśna 3. 5.

416 Muṇḍ. 1. 2. 5, 6, 11 [course to the Brahma-world] see **127.**

417 Muṇḍ. 1. 2. 7—10 [course to 'heaven' and to rebirth] cf. BhG. 9. 21 and see **128.**

418 Muṇḍ. 1. 2. 8 = (var.) Kaṭha 2. 5; Maitri 7. 9.

419 Muṇḍ. 1. 2. 12b *akṛtaḥ* [*lokaḥ*] cf. *akṛtaṃ . . . brahmalokam* Chānd. 8. 13.

420 Muṇḍ. 1. 2. 12c [bringing of fuel as sign of pupilship] see **175.**

421 Muṇḍ. 2. 1. 1 [sparks from fire as analogy of creation] cf. Bṛh. 2.1. 20; Maitri 6. 26, 31. On the creation and reabsorption of beings see **532.**

422 Muṇḍ. 2. 1. 2a [the Puruṣa is formless] cf. Bṛh. 2. 3. 5.

423 Muṇḍ. 2. 1. 2b *sa bāhyābhyantaro* cf. Īśā 5; BhG. 13. 15.

424 Muṇḍ. 2. 1. 3 ⟺ Praśna 6. 4; see **503.**

425 Muṇḍ. 2. 1. 4d *eṣa sarvabhūtāntarātmā* cf. Kaṭha 5. 9c (= 10c, 11c), 12a.

426 Muṇḍ. 2. 1. 5—6 these 2 stanzas seem to be an epitome of Chānd. 5. 4—10: fire whose fuel is the sun, 5. 4; rain from Soma, 5. 5; crops from earth, 5. 6; procreation, 5. 7—8; sacrifices, etc., 5. 10. 3; the year, 5. 10. **2**; worlds of moon and sun [see **127, 128**], 5. 10. 2—3. The course from Soma to earthly embodiment, alluded to in Muṇḍ. 2. 1. 5, appears in fuller form in Chānd. 5. 10. 4—6.

427 Muṇḍ. 2. 1. 8—9 = (var.) Mahānār. 10. 2—3 (Ātharv. rec. 8. 4—5). On the 'seven flames' (8b) see **415**. On *guhāśayā nihitāḥ* (8d) see **349**.

428 Muṇḍ. 2. 2. 1a *āviḥ saṃnihitaṃ* cf. Maitri 6.27. See **535**.

429 Muṇḍ. 2. 2. 1d [Being and Non-being] cf. Praśna 2. 5d, and see also Śvet. 4. 18b. (In Praśna 4. 5 the words have a different meaning.)

430 Muṇḍ. 2. 2. 3—4 [bow and arrow analogy for Yoga] cf. Maitri 6. 24; 6. 28. The technical term *apramatta* recurs at Kaṭha 6.11c; cf. also Muṇḍ. 3. 2. 4b (*pramādāt*).

431 Muṇḍ. 2. 2. 5b *otam* see **50**.

432 Muṇḍ. 2. 2. 5c *tam evaikaṃ jānatha — vimuñca* cf. Bṛh. 4. 4. 21.

433 Muṇḍ. 2. 2. 5d [Ātman a bridge to immortality] see **98**.

434 Muṇḍ. 2. 2. 6 *arā iva rathanābhau — nāḍyaḥ* see **247**. The spoke and hub simile recurs verbatim at Praśna 2. 6a; 6. 6a; and also at Bṛh. 2. 5. 15; Chānd. 7. 15. 1; Kauṣ. 3. 8. (Wheel analogies are found also at Bṛh. 1. 5. 15; Śvet. 1. 4.)

435 Muṇḍ. 2. 2. 6 *sa eṣo 'ntaś carate* see **265**.

436 Muṇḍ. 2. 2. 6 *tamasaḥ parastāt* see **787**.

437 Muṇḍ. 2. 2. 7a = Muṇḍ. 1. 1. 9a; cf. Māṇḍ. 6 (*sarvajña*).

438 Muṇḍ. 2. 2. 7c [Brahma-city] see **231**.

439 Muṇḍ. 2. 2. 7e *manomayaḥ prāṇaśarīranetā* cf. Chānd. 3. 14. 2; see **165**.

440 Muṇḍ. 2. 2. 8a [liberation from the knot(s) of the heart] see **396**.

441 Muṇḍ. 2. 2. 8b [all doubts cleared away] cf. Chānd. 3. 14. 4.

442 Muṇḍ. 2. 2. 8c [cessation of karma] see **449**.

443 Muṇḍ. 2. 2. 8d [the higher and the lower Brahma] see **498**.

444 Muṇḍ. 2. 2. 9a [highest golden sheath] cf. Bṛh. 5. 15. See **122**.

445 Muṇḍ. 2. 2. 9c *jyotiṣāṃ jyotis* cf. Bṛh. 4. 4. 16c.

446 Muṇḍ. 2. 2. 10 = Kaṭha 5. 15; Śvet. 6. 14. See **387**.

447 Muṇḍ. 2. 2. 11 cf. Chānd. 7. 25. 1—2.

448 Muṇḍ. 3. 1. 1—2 = Śvet. 4. 6 [RV. 1. 164. 20]; 4. 7.

449 Muṇḍ. 3. 1. 3a—c = (var.) Maitri 6. 18. With *puṇya-pāpe vidhūya* (pāda c) cf. *vidhūya pāpaṃ* Chānd. 8. 13.

For cessation of karma see also Muṇḍ. 2. 2. 8c and cf. **176**.

450 Muṇḍ. 3. 1. 4c *ātmakrīḍa ātmaratiḥ* ⇕ Chānd. 7. 25. 2.

451 Muṇḍ. 3. 1. 5a—b *tapasā . . . brahmacaryeṇa* cf. *brahmacaryeṇa tapasā* Bṛh. M 4. 4. 22; also Chānd. 2. 23. 1; Praśna 1. 2, 10; 5. 3.

452 Muṇḍ. 3. 1. 5c *antaḥ śarīre jyotirmayo* cf. *yo 'yam . . . hṛdy antar jyotiḥ puruṣaḥ* Bṛh. 4. 3. 7.

453 Muṇḍ. 3. 1. 6 [path to the gods (*devayāna*)] see **127.**

454 Muṇḍ. 3. 1. 7d *nihitaṃ guhāyām* see **349.**

455 Muṇḍ. 3. 1. 8a—b [the Supreme not to be apprehended by the senses] see **394.**

456 Muṇḍ. 3. 1. 8c [a pure nature requisite for mystic attainment] cf. Chānd. 7. 26. 2 (*sattvaśuddhiḥ*); cf. also Muṇḍ. 3. 1. 9, 10; 3. 2. 6.

457 Muṇḍ. 3. 1. 10 [creative power of desire] cf. Bṛh. 1. 4. 15 end; Chānd. 8. 2.

458 Muṇḍ. 3. 2. 1a—b [Brahma-abode] see **231.**

459 Muṇḍ. 3. 2. 2 [he who desires and he who is free from desire] cf. Bṛh. 4. 4. 6.

460 Muṇḍ. 3. 2. 3 = Kaṭha 2. 23. Cf. **354.**

461 Muṇḍ. 3. 2. 4b *pramādāt* cf. the technical term *apramatta* Kaṭha 6. 11c; Muṇḍ. 2. 2. 4.

462 Muṇḍ. 3. 2. 4d [Brahma-abode] see **231.**

463 Muṇḍ. 3. 2. 6 = (var.) Mahānār. 10. 22 (Ātharv. rec. 10. 6).

464 Muṇḍ. 3. 2. 7—8 [unification in the Supreme Imperishable] parallel in thought and simile to Praśna 6. 5; see esp. also Praśna 4. 7—11 and cf. MBh. 12. 219. 42 (C. 7972); 14. 33. 7 (C. 919). Muṇḍ. 3. 2. 7d = (var.) Maitri 6. 18. On the 'fifteen parts' see **501.** On *vijñānamaya ātman* see Tait. 2. 4 and cf. *vijñānātman* Praśna 4. 9.

465 Muṇḍ. 3. 2. 9 *nāsyābrahmavit kule bhavati* = Māṇḍ. 10.

466 Muṇḍ. 3. 2. 9 [*brahmavit*] *tarati śokam* ⇕ Chānd. 7. 1. 3.

467 Muṇḍ. 3. 2. 9 [liberation from the knots of the heart] see **396.**

468 Muṇḍ. 3. 2. 10—11 [restrictions on imparting mystic knowledge] see **133.** With *ekarṣiṃ* (10b) cf. *eka ṛṣir* Praśna 2. 11a.

469 Praśna 1. 1 cf. the similar introduction Chānd. 5. 11. 1—2.

470 Praśna 1.1 [bringing of fuel as sign of pupilship] see **175**.

471 Praśna 1.2, 10 [*tapas, brahmacarya, śraddhā*] see **451**.

472 Praśna 1.5 *ādityo ha vai prāṇo* cf. Praśna 3.8.

473 Praśna 1.8 *viśvarūpaṃ hariṇaṃ* [stanza] = Maitri 6.8.

474 Praśna 1.9—10 [two paths, the southern and the northern] see **127, 128**.

475 Praśna 1.14 [food as the source of creatures] see **728**.

476 Praśna 2.2—4 [superiority of *prāṇa* among the bodily functions] see **124**.

477 Praśna 2.5d [Being and Non-being] see **429**.

478 Praśna 2.6a [spokes fixt in the hub] = Praśna 6.6a; Muṇḍ. 2.2.6a; see **434**.

479 Praśna 2.11a *eka ṛṣir* cf. *ekarṣiṃ* Muṇḍ. 3.2.10b.

480 Praśna 3.3 *ātmana eṣa prāṇo jāyate* cf. Muṇḍ. 2.1.3a; Praśna 6.4.

481 Praśna 3.3 *mano['dhi]kṛtenāyāty asmiñ charīre* (on text and interpretation consult Hume, *Thirteen Principal Upanishads*, p. 383, n. 2) see **192**.

482 Praśna 3.5 [etymological explanation of *samāna*] cf. Praśna 4.4; Maitri 2.6. On the food-offering see Chānd. 5.19, etc.

483 Praśna 3.5 [the seven flames] cf. Muṇḍ. 1.2.4; 2.1.8b.

484 Praśna 3.6 *atraitad ekaśataṃ nāḍīnām* see **247**.

485 Praśna 3.6 *dvāsaptatiḥ — -nāḍīsahasrāṇi* see **25**.

486 Praśna 3.6 *āsu vyānaś carati* cf. Maitri 6.21 (*prāṇa-saṃcāriṇī*).

487 Praśna 3.7 *athaikayordhva udānaḥ* see **249**.

488 Praśna 3.7 [acts determine one's reincarnate status] see **192**.

489 Praśna 3.8 *ādityo — prāṇa udayaty* cf. Praśna 1.5.

490 Praśna 3.9—10 *upaśāntatejāḥ — yuktaḥ* cf. Chānd. 6.8.6; 6.15.2.

491 Praśna 3.10 [thought determines state after death] see **786**.

492 Praśna 4.2 [unification of the functions in sleep] see **319**.

493 Praśna 4.4 [etymological explanation of *samāna*] see **482**.

494 Praśna 4.5 [dream experiences] cf. Bṛh. 4.3.20; Chānd. 8.10. On *sac cāsac ca* see **429**.

495 Praśna 4.7—11 [unification in the Supreme Imperishable] see **464**.

496 Praśna 4.8 [Sāṃkhya enumeration] see **522**.

497 Praśna 4.9 cf. Maitri 6.7 end. On *vijñānātman* see **464**.

498 Praśna 5.2 [the higher and the lower Brahma] = Maitri 6.5; cf. Muṇḍ. 1.1.4; 2.2.8d; Maitri 6.22—23. See also **32**.

499 Praśna 5.3 [*tapas, brahmacarya, śraddhā*] see **451**.

500 Praśna 5.5 [snake freed from its sluf] cf. Kauṣ. Br. 18.7 (see also Ait. Br. 6.1 end); MBh. 12.219.48 (C. 7978—9). The snake-skin simile is used in another application in Bṛh. 4.4.7.

501 Praśna 6.1—2 [the *puruṣa* with sixteen parts] cf. Bṛh. 1.5.14—15; Chānd. 6.7. Cf. the 'fifteen parts', Muṇḍ. 3.2.7a. Cf. also MBh. 12.242.8a—b (C. 8811) = (var.) 14.51.31a—b (C. 1455); 12.304.8 (C. 11324); note also 12.210.33 (C. 7674); and consult Hopkins, *Great Epic*, p. 168. (See Śat. Br. 10.4.1.17; and also VS. 8.36, where Prajāpati is called *ṣoḍaśin*.)

502 Praśna 6.1 *nāham imaṃ veda — nāvakṣyam* ⇕ Chānd. 5.3.5.

503 Praśna 6.4 *sa [puruṣa] prāṇam asṛjata* see **480**.

504 Praśna 6.4 *khaṃ vāyur — pṛthivī-* = Muṇḍ. 2.1.3.

505 Praśna 6.5 [unification in the cosmic Person] see **464**.

506 Praśna 6.6a [spokes fixt in the hub] = Praśna 2.6a; Muṇḍ. 2.2.6a; see **434**.

507 Māṇḍ. 1 *trikālātītaṃ* cf. *paras trikālād* Śvet. 6.5b.

508 Māṇḍ. 3 *saptāṅga ekonaviṃśatimukhaḥ* see **522**.

509 Māṇḍ. 4 *praviviktabhuk* cf. Bṛh. 4.2.3 end.

510 Māṇḍ. 5 *yatra supto — paśyati* = Bṛh. 4.3.19.

511 Māṇḍ. 5 *ekībhūtaḥ* [unification in sleep] see **319**.

512 Māṇḍ. 5 *prajñānaghana eva* = Bṛh. 4.5.13.

513 Māṇḍ. 5 *ānandamayo hy ānandabhuk* see **277**.

514 Māṇḍ. 6 *eṣa sarveśvara* see **98**.

515 Māṇḍ. 6 *eṣa sarvajña* cf. Muṇḍ. 1.1.9a = 2.2.7a.

516 Māṇḍ. 6 *eṣo 'ntaryāmy* cf. Bṛh. 3.7.

517 Māṇḍ. 6 *eṣa yoniḥ sarvasya* see **412**.

518 Māṇḍ. 6 *prabhavāpyayau* cf. Kaṭha 6.11d.

519 Māṇḍ. 7, 12 [fourth, or superconscious, state] cf. Maitri 6. 19; 7. 11, stanzas 7—8. See also the use of *turīya* at Bṛh. 5. 14. 3—7.

520 Māṇḍ. 10 *nāsyābrahmavit kule bhavati* = Muṇḍ. 3. 2. 9.

521[8] Śvet. 1. 2 *kālasvabhāvo* cf. Śvet. 6. 1a—b.

522 Śvet. 1. 4—5 [numerical allusions to series of philosophic terms] cf. Māṇḍ. 3; Śvet. 6. 3; Maitri 3. 3 (*caturjālaṃ caturdaśavidhaṃ caturaśītidhā pariṇatam*); 6. 10; see also BhG. 7. 4 and the Sāṃkhya list at Praśna 4. 8. The 'three paths' are mentioned again at Śvet. 5. 7c. On the 'fifty spokes' see Sāṃkhyakārikā 46. With the wheel analogy cf. Bṛh. 1. 5. 15; MBh. 14. 45. 1—9 (C. 1234—42) and see **602**.

523 Śvet. 1. 8c, 9b, 12c [the soul called 'the enjoyer'] see **360**.

524 Śvet. 1. 8d = Śvet. 2. 15d; 4. 16d; 5. 13d; 6. 13d.

525 Śvet. 1. 14 [Brahma is hidden] see **535**.

526 Śvet. 2. 8—15 [rules for Yoga] cf. Kaṭha 6. 10—17; Maitri 6. 18—30; and esp. BhG. 6. 10—26; 5. 27—28; see also Chānd. 8. 15. With *same śucau* Śvet. 2. 10a cf. Maitri 6. 30 init.; Chānd. 8. 15 (*śucau deśe*). With the 'sixfold Yoga' of Maitri 6. 18 cf. Patañjali's Yoga-sūtras **2. 29**.

527 Śvet. 2. 9c [chariot yoked with vicious horses] clearly an allusion to Kaṭha 3. 3—5; see **359**.

528 Śvet. 2. 12b [earth, water, fire, air, ether] the same cpd. recurs Śvet. 6. 2d; cf. Maitri 6. 4; BhG. 7. 4; and also MBh. 3. 210. 17 (C. 13914); 3. 211. 3 (C. 13922); 12. 311. 10 (C. 11578).

529 Śvet. 2. 15d = Śvet. 1. 8d; 4. 16d; 5. 13d; 6. 13d.

530 Śvet. 2. 16 [VS. 32. 4] = (var.) Mahānār. 1. 13 (Ātharv. rec. 2. 1). *pratyañ janās tiṣṭhati* Śvet. 2. 16d = Śvet. 3. 2c.

531 Śvet. 3. 1d see **541**.

532 Śvet. 3. 2d [creation and reabsorption of the world and of all beings] cf. Tait. 3. 1; Muṇḍ. 2. 1. 1; Śvet. 4. 1a—c; Maitri 6. 15, 17; BhG. 8. 18—19; cf. also MBh. 5. 44. 30 (C. 1713); Manusmṛti 1. 52, 57; Kumārasambhava 2. 8.

---

[8] On quotations from and allusions to Kaṭha in Śvet. see D. p. 289; on parallels between Śvet. and MBh. see Hopkins, *Great Epic*, p. 28.

533 Śvet. 3. 3 [RV. 10. 81. 3 (var.)] = (var.) Mahānār. 1. 14 (Ātharv. rec. 2. 2).

534 Śvet. 3. 4 = (var.) Śvet. 4. 12; Mahānār. 10. 19 (Ātharv. rec. 10. 3). Pāda d recurs as Śvet. 4. 1d. On *viśvādhipo* (pāda b) see **96.**

535 Śvet. 3. 7b [Brahma hidden in all things] cf. Kaṭha 5. 6b; Muṇḍ. 2. 2. 1a (⇕ Maitri 6. 27); Śvet. 1. 14; 6. 11.

536 Śvet. 3. 7c see **553.**

537 Śvet. 3. 8c—d [VS. 31. 18] = Śvet. 6. 15c—d. Śvet. 3. 8b = BhG. 8. 9d; see **787.**

538 Śvet. 3. 9 = Mahānār. 10. 20 (Ātharv. rec. 10. 4). On the 'tree establisht in heaven' see **388.**

539 Śvet. 3. 10b *anāmayam* recurs as an epithet of Brahma-Ātman at Maitri 6. 26.

540 Śvet. 3. 10c—d = Bṛh. 4. 4. 14c—d. On pāda c see also **541.**

541 Śvet. 3. 13a—b [person of the size of a thumb, seated in the heart of creatures] = Kaṭha 6. 17a—b; cf. Kaṭha 4. 12a; 4. 13a; 5. 3c (*madhye vāmanam āsīnaṃ*); Śvet. 5. 8a; Maitri 6. 38 end; cf. also MBh. 3. 297. 17 (C. 16763); 5. 46. 15, 27 (C. 1764, 1786); for *aṅguṣṭhamātraḥ puruṣaḥ* see also MBh. 12. 284. 175a (C. 10450a) and cf. *prādeśamātraḥ puruṣaḥ* MBh. 12. 200. 22c (C. 7351c). Śvet. 3. 13b—d = 4. 17b—d. Śvet. 3. 13c—d = Kaṭha 6. 9c—d [see esp. **390**]; with pāda c cf. MBh. 12. 240. 15 (C. 8748). Śvet. 3. 13d recurs also as Bṛh. 4. 4. 14c; Śvet. 3. 1d; 3. 10c; cf. 4. 20d.

542 Śvet. 3. 16, 17a—b = BhG. 13. 13, 14a—b; see **805.**

543 Śvet. 3. 18 = (var.) MBh. 12. 240. 32 (C. 8765). *navadvāre pure dehī* = BhG. 5. 13; cf. *puram ekādaśadvāram* Kaṭha 5. 1a. (For other epic parallels see Hopkins, *Great Epic,* p. 166 and n. 3.) See also **231.**

544 Śvet. 3. 20 [TA. 10. 10. 1] = Mahānār. 10. 1 (Ātharv. rec. 8. 3); = (var.) Kaṭha 2. 20; ⇕ MBh. 12. 240. 30 (C. 8763). The phrase *aṇor aṇīyān* (pāda a) recurs also BhG. 8. 9b; MBh. 5. 46. 31 (C. 1790). On the doctrine of *prasāda* see **354.**

545 Śvet. 4. 1 [creation and reabsorption of the world] see **532.** Pāda d recurs Śvet. 3. 4; see **534.**

546 Śvet. 4. 5 = (var.) Mahānār. 10. 5 (Ātharv. rec. 9. 2). Cf. *ābhāti śuklam iva lohitam ivātho kṛṣṇam* MBh. 5. 44. 25 (C. 1709); also MBh. 12. 302. 46 (C. 11259).

547 Śvet. 4. 6 [RV. 1. 164. 20] = Muṇḍ. 3. 1. 1.

548 Śvet. 4. 7 = Muṇḍ. 3. 1. 2.

549 Śvet. 4. 11a *yo yoniṃ yonim adhitiṣṭhaty eko* see **412**.

550 Śvet. 4. 11b = Mahānār. 1. 2a.

551 Śvet. 4. 11c—d = (var.) Kaṭha 1. 17c—d.

552 Śvet. 4. 12 = (var.) Śvet. 3. 4; Mahānār. 10. 19 (Ātharv. rec. 10. 3).

553 Śvet. 4. 14 = (var.) Śvet. 5. 13. Pāda c recurs also as 3. 7c; 4. 16c.

554 Śvet. 4. 16 d = Śvet. 1. 8 d; 2. 15 d; 5. 13 d; 6. 13 d.

555 Śvet. 4. 17b—d see **541**.

556 Śvet. 4. 18a [no day or night] see **156**.

557 Śvet. 4. 18c [Sāvitrī stanza] see **130**.

558 Śvet. 4. 19 [VS. 32. 2c—d, 3a—b; TA. 10. 1. 2] = Mahānār. 1. 10; ♀ MBh. 12. 240. 26 (C. 8759).

559 Śvet. 4. 20 = (var.) Kaṭha 6. 9; Mahānār. 1. 11.

560 Śvet. 5. 2a = Śvet. 4. 11a; see **412**. With 5. 2c—d cf. 4. 12c.

561 Śvet. 5. 5a [the One as the source of all] see **412**.

562 Śvet. 5. 5c cf. the similar line Śvet. **6. 4**b.

563 Śvet. 5. 7, 12 [acts determine one's reincarnate status] see **192**.

564 Śvet. 5. 7c [three paths] cf. Śvet. 1. 4d.

565 Śvet. 5. 8a [of the size of a thumb] see **541**.

566 Śvet. 5. 13 = (var.) Śvet. 4. 14. Pāda c recurs also as 3. 7c; 4. 16c. Pāda d = 1. 8d; 2. 15d; 4. 16d; 6. 13d.

567 Śvet. 6. 1a—b *svabhāvam eke . . . kālaṃ tathānye* cf. Śvet. 1. 2a.

568 Śvet. 6. 2 [earth, water, fire, air, ether] see **528**. Pāda b = 6. 16 b.

569 Śvet. 6. 3c [numerical allusions to Sāṃkhya terms] see **522**.

570 Śvet. 6. 4b cf. the similar line Śvet. 5. 5c.

571 Śvet. 6. 5b *paras trikālād* cf. *trikālātītaṃ* Māṇḍ. 1.

572 Śvet. 6. 6a [the world-tree] see **388**.

573 Śvet. 6. 10b [spider and thread analogy for creation] see **27**.

574 Śvet. 6.11 [the one divinity hidden in all things] see **535**.
575 Śvet. 6.12 = (var.) Kaṭha 5.12; see also Kaṭha 5.13c—d.
576 Śvet. 6.13a—b = Kaṭha 5.13a—b. On Śvet. 6.13d see **524**.
577 Śvet. 6.14 = Kaṭha 5.15; Muṇḍ. 2.2.10. See **387**.
578 Śvet. 6.15c—d [VS. 31.18] = Śvet. 3.8c—d.
579 Śvet. 6.16 *kṣetrajña* see **804**. Śvet. 6.16b = 6.2b.
580 Śvet. 6.19c [Brahma a bridge to immortality] see **98**.
581 Śvet. 6.21a [doctrine of *prasāda*] see **354**.
582 Śvet. 6.22 [restrictions on imparting mystic knowledge] see **133**.

583[9] Maitri 1.2 [smokeless fire] see **658**.
584 Maitri 1.2 [ignorance of Ātman confest] cf. Chānd. 7.1.3.
585 Maitri 1.2 [question declared difficult; another choice advised] cf. Kaṭha 1.21b—c.
586 Maitri 1.3 [pessimistic description of the human body] cf. Maitri 3.4; also Manusmṛti 6.76—77 = MBh. 12. 329.42—43 (C. 12463—4); Viṣṇusmṛti 96.43—53.
587 Maitri 1.3 [dissatisfaction with aspects of human life] cf. Manusmṛti 6.62; see also Kaṭha 1.26; and cf. in general Viṣṇusmṛti 96.27ff.; Yājñavalkīya Dharmasūtras 3.63—64.
588 Maitri 2.2 *eṣa samprasādo — etad brahmeti* see **237**.
589 Maitri 2.3—4 [the body like a cart] see **359**.
590 Maitri 2.4 *śuddhaḥ pūtaḥ — sve mahimni tiṣṭhaty* = Maitri 6.28. This passage is referred to in 6.31: *yo 'yaṃ śuddhaḥ pūtaḥ śūnyaḥ śāntādilakṣaṇoktaḥ*. Cf. *sve mahimni [pratiṣṭhitaḥ]* Chānd. 7.24.1; *sve mahimni tiṣṭhamānaṃ* Maitri 6.38.
591 Maitri 2.5 *so 'ṃśo 'yam — prajāpatir* = Maitri 5.2. The group of terms *saṃkalpādhyavasāyābhimāna-* recurs (transposed) in 6.10 and 6.30. On the term *kṣetrajña* see **804**.
592 Maitri 2.6 [Prajāpati alone in the beginning] see **7**.
593 Maitri 2.6 [explanation of *vyāna*] cf. Chānd. 1.3.3.

---

[9] For an elaborate discussion of parallels between Maitri and MBh. see Hopkins, *Great Epic*, p. 33—46; see also D. p. 312—313.

594 Maitri 2.6 *yo 'yaṃ sthaviṣṭho dhātur annasya* cf. Chānd. 6. 5. 1.

595 Maitri 2.6 [etymological explanation of *samāna*] cf. Praśna 3. 5; 4. 4.

596 Maitri 2.6 [universal fire; sound heard on stopping the ears] quoted from Bṛh. 5. 9; see esp. **117.**

597 Maitri 2.6 *nihito guhāyām* see **349.**

598 Maitri 2.6 *manomayaḥ — ākāśātmā* = Chānd. 3. 14. 2. See **656.**

599 Maitri 2.6 *khānīmāni bhittvā* cf. Kaṭha 4. 1a.

600 Maitri 2.6 *pañcabhī raśmibhir viṣayān atti* = Maitri 6. 31.

601 Maitri 2.6 end [the body as a chariot] see **359.**

602 Maitri 2.6 end [the body like a potter's wheel] cf. Maitri 3. 3. See also **522.**

603 Maitri 2.7 *sitāsitaiḥ karmaphalair anabhibhūta iva* see **97.**

604 Maitri 2.7 *prekṣakavad avasthitaḥ svasthaś ca* cf. *prekṣakavad avasthitaḥ susthaḥ* Sāṃkhyakārikā 65.

605 Maitri 3.1 [pairs of opposites] cf. Maitri 3. 2; 6. 29; BhG. 7. 27—28.

606 Maitri 3.2 [acts determine one's reincarnate status] see **192.**

607 Maitri 3.2 [water on a lotus-leaf] cf. Chānd. 4. 14. 3; BhG. 5. 10; see also MBh. 3. 213. 20b (C. 13978d); 12. 187. 24d (C. 6922d); 12. 242. 18b (C. 8821b); and Dhammapada 401.

608 Maitri 3.2 *guṇaughair uhyamānaḥ — khacaraḥ* = Maitri 6. 30.

609 Maitri 3.2 *nibadhnāty ātmanā ''tmānam* cf. *badhnāty ātmānam ātmanā* Sāṃkhyakārikā 63.

610 Maitri 3.3 *yaḥ kartā so 'yaṃ vai bhūtātmā* etc. cf. Manusmṛti 12. 12.

611 Maitri 3.3 [analogy of the transformation of iron] cf. Bṛh. 4. 4. 4.

612 Maitri 3.3 *caturjālaṃ caturdaśavidhaṃ caturaśītidhā pariṇatam* see **522.**

613 Maitri 3.3 [wheel driven by the potter] cf. Maitri 2.6 end.

614 Maitri 3.4 [pessimistic description of the human body] see **586.**

615 Maitri 3. 5 [characteristics of *tamas* and *rajas*] see **810.**

616 Maitri 4. 4 end [chariot-rider] see **359.**

617 Maitri 4. 5 [Agni, Vāyu, Āditya] see **153.**

618 Maitri 4. 6 *brahma khalv idaṃ vāva sarvam* = (var.) Chānd. 3. 14. 1.

619 Maitri 5. 2 *so 'ṃśo 'yam — prajāpatir* = Maitri 2. 5; see esp. **591.** The text calls attention to this reiteration; *asya prāg uktā etās tanavaḥ.*

620 Maitri 5. 2 [the Ātman manifold] cf. Chānd. 7. 26. 2; Maitri 6. 26 end.

621 Maitri 6.1 *atha ya eṣo — puruṣo* = Chānd. 1.6.6; see **149.**

622 Maitri 6. 3 *dve — rūpe mūrtaṃ cāmūrtaṃ ca* see **32.**

623 Maitri 6. 3 *sa tredhā ''tmānaṃ vyakuruta* = Bṛh. 1. 2. 3.

624 Maitri 6. 3 *sarvam idam otam protaṃ caiva* see **50.**

625 Maitri 6. 4 *atha khalu — eṣa praṇava* = Chānd. 1. 5. 1.

626 Maitri 6. 4 *praṇavākhyam — vimṛtyuṃ* recurs with the addition of *viśokam* at Maitri 6. 25; 7. 5.

627 Maitri 6. 4 *nihitaṃ guhāyām* see **349.**

628 Maitri 6. 4 [the Lone Fig-tree with root above] see **388.**

629 Maitri 6. 4 [ether, air, fire, water, earth] see **528.**

630 Maitri 6. 4 *tasmād om ity — upāsīta* see **726.**

631 Maitri 6.4 *etad evākṣaram* [stanza] = (var.) Kaṭha 2. 16.

632 Maitri 6. 5 [the higher and the lower Brahma] quoted from Praśna 5. 2; see **498.**

633 Maitri 6. 6 [Prajāpati produced *bhūr, bhuvaḥ, svar*] see **180.**

634 Maitri 6. 7 [Sāvitrī stanza] see **130.**

635 Maitri 6. 7 [the All-pervader as agent in the bodily functions] cf. Praśna 4. 9.

636 Maitri 6. 7 [duality of knowledge transcended] cf. Bṛh. 2. 4. 14 = 4. 5. 15; also 4. 3. 31.

637 Maitri 6. 8 *eṣa hi khalv ātmeśānaḥ — nārāyaṇo* recurs with the addition of *acyuto* in Maitri 7. 7.

638 Maitri 6.8 *eṣa vāva jijñāsitavyo 'nveṣṭavyaḥ* ⇔ Chānd. 8. 7. 3; cf. Chānd. 7. 23 (etc.); 8. 1. 1.

639 Maitri 6. 8 *viśvarūpaṃ hariṇaṃ* [stanza] = Praśna 1. 8.

640 Maitri 6. 9 *adbhiḥ purastāt* [and infra *upariṣṭāt*] *paridadhati* ⇔ Chānd. 5. 2. 2.

641 Maitri 6. 9 ['Hail!' to *prāṇa, apāna,* etc.] cf. Chānd. 5. 19—23.

642 Maitri 6.10 [the soul called 'the enjoyer'] see **360**.

643 Maitri 6.10 [fourteenfold course] see **522**.

644 Maitri 6.10 *saṃkalpādhyavasāyābhimānā* see **591**.

645 Maitri 6.10 [food and the eater of food] cf. Bṛh. 1.4.6.

646 Maitri 6.11 *na yady aśnāty — draṣṭā bhavati* = (var.) Chānd. 7.9.

647 Maitri 6.11 *annād vai — antataḥ* = Tait. 2.2a—d. See **728**.

648 Maitri 6.12 *annād bhūtāni — ucyate* = Tait. 2.2k—n. See **728**.

649 Maitri 6.13 with the series *anna, prāṇa, manas, vijñāna, ānanda* cf. the series *annarasamaya* to *ānandamaya* in Tait. 2.2—5. See also **690**.

650 Maitri 6.14 end *kālo mūrtir amūrtimān* see **32**.

651 Maitri 6.15 [two forms of Brahma] see **32**.

652 Maitri 6.15 [origin, growth, and death of creatures] see **532**.

653 Maitri 6.15 *kālaḥ pacati bhūtāni* [stanza] = (var.) MBh. 12.240.25 (C. 8758). Pāda d = BhG. 15.1d. Pāda a recurs at MBh. 11.2.24 (C. 69).

654 Maitri 6.16 *ādityo brahmety* = Chānd. 3.19.1.

655 Maitri 6.17 *brahma ha vā idam agra āsīd eko* see **10** and cf. **7**.

656 Maitri 6.17 (*eṣa*) *ākāśātmā* this epithet is found besides only at Chānd. 3.14.2 (quoted Maitri 2.6) and, in a different application, at Kauṣ. 2.14 (9). Cf. *ākāśa-śarīram brahma* Tait. 1.6.2.

657 Maitri 6.17 [creation and reabsorption of the world] see **532**.

658 Maitri 6.17 [the Supreme like a smokeless fire] cf. Kaṭha 4.13b; MBh. 12.250.7 (C. 9044); 12.306.20 (C. 11387). The simile occurs in another connection at Maitri 1.2.

659 Maitri 6.17 [digestive fire in the stomach] cf. Bṛh. 5.9 (quoted Maitri 2.6).

660 Maitri 6.17 *yaś caiṣo 'gnau — sa eṣa eka* = Maitri 7.7. Cf. Chānd. 3.13.7.

661 Maitri 6.18—30 [rules for Yoga] see **526**.

662 Maitri 6.18 *yadā paśyan — vihāya* [stanza, pādas a—c] = (var.) Muṇḍ. 3.1.3a—c; see **449**. On pāda d of this stanza see **464**.

663 Maitri 6.19 [fourth, or superconscious, state] see **519.**
664 Maitri 6.19 *tac ca liṅgaṃ nirāśrayam* [stanza, pāda d] cf. *nirāśrayaṃ liṅgam* Sāṃkhyakārikā 41.
665 Maitri 6.20 *tadā ''tmanā ''tmānaṃ dṛṣṭvā nirātmā bhavati* ✥ MBh. 3. 213. 27c—d (C. 13986c—d).
666 Maitri 6.20 *cittasya hi prasādena* [stanza] = (var.) MBh. 3.213.24 (C. 13983); 12.247.10 (C. 8960); recurs Maitri 6.34. (For discussion see Hopkins, *Great Epic*, p. 42—43.)
667 Maitri 6.21 *ūrdhvagā nāḍī suṣumnākhyā* see **64.**
668 Maitri 6.21 *prāṇasaṃcāriṇī* see **486.**
669 Maitri 6.21 *tālvantarvicchinnā* see **266.**
670 Maitri 6.21 *tayā — ūrdhvam utkramet* see **249.**
671 Maitri 6.22—23 [the higher and the lower Brahma] see **498.**
672 Maitri 6.22 [the spider and his thread] see **27.**
673 Maitri 6.22 [sound heard on stopping the ears] see **117.**
674 Maitri 6.22 [ether within the heart] see **265.**
675 Maitri 6.22 [unified condition of honey] see **209.**
676 Maitri 6.22 *dve brahmaṇī veditavye* [stanza] = MBh. 12. 233. 30 (C. 8540—1); pādas c—d are quoted in Sarvadarśanasaṃgraha p. 147, l. 2 (Bibl. Ind., Calcutta, 1858).
677 Maitri 6.23 *tac chāntam — viṣṇusaṃjñitam* = Maitri 7.3; the words *acalam — viṣṇusaṃjñitaṃ* recur also in Maitri 6.38. See also **362.**
678 Maitri 6.24 [bow and arrow analogy for Yoga] see **430.**
679 Maitri 6.24 [what is not enveloped in darkness] cf. **156.**
680 Maitri 6.24 [Brahma shines in sun, moon, etc.] see **387.**
681 Maitri 6.25 *praṇavākhyam — viśokaṃ* recurs at Maitri 7.5 and, without the last word, at 6.4; see also **235.** Cf. Muṇḍ. 3. 2. 9.
682 Maitri 6.26 *anāmaye 'gnau* see **539.**
683 Maitri 6.26 *viṣṇoḥ paramam padaṃ* see **362.**
684 Maitri 6.26 *aparimitadhā cātmānaṃ vibhajya* etc. see **227.**
685 Maitri 6.26 *vahneś ca yadvat* [stanza] = Maitri 6.31. On the issuance of sparks from fire as an analogy of creation see **421.**

686 Maitri 6.27 [warmth of the body as the heat of Brahma] cf. Chānd. 3.13.8 and see **117**.

687 Maitri 6.27 *āviḥ san nabhasi nihitaṃ* cf. Muṇḍ. 2.2.1 a; see **535**.

688 Maitri 6.27, 28 [ether within the heart] see **265**.

689 Maitri 6.28 [bow and arrow analogy for Yoga] see **430**.

690 Maitri 6.28 [dispersal of the fourfold sheath of Brahma] ⊕ Maitri 6.38. The adj. *caturjāla* occurs also in 3.3. On the 'fourfold sheath' see Tait. 2.1—4 (*annarasamaya, prāṇamaya, manomaya,* and *vijñānamaya ātman*).

691 Maitri 6.28 *śuddhaḥ pūtaḥ — sve mahimni tiṣṭhati* see **590**.

692 Maitri 6.28 [looking down on a rolling chariot-wheel] cf. Kauṣ. 1.4 end.

693 Maitri 6.28 *ṣaḍbhir māsais* [stanza] ⊕ MBh. 14.19. 66c—d (C. 598); cf. 12.241.32c—d (C. 8799). With *nityayuktasya dehinaḥ* (pāda b) cf. BhG. 8.14d. (For discussion see Hopkins, *Great Epic,* p. 45—46.)

694 Maitri 6.29 [pairs of opposites] cf. Maitri 3.1, 2; BhG. 7.27—28.

695 Maitri 6.29 [restrictions on imparting mystic knowledge] see **133**.

696 Maitri 6.30 *śucau deśe* see **526**.

697 Maitri 6.30 [meditation upon the Real, sacrifice to the Real] cf. Maitri 6.9.

698 Maitri 6.30 *puruṣo 'dhyavasāyasaṃkalpābhimānaliṅgo* see **591**.

699 Maitri 6.30 *manasā hy eva paśyati — mana eva* = Bṛh. 1.5.3.

700 Maitri 6.30 *guṇaughair uhyamānaḥ — khacaro* = Maitri 3.2.

701 Maitri 6.30 *atra hi sarve kāmāḥ samāhitā* see **234**.

702 Maitri 6.30 *yadā pañcāvatiṣṭhante* [stanza] see **391**.

703 Maitri 6.30 [northern course to Brahma] see **127**.

704 Maitri 6.30 *dīpavad yaḥ sthito hṛdi* see **265**.

705 Maitri 6.30 *sitāsitāḥ — mṛdulohitāḥ* see **71**.

706 Maitri 6.30 *ūrdhvam ekaḥ sthitas teṣāṃ* see **64**.

707 Maitri 6.30 *yo bhittvā sūryamaṇḍalam — parāṃ gatim* see **249**.

708 Maitri 6.30 *yad asyānyad raśmiśataṃ — prapadyate* see **247, 250.**

709 Maitri 6.31 [the soul as agent in the senses] see **333.**

710 Maitri 6.31 *pañcabhī raśmibhir viṣayān atti* = Maitri 2.6.

711 Maitri 6.31 *yo 'yaṃ śuddhaḥ — -lakṣaṇoktaḥ* see **590.**

712 Maitri 6.31 *vāk śrotraṃ cakṣur manaḥ prāṇa ity eke* cf. Kena 2; see **333.**

713 Maitri 6.31 *dhṛtiḥ smṛtiḥ prajñānam ity eke* cf. Ait. 5.2.

714 Maitri 6.31 *vahneś ca yadvat* [stanza] = Maitri 6.26. See **421.**

715 Maitri 6.32 *sarve prāṇāḥ — satyasya satyam iti* = (var.) Bṛh. 2.1.20.

716 Maitri 6.32 [literature-list] see **41.**

717 Maitri 6.34 [Sāvitrī stanza] see **130.**

718 Maitri 6.34 *cittam eva hi saṃsāraṃ* [stanza] see **192.** Pādas c—d = (var.) MBh. 14.51.27c—d (C. 1451); see Hopkins, *Great Epic,* p. 42—43.

719 Maitri 6.34 *cittasya hi prasādena* [stanza] see **666.**

720 Maitri 6.35 *hiraṇmayena pātreṇa* [stanza] = (var.) Bṛh. 5.15; Īśā 15.

721 Maitri 6.35 [Person in the sun] see **149.**

722 Maitri 6.35 [nectar in the sun] cf. Chānd. 3.1.2; Tait. 1.10.

723 Maitri 6.35 [simile of the solution of salt] see **210.**

724 Maitri 6.35 *atra hi sarve kāmāḥ samāhitā ity* see **234.**

725 Maitri 6.36, stanza [the cosmic egg] see **173.**

726 Maitri 6.37 *tasmād om ity — tejas* = Maitri 7.11. *tasmād — upāsīta* recurs also at Maitri 6.4. Cf. BhG. 17.24 [see **818**]; also **143.**

727 Maitri 6.37 *tat tredhā — prāṇe* = Maitri 7.11.

728 Maitri 6.37 *agnau prāstā* [stanza] = Manusmṛti 3.76; = (var.) MBh. 12.263.11 (C. 9406—7); ⟡ BhG. 3.14; cf. Tait. 2.2 (quoted Maitri 6.11, 12); Praśna 1.14.

729 Maitri 6.38 [cleaving the fourfold sheath of Brahma] see **690.**

730 Maitri 6.38 *acalam — viṣṇusaṃjñitaṃ* see **677.**

731 Maitri 6.38 *sve mahimni tiṣṭhamānaṃ* see **590.**

732 Maitri 6.38 end [person of the size of a thumb] see **541.**

733 Maitri 6.38 end *atra hi sarve kāmāḥ samāhitā ity* see **234**.

734 Maitri 7.3 *tac chāntam — viṣṇusaṃjñitaṃ* see **677**.

735 Maitri 7.5 *praṇavākhyam — viśokam* see **681**.

736 Maitri 7.7 *ātmā 'ntarhṛdaye 'ṇīyān* see **165**.

737 Maitri 7.7 *asminn otā imāḥ prajāḥ* see **50**.

738 Maitri 7.7 *eṣa ātmā — satyakāma* see **235**.

739 Maitri 7.7 *eṣa parameśvara — setur vidharaṇa* see **98**.

740 Maitri 7.7 *eṣa hi khalv ātmeśānaḥ — nārāyaṇaḥ* see **637**.

741 Maitri 7.7 *yaś caiṣo 'gnau — sa eṣa ekaḥ* see **660**.

742 Maitri 7.9 *dūram ete* [stanza] = (var.) Kaṭha 2.4.

743 Maitri 7.9 *vidyāṃ cāvidyāṃ ca* [stanza] = Īśā 11.

744 Maitri 7.9 *avidyāyām* [stanza] = (var.) Kaṭha 2.5; Muṇḍ. 1.2.8.

745 Maitri 7.10 [instruction of gods and devils] cf. Chānd. 8.7—8.

746 Maitri 7.11 *tat tredhā — prāṇa* = Maitri 6.37.

747 Maitri 7.11 [simile of the solution of salt] see **210**.

748 Maitri 7.11 *tasmād om ity — tejaḥ* see **726**.

749 Maitri 7.11, stanza 1 [Indra and Virāj] see **61**.

750 Maitri 7.11, stanza 2 *samāgamas tayor — suṣau* cf. **265**.

751 Maitri 7.11, stanza 2 *tallohitasyātra piṇḍa* ≑ Bṛh. 4.2.3.

752 Maitri 7.11, stanza 3 *hṛdayād āyatā tāvac cakṣuṣy asmin pratiṣṭhitā* see **64**.

753 Maitri 7.11, stanza 6 *na paśyan — sarvaśaḥ* = (var.) Chānd. 7.26.2.

754 Maitri 7.11, stanza 7 [fourth, or superconscious, state] see **519**.

755[10] BhG. 2.13 = Viṣṇusmṛti 20.49.

756 BhG. 2.17b *yena sarvam idaṃ tatam* = BhG. 8.22d; 18.46b; MBh. 12.240.20d (C. 8753d); cf. BhG. 9.4; 11.38.

757 BhG. 2.19, 20 = (var.) Kaṭha 2.19, 18. With BhG. 2.20d cf. *na vadhenāsya hanyate* Chānd. 8.1.5; 8.10.2, 4.

758 BhG. 2.22 ≑ Viṣṇusmṛti 20.50.

---

[10] No note has been taken of the recurrence of a number of pādas of purely formulaic character, and parallels between parts of BhG. are recorded under the first of the passages only.

759 BhG. 2. 23—25, 27, 28 = (var.) Viṣṇusmṛti 20. 51—53, 29, 48.
760 BhG. 2. 29 cf. Kaṭha 2. 7.
761 BhG. 2. 46 = (var.) MBh. 5. 46. 26 (C. 1785).
762 BhG. 2. 61a—b ⇕ BhG. 6. 14c—d.
763 BhG. 2. 70 = Viṣṇusmṛti 72. 7.
764 BhG. 2. 71c *nirmamo nirahaṃkāraḥ* = BhG. 12. 13c; see **803**.
765 BhG. 3. 13 cf. BhG. 4. 31a and see Manusmṛti 3. 118.
766 BhG. 3. 14 ⇕ Maitri 6. 37, stanza; see **728**.
767 BhG. 3. 23c—d = BhG. 4. 11c—d.
768 BhG. 3. 35a—b = BhG. 18. 47a—b.
769 BhG. 3. 42 ⇕ Kaṭha 3. 10; see esp. **363**.
770 BhG. 4. 16d = BhG. 9. 1d.
771 BhG. 4. 21c—d *karma kurvan nāpnoti kilbiṣam* = BhG. 18. 47c—d.
772 BhG. 4. 35c—d *yena bhūtāny . . . drakṣyasy ātmany* see **402**.
773 BhG. 5. 10 [water on a lotus-leaf] see **607**.
773a BhG. 5. 13 [nine-gated citadel] see **543**.
774 BhG. 5. 18 = (var.) MBh. 12. 240. 19 (C. 8752).
775 BhG. 6. 5c—d = (var.) MBh. 5. 34. 64c—d (C. 1158c—d).
776 BhG. 6. 7c, d = BhG. 12. 18c, b.
777 BhG. 6. 10—26 [rules for Yoga] see **526** and note **762**.
778 BhG. 6. 23a—b = (var.) MBh. 3. 213. 33c—d (13992c—d).
779 BhG. 6. 29 ⇕ Īśā 6; see esp. **402**.
780 BhG. 6. 35 cf. Patañjali's Yoga-sūtras 1. 12.
781 BhG. 6. 45 *tato yāti parāṃ gatim* = BhG. 13. 28; 16. 22; cf. 8. 13; 9. 32; Maitri 6. 30 [**707**]; and see **792, 249**.
782 BhG. 7. 4 [earth, water, fire, air, ether] see **528**; cf. also **522**.
783 BhG. 7. 10d = BhG. 10. 36b.
784 BhG. 7. 24 *param bhāvam ajānanto mama* = BhG. 9. 11.
785 BhG. 7. 27—28 [pairs of opposites] cf. Maitri 3. 1, 2; 6. 29.
786 BhG. 8. 5—6 [last thoughts determine state after death] cf. Chānd. 3. 14. 1; Praśna 3. 10. Cf. in general **192, 457**.
787 BhG. 8. 9d = Śvet. 3. 8b. The phrase *tamasaḥ parastāt* recurs Muṇḍ. 2. 2. 6; MBh. 5. 44. 29a (C. 1712a); cf. *tamasas pāraṃ* Chānd. 7. 26. 2. On *aṇor aṇīyāṃsam* in pāda b see **544**.

788 BhG. 8. 11 ⟠ Kaṭha 2. 15.

789 BhG. 8. 14d *nityayuktasya yoginaḥ* see **693**.

790 BhG. 8. 17 ⟠ Manusmṛti 1. 73.

791 BhG. 8. 18—19 [creation and reabsorption of beings] see **532**.

792 BhG. 8. 21b *tam āhuḥ paramāṃ gatim* = Kaṭha 6.10d *(tām)*; see **391** and cf. **781**.

793 BhG. 8. 21c—d ⟠ BhG. 15. 6c—d.

794 BhG. 8. 24—26 [course to the Brahma-world and to the lunar world] see **127, 128**.

795 BhG. 9. 5b = BhG. 11. 8d.

796 BhG. 9. 21 [rebirth when merit is exhausted] cf. Muṇḍ. 1. 2. 10 and see **128**.

797 BhG. 9. 32 = (var.) MBh. 14. 19. 61 (C. 593).

798 BhG. 9. 34 ⟠ BhG. 18. 65.

799 BhG. 10. 35b [Gāyatrī meter] cf. Bṛh. 5. 14. 1—7; Chānd. 3. 12.

800 BhG. 11. 18b = BhG. 11. 38b.

801 BhG. 11. 25d = BhG. 11. 45d.

802 BhG. 11. 34 = Kauṣ. 2. 11 (7).

803 BhG. 12. 13 cf. MBh. 12. 237. 34 (C. 8679—80). BhG. 12. 13c recurs as 2. 71c; cf. also 18. 53 [**816**].

804 BhG. 13. 1—2 = (var.) Viṣṇusmṛti 96. 97—98. The term *kṣetrajña* occurs also at Śvet. 6. 16c; Maitri 2. 5.

805 BhG. 13. 13, 14a—b = Śvet. 3. 16, 17a—b. BhG. 13. 13 = MBh. 12. 240. 29 (C. 8762); = (var.) MBh. 12. 302. 17 (C. 11230); 14. 19. 49 (C. 580—1); 14. 40. 4 (C. 1087).

806 BhG. 13. 14—18 = (var.) Viṣṇusmṛti 97. 17—21.

807 BhG. 13. 15 ⟠ Īśā 5; cf. Muṇḍ. 2. 1. 2b.

808 BhG. 13. 19 cf. MBh. 12. 217. 7c (C. 7848c).

809 BhG. 13. 30 = MBh. 12. 17. 23 (var. in C. 12. 533); cf. Kaṭha 6. 6.

810 BhG. 14. 5—18 [*sattva, rajas, tamas*] cf. Maitri 3. 5; see also Manusmṛti 12. 24—40; Yājñavalkīya Dharmasūtras 3. 137—139; MBh. 12. 194. 29—36 (C. 7094—7102); 12. 219. 25—31 (C. 7955—61).

811 BhG. 14. 18 cf. MBh. 12. 314. 3—4 (C. 11637—8).

812 BhG. 14. 21 [crossing over the Guṇas] cf. MBh. 12. 251. 22 (C. 9085) and see Patañjali's Yoga-sūtras 4. 32.

813 BhG. 15. 1—3 [eternal fig-tree with roots above] cf. Kaṭha 6. 1; Maitri 6. 4; see also Śvet. 3. 9 c; 6. 6 a. BhG. 15. 1d = Maitri 6. 15, stanza, pāda d.

814 BhG. 15. 6, 12 see **387.**

815 BhG. 15. 8 see **320.**

816 BhG. 16. 18 *ahaṃkāram — krodhaṃ* = BhG. 18. 53.

817 BhG. 16. 21 = Viṣṇusmṛti 33. 6.

818 BhG. 17. 24 cf. Āpastambīya Dharma-sūtras 1. 4. 13. 7 and see **143, 726.**

819 BhG. 18. 67 [restrictions on imparting mystic knowledge] see **133.**

TRACES OF EARLY ACQUAINTANCE IN EUROPE WITH THE BOOK OF ENOCH

NATHANIEL SCHMIDT

CORNELL UNIVERSITY

To WHAT EXTENT the literature ascribed to Enoch was known in Europe during the early Christian centuries cannot be determined with certainty. The larger part of Ethiopic Enoch was extant in a Greek translation, as the Syncellus fragments and the Gizeh MSS show. There was also a Latin version, probably of the same portions, and no doubt made from the Greek. Twelve years ago ('The original language of the Parables of Enoch' in *Old Testament and Semitic Studies in Memory of W. R. Harper*, Chicago, 1908) I attempted to show that Book II, comprising chs. 37—71, was translated directly from the Aramaic, and that the strange silence of all Patristic writers as to this remarkable book, whose Christian coloring, at least in its present form, would have been especially tempting to them, renders it doubtful whether it was ever translated into Greek. Some eminent Aramaic scholars, among them Nöldeke, declared themselves convinced so far as my first contention was concerned, but hesitated to accept the *argumentum e silentio*. Charles, in *The Book of Enoch* (Oxford, 1912) and *Apocrypha and Pseudepigrapha of the Old Testament*, II (Oxford, 1913), criticises in detail both of these positions, and finds himself unable to accept either. I reserve for another place a more exhaustive consideration of his arguments than could be given in my articles on Enoch in *The New International Encyclopaedia* ed. 2 (New York, 1915) and the *Encyclopaedia Americana* (New York, 1918). The Slavonic Enoch was a translation of a Greek text which in its earliest form probably goes back to a Hebrew or Aramaic original. No MS. of the Greek text has yet been found, and it seems to have left no important traces in Byzantine literature, though it must have been read in Constantinople as well as in Alexandria. My conclusions in regard to the two recensions of Slavonic Enoch I have already presented to this Society.

The Hebrew Enoch is known to us partly from the *Sefer Hekaloth of R. Ishmael* (Lemberg, 1864), partly from the *Sefer Hekaloth or Book of Enoch,* published from a Munich MS. by Jellinek (Vienna, 1873). A more complete MS. still lies in the Bodleian waiting for the hand of a competent editor and translator. The Hebrew Enoch contains material that appears to have been drawn from both Ethiopic and Slavonic Enoch, possibly in their original Semitic form, as well as from other sources. It is significant that it reveals no signs of acquaintance with the Parables of Enoch. The fact that it is now in Hebrew does not prove that it was originally composed in this language. Books were sometimes translated from Aramaic into Hebrew, when the former had ceased to be the vernacular of the Jews. Kennicott, in his *Vetus Testamentum Hebraicum* II (Oxford, 1780), prints a Hebrew version of the Aramaic portions of Daniel. Aside from the Syncellus excerpts, the Latin fragments, the Hebrew Enoch, known almost exclusively in certain Jewish circles, and the Secrets of Enoch preserved among the Slavs, mediaeval Europe seems to have been ignorant of the works ascribed to the antediluvian patriarch.

But in the humanistic period indications begin to appear among Christian scholars in the western world of acquaintance at least with the existence of some books bearing the name of Enoch. It may not be without its value to pursue these traces. According to Fabricius (*Codex Pseudepigraphus Veteris Testamenti,* Hamburg, 1722, p. 215), it was said by many, on the testimony of Reuchlin, that Pico della Mirandola had purchased a copy of the book of Enoch for a large sum of money. This statement raises a number of questions to which, so far as I am aware, no consideration has yet been given by scholars. What is the nature of Reuchlin's testimony as regards Pico's purchase? Martin (*Le livre d'Énoch,* Paris, 1906, p. cxxxvii) remarks concerning the passage in Fabricius: 'Il ne dit pas où Reuchlin avance ce fait'. Again, does Pico himself say anything on the subject? If he actually bought a copy of the book of Enoch, what was the character of this work, and in what language was it written? What did Reuchlin know about this book, and had he any knowledge of Ethiopic? Finally, it may be of interest to inquire, though this question is not suggested by the words of Fabricius, why Potken, in writing to Reuchlin, spoke of the letters used by Prester John and his people as 'Chaldaean' or 'Chaldic', and why others continued to use these terms.

In Reuchlin's treatise 'De arte cabalistica', published in 1517 (appended to *Opera omnia Johannis Pici Mirandulae*, Basel, 1572), Simon, the Jew, does not question the possible survival of some such books as that of Enoch, but declares that he cannot afford, like Mirandola, to buy at great expense the seventy books of Ezra, among which it may have a place, even if these books had really survived, and were offered for sale. After mentioning that the books of Enoch and Abraham, our father, were cited by men worthy of faith and that others were referred to by Moses and Joshua, in the books of the Maccabees, and by Ezra, he continues: 'pari exemplo innumeri nostro seculo autores periere, tametsi non dubitamus superesse plurima, quae ipsi necdum uidimus, nec istam de me gloriam cum Mirandulo iactare possum, quod quae ille quondam Ezra de cabalisticis secretis septuaginta coscribere uolumina iussit, ea mihi summa impensa conquisierim, cui ne tantidem prope auri et argenti sit, quo eos libros, si superarent, ac offerentur licitari queam' (p. 3028).

Mirandola himself speaks of his purchase and indefatigable study of these seventy books which he unhesitatingly identifies as the seventy books Ezra had been ordered to deliver only to such as were wise among the people (*IV Esdras*, xiv, 46). In his 'Apologia', written in 1489 (*Opera omnia*, p. 178), he quotes this passage in IV Esdras, explains the transmission of secret knowledge, or Cabbala, from Moses to the time of Ezra, when it was 'in plures libros redacta', and adds: 'quos ego libros summa impensa mihi conquisitos (neque enim eos Hebraei Latinis nostris communicare uolunt) cum diligenter perlegerim, uidi' etc. In 'De hominis dignitate' (ib. p. 330) he relates how Pope Sixtus IV (1471—1484) had made great efforts to have them translated, and that at his death three of them had been rendered into Latin. He then declares: 'hos ego libros non mediocri impensa cum comparassem, summa diligentia, indefessis laboribus cum perlegissem, uidi in illis (testis est Deus) religionem non tam Mosaicam quam Christianam'. There can be no doubt that Pico secured an interesting set of books, counted the MSS. carefully to see that they were seventy in number, paid a large sum for them, and devoted much time to their study. But it may perhaps be suggested without discourtesy that he did not read them all. His solemn attestation refers to the Christian, rather than Mosaic, flavor he found in them, not without the aid of the allegorical, tropological, and anagogic methods to which he refers. Modern scholars sometimes make unexpected discoveries even in their own libraries. It is strange that he should have condemned the necromancers for the 'incantations and bestialities' they said they had from Solomon, Adam, and Enoch ('Apologia', p. 181), without confronting them with the authority of the Book of Enoch which he had in his own collection. For the catalogue raisonné of his cabalistic codices given by Gaffarel in 1651 (reprinted in Wolf, *Bibliotheca Hebraica*, I, Hamburg, 1715) in its account of the very first MS. presents extracts from the Book of Enoch. It is possible, therefore, that Pico's collection contained a copy of the Hebrew Enoch. But it is not inconceivable that, besides this book, or parts of it, there may also have been a copy of the Ethiopic Enoch. Gaffarel's list is not likely to have been complete, and would naturally not include any work he could not himself read.

Reuchlin refers directly to the Book of Enoch in *De verbo mirifico*, written in 1494 (Lyon, 1552, p. 92 f.) Here Sidonius lashes the gallows-birds who place splendid titles in front of the volumes they offer, falsely declaring that one is the Book of Enoch, another the Book of Solomon: 'suspendunt furciferi prae foribus uoluminum splendidos titulos et modo hunc esse librum Enoch, quem diuiniorem ante ceteros fuisse uetustas asseruit, modo illum Salomonis mentiuntur, facile indoctis auribus irrepentes'. He prefaces these remarks with the Horatian 'parturiunt montes, nascetur ridiculus mus'. Could he have maliciously included Pico among the 'indoctis'? It is evident that Reuchlin had heard before 1494 of a separate Book of Enoch being offered for sale. Was this the Hebrew or the Ethiopic Enoch? Or was it a late forgery on the basis of Josephus, as Reuchlin thought? His scepticism clearly led him too far afield; but there is no evidence to decide the question.

Johann Potken published at Rome in 1513 his *Alphabetum seu potius Syllabarium literarum Chaldaearum*, *Psalterium Chaldaeum*, etc. In a letter dated 25 Jan., 1515, he wrote to Reuchlin informing him that a very learned man, whose name and position he temporarily withheld, was preparing a dialogue in his (Reuchlin's) defense. 'Id nunc te scire sufficiat', he says, 'quod et latinus et graecus est, etiam quo ad hebraeam et babylonicam, hoc est vulgare chaldaicam, quam Hebraei Europam incolentes, suis, hoc est hebraeis, characteribus effigiant etiam a me Joanne literas veras chaldias, quibus Presbyter Johannes et sui in eorum sacris utuntur non ignaviter didicit' (*Johann Reuchlin's Briefwechsel, gesammelt und herausgegeben von Ludwig Geiger*, Tübingen, 1875, p. 236). The scholar referred to was Georgius Benignus, Nazarene archbishop. Under date of 13. Sept., 1516, Potken wrote again to Reuchlin: 'ero in te linguam ipsam Chaldiam docendo tuus Barnabanus' (ib. p. 258). In 1518 he published at Cologne *Psalterium in quatuor linguis: hebraea, graeca, chaldaea, latina.* Geiger's mistaken notion (*l. c.*, p. 258) that the Chaldaean language of which Potken spoke is what we now call Samaritan, which he supposed at that time was generally designated as 'Chaldiaca' in distinction from 'Chaldaica' or 'Chaldaea', must be due to the fact that he had not seen Potken's earlier edition of the Psalter, and cannot even have examined the Polyglot from whose colophon he quotes some sentences. A glance would have been sufficient to show that Potken's 'Chaldaean' or 'Chaldic' text is Ethiopic in script as well as language.

Geiger was amazed that Potken should have supposed that the Chaldaean, which he himself imagined to be the Samaritan, was spoken in India, and puts an exclamation point after the name of this country. But the archbishop of Cologne was not quite so wrong. In his youth Potken had learned the art of printing from copper-plates; in his old age he used this knowledge to print for the first time Ethiopic texts, and proposed with the aid of his pupil, Johannes Soter, or Heylaffis, to edit also Arabic texts. He may not have known in 1518 that Justiniani had already published the Arabic text of the Psalter in 1516. Before 1513 Potken had lived 'multa lustra', probably therefore during the last decade of the 15th century and the first decade of the 16th, in Rome, where he came in contact with various orders of Abyssinian monks and mendicant friars. He found that their home was 'India major', by which he explains that he meant Ethiopia, south of Egypt. The vast and little known African territory supposed to be ruled by the king of Abyssinia, vulgarly called Presbyter Johannes, and by his vassals, seems to have been designated 'India maior' in distinction from the 'India minor' reached by Vasco da Gama going east and Christopher Columbus going west. From these monks he learned sufficiently what he called the true Chaldaean language to publish, on his return to Germany, the Ethiopic Psalter in neatly cut Ethiopic letters. His words are: 'Statui iam senex linguas externas aliquas discere: et per artem impressoriam, quam adulescens didici, edere, ut modico aere libri in diversis linguis, formis aenaeis excusi emi possint. Cumque maximam Indiae maioris, quae et Aethiopia sub Aegypto est, regis (quem uulgo Presbyterum Johannem appellamus) a puero audissem potentiam: eumque et populos sibi parentes, Christum humani generis redemptorem colere: et non ignorans quod alii septuaginta Reges Christiani ipsius Indiae maioris primario regi, cui ad praesens Dauid nomen est, et Noad hoc est Noe patrem, ac Schendri id est Alexandrum auum, eum in regno praecedentes habuit, uasalli, omnes in tot regnorum ecclesiis, monasteriis, et aliis piis locis Chaldaea in eorum sacris uterentur lingua: magno desyderio: dictorum regnorum diuersorum ordinum monachos, et fratres mendicantes, qui tum Romae pereg(r)inationis causa erant, adii: assiduoque labore non sine temporis iactura quorum idoneum interpretem reperirem minime linguam ipsam Chaldaeam ab eis ad tantam sufficientiam didici, ut mihi persuaderem me posse Psalterium Dauid arte impressoria edere, ut et quinquennio uix exacto, Romae edidi. Sed cum homo Germanus in patriam post multa lustra reuersus, patriae me fatear debitorem: Psalterium ipsum, non modo in hac Chaldaea, per me in Europam importari coepta: sed et Hebraea, et Graeca, ac Latina, linguis, imprimi iuraui' (colophon at the end of *Psalterium,* Cologne, 1518).

How did Potken arrive at the conclusion that Prester John and his people employed the original Chaldaean letters for which the Hebrews in Europe had substituted their own characters, and that the Ethiopic was the true Chaldaean language? Two possible explanations have occurred to me.

In the 14th and 15th centuries numerous magical and astrological works had been translated into Ethiopic, and the Abyssinian monks may have described some of these which Potken associated with the 'Chaldaeans' in the sense of 'Magi' or 'diviners' which it already has in the book of Daniel. Or they may have claimed, as they no doubt rightly could, that some of their books of Chaldaean, meaning thereby Aramaic, origin, had been brought to their far-off country by Aramaic-speaking Jews or Christians. On the whole the latter view is perhaps the more probable. There is no indication that Potken was shown a copy of the book of Enoch. Nor does he seem to have been able to persuade Reuchlin to learn his true Chaldaean. If he had, Reuchlin's interest in the book of Enoch might have led him to make inquiries as to its existence among the Abyssinians.

A few years later Guillaume Postel was actually shown a copy of Ethiopic Enoch in Rome and had its contents explained to him by an Abyssinian priest. In his *De originibus* (Basel, 1553) he relates: 'Audivi esse Romae librorum Enoch argumentum, et contextum mihi a sacerdote Aethiope (ut in Ecclesia Reginae Sabba habetur pro Canonico libro instar Moseos) expositum, ita ut sit mihi varia supellex pro Historiae varietate'. That various parts of the book were explained to him is also indicated by the subtitle: 'ex libris Noachi et Henochi, totiusque avitae traditionis a Moysis tempore servatae et Chaldaicis litteris conscriptae'. Postel visited Rome after his return from Constantinople and Asia Minor c. 1536. He also designated the Ethiopic characters as Chaldaean.

Pierre Gassendi published his *Viri illustris Nicolai Claudii Fabricii de Peiresc, senatoris Aquisextensis, Vita* at the Hague, 1655 (3d ed. by Strunzius, Quedlinburg, 1706—1708). Under the year 1633 he relates (II, iv, p. 284) that at the same time when the Epistle of Clement to the Corinthians and other works were brought from Egypt and Constantinople, Gilles de Loches (Aegidius Lochiensis), a Capucinian monk, also returned from Egypt, where for seven years he had devoted himself to Oriental languages. He now told Peiresc that there were many rare codices in various convents. One contained 8000 volumes, a large part of which had notes from the age of the Antonines. Among others Gilles said that he had seen Mazhapha Einok, or the Prophecy of Enoch, setting forth things that would happen as the end of the world approached, a book hitherto not seen in Europe, written in the letters and language of the Ethiopians, or Abyssinians, among whom it had been preserved. Peiresc was filled with such a desire to buy it at any price that he finally, sparing no expense, was able to secure it. As the title is correct, there can be no doubt today that Gilles de Loches actually had before him the Ethiopic Enoch.

But it has been supposed by many that Peiresc was deceived. Martin voices the generally accepted opinion when he says: 'Malheureusement Peiresc avait été trompé par des vendeurs malhonnêtes ou ignorants. Le manuscrit qu'il s'était procuré fut acheté après sa mort par Mazarin, et déposé à la Bibliothèque Mazarine. Après beaucoup d'efforts pour en obtenir une copie exacte, le célèbre Ludolf se rendit a Paris pour l'étudier, en 1683, et il constata, en le comparant aux fragments du Syncelle, qu'il ne contenait pas le Libre d'Henoch' (*op. l.*, p. cxxxviii). But Ludolf's own words clearly show that he had before him a MS. which at least contained long excerpts from the Ethiopic Enoch. He says: 'Tandem sub finem anni 1683, ipse Lutetiam Parisiorum veni, atque librum hunc in Bibliotheca Regia, quo ex Mazariniana translatus fuerat, reperi, deaurato involucro, tamquam egregius aliquis liber esset, obtectum, cum titulo: Revelationes Enochi Aethiopice. Sed Henochi non esse ex ipso statim titulo apparet, in quo autor libri Bahaila-Michael, diserte nominatur: qui ex veteribus fragmentis has quisquilias compilavit, quales nobis Josephus Scaliger de Egregoriis e libro Georgii Syncelli, qui etiam titulum Enochi habuit, publicavit. Contuli locum illius, et ibi multo plures artes, quas Angeli homines docuisse dicuntur, quam in fragmento Scaligeri reperi, Henochus passim citatur. Continet etiam peculiarem tractatum de nativitate Henochi, unde fortassis libro nomen. Verum tam crassas ac putidas fabulas continet, ut vix legere sustinuerim' (*Historia Aethiopica*, Francfort, 1681, p. 347). He then gives the exordium by Baba Bahaila-Michael, a description of Setnael and his war with the archangel Michael, adding: 'judicent jam lectores, quam pulchrae hae sint revelationes Enochi, tam pulchro involucro, tantisque sumptibus dignae; libentius de stultissimo hoc libro tacuissemus, nisi jam apud tot claros viros hic illic mentio illius facta fuisset'. Ludolf, who did not believe that there ever was a book of Enoch, may be pardoned for being as sceptical about this MS. as Sir William Jones was in regard to Anquetil Duperron's *Zend Avesta.* Better things were expected of Enoch and Zoroaster. There is less excuse for modern editors and commentators repeating with approval the disdainful remarks of Ludolf. It should be obvious to them that Bahaila-Michael was not obliged to translate Scaliger's edition of the Syncellus fragments into Ethiopic, and that he had no difficulty in securing a copy of Ethiopic Enoch, which he provided with a preface and expanded. It is no more remarkable that the story of Setnael and the account of the birth of Enoch should have been added in this MS. than that some extant MSS. contain the story of Methuselah. Some scholar ought to imitate Ludolf's zeal by searching the Bibliothèque Nationale for this MS. and publishing it, if it is still in existence. It is fair to conclude that before Bruce brought back from Abyssinia three copies in 1773 Ethiopic Enoch had been seen by Guillaume Postel, Gilles de Loches, Claude Peiresc, and even Job Ludolf; and that it may have been in the library of Pico della Mirandola and at least heard of by Johann Reuchlin.

THE RECEPTION OF SPRING

Observed in Foochow, China

Lewis Hodous

Kennedy School of Missions, Hartford, Connecticut

One of the joyful days of the year was that on which the new spring was received in the eastern suburb of the city. The Chinese divide their year not only into four seasons, the eight seasons, the twelve months, but they also have twenty-four solar periods or breaths. The first of these twenty-four periods is called the commencement of spring. The day is fixed by the time when the sun is fifteen degrees in the constellation Aquarius.

The ceremony of receiving the spring is a very ancient one. In the Li Chi, in the rescripts for the first month of the year, we read: 'This is the month in which the reign of spring is inaugurated. Three days before the inauguration of spring, the chief secretary informs the son of heaven of the fact saying: "On a certain day spring will commence. The great power of spring is manifested in the element wood (i. e. vegetation)." The son of heaven thereupon practices abstinence. On the day when spring arrives, the son of heaven conducts the three superior ministers of state, the nine secondary ministers of state, the princes and the grand prefects to meet the spring in the eastern suburb. Upon his return he distributes gifts in the court of the palace to the superior ministers, the secondary ministers, the princes and the grand prefects.'

In China the reception of spring was a state ceremony, but it was perhaps the most popular state ceremony, for all the people entered very heartily into it. The customs described in this article belong to the Ch'ing dynasty which has passed away. The new ceremonial in harmony with republican ideas has not been established yet. On the day before the commencement of spring the marine inspector, the two magistrates of Foochow and their deputies met together in the yamen of the prefect in Foochow City. They were dressed in fur-lined garments. On their heads they had caps with a button in the form of a crane. They rode in open sedan chairs. At the prefect's yamen they found a bountiful feast and after the feast they started with their retinue toward the eastern suburb. The procession was headed by a band of musicians. There were the tablets with the titles and offices of the magistrates. There were one or more umbrellas with ten thousand names given to a popular official when he leaves his post. All official decorations were exhibited on this occasion which was made as magnificent as possible. Behind the open sedan chairs of the officials followed a long line of attendants each carrying a bouquet of artificial flowers belonging to the spring season. On this day the prefect had the right of way through the streets, and so the viceroy and the higher officials residing in Foochow made this their at-home day, in order to avoid the unpleasantness of yielding the right of way to an inferior official.

The procession filed through the crowded streets, through the east gate to a pavilion called the pavilion of the spring bull. Here on an altar stood the spring bull. His ribs were made of mulberry wood plastered over with clay and covered with colored paper. Beside the bull was an image of the tutelary god of the current year, called T'ai Sui, the Great Year. In the monthly rescripts of the Li Chi he is called Kou Mang. The god is connected with the star Jupiter, whose revolution in twelve years gives it great power over the years on earth and the events which happen in them. Before these two images was a table with candles, an incense burner, fruits, and cups of wine. In front of the table were mats for the officials. Only the civil officials take part in this ceremony. The prefect stands before the table, the others take places behind him. On each side is a ceremonial usher who directs the ceremony. The ceremonial usher gives the order to kneel. The officials all kneel and bow three times. They arise. An attendant at the left of the prefect hands a cup to him and then pours the wine into it. The official raises it three times up to his forehead and then gives it to the attendant. Then the prefect bows three times, the others likewise bow. Then the musicians form into line, the music strikes up. The clay bull and the image of T'ai Sui are carried on a float into the city. The officials bring up the rear. As the bull passes through the streets the people throw salt and rice at it. This is said to avoid the noxious vapours called *shach'i*. This throwing of salt and rice may possibly correspond to the custom mentioned in the Li Chi. 'The son of heaven ordered the officers to perform the great ceremonies for the dissipation of pestilential vapours, to dismember the victims and disperse them in the four directions, to take out the clay bull and thereby escort the cold vapours.'

When the procession arrives at the yamen of the prefect, the officials form a circle about the bull. Each one strikes the bull with a varicolored stick three times, breaking off pieces of clay. The sound for the character three also means to produce and hence is regarded as propitious. The bits of clay and other parts of the bull are picked up by the crowd. Some people throw lumps of clay to their pigs to stimulate their growth to attain the size of the bull.

Besides this public ceremony there is a reception to spring in each household. A table is placed in the main reception hall at the edge of the court. On it are put an incense-burner, candles, flowers, and three cups of wine. The head of the family takes three sticks of incense, lights them, raises them to his forehead, and then places them into the burner. Then he kneels and bows thrice. Fire-crackers are let off, idol paper is burned. Some families invite Taoist priests to recite incantations on this day.

On this day the children are not whipped, nor scolded. All unpleasant things are avoided, the nightsoil is not removed. All things with strong odors are avoided.

What is the significance of the bull and the image of T'ai Sui? They contained an epitome of the coming year. All the details of their anatomy were carefully fixed the year before in the sixth month by the Imperial Board of Astronomy in Peking. The bull was made after the winter solstice on the first day denoted by the cyclical character *shen*. The ribs were made of mulberry wood because this is one of the trees which bud very early and hence possess much of the *yang* principle. The clay was taken from before the temple of K'ai Ming Wang who was at one time ruler in Fukien. The bull was four feet high to represent the four seasons. He was eight feet long in imitation of the eight seasons into which the Chinese divide the year. The tail was one foot and two inches long to represent the twelve months of the year. The Chinese count ten inches to the foot.

Thus far the anatomy of the bull is readily understood. What follows is very simple if we once obtain the key. The Chinese have ten characters which are called stems, and twelve other characters which are called branches. The first stem character is placed before the first branch character and the second stem character before the second branch character and so on until all the combinations have been made. They number sixty in all and are called the *Chia tzu*, the cycle. The cyclical signs were early applied in numbering days. Probably during the Han dynasty the cycle was applied to the years. The twelve branches are employed as names of the twelve hours into which the Chinese day is divided. Now these stem characters and branch characters belong to one of the five elements, or primordial essences, water, fire, wood, metal, and earth. These primordial essences are attached to certain colors. These essences either repress one another as water does fire, or they produce one another as water produces wood. Here then we have the simple principles of a profound science. In order to understand the application we must remember that a character is not a mere sign of an idea. The character is the double of the object which it signifies. It has a very real power over the object.

The different parts of the bull's anatomy are colored with various colors. These colors are determined by the cyclical characters. For example, the cyclical characters for the year 1911 were *Sing hai*. The head of the bull is determined by the first character *sing*. *Sing* belongs to metal. Metal is white. Hence the head of the bull in 1911 was white. The color of the body is determined by the second character in the cycle, namely, *hai*. Now *hai* belongs to water and water is black and hence in 1911, the last celebration under the dynasty, the body of the bull was black.

Each important part of the bull's anatomy corresponds to the cyclical character of the day, or the branch character for the hour of the day at which the procession takes place. We can readily imagine the refinement to which this can be carried. Once grant the premises, and the whole system is very logically developed.

The year many belong to the male principle or it may belong to the female principle. In case the year belongs to the male principle, the mouth of the bull is open. If the year belongs to the female principle the mouth of the bull is closed. If the year belongs to the male principle the tail of the bull is on the left side, because the left side belongs to the male principle. The reason for this is that the male principle belongs to the east. The emperor sits facing the south or is supposed to sit that way. His left is toward the east and hence the left belongs to the male principle.

As to the image of Kou Mang, who is the tutelary god of spring and is regarded as the tutelary god of the year, there are definite regulations. The image of this tutelary god is three feet, six inches, and five tenths of an inch high. If we remember that a Chinese foot has ten inches, we shall see that his height represents the three hundred and sixty five days of the year. He holds a whip in his hand which is two feet four inches long and represents the twenty-four seasons. The age of the image, the color of his clothing, the color of his belt, the position of his coiffure, the holding of his hand over his left ear, or his right ear, his shoes, his trousers, in short every detail of his image is determined by the cyclical characters for the year, the day, the hour and the elements and colors which correspond to them, and by the quality which the five elements possess of either repressing or producing one another.

The nose of the bull has a ring of mulberry wood. In Kou Mang's hand is a whip. The rope may be made of flax, grass-cloth fiber, or silk according to the cyclical characters of the day. If the inauguration of spring takes place before the new year, the tutelary god of the year stands in front of the bull. If the inauguration of spring takes place five or more days after the New Year, the image is behind the bull. If it takes place between these dates, the image stands at the side of the bull. This position of the tutelary god of the year tells the husbandman whether to begin planting early or late. If the image stands in front of the bull the planting will be early in the New Year. The popular view held that if the image had both hands over his ears there would be much thunder. If he held his hand only over one ear there would be less thunder.

It is unnecessary to go into further details. The bull and the image of the guardian deity of the year epitomized the great events in the year to be. The ceremony was not only symbolic of the sun's power to bring the blessings of the year. It was a method of inducing the sun to return and dispense his gifts to expectant men. It left behind it a confidence and hope that the spring thus well begun would issue forth into summer and be crowned with bountiful harvests in the autumn.

This ceremony, so simple and beautiful, connects the Chinese with Europe with its May day and various other customs of ushering in the Spring of the Year.

STUDIES IN BHĀSA

V. S. Sukthankar

Formerly with Archaeological Survey of India

(Continued from *JAOS* 41. 107 ff.)

III. *On the relationship between the Cārudatta and the Mṛcchakaṭika.*[1]

The close correspondence between the anonymous fragment[2] Cārudatta and the celebrated Mṛcchakaṭika,[3] attributed to King Śūdraka, inevitably necessitates the assumption of a genetic relationship, and indisputably excludes the possibility of independent origin.

It is commonly taken for granted[4] that the Cārudatta is the original of the Mṛcchakaṭika, a relation which does not, however, necessarily and immediately follow from the terseness or brevity of one, nor from (what amounts to the same thing) the length and prolixity of the other; for, in adaptation, abridgment is as common and natural a determining principle as amplification.[5] In view of the intrinsic importance of the question, it seemed,

---

[1] A paper presented at the One Hundred Thirty-third Meeting (Baltimore, 1921) of the Amer. Or. Soc., under the title: 'The Cārudatta and the Mṛcchakaṭika: their mutual relationship'.

[2] See thereon my article, '"Charudatta"—A Fragment' in the *Quarterly Journal of the Mythic Society* (Bangalore), 1919.

[3] Ed. N. B. Godabole, Bombay, 1896.

[4] For instance, Gaṇapati Sâstrî in the Introduction to his editions of the Svapnavāsavadattā (p. xxxviii), and the Cārudatta (p. i); Lindenau, *Bhāsa-Studien* (Leipzig, 1918), p. 11; and Barnett (hesitatingly) *Bulletin of the School of Oriental Studies*, vol. I, part III (1920), pp. 35 ff.

[5] Some attempt has already been made in India to discredit the authenticity of the Cārudatta; see, for instance, Raṅgācārya Raḍḍī, *Vividha-jñāna-vistāra* (Bombay), 1916, and P. V. Kāṇe, *ibid.* 1920; Bhattanatha Svamin, *Indian Antiquary*, vol. 45, pp. 189 ff.

therefore, desirable to undertake an unbiased and exhaustive investigation so as to remove (if possible) the haze of uncertainty surrounding the subject.

Only the resemblances between the two plays appear hitherto to have attracted any attention;[6] the differences between them are, however, equally remarkable and much more instructive. A careful comparative study of the two versions produces highly valuable text-critical results, which help further the understanding of the plays and throw unexpected light on the subject of our inquiry.

Regarding their relationship there are only two logical possibilities: either, one of the plays has formed directly the basis of the other, or else both of them are to be traced to a common source. In the former case we are called upon to answer the question, which of the two plays is the original; in the latter, which of them is closer to the original.

We cannot be too careful in deciding what is original and what is not. The original may have been concise and well-proportioned, and later clumsy attempts at improvement may have introduced digressions, tiresome repetitions and insipid elaborations; on the other hand, the original may have been prolix and loose, and subsequent revision may have pruned away the redundancies. Again, one may feel justified in assuming that the inaccuracies and inconsistencies of the original would be corrected in a later revised version; but one must also readily concede that a popular dramatic text like the Mṛccha-kaṭika, after it had been written down, during its migrations through centuries over such a vast territory as India, may have undergone occasional distortion and corruption.

Every change, however minute, presupposes a cause; even the worst distortion was ushered in with the best of intentions, and though it may not always be possible to trace a given change to its proper cause, we are safe in assuming that in a limited number of favorable instances the intrinsic character of the passages under consideration may spontaneously suggest the cause for the change, and readily supply a clue to the relative priority and posteriority of two variations. In isolated

---

6 See particularly Gaṇapati Sâstrî, Svapnavāsavadattā, Introduction, pp. xxxviii-xlii.

instances we could say no more than that the change in a certain direction appears more probable than a change in the contrary direction. But the cumulative force of a sufficient number of analogous instances, all supporting one aspect of the question, would amply justify our giving precedence to that particular alternative and treating it as a working hypothesis. The problem, therefore, before us is to collect such instances, in which the motive for the change is directly perceptible and capable of objective verification. The cumulative effect of the indications of these scattered traces should not fail to give us the correct perspective. This digression was necessary in order to explain the methodology underlying the present investigation.

The textual differences between the two versions comprise a large mass of details of varying importance. The selection presented below, though conditioned on the one hand by the requirements of the present inquiry, is by no means exhaustive; for lack of space, only a few typical examples have been singled out for discussion.

A Selection of Significant Textual Differences.

We shall now proceed to a discussion of the textual variations, roughly classified here under four headings: 1. Technique; 2. Prakrit; 3. Versification; and 4. Dramatic incident.

1. *Technique.*

In point of technique the Cārudatta differs from the Mṛccha-kaṭika (as from other classical dramas) in two striking particulars. In the first place, the usual nāndī is missing, in both the available manuscripts of the Cārudatta; in the second place, there is no reference to the name of the author or the play in the sthāpanā, which does not contain even the usual address to the audience.

The Mṛcchakaṭika, as is well known, begins with two benedictory verses; the name of the play is announced in the opening words of the sūtradhāra; then follow five verses which allude to the play, the playwright,[7] and other details not directly connected with the action.

---

[7] The verses in the prologue which refer to the death of the alleged

Elsewhere[8] I have tried to show that the Cārudatta is a fragment. I hold, accordingly, that we should not be justified in basing our conclusions regarding the technique of termination on the data of the fragment preserved.

Worth noting appears to be the fact that in the stage directions of the Cārudatta, the hero is never called by his name or his rank, but merely by the character of the rôle he plays, nāyaka. Professor Lüders[9] has already drawn attention to two other instances of this usage (if it may be called a usage), namely, a drama belonging to the Turfan fragments, and the play Nāgānanda attributed to Harṣa. Prof. Lüders sees in it an archaism intentionally copied by the author of of the Nāgānanda. At present we can, it seems to me, do nothing more than record this third instance of its occurrence in a play of uncertain age and authorship.

2. *Prakrit.*

In the first article of this series, it was shown in a general way that the Prakrit of the whole group of plays under consideration was more archaic than the Prakrit of the classical plays.[10] This statement holds good also in the particular case of the Cārudatta and the Mṛcchakaṭika. A comparison of parallel passages in the two plays shows that the Mṛcchakaṭika invariably contains Middle-Prakrit[11] forms in place of the Old-Prakrit forms of the Cārudatta. Here are the examples.

The Absolutive of the roots *gam* and *kṛ*. Cāru. has the Old-Prakrit *gacchia* and *karia* (*kaḷia*): Mṛccha. *gadua* and *kadua*. Cf. in particular Cāru. 1 *gehaṁ gacchia jāṇāmi* with the corresponding passage, Mṛccha. 7 *gehaṁ gadua jāṇāmi*. The form *gadua*, which never occurs in the Cāru., is used uniformly in the Mṛccha.—For the absolutive of *kṛ*;[12] *karia*

author are palpably later additions. This self-evident fact does not, however, necessarily justify the assumption that there was no reference whatsoever to the author in the prologue of the original draft.

[8] See above, footnote 2.

[9] *Bruchstücke Buddhistischer Dramen (Kleinere Sanskrit-Texte, Heft I)*, Berlin, 1911, p. 26.

[10] Above, vol. 40, pp. 248 ff.

[11] Lüders, *op. cit.*, p. 62.

[12] See above, vol. 40, p. 254.

(Śaurasenī) Cāru. 46, *kaḷia* (Māgadhī) Cāru. 23: *kadua* (Śaurasenī and Māgadhī) Mṛccha. 53, 212, 213, etc. In the Cāru. *kadua* never occurs; conversely *karia* is never met with in the Mṛccha.

Pronoun of the 1st Person; nom. sing. Cāru. 23 we have the Old-Māgadhī *ahake*[13] (but never *hage* or *hagge*): Mṛccha. (passim) *hag(g)e* (but never *ahake*). Noteworthy is the following correspondence. Cāru. I. 12c *ahaṁ tumaṁ gaṇhia*: Mṛccha. I. 29c *eśe hage geṇhia.*—Nom. plu. Cāru. 49. has the Old-Prakrit *vaaṁ*:[14] Mṛccha. (passim) *amhe.* The form *amhe* (nom. plu.) is never met with in the Cāru., and conversely *vaaṁ* never occurs in the Mṛccha.

Pronoun of the 2nd Person; nom. sing. Cāru. (passim) we have Old-Prakrit *tuvaṁ*:[15] Mṛccha. (passim) *tumaṁ.* Cf. especially Cāru. 34 *kiṁ tuvaṁ,* etc., with the corresponding passage Mṛccha. 79 *hañje tumaṁ mae saha,* etc.—Gen. sing. Cāru. uniformly *tava*:[16] Mṛccha. sometimes *tuha.* Cf. in particular Cāru. 25 *tava gehaṁ paviṭṭhā* with Mṛccha. 59 *tuha gehaṁ paviśṭā.*

The Neuter plu. of nom. and acc. of thematic stems ends in the Cāru. invariably in *-āṇi* (*-āni* in the Aśvaghoṣa fragments): in the Mṛccha. it ends in *-āiṁ.*

Treatment of the assimilated conjunct. Retained in Cāru. 16 *diśśadi*[17] (as in the Turfan fragments): simplified in Mṛccha.

---

[13] See above, vol. 40, p. 253. Dr. Truman Michelson has drawn my attention to an article of his (*Indogermanische Forschungen,* vol. 23, p. 129) in which he points out that the Māgadhī *ahake* occurs several times in the Devanāgarī recension of the Śakuntalā. The paragraph on this word in my article cited above needs modification in view of this fact. The statement that *ahake* is archaic is none the less correct.

[14] See above, vol. 40, p. 258.

[15] See above, vol. 40, p. 257. In the references under no. 9 the last item 'Cāru. 2 (Naṭī)' is a mistake. Here *tuvaṁ* is used for the *acc.* sing., and not for the nom. sing. as implied. Accordingly, on the same page, in l. 6 from bottom, read 'thrice' instead of 'twice', and add this instance. Cāru. instances of *tuvaṁ* (*nom.* sing.) are Cāru. 34 (Gaṇikā), 47 (Ceṭī), etc.

[16] See above, vol. 40, p. 257.

[17] See above, vol. 40, p. 258.—The form *diś-*, with the simplified conjunct, is met with on the same page (Cāru. 16), spoken by the same character, Śakāra.

41 *dīśantī*. The root-form *diśś-* (*diss-*) is never met with in the Mṛccha., which shows uniformly *dīś-* (*dīs-*).

Vocabulary. Cāru. uniformly *geha* (Skt. *gṛha*): Mṛccha. 39 *ghala*. Cf. especially Cāru. 16 *edaṁ tassa gehaṁ* with Mṛccha. 39 *vāmado taśśa ghalaṁ*.—The Old Prakrit affirmative particle *āma*,[18] which occurs in Pali and the Turfan fragments and which figures so conspicuously in Cāru. (e.g. pp. 4, 20, 64, etc.), is never met with in the Mṛccha.—There is one other thing to be noted about the difference in the vocabulary of the two versions. While the Mṛccha. contains a number of Deśī words (not found in the Cāru.), the vocabulary of the Cāru. consists notably of pure tatsamas and tadbhavas. Here follow some of the Deśī words which occur in the Mṛccha. Mṛccha. 17 *chivia*, 'having touched', from root *chiv* (Hem. 4. 182) with the reflexes in the Tertiary Pkts., Hindi *chūnā*, Marathi *śivaṇe*, 'to touch'; Mṛccha. 104 *ḍhakkehi*, 'shut', from *ḍhakkai*, *ḍhakkei*, traced by Pischel (*Grammatik* 221) to a root **sthak*, with reflexes in the Tertiary Pkts., Hindi *ḍhāknā*, Marathi *ḍhākṇe*, 'to cover'; Mṛccha. 134 *uḍḍhehi*, 'open', for which in the corresponding passage of the Cāru. (p. 19) we have a tadbhava of the root *apā* + *vṛ*,[19] and which for that reason is particularly worthy of note; Mṛccha. 207 *karaṭṭa-ḍāiṇī*, 'malevolent ogress' (cf. Marathi *kāraṭā*, a term of abuse, and *ḍākiṇ*, 'ogress').

3. *Versification.*

In the verses common to the two plays the Mṛcchakaṭika almost always offers better readings, of which a few are cited below.

For Cāru. I. 3b *yathāndhakārād iva dīpadarśanam*, we have Mṛccha. I 10b, *ghanāndhakāreṣv iva*, etc., in which *ghana-* is substituted for the tautologous *yathā*.

Similarly, instead of the Prakrit line Cāru. I. 10b *jahā śigālī via kukkuḷehi*, containing the same fault, we have Mṛccha. I. 28b *vaṇe śiālī via kukkulehiṁ*, in which *vaṇe* takes the place of *jahā*.

---

[18] See above, vol. 40, p. 254.

[19] The text reading is *avāvuda*, imp. 2nd sing., which is evidently incorrect. What the correct form should be I am unable to say. The initial letters *avāvu* of the word show unmistakably that the root is *apā* + *vṛ*.

For Cāru. I. 3c *yo yāti daśāṁ daridratām,* we have Mṛccha I. 10c *yo yāti naro daridratām.* It is correct to say *daśāṁ daridrām,* but *daśāṁ daridratām* is clumsy, to say the least.

Cāru. I. 23a begins *eśā hi vāśū;* instead, we have Mṛccha. I. 41a *eśā śi vāśū.* The *śi* which takes the place of *hi* eliminates the expletive *hi,* and adds moreover another sibilant to the row of alliterating syllables. In the same verse, for *kūjāhi kandāhi* of the Cāru., we have *akkośa vikkośa* in the Mṛccha., which serves better the purpose of the anuprāsa, the dominating alaṁkāra of this verse. Similarly in d, instead of *maheśśaḷaṁ* of the Cāru., we have *śaṁbhuṁ śivaṁ* in the Mṛccha., which latter reading contains an additional sibilant as well as a pleonasm.[20] These are minor details, but they all tend in the same direction.

For Cāru. I. 25a *akāmā hriyate 'smābhiḥ,* we have Mṛccha. I. 44a *sakāmānviṣyate 'smābhiḥ.* The reason for the change is not obvious, as in the foregoing instances. But a closer examination of the context will show that the reading of the Mṛccha. marks a distinct improvement, in so far as it implies a more minute analysis of character. In the Cāru. the ingenuous Viṭa inculpates Śakāra and himself by admitting that they were engaged in carrying away forcibly an unwilling maiden. In the Mṛccha. the artful Viṭa, readily inventing a plausible lie and explaining that they were following a girl who was willing, offers undoubtedly a much better excuse.

Cāru. I 29a describes the moon as *klinnakharjūrapāṇḍu,* 'pale as the moistened fruit of the date': Mṛccha. I. 57a has *kāminīgaṇḍapāṇḍu,* 'pale as a maiden's cheek'. The former is original and naïve, the latter polished but hackneyed; the latter harmonizes better with the sentiment of śṛṅgāra which pervades the last scene of the first act, and is more in keeping with the tradition of the later enervated rasa theory.

For Cāru. III. 3d *viṣāṇakoṭīva nimajjamānā,* 'like the tip of a tusk sinking in the water', the Mṛccha. (III. 7d) has *tīkṣṇaṁ viṣāṇāgram ivāvaśiṣṭam,* 'like the sharp tip of a tusk that alone remains visible'. As far as the sense goes there is not much to choose between them; but the line from the Cāru.

---

[20] According to Lalla Dikshita, commentator of the Mṛcchakaṭika: *vyarthaikārtham apārthaṁ bhavati hi vacanaṁ śakārasya* (Mṛccha. 28).

contains one serious defect. In classical Skt. the root *ni-majj* is used exclusively with Paras. terminations; *nimajjamānā* is, in other words, nothing less than a gross grammatical blunder.[21]

With Cāru. III. 6b *śauryaṁ na kārkaśyatā*, cf. Mṛccha. III. 12b *cauryaṁ na śauryaṁ hi tat*. *kārkaśyatā* of the Cāru. is an anomalous word, being a double abstract formation. The Mṛccha. eliminates this anomaly by substituting instead *caurya*, which, incidentally, rhymes with the succeeding *śaurya*.

These few instances[22] must suffice to illustrate the statement made above, that the Mṛccha. verses are largely free from the flaws of the corresponding verses of the Cāru. It should, however, be remarked that in a vast number of cases it is not possible to assign an adequate reason for the change: the different readings appear to be just arbitrary variations.

4. *Dramatic Incident.*

The Mṛcchakaṭika shows a marked improvement in the selection and arrangement of the incidents of the action.

The action of the Cārudatta begins with a soliloquy of the Vidūṣaka followed by a lengthy dialogue between the Nāyaka and the Vidūṣaka. The hero is conversing with his friend, deploring his poverty. This dialogue is brought to an abrupt end by the scene introducing Vasantasenā, who appears on the street outside pursued by the Śakāra and the Viṭa (Cāru. 10). In the Mṛcchakaṭika (p. 25) the abruptness of the change of scene is skillfully avoided by the addition of the following words placed in the mouth of Cārudatta:

bhavatu | tiṣṭha tāvat | ahaṁ samādhiṁ nirvartayāmi,

'Very well. Wait awhile and I will finish my meditation.'

These words of Cārudatta serve admirably to adjust the time relation of the different events. The playwright here unmistakably indicates that the succeeding scene, which introduces the offers of love by Śakāra, their indignant rejection by Vasantasenā, and her subsequent escape, develops during Cārudatta's

---

[21] Similar solecisms, met with in other dramas of this group, are discussed by me in the second article of the series (above, vol. 41, pp. 121 ff.).

[22] It may be remarked that there are no verses in the second act of the Cārudatta, and only seven in the fourth act.

samādhi. Furthermore, as indicated by the subsequent words of Cārudatta (Mṛccha. 43): *vayasya samāptajapo 'smi*, 'Friend, my meditation is over', Vasantasenā's reaching the door of Cārudatta's house coincides exactly in point of time with the emergence of Cārudatta from his samādhi. The words of Cārudatta quoted above, which serve to link together these various groups of incidents, are missing in the Cārudatta.

Here is another example. In the fourth act of the Cārudatta (p. 72), Sajjalaka comes to the house of the Gaṇikā to buy Madanikā's freedom. He stands outside the house and calls out for Madanikā. Madanikā, who is waiting on the heroine, hears him and, seeing that her mistress is musing on other things, slips away and joins Sajjalaka. The defect of this arrangement is obvious: it is inconsistent and illogical. With stolen goods in his possession Sajjalaka sneaks to the house of the heroine with the object of secretly handing over the spoils of his theft to Madanikā. Under these circumstances it is the height of indiscretion to stand outside the house of the heroine and shout for his mistress at the top of his voice. Again, if Madanikā is able to hear Sajjalaka, so should Vasantasenā, who is sitting close by, be able to hear him. Apparently she fails to do so owing to her preoccupation; but this is a circumstance that could not have been foreseen even by a scientific burglar like Sajjalaka. The situation in the Mṛcchakaṭika (p. 169) is much more realistic. On reaching Vasantasenā's house, Śarvilaka, instead of calling out for Madanikā, hangs about outside the house waiting his opportunity. The meeting of the lovers is brought about in the following manner. Soon after Śarvilaka reaches the house of Vasantasenā, the latter sends away Madanikā on an errand; on her way back, Madanikā is discovered by Śarvilaka, whom she thereupon naturally joins.

One more instance, which is the last. A time analysis of the first three acts of the Cārudatta will show that the incidents developed in these acts are supposed to take place on three *consecutive* days, the sixth, seventh and eighth of a certain lunar fortnight. Here are the specific references. Cārudatta 7, the Vidūṣaka, in speaking of the Nāyaka, applies the adjective *saṭṭhīkidadevakayya* to him, which incidentally shows that that day was the sixth. Latter on in the same act (Cāru. 30), addressing the Ceṭī, the Vidūṣaka says:

saṭṭhīe sattamīe a dhārehi | ahaṁ aṭṭhamīe aṇaddhāe dhāraïssaṁ.

The arrangement he proposes is that the Ceṭī should guard the jewels of the Gaṇikā on the sixth and the seventh, and that he should take over the charge of them on the eighth. In the third act we have a confirmation of the same arrangement. Cāru. 53, Ceṭī remarks:

iaṁ suvaṇṇabhaṇḍaṁ saṭṭhīe sattamīe (pariveṭṭhāmi?) | aṭṭhamī khu ajja.

The Ceṭī, appearing before the Vidūṣaka, with the jewels, on the night of the eighth, points out that she has guarded them on the sixth and the seventh, and adds that that day being the eighth it is the turn of the Vidūṣaka. Later on in the same act (Cāru. 65), the Brāhmaṇī, the hero's wife, incidentally mentions that she was observing on that day the Fast of the Sixth[23], to which the Vidūṣaka pointedly retorts that that day was the eighth and not the sixth[24]. These various references leave no doubt that the events that form the action of the first three acts are supposed to take place within the span of three consecutive days.

There are in the play some further chronological data, which we must also take into consideration. They comprise two lyrical stanzas which describe respectively the rising and the setting of the moon. In that elegant little verse (Cāru. I. 29) beginning with

udayati hi śaśāṅkaḥ klinnakharjūrapāṇḍuḥ

the moon is described as *rising*, late in the evening, after the lapse of a short period of darkness following upon sunset, during which Vasantasenā escapes from the clutches of the evil Śakāra. In the third act, on his way home from the concert, Cārudatta, in a lyrical mood, recites another verse (Cāru. III. 3), beginning with

asau hi dattvā timirāvakāśam
astaṁ gato hy aṣṭamapakṣacandraḥ,[25]

and having for its theme the *setting* moon.

---

[23] The words of the Brāhmaṇī are: *ṇaṁ saṭṭhiṁ uvavasāmi.*

[24] The Vidūṣaka observes: *aṭṭhamī khu ajja.*

[25] Translation: 'For yonder the Moon of the Eighth, giving place to darkness, has sunk behind the western mount.'

This is the chronological material of the Cārudatta. Let us turn for a moment to the Mṛcchakaṭika and examine its data. Here also apparently the same conditions prevail. Apparently the events of the first three acts take place on three consecutive days, but only apparently so. There is nothing in the play itself from which the duration of the action could be precisely computed.

To begin with, the reference to the *ṣaṣṭhī* is missing from the opening words of the Vidūṣaka in the first act. In place of *saṭṭhīkidadevakayya* of the Cārudatta, we have the reading *siddhīkidadevakajja*, in which *siddhī* takes the place of *saṭṭhī*. Likwise we find that all subsequent references to the lunar dates are missing from the succeeding speeches of the Vidūṣaka and the Servant. An entirely different scheme has been adopted for the division of labor between the Vidūṣaka and the Servant. The Servant explains in the third act (Mṛccha. 137) the arrangement arrived at as follows:

ajja mittea edaṁ taṁ śuvaṇṇabhaṇḍaaṁ mama divā tuha lattiṁ ca,

'Maitreya, here is the golden casket, that's *mine by day and yours by night*'; no reference here to the *saṭṭhī*, *sattamī* and *aṭṭhamī* of the Cārudatta. This is not all. The verse from the third act of the Cāru. cited above, containing a reference to the date, has also been substantially modified. Cāru. III. 3b specifically states the date to be eighth: *astaṁ gato hy aṣṭamapakṣacandraḥ*. In the Mṛcchakaṭika version the line reads (Mṛccha. III. 7b): *astaṁ vrajaty unnatakoṭir induḥ*. The phrase *unnatakoṭi* has taken the place of *aṣṭamapakṣa*, which brought in its train, naturally, the change of *gato* to a word like *vrajati*.[26] It is true that later on, in the same act of the Mṛcchakaṭika (p. 159), the Vadhū, Cārudatta's wife, refers to *saṭṭhī*, saying that she is observing the *raaṇasaṭṭhī* (*ratnaṣaṣṭhī*).[27] But here also a significant omission confronts us. The Vidūṣaka, instead of correcting her, accepts her statement with the necklace, and there the matter rests.

---

[26] The present tense *vrajati* gives better sense than the past *gato*, in regard to the simile contained in lines c and d.

[27] Instead of the vague *saṭṭhī* of the Cārudatta we have the more specific *raaṇasaṭṭhī* in the Mṛcchakaṭika.

As remarked above, apparently the joint duration of the first three acts of the Mṛcchakaṭika is also three days. But I have grave doubts whether any strict proof can be brought forward to support such an assumption. I have read the drama carefully and I have failed to find any allusion that necessitates such a time scheme. However that may be, it is absolutely certain that the specific references of the Cārudatta to the lunar dates are conspicuous by their absence in the other play.

At this place it may be observed that the tithi-scheme of the Cārudatta taken in conjunction with the references to moon-rise and moon-set in the verses already cited involves a chronological inconsistency, so minute and so latent as to be hardly noticeable. But the inconsistency is, nevertheless, an undeniable fact. For, the rising of the moon late in the evening and the setting of the moon at or about midnight[28] are phenomena that inherently belong to two *different* lunar fortnights. Only in the dark fortnight does the moon rise late in the evening: and only in the bright fortnight does the moon set at or shortly after midnight. In other words, if the moon is seen rising late in the evening on any particular day, it is nothing less than a physical impossibility that after an interval of forty-eight hours the moon should be seen setting at or about midnight.

The general time-scheme of the Cārudatta has thus been shown to contain a latent contradiction from which the Mṛcchakaṭika is wholly free owing to the absence therein of any specific references to the days on which the action takes place.

Are these variations arbitrary; or are they directly or indirectly related; and if so how?

Summary and Conclusion.

Briefly summarized, the significant differences between the two versions discussed above are the following. Firstly, in point of technique, the Cārudatta differs conspicuously from the other play in the absence of the nāndī, and in having a rudimentary sthāpanā. Secondly, the Prakrit of the Cārudatta is more archaic than that of the Mṛcchakaṭika, in so far that the

---

[28] According to the words of the hero, just preceding the verse *asau hi dattvā*, etc. (Cāru. III. 3): *upārūḍho 'rdharātraḥ* (Cāru. 50).

former contains a number of Old-Prakrit forms not found in the latter. Thirdly, as regards versification, the text of the Mṛcchakaṭika marks an advance upon the other play in the following directions: rectification of grammatical mistakes; elimination of redundancies and awkward constructions; and introduction of other changes which may be claimed to be improvements in the form and substance of the verses. Fourthly and lastly, because of suitable additions and omissions the Mṛcchakaṭika presents a text free from many of the flaws, such as unrealities and inconsistencies, in the action of the Cārudatta.

These are the facts of the case. Do these facts enable us to decide the question of priority and anteriority?

Let us assume first, for the sake of argument, that the Cārudatta contains older material (at least in respect of the passages discussed above) which was worked up later into the Mṛcchakaṭika.

The differences in the technique neither support nor contradict definitely such an assumption. The nāndī, for all we can say, may have been lost. The words *nāndyante tataḥ praviśati sūtradhāraḥ* do not militate against such a supposition: they could be used with or without a nāndī appearing in the text. Moreover, we cannot, in the present state of our knowledge, rightly evaluate the absence of all reference to the name of the play and the playwright in the sthāpanā.[29] To say that in pre-classical times that was the practice is begging the question. The only technique of introduction with which we are familiar is the well-known classical model. Again the only play which is definitely known to antedate the classical plays is the Turfan fragment of Aśvaghoṣa's drama. Unfortunately, as the beginning of the Śāriputraprakaraṇa[30] is missing, we we are not in a position to say whether the prologue of the dramas of Aśvaghoṣa conformed to the standard of the classical dramas, or that of the dramas of the group under consideration. We are therefore bound to admit that at present we have no clear evidence that can aid us in placing with any degree of assurance,

---

[29] The references in the text-books of rhetoric and dramaturgy are obscure and partly contradictory.

[30] Ed. Lüders, *Sitzungsberichte d. kgl. preuss. Ak. d. Wiss.* 1911.

chronologically or topographically, a drama with the technical peculiarities of the Cārudatta.

But the priority of the Cārudatta version would explain, and satisfactorily explain, all the other differences between the two plays. It would explain the presence of archaisms in the Prakrit of the Cārudatta. It would explain why many of the verses of the Mṛcchakaṭika are free from the flaws of the corresponding verses of the Cārudatta; the grammatical corrections one may be justified in regarding as an indication of an increasingly insistent demand for scrupulous purity of language. The hypothesis would lastly explain the reason for the differences in the incidents of the action of the play. All this is legitimate field of 'diaskeuasis', and is readily intelligible.

Let us now examine the other possibility, and try to explain the divergences on the assumption of the priority of the Mṛcchakaṭika version.

The question of the technical differences between the plays has been dealt with already. It was submitted that this part of the evidence was inconclusive; it supported neither one side nor the other.

We will proceed to the next point, the Prakrit.[31] On the assumption of the priority of the Mṛcchakaṭika version, it is at first sight not quite clear, how the Cārudatta should happen to contain Prakrit forms older than those found in (what is alleged to be) a still older play. But a little reflection will suffice to bring home to us the fact that it is not impossible to account for this anomaly. We have only to regard the Cārudatta as the version of a different province or a different literary tradition, which had not accepted the innovations in Prakrit that later became prevalent. In other words we have to assume merely that the Prakrit neologisms of the Mṛcchakaṭika are unauthorized innovations and that the Cārudatta manuscripts have only

---

[31] Until we have before us most carefully edited texts, any linguistic conclusion based upon minute differences in the form of Pkt. words, as appearing in the text-editions employed, must needs be regarded as tentative, a point not sufficiently emphasized in my article dealing with Prakrit archaisms (above, vol. 40, pp. 248 ff.). It may, however, be pointed out that no amount of critical editing can disturb the general inference that the dramas of this group contain quite a number of Old-Pkt. forms.

preserved some of the Old-Prakrit forms of the original Mṛcchakaṭika.[32] This does not, however, necessarily make the Cārudatta version older than the Mṛcchakaṭika version. The Cārudatta would become a recension of the Mṛcchakaṭika with archaic Prakrit. Thus the Prakrit archaisms of the Cārudatta may be said to be not irreconcilable with the general priority of the Mṛcchakaṭika version.

It is much more difficult to explain why the Mṛcchakaṭika should consistently offer better readings of the verses. Some of the discrepancies could perhaps be explained away as the result of misreading and faulty transcript, but not all. We could not explain, for instance, why the excellent pāda: *tīkṣṇaṁ viṣāṇāgram ivāvaśiṣṭam* should have been discarded, and another, *viṣāṇakoṭīva nimajjamānā,* be substituted, forsooth with the faulty *nimajjamānā.* Why should there be a change in the first place, and *why should the change be consistently for the worse?* We could not reasonably hold the copyists guilty of introducing *systematically* such strange blunders and inexcusable distortions.

Let us combine the archaisms of the Prakrit with the imperfections of the Sanskrit verses. On the assumption of the posteriority of the Cārudatta, we are asked to believe that while the compiler of the Cārudatta had carefully copied out from older manuscripts all the Prakrit archaisms, he had systematically mutilated the Sanskrit verses, which is a reductio ad absurdum!

Let us proceed to the fourth point. The theory of the priority of the Mṛcchakaṭika, which could with difficulty be supported in the case of the divergencies already considered, breaks down altogether when we try to account for the inconsistencies in the action of the Cārudatta in general, and in particular the presence of the tithi-scheme, which latter serves no purpose, aesthetic or didactic, but on the other hand introduces gratuitously an indisputable incongruity. The deleting of the whole tithi-scheme admits of a simple, self-evident explanation, acceptable to every impartial critic. But, assuming

---

[32] Or that the Old-Prakrit forms had been substituted for the Middle-Prakrit forms, because the local tradition demanded the use of Old-Prakrit forms.

that the original play contained no trace of it, can any one pretend to be able to give a satisfactory reason for the deliberate introduction of the tithi-scheme?

Taking all things into account, we conclude, we can readily understand the evolution of a Mṛcchakaṭika version from a Cārudatta version, but not vice versa. The special appeal of this hypothesis lies in the fact that it explains not merely isolated variations, but whole categories of them: it implies the formulation of a single uniform principle to explain divers manifestations.

It may be that I have overlooked inconsistencies and flaws in the Mṛcchakaṭika version, absent from the other, which could be better explained on the contrary supposition of the priority of the Mṛcchakaṭika version. If so, the problem becomes still more complicated, and will need further investigation from a new angle. I merely claim that I have furnished here some prima facie reasons for holding that the Cārudatta version is on the whole older than the Mṛcchakaṭika version; hence (as a corollary) if our Cārudatta is not itself the original of the Mṛcchakaṭika, then, we must assume, it has preserved a great deal of the original upon which the Mṛcchakaṭika is based.

SOME ALLUSIONS TO MAGIC IN KAUṬILYA'S ARTHAŚĀSTRA

VIRGINIA SAUNDERS

NEW YORK CITY

THROUGH AN INTEREST in magic in general I have been led to undertake an extended study of the subject in early Sanskrit literature. In the course of my research, upon looking through Kauṭilya's Arthaśāstra, to see if by chance there might be a mention of magic, I was surprised to find a remarkable number of references to the subject—some of it very black. This is indeed surprising when we consider the fact that this book is a work on the Science of Government written by the Prime Minister of Chandragupta.[1]

Throughout the work there are frequent allusions to sorcery, demons, obsessed persons, incantations, witchcraft, etc. To select a few instances: an obsessed person (*upagṛhīta*) may not make legal agreements;[2] a plaintiff in a lawsuit, if he is not a Brahman, may, on failure to prove his case, be caused to perform such acts as drive out demons;[3] witchcraft employed by a husband to arouse love in a wife or by a lover to win the affections of a maiden is no offence, but the practice must not be indulged in if it is injurious to others.[4] Special spies may pretend to use witchcraft in an effort to detect criminal tendencies in youths.[5]

The third chapter of the fourth book is headed 'Counter-action

---

[1] Text, R. Shama Śastri, *Arthaśāstra of Kauṭilya*, revised edition, Mysore, 1919. Transl. id. *Kauṭilya's Arthaśāstra*, Bangalore, 1915.

[2] Text, p. 148, l. 13. *upagṛhīta* here seems to have the sense of obsession by an evil spirit. Transl. p. 188.

[3] Text, p. 150, l. 3; tr. p. 191.

[4] Text, p. 235, l. 17; tr. p. 295.

[5] Text, p. 212, l. 16; tr. p. 266.

against sudden attacks' (*upanipāta-pratīkāraḥ*).[6] These possible attacks are eight in number and are called 'great perils through divine decree' (*daivāni mahābhayāni*), consisting in fire, flood, plague, famine, rats, tigers, snakes, and demons. In the case of flood, plague, rats, snakes, and demons, magic is used in the following ways:

When the floods come, in addition to the very practical use of planks, bottle-gourds, trunks of trees and canoes, recourse shall be had to ascetics with a knowledge of magic (*māyāyogavidas*), and persons learned in the Vedas shall perform incantations against rain.[7]

In the case of plague, besides the aid of physicians with their medicines and spending the nights in devotion to the gods, ascetics endowed with supernatural powers (*siddhatāpasās*) shall perform auspicious and purificatory ceremonials, cows shall be milked on cremation grounds, and the trunk of a corpse shall be burned. If the disease has attacked the cows a 'half nīrājana' (*ardhanīrājana*) should be performed in the cow stalls. This swinging of lights was apparently for the purpose of placating the demons causing disease in the cattle.[8]

In danger from rats, beside the resorting to poison, auspicious ceremonials by magicians may be employed.[9] These magical performances are unfortunately not described.

In the case of snakes, those persons having a knowledge of poisons shall proceed with *mantras* and herbs, or there may be employed the very practical means of assembling and killing the snakes (*sambhūya vopa sarpān hanyuḥ*).[10] Also those who are learned in the Atharvaveda may perform auspicious rites.[11] The reader who is familiar with the Atharvaveda will recall the incantation hymns against snakes.[12]

In danger from demons, experts in magic and those acquainted with the Atharvaveda shall perform demon-destroying rites

---

6 Text, p. 207; tr. p. 261.

7 Text, p. 208, l. 2; tr. p. 262.

8 Text, p. 208, l. 9; tr. p. 262.

9 Text, p. 209, l. 1; tr. p. 262.

10 Text, p. 209, l. 16; tr. p. 263. The text seems dubious and may be corrupt.

11 Text, p. 210, l. 1; tr. p. 262.

12 Av. 10. 4; 7. 56; 6. 56; 6. 12; 5. 13.

(*rakṣoghnāni karmāṇi*).[13] To ward off demoniacal influences special acts of worship at a shrine (*caitya-pūjāḥ*) should be performed at the changes of the moon, with an offering of a goat, a banner, an umbrella, and something which seems to be some kind of representation of a hand.[14] Also the incantation, which begins *vaś carāmaḥ* ('we worship you'), should continually be performed.[15] I have not been able to identify the quotation indicated by this catch-phrase, *vaś*, etc. At the end of this chapter it is stated that those who are experts in magical arts and have supernatural powers should be honored by the king and caused to dwell in his kingdom.

The fourteenth book contains the principal magic of the whole work.[16] This book is divided into four chapters. The first, entitled 'Means of injuring an enemy', is composed mainly of formulas for the use of materials which, when burned, will cause smoke that is poisonous to men and beasts, bringing either death or disease. From the ingredients I should judge these devices would do all claimed for them. With these poison-gas recipes there are also two or three rather magical-sounding suggestions, but this chapter mainly contains purely material devices to be employed.

The second chapter of this book has all sorts of formulas for deceiving the enemy.[17] Some of them would probably succeed but there is doubt about the others. The idea seems to be to cause the enemy to believe that his opponent has great magical power. There is a paste to turn the hair white and one to turn the body black; mixtures to rub on the body which can be set fire to without burning the skin; oil to put on the feet so that a man may walk over hot coals without being burned; the method of making a ball, with fire inside, which can be put in the mouth and cause a man to seem to be breathing out fire and smoke; one may walk fifty yojanas unwearied if he wears camel-skin shoes covered with banyan leaves and smeared with the serum of the flesh of an owl and

---

13 Text; p. 210, l. 3; tr. p. 264.
14 Text, p. 210, l. 4; tr. p. 264.
15 Text, p. 210, l. 6; tr. p. 264.
16 Text, p. 410; tr. p. 495.
17 Text, p. 414; tr. p. 500.

a vulture. Also, one can prevent any other fire burning in a certain place by producing a fire in the following manner: by the friction of a black-and-white bamboo stick on the rib bone of the left side of a man who has been slain with a sword or impaled, or by rubbing a human bone on the rib bone of another man or woman. This fire must then be circumambulated three times from right to left as is usual in black magic.[18] At the end of this chapter the author says one may bring about peace by causing fear in the enemy through exhibiting these marvels which he has mentioned.

The third chapter in the fourteenth book is pure, unmixed magic.[19] In order to see clearly in the dark the following method should be used: Having taken the left and the right eye of a cat, a camel, a wolf, a boar, a porcupine, a *vāguli,* a *naptṛkā* (some kind of night-bird) and an owl, or of one or two or many such nightroving animals, one should make two kinds of powder. Then having anointed his right eye with the powder from the left eyes and his left eye with the powder from the right eyes he can see in the darkest night.[20]

Or if invisibility is desired, having fasted three nights one should, on the day of the star Pushya, sprinkle with the milk of goats and sheep, barley planted in soil placed in the skull of a man who has been killed by a sword or has been impaled. Then, having put on a garland of the barley which sprouts from this, he may walk invisible.[21]

The skin of a snake filled with the ashes of a man bitten by a snake will cause beasts to be invisible.[22]

There are five sets of *mantras* in this chapter, to be used in connection with certain of the magical performances, and the names of many demons are called upon. There is much preparation to be made before the use of the *mantras.* For example, having fasted for three nights one should, on the dark fourteenth day of the month of the star Pushya, purchase from a woman of an outcast tribe some fingernails. Then,

---

18 Text, p. 418, l. 1; tr. p. 504.
19 Text, p. 418; tr. p. 505.
20 Text, p. 418; l. 11; tr. p. 505.
21 Text, p. 418, l. 17; tr. p. 505.
22 Text, p. 419, l. 14; tr. p. 506.

together with some beans, having kept them unmixed in a basket, one should bury them in the cremation grounds. Having dug them up on the second fourteenth day, and having pounded them up with aloes, one should make little pills. Wherever one of the pills is thrown, after chanting the *mantra,* all will sleep.[23]

The aims of the other magical formulas with *mantras* attached are: to cause a door to open of itself, to cause a cart drawn by bullocks to appear and to take the invoker travelling through the sky, to cut a bowstring without touching it.

A different method of procedure is used in the following rite: when the image of an enemy is bathed in the bile of a brown cow which has been killed with a sword on the fourteenth day of the dark half of the month, the enemy becomes blind.[24]

The ingredients mentioned in some of the formulas are almost equal to those of Macbeth's witches. If the nail of the little finger, some part of the nimb tree and of the mango tree, honey, the hair of a monkey, and the bone of a man, are wrapped in the garment of a dead man and are buried in the house of a certain man or are walked over by him, that man, his wife and children and his wealth will not last three fortnights.[25]

This chapter ends with the statement that one should by means of *mantras* and medicines protect one's own people and do injury to those of the enemy.

Evidently the enemy was expected to use some of the same methods, for the fourth and last chapter of the fourteenth book is composed of antidotes for poisons employed by him.

The magic in this work seems to me to be of enough interest aud importance to lead one to go into it more deeply in connection with the magic contained in the better known Sanskrit literature, and this I hope to do.

---

[23] Text, p. 420, l. 12; tr. p. 507. In this connection cf. RV. 7. 55.

[24] Text, p. 423, l. 11; tr. p. 510.

[25] Text, p. 423, l. 18; tr. p. 510.

THE BABYLONIAN PRACTICE OF MARKING SLAVES

Beatrice Allard Brooks

Wellesley College

A practice connected with Babylonian slavery, knowledge of which is involved in considerable obscurity, is that of the method of marking slaves. The interpretation of this custom depends largely upon the meaning assigned to *galabu*,[1] *abuttu*, and *muttatu*. Laws I and II of the *Sumerian Family Laws* provide as the penalty to be imposed on a child who repudiates his parents: DUBBIN MI-NI-IN-ŠA-A, for disloyalty to father, and MUTTATI-A-NI DUBBIN ŠA-NE-IN-SI-EŠ, for disloyalty to mother. The sign transliterated DUBBIN may mean 'a sharp pointed instrument', 'finger', or 'nail-mark' (OBW 104). But DUBBIN MI-NI-IN-ŠA-A is translated in the Akkadian text, *u-gal-la-ab-su*. This part of the law has been translated by Lenormant (*EA* 3, p. 22), 'ils lui rasent'; by Sayce (*Records of the Past* 3, p. 24) 'confirming it by (his) nailmark (on the deed)'; by Oppert (*Doc. Jur.* 56, l. 26) 'et confirmat ungue impresso'; by Müller (*Gesetze Ham.* 270) 'macht er ihm ein Mal'; and Winckler (*Gesetze Ham.* 85), 'soll er ihm die Marke schneiden.' Haupt in his *Sumerische Familien-Gesetze* (p. 35) stated that the expression should not be read 'er legt ihm den Fingernagel an,' but 'er scheert es.' Jensen (*KB* 6, p. 377, l. 11) believed *galabu* to mean 'cut', referring to incised marks, and DUBBIN to be the instrument of cutting. MUTTATI-A-NI DUBBIN ŠA-NE-IN-SI-EŠ is translated in the Semitic text *mu-ut-ta-aš-šu u-gal-bu-ma*, which Sayce translated 'his hair is cut off'; Oppert (*Doc. Jur.* 57, l. 31) 'et

[1] For an early interpretation of *galabu* and *muttatu*, see *ZA* 3, pp. 101, 231.

sigillo impresso confirmat'; Bertin (*TSBA* 8 p. 255), 'his phallus and nails also they shall cut him'; Müller (*Gesetze Ham.* 271), 'ihm ein Mal auf sein Gesicht macht'; and Winckler (*Gesetze Ham.* 85), 'so soll man ihm seine Marke schneiden'. The sign  is, according to Barton, of unknown origin (*OBW.* 426), and is usually read *muttatu* (Br. 9861, M. 7487). The phonetic ŠU-I in the Code has been read *galabu* (Br. 7148, M. 5143), and appears only in Col. XXXV, §§ 226, 227, where it refers both to the agent of the operation and the operation itself. These laws provide that if a ŠU-I, without the consent of the owner of a slave, *ab-bu-ti warad la še-e-im u-gal-li-ib,* his hand should be cut off; and if any one deceive a ŠU-I and induce him to *ab-bu-ti warad la še-e-im u-gal-li-ib,* that man should be put to death, and the ŠU-I upon swearing he did not mark the slave knowingly, should go free. *Ab-bu-ti* has been interpreted in these laws as 'a mark'.[2] The expression *la še-e-im* has been translated: Scheil (*DP* 4, p. 156), 'inaliénable'; Winckler (*Gesetze Ham.* 63) 'unverkäuflich (?)'; Peiser (*KU* 1, p. 63), 'unsichtbar'; Harper (p. 81), 'that he cannot be sold', and Barton,[3] 'unsalable'. § 127 provides that if a man falsely accuse a sacred woman, he shall be brought before the judge and *mu-ut-ta-zu u-gal-la-bu.*

The word *abuttu* is employed also in § 146 which states that if an *amtu* who has borne children attempt to take rank with her mistress, the mistress may *ab-bu-ut-tam i-sa-ak-ka-an-ši-ma,* and count her among the maid servants. This has been interpreted by Scheil (*DP* 4, p. 71), 'une marque elle lui fera'; Winckler,[4] 'zur Sklavenschaft soll sie sie tun'; Peiser (*KU* 1, p. 42), 'Fesseln legt sie ihr an'; Harper (p. 51) and Barton,[5] 'she may reduce her to bondage'. That the Sumerian laws remained in force for a long period, we have evidence from documents requiring this same type of punishment in the case of a child who repudiates his adoptive father (Schorr 9), a woman her sister (*op. cit.* 5), a slave her mistress (*op. cit.* 77), a slave his mistress who has adopted him (*op. cit.* 35), the daughter of a

[2] Scheil, *DP* 4, p. 156; Johns, *Bab. and Ass.* 63; *KU* 1, p. 63; Barton, *Arch. and Bible,* 335; Müller 60, Winckler 63.

[3] *Arch. and Bible,* p. 335.

[4] *Gesetze Ham.* 42, cf. n. 2.

[5] *Arch. and Bible,* p. 327.

sacred woman her adoptive mother (*op. cit.* 83), and a son his adoptive parents (*op. cit.* 8). In all these documents the custom is expressed by use of the word *galabu* alone. *Muttatu galabu* appears as the penalty inflicted on the loser of a law-suit (*op. cit.* 263, 264).

Galabu is related to the Hebrew *gallâb*, 'barber' cf. Ez. 5 1. Johns (*ADD* 2, § 174) believes the *amêl* ŠU-I or *galabu* to be a haircutter, who 'cut, or scratched, a mark on the skin of a slave, to serve as a mark of ownership'. The ŠU-I is mentioned with lists of officials.[6] Meissner (*MAP* p. 152), would read *galabu* in the contract literature 'ein Mal machen', rather than 'scheeren' (Haupt, *Sum. Fam. Ges.* 35). It is used not only in contract literature, but in omen and magical texts. *Galabu* describes the treatment to be practised on a snake if he appeared to a man at a certain time as an ill-omen;[7] and it is used with *zimri* to indicate bodily injury (*op. cit.* 1, p. 369). The word occurs in a Cappadocian tablet, where it has been translated 'castration'.[8] The custom of castrating slaves has been common, as for example, among the Romans.[9] According to Xenophon,[10] such treatment was thought to make them better servants because they had no family ties. It would however be absurd to suppose that this was a customary mark of slavery in Babylonia.

Abuttu, according to Delitzsch (*HWB* 13) and Muss-Arnolt (*Dict.* 12), means 'fetter'. Haupt (*Sum. Fam. Ges.* 35) identifies it with עֲבֹדָה, 'service', and Zimmern (*BB* 59) with עבט, 'to bind'. Besides the occurrences above quoted, *abuttu* is used in a birth-omen text which states what will happen if a woman bear a child *ab-bu-ut-ta* (Jastrow, *Rel.* 2, p. 928). With this text Jastrow compares another line which interprets an omen in case a woman bears a child *bi-ir-tum*, which he translates 'with a fetter', but which Frank (*Studien* 152, l. 20) leaves

---

6 *MAP* p. 130; *AJSL* 21, p. 75.

7 Jastrow, *Rel.* 2, p. 778. The snake's head is to be covered and his sides *galabu*.

8 *Babylonica* 2, p. 29 and note.

9 Cf. Buckland, W. W., *The Roman Law of Slavery* p. 8 etc.

10 *Cyrop.* 7 vs. 60—65. Cf. also Haupt's interpretation of DUBBIN in some passages as signifying 'castrate', *ZK* 2, p. 271, *ASKT* 86, l. 62; 60, l. 3.

untranslated. In the birth omen texts *abuttu* has been interpreted 'Fessel' by Jastrow, and 'Sklavenmal' by Dennefeld.[11] *Abuttu* is employed with *sabatu* and the expression is translated by Zimmern (*BB* 59) and King,[12] 'to go security for', 'to intercede for'.

Muttatu, commonly translated 'forehead', appears in a Neo-Babylonian sign list translated by Haupt (*Sum. Fam. Ges.* p. 71); a brief bilingual vocabulary in the same work has *muttum.*[13] Holma[14] stated that *muttatu* referred to the head, probably the forehead, and that it was at least one of the seats of the mark put on slaves. It occurs also in birth omen texts (Jastrow *Rel.* 2. 913). *Muttatu* appears more frequently than the other words involved in this discussion, but in some cases it is clearly to be interpreted other than 'forehead' or 'hair'. In one instance it is an object offered as a gift to a deity, probably meaning a head-band.[15] In K. 2007, Ob. 18 we find *muttat mâti,* here interpreted by Jastrow (*Rel.* 2, 921. n. 8) as 'the front side' of a piece of land, and by Dennefeld (*op. cit.* 54) as a 'part' of the land, but by Frank (*Studien,* 149) as 'Stirne'. Likewise in the birth omen text occurs the expression *muttat lisâni-šu ša imitti la baši,* here referring to a part of the tongue. It has been considered a synonym for *labâru* (*BA* 1, p. 513).

Connected with this discussion is the problem of the interpretation of *bukânu.* This has been supposed to refer to a ceremony which took place at the time of the transaction of a sale, originally a slave sale. Meissner (*MAP* 120) suggests its connection with Talm. בּוּכְנָא '(Mörser)-Stöpsel, Pistill', and denies its connection with βυκάνη. Daiches[16] follows Meissner and Delitzsch (*HWB* 172^b); Schorr (*ABR* No. 17, l. 10) follows Meissner and Daiches. Langdon (*ZA* 25, p. 208), in discussing the expression *iṣu tag,* Semitic *bukanan šutak*

[11] *Bab.-Ass. Geburtsomina* 64, l. 20; 109, l. 5; 195, l. 4; cf. also Holma, *Die Namen der Körperteile im Assyrisch-Babylonischen,* p. 18, n. 2.

[12] *Bab. Magic and Sorcery* 169.

[13] P. 73 (Text II R 36, 63—66), cf. Haupt's comparison with Syriac.

[14] *Die Namen der Körperteile,* p. 35.

[15] Cf. Langdon, *Neubab. Königsinschriften,* p. 70, l. 15. But it may mean 'hair', and be analogous to Nu. 6 18.

[16] *Altbabylonische Rechtsurkunden,* No. 1.

(*CT* 4, 33^b, 10; 6, 40^b, 8), states that the earlist occurrence of the phrase is in a record of a slave purchase by Lugalušumgal[17], where the expression is *giš-a ib-ta-bal-eš*. He concludes that because the phrase occurs in a grammatical text (K. 46) in a section concerning slavery, it was originally connected with slave sales, and that the *bukânu* may have been a die or stamp with a short handle. The beginning of Col. IV of K. 46 is unfortunately destroyed, but these lines evidently relate to the punishment to be inflicted on a runaway slave.[18]

3. *DUBBIN mi-ni-in-kud*	*u-(gal-la-ab-šu)*
a mark they shall cut(?) on him,	they shall brand him,
4. *GAR in-ni-in-sar*	*ab-bu-ut-tum i-ak-ka-an-šu*
in fetters they shall place him,	a fetter they shall put on him.
5. *azag-kù in-ni-in-si*	*a-na kaspi (i-nam-din-šu)*
for money they shall sell him,	for money they shall give him
6. *šar-a-ni nu uk-si-in-gin*	*a-na bêl-šu (ul u-tar)*
to his lord he shall not go back,	to his lord he shall not return,
7. *é šar-a-ni-ta ba-da-ǵa-a*	*is-tu bit bêl-šu*
from the house of his lord he disappeared.	from the house of his lord he disappeared.
8. *ba-da-ǵa-a-ta im-ma-an-gur-eš*	*is-tu iḫ-li-ku (ú-te-ru-šu)*
On account of his flight they shall return him:	On account of his flight they shall turn him:
9. *ba-da-ǵa-a-ta im-ma-an-si-eš a-ta*	*is-tu iḫliku u-te-ru-(?)*
On account of his flight they shall turn him from mankind.[19]	on account of his flight they shall turn him (from mankind.)

---

[17] *RA* 4 (3), Pl. X, No. 32.

[18] K. 46 in II R 12—13; *ASKT* 60; AL^3 91 f.; Lenormant, *Choix*, No. 12 p. 20. Earlier interpretations: Oppert *Doc.* p. 10, *EA* 2 p. 4 ff., 3 p. 1 ff., 223, 226, 232.

[19] *OBW* 521^4. Or 'from sonship'.

10.	*giš gir-gir na-in-gar*	*kur-ṣa-a ṣa-na se-pi-šu*
	In bonds they shall place him,	A fetter on his feet they shall put,
11.	URUDU *keš-keš im-ni-in-sig*	*šar-šar-ra-ta*[20] *i-pa-ir*
	bonds of bronze they shall appoint,	bonds they shall put on,
12.	*giš i-na ib-ta-an-bal*[21]	*bu-kan-na u-še-ti-ik*
	a wooden shackle he shall drag.	a shackle he shall drag.
13.	*lù-da*[22](?) *-ǵa-a giš-e-lu*	*ḫa-laq ṣa-bat*
	An escaped man, verily he was captured,	(As) a fugitive captured,
14.	*igi-ni-na ni-in-bal*	*i-na pa-ni-šu ik-kur*
	on his face shall be made (the mark of) a foreigner.	on his face he shall be made strange.[23]

The first lines of this text show similarity with the *Sumerian Family Laws.* The text seems to indicate that the *bukânu* was a shackle worn on the foot. But Schorr (p. 116) states that this expression is found in land as well as slave sales of northern Babylonia (Babylon, Sippar, Dilbat) from the earliest time to Samšuiluna. The so-called 'slave tags' were of clay, not of wood, else we should be tempted to establish their identity with the *giš* GAN-NA (*bukânu*). Whether the *bukânu* represented the handing over of a staff by the seller to the purchaser as a symbol of agreement is not certain.[24] If the *bukânu* was an instrument used for marking a slave it is not likely that it would have been used in land deals.

Langdon finds evidence of a real mark made on a slave in the use of *šindu* = *šimtu,* Code Col. XXII 67, pointing out the suggestion of Ungnad in *OLZ* which offers the interpretation, 'a mark burned into the flesh'. But Langdon concludes that since the Code has a law concerning the *changing*

---

20 *MA* 1121^{b}.

21 *OBW* 9^{5}; cf. also *MA* 152^{b}.

22 Haupt reads *zu.*

23 I am indebted to Professor Barton for this interpretation of lines 9, 13, 14.

24 Jastrow, *Civilisation*, 342.

of a slave-mark, the custom might well have been that of painting (*OLZ* 12, p. 113). With this may be compared a document containing the phrase *ši-in-du ša amtu-u-tu,* 'sign of her slavery' (*BA* 4 p. 11).

Keiser[25] calls attention to a class of temple officials, the *širaqu,* mentioned in a number of tablets belonging to the Yale Babylonian Collection, — a class of persons who bore a mark with which they were perhaps branded. From No. 120 l. 4, Keiser suggests that this mark, used also on animals, may have been a star. But what function these *siraqu* had, we do not know. It is possible, if *širaqu* is to be identified with the root *šaraqu,* 'to give', that they may have been slaves handed over to the temple as donations. This, however, is purely conjectural.

The slave-mark may have been on the hand (Holma, *op. cit.* p. 120). According to Clay[26] a slave was said to be twice branded on the right hand, the expression being *šaṭ-rat.* A mark may, according to Holma (*op. cit.* p. 28), have been made on the ear, similiar to the Hebrew custom, Ex. 21 6.

Do any of these theories adequately explain the laws? There appears to be no reason for doubting that *galabu* means *cutting* or *scraping* of some kind, but the real nature is not clear. Code §§ 226, 227 indicate that the operation was performed by a special person who made it his business, and it is to be noted that these laws directly follow those dealing with physicians and their practice. They further indicate, from the seriousness of the penalty attached, that the operation was of importance. Whether *la še-e-im* in this law is to be read 'unsalable' or 'unsightly' has been questioned. The root שים may mean 'fixed', 'decreed', 'purchased'. If all slaves were *galabu,* it is not clear why anyone would want to submit a slave to this operation again; it is therefore more reasonable

---

25 *Bab. Inscrip. in Collection of J. B. Nies,* 1, p. 9.

26 J. P. Morgan 2, p. 35. With this it is interesting to compare No. K. (dated 411 B. C.) in Sayce-Cowley *Assouan-Papyri,* which refers in ll. 4 and 5 to the marking of a slave. Whether *Yod* of the Aramaic is to be interpreted 'hand' has been questioned (p. 48, no. 4). If the real meaning were known, we might find here an interesting analogy between Babylonian and Egyptian Jewish custom.

to suppose that the law refers to a mark of mutilation which would render the slave of no commercial value. And since a Babylonian slave might, if he had sufficient funds, buy his way out of slavery, one questions whether this 'slave-mark' was of a permanent nature, if applied to all slaves. The custom may have been merely the shaving of the head and beard. The prevalence among the Semites of shaving the head, not only as a badge of slavery, but as a sign of mourning, and as a penalty for breaking marriage vows,[27] furnishes a strong argument for the existence of the custom among the Babylonians. But this treatment would not be lasting and archaeological evidence shows no uniformity in the representation of headdress or beards of slaves, nor would it seem probable that the shaving of a slave's head without the permission of the owner would require so severe a penalty. Further, the generally accepted theory of Meyer[28] that the Sumerians shaved their heads close while the Semites did not, precludes the theory that the slave-mark was merely a cutting of the hair. If the process was that of incising or tattooing on the forehead, it is curious that there is no evidence in the sculpture, even though the human head is usually rendered in profile, of an attempt to distinguish slaves by representing such markings. There is no evidence that incision was made in the ear; the sculptures show that the servile classes wore no ear-ring, while the king and official attendants are seldom depicted without it. It might be conjectured that the incising was done on the top of the head and the hair allowed to grow over it; this would in part satisfy the objection that a freed slave would have to bear his marks for life, always failing to be recognized as a freeman. The testimony of the monuments of the custom of leading captives by means of a hook through the lip, together with the fact that *abuttu* may mean 'fetter', suggests the possibility that a metal ring was attached to a slave, which, upon his being freed, was cut off. K. 46, Col. IV, mentioned above, suggests that a metal fetter was attached to the feet of a fugitive slave as punishment. In this connection

---

[27] *WZKM* 19, p. 91 f.; cf. also Wellhausen, *Reste Arab. Heid.* 195 f.
[28] *Sum. und Sem.* p. 24, n. 3.

may be noted a letter of Nebuchadrezzar[29] which appears to be a reply to a letter of appeal made by some prisoners of consequence who were held in durance and compelled to go under service. The prisoners had protested against their fetters.

A document which more than any other seems to shed light on this problem is from the time of Ammîditana, and cites the case of a man who was bought as a slave in a foreign land and later returned to Babylon, his native city (Schorr, 37). After five years, he was summoned and told, *el-li-ta ab-bu-ut-ta-ka gu-ul-lu-ba-at.* The document further states that he was told he could enter the *ridûti*, but that he refused and said he would claim share in his father's estate. It provides that the brothers shall not refuse him this share, even though he has been temporarily reduced to slavery. But the meaning of *el-li-ta ab-bu-ut-ta-ka gu-ul-lu-ba-at* has been thus interpreted: Schorr, 'Du bist frei, deine Sklavenmarke ist (hiermit) abgeschnitten'; Peiser (*KU* 740), 'Deutlich(?) ist Dein Sklavenmal geschnitten'; Johns (*Bab. and Ass.* 176), 'thy *abuttu* is clearly branded'. *Ellita,* from *ellû,* usually means 'bright', 'clean', and is employed in adoption documents to express the ceremony which symbolized the adoption of slaves. It is not clear what the ceremony was, but it seems intended to represent a cleansing. This phrase of our document might mean, 'thou art cleansed, thy mark is cut off'. The fact that this man had been a slave in a foreign land would require his reinstatement as a free citizen, and allow the use of the same word as in an adoption tablet. Now if we interpret this either 'thou art free', or 'thou art cleansed', the whole phrase would imply that the *abuttu* was of such a character that it could be obliterated. If we accept the interpretation of *ellita* as 'clearly', the document becomes more intelligible and offers a partial solution of the question of the nature of the custom.

According to the text of this document, which is published only in *C. T.* 6, 29, the  told the slave he could go with the UḲU-UŠ (= *ridu ša ṣabe* pl.). 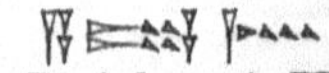 has been read by Schorr *a-bi ṣabe meš,* and by Daiches A-KAR

[29] *YBC* Vol. 3, No. 1. cf. ll. 13—16. Cf. *Bibliotheca Sacra,* 77, No. 307, p. 362.

meš. But Meissner[30] read A. EDIN *meš.* It is not certain what class of society these persons belonged to, but in Nikolsky, *Documents,* No. 32, l. 6 the expression designates an official. So far as we now know, the *ṣabe* was one of the lowest classes of society. This man was told that his *abuttu* was clear and that he could go with the *ridûti,* or overseers of the *ṣabe*; it was evidently because his *abuttu* was visible that he was classed with the *ṣabe.* Code § 16 would imply that a fugitive slave was liable to be called to serve as a public slave and K 46 quoted above shows that a fugitive slave was liable to receive a mark which would make him an outcast. § 280 provided that a slave bought in a foreign land, if he returned later to his native city, must be released.[31] The man mentioned in this document had been a freeman in Babylon, had gone to a foreign country and been reduced to a *warad,* but still bore a mark of slavery. Returning to Babylon, as a *warad* who had been free-born he wished to claim share in his father's estate, but as he had a slave-mark he was assigned to the *ridûti.* It would therefore appear that only the *ṣabe* had a permanent 'slave-mark'. This theory accounts for the occurrence of the custom in the *Sumerian Family Laws* and the contracts; it accounts for the severity of the punishment inflicted on one who *galabu* a slave without the owner's permission, — such a mark would render him unsalable by a private individual for the mark would make him a public slave, or state property; and it explains § 146 of the Code, for it is to be assumed that women as well as men belonged to the *ṣabe* class. We still lack evidence to prove the real character of this mark; while archaeological data are wanting to establish what the mark was, documentary evidence strongly indicates that whatever it was, it was of a comparatively permanent nature.

Additional Note: The publication of the newly discovered Assyrian Law Code (Jastrow, *JAOS* 41. 1ff.) presents a few points for discussion in connection with the problem of the marking of slaves. The practice of boring the ear seems definitely to appear in this code. But here it is a penalty, imposed in the one case upon a man who allows a harlot to

---

[30] M 8813, and cf. *HWB* 79a.

[31] Cf. *WZKM* 22, pp. 385—98.

appear veiled, § 39, and in the other upon a person who holds another for debt, § 43. In the former law it is further stipulated that the offender shall serve one month's royal service. Does the connection of these two penalties imply that the infliction of the one made suitable the performance of the latter? Attempt has been made in this article to indicate the possibility that since not all who were slaves had a mark, and since the mark appears to have been permanent and something of a disgrace, it was only persons of the lowest class of slaves who bore a real mark. It may be, therefore, that § 39 tends to corroborate this theory. But the statement of the custom of boring the ear, analogous to the Hebrew practice of the Covenant Code, does not prove that this was the method of marking slaves in general or public slaves in particular. Furthermore, § 4 legislates that the penalty imposed upon a male or female slave who receives stolen goods be the cutting off of the nose and ear. This same penalty is imposed in other instances, cf. §§ 4, 5, 39, where the offender is not a slave. The purpose of the penalty seems to be to inflict punishment and disfiguration. If the ear was the member that bore the sign of servitude, is it probable that it would have been cut off? If the boring of the ear in the manner designated was practised on a large group of persons, and not merely on the occasional offender, again we ask, why do we find no trace of it in sculpture? The Assyrian Code unfortunately does not throw any new light on the Mesopotamian custom in question.

DIVINE SERVICE IN EARLY LAGASH

SAMUEL A. B. MERCER

WESTERN THEOLOGICAL SEMINARY, CHICAGO

THE OBJECT of this study is to describe as clearly as possible the elements of divine service in early Sumeria. The elements are taken to be gods, temples, priests, sacrifices, altars, dedications, ritual, and festivals. Our study will be confined to early Lagash, that is, from the earliest times in Lagash to the end of the reign of Urukagina, when Lagash was captured by Lugalzaggisi. It will be based upon only those inscriptions which can be dated with certainty. They are the royal inscriptions, the numerous business tablets, and seal cylinders and other similar works of art.[1]

At an early date in the development of Southern Babylonia the city of Lagash became an important centre, and consequently its god became powerful.[2] Lagash must have been

---

[1] Abbreviations of less common use in this article are: *Amherst* = T. G. Pinches, The Amherst Tablets, Pt. I, London, 1908; *CMI* = Clay, *Miscellaneous Inscriptions in the Yale Babylonian Collection,* New Haven, 1915; *Déc.* = Heuzey, *Découverts en Chaldée,* Paris, 1887 ff.; *DP* = Allotte de la Füyé, *Documents présargoniques,* Paris, 1908 ff.; *KSA* = King, *A History of Sumer and Akkad,* N. Y., n. d.; *KSTD* = Keiser, *Selected Temple Documents of the Ur Dynasty,* New Haven, 1919; *KU* = Kohler und Ungnad, *Hammurabi's Gesetz,* Leipzig, 1904 ff.; *Nik.* = Nikolski, *Drevnosti Vostochniya,* S. Petersbourg, 1908; *Nou. Fouill.* = Cros, Heuzey, Thureau-Dangin, *Nouvelles Fouilles de Tello,* Paris, 1910 f.; *RTC* = Thureau-Dangin, *Recueil de Tablettes Chaldéennes,* Paris, 1903; *SAK* = Thureau-Dangin, *Die Sumerischen und Akkadischen Königsinschriften,* Leipzig, 1907; *TSA* = de Genouillac, *Tablettes Sumériennes Archaiques,* Paris, 1909; Ward in Curtiss = Curtiss, *Primitive Semitic Religion of To-day,* Chicago, 1902.

[2] For the idea of god in Sumeria and early Babylonia, see Mercer, *Religious and Moral Ideas in Babylonia and Assyria,* Milwaukee, 1919, ch. 2.

connected with Nippur, for Ningirsu, the god of Lagash, is often called the warrior god of Enlil of Nippur.[3] Ningirsu's name means lord, or lady, of Girsu, one of the four quarters of the city of Lagash. He was considered the son of Enlil, and his consort was the goddess Bau. Three of his daughters are mentioned in the inscriptions of early Lagash,[4] and four others are named in the inscriptions of the reign of Gudea.[5] Besides these there grew up around Ningirsu a regular family of gods. There were DUN-x,[6] Ninsar, the sword-bearer of Ningirsu,[7] Ninšaḫ,[8] Ninḫarsag,[9] and Ninâ,[10] a water-goddess and deity of oracles and dreams, after whom one of the earliest kings of Lagash, Ur-Ninâ, was named. There were other deities who associated themselves with Ningirsu, such as, Dumuziabzu,[11] DUN-šag-ga,[12] son of Ningirsu, Impae,[13] Lama,[14] Lugaluru,[15] Ninki,[16] Innina,[17] Urnuntaea,[18] and Zazari.[19] Enlil, king of lands, was also associated with Ningirsu.[20] But while there were many temples and shrines in Lagash and many deities were worshipped, nevertheless Ningirsu and his great temple, E-ninnû, were the centre of the city's worship. As prince, lord, king, and god, Ningirsu received the adoration of gods and men. His special emblem was Imgig, the lion-headed mythological eagle, which was usually represented as standing on two lions.[21] These early Sumerian gods are represented with flowing hair, bound with a double fillet; with cheeks and upper lip shaven, with a long beard, and nude to the waist, the legs being clad in a close-fitting garment. They usually carry a war-mace, and are often equipped with a great net (*šuš-gal*) in which they trap their enemies.

Around Ningirsu and his associated deities clustered all the details of official worship, and they were the object of the people's veneration. Divine worship was the most compelling force in early Sumeria, and we shall find that it and its

---

[3] *SAK* 38; *CMI*, No. 4, Col. 1.
[4] *SAK* 44 *g* 2, 10—12. [5] Cyl. B 11, 3 ff. [6] *SAK* 36 *l* 3.
[7] *SAK* 42 *c* 21 ff. [8] *SAK* 42 *a* 4. [9] *SAK* 20 *b* 2.
[10] *SAK* 2 *a*. [11] *SAK* 20 *b* 2. [12] *SAK* 44 *g* 2.
[13] *SAK* 44 *g* 2. [14] *SAK* 56, 20. [15] *SAK* 18, 6.
[16] *SAK* 18, 3. [17] *SAK* 20 *b* 2. [18] *SAK* 44 *g* 2.
[19] *SAK* 44 *g* 2. [20] *SAK* *l* 1. [21] *SAK* 44 *e*; *KSA* 98.

influence permeated and controlled society. There was nothing more real than the existence of the gods, and their worship was the people's most serious duty.

The central and most important building in a Sumerian city was the temple. The exact form and arrangement of the Sumerian temple as it existed in Early Lagash are unknown. There are only very scanty remains of Ningirsu's temple, and these date from the time of Ur-Bau and Gudea. But judging by our knowledge of the temple and temple-area at Nippur in the time of Ur-Engur, the temple itself was in the form of a rectangle with inner and outer chambers, and with a great tower or ziggurat.[22] The temple-area was irregular in form, but covering about six times as much ground as the temple. The Sumerian sign for temple is a rectangle with cross-bars, which points to the usual form of the earliest temples.

In Lagash there were, as we shall see, many temples, but the most important one stood in Girsu and was called É-ninnû. It was the temple of Ningirsu. In the other three quarters of the city, Ninâ, Uruazagga, and Uru, were important temples. But shrines and smaller temples were numerous.

Temples were usually constructed at the command of the gods. Thus Gudea was directed by his god to build a temple, and an interesting plaque[23] shows Ur-Ninâ, of Lagash, carrying a basket filled with material probably for the building of Ningirsu's temple. The historical inscriptions are full of references to the building or restoring of temples by the kings for various gods.[24]

Archaeological excavations teach us that the Sumerian temple was built of brick, but it was finished inside with wood.[25] It is likely that a temple could contain a chapel, for the term *êš* (e. g. *êš Gir-zu* *SAK* 6 *i*, etc.) is used in such a way, in relation to the regular term for temple, *é* (e. g. *é* *^{d}Ninâ*, *SAK* 4 *e*, 2), that it seems to indicate a chapel.[26] There is

---

[22] If *é-PA* means temple tower (cf. Gudea St. G 1, 15) there is evidence that the tower was common in Early Lagash, e. g., *SAK* 2*a* 4, 3; 6*l* 23.
[23] *Déc.* pl. 2 *bis.* [24] E. g. *SAK* 2 etc. [25] *SAK* 2*a* 5, etc.
[26] Contrast, however, *éš-DUG-RU* and *êš-gi gi-KA-na*, *SAK* 30*a* 2–3; 32*b*.

however no doubt about the meaning of *bár*. We read of the *bár* ᵈ*Enlil, bár* ᵈ*Ninḫarsag, bár* ᵈ*Ningirsu*, and *bár* ᵈ*Babbar* (*SAK* 38, 2, 14—18) in connections which leave the meaning doubtless. The Sumerian sign for *bár* is a square with strokes across the four sides, and indicates a simple square hut built of reeds. Another word used in a similar connection, *ti-ra-aš*, seems to indicate a palace chapel. Thus we meet not only with the phrase *é ti-ra-aš* (*SAK* 24*d* 2, 4) but also with *é-gal ti-ra-aš*. Now, while *é* may mean either a temple or room in a temple (*SAK* 42*b* 4, 2—4), yet the term *é-gal* always means palace, and the phrase *é-gal ti-ra-aš* would seem to mean palace-chapel (*SAK* 22, 7, 19).[27] The *bur-sag* was also a chapel. We read of a *bur-sag* of ᵈBau to which offerings were brought for her (*SAK* 46*h* 2, 1—3) and it is called an *é* temple, or room in a temple.[28] Still another word which may have been used for chapel is *mal-lu-ur*, although the context leaves the matter uncertain (*SAK* 46*h* 2, 4—6).

The more important temples had spacious yards or fore-courts, where was usually to be found a well (*SAK* 28*i* 3), where, if we can judge from later use, a part of the service was performed.[29] Each temple had its store-houses and magazines, where dates (*é-engur-ra-kalumma*),[30] wine (*é-KAŠ-GAR*),[31] and corn (*kīrmaḫḫu*, Gudea, Cyl. A 28, 5—6) were kept.[32] From the account of Urukagina's reform we learn indirectly of the lands, oxen, and asses which the temples possessed, and how the priests had become rich and powerful.

Associated with some of the temples of important deities there was a sacred grove (*tir-azag*). Thus, Entemena built one for Ninḫarsag and also for Ninâ and for Ninmaḫ.[33] But whether any part of the temple service was conducted there it is impossible to say. It would seem, from inscriptions of the time of Gudea, that the grove was a garden where vines, palms and flowers were cultivated for use in the services of the temple.

In the temple itself were various objects the exact use of

---

[27] Contrast, however, Gudea, Cyl. A 10, 15—18.
[28] *SAK* 42*b* 4, 2—4. [29] Gudea, Stat. E 4, 12f. [30] *SAK* 30*a* 4, 2ff.
[31] *SAK* 42*b* 2, 6. [32] *SAK* 38*n* 2, 19f. [33] *SAK* 30*a* 5; 32*a* 2; 32*f* 29—30.

which cannot be always ascertained, although they were most likely used in connection with the services. Many of these objects were dedicated to the gods. Thus, in the temple of Ningirsu, in the time of Urukagina, was a *ki-AB*, which may have been a chapel (*SAK* 58*k* 5, 3f); and in the same reign a *ki-KU-akkil-lí-ni* was dedicated to Dunšagga (*SAK* 42*b* 2, 9), Other similar objects are referred to, e. g., *Ḫi-en-da-ka* (*SAK* 58. 5, 1), *Im-dub-ba* and *nam-nun-da-ki-gar-ra* (*SAK* 38, 2 and 4), *íb-gal-KA-KA-a-DU* (*SAK* 10*a* 4), *a-ḫus* (*SAK* 30a 3), *a-EDIN* and *nin-gar* (*SAK* 2*a* 3—4) *íb-gal* (*SAK* 2*b* 2—3), *ki-nir* (*SAK* 4*e* 3), and *URU-NIG* (*SAK* 4*f* 2). Besides these objects that cannot be identified, there were many others that were dedicated for use or for ornamentation in the temples. Such were, an onyx bowl dedicated to Bau by Ur-Ninâ (*SAK* 8*p*), the famous silver vase dedicated by Entemena to Ningirsu (*SAK* 34*h*), a stalagmite vessel dedicated to Dun-x by Entemena (*SAK* 34*g*); and various other vessels were dedicated to such deities as Ningirsu and Ninâ.[34] It was customary to dedicate war maces,[35] and plaques as votive offerings were probably attached to the walls of shrines and temples. Votive pillars and blocks of stone were also common,[36] and they may have been considered especially sacred because of some association with a deity or with some ceremonial act. Statues of deities were sometimes dedicated and erected in temples, where such deities were venerated.[37] Some of the objects in the temple bore names, such as, '^{d}Ningirsu interceded in the temple of Uruk with ^{d}Bau for Urukagina',[38] and the furnishings of the temple were adorned with gold and silver.[39]

The chief temples of Lagash, in this early period, were:

é-ninnû of Ningirsu (*SAK* 34*h* 18—19)
é-giš-pu-ra of Ningirsu (*SAK d*)
é-unug^{ki} of Ningirsu and Bau (*SAK* 44*d*)
é-ad-da of *im-šagga* of Enlil (*SAK* 30*a* 1 [Rückseite])
é-an-na of Innina (*SAK* 58*k* 5, 5)
é-me-ḫuš-gal-an-ki of Galalim (*SAK* 42*b* 3)
é-engur of Ninâ (*SAK* 58, 1 [Rückseite], 6—7)

---

[34] E. g. to Ningirsu by Enannatum, a *bur-sum-gaz* (*SAK* 28*a*); to Ninâ a *ḳum-maḫ* (*SAK* 28*k*). [35] E. g. *SAK* 31*c*; 34*i*.
[36] *SAK* 6*k*; 26*g*. [37] E. g. *SAK* 2*b*, *c*; 4*c*. [38] *SAK* 44*d*.
[39] *SAK* 36*m* 2; CMI No. 4, cols. 1—11.

There are other references to temples in Lagash which bore no specific name. Such as:

é-Ningirsu (*SAK* 4*f* 1)
é-Bau (*SAK* 42*b* 3)
é-Ninâ (*SAK* 2*a* 1)
é-Babbar (*SAK* 44*f*)
é-Ama-geštin (*SAK* 58*k* 2)
é-Dumuzi-abzu (*SAK* 58*k* 5)
é-Gatumdug (*SAK* 4*e* 4)
é-Ḫegir (*SAK* 44*c* 26—30)
é-Impae, é-Urnuntae, and é-Zazari (*SAK* 44*g* 2)
é-Anna (Innina) (*SAK* 10*a* 4)
é-Lama (*SAK* 44*g* 2, 6—8)
é-Lugaluru (*SAK* 58*k* 1)
é-Nindar (*SAK* 58*k* 5)
é-Nimmaḫ (*SAK* 32*f* 27)
é-Ninmarki (*SAK* 4*c* 3)
é-Ninšar (*SAK* 42*c* 21—24)

The king among the early Sumerians, as elsewhere, was the representative of the gods, and as such was the priest *par excellence*. In fact, the Sumerian king bore a title which marked him as the man of his god. He was called *patesi*. In Early Lagash this term was interchangeable with *lugal*, the word for king, for while we read of the *patesi* of a town or the *patesi* of a god we never find the phrase *patesi* of a king. Eannatum invariably styled himself *patesi*. Later it was looked upon as less kingly.[40] Sometimes the king was called *patesigal*, the great *patesi*, to represent his office as ideal high priest.

With the multiplication of royal duties, the king was gradually obliged to delegate his priestly acts to others. This began to be so before the earliest date of which we have historic records. Then there arose an official priesthood. But always the office of the priest remained a high one, and sometimes a royal person acted as an official priest. Thus, both Enetarzi and Enlitarzi were priests before they became *patesi* and king. Both were

---

[40] C. Frank, *Studien zur Babylonischen Religion*, Strassburg, 1911, 38—42; *KSA* 106*n* 1.

priests of Ningirsu.[41] And Ili, priest of Ninab or Ninni-eš, was appointed by Entemena as *patesi* of Umma.[42] So important and influential was the priesthood that events were dated according to the time of their installation, e. g., *mu en maš-e-ni-pád,* the year the priest was installed;[43] *mu en ba-túg,* the year the priest was invested.[44] But their influence was often used to further their own interests, so much so that Urukagina's reform centered mainly around the excesses of the priesthood.

There were many classes of priests. The commonest priestly class was the *šangu* (Ideog. *ŠID*). The *šangu* was always the servant of some deity, such as Lugalkigalla, priest of Ningirsu,[45] Luenna, priest of Ninmarki;[46] or of some temple, such as the high priest of Girsu.[47] There were also palace priests.[48] At the head of the *šangu* stood the *šangu-maḫ,* or high priest. He was usually a very influential man. Thus, Dudu, high priest of Ningirsu, was called the servant of Entemena,[49] dates referred to him, and he was represented on bas reliefs.[50] Another priestly class was the *mušlaḫḫu.* The word means serpent-driver, and points to some species of serpent-worship. There was a chief serpent-priest (*mušlalaḫ-gal*),[51] and he is represented on the so-called family-bas relief,[52] wearing a short dress with plain body. He must have been a very important man to have been thus pictured with the royal family. A third class of priests was the *kalû,* whose fees were reduced by Urukagina.[53] And there was likewise a *kalamaḫ* or chief *kalû.*[54] What their particular function was is not yet clear, although they would seem to have been connected with the musical department of the temple.[55] Other priestly classes were the *šutug,*[56] or anointers, at whose head stood the *šutug-nun-ne,* or great *šutug* (*pašišu*);[57] the *abarakku,* a kind of anointing priesthood;[58] and the *nâru,* a musical

---

[41] *Nou. Fouill.* I 52—53; *RTC* 16. [42] *SAK* 38, 3—4.
[43] *KSTD* 103. [44] *KSTD* 107. [45] G. A. Barton, *Sumerian Business and Administrative Documents,* Philadelphia, 1915, No. 2, rev. II.
[46] *Nou. Fouill.* I 52—53. [47] *Amherst,* tablets in Brussels p. 12.
[48] *RTC* 61, 6. [49] *CMI* No. 4, Col. III. [50] *Déc.* pl. 5 *bis,* fig. 2 et p. 205. [51] *SAK* 8 γ 2. [52] *Déc.* 2 *ter* 1; 2 *bis* 1.
[53] *SAK* 46*g* 4, 2; *TSA* 9 I 72. [54] *TSA* 2 rev. I. [55] *SAK* 50, 10, 22; cf. Frank, op. cit. 6—7. [56] *SAK* 46*l.* [57] *SAK* 44*g* 4, 12.
[58] *SAK* 48*h* 4, 4; cf. Frank, op. cit. 12ff.

order.[59] There were also seers and diviners (*šul-dumu*),[60] but the *âšipu* and *bârû*, who became so famous later, as incantation priests, do not appear in the Early Lagash period. Some priests sacrificed and some took care of the food, etc., of the temple, but no distinguishing mark between them has as yet been discovered.

There were also priestesses, but they were not as common as the priests. The *nin-dingir*[61] priestesses were, in the Hammurapi period, cloistered nuns.[62] Priestesses were sometimes of royal blood, if we may judge from Lidda, the daughter of Ur-Ninâ, who held a high rank in the temple hierarchy.[63]

Very little can be learned about the personal habits and practices of Sumerian priests of this early period. It is, however, certain that they married (*RTC* 16), and that they kept servants (*RTC* 16). It is probable that they lived on the lands of the temple.[64] A bas relief gives us a fair idea of the appearance of a priest.[65] It shows a beardless man, with upper part of the body and feet naked. Another plaque, but perhaps later than the period under consideration, has a bearded priest, dressed in a long mantle hanging from his left shoulder. His upper lip is shaven, and he wears a turban, similar to those known to have been worn during the Hammurapi period.[66]

The central act of worship in Early Lagash was the sacrifice. This was so much so that the temple was sometimes referred to as a place of offering.[67] In fact, the temple was the home of sacrificial worship.[68] The *res sacrificii* varied. Eannatum offered to Enzu of Ur a sacrifice of four doves,[69] to Babbar of Larsa two doves and bulls,[70] and to Ninḫarsag of Kish two doves.[71] To Enki of Eridu and to his daughter Ninâ fish were offered in sacrifice.[72] But the material of

---

[59] *SAK* 2, note a, no. 4. [60] *RTC* 16. [61] *SAK* 5, 10, 12. [62] *KU* II 120 b. [63] Plaque of Ur-Ninâ, *Déc.* pl. 2 *bis*. [64] *RA* 7, 182. [65] *Déc.* pl. I, fig. 2, et p. 87—91. [66] *Déc.* p. 251. [67] E. g. *ê sá-dúg-ka-ni*, temple of her (Bau) offering, *SAK* 46 *h* 2, 2. [68] E. g. *ê sá-dúg an-na il-a-ni*, the temple where heavenly offerings are presented, *SAK* 44 *c* 32. [69] *SAK* 16, 21. [70] *SAK* 16, 1, 33—40. [71] *SAK* 14, 18. [72] *SAK* 14, 19; *Amherst*, 1.

sacrifice was almost limitless. Animals, fish, birds, cakes, clothes, metals etc., were offered on various occasions.

Liquid offerings, or libations, were likewise common. Water was often offered[73] and fonts were built to contain such water (*SAK* 2*b* 5), of which there were several varieties, the *abzu* (*SAK* 2*b* 5), the *abzu-banda* (*SAK* 4*f* 4, 6) and the *abzu-pasirra* (*SAK* 30*a* 5). The water contained in these fonts may have been also used for other purposes. Libations of oil were common,[74] and in later times wine was offered in libation (Gudea Cyl. B 5, 21).

It is not possible to say with certainty whether or not the people of Early Lagash offered human sacrifice. There is, however, a significant picture on a plaque published by Ward in Curtiss, fig. 6, which depicts a sacrificial service. There is an altar with flames rising from the oil(?) offering. A kid and a bird are offered. Besides that there is a man seized by two others and brought towards the altar. There is no legend, but the scene suggests that the seized man is to be offered as a sacrifice. So far as I am aware, this is the only evidence for human sacrifice in Early Lagash. But this is far from conclusive.

In the inscriptions of Early Lagash there are a few places where offerings are mentioned in connection with the statues of human beings.[75] But there is here no evidence that such human beings are deified. There is nothing to show that these offerings were anything else than gifts placed beside the statue of human beings in their honour, in much the same way that we place wreaths on a statue. Otherwise, the offerings were made in the same way and for the same reason that the Sumerians of this early time placed drink, food, and a bed in the graves of the dead.[76]

Memorial or votive offerings were often placed in the temples. These usually took the form of inscribed plaques, with a hole

---

[73] Ward in Curtiss, fig. 8.

[74] Ward in Curtiss, fig. 7, where the flame indicates the burning oil.

[75] Thus, offerings were made in the reign of Lugalanda in connection with the statue of Ur-Ninâ, *KSA* 169; offerings were also made for the statue of Šagšag, wife of Urukagina, *TSA* 34 VI and rev. VI.

[76] *SAK* 46*g* 5–6; 50, 9.

in the centre, whereby they were suspended vertically on the walls. Other objects were offered as memorials, such, for example, as the clay object in the form of an inscribed olive offered in honour of Ningirsu by Urukagina (*SAK* 44).

Related to the sacrificial service, but not a sacrifice, was the service of dedication. Exactly what the form of this service was, it is impossible to say; even as it is impossible to say what were the details of the service of sacrifice. But the inscriptions are full of references to objects that were dedicated to the gods in the great temples of Lagash. We think at once of the great silver vase which Entemena dedicated to Ningirsu in É-ninnû to ensure the preservation of his own life (*SAK* 34*h*). It is one of the most precious objects which archaeology has recovered from the graves of the past. Ur-Ninâ dedicated a canal to Ninâ (*SAK* 2), and one to Enlil of Nippur (*KSA* 107); and a warrior dedicated his arms to Ningirsu.[77] The pouring of a libation sometimes accompanied a dedication service.[78]

The central object in divine service was the altar, which itself was a dedicated object. The earliest Sumerian altar was a square boxlike object with one high shelf at the back. On the altar was placed the material of sacrifice and on the shelf was usually set a vase. Ward in Curtiss, fig. 1, shows two flat cakes on the altar, with a vase, over which a libation is poured; fig. 2 represents an altar with a pile of cakes and a bird, probably a dove; fig. 3 shows an altar with cakes and the head of a goat, and a worshipper approaching with a goat in his arms; and fig. 4 depicts an altar with a cup, from which rises a flame, an indication of burning oil. A later, but still early, form of Sumerian altar was what has been called the hour-glass altar—an altar in the shape of an hour-glass. Ward in Curtiss, fig. 5, represents a marble altar from which rise two flames (or branches) and a worshipper approaches with an animal in his arms; fig. 6 shows an hour-glass altar with two flames (or branches), a kid, a bird, and a man being brought by two other men towards the altar; fig. 7 represents an altar with flames, and a worshipper who holds a goat on one arm and with the other pours a libation. He is attended

---

[77] *Déc.* pl. 1 *bis*, fig. 1, and p. 164—166. [78] *KSA* 112.

by two persons, one with a pail, the other with cakes. Fig. 8 shows a double hour-glass altar, and a worshipper, who pours a libation from a slender vase. All these plaques with the exception of figures 5 and 6 show a god or goddess to whom the sacrifice is being offered. What have been called flames in some of these scenes may have been palm branches or flowers.[79] The hour-glass altar was very old; indeed, it may have been quite as old as the square altar, for it is the hour-glass altar which is seen in the oldest script. There it is represented with fire burning on the top.[80]

The ritual of the temple centered around the altar. There the deity was present with his symbols of office. The altar is usually represented as standing before the deity, and between him and the worshipper. In his presence the suppliant pours his libation or offers his sacrifice. The material of libation, water, oil or wine, is kept in a vase, but the material for sacrifice lies on the altar, or, in the case of animals, is brought to the altar by the worshipper. The suppliant is sometimes attended by servers who carry material for the sacrificial service. Sometimes the worshipper is led into the presence of the deity by a priest.[81]

The central figure in divine service is the priest. Ur-Ninâ, as *patesi*, presents his offerings to his god with bare feet and body, and when such high officials appear as suppliants on their own behalf they are led before the deity by a goddess. The priest, however, usually leads the ordinary worshipper before the altar, and it is the priest who does the manual acts. He stands nude before the altar, and presents the oblations, which he receives from the suppliant and his attendants, and reads the prayers.[82] The worshipper then stands with hands clasped upon the breast, or folded at the waist, or in a perpendicular position before the face, palms inward, in an attitude of humility, while the priest raises his hand in the attitude of adoration and prayer.[83] In some parts of the

---

[79] *Déc.* p. 211. [80] Barton, *op. cit.* No. 1, Cols. II. 5, II. 6.
[81] These points are illustrated on the figures in Ward in Curtiss.
[82] *CMI* No. 4, Col. IV. [83] *Déc.* pl. 1 *bis*, fig. 1. See also S. Langdon, 'Gesture in Sumerian and Babylonian Prayer', *JRAS* 1919, 531—556, which came to hand after this article was composed.

service there is probably kneeling and bowing, if we may so conclude from the fact that even the god Ninsaḫ kneels and bows before Ningirsu when he intercedes for the life of Urukagina.[84] When Eannatum prayed to Ningirsu for victory over Umma, he lay flat upon his face and saw in a dream his god who assured him that Babbar would advance at his right hand. Whether such prostrations were common in liturgical worship cannot at present be ascertained.

Music must have played a part in the temple ritual for we read of the 'chief temple singer'[85] in the time of Urukagina, and by the time of Gudea it was common. There may have also been religious processions, for from the time of Gudea we have detailed evidence of such a procession.[86] In this procession were four sacred ministers. The first carried in his hands a musical instrument, the second held a sort of adze, the third had his hands joined and in the attitude of prayer, and the fourth had his hands crossed on his breast. Following these was another person, with hands crossed, and a singing woman carrying a musical instrument. The deity is also depicted, as well as the bull for sacrifice. This scene may well have been often duplicated long before the time of Gudea and perhaps during the period of Early Lagash.

What use was made of onions in the temple service cannot be determined, but there is an account of Eannatum's presenting a mortar to the temple of Ningirsu for pounding onions in connection with the temple ritual (*SAK* 28*a*).[87] It is also uncertain whether the burial service was held in the temple. But considering the fact that the temple was the centre of all religious and civil life of the community, it is most likely that it was there that such important services were held. We gain a good idea of the ritual of a funeral ceremony from the Stela of the Vultures.[88] A bull, lying on his back and bound to a stake driven in the ground, is depicted, with a row of six lambs, or better, kids, decapitated. Then there are two large water pots in which are standing palm branches. A

---

[84] *SAK* 42*a* 5; *b* 5. [85] *TSA* No. 2, rev. I; No. 5, obv. II. [86] *Déc.* p. 219—221. [87] For the oath as a temple ceremony and its ritual, see Mercer, 'The Oath in Sumerian Inscriptions', *JAOS* 33, 33—50. [88] *Déc. passim.*

youth pours water for a libation, and bundles of faggots are near for the burning of the sacrifice. It is probably Eannatum himself who presides as priest. At any rate such ceremonies must have been quite elaborate, and have taken place before the altar in the temple.

A festival is usually the occasion of most elaborate ceremonies in divine service. There is abundant evidence that the Sumerians of Early Lagash observed many festivals. There was the Feast of Bau (*DP* 96, 5), the Feast of Dím-kú (*Nik.* 183, 2; *RTC* 35, 6), the Feast of Se-kú (*RTC* 35, 6), the Feast of Lugal-uru (*DP* 105, 7), the Feast of Ne-[gun]-ka (*Nik.* 187, 2) and the Feast of Ninâ (*RTC* 30, 2). When Ur-Ninâ built the Tirash, a festival in honour of Ningirsu was celebrated on the day of the New Moon. Then there were festivals of increase and of eating of grain (*RTC* 33). But of the ritual and ceremonial detail of these festivals we have no knowledge. In later times a New Year's feast was celebrated in Lagash in honour of the marriage of Ningirsu and Bau, when processions were held; in Babylonian and Assyrian times the *akitu* or Feast of the New Year was held with great ceremony; and in Assyrian times there was a 'Festival House', in which such ceremonies were probably held (*MDOG* Nr. 33). It may be assumed that the people of Early Lagash had their festivals on which processions and divine service were held, but for detailed information about them we must await further work of the archaeologist and linguist.

Divine service in Early Lagash was held in honour of many deities, but especially in that of Ningirsu and his consort Bau, in the great temple, É-ninnû, the cathedral of Lagash. There were other temples in Lagash; there were many priests and priestesses; but in É-ninnû we can safely suppose that the *patesi,* or priest-king, often pontificated as patriarch or archbishop. Under him served a whole hierarchy, beginning with the *Šangu-maḫ,* high-priest or bishop, and ending with the humblest of the clergy. They all had their part to play in the divine service, the details of which we may know better in the future. The central act of worship was the sacrifice, though there were also libations and other minor services of prayer, praise and dedication. Services varied in ritual according as they were more or less solemn, and we may be sure that on great festivals the ceremonial was rich and varied. The norm of correct ceremonial was probably to be found in the great É-ninnû, where Ningirsu appeared in all his divinity, and where the royal *patesi* sometimes celebrated. Imagination must suffice, for the present, to enable us to see the stately procession of sacred ministers and choristers move in solemn manner towards the great altar, the presence of Ningirsu; to watch the genuflections, bowing, and prostrations; to see the sacrificial elements offered up with suiting dignity; to hear the music and solemn words of dedication and consecration; to see those varied colours, to hear those strange sounds and to experience the sensations which those far-off people felt as they took part in their service of prayer and praise, adoration and dedication, worship and sacrifice. The corner of the veil which separates us from a full knowledge of the life of the Ancient Orient has been raised, and we await with patience, but deep interest, its gradual lifting that we may attain a clearer and still clearer vision of it all.

THE KASHMIRIAN ATHARVA VEDA, BOOK NINE

EDITED WITH CRITICAL NOTES

LeRoy Carr Barret

Trinity College, Hartford, Connecticut

Introduction

Twenty years ago at this writing my work on the Pāippalāda was begun; including this book nearly one half of the manuscript has been published. The Pāippalāda has been a disappointment because of its corrupt text, which is worse than was at first realized. The somewhat informal mode of presenting the text has drawbacks as well advantages but it is necessary: the transliterated text is the most important feature and with it in hand any one can test the suggested emendations. In emending it has been my endeavor at all times to keep as close to the ms. as possible and to make only such suggestions as can be explained by principles of textual criticism. The treatment of several hymns in this book is not out of accord with this endeavor. The appearance of a given passage in other texts does not change the problem tho complications may be added: it remains a problem of textual criticism.

The Pāippalāda has not as yet furnished any important new material to enrich Atharvan literature. It probably will add to our understanding of the relations of Vedic schools and texts, and in this respect it may indeed prove itself of great worth.[1] Some of the possibilities in this direction are suggested in my article *Pāippalāda and Rig Veda.*[2]

Just here I desire to record my thanks for the kindly expressions of encouragement received from a number of scholars

---

[1] Roth, *Der AV in Kaschmir*, pp. 19, 20.

[2] *Studies in honor of Maurice Bloomfield*, pp. 1—18.

who are interested in Sanskrit studies: and in particular my thanks to Maurice Bloomfield, teacher, and Franklin Edgerton, fellow-student, and editor of Book Six of this text, who have been ever generous with helpful and valuable advice.

Of the ms.—This ninth book in the Kashmir ms. begins f. 111b 20 and ends f. 133b 7, covering slightly more than eleven and one half folios: the numbers just quoted are those which stand in the upper right corner of each page of the facsimile, '120ab—129ab' being omitted. On the birchbark the numbers are at the lower left corner of the reverse of each folio; the birchbark omits the numerals '102—111': all my references are by the numbers in the upper right corner. There is but one slight defacement in this book: most of the pages have 18 or 19 lines, a few 20 or 21.

Punctuation, numbers, &c.—Within the individual hymns punctuation is most irregular; the colon mark is occasionally placed below the line of letters rather than in it. At f. 132a 3 accents are marked on two pādas. The hymns are grouped in anuvākas: the first has five kāṇḍas all properly numbered, with 'anu 1' after the fifth; the second has six kāṇḍas all properly numbered, with 'anu 2' after the sixth; the third has nine kāṇḍas all properly numbered, but 'anu 3' is lacking after the ninth; for the fourth anuvāka the ms. seems to give nine kāṇḍas but the numbering is confused for '1' appears thrice ('2' does not appear), '3—8' appear next consecutively, and at the very end is 'zz zz anu 7 zz', which should doubtless be 'zz 9 zz anu 4 zz'. In the edited text however anuvāka 4 has five hymns. In the case of hymn 21 the material belongs together and regardless of kāṇḍa numbers the edited form will surely be approved: so also for hymn 23. The unity of the material edited as hymn 22 is not quite so distinct, but the habit of this ms. in dealing with a refrain was the deciding influence in making the arrangement given; in hymn 25 the situation is similar but the indications of a refrain are clear. There are only a few corrections, marginal or interlinear; one omitted pāda is supplied in the margin.

Extent of the book.—The book as edited has 25 hymns, of which one is all prose, one partly prose, and one is a group of brāhmaṇa passages with quasi mantras. The normal number of stanzas is probably 12, continuing the progression of preceding books: 8 hymns are edited as having 12 stanzas each. Assuming the correctness of the stanza division as edited we make the following table.

1	hymn	has	6 st	= 6	stanzas
3	hymns	have	7 st each	= 21	"
1	hymn	has	8 st	= 8	"
4	hymns	have	10 st each	= 40	"
1	hymn	has	11 st	= 11	"
8	hymns	have	12 st each	= 96	"
1	hymn	has	13 st	= 13	"
2	hymns	have	14 st each	= 28	"
1	hymn	has	15 st	= 15	"
1	"	"	17 st	= 17	"
1	"	"	21 st	= 21	"
1	"	"	28 st	= 28	"
25	hymns	have		304	stanzas

New and old material.—There are 17 hymns in this book which may be called new tho some of these contain several stanzas appearing in other texts. The number of essentially new stanzas is 184, and the new pādas are 692 (repetitions not subtracted); new also are the 12 formulae of hymn 20, and the 12 brāhmaṇas and quâsi mantras of hymn 21.

Of the hymns in Ś. 5 seven are represented here more or less completely; one hymn of Ś. 19 appears here.

ATHARVA-VEDA PĀIPPALĀDA ŚĀKHĀ
BOOK NINE

1
(Ś. 5. 27.)

[f. 111 b 20] **navamaṁ ārambhaṣ kṛtāḥ z** [f. 112 a] **oṁ namo nārāyaṇāya z oṁ namaś śārikābhagavatyāiḥ oṁ namas sarasvatyāiḥ zz zz** [2] **oṁ ūrdhvā asya samidho bhavanty ūrdhvā śukrā śucīṅṣy agneḥ dyūmattamā supratīkasya sū-**[3]**nos tanūnapād ambhasuro viśvevedāḥ devo devaṣu devaṣ patho yukta madhvā ghṛtena | ma**[4]**dhvā yajñaṁ nakṣati prīṇāno nurāśaṅsas sukṣad devas savitā viśvavārah aśchā-ya**[5]**m eti śavasā ghṛtena īḍe vahniṁ namasādhriṁ sruco dhvareṣu | prayutsu sruve kṣatasya** [6] **mahimānam agne-**

svenamindrasu prayutsu | vasuś cetiṣṭho vasudhātamaś ca | dvāro [7] devīr anyasya viśved vratā dadaṅte gneḥ | uruvyacasva dhāmnā pacyamānā te sya vṛṣaṇo [8] divyā na yonā | uṣasānaktesaṁ yajñam avatām adhvaraṁ naḥ dāivā hotāra imam a[9]dhvaraṁ no agner jihve bhi gṛṇītaḥ kṛṇutā na sviṣṭiṁ tisro devīr barhir edaṁ [10] sadaṅtv iḍā sarasvatī | mahābhāratī gṛṇānā | taṁ nas turīṣam adbhutaṁ purukṣu [11] tvaṣṭā suvīryaṁ rāyas poṣaṁ viśvata nābhim asmahe | vanaspate va sṛjā rarā[12]ṇas sumanā devebhyaḥ | agnir havyaṁ śamitā sūdayati agne svāhā kṛṇu[13]hi jātaveda indrāya bhāgaṁ | viśve devā havir idaṁ juṣantāṁ z ɪ z

For the introductory phrases read: navamam ārambhaṣ kṛtaḥ z oṁ namo nārāyaṇāya z oṁ namaś cārikābhagavatyāi z oṁ namas sarasvatyāi zz zz

For the hymn read: ūrdhvā asya samidho bhavanty ūrdhvā śukrā śocīṅṣy agneḥ | dyumattamā supratīkasya sūnoḥ z 1 z tanūnapād asuro viśvavedā devo deveṣu devaḥ | patho 'yukta madhvā ghṛtena madhvā yajñaṁ nakṣati prīṇānaḥ z 2 z narāśaṅso 'gnis sukṛd devas savitā viśvavāraḥ | acchāyam eti śavasā ghṛtena z 3 z īḍe vahniṁ namasāgniṁ sruco 'dhvareṣu prayatsu | sruve yakṣad asya mahimānam agneḥ z 4 z †svena mindrasuprayutsu† | vasuś cetiṣṭho vasudhātamaś ca z 5 z dvāro devīr anv asya viśved vratā dadante 'gneḥ | uruvyacasā dhāmnā patyamānāḥ z 6 z te asya vṛṣāṇāu divyā na yonā uṣasānaktā | imaṁ yajñam avatām adhvaraṁ naḥ z 7 z dāivā hotārā imam adhvaraṁ no agner jihvayābhi gṛṇītam | kṛṇutaṁ nas sviṣṭim z 8 z tisro devīr barhir edaṁ sadantv iḍā sarasvatī mahābhāratī gṛṇānāḥ z 9 z tan nas turīpam adbhutaṁ purukṣu | tvaṣṭā suvīryaṁ rāyas poṣaṁ vi ṣyatu nābhim asme z 10 z vanaspate 'va sṛjā rarāṇas sumanā devebhyaḥ | agnir havyaṁ śamitā sūdayāti z 11 z agne svāhā kṛṇuhi jātaveda indrāya bhāgam | viśve devā havir idaṁ juṣantām z 12 z 1 z

In editing this I have followed KS to some extent, particularly in the division of stanzas. In 2c possibly 'nakti should be read. In 4a Ppp is unique and so doubtful; its sruve in 4c is also unique, but Edgerton would read sa yakṣad with other texts. In 7a vṛṣāṇāu does not give a good comparison and perhaps should not be suggested; all others yoṣaṇe.

2

(Ś. 5. 28.)

[f. 112a 14] yajuṅṣi yajñe sami svāhāgneṣ pravidvān iha vo yunaktu yunaktu devas sa[15]vitā prajānan yasmin yajñe sayuja svāhā | indra yukthāmadāni ya[16]jñe asmin pravidvān pranaktu sayujas svāhā chandāṅsi yajñaṁ marutas svā[17]hā | māteva putraṁ pipṛteṣyuktva **āiṣā navidā priyo yajūṅṣi śiṣṭāḥ | [18] patnībhir vātehi yuktā yem agaṅ barhiṣā prokṣaṇebhir yajñaṁ tanvānādi[19]tis svāhā | viṣṇur yunaktu bahudhā upāsmin yajñe sayuja svāhā | tvaṣṭā [20] yunaktu bahudhā virūpāsmin. indro yunaktu bahudhā vīryāṇy asmin. so[f. 112b]mo yunaktu bahudhā payāṅsy asmin. | bhago yunaktv āśiṣo ny asmāsmin yajñe sa[2]yuja svāhā | aśvinā vrahmaṇetam arvāg vaṣaṭkāreṇa yajñaṁ vardhayantāu svāhā | [3] vṛhaspate vrāhmaṇoṣy arvān yajñaṁ vayaṁ svaritaṁ yajamānāya dhehi svāhā | [4] z 2 z

Read: yajūṅṣi yajñe samidhas svāhāgniṣ pravidvān iha vo yunaktu z 1 z yunaktu devas savitā prajānann asmin yajñe sayujas svāhā z 2 z indra ukthāmadāni yajñe asmin pravidvān yunaktu sayujas svāhā z 3 z chandāṅsi yajñe marutas svāhā māteva putraṁ pipṛteha yuktāḥ z 4 z prāiṣā nivida āpriyo yajūṅṣi śiṣṭāḥ patnībhir vahateha yuktāḥ z 5 z eyam agan barhiṣā prokṣaṇībhir yajñaṁ tanvānāditis svāhā z 6 z viṣṇur yunaktu bahudhā tapāṅsy asmin yajñe sayujas svāhā z 7 z tvaṣṭā yunaktu bahudhā virūpāsmin ° ° ° z 8 z indro yunaktu bahudhā vīryāṇy asmin ° ° ° z 9 z somo yunaktu bahudhā payāṅsy asmin ° ° ° z 10 z bhago yunaktv āśiṣo nv asmā asmin yajñe sayujas svāhā z 11 z aśvinā vrahmaṇetam arvāg vaṣaṭkāreṇa yajñaṁ vardhayantāu svāhā | vṛhaspate vrahmaṇehy arvāñ yajño ayaṁ svar idaṁ yajamānāya dhehi svāhā z 12 z 2 z

The edited text is assimilated to that of Ś.: the greatest difficulty is in 12d, where it might be possible to read yajñam āyan ° °: dhehi at the end of the pāda is somewhat open to suspicion. In 12a and 12c the Ś. readings vrahmaṇā yātam and vrahmaṇā yāhy might be intended.

3

[f. 112b 4] āpaṣ punantu varuṇaṣ punātv aya ca yaṣ pavate viśvadānīṁ | yajño [5] bhago adhivaktādhivantāgniś ca naṣ pāvayetām sūryasya | daśaśīrṣo daśaji[6]hvārabhe vīruko bhiṣak. | mā te riṣaṅ khanitāsmāi ca tvā khanāmasi | daśarā[7]treṇa kilamasya vīrudhā veda bheṣajaṁ yatas tud abhriyākhanaṁ kilāsaṁ nā[8]śayāmasi te | apsv anyā virohati dhatvaṁn anyādhi tiṣṭhati | kilāsam anyā nī[9]nīnaśad varcasānyā sam añjatu | ājyena ghṛtena juhomi kilāsabheṣajaṁ [10] vīrudhān agnes samkāśe kilāsaṁ nānu vidyate | piśaṅgaṁ rūpaya bhavati ka[11]kalmāṣam uta saṁdṛśi | kilāsa naśyetaṣ paraṣ pra tvā dakṣāmi vīru[12]dhā yāni pṛthag utpatanti nakṣattrāṇīva saṁdṛśi | kilāsaṁ sarvaṁ nā[13]śayaṁ no bhīvādyema vīrudhā yadi vā puruṣeṣitāt kilāsa pary āja[14]gaṅ namo namasyāmo devān pratyak kartāram ṛśchatu | śīrṣṇas te skandebhyo lalā[15]ṭāt pari karṇayoḥ oṣadhyā kilāsaṁ nāśayāmi te | śastā varṇā itya[16]n arātis sahoṣadhī grīvābhyas tā uṣṇihābhyaṣ kīkasābhyo anūkyāt. | [17] aṅsābhyāṁ te dorbhyāṁ bāhubhyāṁ pari hastayoḥ pṛṣṭibhyas te pārśvābhyāṁ śro[18]ṇibhyāṁ sasa | ūrūbhyāṁ dve ṣṭhīvadbhyāṁ prāpadābhyāṁ | oṣadhyā [19] varṣajūtayā kilāsaṁ nāśayāma te | śastā varṇā ityan arātis saho[f. 113a]ṣadhī | gravābhyas ta uṣṇihābhyaṣ kīkasābhyo anūkyāt. aṅsābhyāṁ te dobhyāṁ bā[2]hubhyāṁ pari hastayoḥ | pṛṣṭibhyas te pārśvabhyāṁ śroṇibhyāṁ pari bhaṅsase | ūrū[3]bhyāṁ dve ṣṭhīvadbhyāṁ pārṣṇibhyāṁ prāpadābhyāṁ | oṣadyā varṣajūtayā kilāsaṁ nā[4]śayāmase | śastā varṇā ityanurotis sahāuṣadhi z 3 z

Read: āpaṣ punantu varuṇaṣ punātv ayaṁ ca yaṣ pavate viśvadānīm | yajño bhago adhivaktādhivaktāgniś ca naṣ pāvayetāṁ sūryaś ca z 1 z daśaśīrṣo daśajihva ārabhe vīrudho bhiṣak | mā te riṣan khanitā yasmāi ca tvā khanāmasi z 2 z daśarātreṇa kilāsasya vīrudhā veda bheṣajam | yatas tad abbriyākhanaṁ kilāsaṁ nāśayāmasi z 3 z apsv anyā vi rohati dhanvany anyādhi tiṣṭhati | kilāsam anyā nīnaśad varcasānyā sam añjatu z 4 z ājyena ghṛtena juhomi kilāsabheṣajam | vīrudhām agnes saṁkāśe kilāsaṁ nānu vidyate z 5 z piṣaṅgaṁ rūpe bhavati kalmāṣam uta saṁdṛśi | kilāsa naśyetaṣ paraṣ pra tvā dhakṣāmi vīrudhā z 6 z yāni pṛthag utpatanti nakṣatrāṇīva saṁdṛśe | kilāsaṁ sarvaṁ nāśayan †no bhīvādyema† vīrudhā z 7 z yadi vā puruṣeṣitāḥ kilāsaṁ pary ājagan | namo namasyāmo devān pratyak kartāram ṛcchatu z 8 z śīrṣṇas te skandhebhyo lalāṭāt pari karṇayoḥ | oṣadhyā varṣajūtayā kilāsaṁ nāśayāmi te | śastā varṇā ity †an arātis† sahāuṣadhiḥ z 9 z grīvābhyas ta uṣṇihābhyaṣ kīkasābhyo anūkyāt | oṣadhyā ° ° ° | śastā ° ° ° z 10 z aṅsābhyāṁ te dorbhyāṁ bāhubhyāṁ pari hastayoḥ | oṣadhyā ° ° ° | śastā ° ° ° z 11 z pṛṣṭibhyas te pārśvābhyāṁ śroṇibhyāṁ pari bhaṅsasaḥ | oṣadhyā ° ° ° | śastā ° ° ° z 12 z ūrubhyāṁ te 'ṣṭhīvadbhyāṁ pārṣṇibhyāṁ prapadābhyām | oṣadhyā varṣajūtayā kilāsaṁ nāśayāmi te | śastā varṇā ity †an urotis† sahāuṣadhiḥ z 13 z 3 z

Our 2cd is edited to the form given in Kāuś. 33. 9ab; our division of stanzas may be wrong here. For 10ab and 13ab see Ś. 2. 33. 2ab and 5ab (Pāipp. 4. 7. 2 and 6). The arrangement of stt. 9—13 seems correct but it is possible that 13 is not the correct total number of stanzas in the hymn.

4

[f. 113a 4] **sahāi**[5]**va vo hṛdayāni saha vijñānam astu vaḥ sendro vṛttrahā karat saha devo vṛha**[6]**spatiḥ |**
Read sahendro vṛtrahā in c.

samānam astu vo hṛdayaṁ samānam uta ro manaḥ samānam agnir vo deva[7]**s**
The right-hand margin has samānā hṛdayaṁ manaḥ pāṭhaḥ, with indication that it is to be read after devas.

Read vo in b, and samānaṁ in d; it would be an improvement if we could read for d samānā hṛdayāni vaḥ (Ś. 6. 64. 3c).

sā rāṣṭram upādhvaṁ | saṁ jānīdhvaṁ sahahṛdayāt sarve saṁmanam asta va |
Read: samānaṁ rāṣṭram upādhvaṁ saṁ jānīdhvaṁ sahṛdayāḥ | sarve * * * samānam astu vaḥ z 3 z
This has some similarity to Ś. 6. 64. 1.

naṣṭo [8] **vo manyur jīrṇe ṛṣyāt saha | jīvātha bhadrayaḥ yathā putraṣ pravāvada pitṛ**[9]**bhyāṁ vadatu priyaṁ |**
In a I would read syāt, tho riṣyāt might be considered; in b remove colon after saha and read bhadrayā; in c pravāvadaḥ (= prattling?).

sahāiva vo dhānyāni samānāṣ paśavaś ca vaḥ saha pṛthivyāṁ [10] **vīrudhas saha vas santv oṣadhīs**
Read oṣadhīḥ at the end of d, and punctuate.

saha dīkṣā saha yajño vivāho vas sahāma[11]tiḥ saha prapharvā nṛtyanti saha vastriyasatāṁ |

In b read sahamatiḥ, in c probably nṛtyantu: for d we might read saha vas striya āsatām. This is st. 6.

sahāivo vīryāṇi sātyā[12]ni randhayādhvāi sā patattriṇīm iṣum anyassāi hetis asyata

In ab read sahāiva vo vīryāṇy asatyāni, tho the last word is somewhat doubtful; also °dhve is probable. In c read saha patatriṇīm, in d anyasmāi hetim.

saṁ vaśyāmi su[13]matiṁ madhunā vācamāṁ riraṣaṁ yuṣmākam anye śṛṇvantūditaṁ saṅgathe jane |

Read vāśayāmi in a, and in b possibly vacasā rīrasan.

[14] **yuṣmān amittrā vṛṇutān iṣmān apratijanā uta | yuṣmāi jñātitvaṁ preṣṭhaṁ tv a[15]mṛtaṁ martyāya ca |**

In ab read amitrā vṛṇutāṁ yuṣmān prati°, in c yuṣme; perhaps the rest can stand, but a verb at the end of c would seem better; possibly preṣyantu.

saṁ samidyas samākaraṁ sā yūthā gavām iva | samā[16]nam astu vo mano jyeṣṭhaṁ vijñānam anvataḥ

In a samidhas may be possible, with samākaran; in b read saha; at the end of d perhaps anvita, but invata might also be considered.

yad iṁ yad eṣāṁ hṛdayaṁ tad eṣāṁ [17] hṛdaye bhavat. | atho yad eṣāṁ hṛdaṁ tad eṣāṁ hṛdi śrutaṁ |

Read īṁ in a, probably hṛdayaṁ in c; śritam in d.

samānam astu vo [18] manaś śreṣṭhaṁ vijñānam anvataḥ yad iṁ yad eṣāṁ mana eṣaṁ yāni manāṅsi ca madhri[19]yagendra taś chṛṇu rathe pādāv ivāhitāu z 4 z

Read: samānam astu vo manaś śreṣṭhaṁ vijñānam anvita | yad īṁ yad eṣāṁ mana eṣāṁ yāni manāṅsi ca | madryag endra tac chṛṇu rathe pādāv ivāhitāu z 12 z 4 z

The general arrangement of the last three stanzas is not wholly satisfactory, but it appears fairly certain that the hymn has 12 stanzas.

5

(Ś. 19. 6.)

[f. 113a 19] sahasrabāhu-[20]ṣ puruṣas sahasrākṣās sahasrapāt. | sa bhūmiṁ viśvato vṛtvāty atiṣṭhad daśā-[21]ñgulam. tribhiṣ padbhir dyām arohat pād asyehābhavat punaḥ tathā vyakrāmud viṣyaṁ [f. 113b] aśanāśayan. | tāvanto sya mahimānas tato jyāyāṅś ca puruṣaḥ pād asya viśvā [2] bhūtāni tripād asyāmṛtaṁ divi | puruṣa evedaṁ sarvaṁ yad bhūtaṁ yaś ca bhavyaṁ | u[3]tāmṛtatvasyeśvaro yad anyenābhavat sahaḥ yat puruṣaṁ vyadadhuṣ katidhā vyam akalpa[4]yan. mukhaṁ kim asya kiṁ bāhū kim ūrū pādāv ucyete | vrāhmaṇo sya mukham ā[5]sīta bāhū rājanyo bhavat. madhyaṁ tad astu yad vāiśyaṣ padbhyāṁ śūdro ajāyata | [6]virāḷ āgre samabharad virājo adhi pāuruṣāt. | sa jāto abhy aricyata paścā[7]d bhūmim atho purā | yat puruṣeṇa haviṣā devā yajñam atanvata | vasanto a[8]syāsīd ājyaṁ grīṣma idhmāś śarad dhaviḥ | taṁ yajñaṁ prāvṛṣāt prāukṣaṁ puruṣaṁ [9] jātam akramaḥ tena devā ayajanta sādhyā vasavaś ca ye | tasmād aśvā a[10]jāyanta ye ca ke cobhayadataḥ gāvo ha jajñire tasmāt tasmāj jātā ajā-[11]vayaḥ tasmād yajñāt sarvahuta ṛcas sāmāni jajñire | chando ha jajñi[12]re tasmād yajus tasmād ajāyata | tasmād yajñāt sarvahutas saṁbhṛtaṁ pṛṣadājyaṁ [13] paśūs tāṅ cakrire vāyavyān āraṇyān gramyāś ca ye | saptāsyāssan pa[14]ridhayas tri sapta samidhāṣ kṛtāḥ devā yajñaṁ tanvānā abadhnan puruṣaṁ [15] paśuṁ | mūrdhno davasya vṛhato aṅsavas saptatī rājas somasyājāyanta jā[16]tasya puruṣād adhi zz 5 zz anu 1 zz

Read: sahasrabāhuṣ puruṣas sahasrākṣas sahasrapāt | sa bhūmiṁ viśvato vṛtvāty atiṣṭhad daśāñgulam z 1 z tribhiṣ padbhir dyām arohat pād asyehābhavat punaḥ | tathā vyakrāmad viṣvaññ aśanānaśane anu z 2 z tāvanto 'sya mahimānas tato jyāyāṅś ca pūruṣaḥ | pād asya viśvā bhūtāni tripād asyāmṛtaṁ divi z 3 z puruṣa evedaṁ sarvaṁ yad bhūtaṁ yac ca bhavyam | utāmṛtatvasyeśvaro yad anyenābhavat saha z 4 z yat puruṣaṁ vy adadhuṣ katidhā vy akalpayan | mukhaṁ kim asya kiṁ bāhū kim ūrū pādāv ucyete z 5 z vrāhmaṇo 'sya mukham āsīd bāhū rājanyo 'bhavat | madhyaṁ tad asya yad vāiśyaṣ padbhyāṁ śūdro ajāyata z 6 z virāḷ agre sam abhavad virājo adhi pūruṣaḥ | sa jāto aty aricyata paścād bhūmim atho puraḥ z 7 z yat puruṣeṇa haviṣā devā yajñam atanvata | vasanto asyāsīd ājyaṁ grīṣma idhmaś śarad dhaviḥ z 8 z taṁ yajñaṁ prāvṛṣā prāukṣan puruṣaṁ jātam agraśaḥ | tena devā ayajanta sādhyā vasavaś ca ye z 9 z tasmād aśvā ajāyanta ye ca ke cobhayādataḥ | gāvo ha jajñire tasmāt tasmāj jātā ajāvayaḥ z 10 z tasmād yajñāt sarvahuta ṛcas sāmāni jajñire | chando ha jajñire tasmād yajus tasmād ajāyata z 11 z tasmād yajñāt sarvahutas saṁbhṛtaṁ pṛṣadājyam | paśūṅs tāṅś cakrire vāyavyān āraṇyān grāmyāś ca ye z 12 z saptāsyāsan paridhayas triḥ sapta samidhaṣ kṛtāḥ | devā yad yajñaṁ tanvānā abadhnan puruṣaṁ paśum z 13 z mūrdhno devasya vṛhato aṅśavas sapta saptatīḥ | rājñas somasyājāyanta jātasya puruṣād adhi z 14 z 5 z anu 1 z

This version of this hymn is almost identical with that of Ś.; the omission of stanzás 7 and 8 of Ś. is almost surely due to accident. When the AV versions are compared with the others the similarity of Ś. and Ppp. is the more impressive; note particularly our 4c and 11c. Whitney reports some variants from two recensions of this hymn given in the ṛcaka of the Kaṭhas; in 5b he reports enam for vi of Ś.: note our ms. reading vy enam°; and I have allowed cakrire to stand in our 12c because it is reported from the ṛcaka; these readings are further indications of close connection between Ppp. and Kaṭha texts. In 5d I think the ms. intends ucyete, tho Roth (quoted by Whitney) read it ucyate, which is said to be the Kaṭha reading.

6

[f. 113b 16] **imāṁ khanāsy oṣadhi**[17]**m adṛṣṭamahanīm ahaṁ | aśvasyāvo dadāti tvā vāirūpo vājinīvati |**

Read khanāmy in a, and probably °dahanīm aham in b; the rest seems good, tho there may be a corruption at the beginning of c.

[18] **nādṛṣṭā vo jihvās santi na dantā haṁnor adhi nāpi madhyanyaṁ śiras te yū**[19]**yaṁ kiṁ kariṣyataḥ zz zz oṁ te yūyaṁ kiṁ kariṣyataḥ**

Read hanvor in b, and kariṣyatha in d; delete oṁ &c.; madhyanyam is given only by native lexicons and may not be correct here.

oṁ indrāmittrā [20] indraṁ hatā nu va hyāsti nuñcanaṁ indro vas sarvāsāṁ sākaṁ śakras tṛṇeṣu [21] vṛttrahā

For a we may read indrāmitrā indrahatā; for b I would adopt Bloomfield's emendation of Kāuś 116. 7c na va ihāstu nyañcanam; in d read tṛṇeḍhu vṛtrahā.

aśvatarāṅ | ayaśśaphān yā indro adhi tiṣṭhati tvāir vo pi nahye[f. 114a]te mukhānyad uca sarpiṇaḥ

Without the colon pāda a can stand; read yāṅ in b. In c read tāir vo 'pi, and for d probably mukhaṁ yad uta sarpaṇam. In c a subject for nahyete is needed. In d Edgerton would read sarpiṇām.

apinaddham adṛṣṭānā mukhaṁ pāda dṛter iva | utāi[2]ṣāṁ jihvā jiṣūntā na dantā haṁnor adhi |

Read adṛṣṭānāṁ in a, pādaṁ in b, and hanvoṛ in d; for jiṣūntā I can see nothing.

avadhikam asṛgādā nyakroḍādā[3]lipsata | abhītsaṁ sarveṣām āṁtvāni ye dṛṣṭāṣ pṛthivīkṣikaḥ

I am inclined to accept avadhikam (from a-vadha); for b read ni kroḍādā alipsata. In c read abhāitsaṁ, for d ye 'dṛṣṭāṣ pṛthivīkṣitaḥ: aṅkān is the best suggestion I can make for āṁtvāni. This is st 6.

ṛṣyā[4]saṣ pāuruṣākṣo darbhāso vīraṇā uta māuñjā adṛṣṭās sāiryās sarve sā[5]kaṁ ni jāsyaca |

With pūruṣākṣāso we would have a possible form for pāda a; in b read vāiriṇā, in d jasyata. Cf. RV 1. 191. 3bc and 7d.

adṛṣṭānāṁ sapta jātā pṛthivī niṣase mahī | tān indro [6] bāhubhyāṁ sarvāṅ śakro nupāvapat.

Read jātān in a, and possibly nirmame in b: sarvāñ in c, nv apāvapat in d.

vayasyantu sapta jātādṛṣṭāṣ puruṣā[7]disa | grāvṇāṅsūn iva somasya tayāhaṁ sarvān pra mṛṇīmasi |

For ab read vy asyantu sapta jātā adṛṣṭāṣ puruṣādaś ca; in c -āṅśūn; in d tān, tho tayāha would seem good save for the sudden change of meter; the echo of several AV pādas beginning tayāhaṁ may have been at work.

ātmājā ye va[8]stijāruṣā ya utodima tebhyaḥ khanāmy oṣadhiṁ tebhyo bimbī vadhaṣ kṛta |

Read in ab ya ātmajā ye vāsthijā aruṣā; in d kṛtā.

adṛ[9]ṣṭebhyas taruṇebhyo dhavabhya sthavirebhyaḥ aharṣam ugrām oṣadhiṁ tebhyo bimbī vadhaṣ kṛta z

In b we might perhaps read dhavebhyas (from dhū); read ahārṣam in c, and kṛtā in d.

[10] ye ca dṛṣṭā ye cādṛṣṭās titīlāmbhyalunāṅś ca ye | tenāgne sarvān sandaha [11] krimīn anejito jahi z ı z

Read: ye ca dṛṣṭā ye cādṛṣṭās titīlāś cālinaś ca ye | tenāgne sarvān sandaha krimīn anejato jahi z 12 z 1 z

7

[f. 114a 11] śītajalāyata śītāvāta [12] upāgantu himenāgnināvṛto himenāgniṣ parīvṛtā ta tvā devā uru[13]ndhaṁnāt samudriyam ajāvayaḥ

In ab we may read without much hesitation śītajala upāyata śītavāta; in d parīvṛtaḥ; in e taṁ tvā ∘ urudhārāḥ, and in f ajāvayan.

himo jaghāna vo jaṁ himo vakṣaṁ hi ma[14]tsati | himād adhi prayāmasi hime gyavimocanaṁ |

In a read 'jaṁ, in b vakṣan, in d 'gnivimocanam.

himavaṭaṁ śadhara[15]nardhendras saptavadhre | avakā tatra rohatu khale pari bilaṁ tava |

In a himavantaṁ unless himavāṭaṁ be possible, and śatadhāraṁ seems probable; in b possibly ānardhendras: in d read śāle.

arci[16]ṣ ṭe agne prathamam aṅgānāṁ aparāṁ uta | gṛbṇāmi vrahmaṇā nāma dhāma[17]dhā paruṣṣaruḥ

In b read aṅgānām aparam, in c gṛbhṇāmi, for d dhāmadhāma paruṣ-paruḥ.

śītikā nāma te mātā jalāṣo nāma te pitā i[18]ha tvam antarā bhava bāhīkum astu yad rapā

In d read bāhīkam and rapaḥ. This is st. 5.

hime jātodake vṛddhā sindhu[19]tas paryābhṛta | tayā te agrabhaṁ nāmāśvam ivāśvāpidhānyā

In b read ∘bhṛtā, in d ∘ābhidhānyā.

āmā [f. 114b] nāmāsy oṣadhe tasyās ta nāma jagrabhaḥ | agastyasya putrāso mā vidhātu puruṣā[2]n mama |

In b read te and jagrabha; vidhyantu would give a good sense to pādas c d.

mā no agne tanvaṁ sā vāsaṁ sya rīriṣaḥ |

Reading mā vāsam asya we have a fairly good meaning. This is all the ms. offers for this stanza, I think; it does not seem to belong with what precedes or follows.

yaṁ tā samudraja vayam ārohā[3]ma svastaye | divas tādāvāpad rundhārāt samudriyā

In a probably tvā; in c I can only suggest devas tvām avāvapad; for d probably urudhārāt samudriyāt.

apa hiraṇakumbho ha[4]rito vakābhiḥ | parivṛte tenāgnīṁ śamayāmasi |

Read hiraṇyakumbho, 'vakābhiḥ and tenāgniṁ; In can do nothing more towards restoring the stanza. This is st. 10.

śamayāmy arcir agne śi[5]ṣas tastumāvidhā | gṛbhīte dyāvāpṛthivī gṛbhītaṁ pārthivaṁ rajaḥ

For b I can offer nothing; the rest is correct.

ni mu[6]ñjeṣu yad udakaṁ ni nadreṣu yad antaraṁ | yat samudre yat sindhāu tenāgnyaṁ śamayāma[7]si |

The margin corrects to nabhreṣu. I would suggest nir for ni in a and b with abhreṣu in b; a form such as gantu would then have to be understood. In d read tenāgniṁ.

vetamasyāvakāyā naḍasya vīraṇasya ca | rohītakasya vṛkṣasyā[8]gniśamanam ud dhare |

Read vetasasyā° in a.

āyatī uta jāryo vi te harantu yed rapaṣ parāyatī[9]ṣ parāvataṁ parā vahantu yat tapaḥ

In a āyatīr seems necessary, and after it something like udadhārā; in b yad rapaḥ before colon.

himasya tvā jarāyuṇāgne para vya[10]yāmasi | śītike śītim it karo himake himam it kira z 2 z

Read: himasya tvā jarāyuṇāgne parā vyayāmasi | śītike śītam it karo himake himam it karaḥ z 15 z 2 z

Pādas ab appear Ś. 6. 106. 3ab and elsewhere; Ś. has in b śāle pari.

8

[f. 114b 11] **akṛṇvatā lāñgalena padvatā pathayiṣṇunā | lāñgūlagṛha** [12] **carakraṣur vṛkeṇāivam aśvinā |**

In a read akṛṇvata; for cd °gṛhyācarkṛṣur vṛkeṇa yavam aśvinā. But a dual in c would be smoother, and we might consider carkarṣathur.

devā etaṁ madhunā saṁyuktaṁ yavaṁ sa[13]rasvatyām adhu maṇāv acarakraṣu | indra āsīt serapatiś śatakratuṣ kī[14]nāśāman marutas sudānavaḥ

In b read adhi and acarkṛṣuḥ, in c sīrapatiś, in d kīnāśā āsan. This stanza appears in Ś. 6. 30. 1, and elsewhere.

hiraṇmayaṁ kalamaṁ sudānavo divya[15]yā kṛtaṁ | avabhṛtam aśvinā sāraghaṁ madhu | tato yavo virohat so bhava[16]d viṣadūṣaṇā |

Omitting sudānavo we would get a good pāda a, but how it got in is not clear; remove colon and read kṛtam: the next pāda is good if avabhṛtam is acceptable as an aorist. In cd read ° vy arohat so 'bhavad viṣadūṣaṇaḥ. I suspect that we have here the remains of two stanzas, tho I edit them as one.

yavārvāyāṁ saraghāyaṣ pṛṣāya maśv ābharat. |

Read: yavamayas saraghāyāṣ poṣāya madhv ābharat | tato ° ° z 4 z

I feel fairly certain that the refrain should be understood here as indicated; cf. below, hymn 11 st. 11, for a variant of the stanza. The emendation to poṣāya is somewhat unsatisfactory.

[17] **yad vṛkaṁ madhupāvāna savārdhayattam aśvinā |**

Read: yad vṛkam madhupāvanaṁ saṁ vardhayatam aśvinā | tato ° ° z 5 z

This restoration I think is in the right direction.

kāiraṇḍā nāma saratho [18] **vṛkasya saṁsyādhi | tato yato virohat so bhavad viṣadūṣaṇāḥ**

With saragho pāda a can stand; in b māṅsād adhi is the only possibility that occurs to me. Read cd as above.

yad asya [f. 115a] **bharatho madhu saraghā sarthaś carat. sadyas tu sarvato yuvaṁ punar ā dhattam aśvinā**

Pāda a can stand; in b sarathā for sarthaś might be considered but it has little to commend it. In c read yavaṁ. Edgerton would read for pāda a yad asyās saragho madhu.

yo vaṁ digdha[2]viddho hideṣṭopācarat. tīrthe radhram iva majjantam ut taṁ bharatam aśvināḥ z 3 z

Read: yo vāṁ digdhaviddho 'hidaṣṭa upācarat | tīrthe radhram iva majjantam ut taṁ bharatam aśvinā z 8 z 3 z

9

[f. 115a 3] **sa yaṁ vahanty aṣṭāyogā ṣaḍyogā yaṁ caturgavā | sarve te viṣaṁ vidhātām ugro madhyama[4]śīr iva | yasyāiva prasarpasy aṅgam-aṅgaṁ paruṣ-paruḥ tasmād viṣaṁ vi bādhasva ugro ma[5]madhyamaśīr iva | śakaṁlaṁ cana te yuvānyān hanty oṣadhīḥ yavāid yāvayāyad go[6]r aśvāt puruṣād viṣaṁ yavo rājā yavo bhiṣag yavasya mahimā mahān. yavasya [7] manthaṁ papivān indraś cakāra vīryaṁ | ā bharāmṛtaṁ ghṛtasya puṣpam ā rabha | [8] anabhriṣātoṣadhāi idaṁ dūṣayad viṣaṁ ihā yantu digdhaviddhā śūdrā rā[9]janyā uta | cakṣur me sarvā dṛśyate yaṁtu kadā punaḥ z 4 z**

Read: sa yaṁ vahanty aṣṭāyogā ṣaḍyogā yaṁ caturgavāḥ | sarve te viṣaṁ vi bādhantām ugro madhyamaśīr iva z 1 z yasya yava prasarpasy aṅgam-aṅgaṁ paruṣ-paruḥ | tasmād viṣaṁ vi bādhasa ugro madhyamaśīr iva z 2 z śakalaṁ chinatti yavo 'nyān hanty oṣadhīḥ | yavo ya āyad yāvayad gor aśvāt puruṣād viṣam z 3 z yavo rājā yavo bhiṣag yavasya mahimā mahān | yavasya manthaṁ papivān indraś cakāra vīryam z 4 z ā bharāmṛtaṁ ghṛtasya ghṛtasya puṣpam ā rabha | anabhrikhātāuṣadhir idaṁ dūṣayad viṣam z 5 z ihā yantu digdhaviddhāś śūdrā rājanyā uta | cakṣur me sarvā †dṛśyate yāyanti kadā cana z 6 z 4 z

In 1c vi might well be omitted. St. 2 has appeared as Ppp. 8. 3. 11, and Ś. 4. 9. 4, with variants: in c I have followed Ś. tho we might of course read bādhasvogro. The emendations in 3a and 3c are rather violent but not improbable. In 6cd perhaps sarvān and ya āyanti. In 5b bhara might be read for rabha.

10

[f. 115a 10] **jīvātave na martave śiras tārabhāmahe | rasaṁ viṣasya nāvidam udhnaṣ phe[11]na madann iva**

Read ta ā° in b, and ūdhnaṣ phenaṁ in d. Pāda a as here appears Ppp. 5. 17. 8e, and PB. 1. 5. 18d; RV. 10. 60. 9c has mṛtyave. Pādas cd have appeared Ppp. 2. 2. 3.

bhūmyā madhyād divo madhyā bhūmyāṁtvād atho divaḥ madhye pṛ[12]thivyā yad viṣaṁ tad vācā dūṣayāmasi |

In ab read divo madhyād bhūmyā madhyād.

aśvatthe nihataṁ viṣaṁ kapagle [13] nihataṁ viṣam. śilāyāṁ jajñe tāimātaṣ prathamo viṣadūṣaṇī |

In a and b nihatam is possible tho nihitam would seen better. In d read °dūṣaṇaḥ; Edgerton would retain °dūṣaṇī, thinking that tāimātaṣ is corrupt.

vi[14]ṣasyāhaṁ vāirdakasya viṣasya dālbhyasya ca | atho viṣasya māittrasya sāmānīṁ [15] vācam agrabhaṁ |

Read bāindakasya in a, and śamanīṁ in d.

tad id vadaṁtv arthita uta śūdrā utārya viṣāṇāṁ viśva-[16]gartānāṁ sarvathāivārasaṁ viṣaṁ

Read in ab vadantv arthitā° °utāryāḥ; in d viṣam.

puruṣas tvāmṛta kaṇvo viṣa prathama[17]m āvayam. | yathā tanvāropayas tathāsy arasaṁ viṣaṁ |

With āvayat in b the first hemistich can stand, but I have some doubts about pāda a; pāda b = Ś. 4. 6. 3b (cf. Ppp. 5. 8. 2b). In c tanvo aropayas (nom. pl. of aropi) seems probable to me. This is st. 6.

yad vo devā [18] upacīkā ud vehaṁ śuśiraṁ dadhuḥ tatrāmṛtamyāsiktaṁ uś cā[f. 115b]kārārasaṁ viṣaṁ

In b read yad vedhaṁ suṣiraṁ, in c °mṛtasy°; for d tac cakārārasaṁ viṣam. For pāda a cf. Ś. 6. 100. 2a; on upacīka see Ppp. 1. 8. 4. Our cd have appeared as Ppp. 5. 8. 8cd.

śakuntika me vravīd viṣapuṣpaṁ dhayantikā na ropayati na sāda[2]yaty arasaṁ sārvyaṁ viṣaṁ z abhy apaptāni durgāṇi sārīś śakunayo yathā |

For a read śakuntikā me 'vravīd, in d śaravyaṁ viṣam; in e probably apaptan. The last two pādas seem best placed in this stanza. Pādas abc have appeared Ppp. 4. 19. 6.

[3] **ihendrāṇīṁ varuṇānīṁ sinīvālīṁ krukoṣyāṁ gṛhāñ śūraputrāṁ de[4]vaṁ yācāmo viṣadūṣaṇaṁ |**

For krukoṣyāṁ at the end of b I see nothing, unless it might be a form kruś: in c read śūraputrān, and in d °dūṣaṇam.

ālakaṁ vyālakaṁ yāvaṁ jālpa jigī[5]mahe | carad viṣaṁ yavā bhiṣag vayam iśchāsāmahe

Probably pāda a can stand; in b we might read kalpaṁ and take jigīmahe as a formation from gā (to go) after the manner of mimīte from mā. In c śarād and yavād seem probable; in d possibly ic chāsāmahe, but this is very doubtful.

astā dyāur athāt pṛthi[6]vy asthād viśvam idaṁ jagat. | asthur viśvasyāropayo anaḍvāhaṣ kṛṣā[7]yavaḥ

Read asthād and asthāt in a; in c I would read viṣasyā°, which is supported by the reading of a similar stanza on f. 251b whose pādas cd are asthur viṣasya bhītayaṣ pratikūla ivābalaḥ. For pādas ab see Ś. 6. 44. 1; 77. 1; Ppp. 3. 40. 6.

yāvat sūryo vitapati yāvaś cābhi va paśyati | tenāham indra [8] tat tena kṛṇomy arasaṁ viṣaṁ ud viṣam arasam viṣam adhobhāge rasaṁ viṣaṁ z [9] z 5 z

Read: yāvat sūryo vitapati yāvac cābhi vipaśyati | tenāham indra tat tena kṛṇomy arasaṁ viṣam | tad viṣam arasaṁ viṣam adhobhāge 'rasaṁ viṣam z 12 z 5 z

The division into stanzas is not wholly satisfactory; in particular one may suspect that two pādas have been lost before yāvat sūryo.

11

[f. 115b 9] **mātariśvā sam abharad dhātā sam adhāt paruḥ indrāgnī a[10]bhy arakṣatāṁ tvaṣṭā nābhim akalpayat. bhagas tvābhy anakṣad rudras te asu[11]m ābharat. rātrīs tvābhy agopāya sā tvaṁ bhūte ajāyatām. | dyāu[12]ṣ ṭāyur gopāyad antarikṣam amuṁ tava | mātā bhūtasya bhavyasya pṛthi[13]thivī tvābhi rakṣatu | yāṁ tvā devās sam adadus sahasvapuruṣaṁ sa[14]tīṁ | sāje vittam asyejam apāja vyajā viṣaṁ yāṣ purastāt pra[15]syandante divā naktaṁ ca yoṣitaḥ āpaṣ puras sravantīs tā ubhe vi[16]ṣadūṣaṇī | ātaṣpas te varṣam āsīd agniś chāyābhavat tamaḥ | [17] ulvaṁ te abhram āsīt sā tvaṁ bhūte ajāyatām. | | gandharvas te mūlam āsīś**

chākhāpsarasas tava | [f. 116a] marīcīr āsaṁ pūrṇāni sinīvālī kulaṁ tava | ajarā devādadur amṛ[2]taṁ martyeṣv ā | tasyāitad agram ādade tad u te viṣadūṣaṇaṁ z anabhrāu khanamā[3]naṁ vipraṁ gambhīrepsaṁ bhiṣak cakṣur bhiṣak khane tad u te viṣadūṣaṇaṁ | yāṣ pu[4]rastād vitiṣṭhanti gāvaṣ pravrājinīr iva | amṛtasyeva vāsy ato hāsy a-[5] rundhatī yomayas svaraghāyā pṛṣāya madhv ābharat. | tato yavaṣ prajā[6]yatas so bhavad vimadūṣaṇā | yavasyāitat palālino godūmasya ti[7]lasya ca | vrīher yavasya vasadāivena kṛṇomy arasaṁ viṣaṁ | mahī[8]yonyo samudras syān na nirdaṁ nṛcāyava | tāṁ devā guhyām āmī[9]nāṁ samudrāś ca ud ābharaṁ | samudrāś ca udābhṛtya utāma puṣka-[10]rādaduḥ asyāṣ pṛthivyā devyāś cakṣur ākāśyam asi viṣadū[11]ṣaṇaṁ z 6 z anu z 2 z

Read: mātariśvā sam abharad dhātā sam adadhāt paruḥ | indrāgnī abhy arakṣatāṁ tvaṣṭā nābhim akalpayat z 1 z bhagas tvābhy arakṣad rudras te asum ābharat | rātrīs tvābhy agopāyan sā tvaṁ bhūte ajāyathāḥ z 2 z dyāuṣ ṭa āyur gopāyad antarikṣam asuṁ tava | mātā bhūtasya bhavyasya pṛthivī tvābhi rakṣatu z 3 z yāṁ tvā devās sam adadhus sahasrapuruṣāṁ satīm | sāje vittam āsyejam apāja vyaja viṣam z 4 z yāṣ purastāt prasyandante divā naktaṁ ca yoṣitaḥ | āpaṣ purastāt sravantīs tā u te viṣadūṣaṇīḥ z 5 z ātapas te varṣam āsīd agniś chāyābhavat tava | ulbaṁ te abhram āsīt sā tvaṁ bhūte ajāyathāḥ z 6 z gandharvas te mūlam āsīc chākhāpsarasas tava | marīcīr āsan parṇāni sinīvālī kulaṁ tava z 7 z ajarā devā ādadhur amṛtaṁ martyeṣv ā | tasyāitad agram ādadhe tad u te viṣadūṣaṇam z 8 z anabhrayaḥ khanamānā viprā gambhīre 'pasaḥ | bhiṣak cakṣur bhiṣak khanaṁ tad u te viṣadūṣaṇam z 9 z yāṣ purastād vitiṣṭhanti gāvaṣ pravrājinīr iva | amṛtasyeva vā asy ato hāsy arundhatī z 10 z yavamayas saraghāyāṣ poṣāya madhv ābharat | tato yavaṣ prājāyata so 'bhavad viṣadūṣaṇaḥ z 11 z yavasyāitat palālino godhūmasya tilasya ca | vrīher yavasya dāivena kṛṇomy arasaṁ viṣam z 12 z mahīyonāu samudras syān †na nirdaṁ nṛcāyava† | tāṁ devā guhyām āsīnāṁ samudrāc cod ābharan z 13 z samudrāc codābhṛtyot tāṁ puṣkarā adadhuḥ | asyāṣ pṛthivyā devyāś cakṣur ākāśyam asi viṣadūṣaṇam z 14 z 6 anu 2 z

With our 9ab cf. Ppp. 8. 8. 9ab (= Ś. 19. 2. 3ab); it would seem that somewhere in the transmission of the text an attempt was made to put the adjectives of these pādas into the neuter, harking back perhaps to the previous stanza. St. 11 here is almost identical with st. 4 of hymn 8. I feel doubtful about several of the suggestions offered, particularly in 13a. Edgerton would suggest for 14ab samudrāc codabhratota tāṁ puṣkaraṁ dadhuḥ, or something similar.

12

[f. 116a 11] **samānam arthaṁ pāryanti** [13] **devā rūpo rūpaṁ tapasā vardhamānā | ud āditām abhi maṁ vi**[14]**ṣanti tad eko rūpam amṛtatvam eṣāṁ**

In a read pārayanti, in b rūpaṁ-rūpaṁ and vardhamānāḥ: in c read tad ādityam and saṁ viśanti, in d ekarūpam and eṣām.

devo devebhir āgamaṁ maṅ[15]**haṁ no aditiṣ pitā suprīta jātavedasam ekarūpo guhā bhavaṁ**

In a read āgaman, in b maṅhan: for c probably suprīto jātavedās san, in d bhavan.

[16] **ātithyam agnir avatu deva ubhayebhiṣ pitṛbhis saṁvidānaḥ | mahā**[17]**n marīyā upa bhakṣam āgaṁ maṁ gurbhādityāṁ niviṣṭavahniḥ**

In c possibly varīyāṅ may be read, and āgan; pāda d probably begins with saṁ and has °ādityān, but I cannot make any thing of gurbh unless gūrta (aorist) is acceptable.

tāvi[18]**śanti puruṣaṁ śayānaṁ prāṇā niṣṭvā niṣasanty enaṁ te no rātryā** [19] **sumanasyamānāḥ ahvā rakṣāṁtv ahṛṇīyamānāṁ |**

Read: ta āviśanti puruṣaṁ śayānaṁ prāṇā viṣṭvā ni śamayanty enam | te no rātryā sumanasyamānā ahnā rakṣantv ahṛṇīyamānāḥ z 4 z

The suggestion in b is somewhat bold but I have considerable confidence in it.

paśubhyo na[20]**ṣ paśupataye mṛḍas sarvasyo nir hāyatāṁ mā naṣ prāṇo pu rī**[f. 116b]**riṣaḥ**

In a I think we should read paśupate: in d read prāṇopa. The remainder I cannot restore; there are only nine syllables out of which to make two(?) pādas.

vāyus satye dhiśrutaḥ prāṇāpānām abhirakṣaṁ pradāyur edi [2] māṁ | devā yattā prajāpatā sādityāś ca yemire |

In a read 'dhiśritaḥ for b possibly prāṇāpānāv abhirakṣan; for c possibly pradadad āyur eti mām; in d yatāḥ prājāpatyāḥ. The grouping of these pādas into one stanza is not wholly certain, and throughout the rest of the hymn there are difficulties in the division into stanzas.

pūṣā raśmiṣu [3] yattādityo viṣṇur ākrame sva rohaṁ diva rohati |

Read: pūṣā raśmiṣu yataḥ | āditya viṣṇur ākrame svā rohan divaṁ rohati z 7 z

pra yātu devas savi[4]tu sarve tvaṣṭā rūpāṇi piṅśatu aṁjanto madhunā payo

Read savitā in a; I would delete sarve, and have the next three words stand as pāda b (= Ś. 5. 25. 5b). For c perhaps we may read añjanto madhunā payaḥ, but yuñjanto would be better.

atandraṁ yātu[5]m aśvināṁ viśve devāḥ prayātanādityāssas sajoṣasaṣ puraṣ pa[6]ścāt svastaye |

Read: atandraṁ yātam aśvināu viśve devāḥ prayātana | ādityāsas sajoṣasaṣ puraṣ pascāt svastaye z 9 z

vrahma varma vṛhaspatis saṁgavo no bhi rakṣatu | devo de[7]vāiṣ purohitā | maruto vṛṣṇyā nāgamat satyadharmāṇa ūtaye |

In b read 'bhi; in d possibly na āgamant; I would remove the colon after pāda c. In b saṁgave would be somewhat smoother.

a[8]parāhneṣu jindhataḥ indro rājā divas pari rahan mimāya tiṣṭhasi | [9] sa nāimāṣ kalpayād diśaḥ z ɪ z

Read: aparāhneṣu jinvita indro rājā divas pari | rohan mimāya †tiṣṭhasi sa na imāṣ kalpayād diśaḥ z 11 z 1 z

Pāda d would be improved by omitting na.

13

Ś. 5. 30. 1—10.

[f. 126b 9] **āvatas te parāvataṣ pa[10]rāvatas ta āvata | iheva bhava mā nu ga mā pūrvāṅ anu gā gatā | na [11]**

muṁ badhnāmi te ḍuḍhaṁ yas tvābhi ceruṣ puruṣaḥ so yad aruṇo danaḥ [12] unmocanapramocane ubhaya vādā vadāmi te | yadadrohita śepi[13]ṣe strī puṁse cityā z yad enaso mātariktāś cheṣe pitṛṣutād uta | [14] unmocanapramocane | ubhaya vācā vadāmi te | yat te mātā ya[15]t te pitā jāman bhrātā ca sarjata | pratyak chevasya bheṣajaradaṣṭiṁ [16] kṛṇomi te | yehi yehi punar ehi sarveṇa sanasā saha | śa[17]to yamasyasānu gādhi jīvapurā hi | anuhataḥ punar ehi vidvā[18]udayanaṁ pathaḥ ārohaṇas ākramaṇaṁ jīvato jīvato yanaṁ sā [19] bibhen na pariṣyasi jaradaṣṭir bhaviṣyasi nir vocamaṁ yakṣmas añge[20]bhyo añgajvaraṁ tava | śīrṣarogam añgarogaṁ yaś ca te hṛdayāmaya | ya-[f. 117a] yakṣma śyenāiva prāpattatad vācānuttaḥ parastaṁ ṛṣī bodhapratībodhāv asva[2]pno yaś ca jāgavi | te te praṇamya goptāro divā svapnaṁ ca jāgratu z 2 z

Read: āvatas te parāvataṣ parāvatas ta āvataḥ | ihāiva bhava mā nu gā mā pūrvāñ anu gā gatān asuṁ badhnāmi te dṛḍham z 1 z yat tvābhiceruṣ puruṣaḥ svo yad araṇo janaḥ | unmocanapramocane ubhe vācā vadāmi te z 2 z yad dudrohitha śepiṣe striyāi puṁse acittyā | unmo° • • z 3 z yad enaso mātṛkṛtāc cheṣe pitṛṣutād uta | unmocanapramocane ubhe vācā vadāmi te z 4 z yat te mātā yat te pitā jāmir bhrātā ca sarjata | pratyak chevasya bheṣajaṁ jaradaṣṭiṁ kṛṇomi te z 5 z ehy ehi punar ehi sarveṇa manasā saha | dūtāu yamasya mānu gā adhi jīvapurā ihi z 6 z anuhūtaḥ punar ehi vidvān udayanaṁ pathaḥ | ārohaṇam ākramaṇam jīvato-jīvato 'yanam z 7 z mā bibher na mariṣyasi jaradaṣṭir bhaviṣyasi | nir avocam ahaṁ yakṣmam añgebhyo añgajvaraṁ tava z 8 z śīrṣarogam añgarogaṁ yaś ca te hṛdayāmayaḥ | yakṣmaś śyena iva prāpatad vācānuttaḥ parastarām z 9 z ṛṣī bodhapratībodhāv asvapno yaś ca jāgṛviḥ | tāu te prāṇasya goptārāu divā svapnaṁ ca jāgratuḥ z 10 z 2 z

The text is edited to a fairly close accord with that of Ś. In 1a Ppp. is better; in 4b Ś. has pitṛkṛtāc ca yat; 5c seems possible as given, but might well be only a corruption of the Ś. form; in 6c sado would seem good and nearer to our ms.; in 10cd Edgerton would read te te • goptāro • • • jāgratu; in 10d Ś. has naktaṁ ca jāgṛtām. Other variants are not striking.

The ms. clearly indicates the end of a hymn here, and

there seems to be justification for it in that the next stanza (Ś. 11) has somewhat the tone of an opening stanza. With some hesitation I keep the division.

14

(Ś. 5. 30. 11–17.)

[f. 117a 3] **ayam agnir upasadya iha sūrya ud etu te | ud ehi mṛtyor gambhīrat kṛśchrā[4]ś cit tamasas pari | namo yamāya namamo stu mṛtyave namaṣ piturbhyaḥ uta** [5] **ye nayanti | utapāriṇasya yo veda tvam agniṁ puro dadhe | āitu prāṇa āi**[6]**tu mana āitu cakṣur atho balaṁ | śarīramam asya saṁ vidā tat padbhyāṁ** [7] **pratiṣyatu | prāṇenāgnaya cakṣuṣā saṁ sṛjemaṁ samīraya | tanvā** [8] **saṁ sṛjanena votthāmṛtasya mā mṛta mo ṣu bhūmigṛho bhuvat. | mā te prāṇa** [9] **upa dasaṁ māpāno pa dhāya te | sūryas tvādhipatir martyor ud āyaśchāti raśmi**[10]**bhiḥ | imaṁtar vadaty ugrā jihvā maṇiṣpadā tātayā romaṁ vi nayāsaḥ |** [11] **śataṁ romīc ca uksanā | ayaṁ lokaṣ priyatamo devānām aparājitaḥ** [12] **tasmāi tvam iha jajñiṣe adṛṣṭaṣ puruṣa mṛtyave | tasmāi tvāni hveyāma**[13]**si mā purā jaraso mṛdhā z 3 z**

Read: ayam agnir upasadya iha sūrya ud etu te | ud ehi mṛtyor gambhīrāt kṛcchrāc cit tamasas pari z 1 z namo yamāya namo 'stu mṛtyave namaṣ pitṛbhya uta ye nayanti | utpāraṇasya yo veda tam agniṁ puro dadhe <smā ariṣṭatātaye> z 2 z āitu prāṇa āitu mana āitu cakṣur atho balam | śarīram asya saṁ vidāṁ tat padbhyāṁ pra tiṣṭhatu z 3 z prāṇenāgne cakṣuṣā saṁ sṛjemaṁ samīraya tanvā saṁ sarjanena | vetthāmṛtasya mā mṛta mo ṣu bhūmigṛho bhuvat z 4 z mā te prāṇa upa dasan māpāno 'pi dhāyi te | sūryas tvādhipatir mṛtyor ud āyacchatu raśmibhiḥ z 5 z iyam antar vadaty ugrā jihvā paṇiṣpadā | tayā rogaṁ vi nayāmaś śataṁ ropīś ca takmanaḥ z 6 z ayaṁ lokaṣ priyatamo devānām aparājitaḥ | yasmāi tvam iha jajñiṣe diṣṭaṣ puruṣa mṛtyave | tasmāi tvānu hvayāmasi mā purā jaraso mṛthāḥ z 7 z 3 z

The variations from Ś. here are few and not important; the restoration of the end of 2d seems necessary. In 3d we might well read prati as in Ś.; in 7d adṛṣṭaṣ as in our ms. does not seem possible.

15

(Ś. 5. 17. 1–7, 10, 11.)

[f. 117a 13] taṁ vadaṁ prathā vrahmakilvi[14]ṣe kūpāras salilo mātariśvā | vīḍūharas tapa ugraṁ mayobhuva apo [15] po devīṣ prathamajā ṛtasya somo rājā prathamo vrajāyāṁ punaḥ prāyaścha[16]d ahṛṇīyamānaḥ anvantitvā varuṇo mittro āsīd agnir hotā hasta[17]gṛhṇā ināya | hastenāiva grāhya ādir asyā vrahmajāyeti ced avocat. [18] na dūtāya prahyātasta eṣā tathā rāṣṭe gupitaṁ kṣattriyasya | yām ā[19]hus tārakāṁ vikeśīḍat prāgāmam avapabhyamānā sā vrahmajāyā pra [f. 117b] tinotu rāṣṭraṁ yatra prāpāddi śamu ulkakhīmāṁ vrahmacārī carati veviśa[2]d viṣas sa devānāṁ bhāvaty ekam aṅgaṁ tena jāyām anv avindad vṛhaspatis so[3]mena nihatāṁ juhvaṁ na devāḥ devā etasyāpajayaṁtu pūrve saptarṣaya[4]s tapas te ye niṣeduḥ bhīmā jāyā vrahmaṇasyāpinihitā dugdhāṁ da[5]dāti parame vyoman. | ya garbhāvapabhyante jagad yaś cāpilupyate | vīrā [6] ye hanyonte mitho vrahmajāyā hinasti tām. | sarva garbhāṣ pra vyathante ku[7]mārā daśamāsyā asmin rāṣṭre niruddhyate vrahmajāyādityā punar vāi de[8]vā adaduṣ punar manuṣyā uta | rājānas satyaṁ kṛṇvāno vrahmajāyāṁ na pu[9]nar daduḥ | yo punardāya vrahmajāyāṁ kṛtvā devāir nakilviṣaṁ ūrjaṁ pṛ[10]pṛthivyā bhaktobhagāyam upāsate z 4 z

Read: te 'vadan prathamā vrahmakilbiṣe 'kūpāras salilo mātariśvā | vīḍuharās tapa ugraṁ mayobhuva āpo devīṣ prathamajā ṛtasya z 1 z somo rājā prathamo vrahmajāyāṁ punaḥ prāyacchad ahṛṇīyamānaḥ | anvartitā varuṇo mitra āsīd agnir hotā hastagṛhyā ināya z 2 z hastenāiva grāhya ādhir asyā vrahmajāyeti ced avocat | na dūtāya praheyā tastha eṣā tathā rāṣṭraṁ gupitaṁ kṣatriyasya z 3 z yām āhus tārakāṁ †vikeśīḍat prāggrāmam avapadyamānām | sā vrahmajāyā pra dunoti rāṣṭraṁ yatra prāpādi śaśa ulkaṣīmān z 4 z vrahmacārī carati veviṣad viṣas sa devānāṁ bhavaty ekam aṅgam | tena jāyām anv avindad vṛhaspatis somena nītāṁ juhvaṁ na devāḥ z 5 z devā etasyām ajāyanta pūrve saptarṣayas tapas te ye niṣeduḥ | bhīmā jāyā vrāhmaṇasyāpanītā durdhāṁ dadhāti parame vyoman z 6 z ye garbhā avapadyante jagad yac cāpalupyate | vīrā ye hanyante mitho vrahmajāyā hinasti tān z 7 z sarve garbhāṣ pra vyathante kumārā daśamāsyāḥ | yasmin rāṣṭre nirudhyate vrahmajāyācittyā z 8 z punar vāi devā adaduṣ punar manuṣyā uta | rājānas satyaṁ kṛṇvānā vrahmajāyāṁ punar daduḥ z 9 z punardāya vrahmajāyāṁ kṛtvā devāir nikilbiṣam | ūrjaṁ pṛthivyā bhaktvorugāyam upāsate z 10 z 4 z

This text agrees almost entirely with that of Ś.; our 8ab are new, and 8cd = Ś. 12cd. In 4a Ppp. probably has a variant from the Ś. text tārakāiṣā vikeśiti; except for the lack of iti, vikeśī ruk would seem good; in 4b Ś. has duchunāṁ grāmam. In 6a Ś. has avadanta.

The fact that RV. 10. 109 has seven of these stanzas (lacking our 4, 7, and 8) makes it reasonable to follow the Ppp. ms. in counting this as a separate hymn. Ś. 5. 17 has been recognized as a composite hymn.

16

[f. 117b 10] **na tatra dhenu drohe [11] nānaḍvān sahate dhuraṁ vijāni yatra vrāhmaṇo rātiṁ vasati pāpayā | [12] na varṣaṁ māitträvaruṇaṁ vrahmajyām abhi varṣati | āsmāi samitiṣ kalpate [13] na mittraṁ nayate vaśaṁ | asuñmatī carati vrahmajāyāṁ śālaṁ pañktīṣ pra[14]diśaś catasraḥ yaḥ kṣattriyaṣ punar enāṁ dadātu sa divo dārāṁ yayā[15]tu prapīṇāṁ | yo punardāya | vrahmajāyāṁ rājā kalpe na padyate | du[16]ryoṇo smā oṣadhīr yākāśyābhivapaśyatī viṣam uṣṇāty apā vi[17]ṣam uṣṇāti vīrudhāṁ yo vrahmajāyāṁ na punar dadāti tasmāi devās su[18]dhiyaṁ digdham asyāṁ | tat padayo diśa striyāṣ pūrve vrāhmaṇā vrahmā [f. 118a] ced dham agrahīt sa eva patir ekadhā vrāhmaṇeva patin na rājā nota vāiśyat tat sū[2]ryaṣ pravruvann ayatu pañcabhyo mānavebhyaḥ z 5 z**

Read: na tatra dhenur dohyā nānaḍvān sahate dhuram | vijānir yatra vrāhmaṇo rātriṁ vasati pāpayā z 1 z na varṣaṁ māitrāvaruṇaṁ vrahmajyam abhi varṣati | nāsmāi samitiṣ kalpate na mitraṁ nayate vaśam z 2 z †asuñmatī carati vrahmajāyā śālaṁ pañktīṣ pradiśaś catasraḥ | yaḥ kṣatriyaṣ punar enāṁ dadātu sa divo dārāṁ yayātu prapīṇām z 3 z punardāya vrahmajāyāṁ rājā kalpe na padyate | duryoṇe 'smā oṣadhir yākāśyābhivipaśyatī z 4 z viṣam uṣṇāty apāṁ viṣam uṣṇāti vīrudhām | yo vrahmajāyāṁ na punar dadāti tasmāi devās svadhitiṁ digdhaṁ asyān z 5 z uta yat patayo daśa striyāṣ pūrve 'vrāhmaṇāḥ | vrahmā ced dhastam agrahīt sa eva patir ekadhā z 6 z vrāhmaṇa eva patir na rājā nota vāiśyaḥ | tat sūryaṣ pravruvann eti pañcabhyo mānavebhyaḥ z 7 z 5 z

St. 1 is Ś. 5. 17. 18; st. 2 is Ś. 5. 19. 15; stt. 6 and 7 are Ś. 5. 17. 8 and 9. In 1a Edgerton suggests dohāya which is in some ways better than dohyā; in 3c he would read dive, and perhaps dhārāṁ. In 3c dadāti might be read; the whole stanza is unclear to me.

17

(Ś. 5. 18, in part.)

[f. 118a 2] nāitāṁ te devādadu[3]s tubhyaṁ nṛpate attave mā vrāhmaṇasya rājanya gāṁ jighatso nāḍyāḥ akṣa[4]dugdho rājanyaṣ pāpānmam aparājitaḥ | sa vrāhmaṇasya gām adyatadvya [5] jīvāni ma śvā nir vāi kṣattraṁ nayati hanta varco gnir vālabdhaḥ pṛtannotu rāṣṭraṁ [6] yo vrāhmaṇaṁ devabandhuṁ hinasti tasya pitṝṇām apy etu lokam. | devapī[7]yūṅś carati martyeṣu garagīrtyo bhavaty asthibhūyāṁ yo vrāhmaṇaṁ manyate anna[8]m eva sa viṣasya pivati tāimātasyā viṣaṁ sa pivati tāimātaṁ paśyann agniṁ pra [9] sīdati | yo vrāhmaṇasya śraddhanam abhi nāra manyate satāpāṣṭhā ni ṣīda[10]ta tāṁ na śikhanota niṣkidaṁ anna yo vrahmaṇā nandas sādv anamīta manya[11]te | ya enāṁ hanya mṛda manyamāno devapī banakāmo na cintā san taśce [12] andho hṛdaye agni bandho ubhāinaṁ daṣṭo nabhasī carantaṁ | na vrāhmaṇo [13] hiṅsitavāgneṣ priyatamā tanūḥ somo hy asya dāyāda indro syābhiśa[14]stipāt. | agnir vāi naṣ padavāya somo dāyāda ucyate | jayatābhi[15]śasta indras tat satyaṁ devasaṁhitaṁ | āviṣṭitaghahaviṣā prajākūr i[16]va śarmaṇā | vrāhmaṇasya rājanyas tṛpsīṣā gāur anāḍyaḥ z 6 z

nāitāṁ te devā adadus tubhyaṁ nṛpate attave | mā vrāhmaṇasya rājanya gāṁ jighatso 'nādyām z 1 z akṣadrugdho rājanyaṣ pāpa ātmaparājitaḥ | sa vrāhmaṇasya gām adyād adya jīvāni mā śvaḥ z 2 z nir vāi kṣatraṁ nayati hanti varco 'gnir ivālabdhaḥ pra dunoti rāṣṭram | yo vrāhmaṇaṁ devabandhuṁ hinasti na sa pitṝṇām apy etu lokam z 3 z devapīyuś carati martyeṣu garagīrṇo bhavaty asthibhūyān | yo vrāhmaṇaṁ manyate annam eva sa viṣasya pibati tāimātasya z 4 z viṣaṁ sa pibati tāimātaṁ paśyann agniṁ pra sīdati | yo vrāhmaṇasya sad dhanam abhi nārada manyate z 5 z śatāpāṣṭhā ni ṣīdata tāṁ na śaknoti niṣkhidam | annaṁ yo vrahmaṇāṁ nandan svādv admīti manyate z 6 z ya enāṁ hanyān mṛduṁ manyamāno devapīyur dhanakāmo na cittāt | saṁ tasyendro hṛdaye agnim indha ubhe enaṁ dviṣṭo nabhasī carantam z 7 z na vrāhmaṇo hiṅsitavyo 'gneḥ priyatamā tanūḥ | somo hy asya dāyāda indro 'syābhiśastipāḥ z 8 z agnir vāi naṣ padavāyaḥ somo dāyāda ucyate | jayate 'bhiśasta indras tat satyaṁ devasaṁhitam z 9 z āviṣṭitāghaviṣā pṛdākūr iva carmaṇā | vrāhmaṇasya rājanya tṛṣṭāiṣā gāur anādyā z 10 z 6 z

The text as edited is verbally fairly close to that of Ś. For 6a Ś. has śatāpāṣṭhaṁ ni girati, and 6c has malvas for our nandan (ms. nandas). For 9cd Ś. has (in its st. 14) hantābhiśastendras tathā tat vedhaso viduḥ; it would improve our text to read 'bhiśastim. St. 5ab is new; cd = Ś. 5. 19. 9cd. Ś. 5. 18. 8—12 and 15 do not appear in this hymn according to our ms.; all but 12ab appear in the next hymn. There is no reason to object to the Ppp. arrangement except that the number of stanzas in the hymn is less than the norm for this Book 9.

18

(Stanzas from Ś. 5. 18 and 19.)

[f. 118a 17] **iṣur iva digdhā nṛpate pṛdākūr iva gopate | sā vrāhmaṇasyeṣun di[18]gdhā tayā vidhyatu pītayā | tīkṣṇa iṣavo vrahmaṇā hetisanto yām assa[19]nti śarvyāṅ ni sā mṛṣāṁ | anūhāyati tapasā manyunā cota d*rād abhinda[f. 119a]nti te tayā | jihvā bhyā bhavati kunmalaṁ vāñ naḍīkā dantā tapasāsiddhi[2]gdhā tebhir vrāhma vidyātu devapīyaṁ nirjalāi vanurbhir devajūteḥ ye vrā[3]hmaṇaṁ hiṅsitāras tapasvinaṁ manīṣiṇaṁ vrahmacaryeṇa śrāntaṁ ava[4]ntimad bhavitā rāṣṭram eṣāṁ tapasāiva nihataṁ nānu vetu ye sahasram arā[5]jaṁn āśaṁ daśatād uta tebhyaṣ pra vravīmi tvā vāitahavyāṣ parābhuvaṁ gāu[6]r eva tāñ hanyamano vāitavyāṅ ivācarat. | ye keśaraprāpuṁdāyaś carumā[7]dā upecaraṁ abhimātrā jāyanti nod ivi divi paspṛśaṁ sṛga hiṅ[8]satvā vrahmīm amuṁbhavyaṁ parābhuvaṁ | ye vṛhatsāmānam āñgirasam ālpa[9]yaṁ vrāhmaṇaṁ janāḥ |**

tetvak stokām ubhayādan yat stokāny āmayat. | [10] ye vrāhmaṇaṁ pratyuṣṭhīvaṁ yaś cāsmāi śulkam īśire | astras te madhye kūlyā[11]yāṣ keśān akhādantāsate | aṣṭāpadī caturakṣī catuśśrotā ca[12]turhanuḥ dvijihvā dviprāṇā bhūtvā sā rāṣṭram avi dhūnute z [13] z 7 z

In f. 119a 1 the margin corrects bhyā to dyā and ddhi to di.

Read: iṣur iva digdhā nṛpate pṛdākūr iva gopate | sā vrāhmaṇasyeṣur digdhā tayā vidhyati pīyataḥ z 1 z tīkṣṇeṣavo vrāhmaṇā hetimanto yām asyanti śaravyāṁ na sā mṛṣā | anuhāya tapasā manyunā cota dūrād ava bhindanti te tayā z 2 z jihvā jyā bhavati kulmalaṁ vāñ nāḍīkā dantās tapasā sudigdhāḥ | tebhir vrahmā vidhyāti devapīyuṁ nirjalāir dhanurbhir devajūtāiḥ z 3 z ye vrāhmaṇaṁ hiṅsitāras tapasvinaṁ manīṣiṇaṁ vrahmacaryeṇa śrāntam | avartimad bhavitā rāṣṭram eṣāṁ tapasāiva nihataṁ †nānu vetu† z 4 z ye sahasram arājann āsan daśaśatā uta | tebhyaṣ pra vravīmi tvā vāitahavyāṣ parābhavan z 5 z gāur eva tān hanyamānā vāitahavyāñ ivācarat | ye †kesaraprāpuṁdāyaś caramājām apeciran z 6 z atimātrā ajāyanta nod iva divam aspṛśan | prajāṁ hiṅsitvā vrāhmaṇīm asaṁbhavyaṁ parābhavan z 7 z ye vṛhatsāmānam āṅgirasam ārpayan vrāhmaṇaṁ janāḥ | †tetvak stokām ubhayādan yat stokāny āmayat† z 8 z ye vrāhmaṇaṁ pratyaṣṭhīvan ye cāsmāi śuklam īṣire | asnas te madhye kulyāyāṣ keśān khādanta āsate z 9 z aṣṭāpadī caturakṣī catuśśrotrā caturhanuḥ | dvijihvā dviprāṇā bhūtvā sā rāṣṭram ava dhūnute z 10 z 7 z

St. 4 is new. Ś. 5. 18. 11b has avātirat which perhaps should be read in Ppp. 6b; and 6c looks very like a corruption of the form in Ś. The Ś. reading of 5. 19. 2cd is petvas teṣām ubhayādam avis tokāny āvayat; perhaps this should be read in Ppp. st. 8, with ubhayādann as emended by Whitney.

19

(Cf. Ś. 5. 19.)

[f. 118b 13] **vrahmagavī paśyamānā yāvat sābhi vajaṅgahe | te[14]jo rāṣṭrasya nir hanti na vīro jāyate pumān. ākramaṇena vāi devā [15] dviṣanto ghnanti pāuruṣaṁ te ājaṁ vrahmajaṁ kṣettre tā anṛtavādi[16]nam. | viṣam etad devakṛtaṁ rājā varuṇo avravīt. | te vrāhmaṇasya [17] gāṁ dugdhvā rāṣṭre jāgara kaś cana | tad vāi rāṣṭram ā sravati**

bhinnāṁ nā[18]vam ivodakaṁ | vrāhmaṇo yatra jīyate tad rāṣṭram ā sravati chinnāṁ [19] nāvam ivodakaṁ | vrāhmaṇo yatra jīyate tad rāṣṭraṁ havi duśchunā | [20] ekaśataṁ vāi javatā bhūmir yā dvidhūnataṣ prajā hiṅsatvā vrāhmī[f. 119a]m amūṁbhavyaṁ parābhuvaṁ | yām ud ājaṁ gṛṣayo maṇīṣiṇaś śapusātāṁ vṛhatīṁ [2] devajūtāṁ | sā vrahmajyaṁ pacati padyamānā rāṣṭram asya vṛhatī yaś ca varcaḥ [3] vācā vrāhmaṇam iśchati jāmiyaṁ hanti cibhyā mittrāya satye druhyati yaṁ devā ghnanti pāuruṣam. z 8 z

In the top margin of f. 119a stands pacyamā above padyamānā of line 2.

Read: vrahmagavī pacyamānā yāvat sābhi vijaṅgahe | tejo rāṣṭrasya nir hanti na vīro jāyate pumān z 1 z ākramaṇena vāi devā dviṣanto ghnanti pūruṣam | te ajan vrahmajyaṁ kṣetre 'thānṛtavādinam z 2 z viṣam etad devakṛtaṁ rājā varuṇo avravīt | na vrāhmaṇasya gāṁ jagdhvā rāṣṭre jāgāra kaś cana z 3 z tad vāi rāṣṭram ā sravati bhinnāṁ nāvam ivodakam | vrāhmaṇo yatra jīyate tad rāṣṭraṁ hanti ducchunā z 4 z ekaśataṁ vāi janatā bhūmir yā vyadhūnuta | prajāṁ hiṅsitvā vrāhmaṇīm asaṁbhavyaṁ parābhavan z 5 z yām ud ājan ṛṣayo manīṣiṇaś †śapusātāṁ vṛhatīṁ devajūtām | sā vrahmajyaṁ pacati pacyamānā rāṣṭram asya vṛhatī yac ca varcaḥ z 6 z vācā vrāhmaṇam icchati †jāmiyaṁ hanti cittyā | mitrāya satye druhyati yaṁ devā ghnanti pūruṣam z 7 z 8 z

Stt. 2, 6, and 7 are new; st. 5 = Ś 5.18.12. Edgerton suggests saptaśatāṁ in 6b. In st. 7 we need an accusative; jāmim ayam is the only suggestion I have.

20

[f. 119a 4] **ekapāś chanda ekakāsū[5]ñ ca ta āpnoti cāva ca rundhe prathamayā rātnyā prathamayā samidhā dvipā[6]ś chando dvipadaś ca paśūn. tad āpnoti cava ca rundhe dvitīyayā rātnyā [7] dvitīyayā samidhā z tripāś chandas trīṅś ca lokān. sa tad āpnoti cā[8]va carundhe tṛtīyayā rātnyā tṛtīyayā samidhā | catuṣpāś chandaś catuṣpa[9]daś ca paśūn. tad āpnoti cava ca rundhe caturthyā rātnyā caturthyā samidhā | pañca [10] diśaṣ pañca prediśas tad āpnoti cāva ca rundhe pañcamyā rātnyā pañcamyā sa[11]midhā | trāiṣṭubhaṁś chando virājaṁ svarājaṁ samrājaṁ tad āpnoti cāva ca** rundhe [12] ṣaṣṭhyā rātnyā ṣaṣṭhyā samidhā | sapta prāṇāṁ saptāpānāṁ saptarṣīś ca tad āpno[13]ti cāva cā rundhe saptamyā rātnyā saptamyā samidhā | ojaś ca tejaś ca saha[14]ś ca balaṁ ca tad āpnoti cāva ca rundhe aṣṭamyā rātnyā aṣṭamyā samidhā | [15] ambhaś ca mahaś ca annaṁ ca annādyaṁ ca tad āpnoti cāva ca rundhe navamyā rā[16]tnyā navamyā samidhā | vrahma ca kṣattraṁ cendriyaṁ ca vrāhmaṇavarcasaṁ ca tad ā[17]pnoti cāva ca rundhe daśamyā rātnyā daśamyā samidhā | viśvāvasu ca sarva[18]vasu ca tad āpnoti cāva ca rundhe ekādaśā rātnyekādaśyā samidhā [19] pāñktaṁś chandaṣ prajāpatiṁ saṁvatsaraṁ tad āpnoti cāva rundhe dvādaśyā rātnyā dvā[f. 119b]daśyā samidhā z 9 z

Read: ekapāc chanda ekapadaś ca paśūn sa tad āpnoti cāva ca rundhe prathamayā rātryā prathamayā samidhā z 1 z dvipāc chando dvipadaś ca paśūn ◦ ◦ ◦ rundhe dvitīyayā rātryā dvitīyayā samidhā z 2 z tripāc chandas trīṅś ca lokān sa ◦ ◦ ◦ rundhe tṛtīyayā rātryā tṛtīyayā samidhā z 3 z catuṣpāc chandaś catuṣpadaś ca paśūn sa ◦ ◦ ◦ rundhe caturthyā rātryā caturthyā samidhā z 4 z pañca diśaṣ pañca ca pradiśas sa ◦ ◦ ◦ rundhe pañcamyā rātryā pañcamyā samidhā z 5 z trāiṣṭubhaṁ chando virājaṁ svarājaṁ samrājaṁ sa ◦ ◦ ◦ rundhe ṣaṣṭhyā rātryā ṣaṣṭhyā samidhā z 6 z sapta prāṇān saptāpānān saptarṣīṅś ca sa ◦ ◦ ◦ rundhe saptamyā rātryā saptamyā samidhā z 7 z ojaś ca tejaś ca sahaś ca balaṁ ca sa ◦ ◦ ◦ rundhe aṣṭamyā rātryāṣṭamyā samidhā z 8 z ambhaś ca mahaś cānnaṁ cānnādyaṁ ca sa ◦ ◦ ◦ rundhe navamyā rātryā navamyā samidhā z 9 z vrahma ca kṣatraṁ cendriyaṁ ca vrāhmaṇavarcasaṁ ca sa ◦ ◦ ◦ rundhe daśamyā rātryā daśamyā samidhā z 10 z viśvāvasu ca sarvavasu ca sa ◦ ◦ ◦ rundha ekādaśyā rātryāikādaśyā samidhā z 11 z pāñktaṁ chandaṣ prajāpatiṁ saṁvatsaraṁ sa tad āpnoti cāva ca rundhe dvādaśyā rātryā dvādaśyā samidhā z 12 z 9 z anu 3 z

21

[f. 119b 1] oṁ yo vā ekaśarāvaṁ nirvaped ekarṣim evā[2]nu nivapet. | eṣa vā eka ṛṣir yad agniḥ eka ṛṣiṁ cāiva lokaṁ cā[3]va rundhe | eka ṛṣir iva tapatye eka ṛṣir iva dīdāya eka ṛṣi[4]r ivānnādo bhavati | ya evaṁ vada | sa evaṁ vidvān prāśnīyād etām eva [5] devatāṁ manasādhyāyed eka ṛṣes tvā cakṣuṣā paśyāmi eka ṛṣes tvā [6] hastābhyām ārabhed eka ṛṣes tvāsyanu prāśnāmy eka ṛṣes tvā jaṭhare sā[7]dhayāmīti sa yathā hutam iṣṭaṁ prārśnīyād evāinaṁ prāśnāti vāi dviśa[8]rāvaṁ nirvapet prāṇāpānāv evavānu nirvaped ete ve prāṇāpānāu [9] yan mātariśvā cāgniś ca | prāṇāpānāu cāiva lokaṁ cāva rundhe jyog jī[10]vati sarvam āyur eti na purā jarasaḥ pramīyate yaḥ prāśnīyā[11]d etām eva devatāṁ manasādhyāyet prāṇāpānayos tvā cakṣuṣā pa[12]śyāmi | prāṇāpānayos tva hastābhyām ārabhet prāṇāpānayos tvāsya[13]nu prāśnāmi prāṇāpānayos tvā z vāi triśarāvaṁ nirvapet trīṇy eva [14] trikādrukādrukāny anu nirvaped etāni vāi trīṇi trikādrukāny anu [15] nir vaped etāni vāi trīṇi trikādrukāṇy ajuryajus sāmāni ya[16]jūṅṣi vrāhmaṇaṁ vrahma cāiva lokaṁ cāva rundhe vrāhmaṇavarcasī [17] bhavati yaṣ prāśnīyād etām eva devatāṁ manasādhyāyed vrāhmaṇas tvā [18] cakṣuṣā paśyāmi vrahmanas tvā hastābhyām ārabhed vrahmaṇas tvāmyena prā[19]śnami vrāhmaṇas tvā z vāi catuśarāvaṁ nirvapeś catasra evorvīr anu ni[20]rvaped etā vāi ścatasra urvīr yad diśo diśaś cāiva lokaṁ cāva rundhe ka[f. 130a]lpante smāi diśo diśāṁ priyo bhavati yaṣ prāśnīyād etām eva devatāṁ mana[2]sādhyāyed diśānāṁ tvā cakṣuṣā paśyāmi diśānāṁ tvā hastābhyām ārabhed di[3]śānāṁ tvā cakṣuṣā paśyāmi diśānāṁ tvā hastābhyām ārabhed diśānāṁ tvāmye[4]na prāśnāmi diśānāṁ tvā z vāi pañcaśarāvaṁ nirvaped vāiśvānaram eva pañca[5]mūrdhānam anu nirvaped ete vāi vāiśvānaraṣ pañcamūrdhā yad dyāuś ca pṛthivī ca [6] rasāvatipaṁ vāiśvānaraṁ cāiva lokaṁ cāva rundhe vāiśvānaraṁ tapati vāiśvānarīva [7] dīdāya vāiśvānarīvānnādo bhavati yaṣ prāśnīyād etām eva devatāṁ mana[8]sādhyāyad vāiśvānarasya tvā cakṣuṣā paśyāmi vāiśvānarasya tvā hastābhyā[9]m ārabhed vāiśvānarasya tvāsyena prāśnāmi vāiśvānarasya tvā hastābhyām āra[10]bhed vāiśvānarasya tvāsyena prāśnāmi vāiśvānarasya tvā z vāi ṣaṭśarāvaṁ nirvape[11]t ṣaḍyāmna eva devān anu nirvaped ete vāi ṣaḍyāvāno devā yad ṛtava ṛtūṅś cāi[12]va lokaṁ cāva rundhe kalpantāismāi ṛtavo nartūṣv āvṛścatu ṛtūnāṁ [13] priyo bhavati yaṣ prāśnīyād etām eva tāṁ manasādhyāyed ṛtūnāṁ tvā [14] cakṣuṣā paśyāmi ṛtūnāṁ tvā hastābhyām ārabhed ṛtūnāṁ tvāsyena prā[15]śnāmi ṛtūnāṁ tvā vāi saptaśarāvaṁ nirvape saptarṣīn evānu nirvape[16]d ete vāi saptarṣayo yat prāṇāpānāvyānā saptarṣīṅś cāiva lokaṁ cāva [17] rundhe saptarṣir iva tapati saptarṣir iva dīdāya saptarṣīvānnādo [18] bhavati yaṣ prāśnīyād etām eva devatāṁ manasādhyāyet saptarṣīṇāṁ [19] tvāṁ cakṣuṣā paśyāmi saptarṣīṇāṁ tvā hastābhyām ārabhet saptarṣīṇā[20]syena prāśnāmi saptarṣīṇāṁ tvā z z yo vā aṣṭaśarāvaṁ nirvape[f. 130b]d virājas evāṣṭāpadīn anu nirvaped eṣa vāvā virāḍ aṣṭāpadir yad dyāuś ca [2] pṛthivī cāpaś coṣadhayaś ca virājad yasmiṅś ca loke muṣmiṅś ca vāi[3]rāja ṛṣabha ity anem āhur yaṣ prāśnīyād etām eva devatāṁ manasā[4]dhyed virājas tvā cakṣuṣā paśyāmi virājas tvā hastābhyām ārabhed virā[5]jas tvā cakṣuṣā paśyāmi virājas tvā hastābhyām ārabhed virājas tvā[6]syena prāśnāmi virājas tvā z ɪ z vāi navaśarāvaṁ nirvapen navayā[7]mna eva devān anu nirvaped ete vāi navayāvāno devā yan māsā māsa[8]ś cāiva lokaṁ cāva rundhe kalpante smāi māsā māsānāṁ priyo bhavati [9] yaṣ prāśnīyād etām eva devatāṁ manasādhyāyen māsānāṁ tvā ca[10]kṣuṣā paśyāmi māsānāṁ tvā hastābhyām ārabhen māsānāṁ tvāsyena [11] prāśnāmi māsānāṁ tvā z vāi daśaśarāvaṁ nirvapeḍām eva dhenum a[12]nu nirvaped eṣa vāvāv iḍā dhenur yad yajñaṣ paśava iḍāṁ cāiva dhe[13]nuṁ ca yajñaṁ ca lokaṁ ca paśūś cāva rundhe kalpante smāi iḍo iḍāṁ [14] priyo bhavati yaṣ praśnīyād etām eva devatāṁ manasādhyāyed i[15]ḍāyās tvā cakṣuṣā paśyāmīḍāyās tvā hastābhyām ārabhed iḍā[16]yās tvāsyena prāśnāmīḍāyās tvā z z yo vā ekādaśaśa[17]rāvaṁ nirvaped rohitām evānu nirvaped eṣa vāi rohito yad indra indraṁ [18] cāiva lokaṁ cāva rundhe kalpante smāi indriyā vāi priye indraś ca bhava[19]ti yaṣ prāśnīyād etām eva devatāṁ manasādhyāyed indrasya tvā [f. 131a] cakṣuṣā paśyāmīndrasya tvā hastābhyām ārabhed indrasya tvāsyena prāśnāmīndra[2]ndrasya tvā jaṭhare z z yo vāi dvādaśaśarāvaṁ nirvaped viśvāmni eva [3] devān anu nirvaped ete vāi viśve devā yad idaṁ sarvaṁ viśvāṅś cāiva deva lo[4]kaṁ cāva rundhe kalpante smāi viśve devāḥ priyo viśveṣāṁ devānāṁ bhava[5]ti ya evaṁ veda | sa evaṁ vidvān prāśnīyād etām eva devatāṁ manasādhyā[6]yed viśveṣāṁ tvā devānāṁ cakṣuṣā paśyāmi viśveṣāṁ tvā devānāṁ hastā[7]bhyām ārabhed viśveṣāṁ tvā devānām

āsyena prāśnāmi viśveṣāṁ tvā devānāṁ [8] tvā jaṭhare sādayāmīti sa yathā humam iṣṭaṁ prāśnīyād evāinaṁ prāśnā[9]ti z I z

Read: yo vā ekaśarāvaṁ nirvaped ekarṣim evānu nirvapet | eṣa vā ekarṣir yad agniḥ | ekarṣiṁ cāiva lokaṁ cāva rundhe | ekarṣir iva tapaty ekarṣir iva dīdāyāikarṣir ivānnādo bhavati ya evaṁ veda | sa evaṁ vidvān prāśnīyād etām eva devatāṁ manasādhyāyet z

ekarṣes tvā cakṣuṣā paśyāmy ekarṣes tvā hastābhyām ārabhe | ekarṣes tvāsyena prāśnāmy ekarṣes tvā jaṭhare sādhayāmī z iti sa yathā hutam iṣṭaṁ prāśnīyād evāinaṁ prāśnāti z 1 z

yo vāi dviśarāvaṁ nirvapet prāṇāpānāv evānu nirvapet | ete vāi prāṇāpānāu yan mātariśvā cāgniś ca | prāṇāpānāu cāiva lokaṁ cāva rundhe | jyog jīvati sarvam āyur eti na purā jarasaḥ pra mīyate ya evaṁ veda | sa ◦ ◦ ◦ z

prāṇāpānayos tvā cakṣuṣā paśyāmi prāṇāpānayos tvā hastābhyām ārabhe | prāṇāpānayos tvāsyena prāśnāmi prāṇāpānayos tvā jaṭhare sādhayāmi z iti sa ◦ ◦ ◦ z 2 z

yo vāi triśarāvaṁ nirvapet trīṇy eva trikadrukāṇy anu nirvapet | etāni vāi trīṇi trikadrukāṇi yad ṛcas sāmāni yajūṅṣi vrāhmaṇam | vrahma cāiva lokaṁ cāva rundhe | vrāhmaṇavarcasī bhavati ya evaṁ veda | sa ◦ ◦ ◦ z

vrahmaṇas tvā cakṣuṣā paśyāmi vrahmaṇas tvā hastābhyām ārabhe | vrahmaṇas tvāsyena prāśnāmi vrahmaṇas tvā jaṭhare sādhayāmi z iti sa ◦ ◦ ◦ z 3 z

yo vāi catuśśarāvaṁ nirvapec catasra evorvīr anu nirvapet | etā vāi catasra urvīr yad diśaḥ | diśaś cāiva lokaṁ cāva rundhe | kalpante 'smāi diśo diśāṁ priyo bhavati ya evaṁ veda | sa ◦ ◦ ◦ z

diśānāṁ tvā cakṣuṣā paśyāmi diśānāṁ tvā hastābhyām ārabhe | diśānāṁ tvāsyena prāśnāmi diśānāṁ tvā jaṭhare sādhayāmi z iti sa ◦ ◦ ◦ z 4 z

yo vāi pañcaśarāvaṁ nirvaped vāiśvānaram eva pañcamūrdhānam anu nirvapet | eṣa vāi vāiśvānaraṣ pañcamūrdhā yad dyāuś ca pṛthivī ca †rasāvatipaṁ | vāiśvānaraṁ cāiva lokaṁ cāva rundhe | vāiśvānara iva tapati vāiśvānara iva dīdāya vāiśvānara ivānnādo bhavati ya evaṁ veda | sa ◦ ◦ ◦ z

vāiśvānarasya tvā cakṣuṣā paśyāmi vāiśvānarasya tvā hastābhyām ārabhe | vāiśvānarasya tvāsyena prāśnāmi vāiśvānarasya tvā jaṭhare sādhayāmi z iti sa ◦ ◦ ◦ z 5 z

yo vāi ṣaṭśarāvaṁ nirvapet ṣaḍyāmna eva devān anu nirvapet |

ete vāi ṣaḍyāmāno devā yad ṛtavaḥ | ṛtūṅś cāiva lokaṁ cāva rundhe | kalpante 'smā ṛtavo nartuṣv āvṛścyatartūnāṁ priyo bhavati ya evaṁ veda | sa ° ° ° z

ṛtūnāṁ tvā cakṣuṣā paśyāmy ṛtūnāṁ tvā hastābhyām ārabhe | ṛtūnāṁ tvāsyena prāśnāmy ṛtūnāṁ tvā jaṭhare sādhayāmi z iti sa ° ° ° z 6 z

yo vāi saptaśarāvaṁ nirvapet saptarṣīn evānu nirvapet | ete vāi saptarṣayo yat prāṇāpānavyānāḥ | saptarṣīṅś cāiva lokaṁ cāva rundhe | saptarṣir iva tapati saptarṣir iva dīdāya saptarṣir ivānnādo bhavati ya evaṁ veda | sa ° ° ° z

saptarṣīnāṁ tvā cakṣuṣā paśyāmi saptarṣīṇāṁ tvā hastābhyām ārabhe | saptarṣīnāṁ tvāsyena prāśnāmi saptarṣīnāṁ tvā jaṭhare sādhayāmi z iti sa ° ° ° z 7 z

yo vā aṣṭaśarāvaṁ nirvaped virājam evāṣṭāpadīm anu nirvapet | eṣā vāi virāḍ aṣṭāpadīr yad dyāuś ca pṛthivī cāpaś cāuṣadhayaś ca | virājaty asmiṅś ca loke 'muṣmiṅś ca | vāirāja ṛṣabha ity enam āhur ya evaṁ veda | sa ° ° ° z

virājas tvā cakṣuṣā paśyāmi virājas tvā hastābhyām ārabhe | virājas tvāsyena prāśnāmi virājas tvā jaṭhare sādhayāmi z iti sa ° ° ° z 8 z

yo vāi navaśarāvaṁ nirvapen navayāmna eva devān anu nir vapet | ete vāi navayāmāno devā yan māsaḥ | māsaś cāiva lokaṁ cāva rundhe | kalpante 'smāi māsā māsānāṁ priyo bhavati ya evaṁ veda | sa ° ° ° z

māsānāṁ tvā cakṣuṣā paśyāmi māsānāṁ tvā hastābhyām ārabhe | māsānāṁ tvāsyena prāśnāmi māsānāṁ tvā jaṭhare sādhayāmi z iti sa ° ° ° z 9 z

yo vāi daśaśarāvaṁ nirvaped iḍām eva dhenum anu nirvapet | eṣā vā iḍā dhenur yad yajñaṣ paśavaḥ | iḍāṁ cāiva dhenuṁ ca yajñaṁ ca lokaṁ ca paśūṅś cāva rundhe | kalpante 'smā iḍa iḍāṁ priyo bhavati ya evaṁ veda | sa ° ° ° z

iḍāyās tvā cakṣuṣā paśyāmīḍāyās tvā hastābhyām ārabhe | iḍāyās tvāsyena prāśnāmīḍāyās tvā jaṭhare sādhayāmi z iti sa ° ° ° z 10 z

yo vā ekādaśaśarāvaṁ nirvaped rohitam evānu nirvapet | eṣa vāi rohito yad indraḥ | indraṁ cāiva lokaṁ cāva rundhe | kalpante 'smā indriyā vāi priya indrasya bhavati ya evaṁ veda | sa ° ° ° z

indrasya tvā cakṣuṣā paśyāmīndrasya tvā hastābhyām ārabhe | indrasya tvāsyena prāśnāmīndrasya tvā jaṭhare sādhayāmi z iti sa ° ° ° z 11 z yo vāi dvādaśaśarāvaṁ nirvaped viśvān eva devān anu nirvapet | ete vai viśve devā yad idaṁ sarvam | viśvāṅś cāiva devān lokaṁ cāva rundhe | kalpante 'smāi viśve devāḥ priyo viśveṣāṁ devānāṁ bhavati ya evaṁ veda | sa evaṁ vidvān prāśnīyād etām eva devatāṁ manasādhyāyet z

viśveṣāṁ tvā devānāṁ cakṣuṣā paśyāmi viśveṣāṁ tvā devānāṁ hastābhyām ārabhe | viśveṣāṁ tvā devānām āsyena prāśnāmi viśveṣāṁ tvā devānāṁ jaṭhare sādhayāmi z iti sa yathā hutam iṣṭaṁ prāśnīyād evāinaṁ prāśnāti z 12 z 1 z

The ms seems to count this as two hymns, the first ending being indicated in f. 130b 7, but the unity of these groups has induced me to count them together as one hymn: moreover the norm in this book seems to be 12 stanzas. The ms at f. 130b 14 has kalpante smāi iḍo iḍāṁ as if from stem iḍ, but elsewhere in the immediate context the stem is clearly iḍā so we might emend to iḍā iḍānāṁ.

22

[f. 131a 9] imāṁ sātāṁ nir vapa odanasya tasya panthā mucyatāṁ kilvi[10]ṣebhyaḥ abhi drohād enaso duṣkṛtāś ca punātu mā pavanāiṣ pavitraḥ bhadrāu [11] hastāu bhadrā jihvā bhadraṁ bhavatu me vacaḥ mahyaṁ pavitram odanaṁ vrahmaṇā ni[12]r vapāmasi | hastābhyāṁ nir vapāmasi | yan me garbhe sati mātā cakāra [13] duṣkṛtaṁ ayaṁ mā tāssad odanaṣ pavitraṣ pātv aṅhasaḥ | yad urvācīnam āi[14]kahāyanād anṛtaṁ kiṁ codimaḥ yad duṣkṛtaṁ yaś chamalaṁ yad enaś cakṛmā [15] vayaṁ yan mātaraṁ yat pitaraṁ yad rājāmadriyaṁśisaḥ yan mātṛghnā [16] yat pitṛghna bhrūṇaghnā yat sahāśimaḥ cyāvadatā kunakhinā stenena [17] yaś cahāśimaḥ śuśuṇḍānāṁ pāuścalānāṁ tat kṛṇāṁ yad annam āśimaḥ [18] yad apām api jahur munmṛjy apapi sodakam. z ɪ z yad ukta [19] vāmanyato vayaṁ vrahmaṇasya nijaghnunsu padāvāgām upedima | yad vra-[f. 131b] hmacarye snātacarye anṛtaṁ kiṁ codima kilāsena duścarmaṇā vaṇḍe yat sahā[2]śimād dhārābhiṣiktena mā | yatra kṣettram abhi tiṣṭhātāśvaṁ vā yaṁ nir emi[3]ṣe yad akṣeṣu hiraṇyaye goṣv aśveṣu yad dhane anṛtaṁ kiṁ codima cakṣu[4]r jāyāṁ svāṁ dāsīṁ sūtikāṁ lohitāvatīm aśuddhāṁ yad ipeyima | [5] parividyaṣ parividānenābhyavastrā tena

paribhakṣatena dviduṣūpatyā [6] yat sahāśima | yad uktasīdaṁ vimejamad vimeyaṁ dhanakāmyā ya [7] dvaye kaṁ ya traye kam upayāi kam iti yad dadāu yat paramāṇā śa-[8]valam apakvaṁ māṅsam āśimaḥ z 2 z yad annam āśimā va[9]yam ad annam annakāmyodanasyāpi śācyā | yad vidvāṅso yadi [10] vidvāso anṛtaṁ kiṁ codimaḥ ayaṁ mā tasmād odanaṣ pavitra[11]ṣ pātv aṅhasaḥ yed devasya savituṣ pavitraṁ sahasradhāraṁ vitathaṁ hi[12]raṇmayaṁ yenendrav apunaṁnārtisartyās tenāyaṁ māṁ sarvapaśuṁ punā[13]tu | yenāpunāt savitā revatīr atho yenāpunīta varuṇasya vāyaḥ [14] yenemā viśvā bhuvanāni pūtās tenāyaṁ māṁ sarvapaśuṁ punā[15]tu | atikrāmāsi duritaṁ yad eno jahāmi ripuṁ [16] parame sadhasthe | yenendrava punaṁnāti duritaṁ yad eno jahāmi [17] ripuṁ parame sadhasthe yenendrava punaṁnāti duṣkṛtas tham ā ruhe[18]ma sukṛtāsu lokaṁ mā yakṣmaṁm ihāmiṣṭam ārihanto vi-[19] gātu naḥ samāiva puṇyam astu no tṛṇaṁ nayatu duṣkṛtaṁ imaṁ pa[20]cāmy odanaṁ pavitraṁ pacanāya kaṁ sa mā muñcatu duṣkṛtād viśma[f. 132a]śmasmāś cāinasas pari z 4 z

Read: imāṁ †sātāṁ nir vapa odanasya tasya panthā mucyatāṁ kilbiṣebhyaḥ | abhi drohād enaso duṣkṛtāc ca punātu mā pavanāiṣ pavitraḥ z 1 z bhadrāu hastāu bhadrā jihvā bhadraṁ bhavatu me vacaḥ | mahyaṁ pavitram odanaṁ vrahmaṇā nir vapāmasi hastābhyāṁ nir vapāmasi z 2 z yan mayi garbhe sati mātā cakāra duṣkṛtam | ayaṁ mā tasmād odanaṣ pavitraṣ pātv aṅhasaḥ z 3 z yad arvācīnam āikahāyanād anṛtaṁ kiṁ codima | • • • z 4 z yad duṣkṛtaṁ yac chamalaṁ yad enaś cakṛmā vayam | • • • z 5 z yan mātaraṁ yat pitaraṁ yad vā jāmātaraṁ hiṅsmaḥ | • • • z 6 z yan mātṛghnā yat pitṛghnā bhrūṇaghnā yat sahāsima | • • • z 7 z śyāvadatā kunakhinā stenena yat sahāsima | • • • z 8 z śuṇḍānāṁ pāuṣkalānāṁ tat †kṛṇāṁ yad annam āśima | • • • z 9 z yad apām api †jahur munmṛjy apapi† sodakam | • • • z 10 z yad uktāv āmanyato vayaṁ vrāhmaṇasya nijaghnatsu †padāvāgām u† pedima | • • • z 11 z yad vrahmacarye snātacarye 'nṛtaṁ kiṁ codima | • • • z 12 z kilāsena duścarmaṇā baṇḍena yat sahāsima | • • • z 13 z yad dhārābhiṣiktena * * sahāsima | • • • z 14 z yatra kṣetram abhitasthāthāśvaṁ vā yan niremiṣe | • • • z 15 z yad akṣeṣu hiraṇyaye goṣv aśveṣu yad dhane 'nṛtaṁ kiṁ codima | • • • z 16 z †cakṣur jāyāṁ svāṁ dāsīṁ sūtikāṁ lohitavatīṁ aśuddhāṁ yad upeyima | ° ° ° z 17 z parividya †parivedanenābhyavastrātena paribhakṣitena didiṣūpatyā yat sahāsima | ° ° ° z 18 z yad †uktasīdaṁ vimejaṁ† yad vimeyaṁ dhanakāmyāḥ | ° ° ° z 19 z yad dvaye kam yat traye kam ubhaye kam iti yad dadāu | ° ° ° z 20 z yat paramāṇāṁ śevalam apakvaṁ māṅsam āśima | ° ° ° z 21 z yad annam āśima vayaṁ yad annam annakāmyā odanasyāpi śacyā | ° ° ° z 22 z yadi vidvāṅso yadi vāvidvāṅso 'nṛtaṁ kiṁ codima | ayaṁ mā tasmād odanaṣ pavitraṣ pātv aṅhasaḥ z 23 z yad devasya savituṣ pavitraṁ sahasradhāraṁ vitataṁ hiraṇmayam | yenendro apunād anārtam ārtyās tenāyaṁ māṁ sarvapaśuṁ punātu z 24 z yenāpunat savitā revatīr atho yenāpunīta varuṇaś ca vayaḥ | yenemā viśvā bhuvanāni pūtā tenāyaṁ māṁ sarvapaśuṁ punātu z 25 z ati krāmāmi duritaṁ yad eno jahāmi ripraṁ parame sadhasthe | yenendra eva punāti duṣkṛtas tam ā ruhema sukṛtām u lokam z 26 z †mā yakṣmaṁm ihāmiṣṭam ārihanto vigātu† naḥ | samāiva puṇyam astu nas tṛṇaṁ nayatu duṣkṛtam z 27 z imaṁ pacāmy odanaṁ pavitraṁ pacanāya kam | sa mā muñcatu duṣkṛtād viśvasmāc cāinasas pari z 28 z 2 z

The restoration of a refrain in the edited text is done with confidence altho it involves making one hymn where the ms indicates three, as shown by the numerals in f. 131a 19, f. 131b 8; the unity of the material as edited is clear. For our 4ab see Ś. 10. 5. 22ab; 5a=Ś. 7. 65. 2a; for 6ab cf. Ś. 6. 120. 1b; for 8ab cf. Ś. 7. 65. 3ab; 13b=Ś. 7. 65. 3b; for st. 26 see TB. 3. 7. 12. 5.

23

[f. 132a 1] sahasrākṣaṁ śatadhāram ṛṣibhiṣ pāvanaṁ [2] kṛtaṁ | tenā tenā sahasradhāreṇa pavamānaṣ punātu māṁ yena pūtam antarikṣaṁ [3] yasmin vāyur adhiśrutaḥ yená pūté dyāvapṛthívī āpáṣ pūtā átho sváḥ yena [4] pūte ahorātre diśaṣ pūtā uta yena pradiśaḥ yena pūtāu sūryāścandramasāu [5] nakṣattrāṇi bhūtakṛtas saha yena pūtā | yena pūtā vedir agnayaḥ paridhaya[6]s saha yena pūtā yena pūtaṁ barhir ājyam atho haviḥ yena pūtāu yajño vasa[7]ṭkāra hutāhutiḥ yena pūtāu vrīhiyavābhyāṁ yajño adhinirmitāḥ yena pū[8]tāśvā gāvo atho pūtā ajāyavaḥ z 5 z yena pūtā ṛcās sā[9]māni yajur vrāhmaṇa saha yena pūtaṁ yena pūtān ātharvāñgiraso devatā[10]s saha yena pūtā | yena pūtā ṛtavo yenāntavā yebhyas saṁvatsaro adhini[11]rmitaḥ | yena

pūtā vanaspatayo vānaspatyā oṣadhayo vīḍadha[12]s saha yena pūtā | yena pūtā gandharvāpsarosas sarpapuṇyajanāḥ saha [13] yena pūtāḥ yena pūtāṣ parvatā himavanto vāiśvānaraṣ paribhavas saha ye[14]na pūtāḥ yena pūtā nadyas sindhavas samudrās saha yena pūtāḥ yena pūtā [15] viśve devāṣ parameṣṭhī prajāpatiḥ yena pūtaṣ prajāpatiḥ lokaṁ viśvaṁ [16] bhūtaṁ svar ājabhāra | yena pūtas sthanayitnur apāṁ vatsaṣ prajāpatiḥ yena pū[17]tam ṛtaṁ satyaṁ tapo dīkṣā pūtayate | yena pūtam idaṁ sarvaṁ yad bhūtaṁ yaś ca [18] bhavyaṁ yena sahasradhāreṇa pavamānaṣ punātu māṁ z 6 z

Read: sahasrākṣaṁ śatadhāram ṛṣibhiṣ pāvanaṁ kṛtam | tenā sahasradhāreṇa pavamānaṣ punātu mām z 1 z yena pūtam antarikṣaṁ yasmin vāyur adhiśritaḥ | tenā ° ° ° z 2 z yena pūte dyāvāpṛthivī āpaṣ pūtā atho svaḥ | tenā ° ° ° z 3 z yena pūte ahorātre diśaṣ pūtā uta yena pradiśaḥ | tenā ° ° z 4 z yena pūtāu sūryācandramasāu nakṣatrāṇi bhūtakṛtas saha yena pūtāḥ | tenā ° ° ° z 5 z yena pūtā vedir agnayaḥ paridhayas saha yena pūtāḥ | tenā ° ° ° z 6 z yena pūtaṁ barhir ājyam atho havir yena pūto yajño vaṣaṭkāro hutāhutiḥ | tenā ° ° ° z 7 z yena pūtāu vrīhiyavā yābhyāṁ yajño adhinirmitaḥ | tenā ° ° ° z 8 z yena pūtā aśvā gāvo atho pūtā ajāvayaḥ | tenā ° ° ° z 9 z yena pūtā ṛcas sāmāni yajur vrāhmaṇaṁ saha yena pūtam | tenā ° ° ° z 10 z yena pūtā atharvāṅgiraso devatās saha yena pūtāḥ | tenā ° ° ° z 11 z yena pūtā ṛtavo yenārtavā yebhyaḥ saṁvatsaro adhinirmitaḥ | tenā ° ° ° z 12 z yena pūtā vanaspatayo vānaspatyā oṣadhayo vīrudhas saha yena pūtāḥ | tenā ° ° ° z 13 z yena pūtā gandharvāpsarasas sarpapuṇyajanāḥ saha yena pūtāḥ | tenā ° ° ° z 14 z yena pūtāṣ parvatā himavanto vāiśvānarāṣ paribhavas saha yena pūtāḥ | tenā ° ° ° z 15 z yena pūtā nadyas sindhavas samudrās saha yena pūtāḥ | tenā ° ° ° z 16 z yena pūtā viśve devāṣ parameṣṭhī prajāpatiḥ | tenā ° ° ° z 17 z yena pūtaṣ prajāpatir lokaṁ viśvaṁ bhūtaṁ svar ājabhāra | tenā ° ° ° z 18 z yena pūtas stanayitnur apām utsaṣ prajāpatiḥ | tenā ° ° ° z 19 z yena pūtam ṛtaṁ satyaṁ tapo dīkṣā pūtayate | tenā ° ° ° z 20 z yena pūtam idaṁ sarvaṁ yad bhūtaṁ yac ca bhavyam | tenā sahasradhāreṇa pavamānaṣ punātu mām z 21 z 3 z

The arrangement made for st. 7 may not be correct, as the ms. reading haviḥ may indicate the end of a hemistich. At the end of 19b pūtayate for prajāpatiḥ would be much better, and possibly it should be read.

24

(Ś. 5. 20.)

[f. 132a 18] uścāirghoṣo [19] dundubhis satvanāthaṁ vānaspatyas saṁbhṛta usriyābhiḥ vācaṁ khaṇvāno [f. 132b] damayan sapattrān siṅhāiva dveṣaṁn abhi taṅstanayati | siṅhāivāttānīdravayo vi[2]baddho abhikrandaṁn ṛṣabho vāśitam iva | nṛṣā tva vadhrayas te sapatnān indra[3]s te śuṣmo bhimātiṣāhaḥ saṁjayaṅ pṛtanā ūrdhvamāyu gṛhyā gṛhṇāno [4] bahudhā vi cakṣaḥ z devīṁ vācasāgurassu medhā śatṝṇām upa bha[5]rassu vedāḥ vṛṣeva yūthaṁ sahasaṁ vidāno gavyaṁn abha roha saṁdhanājit su[6]mā viddhi hṛdayaṁ pareṣām. hutvā grāmān pracyutā yantu śattravaḥ [7] dundubhir vācaṁ prayatāṁ vadantīm āśṛṇvatī nāthitā gho-[8]ṣabuddhā nārī putraṁ dhāvatu haṁgṛhyāmittre bhītāḥ samare vadhānaḥ dhī[9]bhiṣ kṛtaṣ pū bharassu vācam ud dharṣayas saptanām āyudhāni amittrase[10]nānām abhijajabhāno dimad vala dundubhe sūnṛtāvat. | pūrvo du[11]ndubhe viṣahasva śatrūn bhūmyās pṛṣṭhe vada bahu rocamānāḥ indrase[12]dīn satvanas saṁhuyasva | amittrāir amittrān ava jaṁghanīhi antareso [13] nabhasī ghoṣo astu pṛthak te ddhanayo yantu śībhaṁ | abhi kranda stanayoya[14]tpipānā ślokakṛtraturyāya śraddhī saṅkrandanaṣ prasraveṇo dhṛṣṇu[15]ṣeṇaṣ pravedakṛd bahudhā grāmaghoṣī | śrayo vadhvāno vayunāni [17] vidvān kīrti bāhubhyo vi bhaja dvirāje z śriyaṣketo vasudhis sahī[17]yān mittraṁ dadhānas tviṣito vipaścit. | aṅśūn iva śrāvā vṛṣaṇe [18] drir gavyaṁ dundubhe adhi nṛtya vedaḥ śatrūṣāṁ ṇīṣāḍ abhimātiśā-[f. 133a]ho gaveṣaṇaḥ sahamānodabhṛt. | vāgvī mindraṁ pṛtanayassu vācaṁ saṅgāma[2]jibhyā eṣam ud vadehaḥ abhyuduśyan samatho gamiṣṭha madho jayatā pṛtanā[3]ṣaḍ ayodhyaḥ indreṇa klipto vitathā nicikyud yubhyotano dviṣatāṁ yāhi śī[4]bham. z 7 z

Read: uccāirghoṣo dundubhis satvanāyan vānaspatyas saṁbhṛta usriyābhiḥ | vācaṁ kṣṇuvāno damayan sapatnān siṅha iva dveṣann abhi taṅstanīti z 1 z siṅha ivāstānīd druvayo vibaddho abhikrandann ṛṣabho vāśitām iva | vṛṣā tvaṁ vadhrayas te sapatnā indras te śuṣmo 'bhimātiṣāhaḥ z 2 z saṁjayan pṛtanā ūrdhvamāyur gṛhyā gṛhṇāno bahudhā vi cakṣaḥ | dāivīṁ vācam ā gurasva vedhāś śatrūṇām upa bharasva vedaḥ z 3 z vṛṣeva yūthaṁ sahasā vidāno gavyann abhi roha sandhanājit | śucā vidhya hṛdayaṁ pareṣāṁ hitvā grāmān pracyutā yantu śatravaḥ z 4 z dundubher vācaṁ prayatāṁ vadantīm āśṛṇvatī nāthitā ghoṣabuddhā | nārī putraṁ dhāvatu hastagṛhyāmitrī bhītā samare vadhānām z 5 z dhībhiṣ kṛtaṣ pra bharasva vācam ud dharṣaya satvanām āyudhāni | amitrasenām abhijañjabhāno dyumad vada dundubhe sūnṛtāvat z 6 z pūrvo dundubhe vi ṣahasva śatrūn bhūmyās pṛṣthe vada bahu rocamānaḥ | indramedī satvanas saṁ hvayasva mitrāir amitrān ava jaṅghanīhi z 7 z antareme nabhasī ghoṣo astu pṛthak te dhvanayo yantu śībham | abhi kranda stanayotpipānaś ślokakṛn mitratūryāya śraddhī z 8 z saṅkrandanaṣ prastāvena dhṛṣṇuṣeṇaṣ pravedakṛd bahudhā grāmaghoṣī | śreyo vanvāno vayunāni vidvān kīrtiṁ bahubhyo vi bhaja dvirāje z 9 z śreyaṣketo vasudhitis sahīyān mitraṁ dadhānas tviṣito vipaścit | aṅśūn iva grāvā †vṛṣaṇe 'drir gavyaṁ dundubhe adhi nṛtya vedaḥ z 10 z śatrūṣāṇ nīṣāḍ abhimātiṣāho gaveṣaṇaḥ sahamāna udabhṛt | vāgvī mandrāṁ pra tanayasva vācaṁ sāṁgrāmajityāyeṣam ud vadeha z 11 z acyutacyut samado gamiṣṭho mṛdho jetā pṛtanāṣāḍ ayodhyaḥ | indreṇa kḷpto vidathā nicikyad dhṛdyotano dviṣatāṁ yāhi śībham z 12 z 4 z

In 3b if vi cakṣaḥ is not acceptable perhaps vicakṣaḥ would be good. In 10c Ś has grāvādhiṣavaṇe, which might be restored here. The hymn shows a number of interesting variants from the text of Ś. Edgerton would read svardhī with Ś in 8d.

25

[f. 133a 4] **imās tapantv oṣadhīr oṣadhīnām ayaṁ rasaḥ aśvatthas te yaṁ hṛ[5]dy agnir bhūto vy oṣatu pra patāno mamādhya**

In c read 'yaṁ, for e probably pra patānu mamādhyaḥ.

yathā sūtaṁ lākṣā rakta mājyenānu ṣi[6]ṣyadhyate | evā te kāma sarpantv aṅtv arthasu majjasu prā

In a sūtraṁ seems probable, and raktaṁ; for b I would suggest madhyenānu ṣiṣyadāti: in cd read kāmaḥ sarpatv antar artheṣu; read for e as in st 1.

yathā kuṣṭhaṣ prayasyati yathā [7] **dahyate arciṣā | evā te dahyatāṁ manaḥ pra**

In a kuṣṭhaṣ seems a little suspicious but I can suggest nothing else; for d read as st. 1e.

puṁsaṣ kuṣṭhaṁ pra kṣarati stokādhībhir ā[8]**bhṛtaḥ sa te hṛdaye vivarta tān manādhībhis tava pra |**

Again kuṣṭhaṁ is suspicious; in b read stoka ā°: in c I would suggest vavartti, in d tan mana ā°, and e as in st. 1.

eṣa te stoko hṛdayaṁ digde[9]**veṣu pra padyatā | astrakhaṇaṁ yatheṣṭā kāmo vidyatu tāmava prā** *z*

Read: eṣa te stoko hṛdayaṁ digdheveṣuḥ pra padyatām | astrākhaṇaṁ yatheṣitā kāmo vidhyatu tvā mama pra patānu mamādhyaḥ z 5 z

hariteti śu[10]**ṣkākṣas sarvadā hṛdayāmayī trihaste anyām aśchāṅsur atho tvā śābhi śocatu pra** *z*

Read °kṣā in a; I can do nothing with pāda c; in d read sābhi, or perhaps cābhi. Read e as in st. 1.

[11] **śocīnud astu te śayanaṁ śocānud apa veśanaṁ | śucīm astu te mano yathā tvanaramā**[12]**sā**

Considering merely the letters we might emend to śocinud and śokanud, but śocivad and śokavad would seem better in the context; in b read api. In c śucīdam would seem possible but I would suggest śoṣīdam; in d possibly tvam araso 'saḥ. Only here is 'pra' (indicating repetition of 1e) lacking, and I would restore the pāda.

vācīna manas sapro nir mām aya maṁgatheṣu capānaṁ tvābhi śocatu | stoka sto[13]**ka uttarottara prā**

In a probably arvācīnaṁ manas, in b saṁgatheṣu, but for the rest of ab I can suggest nothing. In c tapanaṁ seems probable; for d read stokaḥ stoka uttarottaraḥ, for e as in st. 1.

antar mahatu carmaṇosthivāṅsebhir ābhṛtaṁ sarvān yajñaḥ pra yā[14]**śayād iḍādhībhis tava pra**

In pādas ab I can make no suggestion: in c possibly yāsayād; the rest seems possible, with e as in st. 1. The margin suggests itā for iḍā.

hṛdaye tu sam ṛddhyatāṁ śvāir dāṅsebhir eṣatę | agniṣ kā[15]**masya yo mahān sa mahyaṁ rundhayātu tvā prāḥ** *z* **8** *z*

Read: hṛdaye tu sam ṛddhyatāṁ svāir daṅsebhir eṣate | agniṣ kāmasya yo mahān sa mahyaṁ randhayatu tvā prapatānu mamādhyaḥ z 10 z

The numeral '8' given in the ms. indicates the 8th kāṇḍa of the 4th anuvāka, thus ending this hymn here; but the abbreviations (here prāḥ) indicating the refrain pāda continue to st. 15 of my arrangement and then in st. 16 the pāda is given in full; this fact and the subject-matter induce me to edit the next seven stanzas as part of this hymn.

aśvam agnim ājyaṁ [16] dra tāni kṛṇve manojavāṁ | agniś carum ivārciṣā kāmo vidhyatu tvā mama prāḥ

In ab we may probably read ājyam indraṁ tān u and °javān; pāda e as in st. 1.

[17] z **śayānam agnāmīnam aśvatthasya savāsināu caratum upatiṣṭhanta samādhībhi**[18]**r vi viddhyataṁ pra |**

In a I would suggest agna āsīnam, in c possibly carantam uta tiṣṭhantaṁ; in d mamā°, and possibly vidhya taṁ; pāda e as in st. 1.

carantiṁ stha tiṣṭhantam āsīdam upa saṁsati | reṣmā tṛṇam eva ma[f. 133b]**ttvātu vahaṁ kāmaratho mama prā z**

The following suggestions may be possible; for a carantaṁ ca tiṣṭhantaṁ cā°, in b upamaṁ satī; in c iva mathnātu, in d vahan; pāda e as in st. 1.

yathendrāyāsurān arundhayatu vṛhaspa[2]**tiḥ evā tvam agne aśvatthān amūn amayam ihā naya prāḥ**

Read arandhayad in b, and probably mahyam in d; e as in st. 1.

ahaṁ te manāda[3]**dhe guḍena saha medinā | devā manuṣyā gandharvās te mahyaṁ randhayātu tvā praḥ**

Read mana ā dade in a, randhayantu in d; e as in st. 1.

[4] **yathāśvatthasya parṇāni nīlayanti kadā cana | evāsāu mama kāme**[5]**na māva svāpsīt kadā cana | pra patatāto pamādhyaḥ**

Read nilayanti in b; I believe that pāda e here is intended to be the same as st. 1c.

kuṣṭhaṁ tapanta marutas sā[6]**dhyaṁ dvarājānaṁ svarayanto arciṣā yathā nas svapāt katamaś canāhavāiva ga-**[7]

śchān mamādhyāḥ zz zz anu 7 zz ity atharvaṇika[8]pāi-palādaśākhāyāṁ navamaṣ kāṇḍa samāptaḥ zz zz

Read: kuṣṭhaṁ tapanta marutas sādhyaṁ †dvarājānaṁ svarayanto arciṣā | yathā na svapāt katamaś canāhāvāiva gacchān mamādhyaḥ z 17 z 5 z anu 4 z

ity atharvaṇikapāippalādaśākhāyāṁ navamaṣ kāṇḍas samāptaḥ zz

In pāda b we might read svarājānaṁ, but the first two pādas are not clear; the general intent of the hymn is however clear enough.

THE PART PLAYED BY THE PUBLICATIONS OF THE UNITED STATES GOVERNMENT IN THE DEVELOPMENT OF PHILIPPINE LINGUISTIC STUDIES[1]

FRANK R. BLAKE

JOHNS HOPKINS UNIVERSITY

WHEN THE UNITED STATES took possession of the Philippine Islands at the close of the Spanish-American War in 1898, a great amount of work on the native languages had already been done, chiefly by the Spanish missionaries of the various religious orders, who compiled grammars, dictionaries, phrase-books, and religious manuals for the purpose of bringing the natives into the fold of the Roman Catholic Church. Of the forty or fifty different languages spoken in the Archipelago about two dozen had up to that time received more or less treatment, and were more or less familiar to students of Philippine matters.

The seven principal languages, Tagalog, Bisaya (in its three chief dialects, Cebuan, Hiliguayna or Panayan, and Samaro-Leytean),[2] Iloko, Pampanga, Bikol, Pangasinan, and Ibanag,

---

[1] My *Bibliography of the Philippine Languages*, Part I, *JAOS* 40 (1920) pp. 25—70, will be referred to in this article as *BB*. Since the publication of this work, my friend, Prof. Otto Scheerer of the University of the Philippines at Manila, has sent me a type-written list of over a hundred additional titles (including 16 MSS), at least half of which are important works. These additional titles, which will furnish the basis for a supplement to *BB* to be published later, will be referred to in this article as *S*.

[2] The less known Bisaya dialects are the Haraya of the island of Panay, Bisaya of Mindanao, the dialect of Bohol, and the dialect of Masbate and Ticao. The Aklán dialect, mentioned by Beyer, *Population of the Philippine Islands in 1916*, pp. 24, 27, 40, as spoken on the island

were set forth in fairly good dictionaries and grammars,[3] and were each represented by a considerable number of texts, chiefly of a religious character.[4] Grammars and dictionaries of some sort, and a certain amount of text, also existed for the two Moro languages, Magindanao and Sulu, and for the Tiruray of Mindanao.[5] Dictionaries and texts were available for the study of the Chamorro language of Guam (including a Spanish grammar in Chamorro), for the language of the Caroline Islands (also some few grammatical notes), and for the Gaddan(g) of North Luzon. For the Bagobo of Mindanao there was a fairly good dictionary, Bagobo-Spanish and Spanish-Bagobo with a few grammatical remarks. For the following there were short word-lists with some text or some brief grammatical discussion, or both, viz., Tagbanua (text, gram. remarks), Zambal (text), Kalamian (text),[6] Negrito (gram. remarks), Palau (gram. remarks). The following were represented only by brief word-lists, viz., Atás, Bilaan, Ginaan, Igorot dialects (Banawe, Bontok, Benget, Lepanto), Manobo, Samal, Tagakaolo. Texts without word-lists or grammar were in existence for the

---

of Panay, is perhaps the same as Haraya, which does not appear in Beyer as a Bisaya dialect. Scheerer in *S* mentions a dialect Aklanón in the list of those languages of which he has collected stories, etc. Otherwise the name is entirely unknown to me. For the material available for the study of these dialects both before and after 1898, cf. table on p. 166 f.

[3] Cf. my 'Contributions to Comparative Philippine Grammar', *JAOS* 27 (1906) p. 323, n. 2; also *BB* under the various languages.

[4] Cf. my article 'Philippine Literature', *American Anthropologist*, 13 (1911) pp. 449—457.

[5] For the bibliography of these languages and those mentioned subsequently in this paragraph, cf. *BB*, under language in question.

[6] The language here called Kalamian is the language so called by Jerónimo de la Virgen de Monserrate (cf. *BB* 190). Whether the text *BB* 103, said by Retana to be in Agutayna = Kalamian, and the MS texts *BB* 453, 454, none of which I have seen, are in the same language, is not certain, as there is apparently more or less confusion between the names Kalamian and Kuyo (cf. next note). Beyer in *Population of the Philippine Islands in 1916*, Manila, 1917, p. 49, says Kalamian 'is related to the Bisayan dialects, but is more like the Tagbanúa speech of Palawan than anything else. A special dialect called Agutaino is said to be spoken on the small island of Agutaya'. Scheerer in his treatise on the Batan dialect (cf. below p. 151, No. 15) on p. 15 says he has reason to believe Kalamian is a Tagbanúa dialect: so also in *S*.

Batan of the Batan Islands (also some grammatical remarks), for the Isinay of North Luzon (including a Spanish grammar in Isinay) and for the Kuyo[7] of the Kuyo Islands. The same is also true of the Ilongot or Egongot of North Luzon, tho an otherwise unknown grammar of this language is listed by Barrantes (*BB* 218). References to the Tingyan of North Luzon are said by Conant to be contained in H. Meyer's *Eine Weltreise* (*BB* 246), and the Igorot dialect of Abra province in North Luzon was represented by a single poem (*BB* 151).

In addition to these works there were also a number of books or articles on special linguistic topics, and some in which the languages were treated from a comparative point of view. The most important of these special topics are, viz., the native alphabets, native poetry, the numerals, the Sanskrit element in Tagalog and Bisaya, the Chinese element in Malay, plant names, names of persons, and the Spanish of the Philippine Islands.[8] Most of the works of a comparative character were merely comparative word and phrase lists, tho there were a few of some importance, viz., the general account of the languages of the Philippine group in Friedrich Müller's *Grundriss der Sprachwissenschaft* (*BB* 258); Gabelentz (G. von der) and Meyer's contributions to our knowledge of the Melanesian, Micronesian, and Papuan languages (*BB* 157); H. C. von Gabelentz' article on the passive (*BB* 158); and Kern's treatment of the connective particles (*BB* 197).[9] Finally special linguistic bibliographies had been prepared by Blumentritt and Barrantes (cf. *BB*, pp. 25–28).

Since the occupation of the Philippine Islands by the United States in 1898, the following five steps forward in Philippine

---

[7] Whether the texts given under Kuyo in *BB* are all in the same language, I cannot say. According to the *Report of the Philippine Commission*, 1900, vol. 3, p. 79, Calamian, Agutiano (*sic!* = Agutayna), and Coyuno (= Kuyo) are distinct languages or dialects; Beyer, *op. cit.*, p. 25, seems to identify Kalamian and Kuyonon (= Kuyo).

[8] Cf. *BB* under Alphabets, Chinese, General Philippine Linguistics, Literature, Malay, Malayo-Spanish, Names, Numerals, Poetry, Sanskrit, Spelling.

[9] Cf. *BB* under Comparative Philippine Grammar and Vocabulary, and General Philippine Linguistics.

linguistic studies may be noted. 1) Our knowledge of some of the better known languages, particularly Tagalog, has been increased and deepened: 2) additional texts in the native tongues, particularly portions of the Bible, have been published: 3) a number of grammatical sketches and grammars of languages not before treated to any extent have appeared: 4) a complete Bibliography of Philippine languages is in process of compilation: 5) considerable progress has been made in the scientific and comparative study of the languages.

The object of the present article is to give some account of those government publications which deal either directly or indirectly with Philippine languages, and to consider to what extent the present status of Philippine linguistic studies is due to the activities of the United States government either in this country or in the Philippine Islands.

The following is a list of books and articles of a more or less linguistic character, whose publication is the result of government support, arranged in the order of their publication: the numbers in parentheses are the numbers of the titles in *BB*; *ESP* = Ethnological Survey Publications, Department of the Interior (Philippines); *BS* = Government Bureau of Science, Division of Ethnology Publications, Manila (a continuation of *ESP*); *PJS* = Philippine Journal of Science, published by the Bureau of Science, Manila.

1. El archipiélago filipino: Colleción de datos . . . Washington, 1900, Tom. I, pp. 26—147 *passim* and pp. 221—238 (translated in *Report of Philippine Commission for 1900,* vol. III, pp. 14—128 *passim* and pp. 397—412). (8)
2. Mason, O. T. — Blumentritt's list of the native tribes of the Philippines and the languages spoken by them. *Report of the Smithsonian Inst. for 1899* (1901), pp. 527—547. (236)
3. The geographic names in the Philippine Islands. *Special report of the U.S. Board on Geographic names,* Washington, 1901, pp. 59. (164)
4. Merrill, E. D. — A dictionary of the plant names of the Philippine Islands. *Publications of Bureau of Government Laboratories,* Manila, 1903, pp. 193. (240)
5. Porter, R. S. — A primer and vocabulary of the Moro dialect (Magindanau). Washington, 1903, pp. 77. (289)

6. Reed, W. A. — Negritos of Zambales. *ESP*, II, 1, Manila, 1904. (293)
7. Jenks, A. E. — The Bontok Igorot. *ESP*, I, Manila, 1905. (189)
8. Scheerer, O. — The Nabaloi dialect. *ESP*, II, 2, Manila, 1905, pp. 97—178. (335)
9. Saleeby, N. M. — Studies in Moro history, law, religion. *ESP*, IV, 1, Manila, 1905. (312)
10. MacKinlay, W. E. W. — A handbook and grammar of the Tagalog language. Washington, 1905, pp. 264 + 6 charts. (217)
11. Census of the Philippine Islands, vol. I, Washington, 1905. (91)
12. Worcester, D. C. — The Non-Christian tribes of Northern Luzon. *PJS*, I, 1906, pp. 791—875. (377)
13. Smith, C. C. — A grammar of the Magindanao tongue. Washington, 1906, pp. 80. (353)
14. Saleeby, N. M. — History of Sulu. *BS*, IV, 2, 1908. (313)
15. Scheerer, O. — The Batan dialect as a member of the Philippine group of languages. *BS*, V, 1, Manila, 1908, pp. 9—131. (337)
16. Conant, C. E. — "F" and "V" in Philippine languages. *BS*, V, 2, Manila, 1908, pp. 135—141. (105)
17. Clapp, W. C. — A vocabulary of the Igorot language as spoken by the Bontok Igorots: Igorot-English and English-Igorot. *BS*, V, 3, Manila, 1908, pp. 141—236. (99)
18. Swift, H. — A study of the Iloko language. Washington, 1909, pp. 172. (354)
19. Christie, E. B. — The Subanuns of Sindangan Bay. *BS*, VI, 1 Manila, 1909. (97)
20. Barton, R. F. — The Harvest-feast of the Kiangan Ifugao. *PJS*, VI, D, 1911, pp. 81—103. (*S*)
21. Beyer, H. O. and Barton, R. F. — An Ifugao burial ceremony. *PJS*, VI, D, 1911, pp. 227—252. (*S*)
22. M(iller)?, M. L. — *Review of* Allin's 'Standard English-Visayan dictionary'. *PJS*, VI, D, 1911, p. 281. (213)
23. Scheerer, O. — On a quinary notation among the Ilongots of Northern Luzon. *PJS*, VI, D, 1911, pp. 47—49. (338)
24. — *Review of* C. W. Seidenadel's 'The first grammar of the language spoken by the Bontok Igorot'. *PJS*, VI, D, 1911, pp. 271—281. (341)

25. Miller, M. L. — The Mangyans of Mindoro, *PJS*, VII, D, 1912, pp. 135—156. (248)
26. Schneider, E. E. — Notes on the Mangyan language. *PJS*, VII, D, 1912, pp. 157—178. (343)
27. Waterman, M. P. — A vocabulary of Bontok stems and their derivatives. *BS*, V, 4, Manila, 1913, pp. 239—299. (374)
28. Elliott, C. W. — A vocabulary and phrase book of the Lanao Moro dialect. *BS*, V, 5, pp. 301—328, Manila, 1913. (137)
29. Robertson, J. A. — The Igorot of Lepanto. *PJS*, IX, D, Manila, 1914, pp. 465—529. (*S*)
30. Vanoverbergh, M. — A grammar of Lepanto Igorot as it is spoken at Bauco. *BS*, V, 6, Manila, 1917, pp. 331—425. (362)
31. Reyes, F. D. — *Review of* H. O. Beyer's 'Population of the Philippine Islands in 1916'. *PJS*, XIII, D, 1918, pp. 41—42. (301)

In addition to these works and articles there are a few remarks in certain government reports on the general character and future of the native languages, and with regard to their use in the schools, viz.:

32. Reports of Philippine Commission for 1901 and 1908. Washington, 1901, p. 539 f.; 1909, pp. 817—819. (*S*)
33. Fifteenth, Seventeenth and Eighteenth annual reports of Director of Education. Manila, 1915, pp. 68—70; 1917, p. 20; and 1918, p. 54. (*S*)
34. Report of Governor General for 1918. Washington, 1919, p. 110. (*S*)

Of these, Nos. 22, 24, 31 are reviews; Nos. 2, 3, 4 are lists of names; Nos. 1, 6, 7, 9, 11, 12, 14, 19, 20, 21, 25, 29, to which must be added Nos. 32, 33, 34, treat of languages only incidentally, their chief interest being ethnological or general; Nos. 15, 16, 23 are special treatises on linguistic points; Nos. 17, 26, 27 are word lists or dictionaries; Nos. 5, 8, 10, 13, 18, 28, 30 are grammars or grammatical sketches.

Of the reviews, Nos. 22 and 31 are brief and unimportant: No. 24 contains a long review of Seidenadel's very creditable Bontok grammar, over three pages of which are devoted to an approbation of the author's futile attempt to show that the so-called passive verbs of the Philippine languages are not to be regarded as passive, but as active, because of the perfectly familiar fact that they correspond in meaning to the active verbs of other languages.[10]

Of the lists of names the only one that has any direct bearing on languages is No. 2, which is a list of the names of the chief tribes of the Archipelago with an indication of their habitat and language. This was very useful for a time, but is now superseded for the most part by H. O. Beyer's *Population of the Philippine Islands in 1916*, published by the Philippine Education Co., Inc., Manila, 1917.

The linguistic material in the third group of titles may be described as follows. No. 1, *El Archipiélago filipino,* contains, in the discussion of the geography of the islands, a statement in the case of each island or district of the name or names of the language or languages spoken there. In addition to this there are about fifteen pages dealing with the native alphabets and general character of the Philippine languages, illustrated by a number of examples taken from the most important tongues. No. 6, Reed's *Negritos of Zambales,* contains in an appendix about four pages of comparative vocabularies of a hundred Zambal and Negrito words. Some words used by the Negritos are also discussed in the main body of the work. No. 7, Jenks's *Bontok Igorot,* contains a final chapter of twenty-two pages on language, chiefly a topically arranged vocabulary of Bontok. This chapter includes also a comparative vocabulary of about eighty English, Malay, Sulu, Benget Igorot and Bontok Igorot words. The preceding chapters serve to some extent as a commentary on the Bontok words in the vocabularies. No. 9, Saleeby's *Studies in Moro history, etc.,* contains a number of plates giving specimens of native Moro texts, together with translations of the same in the body of the work; No. 14, his *History of Sulu,* gives the translations of a number of Moro historical documents. No. 11, *The Census,* has on pp. 412, 448, 449, 461, 515, and 516, some remarks on the languages. No. 12, Worcester's *Non-Christian Tribes,* has on p. 861 f. a few remarks on dialect groups. No. 19,

---

[10] Cf. my review of this work in *American Journal of Philology,* vol. 31, 3, whole No. 123, 1910, pp. 341—344.

Christie's *Subanuns,* gives a good account of the region occupied by the Subanuns and of their subdivision into groups, and contains, moreover, about nine or ten pages of word lists and about four pages of native text and translation. Some words and phrases are also explained in the body of the work. No. 20, Barton's *Harvest-feast of the Kiangan Ifugao,* contains several pages of Ifugao texts, and explains a number of Ifugao words. No. 21, Beyer and Barton's *Ifugao burial ceremony,* gives the explanation of a number of Ifugao words and expressions as well as the text and translation (about a dozen lines) of an Ifugao song. No. 25, Miller's *Mangyans,* devotes two pages to a discussion of the native alphabet. No. 29, Robertson's *Igorot of Lepanto,* gives the meaning of a number of Igorot terms including the names of the months. The government reports, Nos. 32—34, deal briefly with the topics already mentioned above p. 152.

Of the three treatises on special grammatical points, No. 15, Scheerer's *Batan dialect,* investigates the relationship between Batan and the other Philippine languages and the Formosan dialects. It consists of four parts. First is given a lexical comparison of 113 Batan words with their semantic correspondents in 19 Philippine languages and in the chief Formosan dialects, preceded by a brief introductory description of the languages and a brief bibliographical list. Second there follows a discussion of the results of the lexical comparison, the general conclusion being that while Batan is undoubtedly a member of the Philippine group, it shows no special closer relationship with any of the other Philippine languages compared. There is also some brief comment on the Formosan dialects. The third part shows how Batan conforms to the general principles of word formation and derivation common to the Philippine languages, while part four discusses in some detail from a comparative point of view the important verbal derivatives made with the prefix *i* and with the suffixes *en* and *an.* The work has two appendices; the first giving the Apostles' Creed in Batan preceded by the English and Spanish versions, and followed by the text a second time with interlinear English translation; the second adducing evidence to show that the Ilocano (Iloko) language is practically uniform thruout the territory in which it is spoken, with only slight dialectic differences. No. 23, Scheerer's *Quinary Notation*, is an interesting treatment of the peculiar system of counting by fives instead of by tens, employed by the Ilongots of North Luzon. The article is based on an old catechism, the only Ilongot text available (*BB* 53). No. 16, Conant's *F and V*, discusses the various cases of the occurrence of these sounds, which are comparatively rare in the whole Malayan group, in the Philippine languages.

Of the three word lists, No. 26, the Mangyan list of Schneider, is very brief, containing 109 words and the chief numerals compared with their cognates in other Philippine languages. The two Bontok Igorot vocabularies of Clapp, No. 17, and Waterman, No. 27, are much more extensive. The two works are complementary in character, Clapp's containing the words arranged alphabetically without regard to root, in two parts, Igorot-English and English-Igorot; Waterman's grouping the various Bontok words under the roots from which they are derived. As is usually the case with vocabularies prepared by those who have no special scientific linguistic training, the treatment of symbolic words (i. e. such words as pronouns, prepositions, adverbs, particles, etc.) is very poor and incomplete. The treatment of the verb is also unsatisfactory, no effective attempt being made to distinguish between active and passive, tho the notes on the verbal prefixes which precede Waterman's vocabulary partly compensate for this defect. On the whole the two vocabularies are little more than word lists with English translation, but in conjunction with Seidenadel's Bontok grammar, English-Bontok vocabulary, and Bontok texts (*BB* 345), they furnish good material for the study of Bontok Igorot.

Of the seven grammars, only three can properly be called by that name, viz., No. 30, the Lepanto Igorot grammar of Vanoverbergh, No. 13, the Magindanao grammar of Smith, and No. 18, the Iloko grammar of Swift, and of these the last two are respectively a word for word translation, and an adaptation, of previous Spanish works. The other four works are only imperfect grammatical sketches, consisting very largely of lists of words and phrases, but with some meager grammatical comment interspersed.

Vanoverbergh's grammar of Lepanto Igorot is a fairly good sketch of the dialect spoken at Bauco, tho it is admittedly very incomplete, and intended by the author to form a groundwork for further study of the dialect. It is divided into eleven chapters treating respectively of phonology, articles, nouns, adjectives, pronouns, numerals, verbs, adverbs, prepositions, conjunctions, and interjections. The work suffers from a lack of examples, particularly of examples in complete sentences, but furnishes a welcome addition to the material available for the study of Igorot dialects.[11]

Smith's translation of Juanmarti's Magindanao grammar (*BB* 194) is a great improvement in type and in page arrangement over the older Spanish work, but it contains nothing original except one page (8), which purports to give the pronunciation of the letters, but in reality gives for the most part only the Spanish names for the letters, and the pronunciation of the vowels in those names, e. g., **G — He** (e as in *end*), **J — Hota** (o as in *note*, and a as in *arm*).

Swift's Iloko grammar, which is based on the *Gramática hispano—ilocana* of Naves (*BB* 259), is an excellent little work, consisting of a convenient rearrangement of the grammatical material contained in Naves, without the Iloko exercises. While, as the author states, there is nothing original in the material, he has produced as the result of his efforts what is practically a new grammar, and what is moreover the best hand-book treating any of the languages that has been issued by the government. About half the grammar is devoted to the treatment of the verb, pp. 57—112, but the author does not succeed in making entirely clear the difficult question of the verbals (or formulas as he calls them). The grammar is followed by a vocabulary, pp. 115—161, of words and roots occurring in the work. This is more than a mere word list, as it contains many examples and explanations. An index, pp. 163—172, completes the work.

MacKinlay's Tagalog Handbook, No. 10, is perhaps the most pretentious work issued by the government. Its author is a man of evident scholarly attainments who has spent considerable time in the islands, and who, besides having a conversational command of Tagalog, is familiar with several other Philippine languages, e. g., Iloko and Bikol. The book

---

11 Cf. my extended review of this work in the *American Journal of Philology*, vol. 39, 4, whole No. 156, 1918, pp. 418—420.

is divided into eight sections, treating respectively the articles; pronouns; nouns; adjectives; numerals; adverbs, prepositions, and conjunctions; verbs; and contracted verbal forms. The seventh section, verbs, pp. 105—247, occupies more than half the work; section eight is simply a table covering about two pages. These eight sections are preceded by an introduction giving a fairly complete bibliography of grammatical and lexicographical works on Tagalog, some discussion of the general features of the language, some remarks on pronunciation, and a number of the most common and indispensable conversational phrases. The last section is followed by a series of folders designed to give, by a peculiar type scheme, a clear and comprehensive idea of the Tagalog verb, and a number of indexes complete the work. In spite of the erudition of the author and of the special advantages which he has enjoyed, the work is distinctly disappointing. The grammatical remarks are very meager and unsatisfactory, and refer for the most part to morphology, little attention being paid to syntax. The book adds practically nothing to the grammatical knowledge which was already available in the various Spanish grammars, and is indeed inferior to many of them in this respect. It is really little more than a collection of words, phrases, and sentences, arranged with some appearance of order under various grammatical categories or topics. Its chief value lies in the lists of the different classes of words, which are in many cases excellent, and in the material it furnishes for the study of Tagalog idioms.

Porter's Magindanao primer, No. 5, consists chiefly of an English-Moro vocabulary, pp. 19—71, to which is prefixed about eight and a half pages of grammatical remarks and paradigms, and four and a half pages of conversational phrases. At the end of the book are about four and a half pages dealing with the writing of the language. The work is crude and unscientific, but contains a considerable amount of useful material for the study of Magindanao in the conversation and in the numerous examples of phrases and complete sentences which are given in the vocabulary.

Scheerer's Nabaloi dialect, No. 8, is a grammatical sketch devoted mainly to an exposition of the elementary grammatical facts of the language, arranged under the heads of the various parts of speech. This is followed by about two pages of conversational phrases, some account of the popular songs of the Nabaloi, a topically arranged vocabulary, pp. 157—171, and an appendix giving a translation of an account of a Spanish expedition into the Nabaloi country in 1829. The work is weak in the discussion of the verbal forms. Aside from the recording of the elementary facts of the language, and the registering of some of its most common words, the chief importance of the work lies here again in the considerable number of examples of the use of words, particularly of verbs, which it contains.

Elliott's Lanao Moro vocabulary, No. 28, contains a brief statement of some of the grammatical features of the dialect. After an introduction of about a page and some treatment of the spelling, pronunciation, and parts of speech (about 8 pp.), there follow about seven pages of word lists topically arranged, and three pages of idioms and sentences. The grammatical part of the work is entirely unsatisfactory, the most important part of speech, the verb, being given up by the author in despair. His lists of words and sentences, however, have their value.

The Government in its policy towards the native tongues has apparently centered its attention chiefly on three groups of languages, viz., 1) Tagalog, the language of Manila, and the most important language of the archipelago, and Iloko, the most important language of the civilized Filipinos in Northern Luzon; 2) the languages of the Moros or Mohammedan tribes of Mindanao and the Sulu Islands; and 3) the languages of the Igorots of Northern Luzon. As a beginning, such a policy is excellent, but unfortunately it gives no promise of advancing beyond this initial stage. The treatment of the languages in question has been very superficial, and other languages that have just as good a claim to consideration, e. g., Bisaya, have so far been entirely ignored.

On the whole the work done under government auspices has added comparatively little to our knowledge of the languages of the Philippine Islands. The government has produced a few incomplete grammatical sketches and vocabularies, some lists of geographical and botanical terms, and has given some brief treatment of the general features of the languages, and a considerable amount of linguistic information in publications devoted primarily to ethnology, but in the aggregate this does not amount to a great deal. Little has been done besides furnish a rather small body of linguistic raw material, which can be utilized by later workers in the Philippine field. The most important works on Philippine languages published since 1898 have been printed without government assistance.

The chief of these works published independently of the government, grouped under the five heads enumerated above (p. 150), are the following.

Of works which add to our knowledge of languages already well known, the most important are those which deal with Tagalog. Here may be mentioned a number of new dictionaries, Neilson, English-Tagalog and Tagalog-English (*BB* 260[a], 260[b]); Nigg, Tagalog-English and English-Tagalog (*BB* 262); Serrano Laktaw, Tagalog-Spanish (*BB* 352): several new grammars, e. g., Lendoyro's (*BB* 206), L. Bloomfield's (*BB* 47): and some conversation and phrase books (*BB* 124, 136, 203).[12] In the other languages the most important works are as follows, viz.:

Batan — The Spanish-Batan dictionary prepared by various Dominicans, assisted by O. Scheerer (*BB* 131).

Bikol — Vera — Gramatica hispano-bikol (*BB* 363).

Bisaya — 1) Guillén's Cebuan grammar, published 1898 (*BB* 170).
2) Romualdez' Samaro-Leytean grammar (*BB* 306).
3) P. de la Rosa's manual of Spanish in the dialect of Masbate and Ticao (*BB* 308).

Caroline Is. — Fritz's grammar of the language of the Central Carolines (*BB* 153[b]).

Chamorro — 1) Fritz's Chamorro grammar and dictionary (German-Chamorro and Chamorro-German) (*BB* 152, 153[a]).
2) Safford's Chamorro grammar (*BB* 311).

---

[12] The following are the chief titles after 1898 dealing with Tagalog that are given by Scheerer in *S*, viz.:

1. Calderon, S. G.—Munting diccionario na Inglés-tagalog. Manila, 1916, pp. 279, 16×11.5 cm.
2. — Diccionario inglés-español-tagalog (con partes de la oracion y pronunciacion figurada). Manila, 1915, pp. 654, 23.5×17 cm.
3. Daluz Torres, E.—Manga unang hakbang sa ikadudunong (a Tagalog primer). Manila, 1905, pp. 95, 17.5×12.5 cm.

Iloko — 1) Floresca's English-Iloko vocabulary (*BB* 150).
2) Williams' grammatical sketch of the language (*BB* 375).
Pampanga — 1) Parker's English-Spanish-Pampanga dictionary (*BB* 280).
2) G. Magat—Gramatica qng sabing castila, t capampangan. Manila, 1915, pp. 281, 18.5×13 cm (*S*).

There are also some new editions of works published prior to 1898, which in some cases at least are probably only reprints of former editions, e. g., Campomanes' Tagalog grammar (*BB* 81), Pellicer's Pangasinan grammar (*BB* 282), Sanchez de la Rosa's Samaro-Leytean dictionary (*BB* 321, 322), R. Serrano's dictionary of terms common to Spanish and Tagalog (*BB* 349; *S*.)

Under the head of new texts are especially to be mentioned L. Bloomfield's Tagalog texts with accompanying English translation on the opposite page (*BB* 47) and Seidenadel's Bontok texts with interlinear translation (*BB* 345). Other texts are translations of the Gospels in Tagalog, Iloko, Bikol, Pangasinan, Bontok, Ifugao and probably other languages; a number of Batan texts (*BB* 264, 366); and Buffum and Lynch's Sulu primer (*BB* 75).[13]

Of languages which were unknown or practically unknown in 1898, only two, Bontok and Palau, have received any attention from persons not connected with the government. Bontok is treated in Seidenadel's grammar of Bontok (*BB* 345), which, in spite of some defects, is the best grammar of a Philippine language yet published;[14] Palau or the language of the Pelew

---

4. Fernandez, E. and Calderon, S. G.—Vocabulario tagalog-castellano-inglés con partes de gramatica y frases usuales. 2ª ed., Manila, 1917, pp. 269, 13×19 cm.
5. Ignacio, R.—Vocabulario bilingue español-tagalo-tagalo-español. Manila, 1917, pp. 212+3, 18.5×13 cm.
6. Oelpz (= Lopez), M. H.—Dictionary—pahulugan (Diccionario) English-Tagalog. Manila, 1909, pp. 136, 18.5×13.5 cm.
7. Paglinawan, M.—Gramaticang kastila-tagalog. Manila, 1914: 1er tomo, pp. 301; 2o tomo, pp. 275: 18.5×13.5 cm.
8. — Bagong bokabulario at aklat ng mga salitaan, sa kastila at tagalog ó Nuevo vocabulario y manual de conversacion en español y tagalog. Maynila, 1915, pp. 236.

[13] Additional texts are mentioned by Scheerer in *S*.

[14] Cf. my review of this work already mentioned above, n. 10; also the various other reviews cited in *BB* 110, 202, 290, 341. Scheerer in *S* cites

Islands is set forth in the grammar and dictionary of Walleser (*BB* 372, 373).

Of bibliographical works dealing specifically with Philippine languages the only one of any extent since 1898 is *BB*; for general Philippine bibliographies dealing with the languages only as one of many topics, and some brief lists of linguistic titles, subsequent to 1898, cf. *BB*, pp. 27, 28.

In comparative grammar the chief work has been done by Scheerer, Conant, and myself. Scheerer's *Particles of relation in Isinay,* Conant's treatment of the Pepet vowel and of the RGH and RLD consonants, and my own articles on Philippine pronouns and numerals, and on various points of Philippine syntax are especially important. Brandstetter's monographs on general Indonesian (Malayo-Polynesian) grammar may be added here as they usually treat to some extent the languages of the Philippines. Two articles by former students of mine are also worthy of mention, W. G. Seiple's *Polysyllabic roots with initial* P *in Tagalog,* and L. B. Wolfenson's *The infixes la, li, lo in Tagalog* (*BB* 347ᵇ, 376).[15]

Of works of a miscellaneous or general character not falling under any of the five heads just enumerated, may be mentioned

---

an additional one by Adriani in *Tijdschrift van het Bataviaasch Genootschap van Kunsten en Wetenschappen,* Deel LV, afl. 4, 5 en 6, Batavia, 1913, pp. 601–617.

[15] For a practically complete list of articles by these six authors cf. *BB* under their names. Scheerer's supplement furnishes the following additional titles, viz.,

1. Brandstetter, R.—Die Lauterscheinungen in den indonesischen Sprachen. Luzern, 1915, pp. 99, 8º.
2. — Die Reduplikation in den indianischen, indonesischen und indogermanischen Sprachen. Luzern, 1917, pp. 33, 8º.
3. Conant, C. E.—Indonesian *l* in Philippine languages, *JAOS*, vol. 36, 1916, pp. 181—196.
4. Scheerer, O.—The languages of the Philippines. *Cablenews-American Yearly Review Number*, Manila, 1911, pp. 98–99.
5. — Outlines of the history of exploration of the Philippine languages and their relatives in East and West. *The Philippine Review*, vol. 3, No. 1—2 (Jan.—Feb., 1918), pp. 59—67.

Several other works which treat Philippine languages from a comparative point of view are given by *S,* the most important being Brandes, J.—Het infix I N... *Album Kern*, Leiden, 1903, pp. 199–204.

two treatises on Sulu and Tagbanua writing (*BB* 79, 307); my own brief sketches of Philippine Literature (*BB* 40), and of the Sanskrit element in Tagalog (*BB* 28); and a number of reviews (cf. Reviews in *BB*).

What numerical relation the works resulting from government activities bear to the whole body of works published both before and after 1898 will appear from the following table. This contains a complete list of the numbers of all works given in *BB*[16] which were published in 1898 or after, (MSS, of course, are not included), arranged in the order of the topics of the general index in *BB*; the numbers referring to government publications are starred; the total number of printed titles (both before and after 1898) in *BB* is indicated by a small subscript number following the name of the topic; (l. e.) = later edition of work first published before 1898, (r) = review, (?) = date of publication uncertain; works published in 1898 are followed by ('98).

Alphabets$_{23}$—79, 307.[17]
Batan$_{6}$—131, 264, 336, *337, 366.
Bikol$_{12}$—363.
Bisaya
  in general$_{5}$—30, 31, 107.
  dialect not stated$_{15}$—100, *213 (r).
  Cebuan$_{13}$—170 ('98).
  Masbate and Ticao$_{1}$—308.
  Samaro-Leytean$_{8}$—306, 321 (l. e.), 322 (l. e.).
Caroline Is.$_{7}$—153^{b}.
Chamorro$_{8}$—109, 152, 153^{a}, 311.

---

[16] The additional titles given in *S* fall under the following heads, viz., Batan, Bikol, Bontok, Caroline Is., Comparative Grammar and Vocabulary, General Linguistics, Ifugao, Iloko, Kuyo, Literature, Negrito, Pampanga, Poetry, Reviews, Spanish grammars in native dialects, Spelling, Sulu, Tagalog, Tingyan. The effect of adding these to the list would simply be to increase the disparity between the numbers of governmental and non-governmental publications, as very few of these are due to government activity. For those which are, cf. the list of government publications above, p. 150 ff., Nos. 20, 21, 29, 32—34.

[17] *248, not listed under this head in *BB*, should be added here, as the two page account of Mangyan is almost exclusively occupied with the Mangyan alphabet.

Comparative Grammar and Vocabulary $_{61}$ — 29, 30, 31, 33, 34, 35, 36, 41 (r) 42, 64, 65, 66, 67, 68, 69, 70, 71, 72, 73, 74, *105, 108, 109, 111, 112, 113, 114, 115, 145 (l. e.), *189, 227, *337, 340, 347[b], 376, 378 (r), 379 (r) [37 titles].
English Grammar in Tagalog $_{1}$ — 159.
General Philippine Linguistics $_{50}$ — *8, 16, 26, 27, 38, 40, 60, 91, 93, 106, 135, *164, 207(?), 215, 216, *236, *240, 268(?), 279, 299, *301 (r), 303, 339, 377, 380 [25 titles].
Ifugao $_{1}$ — 222[b].
Igorot
  in general $_{4}$ — 98.
  Benget $_{2}$ — *189.
  Bontok $_{10}$ — 37 (r), *99, 110 (r), *189, 202 (r), 290 (r), *341 (r), 345, *374 [9 titles].
  Inibaloi $_{1}$ — *335.
  Kankanai $_{1}$ — *337.
  Lepanto $_{3}$ — 45 (r), *362.
Iloko $_{16}$ — 150, *354, 375.
Ilongot $_{4}$ — *338.
Isinay $_{5}$ — 115, 340.
Lanao $_{1}$ — *137.
Literature $_{5}$ — 40, 228.
Madagascan $_{2}$ — 64, 227.
Magindanao $_{11}$ — *289, *312, *353.
Malay $_{11}$ — *313.
Mangyan $_{4}$ — *248, *343.
Names (Personal, Race, Place) $_{13}$ — 92, 93, 95, 106, *164, *236, 268(?), 279 [8 titles].
Names (Plant) $_{2}$ — *240.
Names (Utensils, Animals) $_{1}$ — 60.
Negrito $_{10}$ — 92, *293.
Numerals $_{6}$ — 34, *338, 347[a].
Pampanga $_{13}$ — 111, 280.
Pangasinan $_{4}$ — 282 (l. e.).
Pelew Is. (Palau) $_{6}$ — 114, 372, 373.
Poetry $_{4}$ — 346.
Reviews $_{13}$ — 37, 41, 45, 46, 110, 202, *213, 290, *301, *341, 378, 379, 380 [13 titles].
Sanskrit $_{6}$ — 28.
Semitic $_{1}$ — 29.

Spanish grammars in native dialects $_{15}$—*none.*[18]
Spelling$_{3}$—268(?).
Subanun$_{2}$—*97, 149.
Sulu$_{10}$—75, 79, *189, *312, *313.
Tagalog$_{95}$—28, 29, 30, 32, 35, 39, 43, 44, 46 (r), 47, 64, 78, 81 (l. e.), 94, 95, 124, 134, 136, 145 (l. e.), 159, 203, 206, *217, 227, 228, 229, 260^{a}, 260^{b}, 262, 272, 346, 347^{a}, 347^{b}, 352, 376 [35 titles].
Tagbanua$_{4}$—307.
Tiruray$_{11}$—113.

In the case of those works which are most important for the study of the chief Philippine languages, the table on pp. 166 f. shows what proportional relation works issued under the auspices of the government bear to those published thru other means. The table gives in compact form the character of the material available for the study of Philippine languages; the name of the author or the first important word of the title when the author is unknown is given in every column but the last (text), with a reference to *BB*; the existence of more or less text for the language in question is indicated by ×; ⊙ in a column indicates that no works of this kind exist for the language; † after a name indicates brief lists or notes only; MS works are indicated by brackets; *S* = Scheerer's supplement; Phil. = a Philippine language. The European language employed in these works is Spanish unless otherwise indicated, in which case **e** = English, **g** = German, **d** = Dutch, **f** = French. Works prepared under government auspices are starred; those published during or after 1898 are in italics: a work first published before 1898, but having one or more later editions after 1898, has the reference number alone in italics. References to texts are given in all instances where there are less than three; also in some other cases.

Of the following languages not given in the adjoining table only brief word lists or brief specimens of text have been published, viz., Atás, Bilaan, Ginaan, Igorot, (Abra, Banawe,

---

[18] None of those listed under this topic in *BB*, are later than 1898; Nos. 193, published 1887, and 308, published 1905, apparently belong here. Scheerer in *S* also lists some published after 1898, viz., in Tagalog by Paglinawan (cf. n. 15, No. 7), in Pampanga by Magat (cf. p. 160, under Pampanga).

Benget, Kankanai[19]), Mangyan, Manobo, Samal, Subanun, Tagakaolo, Tingyan (cf. *BB*, index). Of these the Benget list in Jenks's Bontok Igorot (189), the Mangyan material in Miller (248) and Schneider (343), and the Subanun material in Christie (97), are the result of government activity.

A number of additional languages are treated in unpublished MSS. For Iruli, Igolot (doubtless Igorot, but what dialect is uncertain), Iraya (=Egongot?), Itawi, Ituy (?), Yogad, cf. *BB* 407, 414, 431, 433, 468. Scheerer in *S* mentions the following manuscripts as being in his possession, viz., lists of Mamanua (2 pp.) and Itbayat; a phrase book of Bontok and Kalingga; and a collection of popular stories, etc. in the following dialects, viz., Aklanón, Apayao, Inibaloi, Inivatan (=Batan), Isinay, Itneg (=Tingyan), Itbayat, Ifuntok (=Bontok), Kalingga (partly in press), Katawan (=Kankanáe), Mangyan, Pangasinan, Sambalé, Tagalog.

The printed works listed in the foregoing table are in many cases very good, and it is possible with their assistance to acquire a considerable knowledge of many of the languages, but in the case of no language is it possible to get answers to all the problems which naturally arise in the study of any form of speech, and there is no case in which the arrangement of the material in the various grammars could not be greatly improved. The dictionaries, moreover, are in most cases little more than extensive word-lists, and the material in the phrase books is usually very meager. Briefly stated there is no language in the list, the material for whose study does not stand in great need both of improvement and completion.

On the whole we may say there has been comparatively little progress in the development of our knowledge of Philippine languages in the period of more than two decades since 1898. But this is perhaps not surprising, considering the lack of interest on the part of the government, and taking into consideration the fact that the three chief workers in this country and the Philippines can devote only a limited portion of their time to these subjects, one of them being a teacher of German,

---

[19] A brief MS list of 50 words also exists, cf. *BB* 416, and Scheerer has collected some texts (cf. next paragraph).

Language	*Dictionary Phil.-European*	*Dictionary European-Phil.*	*Grammar*	*Grammar of European Lang. in Phil.*	*Phrase-book*	*Text*
Agta	○	○	Kern, **d** (61)†	○	○	○
Bagobo	Gisbert (167)	Gisbert (168)	Gisbert (167)†	○	○	○
Batan	[Creville]-*S*	*Diccionário* (*131*) [Paula and Castaño] (444)	Retana (298, 87)† **Scheerer* **e** (*337*)† [Creville and Tamayo]-*S*	[Barsana]-*S*	[Scheerer] **e**?-*S*	×
Bikol	Lisboa (208)	Perfecto (285)	San Augustin-Crespo (120)	Herrejón (173) Perfecto (286)	Gayacao (162) Perfecto (284)	×
Bisaya Ceb.	Encarnación (138)	Encarnación (138)	Gonzalez (169) Zueco (381) *Guillén* (*170*)	Abecedario (1)	Zueco (381)	×
Hil.	Méntrida (239) [Santarén] (457)	Martín (231)	Méntrida (238)	○	Gayacao (161)	×
S.-L.	Sanchez d.l. Rosa (*322*)	Sanchez d.l. Rosa (*321*)	Esguerra (141) Figueroa (148) *Romualdez*, **e** (*306*)	Sanchez d. l. Rosa (323, 324)	○	×
Har.	Méntrida (239)	Martín (231)	Méntrida (238)†	○	○	× (329)
Boh.	○	○	Esguerra (141)† Zueco (381)†	○	○	○
Min.	○	○	Zueco (381)†	○	○	× (133, 360)
Masbate and Ticao	○	○	○	*P. d. l. Rosa* (*308*)	○	○
Carolines	○	Ariñez (9)	Valencia (361) *Fritz*, **g** (*153*[b]) Ariñez (9)†	○	○	× (10, 291)
Chamorro	*Fritz*, **g** (*152*)	*Fritz*, **g** (*152*) Ibánez d. Carmen (183)	*Fritz*, **g** (*153*[a]) *Safford*, **e** (*311*)	Ibánez d. Carmen (182)	○	× (181, 274)
Gaddan(g)	*Malumbres* (*222*[a]) [Bermejo] (399)	○	[Arte] (387)	○	○	× (80, 88)
Ibanag	Bugarín-Rodriguez (305) [MS] (428)	Diccionário (130) Payo (281)	Fausto d. Cuevas (126)	Nolasco d. Medio (237) Nepomuceno y Siriban (261)	Gayacao (163)	×
Ifugao	○	*Malumbres* (*222*[b])	○	○	○	×-*S*[20]
Igorot Bon.	**Clapp*, **e** (*99*) **Waterman*, **e** (*374*)	**Clapp*, **e** (*99*) *Seidenadel*, **e** (*345*)	*Seidenadel*, **e** (*345*)	○	[Scheerer] **e**-*S*	× (345)-*S*[20]

		Floresca, **e** (*150*)	**Swift*, **e** (*354*) *Williams*, **g** (*375*)			
Ilongot (Egongot)	[Scheerer] **g**-*S*	○	S.d.l. Madre d. Dios (218)? [Zarza] (470)	○	[Whitney] **e**-*S*	× (53)-*S*[20] [×] (407, 471, 472)
Isinay	○	[Scheerer] **e**-*S*	*Conant* **e**, (*115*)† *Scheerer*, **e** (*340*)†	○	Lázaro (205)	× (304) [×] (407, 408)
Kalamian	Jerónimo d. l. Virgen d. Monserrate (190)	○	○	○	○	× (103) [×] (453, 454)[21]
Kuyo	○	[MS]† (413)	○	○	○	×(11, 122, 165, 166, 177, 223)-*S*[21]
Lanao	○	○	**Elliott*, **e** (*137*)	○	**Elliot*, **e** (*137*)	○
Magindanao	Juanmarti (195)	Juanmartí (195)	Juanmarti (194)	Juanmartí (193)?	**Porter*, **e** (*289*)	× (85, 102, 312)
Negrito	[B. d. Santa Rosa] (459) [Garvan], **e** (426) Meyer, **g** (243)† Schadenberg, **g** (331)†	○	[B.d.SantaRosa] (458) Kern, **d** (200)† Meyer, **g** (242)† Meyer and Kern, **g** (244)†	○	○	[×] (460, 461)
Palau	*Walleser*, **g** (*373*)	*Walleser*, **g** (*373*)	*Walleser*, **g** (372)	○	*Walleser*, **g** (*373*)	○
Pampanga	Bergaño (24)	Bergaño (24)	Bergaño (23)	*Magat* (*S*)	Brabo (63) Fernandez (*145*)	×
Pangasinan	Cosgaya-Villanova (118)	Macaraeg (214)	Pellicer (*282*)	○	○	×
Sulu	○	Cowie, **e** (119) Haynes, **e** (171)	Cowie, **e** (119)	○	*Buffum*, **e** (*75*) Cowie, **e** (119)	× (312)-*S*[20]
Tagalog	Noceda (263) *Nigg*, **e** (*262*) *Neilson*, **e** (*260*[b]) *Serrano Laktaw* (*352*)	Noceda (263) *Nigg*, **e** (*262*) *Neilson*, **e** (*260*[a]) Serrano Laktaw (351)	Totanes (359) Minguella (249) Campomanes (*81*) *Lendoyro*, **e** (*206*) **MacKinlay*, **e** (*217*) *Bloomfield*, **e** (*47*)	Apacible (7) Minguella (250) Pinpin (288) *Garcia and Herrera*, **e** (*159*)	Abella (2) *Cue-Malay* (*124*) *Duran* (*136*) Fernandez (*145*) *Kirk*, **e** (*203*)	×
Tagbanua	○	Everett, **e** (142)	Marche, **f** (224)†	○	○	× (104)
Tiruray	Bennásar (21)	Bennásar (22)	Observaciones (265)†	○	○	× (86, 89, 357)
Zambale	[Rodrigo d. San Miguel]-*S*	**Reed*, **e** (*293*)†	[Rodrigo d. San Miguel]-*S*	○	○	× (90, 128, 172)

another a teacher of Modern Languages, and a third a teacher of Semitic Languages and General History.

It is to be hoped that in future the Government will pursue a more liberal policy towards the study of Philippine languages. In the first place it is important from a scientific point of view that the languages should be registered and studied, just as is being done in the case of our Indian dialects, ere they die out before the advance of English. In the second place from a practical point of view it is essential that a thoro knowledge of the language should be possessed by those who work among the natives in order that these workers may understand the native manners and customs, and in order that communication between whites and natives may be simplified and facilitated.

The chief needs of Philippine linguistic studies may be briefly stated as follows. In the first place those who collect linguistic material among the natives, whether government employees or not, should have some measure of linguistic training. They

---

[20] The titles of native texts given in *S* which are to be added here are —

1. American Bible Society—Nan Evanhelio an inkulit hi Luke (Gospel of St. Luke in Ifugao). Manila, 1915, pp. 126, 13×9.5 cm. [For Ifugao cf. also Nos. 20, 21, p. 151.
2. British and Foreign Bible Society, London—Nan Evanhelio isnan apotaku ya enigtwentaku Jesu Kristo ai naikolit ken Santo ai Marko (Gospel of St. Mark in Bontok-Igorot). Kobe, 1912, pp. 41. 18.5×12 cm.
3. Moss, C. R. and Kroeber, A. L.—Nabaloi (Inibaloi) Songs. *University of California Publications in American Archaeology and Ethnology*, Vol. 15, No. 2, Berkeley, 1919, pp. 187—206.
4. The Sulu News (Ing Kabaytabayta an sug): a monthly newspaper in English and Sulu. Zamboanga, Mindanao, P. I.
5. A MS Egongot (Ilongot) catechism of 51 pp. 8° in possession of O. Scheerer.

[21] All Kalamian and Kuyo texts in *BB* are here cited on account of the ambiguity associated with these names (cf. nn. 6 and 7): *S* gives also the following—

1. Catecismo cuyono. Adalan sa mga cristianos nga insulat sa cuyonon ig sa isarang P. Agustino Recoleto. 2ª ed., Manila, 1904, pp. 72, 14×10.5 cm.
2. (Catecismo cuyono) Parangadien sa mga Cuyonong cristianos nga sinulat sa Padre Exprovincial Fr. Pedro Gibert. Manila, 1907, pp. 32, 12×8.5 cm.

should possess at least an elementary knowledge of the science of Phonetics, and a good working knowledge of general grammatical principles, so that they can know what to look for or ask for in their search for linguistic material.[22]

Secondly, good manuscript works already prepared should be published as soon as possible. Here are especially to be mentioned, e. g., Garvan's work on Negrito (*BB* 426); the Batan and Zambal Grammars, and the word lists, native texts, etc. in the possession of Scheerer (cf. table on p. 166 f., and works mentioned on pp. 165, 168); Conant's Bisaya dictionary (*BB* 412); and others (cf. *BB* 383—473).

Thirdly, numerous texts, especially folk stories and poems, should be collected, particularly in the less known tongues.

Fourthly, really first class grammars and dictionaries of the most important languages of the islands should be prepared, in addition to the imperfect grammars already in existence. At the very least this should be done for Tagalog, Bisaya, Iloko, Magindanao, and Sulu.[23]

---

[22] Where the workers in the field have not these qualifications, it is possible, at least to some extent, to supply this lack by issuing a series of instructions to them covering the matters they are investigating. At the suggestion of one of my Philippine correspondents, Mr. Luther Parker of Laoang, Ilocos Norte, I have recently sent out about a hundred mimeographed circulars of instruction dealing with the construction of coordinated ideas in Philippine languages, for distribution and use in the Islands, and I have already collected in this way much valuable material. It is interesting to note that Dr. Frank Sanders, Chairman of our Committee on Enlargement of Membership, has independently conceived the notion of applying this principle of instructing workers in the Oriental field on a far more extensive scale, and is at present at work on plans for translating his ideas into action.

[23] I have prepared a Tagalog grammar which is intended to furnish a complete account of the linguistic phenomena of the language, and also to serve as a model of arrangement for other Philippine grammars. This grammar has received the endorsement of some of the foremost Malayo-Polynesian scholars in Holland (Profs. Junker and Juynboll of Leyden), and will soon be published as the first of a special series of Oriental Publications by the American Oriental Society. I have also prepared preliminary grammatical sketches for the other languages here mentioned, but much work remains to be done before any other complete grammar will be ready for publication. Conant would probably be prepared to write a Cebuan grammar.

Fifthly, briefer grammatical studies and vocabularies of as many as possible of the other languages should be prepared, based on existing grammars, vocabularies, and texts, where these exist, and supplemented in every case by intercourse with intelligent natives, especially those who understand English.[24]

Sixthly, a complete bibliography of all works written in any Philippine dialect should be published.[25]

Finally, a comparative grammar should be prepared giving a complete account of all the linguistic phenomena of a dozen or more of the principal languages from both a scientific and a practical point of view, and registering the special peculiarities of all the other dialects about which anything is known.[26]

---

[24] I have made preliminary studies of a number of the languages in this group, viz., Pampanga, Pangasinan, Ibanag, Bikol, Chamorro, etc. Scheerer would probably be prepared to write grammars of Batan, Inibaloi, (= Nabaloi), Isinay, and possibly of other languages.

[25] *BB* contains a list of the most important works dealing with Philippine languages, including all texts in any except the seven principal dialects. This will be supplemented shortly by a number of additional titles furnished by Scheerer (cf. *S*) and others in the islands. The work on the second part of my Bibliography, works in the seven principal dialects, has already reached an advanced stage of preparation.

[26] Besides the work of this character done before 1898 (cf. above p. 149), and in addition to monographs by Conant, Scheerer, myself, and others on comparative topics, I have projected a series of Contributions to Comparative Philippine Grammar which are intended to form the basis for a comparative grammar of the type just described. Two of these Contributions have already been published, viz., I. General features, phonology, and pronouns, and II. Numerals. III. Noun formation, is in an advanced stage of preparation. The other Contributions projected, on many of which a considerable amount of preliminary work has been done (cf. Blake in *BB*), are as follows, viz., IV. Verb formation, V. Particles (Adverbs, Prepositions, Conjunctions, and Interjections), VI. The Noun and its modifiers, VII. The ideas 'to be' and 'to have', VIII. Active and Passive constructions, IX. Construction of particles, X. The use of ligatures, XI. The expression of various symbolic ideas (*a.* indefinite pronominal ideas, *b.* modal auxiliary ideas), XII. Verbs derived from other parts of speech, XIII. Elements of comparative vocabulary and conversation in the chief languages.

ALOES

Wilfred H. Schoff

Philadelphia Commercial Museum

Elsewhere I have referred to the early conception of trees and plants as animate, and to the belief that divine life or protection might be transmitted and an offender purified by eating the leaves, bark, gum or wood, or by breathing the smoke of their burning.[1] Notable among products valued for purposes of purification were the lemon grass, senna, myrrh, balsam, and frankincense. The present inquiry has to do with the aloe and the several products, diverse in nature and origin, to which that name has been applied.

Frazer tells of the procedure of a British East African tribe to escape the impurity of bloodshed. For the man-slayer was everywhere considered unclean, and his impurity extended to his tribe. This uncleanness lasted for four days, during which he might not go home and must remain alone eating only specified food. At the end of the fourth day he must purify himself by taking a strong purge made from the leaves of the *segetet* tree, and by drinking goat's milk mixed with blood.[2] In another East African tribe the sorcerer expels the sin by a ceremony, of which the principal rite is an emetic, the sin being conceived in both cases as a sort of morbid substance to be expelled, confession and absolution being, as Frazer observes, a purely physical process of relieving the sufferer of a burden which sits heavy on his stomach rather than on his conscience.

So Robertson Smith remarks that redemption, substitution, purification, atoning blood, and garment of righteousness

---

[1] *JAOS* 40, Part IV, 260—270.

[2] *Taboo and the Perils of the Soul*, 175, 214.

are all terms which in some sense go back to ancient ritual. The fundamental idea of ancient sacrifice is sacramental; communion and all atoning rites are ultimately to be regarded as owing their efficacy to a communication of divine life to the worshipers.[3] In primitive ritual this conception is grasped in a purely physical and mechanical shape, as indeed in primitive life all spiritual and ethical ideas are still wrapped up in the husk of material embodiment. His conclusion was that a ritual system must always remain materialistic, even if its materialism is disguised under the cloak of mysticism. But it may be questioned whether

> Purge me with hyssop and I shall be clean,
> Wash me and I shall be whiter than snow[4]

may not still have a more direct appeal and significance than

> I have blotted out as a cloud thy transgressions,
> And as a mist thy sins.[5]

Perfumes played a similar part, a sweet savor being regarded not only as agreeable to deity, but as proceeding from the divine being animating the tree. Especially among the Semites was perfume, as Pliny remarked,[6] a very holy thing, which Herodotus[7] tells us they used in purification; and clothing worn on sacred or festal occasions was perfumed.[8] In many cases the gums or resins used as medicine would, when burned, give forth a fragrant incense; and this fact may explain the looseness in application of some of their names. Among these is the medicinal aloe, the sacredness of which as a means and sign of purification is indicated to this day by the fact that the Muhammadans regard it as a symbolic plant, and that especially in Egypt those returning from a pilgrimage to Mecca hang it over their street doors as token that they have performed the journey. Curiously the same name has been applied to an Eastern incense in high favor among the Chinese, and to another incense, perhaps not the same, used by the

---

[3] *Religion of the Semites*, 439.
[4] Ps. 51 7.
[5] Isai. 44 22.
[6] H. N. 12 54.
[7] I 198.
[8] Gen. 27 15, 27.

Parsees of India, and variously called aloe wood, *gharu* wood, eagle wood, *calambac*, and by the Chinese, 'sinking incense' (referring to its very high specific gravity), and in India *agar* or *agur*, referred to Sanskrit *a* + *guru*, not heavy—an obvious absurdity unless we allow for another strange grouping of such substances according to aroma rather than appearance, whereby aloe wood and ambergris have been sometimes associated. The subject is important, not solely to the pharmacologist, for it raises questions of early commerce as to which there has been much misunderstanding.

In the Amarna tablets Hommel[9] called attention to a substance, *aigalluhu*, strongly suggestive of the Greek *agallochon*, the name now applied to the incense aloe. In the Hebrew Scriptures are four references which have been a stumbling block to the translators. In the story of Balaam in Numbers is the line 'as *ahalim* planted of the Lord' (24 6). In Proverbs (7 17), 'I have perfumed my bed with myrrh, *ahalim* and cinnamon'. In Psalms (45 9), 'myrrh, *ahaloth* and cassia are all thy garments'. And in the Song of Songs (4 14), 'all trees of frankincense, myrrh and *ahaloth* with all the chief spices'. The last two are passages suggesting the festivals at a royal wedding, or state ritual of some sort. In most modern versions all four are translated 'aloes', and so recent a lexicographer as Loew[10] asserts as a matter beyond question that all four are aloe wood and holds that they are identical with the *almug* (I Kings 10 11-12)—an identification as to which I feel wholly skeptical. *Almug* or *algum*, while identified by some with *agaru* or *laghu*, so strongly suggests an Arabic origin that one need hardly go farther than *al-muġra-(t)*[11], a South Arabian name for myrrh or frankincense; while the analogy of the Egyptian 18th Dynasty temples, with their balustrades set about with frankincense trees brought from Punt, strongly suggests that these trees of the Ophir voyages were incense trees also—a supposition strengthened by the application of the same word to a tree of Lebanon, probably

---

[9] *Expository Times*, 9. 525. Winckler left it unexplained in his Index.

[10] *Aramäische Pflanzennamen*, 295.

[11] Bent, *Southern Arabia*, 446: cf. μοκρότου, Periplus, 10.

the cedar,[12] valued not only as a building timber, but on account of its aromatic wood used in medicine and ceremonial. For *ahalim* or *ahaloth* one's first impulse is again to inquire in South Arabia, the source of so many aromatics, where Bent reports *hal* as a word used in Socotra for perfume generally;[13] but I am rather inclined to follow the thought of Cheyne and Barton that the word *ahalim* is corrupt, and that it was originally ē(i̯)*lim*,[14] terebinth, the difference in old Hebrew script between the *h* and the *i̯* being no more than the shifting of a single stroke.[15] This is supported by the Greek text which assumes *ohalim* and renders *skēnai* 'tents', being followed by the Latin Vulgate, *tabernaculi:* that is, at a time when the Eastern sea trade was admittedly active and aloe wood might have been imported, the best scholarship knew nothing of it, and the assumption of the Indo-Chinese wood did not find its way into the versions until after the Reformation, or after the Portuguese conquests in the East.

As for the two bridal songs, in one the LXX has *staktē* which could mean any fragrant gum, and in the other *alōth* which might be the Arabic *al'ud,* i. e. any fragrant wood: but of the terebinth more anon. It may be well now to recall the nature of these diverse products.

The medicinal aloe is the product of a plant, *Aloe Perryi,* of the lily family (similar in appearance and longevity to the century plant), which grows on the chalky plateau of Socotra and in various districts of South Arabia and Somaliland. The Ptolemies planted colonies in Socotra to stimulate its cultivation. The gatherer punches a little hole in the leaf and inserts a stick, on which the juice exudes. The first product is a watery sap; the second a thicker gum; and the third after six weeks or

---

[12] 2 Chron. 2 7. Cf. Cheyne, *Expos. T.* 9 : 470—473.

[13] *Op. cit.* 448.

[14] *The Jewish Encyclopaedia, sub verbo* 'Aloe'. Hommel (*Expos. T.* 9 : 526) suggests Babylonian *uḫulu,* a vegetable substance often named along with *tabtu,* incense (later also 'salt'; and in modern times al-kali), and connects its ideogram through *ildig,* with *vildig* and *bdolaḥ,* rendered bdellium. Delitzsch (*Paradies* 104) cites *êlammâku* as one of the woods used by Sennacherib in building his palace, which Meissner classifies as cypress.

[15] But the writer of the Epistle to the Hebrews (8 2) quotes from the Septuagint version: 'the true tabernacle which the Lord pitched'.

more of bleeding, a dark hard resinous substance which is the most valuable. But this is not the most productive method of treatment. According to Bent,[16] the aloe gatherers dig a hole in the ground and line it with skin; then they pile leaves, points outward, all around until the pressure makes the juice exude. When it has dried for about six weeks it is nearly hard and is ready for the market, being shipped from time immemorial to the ports of western India, whence it is redistributed. The Socotrans call it *tayif* but the Arabs *ṣabr* or *ṣibar* which has passed into European languages: Spanish *acibar* and Portuguese *azevre*; but this word *ṣabr* the Arabs use also for myrrh, and the two products are not dissimilar, both being dark and of bitter taste. The root meaning seems to be 'to tie up', or in the second stem 'to heap up', and reminds one forcibly of that passage in the Periplus[17] describing the gathering of gums in South Arabia, in which it is said that the gum 'lies in heaps all over the country, open and unguarded, for neither openly nor by stealth can it be loaded on ship without the King's permission'. And a striking feature of the Deir-el-Bahari reliefs are these same heaps of gum which the workmen shovel into bags to be carried on board ship.[18] The association of myrrh and aloes appears in the Song of Songs,[19] which has another curious expression, 'thy lips are as lilies dropping with flowing myrrh'[20]. Both products are covered by the same trade name *ṣabr*,[21] and the aloe is the product of a lily. The same association appears in John 19 39.

The word 'aloe' seems to be derived from an Arabic root, *lawaya*, to bend or twist, and could refer to any product obtained by bending or doubling back a growing branch, or otherwise injuring it whereby an excrescence would be produced charged with accumulated and hardened sap. It could also refer to diseased growths produced by bark-splitting, insect

---

16 *Op. cit.*, 381.

17 Periplus, 32.

18 Cf. Naville's illustration in *Deir-el-Bahari*, Egypt Exploration Fund.

19 4 14.

20 5 13.

21 Cf. the *Sçobr* of Marco Polo.

stings or bacteriological action. It seems quite possible that it included the bent galls which are so characteristic of the Pistacia varieties that produce gum mastic and gum terebinth, also growths on varieties of the cedar and juniper, more specifically alluded to under the term 'thyine wood'. It is not impossible that it included the balsams. Dr. J. B. Nies (*Ur Dynasty Tablets*, 152, 169) gives a cuneiform sign *li* which he connects with *gûb*, cedar, cypress or juniper, and reads the temple name E-bil-li, as 'house of cedar fire'. He thinks that *li* and *šim* were juniper berries used as incense. I am inclined to think that resinous growths, or the resin itself, may also have been included. Dioscorides says that the resin of terebinth was exported from Arabia Petraea, and that it was produced in Judaea, Syria, Cyprus, Libya and the Cyclades.[22] An inscription of Sargon, the Assyrian, in 715 B. C., tells how he received from Egypt, Syria, Arabia, Sabaea, the seacoast and the desert, precious stones, ivory, *ušu* wood, spices of all kinds, horses and camels; and Hirth would identify this *ušu* with the *su-ho-yu* of the Chinese Annals, which he thinks was storax.[23] This storax was a concoction of numerous aromatics, having as its basis the sap of the Syrian sweet gum, as to which the Chinese recorded that it was 'not a natural product, but made by mixing and boiling the juices of various fragrant trees; the natives thus make a balsam and sell the dregs to the traders of other countries. It goes through many hands before reaching China, and when arriving there is not so very fragrant'. Subsequently a sweeter storax from the Java rose-mallow, a near cousin of the sweet gum, won a place of favor in the Chinese market, but never drove out the Arabian product, which Hirth tells us still reaches the ports of China in vessels from Bombay, transshipped from ports of the Persian Gulf or Gulf of Aden. A similar instance is the frankincense, for which a substitute is the benzoin, a corrupt form of *luban jawī*, or Sumatra incense. The 'ointment of spikenard, very precious', mentioned in the Gospels, contained

---

[22] In passing, I wish to testify to the thoroughness of Sprengel's Commentary on Dioscorides. Written a century ago, it still outranks most of its successors.

[23] *China and the Roman Orient*, 266; cf. Delitzsch, *Paradies* 285.

perhaps very little either of spikenard or the better-known lemon-grass nard, which we call citronella; and in Islamic times *nadd* meant something altogether different. The *nadd* for the special use of the caliphs was composed of ambergris, musk, aloes and camphor, and that prepared for perfuming the Ka'ba on Fridays and the sacred rock of the temple at Jerusalem was made of pure Tibetan musk and Shihr ambergris with no aloes or camphor.[24]

So most of these aromatics reached the market after dilution or adulteration. The Arab, Jaubarī, gives a recipe for making aloe wood. He directs that olive wood be steeped in the juice of grapes set on the fire and covered with rose water, into which chips of true aloe wood are placed. Then simmer and dry in the shade and, he says, you get an unmatched aloe. 'Sir John Mandeville' makes the same complaint of balm, for, says he, men sell a gum that they call turpentine instead of balm, and they put thereto a little balm to give good odor, and some put wax in oil of the wood of balm and say that it is balm, for so the Saracens counterfeit by subtilty of craft for to deceive the Christian men';[25] whereby we learn that Poe's mournful lines were literally true:

'Is there—is there balm in Gilead?—tell me—tell me, I implore!
Quoth the raven—"Nevermore".'

The Persian Empire for the first time brought the coasts of India and the Levant within the same commercial system, and the Zoroastrian ritual made of fire and incense perhaps a more general use than any previous cult. That the aromatics of Semitic lands were drawn upon is fully known, and at this time we may infer the first systematic use of aromatics from India, including the *gharu*, eagle or aloe wood, produced to some extent in India proper, but more abundantly and in higher quality in Indo-China and the Archipelago. This substance, which seems to be that described by Dioscorides under the name *agallochon*,[26] belongs to an order of which

---

[24] Cf. Nuwairī, quoting Tamīmī. Most of the Arabic citations in this paper are from Ferrand's *Textes Arabes Persans et Turks relatifs à l'Extrême Orient.* The classical references are conveniently assembled in Coedès, *Textes d'auteurs grecs et latins relatifs à l'Extrême Orient.*

[25] *Travels*, Chap. 7.

[26] *Aquilaria Agallocha*, order *Thymeliaceae.*

many varieties have sweet sap useful in perfumery, but in its natural state the fragrance is insignificant. When the tree is injured or in a diseased condition, its sap collects in dark, hardened masses in the trunk and branches, the resin being somewhat similar in appearance to that of the Socotran aloe, but of much finer fragrance and of very high specific gravity. Medicinally it is useful, not as a purge, but as a febrifuge. To gather the resin, whole trees may be cut down without obtaining anything, while others will be found full of resin pockets, of which no outward sign exists. The tree is cut down and allowed to decay for a few months in the tropical jungle, when little but the heavy resin remains; or to hasten the operation the branches or the trunk itself may be cut into smaller sections and piled together in a pit. Edrīsī says that the roots are dug, then the top taken off and the hard wood scraped until frayed, and then again scraped with glass and put in bags of coarse cloth. Yāḳūt says that the aloe must be hard and heavy: if the cuttings do not sink in the water it is not choice wood. If they sink, it is pure aloe wood—there is none better. The Chinese Chau Ju-Kua calls it *ch'ön hsiang*, 'sinking incense' and observes that the hard wood and joints which are hard and black and sink in water are so called, while those which float on the surface are of less value and are called 'chicken bone perfume'.[27] Marco Polo tells of its use by conjurers in Cambodia. If a man falls sick conjurers dance until one falls in a trance and says what harm the sick man has done to some other spirit. Then the friends bring the things specified for sacrifice and the conjurers come and take flesh broth and drink and aloes wood and a great number of lights and go about scattering the broth and the meat and drink, and when all that the spirit has commanded has been done according to ceremony, then it shall be announced that the man is pardoned and is speedily cured and presently the sick man gets sound and well'.[28]

As to the use of these resins in purification, Plutarch says

---

[27] Hirth, *Chau Ju-Kua,* 204—208.

[28] II. 50. The Cordier-Yule edition has a useful analysis of Marco's classification of the aloe.

that it was 'not considered fitting to worship with sickly bodies or souls'. As an incense to purify the air at dawn they burned resin, and at noon myrrh because its hot nature succesfully dissolved and dissipated the turbid element in the air drawn up from the ground by the force of the sun. These impurities were better driven away if woods of a dry nature were burned, such as cypress, juniper and pine. Aristotle asserts that the sweet-smelling exhalation of perfumes conduces no less to health than enjoyment, and if amongst the Egyptians they call myrrh 'bal' and this word signifies 'sweeping out of impurities', the name furnishes some evidence for Plutarch's explanation of the reason for which it is used.[29]

With the development of philosophic thought, especially after the Persian Empire, ideas regarding the uses of incense would seem to have been modified to make it applicable more especially to the spiritual side of the personality. Plutarch, for example, says of the Egyptian *kyphi* that it 'fans up the fire of the spirit connate with the body;' and Philoponus: 'as this gross body is cleansed with water, so is that spiritual body by purifications of vapors, for it is nourished with certain vapors and cleansed with others'.[30]

This aloe wood, calambac, sinking incense, or honey incense has been in very general use from India eastward. That it was ever anything but a rare exotic in Semitic or Mediterranean countries may be doubted, and that it was ever included in the Hebrew Scriptures among familiar native trees is, as Barton remarks, 'more than doubtful'. It was clearly known at about the Christian era, for the Book of Enoch, where the eastern journeys of Enoch are described, mentions a valley having fragrant trees such as the mastic, and east of them other valleys of fragrant cinnamon, still further eastward valleys of nectar and galbanum, and beyond these 'a mountain to the east of the ends of the earth whereon were aloe trees; and all the trees were full of *stacte*, being like almond trees, and when one burned it, it smelled sweeter than any fragrant odor'.[31]

---

29 De Is. et Osir. 80. 2.

30 In Aristotelis de Anima, 19. 24; cf. Mead, *The Subtle Body*, 67—68.

31 I Enoch 28—31.

But classical writers are notably silent concerning aloe wood. For generation after generation in speaking of the wealth of the East they mention the silk of the Seres, the laurel and sometimes the pepper of India, and the spices of Arabia; but a rather thorough search discloses nothing further about aloe until Cosmas Indicopleustes, the Greek monk of the 6th century, who remarks in his *Christian Topography*[32] that Ceylon received from Tzinista—a combination of Burma and Yün-nan—silk, aloe, cloves and sandalwood.

At this point we may let the Arab writers take up the tale. Ya'ḳūbī, writing in the 9th century, distinguishes between the aloe of Kakula or Khmer and that of Champa, also an aloe of Kita', the best Chinese variety. He refers to another variety, *kašur*, as soft and ashen gray, which we may suspect to have been ambergris. The fifth voyage of Sindbad mentions the Isle of Khmer as producing the *Ṣanfi* or Champa aloe. Ibn Khordadhbeh, in the 9th century, refers to the Kingdom of Jāwaga (Sumatra) as producing aloes and the information is confirmed by Abū Zaid in the 10th century. The Island of Kalah, he says, which belongs to the King of Jāwaga, is the 'center of the commerce of aloes, camphor, sandalwood, ivory, tin, ebony, brazil wood, spices of all kinds, and other things too numerous to mention.' The Digest of Marvels, dating about 1000, gives similar information and extends the aloe trade to the rather fabulous country of Wak, which may have embraced the eastern islands from Japan to the Philippines. Edrīsī mentions several places in the Indo-Chinese peninsula as producing aloe. Yāḳūt, at the end of the 12th century, gives the curious piece of misinformation already referred to, in connection with Kūlam in South India, which he mentions as a center in trade of aloe, camphor, resins and barks. Aloe, he says, 'is brought northward by the sea. It is not drawn, yet it arrives at the shore. The aloe of Khmer begins to dry in its native land and continues to dry at sea. The king levies one-tenth of the aloe upon those who gather it at the beach'. This can hardly be other than floating ambergris (the product of disease or indigestion in whales), but there is

---

[32] XI. 337.

no similarity in the two products, and no connection except that they were ingredients in the strong perfumes favored by the Muhammadans. This confusion of ambergris with aloe can certainly not have been due to appearance. As already stated, ambergris and musk, aloe and camphor, were all ingredients in the *nadd* of the caliphs that no longer contained nard. The confusion may have been due to that cause, or to a plain misreading of the Arabic, for *ṣbr*, aloes or myrrh, and *'nbr*, ambergris, are written so nearly alike that it might take a careful reader to distinguish between them.

Yāḳūt quotes a verse of an Arabian poet, Abū'l-'Abbas aṣ-Ṣufri; 'It exhales a perfume as penetrating as musk rolled in the fingers, or as Kalahi aloe'. Ibn al-Baiṭār, writing in the 13th century, quotes the earlier description of Dioscorides and Galen referring to aloe as an incense, a perfume for the person or clothing, and in medicine as a remedy against fever and congestion. Avicenna enumerates several varieties, the best sorts being those which sink in water, and refers to the custom of burying the wood until it decays and nothing but the resin is left. Ibn Sa'id, also of the 13th century, refers to the aloe of Jāwa, black, heavy and sinking in water as if it were a stone. Waṣṣāf, at the end of the 13th century, waxes poetic about the Island of Mūl Ṣawa, one of the conquests of Kublai Khan: 'The creative power of the Almighty', says he, 'has embalmed this place and its neighborhood in the perfume of the aloe and the clove. The very parroquets cry out in Arabic, "I am a garden, the glory and joy whereof are the envy of Paradise. For jealousy of my wealth the shores of Oman shed tears like pearls. The aloe of Khmer burns in my censers like wood on the fire."'

Abu'l-Fidā tells of the mountains of Kamrun, a barrier between India and China, where aloes grow. Ibn Baṭūṭā, in the 14th century, tells of the gathering of the aloe in Indo-China and notes that in Muhammadan countries the trees are considered private property, but there they are wild and common. He made a visit to the king of Jāwa and was present at the wedding of the king's son, being dismissed thereafter with gifts of aloe, camphor, cloves and sandalwood. Ibn Iyas, in the 16th century, tells of the city of Kabul as exporting grapes, coconuts, aloe of delicate aroma and iron.

Abū'l-Fazl, at the end of the 16th century, speaks of *'ūd* or aloe wood, 'called in India *agar*', as 'the root of a tree which is cut off and buried; that part which is worthless perishes; the remainder is pure aloes. The information of ancient writers to the effect that the tree grows in central India is absurd and fanciful'. All the varieties he mentions come from Indo-China or the Archipelago. The best, he says, 'is that which is black and heavy; put in water it lies at the bottom; it is not fibrous and it readily crumbles; the sort that floats is considered valueless; it centers freely into composition of perfumes. When one eats it one becomes joyous. It is generally used as incense, and in the form of powder its best qualities are used to rub into the skin and dust into the clothing'.

Sulaimān tells of the uses of aloe among the Chinese. When a man dies, says he, 'he is not interred until some subsequent anniversary of his death. The body is placed in a bier and kept in the house, lime being put on it for preservation, but in the case of a prince, aloe and camphor are used instead of lime. The dead are mourned three years. Those who do not mourn are beaten with rods, whether men or women, the people saying, "What, are you not afflicted by the death of your relatives?" Then the body is interred in a tomb as among the Arabs'.

The confusion in these substances is indicated in a passage in Jaubarī, a recipe for making myrobalan. First, he says, take a little true myrobalan, then one part each of gall-nut (terebinth?), myrrh and gum. Instead of myrrh other manuscripts at this passage have *ṣibar as-suḳutrī,* Socotrine aloes; but this word *ṣibar,* as already stated, refers indiscriminately to aloes and myrrh, and there is another word, *kāṭir* or *kuṭar,* which covers both aloes and dragon's blood. The modern Arabic version of the Psalms renders cassia as *salīḥ,* which is the word for myrobalan; which, in turn, means no more than an acorn, or fruit, used in ointments.

Why now the name *agar* or *agur* by which this Eastern resin is generally known in India? The Sanskrit lexicographers give *a+guru,* 'not heavy', and they give as a synonym, *laghu,* 'light'. Professor Edgerton tells me that the latter word is not applied to aloe in the literature, and that while the form *a+guru* is unimpeachable, he will go so far as to say that the derivation looks 'a little fishy'. While the incense is in constant use by the Parsees, Professor Jackson tells me that the word is quite certainly not Persian, and in conversation with a Zoroastrian priest, Jal Pavry, he finds that the incense is prepared by combining *agar* with *luban* (no doubt frankincense) and *bōi*—identification uncertain.[33] Sir Dinshah E. Wacha, a leading Parsee of Bombay, who is a member of the Indian Imperial Council, tells me that *agar* is burned with Zanzibar sandalwood and frankincense, both as incense and for purification of dwellings, and that it comes to Bombay from Arabia While he may possibly be mistaken as to its origin, I incline to accept the statement, and to think that an *agar* usable as incense may have figured in early trade from Arabia, and may still figure, just as Arabian storax still reaches China in competition with the better quality that comes from Java. But the East Indian aloe or eagle-wood is not, and, so far as known, has never been a product of Arabia. What then may it have been? Cedar and juniper are possibilities. Henry Salt,[34] writing about a century ago, before modern transportation had revolutionized commerce, mentions among exports at Aden, coffee, myrrh, aloes, frankincense and mastic. Dioscorides mentions mastic or terebinth as exported from Central Arabia. But in South Arabia and Socotra the name aloe was applied also to the lily family. Chau Ju-Kua correctly describes the Socotrine aloe and transcribes it as *lü hwui*, which is pretty close to an Arabic *luwiyy*.[35]

The derivation of a trade name like this can hardly be more than conjectural. There is a port Agar on the Arabian shore of the Persian Gulf at the upper end of the Bay of Bahrein. Until a century ago the same name was borne by an important trading city a few leagues inland now named Hofhuf. The classical geographers all mention a tribe named Agraei as dominating the Central Arabian caravan routes. In modern

---

[33] According to Dr. Laufer (*Sino-Iranica*, 462) this is a Baluchi name for bdellium, the resin of *Balsamodendron Mukul*. According to E. W. West (Pahlavi Texts, *S. B. E.* Vol. V) in Iranian literature 'whatever root, or gum, or wood is scented, they call a scent (*bod*)'.

[34] *Travels in Abyssinia*, 106.

[35] To the suggestion that *agar* may be a Dravidian word, it can only

Arabic this central region is still El Hejr. The name means merely 'stony', and was correctly Latinized as Arabia Petraea. The district between the valley of Hadramaut and the South Arabian coast is also known as El Hejr. On the Somali coast Drake-Brockman found *hagar* as a variety of incense gum.[36] Ibn Jamī says about rhubarb that 'if one associates with it myrobalan of Kabul, aloes of Socotra and agaric, its action is thereby strengthened'. Agaric was a corky fungus growing on rotten wood, and no doubt would be a dependable emetic, and perhaps in sufficient quantity a positive poison. While Dioscorides would derive its name from a tribe of Agari in Sarmatia, it seems more likely that it goes back to the same root meaning 'to bend', that is, a bump, or excrescence. Finally there is the early Semitic root *'gr* meaning 'to scratch', hence, to scrape up, gather, or collect; hence, from scraping together, to hire for wages, and by transfer to the person hired, a public courier or royal messenger. The writing which the messenger carried was in Persian *engareh*. The word passed into Greek as *angaros*, messenger, hence *angelos* or angel. While this could have had some bearing on the gathering of the resin by scratching the leaf or bark, I do not press the point.

'Perhaps 't is pretty to force together
Thoughts so all unlike each other;'

and this is unavoidable in dealing with ancient commerce. The Jewish Prayer Book, in its 'Blessings on Various Occasions', classifies the fragrant substances for which blessings are to be offered, as Fragrant Woods or Barks, Odorous Plants, Odorous Fruits, Fragrant Spices, and Fragrant Oils. Greater nicety of distinction may not have been expected of priest or people. In the aloe we seem certainly to have an ancient trade name that referred to disease, injury or decay in several trees or plants which appeared in the form of swellings or

---

be said that the synonyms in modern Dravidian languages, supplied by Watt, have no resemblance to such a form.

[36] Cf. *Bulletin of the Imperial Institute*, London 1914, Vol. XII, pp. 11—27. *Habbak hagar* is *Commiphora Hildebrandtii*, a near cousin of the myrrh.

growths, resulting in dark aromatic resins somewhat similar in appearance, bitter in taste and fragrant in the burning, conceived of originally as the dried blood of the in-dwelling divinity, and consequently as a means of purification. The definite limitation of the term in Biblical translations to a Far Eastern product unknown in Biblical times is an unfortunate anachronism for which the responsibility rests, not with the text itself, but with uncritical readers of the accounts of later exploration, too ready to identify new knowledge with ancient records.

TWO LITHUANIAN ETYMOLOGIES

HAROLD H. BENDER

PRINCETON UNIVERSITY

Lithuanian *výdraga* "virago"

UNDER THE suffix *-aga* Leskien, Bildung der Nomina im Litauischen, p. 525, includes "*výdraga* KLD ['eine Furie, besonders von einer bösen Hündin'; N aus BdQu[1] 'eine freche Magd', sieht aus wie ein slav. Fremdwort". But Leskien gives no evidence of Slavic origin, and *výdraga* seems very clearly to be a derivative in *-ga* (for the suffix see Leskien, Nomina, 523) from *výdra* (*vidras* m.) "storm". Lalis, Lithuanian-English Dictionary[3], 419, gives *vydraga* "hag, fury, stormy woman, virago". Lalis's "stormy woman" is an etymologically exact and literal translation, altho Lalis, like Nesselmann and Kurschat, does not know *výdra*, and thus overlooks the rather obvious derivation of *vydraga*. It is unnecessary to give semantic parallels, but one may notice, from the same IE. root, Lith. *áudra* "Flut, Sturm, Stürmen, Toben, Tosen, Getöse" (Lalis, "storm, tempest"; fig. "storm, fury"), and Eng. *to storm* "to give vent boisterously to rage or passion". For the Lith. and IE. belongings of *výdra*, *vidras*, see Leskien, Nomina, 438, 436; Brugmann, Grundriss[2], II. 1. 379; Walde, Lateinisches etymologisches Wörterbuch[2], s. v. *ventus*.

---

[1] Leskien's KLD = Kurschat, Littauisch-deutsches Wörterbuch; N = Nesselmann, Wörterbuch der littauischen Sprache; Bd = Brodowski, Lexicon Lithuanico-Germanicum et Germanico-Lithuanicum (early 18th century MS.); Qu = "ein anonymes, höchst sauber geschriebenes Deutsch-littauisches Wörterbuch in zwei starken Quartbänden, . . . mit Brodowski's Lexikon verwandt, aber nicht identisch" (cf. Nesselmann, p. VI).

Lithuanian *žógis* "meadow-drain, gully"

In Nesselmann Wb., p. 550, appears *žógis* m. "eine vom Wasser verdorbene Stelle auf Wiesen"; no connection is indicated with any other Lithuanian word. Kurschat LDWb. 523 cites *žiõgis, žiogỹs* m. "in poln. Litt. 'ein Wiesenflüßchen, Bach'". Bezzenberger, Litauische Forschungen, pp. 203, (205, 178), quotes from two authorities *žiógys*, which we may render, by following up his cross references and his reference to Nesselmann, as "ein kleiner Sumpfbach, ein Wasserloch auf einer Wiese; Rinne, Rinnsel", with a Lithuanian example (of a synonym) meaning "his tears began to fall in *streams* down his cheeks". Lalis LEDict.[3] 434 has *žiogis* m. "rivulet, streamlet, brook".

Several interesting discussions of the word may be found in the Mitteilungen der Litauischen literarischen Gesellschaft (hereinafter abbreviated as MLG.). Under the title "Litauische Wörter, die im Nesselmannschen Wörterbuche nicht vorfindlich sind" Ziegler (MLG. I. 21) has the following to say of *žogis*: "Die Bedeutung ist nicht richtig angegeben; *žogis* bezeichnet ein Gewässer, welches sich an niedrigen Stellen findet, und nach gewöhnlich kurzem Verlaufe in ein größeres mündet. Nach meiner Meinung kommt es von *žogauju* ["I yawn"] oder *žoju* ["I gape"] her, weil es an seiner Mündung am breitesten, einem aufgesperrten Rachen nicht ganz unähnlich ist." In an article entitled "Bemerkungen zum Vocabularium von Ziegler" Jacoby says (MLG. I. 137): "*žógis* bezeichnet eine Wasserstelle unweit eines Flusses, meistens ein alter Ausriß, der bei hohem Wasserstande vom Flusse aus sich mit Wasser füllt, also bei niedrigem Wasserstande wieder trocken wird; im erstern Falle wird darin gern gefischt *(į žógį žvejóti)*. Verschieden davon ist *dumburỹs*, allerdings auch ein ehemaliger Ausriß eines Flusses, aber von solcher Tiefe, daß das Wasser darin stehen bleibt."

According to Hoffheinz (MLG. IV. 274, 279 — see map opposite 206) *žiogis*, which he translates as "Graben, Bach", appears in proper names about the Krakerorter Lank, a small lake near the mouth of the Memel (Niemen) River. The name of a small stream that empties into an arm of the Memel and thence into the lake, *Lydekžoge* or *Lidekszoge*, is interpreted by Hoffheinz as "Hechtgraben, von *lydeka* und *žiogis*". One of the thirty-two definitely distinguished and named parts of the Krakerorter Lank through which the nature of the bottom permits the fishermen successfully to draw their drag-nets is called *Żiagis*, which Hoffheinz identifies with *żiogis* "Graben, Bach".

I find no citations for *żógis* other than those I have given, and I know of no attempt to explain it etymologically save the unsuccessful one by Ziegler. Leskien, Bildung der Nomina im Litauischen, p. 300, gives no connections for his *żiõgis, żiogỹs* "Bächlein", and includes it in a group in which "keine Beziehung zu einem in der Sprache gebräuchlichen Verbum vorliegt oder die Beziehung nicht klar ist". But an examination of the various conceptions of the word should give us something that is basically common to all. The connotation seems to be that of a runnel or gully which may normally be merely swampy or even dry, but which in time of freshet either pours its water from a meadow into a stream or permits the backwater of the stream partially to inundate the meadow. In either event the rivulet muddies the stream and the adjacent meadow becomes covered with a deposit of silt which tends to make the grass unfit for grazing and to injure the meadow.

This leads us rather directly to the verb *żagiù, żàgti*, which is given the following meanings: "versehren, unrein machen" (Nesselmann Wb. 538); "in Südlitt. 'unrein machen', zunächst vom Wasser" (Kurschat LDWb. 514); "to sully, pollute, impure, defile, debauch" (Lalis LEDict.[3] 428). Notice also Kurschat's (p. 515) *vándenį įżàgti* "das Wasser verunreinigen" and, in Lalis, *żaginti, įżagti, sużagti. żógis* m. may bear the same ablaut relation to *żagiù* as *żódis* m. to *żadù, móżis* m. to *mážas, klónis* m. to *klánas, lóbis* m. to *lábas*, &c. So far as I know, *żagiù* has not been identified outside of Baltic — or in fact outside of Lithuanian, for I am very skeptical as to the relationship to *żagiù* of the Lettish words which Leskien (Ablaut der Wurzelsilben im Litauischen, p. 376) connects with it. But I do propose that *żagiù* be taken out of Leskien's list of primary verbs in *a* without ablaut, and that a new *a-o* ablaut group be formed from *żógis* and *żagiù*.

IGNAZ GOLDZIHER

RICHARD GOTTHEIL

COLUMBIA UNIVERSITY

DR. IGNAZ GOLDZIHER, Professor at the University of Budapest, Hungary, had been an honor to the membership of our Society since the year 1906. His death on November 13, 1921, has removed from the learned world the one who not only had penetrated furthest into the real essence of Islam, but who had also made himself most thoroughly acquainted with every excrescent movement to which it has given life. To many persons, Islam represents a political organization; to others it is merely a religious system. In reality, it is both, and it is something more. It connotes a definite and certain philosophical view of life. As its influence stretches from Morocco to China and to the Malay States, it has come into contact with the most varied forms of government and with every kind and class of man. In this wonderful sweep of its power, it has learned much, and it has taught more. But it has seldom budged from the root ideas in which it was born and nurtured.

To be at home in the mass of deed, thought and writing that this progress has brought forth needs a brilliant and capacious intellect. Such was that of Goldziher. Born in Stuhlweissenburg, Hungary, June 22, 1850, at an early age he was introduced not only into the secular learning of the schools of his day, but also into the Hebrew and Rabbinic dialectics that have grown up around the Bible and the Talmud; and his doctor's dissertation showed his leanings, as it dealt with a certain Tanḥum of Jerusalem, a liberal Arabico-Hebraic exegete of the thirteenth century. It was just this training in argumentation that made it possible for Goldziher to penetrate where others were afraid to tread, and to discern the minute differences which have produced so many so-called sects in Islam and have divided its devotes into so many categories, each category following a specific line of devotion or of action. During his training in Semitics he had the benefit of sitting at the feet of the foremost leaders in France and in Germany — de Sacy and Fleischer (1870). In 1872 he became Privat-docent at the University of Budapest; but, because of his race and of his religion (to which he was attached devotedly), it was not until the year 1894 that he was appointed professor. During this whole time he met his material necessities by acting as secretary of the Jewish Community in the Hungarian capital and as lecturer on Religious Philosophy at the Rabbinical Seminary.

Book-study was, however, not sufficient for him. He felt the need of coming into closer relations with those who professed the religion that he was studying with so much care. In 1873, and once or twice afterwards, he went as a student through a good part of the Mohammedan Near East, drinking deeply at such fountains as the public and private libraries at Damascus, and sitting at the feet of the learned men who had made al-Azhar famous. Nor did he neglect the language of the streets nor the poetry of their denizens. He spoke Arabic very fluently; and I remember well how, at the Congress of Orientalists held in Geneva in the year 1894, he privately rebuked a number of young Egyptians who were hilariously drinking wine, telling them that if only out of respect for the religion they represented, they ought at least to show outward respect for its tenets.

There are few Semitic scholars of our day who have published as much as has Goldziher. But not for one moment did he ever deviate from the high standard of scholarship that he set for himself. He was meticulously exact in all details, in all his proofs, in all his citations. But he never permitted this extreme care to lead him into the blind alley of mere "Gelehrsamkeit" or into the show-window of a pack of citations for citation's sake. As a true scholar, the larger and weightier problems — whether they were of philology, of history, or of philosophy — were continually before his mind.

What all this means one can realize, if one thinks for a moment that there is hardly a volume of the *ZDMG*, since vol. 28, which does not contain one or more contributions from his pen, that many have appeared in the *WZKM*, in *Islam*, in the *JRAS*, in the *JQR*, in the *Denkschriften der Kaiserlichen Akademie der Wissenschaften* — as well as in the *Encyclopedia of Islam* which is now going through the press.

But the great value of Goldziher's numerous works lies in the fact that he levelled new paths for us to walk on in dealing with the evolution of Islam. In the introduction to vol. 26 of the *ZA*, which was dedicated to him upon the occasion of the celebration of the fortieth anniversary of his connection with the University of Budapest, Nöldeke says to him: "Ich hebe hervor, dass erst Sie das Wesen der muslimischen normativen Tradition ins wahre Licht gestellt haben". And, in like manner, it was he who first attacked the problem of Shiism (*WZKM* 13; *KADW* 75) — a subject which had been quite neglected by European scholars. In his "Zahiriten" (1884), Goldziher for the first time brought light into an obscure, though important, drift in the interpretation of the Koran and showed its influence upon the practical workings of Mohammedan law. In his "Muhammedanische Studien", he gives us an insight into the Shu'ubiyyah — which touches upon the delicate question of the relations of Arabs to non-Arabs within the charmed circle of Islam; and in his edition of the writings of Ibn Tumart (1903), together with its learned preface, he has given us the material with which to study the beginnings of the Almohad invasion of Spain in the twelfth century.

A subject of equal interest to all those who deal with Mohammedan questions is that of the Ḥadīth or Tradition concerning the Exegesis of the Koran, which Goldziher has treated in a broad and masterly manner in the second volume of his "Muhammedanische Studien" (1890). With these as a basis he enlarged upon the subject in his lectures at the University of Upsala, which are printed under the title "*Die Richtungen der Islamischen Koranauslegung*" as vol. 7 of the series of the de Goeje Stiftung. Along the same line run his publication and translation of al-Ghazali's attack upon the Bāṭiniyyah sect, the sect of those who looked for hidden meanings in the words of the Mohammedan scriptures (published as vol. 3 in the same series).

One has only to go through the array of Goldziher's many

articles to see the diversity of his interests in matters affecting Islam. From his "Jugend- und Strassenpoesie in Kairo" (*ZDMG* 33) to his edition of the poems of Jarwal ibn Aus al-Ḥuṭai'ah, the wandering poet whose biting sarcasm Omar himself feared (*ZDMG* 46, 47); from his "Eulogien der Muhammedaner" (*ZDMG* 50) to his "Stellung der alten islamischen Orthodoxie zu den antiken Wissenschaften" (*KPAW*, 1915), no subject was strange to him. And, at the same time, he never forgot his own people and their literature. Many articles in Jewish periodicals stand as witnesses to this — and especially his careful edition of the Arabic text in Hebrew characters of the philosophical work entitled "Ma'ānī al-Nafs" ("The Essence of the Soul", *AKGW*, 1907).

By the general public Goldziher will be remembered best by reason of his "Vorlesungen über den Islam" (1910) — the first intelligent and consecutive presentation of the system of Islamic doctrine and tradition, based upon the widest possible study of all its ramifications. The lectures were intended originally to have been delivered under the auspices of the American Committee for Lectures on the History of Religions; but at the last moment the arrangements went awry, and they were published in book form. An English translation of these lectures appeared in this country for a while, but then suddenly hid its head in blushing concealment.

Since the Geneva Congress of Orientalists in 1894, where I made the personal acquaintance of Goldziher, it has been my good fortune to remain in constant connection with him. In 1910 I had the pleasure of spending an evening with him in his own study and of seeing the wonderful collection of books that he had accumulated. Unfortunately, when he came to this country in 1910 for the purpose of attending a congress of religions, I was in the Near East and missed him. In 1921 I had three communications from him; but he complained much about his declining health—especially in the last one, dated May 4th. But up to the very end he showed the same desire to read, to learn, to know. The war had made a serious break in his studies, and had cut him off from his customary learned and literary connections in many lands, especially in America. It is certain that the war had affected him in other ways also; and his end on November 13th, 1921, did not come in the circumstances in which his friends would have wished.

Deeply pious in his own soul, and passionately attached to his own faith, he had a wide breadth of vision that permitted him to approach other religious systems with affectionate care. I am sure that he felt as did the Mohammedan when he wrote: راس العلم الخوف لله (Iḳd I, 202).

BRIEF NOTES

India and Elam

Indologists are aware that when Gautama Buddha lived and preached, Bimbisāra ruled in Magadha. Five Purāṇas, incorporating a dynastic account of the post-Mahābhārata period, namely, Matsya, Vāyu, Brahmāṇḍa, Viṣṇu, and Bhāgavata, agree in pointing to one Śiśunāka or Śiśunāga as the founder of the dynasty to which Bimbisāra belonged.[1] It is true that the Ceylon chronicles place Śiśunāka (whom they call Susunāga) six generations *later* than Bimbisāra.[2] But Purāṇic authority is, in this matter, more to be relied upon than confused recollections conjured up in chronicles of distant Ceylon.

The Purāṇas posit three kings between Śiśunāka and Bimbisāra. The Matsya counts 154 years from the accession of Śiśunāka to the termination of Bimbisāra's reign. The Vāyu reckons the interval between the same two events as one of 164 years, while the Brahmāṇḍa's total is 174 years.[3] Copyists' mistakes are probably responsible for this divergence, the '26' and '28' years assigned respectively to Kākavarṇin and Bimbisāra in the Matsya's original being misread as '36' and '38',—a common enough blunder, occasioned by the similarity between *va* and *tra* which was likely to make *ṣaḍviṁśat* and *aṣṭāviṁśat* appear *ṣaṭtriṁśat* and *aṣṭātriṁśat*.[4] The Matsya total, 154 years, should be preferred to the bigger totals given in the Vāyu and the Brahmāṇḍa, since the Matsya contains the oldest version of the dynastic account.[5]

According to Ceylonese tradition, towards which Western scholars, sceptical at first, are gradually assuming an attitude

---

[1] Pargiter, *Dynasties of the Kali Age* (Oxford, 1913), p. 21.

[2] *Dīpavaṁsa*, ch. V; *Mahāvaṁsa*, ch. IV.

[3] Pargiter, *op. cit.*, p. 21.

[4] *Ibid.*, p. xxiii.

[5] *Ibid.*, p. xiv.

of faith, Buddha died in the 8th year of Ajātaśatru, successor to Bimbisāra, that year corresponding to 544 B. C.[6] Northern tradition represents Buddha to have died in the 5th year of Ajātaśatru.[7] Bimbisāra's last year is thus placed 551 or 548 B. C., and Śiśunāka's accession, being (according to the Matsya Purāṇa) 154 years earlier, falls in the year 705 or 702 B. C.

To Assyriologists the name *Śiśunāka*, *Śiśunāga* or *Susunāga* inevitably recalls the designation *Susinak* or *Susunqa* adopted in those days and earlier still by native kings of Susa (Elam).[8] *Śiśunāka*, if taken as a Sanskrit compound made up of *śiśu* and *nāka*, would mean nothing; and we know that Indian kings of that period, choosing to adopt Sanskritic names, usually selected names with a meaning. In a commentary on the Ceylon chronicle, the Mahāvaṁsa, we find a traditional account of the name *Susunāga*.[9] It is clear from this account, though we need not believe every word of it, that tradition, too, failed to connect the first element *susu* with Sanskrit *śiśu*. Susinak of Elam could be easily transformed into Śiśunāka by metathesis of the first two syllables, and the transformation would come in handy to an Indian *purāṇakāra* naturally disposed to look out for Sanskritic names. The Ceylon form *Susunāga* is nearer still to the Elamite *Susunqa*.

Susinak or *Susunqa* means 'the Susian'. Could a Susinak have come to rule over Magadha about 700 B. C.? No very close examination of the history of Elam is required for a satisfactory answer to this very relevant question. After 720 B. C. when Sargon of Assyria carried out a campaign against Elam, the latter country adopted the policy of helping Babylonia against Assyria. About 704 B. C. the combined forces of Elam and Babylonia were overthrown at Kis. Elam now set herself on a war of revenge. She formed a confederacy, embracing numerous neighboring states, to humble Assyria; but that confederacy was broken by Sennacherib in a battle at Khaluli (691 B. C.).[10] Is it not likely that India was included by the

---

6 *Mahāvaṁsa*, ch. II; Smith, *Oxford History of India* (1919), p. 52. The date 544 B. C. is deduced from data in *Dīpavaṁsa* and *Mahāvaṁsa*.

7 Rockhill, *Life of the Buddha*, p. 91.

8 Sayce, *Records of the Past*, N. S., vol. V, p. 148.

9 Turnour, *Mahawanso* (1837), p. xxxvii.

10 *Encyclopædia Britannica* (11th ed.), article 'Elam'.

Elamite king in this quest of alliance? The territorial limits of Elam are given differently by different classical authors, but some writers define the country as 'lying between the Oroatis and the Tigris, and stretching from India to the Persian Gulf.'[11] Could India be left out, as at any rate a potential ally, by Elam in her life-and-death struggle with Assyria? An Elamite prince of the blood royal, a Susinak, would be the most suitable person to be entrusted with a mission to India. The mission could readily secure hospitality in an Indian Court, and there is nothing strange in the Susinak afterwards carving out a kingdom for himself within the borders of India. Benares, for instance, would form a most convenient centre of political intrigue. The Purāṇic account indicates, in fact, that Śiśunāka, placing his son on the throne of Benares, 'proceeded towards' (*śrayiṣyati*) or 'started an expedition against' (*saṁyāsyati*) Girivraja, the capital of Magadha;[12] and he may have begun his career here as a minister, as the Mahāvaṁsa asserts.[13] The Purāṇas further emphasize that the descendants of Śiśunāka were *kṣatrabandhavaḥ*.[14] The term *rājanyabandhu*, a synonym of *kṣatrabandhu*, is used in early Indian literature to denote a *rājanya* or 'a prince', but usually with a depreciating sense.[15] In later literature, however, *e. g.*, in the Mānava Dharmaśāstra, the terms *kṣatra*, *kṣatrabandhu*, *rājanya* and *rājanyabandhu* are used without discrimination.[16] How did the elevation in meaning of the terms *kṣatrabandhu* and *rājanyabandhu* come about? The answer, I think, is pretty simple. These compounds originally meant, in all probability, 'kinsman of a prince', *i. e.* of a prince native to India. Foreign invaders of a princely origin, even upstart adventurers who rise from the ranks, usually attempt, and succeed in their attempt, to effect matrimonial alliances with ruling dynasties of established dignity. They would not be generally acknowledged as *kṣatriyāḥ* or *rājanyāḥ* at first, and would be designated *kṣatrabandhavaḥ* or *rājanyabandhavaḥ*. Gradually, however, the distinction would

---

11 *Ibid.*

12 Pargiter, *op. cit.*, p. 21.

13 *Mahāvaṁsa*, ch. IV.

14 Pargiter, *op. cit.*, p. 21.

15 Macdonell and Keith, *Vedic Index*, *sub voce* 'Rājanyabandhu'.

16 Cf. Manu, V. 320 and II. 38, 49, 65, with one another.

disappear, and the descendants of a *kṣatrabandhu* would come to be regarded as *kṣatriyāḥ* themselves. In the Mānava Dharmaśāstra the distinction could hardly be observed, since its ethnic outlook on Kṣatriyas was so broad that Śakas, Yavanas, Pahlavas, and even Cīnas, were held by its author to have been Kṣatriyas by race, who had been rendered outcast only by long abstention from Brahminical ways of life and protracted separation from Brahmins.[17] If, therefore, Śiśunāka was originally an Elamite prince who afterwards made himself master of Magadha, he would, in the plenitude of his power, naturally seek the hand of an Indian princess of a Kṣatriya house; and his descendants could very properly be designated *kṣatrabandhavaḥ* in early Sanskrit records. That some of his descendants intermarried with well-established indigenous dynasties is known from literary evidence. Thus, Bimbisāra is stated to have married a sister of Prasenajit of the Ikṣvāku dynasty,[18] and Udayana of Kauśāmbī is represented as having taken to wife a sister of Darśaka, grandson of Bimbisāra.[19]

Our finding throws some light on the fact, long familiar to the scholarly world, that brisk trade began between India and Babylonia about 700 B. C.[20] With the advent of an Elamite dynasty into Magadha, commerce would be fostered between India and Babylonia, Elamite policy being at that time pro-Babylonian. We are also able to understand the presence of so-called Assyrian, but really Babylonian, elements in early Indian art. Babylonian influence, traced in other spheres of Indian cultural activity, receives, too, an intelligible explanation.

HARIT KRISHNA DEB

Calcutta, India

The Name and Nature of the Sumerian God Uttu

JAOS 40, 73 f. the writer discussed the character of the Sumerian god Uttu *(TAG-KU)* and proposed to consider him as the god of commerce and the arts of civilization. Originally,

[17] Manu, X. 44.

[18] Rhys Davids, *Buddhist India*, p. 3.

[19] Bhāsa, *Svapnavāsavadattā*, Act I.

[20] Rhys Davids, *op. cit.*, p. 115.

I thought, he was a god of fertility, perhaps with solar associations, to judge from the similarity between the name *Uttu* and *Utu* = Babbar, as well as from certain analogies. That he was a patron of culture and a god of fertility may be regarded as certain, but the explanation of his name, as well as the consequent deductions, was wrong. The true explanation is furnished by *CT* 19. 17, Col. I. 6 ff. and *CT* 11. 48. 32 ff. In the first passage we have:

KI (u-tu) KI: erṣitim ša[plîtim], "lower world"
kúr-nu-gé-a : „ „ „ „
ki-ùr : *duru[ššu]*, "foundation platform" (*JAOS* 40. 317)
ki-ùr-ra : *nêrib erṣitim*, "entrance to the (under) world".

The second passage has:

kukku: KI-K[I]: mâtu šapl[îtu], "lower world"
„ : „ : [ ]
utte : „ : *[er]ṣitu šapl[îtu]*.

The etymology of the word *utu-utte* has been given by Delitzsch, *SGl* 44, who correctly identifies it with *ut-tu: erêb-šamši*, "sunset", lit. "entrance of the sun (into the underworld)". Delitzsch does not strengthen his position by repeating the hazardous combination of Gr. Ἔρεβος with *erêbu*, but there are excellent parallels in the semantic development of Sum. *edin*, "western desert, underworld" (*AJSL* 35. 171, n. 2) and Egypt. *ỉmnty*, "west, underworld". The word *uttu-utu-utte* then means properly "netherworld", but since our divinity is a god of fertility we must refer it to the subterranean world of life, and not to Hades proper. That *uttu* is associated with the *apsû* appears from its synonym *kukku*, which elsewhere is an equivalent of *gug (LÚ)*, "chaos", from which it is derived. The Babylonians, like the Hellenes, conceived of chaos as an amorphous fluid mass, closely related to the *apsû*, Heb. *tehôm*. In the Flood-poem, line 88, we read: *m'ìr kukkê* (like *âšib-kussê*) *ina lîlâti ušaznanû šamûtu kibâti* = "The regents of the *kukku* will cause the (storm) clouds to rain down hail (Ungnad, *ZDMG* 73. 165) in the evening". Here the idea that the ultimate source of rain is the subterranean ocean is expressed as clearly as in Amos and the Avesta.

If *uttu* is a synonym of *ki*, "underworld" (Zimmern, against Jastrow) we would expect the lord of the *uttu*, the *mu'ìr kukki*, to be called the *En-uttu*, just as *En-ki* is the lord of the *ki*.

Nor are we disappointed. In a very important tetragonal cylinder, published by Keiser in *Babylonian Inscriptions in the Collection of J. B. Nies*, No. 23, this very god En-ut appears. The opening of the text is best preserved, but has been unfortunately misunderstood throughout by the editor, so I will give my own translation:

1. To thee, O *apsû*, O seemly maiden *(ki-sikil [me]-te-gál)*,[1]
2. To the house of the ocean (? *ê-gur* [?]-*ra*) may thy king betake himself,
3. En-ut, king of the *apsû*.
4. Thy quay of malachite he has [ ]
5. [ ] lapis lazuli he has come to thee.
6. The house of Enki, the pure — — —
7. Bull, king [ ] hero endowed with might (*a* for *á*?),
8. In himself *(ni-bi)* he meditated, together *(diš-bi)* he consulted;
9. To the house of the ocean (?), which is Enki's pure sea *([a]-ab-ba kug me-a)*,
10. Where in the midst of the *apsû* a great sanctuary is established,
11. [ ] the pure might(?) of heaven,
12. The *apsû*, the pure place (resp. maiden), the place of determining fates,
13. [ ] the ear of king En-ut,
14. [Enk]i, lord of determining fates,
15. [Nug]immut (so!), lord of Eridu (i. e., the *apsû*),

* * *

20. The *apsû*, life of the land, the beloved of En-ut,
21. The pregnant one,[2] [ ] perfect in fulness *(sukud-da tum-ma)*

* * *

23. The nether sea, the life of the land a rival has not,[3]
24. The mighty river, rushing over the land.

In the badly mutilated second and third columns we read the name En-ut in connection with the various works of fertility

[1] We have here a paronomasia associated with a profound mythical conception. The word *ki-sikil* (so, not *ki-el*, Thureau-Dangin, *RA* 17. 82 f.) means literally "pure place", but also "virgin, maiden".

[2] For this meaning of *si-zag*, or *zag-si*, lit. "full of side", see *AJSL* 35. 181, n. 5.

[3] Or "In the nether sea — — — a rival he has not".

in a number of places; toward the end of the tablet Enki and his *sukkal* Isimu appear (Keiser reads the name Isimu wrongly, and renders "messenger of the yellow scorpion".)

From this text it is clear that En-ut[4] is merely a variant form of Enki or Ea, since both receive the same appellations, and *Nugimmut* is given as a title to En-ut. With Ea, wisdom and fire,[5] from which spring the human arts and crafts of civilization, have their source in his nether ocean; in the myth of Oannes, whose cuneiform original remains to be discovered, the god rises from the sea (properly the *apsû*) and teaches men the amenities of culture. In Uttu, the patron of commerce, we have a third Babylonian figure of the Prometheus type, a true culture-hero.

In our text, the *apsû*, the Sumerian virgin-mother Engur, or Nammu, appears as a virgin, into whose fertile womb her lord, En-ut, pours his fertilizing seed and renders her pregnant. But we have learned that *uttu* is really a synonym of *abzu* and *engur*, so we should expect Uttu to be originally feminine, like Engur-Apsû, and to show the same androgynous tendencies as Apsû-Ti'âmat, Tammuz, Ištar, and the ancient oriental gods of fertility in general. Nor are we misled. Schröder's valuable publication, *Keilschrifttexte aus Assur verschiedenen Inhalts*, No. 63, Col. III. 41 states that [d]*TAK-KU* (No. 65, Col. III. 18 glosses [d]*TAK-KU* by *ut*) is the daughter of Anu *(mârat Anu)*. Uttu is therefore, according to another theory, of even greater antiquity, we may suppose, a form of Ištar, since the latter is also *mârat Anim*, as well as *mârat Šin*. One of the greatest weaknesses in the critical study of Assyro-Babylonian religion is the failure to distinguish sharply between different theories, which were current often simultaneously, and appear, as in Egypt, even in the same composition. It is one of the great merits of Jastrow to have stressed the principle of distinct theories, held originally by special schools of theologians, and later syncretized.

W. F. Albright

American School in Jerusalem

---

[4] It is possible that the divine name *En-ut-ti-la* means "Lord of the nether sea of life", but more likely that the rendering "Lord of the day of life" is correct.

[5] *AJSL* 35. 165.

Sanduarri, king of Kundi and Sizû

In the account of Esarhaddon's expedition against Abdi-milkutti, king of Sidon, Kundi and Sizû are allied with the Phoenician king against the Assyrians. Delitzsch, *Paradies*, p. 283, considered the possibility that these cities were situated near Sidon. He remarked that the name Kundi is reminiscent of the name of the village 'Ain Kundya near Ḥâsbeyâ east of Sidon. KA[3], p. 88 identifies Kundi with Amhiale and Sizû with Sis, in Cilicia. To seek the cities in Cilicia is difficult according to the account of Esarhaddon. The latter assembled the kings of the land of the Ḫatti and all the rulers of the sea-coast into his presence *(upaḫirma šarrani mât Ḫatti ù aḫi tamtim kališunu ina pania)*. The king of Cilicia and his city-chiefs evidently were still at peace with Assyria at the time of the conquest of Sidon and the war against Sanduarri. It is not until the next campaign that Esarhaddon actually warred against the people of Cilicia (*ukabis kišudi nišê mât Ḫi-lak-ki*; IR 1. 45, Col. 2). It is, therefore, more likely to suppose that the allies of Abdi-milkutti were Syrian or Phoenician rather than Cilician towns.

The name of the king of these two cities may probably throw some light on the question. A king of Cilicia was named Sa-an-dar-(š)ar-me, III R 18, II, 113; Ann. II, 75; he gave his daughter in marriage to Ashurbanipal. Other names which have a similar initial element are Sandaksatru (Iranian accord. to Justi, *IN* p. 283) and Sandapî (probl. for Sanda-dapi, Sayce, *PSBA* 28, p. 92). The initial element in these three names is *sanda*. The element is, therefore, not completely the same as that in the name Sanduarri, where it is *sandu*, once written *sa-an-du-ú*, and this has probably nothing whatever to do with the element *sanda*. Therefore another explanation must be sought for. A possibility is the Egyptian origin of the name. *Sa-an-du-(ú)-ar-ri* might well stand for *s'-n-dw'-R*ʿ, i. e., 'the worshipper of Rêʿ'. Two objections might be raised against this interpretation. It might be said that 'the person of the praise of Rêʿ', i. e., 'the worshipper of Rêʿ' is no personal name and, therefore, is improbable. Yet this would not stand without parallel. In K 3082 S 2027 K 3086 the king of Tyre is called *ba-'a-lu*, which is certainly not his name but the

Hebrew בעל. This instance would meet the objections against a name which is rather an epithet. The second objection might be directed against the fact that this puts an Egyptian over two Phoenician or Syrian cities at a time when we should not expect it. Yet it is altogether not improbable that the Egyptian Sanduarri was a man who had been raised to the rank of a chieftain over two rather insignificant places by the king of Sidon, for personal or political reasons. The Phoenician cities were always the good friends of Egypt. Thus the king Tirhakah of Egypt is called a friend of Ba'alu of Tyre (*Ba-'a-lu šar* mât *Ṣur-ri ša a-na Tar-ku-ú šar* mât *Ku-ú-si ip-ri-šu it-tak-lu-ma).*

The Tell el-Amarna letters represent the element Rê' by the syllables *ri-ia* (*nimmuria*, Amenhotep III; *napḫuria*, Amenhotep IV), *a* representing the 'Ain. We would have in Sanduarri the omission of the closing guttural, which, again, is not a point against the Egyptian interpretation of the name.

H. F. Lutz

University of California

The root ידל, edelu *in Egyptian*

Pognon, *Bav.* 131 referred Babylonian *daltu*, 'door' to the root ידל, *edelu*, 'to bar, bolt, lock up, shut up'. He has been followed by Barth, *ZDMG* Vol. 41 (1887), p. 607, and this etymology has been accepted since by most scholars (see the Hebrew dictionaries *sub deleth*). That this etymology indeed is correct is shown by the Egyptian, which has preserved the root ידל, *edelu*, although, as far as I know, no reference has ever been made to it. ידל is preserved in the verb *ỉḏr* (determ., wall and strong arm), *Aeg. Zeitschr.* 1868, p. 112 with the meaning 'to lock up, bolt, bar, fortify'; Sethe, *Urkunden*, 4, p. 1174 *ỉḏr. t* (determ., house), 'a locked up place, a bolted place', thence also 'a fort, a fortress'. The root *ỉḏr (ỉdr, ỉdl)* has undergone metathesis in the word *ḏry*, Copt. ⲧⲏⲣ, 'boundary'. That metathesis took place is shown by the writing *ỉḏr* (Copt. ⲁⲣⲏϫ) with the same meaning 'boundary'. The idea of 'door' is also preserved in this word.

Furthermore, it should be noted that the Egyptian word for 'hand', commonly transliterated *ḏ. t* (Copt. ⲧⲟⲟⲧ) does not merely go back to *ḏr. t* (U. 3, 550, T. 29, 32, P. 6, 113, M. 781, N. 179, 1138) but to *ḏry. t* (so *Recueil de Travaux*, 31, 30), which again in turn goes back to the root *ḏr*, *idr*, *idl*, *edelu*, 'to lock, to close' etc. The same root ידל, *edelu* must, therefore, also underlie the Hebrew יד, 'hand', which underwent practically the same deterioration as the Egyptian *d. t.*

H. F. Lutz

University of California

The etymology and meaning of Sanskrit garútmant

In the post-Vedic literature and in the native lexicons *garútmant* is a noun and signifies sometimes bird in general, and sometimes the mythical bird Garuḍa in particular. The word appears twice in RV., once in VS., and twice in AV. (but AV. 9. 10. 28 is RV. 1. 164. 46). In the Veda it always occurs with *suparṇá*; the latter word is usually taken as a noun, and the *garútmant* as an adjective with the meaning 'winged'. But I consider *suparṇá* the adjective and suggest that in the Veda, as in the later literature, *garútmant* is a noun, and that the phrase should be rendered 'the beautiful-winged (mythical) bird' or 'the beautiful-winged Garutmant (= Garuḍa)'. The adjectival usage of *suparṇá* and its literal meaning were too familiar in the Veda to permit the probability of the meaning 'winged' for *garútmant*: 'the winged beautiful-winged one'. In addition to vs. 46, with its combination *sá suparṇó garútmān*, the word *suparṇá* occurs five times in RV. 1. 164, each time with distinctly adjectival force, modifying nouns like *sákhi*, *hári*, *vāyasá*. Moreover, Garuḍa and Garutmant are united by their common association with the sun, an association that is clear, at least as to the fact.

The Western translators do indeed occasionally render *garútmant* by Garutmant, and the Hindu commentator of the AV. suggests at 4. 6. 3 the equation Garutmant = Garuḍa, but the suggestion is not accepted by Whitney-Lanman, and they, together with Monier-Williams, Uhlenbeck, Brugmann, and other scholars, are inclined to agree, by statement or by inference, upon 'winged *(garútmant)* bird or eagle *(suparṇá)*'. Pet. Lex. is non-committal as to meaning, but considers the Vedic *garútmant* an adjective, as does Grassmann.

The interpretation 'winged', for *garútmant*, apparently owes its persistence, and probably its origin, to the Vedic association of the word with *suparṇá*, which often means 'bird'; to the general predominance of the adjectival use of the suffix *-mant*; to the frequency of the possessive idea in *mant-* derivatives (nearly two-thirds of all examples);[1] and to the fact that wings are the most obvious possession of birds. It is required by Ragh. 3. 57, where flying arrows are likened to winged serpents, but it is not required by any passage in the Veda. And, as Pet. Lex. says, 'die Bedeutung "geflügelt" scheint für den Veda schon deshalb zweifelhaft zu sein, weil sie Nir. 7. 18 ganz fehlt'. It has no linguistic basis unless *garut* means 'wing', and there is no evidence of an independent *garut* 'wing', save as it is assumed to explain *garútmant*.

Grassmann, *RVWb.*, explains *garútmant* as meaning 'die Höhe des Himmels innehaltend, in der Höhe schwebend', and derives the *garut* from **gar*, *gir*, which means 'to praise, honor', and which he takes to mean basically 'to raise, exalt'. Uhlenbeck, *Ai Wb.*, and Brugmann, *Grundriß*², 1. 599, are inclined to compare the word with Lat. *volāre* 'to fly'. But neither of these etymologies is semantically and phonetically convincing. Nir. 7. 18 connects *garútmant* with *garaṇa* 'swallowing', but this derivation has not won any measure of the acceptance that it deserves. There seems to be no reasonable objection to considering *garút* a derivative in *-t* — like RV. *marút(vant)*, *niyút(vant)*, *vidyút (vidyúnmant)*, *vihút(mant)* — from the strong form of the root *gṛ*, *gir (giráti;* Lat. *vorāre*, Gk. *βορά*, Lith. *gérti)* 'to swallow', which one finds in the noun-derivatives *gará*, etc. The force of *-mant* would be that of a noun-suffix of agency,[2] or one expressing the idea 'connected with' or 'relating to'.[3] From this root is usually derived *garuḍa*, which is likewise the name of a mythical bird: 'das alles verschlingende Feuer der Sonne' (Pet. Lex.). *Garuḍa* may even be a corruption of *garútmant*; cf. Roth's *Erläuterungen zum Nirukta*, p. 107.

Harold H. Bender

Princeton University

---

[1] Cf. Bender, *The Suffixes mant and vant in Sanskrit and Avestan*, pp. 60, 61.

[2] Cf. Bender, *op. cit.*, p. 68. [3] *Ibid.*, p. 66.

Scale-Insects of the Date-Palm

Classical Arabic lexicographers describe غَفَا as 'a dust that comes upon unripe dates, spoiling them and rendering them like the wings of the jundab' (a sp. of locust). They describe غَفَى as 'a blight incident to palms, like dust falling upon the unripe dates, preventing them from becoming ripe and rendering them tasteless', or 'a thick crust that comes upon unripe dates'. Finally, to explain اغفر النخل, 'the palms had, upon their unripe dates, what resembled a bark or crust, which the people of al-Madînah call غَفَّا'.

These three words, none of which is defined intelligibly to a date-grower, are probably one and the same thing. I suspect that the original is غفى, from which غفا would come by metathesis; while غفر, an easy mispronunciation of غفى, would easily be ascribed to the root *ġafara* = to cover, veil, or conceal.

The original meaning of *ġafa* is apparently the chaff of wheat.

There can be no doubt, I think, that these terms all refer to attacks of a scale insect, of which there are two that infest the fruit of the date-palm.

One of these *(Phoenicococcus marlatti)* is flesh-colored, and habitually lives at the base of the leaves, far inside the trunk of the palm, but comes out in migration twice a year or oftener. By sucking the juices out of a developing bunch of dates, it causes a shriveling which at Biskra, Algeria, is now called *khâmij* (i. e., debility), while the insect is there called *armud* (i. e., ash-colored). At Baghdâd تَبَضَّع describes a palm attacked by this scale, بضع meaning to butcher or cut meat in pieces, since the insect looks not unlike a tiny piece of raw meat, flattened out.

The other insect *(Parlatoria blanchardi)* is white, and lives on the leaves for the most part. At Baghdâd it is now called *'urrah*, from its resemblance to the droppings of birds. At Biskra it goes by the name of *subbâḥ*, which properly describes a salt efflorescence.

The only clue to the identity of the *ġafa* is the statement that it looks like the wings of the jundab; this conveys nothing to me, however, for I am not acquainted with that species of locust. Possibly the term was applied to both species of scale without distinction. From the description of its effects, however, I believe it refers to the Phoenicococcus or so-called Marlatt scale.

As the classical lexicographers usually admitted only words current before Islâm, it may fairly be said that this scale insect has a written history of more than 1300 years. It would be interesting to know whether any other of these minute pests has such a long record in literature.

PAUL POPENOE

Coachella, Calif.

The meaning of Babylonian bittu

The Assyro-Babylonian Dictionaries are still doubtful as to the meaning of *bittu.* Delitzsch, *HWB* p. 192 does not give any conjecture at all, while Muss-Arnolt, *ABHWB*, p. 204 notes down "according to Ball, *PSBA* XII, 221, a kind of dress".

Bittu (or also *battu*) is ideographically written *ne-ġar-ra*; *ġar*, according to Delitzsch, *Sum. Glossar*, p. 210, having the meaning "einschränken, einengen", *ramâṣu*, "einfassen". *Ne-ġar-ra* is an active participle with prefix *ne* and affix *a* (see Delitzsch, *Sum. Gram.* p. 123) and therefore means "das Einengende, das Umfassende", which, of course, at the first thought would be the girdle. That this is really the case, and that the meaning of *bittu*, *battu* is "girdle, belt", becomes clear when we consider similar words in the cognate languages. *Bittu*, first of all, is a contraction with reduplicated *t*, going back to *bintu* or *bantu*. *Bantu* equals Egyptian *bnt*, "girdle", and Hebrew אַבְנֵט with the same meaning, although here it is generally the "priestly girdle".

The Hebrew and the Egyptian words have often been compared with our own "band", German "Binde, Band", but these words are certainly not borrowings from Indo-European; they are purely Semitic.

The primary meaning of the stem *בנט seems to be "to encircle, to be all around" and this meaning is preserved in the Babylonian adverb *battubatti*, *battibatti*, *battabatta*, which is a reduplication of *bantu*, and has the meaning "circle", "all around", "all about". A goodly number of Semitic words meaning "girdle", by the way, are derivatives of verbs whose meanings express exactly this idea. The fact that "binden, umbinden" comes near to the meaning of the stem *בנט, and has the same consonantic skeleton is merely accidental.

H. F. Lutz

University of California

A note regarding the garment called بَدَنْ *and its etymology*

Ibn-Batutah narrates that "the people of Mecca possess elegance and neatness in their garments. They wear mostly white ones and among their costumes are seen the clean and immaculate بدن garments": واهل مكة لهم ظرف ونظافة فى الملابس واكثر لناسهم البياض فترى من ثيابهم ابدانا ناضعة ساطعة

The بدن is described as a *ǵubbah* (جُبَّة) or *dir'* (دِرْع), being short and sleeveless. This sleeveless tunic may be the one represented already in the Egyptian monuments (*vide* Rosellini, *Monumenti civ.*, I, pl. LXVII), which show a Beduin's garment reaching from the arm-pit to the knees. About the waist down it was wrapped twice, and one lower corner of the wrapping was fastened to the girdle.

The word بدن, of course, has no etymological connection with بدن "body", Hebrew בֶּטֶן, although Lane, in his Dictionary, for instance, discusses the word in one and the same article with بدن "body". The word بدن meaning "a short sleeveless tunic" goes back to a root *bdn* which has been preserved in Egyptian (), and which here has the meaning "to tie, to bind". *Bdn* in its turn is a transposed form of the verb *bnt*, Semitic *בנט, of which I spoke in my note on *bittu*.

The name, therefore, would show that the بدن garment, like the *shimlah*, for instance, which is also represented in the Egyptian monuments, is a very old costume, although there is no doubt that it, like other garments, was subject to development in the course of time.

H. F. Lutz

University of California

The ḥagoroth *of Genesis* 3 7

The *ḥagorah* in later time designates without exception a certain kind of loin-girdle (II Sam. 18 11; I Kings 2 5; II Kings 3 21 etc.); only in one passage, Gen. 3 7, does it apparently denote a kind of apron, which was made of fig-leaves, and which seemingly differed only in regard to material from the ordinary loin-cloth, or the short skirt as worn for instance by the early Sumerians. It would therefore appear that the word *ḥagorah*, as many other words designating garments, has undergone a change of meaning. That this, however, is not the case, it is the object of the following note, to show.

Some of the archaic Babylonian cylinder seals present to us the fact that it was the custom among the early Sumerians simply to tie a cord a few times around the loins. To the front of the cord were attached generally two small pieces of cloth to hide the privy parts; these two flaps serving a similar purpose as the *Phallustasche* among the pre-dynastic Egyptians, and among the Libyans down to a comparatively late period. For this ancient Sumerian custom see for instance Ward, *Seal Cylinders of Western Asia*, p. 43, No. 110 a and p. 55, No. 138 b. The statue of the god Min, discovered at Koptos, and now in the Ashmolean Museum at Oxford, shows as the only garment a girdle which is wound eight times round the body, one end of the girdle falling down the right side and widening toward the base. Among the lower classes in Egypt in the time of the Old and Middle Kingdoms it was often customary to wear only a girdle from which hung a special small piece of cloth, which could be pushed to the side or even to the back in case it was in the way during hard work (see e. g. Davies, *The Mastaba of Ptahhetep*, II, pls. 5, 7, 8, 17, 21, 22, 23; Lepsius, *Denkmäler*, II, 61 b, 69, 70, 101 b, 102). Sometimes the middle piece was drawn between the legs, and the end fastened to the girdle in the back, like an infant's diaper.

These considerations would tend to show that the *ḥagoroth* mentioned in Genesis 3 7 consisted of girdles which were wound once or more often around the loins, and to which were fastened, instead of the pieces of cloth, fig-leaves, which had been sewed together.

In view of the fact, furthermore, that the text reads וַיִּתְפְּרוּ עֲלֵה תְאֵנָה וַיַּעֲשׂוּ לָהֶם חֲגֹרֹת and not וַיִּתְפְּרוּ עֲלֵה תְאֵנָה וַיַּעֲשׂוּ גַּם לָהֶם חֲגֹרֹת it seems most likely that the *ḥagorah*, or *ḥagor* in the other passages where the word occurs, no more means "girdle", than it does "apron" or "loin-cloth" in Genesis 3 7. In every instance it means the girdle plus the additional shame-cover, be it in the form of leaves or in the form of small pieces of cloth. The *ḥagorah* is the oldest piece of garment seen on the monuments both of Egypt and Sumer, and, of course, was the predecessor of the loin-cloth.

The *ḥagorah*, in other words, is very similar to the priestly *mikhnas*, which may be a development of the *ḥagorah*. According to Exod. 28 42 the *mikhnas* serves the purpose לְכַסּוֹת בְּשַׂר עֶרְוָה מִמָּתְנַיִם וְעַד־יְרֵכַיִם יִהְיוּ. Josephus describes the *mikhnas* similarly as "a girdle composed of fine twined linen and is put about the privy parts, the feet to be inserted into them in the manner of breeches, but about half of it is cut off, and it ends at the thighs, and is there tied fast". Brown-Driver-Briggs renders *mikhnas* by "drawers" which of course is absolutely wrong. Notice especially that also Josephus terms the *mikhnas* a "girdle", and his description leaves no doubt what we have to understand by it. Also here as in the case of the "layman's" *ḥagorah* it is primarily a girdle, to which, however, is fastened a piece of cloth which is drawn between the legs and fastened at the back of the girdle; the cloth being wide enough to cover the loins and especially the inner part of the upper legs. It thus resembled somewhat short breeches as indicated by Josephus.

H. F. LUTZ

University of California

Ḳû, "*thread, cord*" *in Egyptian*

In Egyptian the idea of "spinning" is expressed by the word *šty*,  from which the verbal noun *šty.t* , 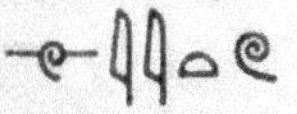 "thread, cord" is derived. The root *šty*, Coptic ⲥⲟⲧⲉ is preserved in Hebrew שְׁתִי "warp", which is given in Hebrew dictionaries under the root שתה. It is rather curious that in Arabic the root appears with ذ and ث in سدى and

ستى, which verbs in the fourth stem mean "to make a warp". The fluctuating writing of the dental may here point to a foreign origin of the stem.

Side by side with *śty* appears in Egyptian the word , also meaning "to spin". This word is of interest. Its real nature has not been detected so far. It is obviously not a causative form of an otherwise unknown verb *tḳ3*, but composed of the verb *śty* "to spin" and *ḳ3* "thread, cord", which of course is the Babylonian *ḳû*, Hebrew קַו. The composite verb should therefore be transcribed by *śtyḳ3* and has the meaning "to spin the thread".

H. F. Lutz

University of California

Nin-Uraš and Nippur

The name of the god Nin-IB has been read in a number of ways; thus the readings Nirig, Ninrag, or Ênu-rêštū have been proposed in addition to the more recent readings of the name Inurta, Inmashtu, and Nin-Uraš. I quite agree with the reading of the name as Nin-Uraš, but I disagree completely with the interpretations of the name as given so far for the following reasons.

In order to explain the name of a god or his attributes he has to be dealt with locally, that is, he has to be studied in relation to the local cult and in relation to the national mythology. If this, of course, can not be done, as a second expediency it becomes necessary to look across the frontiers of the land and explain it by drawing on some foreign pantheon. This, however, is absolutely unnecessary in the case of Nin-Uraš. The name can well be explained from the Babylonian side and mythological considerations show beyond doubt that Nin-Uraš was an older Sumerian god than Enlil, or was at least a god who played a more important rôle in ancient Sumer than Enlil.

Nin-Uraš, let it first be said, gave *his very name* to the city of Nippur, for Nin-Uraššu, which stands for Nin-buraššu, or possibly Nin-puraššu, means the "Lord in Bur"; whatever meaning *bur* or *pur*, which passed into *wur*, and finally into *ur* may have had is irrelevant for the present. Nippur, therefore, goes back to Nin-bur, or Nin-pur, the original name of the god. The name thus was given to the place at a time when the people were still in the animistic stage of religion. Nin-Uraš thus was the oldest and most renowned spirit of the place, and in time gave his name to it. This is in perfect harmony with Babylonian mythology. Nin-Uraš of Nippur in the astral mythology of Babylonia figures as the planet Saturn. Although the particular myth in which Nin-Uraš figures as Saturn has not yet been recovered from the ground of Babylonia, there is absolutely no doubt that, in view of the widespread myth of the elder god slain by the younger, Nin-Uraš the elder god was slain by the younger god Enlil in the same fashion as was Saturn by Jupiter etc.

H. F. Lutz

University of California

Shāhbāzgaṛhī uthānaṃ; *Śaurasēnī locative in* ē

May I supplement Dr. Truman Michelson's remarks on Shāhbāzgaṛhī *uthānaṃ* (*JAOS* 41. 460) by referring to an article on *The Linguistic Relationship of the Shāhbāzgaṛhī Inscription* on pp. 725 ff. of the *JRAS* for 1904? I there pointed out that this inscription was incised in the neighbourhood of what is now the country in which the Modern Piśāca (or, as I now call them, Dardic) languages are spoken at the present day, and that numerous instances of its phonetic peculiarities are paralleled by forms in these tongues. This country was also the home of the Kaikēyā Paiśācikī of Mārkaṇḍēya, with which the Dardic languages closely agree[1].

Even the Paiśācī Prakrit of Hēmacandra (spoken apparently in Central India) shows a weak sense of the difference between dental and cerebral *t* (Hc. 4. 311), and this is much more prominent in the Dardic languages. In Šiṇā, the language of Gilgit, the pronunciation of dentals and cerebrals fluctuates, and my latest authority, a skilled phonetician, who is stationed in the country, informs me that the usual pronunciation of

[1] See *ZDMG* 66. 77 ff. for resemblances between them and Hēmacandra's Paiśācī.

both approaches that of the English alveolars. Even in so Sanskrit-ridden a language as literary Kāshmīrī, there are many instances of the interchange of cerebrals and dentals. As an extreme example, — in poetry *Yindrazīth* (= *Indrajit*) rhymes with *dīṭhü* (= *dṛṣṭā*).

Coming now to Dr. Michelson's *uthānaṃ*, it may be noted that relations of this word are common in Dardic, and that they nearly all agree with Mārkaṇḍēya's Śaurasēnī in preserving the dental *th*. Maiyā̃ has √*uth*-, Kāshmīrī has √*wŏth*-, and Bašgalī Kāfir has √*ut*- or √*ušt*-. So, in the related Sindhī we have √*uth*-, and in Lahndā the word *uthā̃*, up, above. Horn (*Grundriss der neupersischen Etymologie*, § 84) refers the Balōcī √*vušt*- to *ava* + √*stā*-, but it is equally possible that it as well as the above forms come from *ut* + √*sthā*-, like the Śaurasēnī *utthidō*.

I would therefore suggest that the Shāhbāzgaṛhī *uthānaṃ* is to be referred to the ancestor of Dardic, rather than to Śaurasēnī influence.

On page 462 of the same number of the *JAOS* Dr. Michelson refers to Mārkaṇḍēya's rule that in Śaurasēnī, the locative singular of *a*-bases ends only in *ē*, while in the case of *i*- and *u*-bases it ends in *mmi*. For the latter he offers three possible explanations (himself preferring the first), viz. (1) that Mahārāṣṭrī has influenced Śaurasēnī, (2) that Mārkaṇḍēya has made a mistake, and (3) that the manuscripts of his grammar need correction.

Regarding the third suggested explanation, I may state that I have five MSS. of the grammar, and that on this point they all agree with the printed text. Regarding the second suggestion, as Mārkaṇḍēya is entirely borne out by Rāma-śarman (Tarkavāgīśa) in the chapter referring to Śaurasēnī in the *Prākṛta-kalpataru*, (II, x, 14, *ēd ēva ṅēḥ syād, id-ud-antayŏr mmiḥ*), it appears that, at least according to the eastern school of Prakrit grammarians, he has made no mistake, and that Dr. Michelson's preference for his first explanation is amply justified.

George A. Grierson

Camberley, England

NOTES OF THE SOCIETY

The Executive Committee, at a meeting held in New York on June 2, 1922, voted "that Professors Hopkins and Torrey, and the Editors of the Journal, be appointed to act as a provisional committee to supervise the publication of Dr. Blake's Tagalog Grammar and Professor Edgerton's Pañcatantra Reconstructed and to make all contracts requisite for that purpose".

By unanimous vote the Executive Committee has, since the recent meeting of the Society in Chicago, elected the following persons to membership in the Society:

Prof. A. E. Bigelow,
Mr. Dhan Gopal Mukherji,
Rev. Dr. Z. T. Phillips,
Dr. Najeeb M. Saleeby,
Mr. Samuel Seligman.

The names of the new members elected at Chicago will be printed in the Proceedings of the meeting, which will be published in the next number of the JOURNAL.

NOTES OF OTHER SOCIETIES, ETC.

At the meeting of the American Historical Association held in St. Louis in December, 1921, a luncheon conference on the Far East was held, at which Prof. K. S. Latourette presided, and at which papers were presented by Mr. Langdon Warner, of the Philadelphia Museum, on Prince Shotoku of Japan, and by Prof. M. I. Rostovzeff, of the University of Wisconsin, on relations between prehistoric culture in Southern Russia and China as indicated by ornamentation on pottery. The section on Ancient History held a session on the Roman Empire, at which Prof. A. T. Olmstead spoke on the importance of oriental elements in the empire's history and culture. The section on the History of Culture was presided over by Prof. J. H. Breasted of the University of Chicago, who spoke on the oriental basis of all culture and on problems of the future. At a luncheon conference on the History of Science Prof. Breasted spoke on the scientific advancement made by the Egyptians, and Prof. C. H. Haskins of Harvard University spoke on the relations between eastern and western scientific knowledge in the Middle Ages.

The Gypsy Lore Society is resuming its activities, interrupted since 1914, by publishing the first quarterly number of Volume 1 of the Third Series of its Journal. Those who are interested in the work of the Society may apply for further information to the Honorary Secretary, Mr. T. W. Thompson, M. A., Repton, Derby, England. The Editor of the Journal is Mr. E. O. Winstedt, M. A., of 181 Iffley Road, Oxford.

PERSONALIA

A cablegram received on June 18 from Jerusalem announces the death of Rev. Dr. James B. Nies, a former president of the American Oriental Society, and for many years one of its most valued members.

Professor George A. Barton has been appointed to fill the position at the University of Pennsylvania left vacant by the death of Professor Morris Jastrow Jr.

SPECIAL NOTICE

To authors and publishers of books on oriental subjects

The Directors of the American Oriental Society have instructed the editors to enlarge the Journal and to devote approximately one-fourth of its space to reviews of important works on oriental subjects. It is intended to begin publication of such reviews with the next volume, to appear in the year 1923. The editors will be glad to receive for review copies of new publications within the fields which the Journal covers. They reserve the right to decide in the case of each book whether a review of it would be suitable for the Journal. All books for review should be sent to one of the editors (Max L. Margolis, 152 West Hortter Street, Philadelphia, Pa., or Franklin Edgerton, 107 Bryn Mawr Avenue, Lansdowne, Pa.), and should be accompanied by a statement to the effect that they are intended for review in the Journal. It is requested that books on Indo-Iranian and other Indo-European subjects be addrest to Mr. Edgerton, and those on Semitic and allied fields to Mr. Margolis.

215

A COMPARATIVE TRANSLATION OF THE ARABIC KALĪLA WA-DIMNA, CHAPTER VI

W. Norman Brown

Johns Hopkins University

Studies in the Pañcatantra or its 'Western' representative, the Kalīla wa Dimna, suffer greatly from the lack of a definitive text of the Arabic version, and, of course, still more from the total loss of the Pehlevi from which the Arabic is translated. The existing editions of the Arabic are wholly unsatisfactory and should be replaced by a text which aims to give at least the sense of Ibn al-Moqaffa''s version.[1] Such a text would have to be prepared after an examination not only of the known Arabic Mss. but also of the many offshoots of the Arabic, that is, the translations into Hebrew, Syriac, Spanish, Persian, Greek, and other languages. At times it would be necessary to make comparisons with the Old Syriac translation from the lost Pehlevi and with the Sanskrit versions, which latter will soon be most happily accessible in Professor Edgerton's reconstruction of the original Sanskrit Pañcatantra.[2]

It is the lack of some such text that has led me to prepare this paper. When Professor Edgerton first undertook his reconstruction, he began with Book II of the Pañcatantra, and at the time I entered upon the work with him. To render

[1] The difficulties in the way of such a text are enormous (see Nöldeke in *ZDMG* 59. 794—806 or in the Introduction to his *Burzoës Einleitung*), but I understand that Professor Sprengling is hard at work on the proposition; it is to be hoped that he will not find the difficulties insuperable. For a discussion of the literary history of the Kalīla wa-Dimna, see Hertel, *Das Pañcatantra* p. 362 ff., and Chauvin, *Bibliographie des ouvrages arabes*, vol. 2.

[2] This work, announced in *JAOS* 38. 273, is now ready for the press. For an estimate of the relative value of the Sanskrit versions, see Edgerton in *AJP* 36. 44 ff. and 253 ff.

our work more effective I determined to make a translation of some such hypothetical Arabic text as that indicated above, and naturally attacked first that portion of the Arabic which corresponds to Book II of the Sanskrit, this portion being chapter 6 in Cheikho's text.

In dealing with my problem I began with the text of Cheikho, which is the best of the Arabic versions yet published, and this I translated to the best of my ability. I compared this translation with a translation of the text as edited by Khalīl al-Yazijī (Beirut, 1902) which the late Professor Jastrow was kind enough to read in an advanced class during the academic year of 1916—17. These I have further compared with de Sacy's text (Paris, 1816), which is frequently followed by Khalīl, and with various offshoots of the Arabic (see the list below). I have also availed myself of scattered and brief reports of other, unedited, mss. and of the translation of the Old Syriac. At times I have also given critical notes from the Sanskrit, altho in general I avoid this procedure, because the Sanskrit versions often differ widely and no one is to be trusted by itself unless it is given support by others.[3]

At this point I showed my ms. to Professor Jastrow who, altho he could give only a very few hours to the task, made a number of valuable suggestions. Later I showed it to Professor Sprengling of the University of Chicago, who has been studying the Kalīla wa-Dimna for several years, and he most generously went over the whole work minutely, adding a great many notes, some of which affected the translation and others the comparisons. These have been of inestimable value, and I have tried to acknowledge my indebtedness by making a free use of his initials ('M. S.') at those points where he has helped me.

The translation as it here appears aims to reproduce in English the sense of Ibn al-Moqaffa''s text, altho it is possible that I sometimes, tho not intentionally, come closer to the sense of the lost Pehlevi than of the original Arabic. To effect my purpose I have frequently added in square brackets words

---

[3] In the cases where I have quoted the Sanskrit I have done so only after feeling sure that the Sanskrit represents something appearing in the original Pañcatantra.

reproducing ideas which my comparative examination leads me to believe were present in the earliest Arabic but are missing in Cheikho. Similarly, I indicate in the notes those passages in which I think Cheikho's text is expanded. In all cases I quote my authorities.

For convenience I have divided the translation into numbered sections, which are followed in most cases by other numbers in parentheses, the latter referring to corresponding sections in the Sanskrit Reconstruction referred to above.

My translation does not aim to have literary grace, but I trust that my effort to 'be literal' has not been carried to a point where obscurity of meaning is the result.

Unfortunately I have no acquaintance with any Semitic language but Arabic; hence I have trusted to translations of Hebrew and Syriac.

The texts on which my comparisons are based are referred to by the following abbreviations:

Arabic texts

Ch P. L. Cheikho, *La version arabe de Kalilah et Dimnah d'après le plus ancien manuscript daté.* Beirut. 1905.

Kh Khalīl al-Yazijī, *Kitāb Kalīlah wa-Dimnah.* Beirut. 1902.

deS S. de Sacy, *Calila et Dimna ou Fables de Bidpai.* Paris. 1816.

Offshoots of the Arabic, sometimes spoken of herein as 'the versions'

J Hebrew of R. Joël. Text and translation by J. Derenbourg. *Bibliothèque de l'école des hautes études,* vol. 49.

JC John of Capua's Latin *Directorium Vitae Humanae.* Text with notes by J. Derenbourg. *Ibid.,* vol. 72. This is the translation of a text of J.

BdB Anthonius von Pforr's *Das Buch der Beispiele der alten Weisen.* This is the translation of a text of J. It is mostly quoted by M. S.

OSp Old Spanish. I have used the annotated text of J. A. Bolufer, *La antigua versión castellana del Calila y Dimna.* Madrid. 1915.

El Hebrew of Jacob ben Eleazar. Text by J. Derenbourg, *Bibliothèque de l'école des hautes études,* vol. 49. Quoted mostly by M. S.

NS New Syriac. Text by W. Wright, *The Book of Kalilah and Dimnah.* Oxford. 1884. Translation by I. G. N. Keith-Falconer, *Kalilah and Dimnah, or the Fables of Bidpai.* Cambridge. 1885.

Gk Στεφανίτης καὶ Ἰχνηλάτης in the version of Stark. Quoted only by M. S.

ASu Persian Anwar-i-Suhaili. Text by J. W. J. Ouseley. Hertford. 1851. I have used the translation by A. N. Wollaston, *Anwar-i-Suhaili, or Lights of Canopus.* 2d ed. London. 1904.

Syriac translation of the Pehlevi

OS The later edition of the text and translation by F. Schulthess, *Kalila und Dimna.* Berlin. 1911.

The Sanskrit versions of the Pañcatantra are referred to by full name without abbreviations.

CHAPTER OF THE CROW, THE RINGDOVE, THE MOUSE, THE TORTOISE, AND THE DEER

1. The king said to the wise man:[4] I have heard the fable of the two friends whom the false trickster separated [and the termination of his lawsuit afterwards].[5] Now give me a fable concerning sincere friends—how the beginning of their friendship came about, and how they profited, each of them from the other. The wise man said:

2 (vs. 1). The intelligent man[6] thinks nothing equal to sincere friends; for friends are of the greatest help in securing benefits and of the greatest consolation in misfortune. As an example there is the fable of the crow, the ringdove, the mouse, the tortoise, and the gazelle.

3 (2). The king said: How was that?

4 (3, 4, 5). The philosopher said: They say that there was

---

[4] Kh (deS), *Dabshalīm, the king, said to Baidapā, the philosopher*; OS, *Dbšrm sprach;* OSp and NS like Ch, but reading 'philosopher' instead of 'wise man'. (Guidi's ms. F=deS; Guidi's V and M=Ch; Gk like NS. M. S.)

[5] Supplied from Kh (deS), supported by J (JC) and OSp. ASu paraphrases. (NS, Gk, and El omit, with Ch. M. S.)

[6] Ch is mispunctuated: the point should follow العالم not العاقل.

in a certain land[7] a place full of game in which hunters used to hunt; and in this place there was a large tree with great[8] branches covered with leaves. In it was the nest of a crow.

5 (6). One day while the crow was on the tree, he saw a hunter approaching the tree, ugly in appearance and of evil state. On his shoulder he carried a net and in his hand a staff. The crow was frightened by him and said:

6 (7). Assuredly something, [either my destruction or the destruction of someone else,][9] has brought this man to this place, and I shall [remain until I][9] see what he is going to do.

7 (8). The hunter approached, spread his net and scattered [upon it][10] his[11] grain, and hid himself in a place nearby.

8 (9, 10). He waited only a short time until a dove which was called 'the ringdove' passed by him. She was the mistress of many doves, who were with her.[12] The ringdove perceived the grain, but did not perceive the net, and they fell into it [in order to pick up the grain, and they were caught in the net][13] together.

9 (11, 12). Then the hunter came near them quickly,[14] being glad over them; and every dove struggled frantically from her own direction, striving for herself.[15] And the ringdove said to them:

---

[7] The Arabic and its offshoots are hopelessly at sea in handling the place names which the Sanskrit had here. OS, however, is good, reading Dḫšnbt and Mhllḫb, which well represent such forms as dakṣiṇāpatha (the south-land) and Mahilāropya: the reading was, *in the south-land in the city of Mahilāropya.*

[8] Thus Ch and a Ms. in the British Museum against the field which says 'many'. M. S.

[9] Supplied from Kh; similar phraseology in Ms. in British Museum quoted in Ch's note, also in J (JC), OSp, NS, and OS.

[10] Supplied from deS etc., NS, ASu, El; OSp, J (JC), *there*; Gk, *under it.* M. S.

[11] Ch alone; deS and texts that follow him, *the grain;* all others *some grain.* M. S.

[12] DeS (Kh) with J and OS, *the mistress of the doves and many doves were with her.* M. S.

[13] Supplied from Kh, supported by J (JC); other texts briefer and more like Ch.

[14] Thus Ch, supported by OSp and J; deS, Kh, and Gk, *rejoicing.* M. S.

[15] DeS, Kh, etc., *began to struggle in her own snares and to seek deliverance for herself.* M. S.

10 (13, 14). Do not fight with each other[16] as you seek escape, and let not anyone of you be more anxious about her own life than about the life of her companion; but do you all assist each other so that we may perhaps lift up the net, and each of us shall be freed thru the others. They did this and carried off the net, and flew with it into the sky.[17]

11 (15, vs. 2). The hunter followed them,[18] for he thought that they would go a short distance when the net would become too heavy for them and they would fall.

12 (17). The crow said: I shall follow them that I may see what is the outcome of this affair of theirs with the hunter.

13 (16, 18). The ringdove turned around and saw the hunter following them with his hope of them not cut off, and she said to her companions: I see that the hunter is determined to pursue you, and if you keep right on over the fields you will not be concealed from him. But if you direct yourselves to gardens[19] and inhabited regions, it will not be long until your goal is hidden from him, and he will turn back, losing hope of you.[20]

14 (22, 23). And as for this (net) with which we are distressed—near the inhabited regions and the fertile land is a place in which I know is the hole of a mouse. He is a faithful friend to me; and, if we go to him, he will cut the net away from us and the injuries we suffer from it.[21]

---

[16] Keeping the text تجادلن which is supported by OS 'kämpfet nicht einzeln'. Ch's emendation تتخاذلن is suggested by the corruption تخاذلن found in deS and Kh.

[17] Kh, *They all acted together, and sprang up with a single spring, and all of them together carried off the net by their concerted action; and they arose with it into the sky.* Also OS, J (JC), OSp, and NS are fuller than Ch.

[18] Disregarding minor differences in this section, deS 'he did not give up hope' should be noted, borne out by all the versions. Only OS is here defective. M. S.

[19] Emending التخير to الحير.

[20] *And if you keep . . . hope of you*: in this passage Kh, the offshoots of the Arabic and OS use pronouns of the first person, not the second.

[21] OS, *so that we shall become free;* J and OSp, *and he will free us;* Kh omits.

15 (19). They directed themselves[22] as the ringdove had indicated, and became concealed from the hunter. And he turned back, having lost hope of them.

16 (17). But the crow did not turn back, for he desired to see whether they had a trick to employ for extrication from the net, that he might learn it and it might be a resource for him in case this thing should happen to him.[23]

17 (24). And when the ringdove reached [the hole of][24] the mouse with them, she commanded the doves to descend, and they descended,

18 (25). and found around the hole of the mouse a hundred entrances which he had prepared for dangers; for he was experienced and clever.

19 (27—29). The ringdove addressed him by name—now his name was Īzāk[25] —and the mouse answered her from his hole saying: Who are you? She said: I am your friend, the ringdove.

20 (30—32). He approached her quickly, but when he saw her in the net he said to her: How did you fall into this plight? For you are clever.[26] The ringdove said: Do you not know that—

21 (vs. 3). there is nothing good or bad that is not predestined for him upon whom it falls, both as regards its time and its duration?[27]

---

[22] Thus Ch and ASu; deS (with Kh etc), OSp, J (JC), and NS, *and they did.* M. S.

[23] It is curious that with all versions supporting Ch, OS—*the raven went with them to see the finish*—seems nearer deS (with Kh and Mosul ed., which draw upon deS). M. S.

[24] Inserted from J (JC), NS, and OSp (M. S. adds Gk and ASu). Also in OS.

[25] There are a number of variations of this name in the versions, but the significant ones are those of deS, NS, and ASu *(Zīrak)*, OSp *(Zira)*, OS *(Zir* for *Zirg)*. (There is hardly any doubt that *Zīrak* is the correct form. M. S.)

[26] Ch alone against all others, including OS, tho this is foolishly expanded. The phrase recurs in an expansion as stupid as OS here, Ch, p. 140, l. 7 (our section 192). ASu has a similar statement *after* the dove's first sentence about fate. M. S.

[27] Hardly more than a hackneyed phrase, 'in his day and time', in the use of which Ch stands alone, tho precisely here the addition of hackneyed phrases abounds in the versions. M. S. [It probably represents the Sanskrit original, *yāvac ca yadā ca*, etc. F. E.]

22 (vs. 4). And fate has brought me into this plight; for this it was which showed me the grain but blinded my sight in regard to the net until I was entangled in it, I and my companions.

23 (vs. 5). There is nothing strange in my case and my ineffectiveness in opposing fate; for not even he who is stronger and greater than I can oppose fate. Indeed, the sun and the moon are darkened when this is decreed for them.

24 (vs. 6). And indeed fish are caught in the watery deep[28] and birds are brought down from the air. The cause thru which the weak man obtains what he needs is the same as that which separates the clever man from his desire.

25 (34, 35). Then the mouse began to gnaw the meshes in which the ringdove was, but the ringdove said to him: Begin with the meshes of my companions, then come to my meshes.

26 (36, 37). She repeated the speech to him several times, but the mouse paid no regard to her speech. Then he said to her: You constantly repeat this remark to me, as tho you had no pity[29] for yourself. You have no regard for any duty toward it (i. e. your own person or life).[30]

27 (38). The ringdove said: Do not blame me for what I command you, for nothing impels me to this except (the fact) that I bear the burden of rulership over all these doves, and consequently have a duty toward them. And truly they have paid me my due by obedience and counsel; for thru their obedience and their help Allah saved us from the owner of the net.[31]

28 (39, 40). But I feared that, if you should begin by cutting my meshes, you would grow weary, and when you had completed that be negligent of doing this with the meshes of some that were left; but I knew that, if you should begin with them and I should be the last, you would not be content,

---

[28] Ch with OSp, J (JC), Gk, El, ASu, and OS. Guidi's Mss. V and M with NS, *water*. M. S.

[29] Kh, *need;* so also J. (Kh, with Mosul, 4th ed. adds, *nor solicitude;* deS with Ch. NS corresponds more to JC and BdB than to J. M. S.)

[30] The translation of this last sentence is by Dr. Sprengling.

[31] J (JC) and OSp, *hunter;* NS and ASu, *fowler.* (Gk, τῶν τοῦ θηρευτοῦ παγίδων; ASu, ed. Ousely ازدست صیاد; NS has the same word in Syriac letters, which may mean *hunter*, *fowler*, or *fisher*. M. S.)

even tho weariness and lassitude should seize you, to avoid the labor of cutting my meshes from me. The mouse said:

29 (vs. 7). This is one of the things that increase the affection and love of those who love you and feel affection for you.

30 (41, 42). Then the mouse began to gnaw the net (and continued) until he finished it. And the ringdove and her doves went away to their home, returning safely.

31 (43, 44). When the crow saw the deed of the mouse and the rescue of the doves by him, he desired the friendship of the mouse and he said:[32] I am without safety in a situation like that which befell the doves and I have need of the mouse and his love.

32 (45—47, 49). So he approached the mouse's hole. Then he called him by his name, and the mouse answered him: Who are you? He said: I am a crow; affairs have gone so and so with me. I saw your affair (with the doves) and your faithfulness to your beloved friends, and how Allah benefited the doves thru it, as I saw. I longed for your friendship, and I have come to you for this.

33 (51). The mouse said: There is no basis for union between me and you.

34 (vs. 8). For it behooves the wise man to seek only that which is possible, and to refrain from seeking that which may not be, lest he be considered a fool like a man who wishes to make ships run in[33] the land and wagons on[33] the water.

35 (vs. 9). How can there be a way to union between me and you? For I am only food and you the consumer.

36 (52). The crow said:

37 (vs. 10). Consider that my eating you, even tho you are food for me, would not satisfy me in any respect;[34] whereas your continued life and your affection would be more advan-

---

[32] OSp, J (JC), NS, ASu add, *within (to) himself*. M. S.

[33] Ch with NS, ASu, and Gk. Guidi's Mss V and M, OSp, J (JC, BdB) have the same preposition in both places and thus miss the distinction, a fine point of style such as Ibn al Moqaffa' was noted for. OS indeed supports the second group. M. S.

[34] The Arabic idiom corresponds exactly to English, 'is of those things which are of no use at all to me'. M. S.

tageous to me and more conducive to safety as long as I remain alive.

38 (53). You are acting unworthily in sending me away disappointed when I have come seeking your affection. For indeed the beauty of your character has become manifest to me, even tho you do not endeavor to make it manifest yourself.

39 (vs. 13). For the intelligent man—his superiority is not concealed, even tho he strives to conceal it. (It is) like musk which is hidden and sealed; but this does not prevent its odor from spreading.

40 (? 56). Do not disguise[35] your character from yourself[36] and do not deny me your love and your kindliness.

41 (59). The mouse said: The strongest enmity is that of nature, [nam odium accidentale cessat cum cessat accidens, odium vero substantiale non potest cessare,][37] which (enmity of nature) is of two sorts. The one is an enmity which is equal on both sides,[38] like the enmity of the elephant and the lion,

---

[35] The text reads تعيرنّ. I accept Cheikho's conjecture on p. 54, l. 19, of his **text** تغيّرنّ, which is supported in sense by J (JC) and OSp. (Cheikho's second conjecture يتغيّرنّ 'thy nature will certainly not change against thee' seems to correspond better to Hertel, Tantrākhyāyika, translation, p. 64, vs. 24. Cheikho's text seems to have in mind the well-known idiom غَيَّرَ عليه, short for عَيَّرَهُ على فِعْلِه 'he reproached him for his act', but leaves خلقك in the air. The parallelism of the western versions (J, OSp) is more perfect. It is not easy to decide: (1) is the good parallelism original and عليك a scribal error, ك attracted from خلقك, or (2) is the more crude, difficult Ch the original and the change to علّى of the Westerns (J, OSp) a piece of editorial finessing by a clever copyist? M. S.)

[36] J (etc.) and OSp, *against* or *toward me.* M. S.

[37] Supplied from J (JC, BdB), using text of JC, supported by ASu. Cf. Sanskrit in text of Bühler and Kielhorn (Textus Simplicior) II, p. 8, l. 10 ff, *dvividhaṁ vāiraṁ bhavati sahajaṁ kṛtrimaṁ ca . . . kāraṇena nirvṛttaṁ kṛtrimam, tat tadarhopakārakaraṇād gacchati, svābhāvikaṁ ca punaḥ katham api na gacchati,* 'Enmity is of two sorts, spontaneous and artificial. Artificial arises from a cause. Therefore it vanishes on the performance of a benefit that fits it (the cause); the innate (enmity), however, vanishes thru no means whatever.'

[38] Text reads متجاوزة (excessive); I read متجارية as in Cheikho's ms. B; see his note (also the reading of Djāhiẓ, Kitāb al Ḥaiawān. M. S.). The meaning is supported by Mosul, 4th ed. and Kh متكاف, and by OSp, *egual;* (add Gk, ἀντεριστική, and in general ASu and NS. M. S.). Cf. OS, *gegenseitige.*

for often the lion kills the elephant, and often the elephant kills the lion; and the other is an enmity in which the injury is from only one of the two upon the other, like the enmity which exists between me and the cat, and like the enmity between me and you.[39] For the enmity with me exists not in (consequence of) any injury that can come from me to you, but because of what can come from you to me. The natural enmity knows no peace that does not ultimately return to enmity. There is no peace to the enmity, neither by anything inherited nor by any interference from outside.[40]

42 (vs. 15). For water, even tho it is heated and its heating extends for a long time—this does not prevent it from quenching fire when it is poured upon it.

43 (vs. 17). But the man with an enmity[41] which he has tried to reconcile is like a man with a snake which he carries in his palm.[42]

44 (vs. 18). But the wise man never associates with a shrewd foe.

45 (60). The crow said: I have understood what you have said, and you are verifying the excellence of your character. And recognize the truth of my words and do not interpose a difficulty between our relationship by saying 'We have no way to union'.

46 For intelligent and noble men seek union and a way to it for every good purpose.[43]

47 (vs. 22). Friendship between the good is hard to break

---

[39] Djâhiẓ, Kitâb al Ḥaiawân omits, supported by Gk, and reads what follows in 3d pers. instead of 2d. This is supported also by ASu (which inserts 'between wolf and sheep' instead of the very obvious argumentum ad hominem insertion 'between thee and me'). M. S.

[40] 'Neither by . . . outside', translation by M. S. Other Arabic texts omit as do also OSp, NS, ASu, and OS. J says, *sur une paix, succédant à une telle haine, on ne pourrait s'appuyer, ni s'y fier*; JC, *nec est confidendum de pace inimici.*

[41] Kh and deS, *who has an enemy*, probably supported by J (JC), OSp, and OS. (J and OSp may translate Ch as well as deS; ASu directly supports Ch; OS corresponds to J and OSp, but not exactly to deS, renders the sense of, and probably the same Pehlevi as, Ch. M. S.)

[42] DeS, Kh, Cheikho's Ms. B, NS, *sleeve* or *garment*; OSp and OS, *bosom*; but J (JC), *hand*. Confusion between كَفّ and كُمّ.

[43] DeS, Kh, . . . *noble men seek no reward for a kindness.* M. S.

and easy to join: it may be likened unto a golden waterjar, which is hard to break, easy to repair and to restore if a break happens to it. But friendship between the wicked is easy to break, hard to repair, like a waterjar of pottery, which the least injury breaks; and then it can never be pieced together.

48 (vs. 21). The noble man feels love for the noble on meeting him only once or on an acquaintance of (but) a day. But the ignoble does not unite with anyone except on account of fear or greed.

49 (61). You are noble and I need your love; and I shall remain at your door without tasting food [or drinking][44] until you make friends with me.[45]

50 (62, 63). The mouse said: I accept your friendship, for never in any case have I withheld his necessity from one in need. I began with you as I did (merely) thru desire of justifying myself, so that, even tho you should be deceiving me, you should not be able to say, 'I found the mouse weak in good sense, easy to trick'.

51 (64, 65). Then he came out from his hole and stood at the door, and the crow said to him: What keeps you at the door of your hole, and what prevents you from coming out to me and joining me? Have you still doubt?

52 (66). The mouse said: The people of this world give each other two kinds of things and make alliances on the basis of them. They are the heart and property. Those who exchange hearts are true and loyal (friends); but those who exchange property are those who assist and benefit each other that each of them may enjoy the benefit (secured) from the other. Whoever does good merely to secure a return or to win some worldly profit—in what he gives and takes he is like the hunter when he casts grain (upon the ground) for the birds. He does not desire to benefit them thereby, but himself. But the exchange of the heart is superior to the gift of property.

---

[44] Supplied from J (JC) and OSp, supported by OS. (On the other hand NS, ASu, and El support the published Arabic texts, seeming to point to an Eastern as against a Western reading; it seems to me that 'water' could more easily have been added than omitted. ASu expands differently. M. S.)

[45] Kh adds, *and know that if I had wished to injure you, I should have done so while circling in the air above your head, at the time when you were cutting the meshes of the doves.*

53 (67). I feel confident in respect to you of your heart, and I present you with the same from me. It is no evil opinion that prevents me from coming out to you; but I realize that you have friends whose nature is like yours, but whose attitude toward me is not like your attitude toward me. I fear that some of them will see me with you and will destroy me. The crow said:

54 (vs. 24). It is one of the marks of a friend that he is a friend to his friend's friend and an enemy to his friend's enemy. I will have no companion or friend who does not love you. For it would be easy for me to cut off (from my friendship) anyone who is of this sort, just as the sower of sweet basil, when there sprouts among the basil any growth that will injure it and corrupt it, uproots it and uproots some of the basil with it.[46]

55 (68, ?vs. 25, 69, 72). Then the mouse came out to the crow, and they shook hands and made friends, and each enjoyed the company of his companion. They remained thus for some days,[47] or as long as Allah wished.

56 (73, 75). [Until when some days had passed for them][48] the crow said to the mouse: Your hole is near the road of men, and I fear that someone may throw (stones[49]) at me.

57 (76, 77). But I know a secluded place, and (there) I have a friend, a tortoise. (It is) well supplied with fish, and I can find there what (I need) to eat. I desire to go to her (the tortoise) and dwell with her in safety.[50]

58 (78, 79). The mouse said: May I not go with you? For

---

[46] For the translation of the last clause, which is a little obscure, I am indebted to Dr. Sprengling.

[47] At this point J (JC) and OSp add, *relating stories, fables, and histories.*

[48] Supplied from deS, Kh, supported by OSp and ASu; cf. J, *longtemps* (JC, *moram*).

[49] Guidi's Mss. V and M actually supply this word. M. S.

[50] As Dr. Sprengling remarks, Ch is corrupt and cannot be properly translated as it stands, while Guidi unfortunately does not quote the passage. The translation here printed is substantially a translation of deS and Kh, with the exception that 'I can find' is in those texts 'we . . .' As he also points out, 'to her' and 'with her' are supported by OSp and NS; Guidi's V and M say 'go there' but omit 'with her'.

I feel averse to this place of mine. The crow said: Why do you feel averse to your place?

59 (80). The mouse said: I have tales and stories (concerning that[51]) which I shall tell you when we arrive at the place we have in mind.

60 (81). The crow seized the tail of the mouse and flew with him until he arrived at the place he had in mind.

61 (82). When he drew near the place[52] in which the tortoise was and the tortoise saw the crow and a mouse with him, she was frightened at him, for she did not know that it was her friend, and she dived into the water.

62 (83, 84). The crow set down the mouse, alighted on a tree,[53] and called the tortoise by name.

63 (85, 86). She recognized his voice, came out to him and welcomed him, and asked him whence he came.

64 (88). The crow told her his story from the time when he had followed the doves, (including) what had happened thereafter between him and the mouse until they had come to her.

65 (89). When the tortoise heard of the mouse's deed, she was astonished at his intelligence and faithfulness, and she welcomed him, saying: What drove you to this land?

66 (90). The crow said to the mouse: Where are the tales and stories which you said you would tell me? Tell them now that the tortoise asks you for them. For the tortoise in her relation to you is in the same position as I. The mouse began his story and said:

Story 1: Mouse and Two Monks

67 (91). The first place where I dwelt was in a certain city[54] in the house of an ascetic. The ascetic had no family.

---

[51] The words for this phrase appear in Guidi's Ms. V. M. S.

[52] DeS, Kh, OS, OSp, J (add Gk and El, M. S.), *spring*, NS *fen* (*peṣîda* in Syriac means "fountain or spring", M. S.); ASu, *fountain*.

[53] Ms Jos. Derenbourg (see his JC, p. 144, note 1), *Thereupon the crow descended to the earth, deposited the mouse from his mouth, flew up to his nest* (sic! *covert?*) *in the top of the tree.* OSp, J (etc.), Gk, ASu, and OS support Ms. Derenbourg to the extent of adding here, *on the earth* (or, *ground*); NS, *at the water's edge;* El, *mercifully* (i. e. softly), בחמלה, perhaps to be emended to במחלה, 'in a hollow'. M. S.

[54] Of the various names in the Mss. OS is best: Mhllụb, for Sanskrit Mahilāropya̧.

68 (92). Every day there was brought to him a basket of food, of which he ate as much as he needed. Then he put the rest of the food in it and hung it up in his house.

69 (93). I used to watch the ascetic until he went out. When he went out I would jump up into the basket; and I would leave no food in the basket, but I would eat it and throw it to the (other) mice.[55]

70 (94). The ascetic continually tried to hang up this basket in such a way[56] that I could not reach it, but he never succeeded in this.

71 (95). One night a guest came to the ascetic.

72 (96, 97). They ate the evening meal together, until when they engaged in conversation,[57] the ascetic said to the guest: From what land are you, and what place is your present destination?

73 (98). Now the guest was a man who had traveled the world and seen strange sights, and he began to tell the ascetic in what lands he had set foot and what things he had seen.

74 (99, 100). In the midst of this the ascetic clapped his hands from time to time to frighten away the mice.[58] The guest became angry and said:

75 (101). I am telling you my adventures,[59] but you clap your hands as tho ridiculing my account. What made you ask me?

76 (102, 103). The ascetic apologized to the guest and said: I have been paying attention to your account, but I clapped my hands to frighten away the mice,[60] for they annoy me.

---

[55] J (JC, BdB), NS, Eleazar add, *which were in the house;* OS, *which were with me.* The word 'other' appears in all the versions (except El) and OS. DeS Ms. 1489, *my companions among the mice;* ms. 1502, *his companions.* M. S.

[56] DeS, Kh, *in a place I could not reach;* similarly OSp, J (JC).

[57] The text in Ch needs a slight correction, see Cheikho's note on p. 54 of his edition.

[58] DeS, Kh, *to frighten me away from the basket;* so also OSp, and similarly J (JC); NS, *to scare the mice lest they come near the basket;* ASu similar to Ch and NS. (Gk, ἐμὲ δεδιττόμενος; Schulthess, note 226 to OS, quotes from Puntoni's ed: ἡμᾶς, var. ἐμὲ ἐκφοβίζων. M. S.)

[59] NS, *you have asked me to tell you my history, and now that I begin to tell it . . .* Cf. OS, *Da erzähle ich dir, was du mich gefragt hast.*

[60] DeS (Kh), Gk, NS, El, and OS, *a mouse.* M. S.

I cannot put food (anywhere) in the house that they do not eat it.

77 (104). The guest said: Is it a single mouse or many?

78 (105). The ascetic said: Truly, the mice [of the house][61] are many, but it is a single mouse among them that outwits me, and I cannot circumvent him with any device.

79 (106). The guest said: This is not without a reason.[62] Verily you bring to my mind the remark the man made to his wife.

80 (vs. 27). There is surely a reason why this woman sells (exchanges) husked sesame for unhusked.

81 (107). The ascetic said: How was that? (*Fable.*)[63] The guest said:

Story 2: Husked for Unhusked Sesame

82 (108). I once stayed with a man in such and such a city. We ate the evening meal together.

83 (109). Then he spread a carpet for me, and the man retired to his own carpet and to his wife. Between me and them was a lattice of reeds, and once during the night[64] I heard the man and his wife talking, and I listened to their conversation. Then the man said:

84 (110). I wish to invite a company to take a meal with us to-morrow.

85 (111). His wife said: How can you invite people to your table when there is no more (food) in your house[65] than is necessary for your family? For you are a man who never saves anything and lays it by for the future.

86 (112). The man said: Have no regret for what we have given away and eaten up!

87 (vs. 28). For saving and laying up--often the end of him who practises them is like the end of the wolf.

---

[61] Supplied from deS and Kh, supported by J (JC) and OSp; cf. OS, *hier sind viele Mäuse.* (Ch is supported by Gk and NS; El, *many mice frequent mouseholes;* ASu indecisive. M. S.)

[62] Emending Ch (امر) from ms. Jos. Derenbourg (JC, p. 145, note 7) to read لامر; supported by OSp, ASu, and (weakly) NS. M. S.

[63] Word inserted in text of Ch as the introduction to a new story.

[64] DeS, Kh, *toward the end of the night;* so also J; but JC, *circa mediam noctem* (add BdB, *nachtes.* M. S.).

[65] Emending يديك to بيتك; sense supported by J (JC), OSp, and ASu (also El, *in my house;* NS and OS indecisive. M. S.).

88 (113). The wife said: What was it that happened to the wolf?[66] *(Fable)*[63] The man said:

Story 3: Too Greedy Wolf (Sanskrit, *Jackal*)

89 (114). A[67] hunter went out one morning with his bow and arrows, desiring to hunt and to indulge in the chase.

90 (115). He had not gone far before he shot a gazelle and struck it down. He carried it off, returning homeward with it.

91 (116). A boar[68] met him on the way; and the boar came on against the man when he saw him.[69]

92 (117, 118). The man threw down the gazelle, took his bow, and shot the boar so that (the arrow) passed thru his middle.

93 (119). The boar [. . .][70] charged the man, and struck him a blow with his tusk that knocked the bow and arrows from his hand, [and ripped open his belly],[71] and they (both) fell down together dead.

94 (120—122). A hungry wolf came upon them, and when he saw the man, the gazelle, and the boar [dead][72] he felt assured within himself of an abundance of food, and said: It is fitting that I lay by what I can for the future.

95 (vs. 29, 123). For that man is without will-power who neglects to save and to lay by. I propose to save and heap

---

[66] Ch (and NS?) against the field. DeS (with Mosul, 4th ed. and Kh), *and how was that;* supported by OSp, J (JC, BdB), El, ASu, and OS. Gk omits; NS, *and what befell him.* M. S.

[67] DeS (with Mosul, 4th ed. and Kh), OSp, J (JC, BdB), Gk, NS, ASu add, *They say that* . . . With Ch only El and OS. M. S. (However, the Sanskrit agrees with Ch. W. N. B.)

[68] DeS, Kh, NS, and OS, *wild boar* (also J etc. M. S.).

[69] Ch's text seems corrupt here. It should read 'When the man saw him, he threw down . . .' This would make it conform to OS, JC, and the Sanskrit versions.

[70] Some phrase, just what is uncertain, is missing here. The versions J, JC, and ASu have phrases such as 'maddened by the pain of the wound' (JC) or 'tho mortally wounded' (ASu). (J, in spite of Derenbourg's translation, supports ASu. M. S.) The Sanskrit versions also vary in their phraseology.

[71] Supplied from J (JC), supported by Sanskrit. ASu says 'hunter's breast'.

[72] Supplied from J (JC), OSp (add Gk and El. M. S.), and ASu; supported by OS. (Slightly different phrase in NS. M. S.)

up what I have found, and content myself for to-day with this bow-string.[73]

96 (124). Then he approached the bow to eat its string.

97 (125). When he cut the string, the bow unbent and rebounded and struck the mortal spot in his neck,[74] and he died.

98 (126). I have told you this story merely that you may know that greed in saving [and laying by][75] is disastrous in the end.

99 (127). The woman said: What you have said is right. We have some rice and sesame which will be food (enough) for a company of six or seven.

100 (128). I shall prepare the food to-morrow, and do you invite whom you wish for dinner.[76]

101 (129). The woman arose at dawn, took the sesame, and husked it. Then she spread it out in the sun to dry, and said to her husband ['s boy]:[77] Drive away the birds and the dogs from this sesame.

102 (130). The woman went away on some business and work of her (own). The man[78] was negligent, and a dog came to the sesame and began to eat it.[79]

---

[73] DeS and Kh, *This man, the deer, and the boar—the eating of them will suffice me for a long while. But I shall begin with this bow string and eat it, for it will be nourishment for to-day;* (Kh only), *and I shall save the rest for to-morrow and the following (days)*. ASu similar, but fuller.

[74] Text very uncertain. OS and NS (JC?) make *the string* strike *him;* deS (Kh), supported by OSp, El, ASu, ms. Jos. Derenbourg say, *the end or point of the bow;* Gk, τὸ βέλος (bow?); BdB, 'der stral' of an 'armbrost' (crossbow). With Ch, J seems to name simply the bow. Ch and ms. Jos. Derenbourg, *vital part;* Ch and deS (Kh), J, *of the neck;* ms. Jos. Derenbourg, *vital part of the wolf;* Gk, ASu, *heart;* El, *gullet;* OSp, *head;* NS, according to Keith-Falconer, *testicles,* but very uncertain, may be neck or vital spot or vital spot of neck; OS *mouth.* M. S.

[75] Supplied from deS (Kh), supported by OSp, NS, and ASu.

[76] Note distinction between غدا ('to-morrow') and غداء ('dinner'). M. S.

[77] DeS and Kh, *boy* or *slave* (غلام); J and JC, *boy;* OSp, *esclavo pequeño;* but NS and ASu (add El. M. S.), *husband.* Note OS, *husband's pupil,* corresponding to Sanskrit *śiṣya,* pupil.

[78] DeS and Kh, correctly, *boy.* See preceding note.

[79] J (JC etc.), ms. Jos. Derenbourg (add El and a possible reading of deS and Kh. M. S.) add, *and staled upon it.* OSp supports this but omits the words 'to eat it' (so also Gk. M. S.). OS says merely, *frass davon,* as does Ch (also NS; ASu, *put his mouth in it.* DeS and Kh may also be read, *disturb it.* M. S.).

103 (131). The woman saw this, considered it (the sesame) defiled, and was loath that any of her guests should eat it.

104 (132). She took it to the market and exchanged it for unhusked sesame, measure for measure.

105 (133). This she did while I was in the market seeing what she did.

106 (134). I heard a man say: There is surely a reason why she gives this husked sesame for unhusked sesame.

107 (135). Just such is my opinion of this mouse, which you tell me jumps to the basket wherever you place it. There is surely a reason why he is able to do this, but not his companions.

108 (136). Get me an ax [that I may dig out his hole and investigate his circumstances to some extent. The ascetic borrowed an ax from one of his neighbors][80] and he brought it to the guest.

109 (138). At that time I was in a hole that was not mine, listening to their conversation.

110 (140). Now my hole was in a place in which were a thousand dinars—I do not know who put them (there). I used to spread them out and exult over them, and waxed strong thru their strength[81] whenever I thought of them.

111 (141). The guest dug out my hole until he reached the dinars. Then he took them and said to the ascetic: This it was that empowered that mouse to jump where he did.[82]

112 (vs. 30). For wealth brings increase of power and intelligence.

113 (150). And you will see that after to-day the mouse will never regain the power and daring for (accomplishing) that which used to be possible for him in times past.[83]

---

[80] Supplied from deS and Kh, supported in general by OSp, J, JC, NS, ASu, and OS.

[81] I am indebted to M. S. for this translation of بمكانيها.

[82] DeS and Kh, *This mouse has not been able to jump where he has been accustomed except thru the aid of these dinars.* So also OSp (add J etc. M. S.) OS similar both to these and to Ch.

[83] This section in deS and Kh, *You will see that hereafter he will not be able to spring up to the place to which he used to spring.* OSp, NS, and OS similarly. JC reads, *Nunc vero videbis ipsum nihil posse, nec habebit prerogativam ceteris muribus* (so also J). (Gk supports the general

114 (151). I heard the guest's remark and recognized [that it was true (and I felt)][84] in my soul despondency and a diminution of the pride in myself.

115 (142). I went from my hole to another hole.

116 (143, 144). And I realized[85] the degradation of my position among the mice and diminution of their respect for me. For they imposed upon me the task of jumping to the basket to which I had accustomed them.[86]

117 (149). [I tried this often, but][87] I was too weak for this.

118 (152). [The weakness of my state became apparent to the mice,][88] and they avoided me and began to say among themselves: The brother of luck has come to nought.[89] [Leave him and covet no more what he has to offer, for we see that][88] he is rapidly approaching a state in which he will have need that some of you feed him.

---

statement of Ch and has nothing else. OS has the specific 'springing' statement only, but adds comparison with other mice. J (with JC and BdB) have the general statement (like Ch) and the comparison. El and NS have the specific 'springing', the general statement, and the comparison. ASu is too freely translated to make sure. M. S.)

[84] Supplied from J (JC), OSp, and NS; OS similar. (Gk and ASu similar to Ch. M. S.)

[85] Text, اصبحت اعرف; translation that of M. S. This makes better sense in view of section 136, but the translation 'At dawn I realized' is perhaps supported by other texts; see the next note.

[86] DeS and Kh, *When it was the next day* (or *morning) the mice that were with me assembled* (J, JC, OSp, and NS, add *according to their custom) and said: Hunger has come upon us, and you are our hope* (J, JC, OSp, and NS add, *do what you are accustomed to do). And I went with the mice to the place from which I used to jump up to the bag.* OS is similar.

[87] Supplied from deS and Kh, supported by OSp; cf. J, *malgré mes efforts.* (J's translation is free. As literal as possible, JC, *nisus fui illuc ascenderc,* equivalent to NS, *strove with all my might.* Gk, *καὶ μέλλων τῇ ἑξῆς εἰσπηδῆσαι τῇ χύτρᾳ τῶν ἐδεσμάτων οὐκ ἐδυνήθην*; OS has not the 'many times' or 'several times'. M. S.)

[88] Two insertions from deS and Kh, supported by J (with JC and BdB); (add OSp, which is the nearest to the Arabic. M. S.)

[89] Ch literally, *The brother of the epoch* (age, lifetime) *has perished* (come to nought). I do not know this, nor can I find it, as an idiom, which it may well be. It might mean, *the lifelong friend, the peer of the age, the matchless one,* or, *the brother of luck* (Bolufer, *el hermano de la fortuna).* M. S.

119 (153). So they all repudiated me and attached themselves to my enemies and they began [to divulge][90] my faults and defects to everyone to whom they spoke of me.[91] I said to myself:

120 (vs. 31). I see no followers or brothers or family or friends or helpers except as an adjunct to wealth. I see nothing that makes virtue manifest except wealth, and there is no judgment or power except thru wealth.

121 (vs. 32). I have found that whoever is without wealth—when he strives for anything, poverty prevents him from (attaining) what he desires and hinders him from realizing his aim, just as the water of the rains of summer is cut off in the wadis. It cannot reach the sea or a river before the earth absorbs it, and has not[92] the capacity thru which to reach its goal.

122 (vs. 34). And I found that whoever has no friends has no family; whoever has no child has no memorial; whoever has no intelligence has nothing in this world or in the next world; and whoever has no wealth has nothing at all.[93]

---

[90] Supplied from Ms. Jos. Derenbourg. M. S.

[91] This section is mostly translated by M. S., who also notes that deS, Kh, OSp, and OS say, . . . *defects to my haters and enviers.*

[92] The word 'not' is not in the text but obviously belongs there.

[93] This rendition is from the version quoted by Ibn 'Abd Rabbihi I. 313 (see Cheikho's note). It comes nearer the Sanskrit original than does any other Arabic version. The Sanskrit (best in Pūrṇabhadra II, vs. 80) says: 'Empty is the house of him who has no son; empty is the heart of him who has no true friend. The directions (i. e. the world) are empty for the fool; everything is empty for the poor man.' Kh says, 'And I found that whoever has no friends has no family; whoever has no child has no memorial; whoever has no wealth has nothing in either this world or the next'. So OSp and, with some transpositions and corrections, OS. J says, 'Puis j'ai trouvé, que tous ceux qui sont sans fortune, n'ont pas de frères; qui n'a pas de frères est privé de famille; s'il n'a pas de famille, il n'a pas d'enfants; sans enfants, on ne perpétue pas sa mémoire; celui dont personne ne conserve la mémoire, est comme s'il n'avait pas d'intelligence; et sans intelligence, on n'a rien en ce monde, ni dans le monde à venir; on n'a ni passé ni avenir'. So also JC. Ch is badly garbled. (Ch, 'And I found some of the brethren, who had neither wealth, nor kinsfolk, nor offspring, nor memorial (or fame), and he who has no wealth, has no brains in the estimation of men (or, has no bloodwit or stronghold among men), and neither this world nor the next.' This is a very simple corruption, by the insertion of من لا مال,

123 (vs. 33). For a man—when need afflicts him, his friends desert him and he is despised among his relatives. Often he lacks the means of subsistence and (lacks) those things which he needs for himself and his family.

124. Until he seeks that which will make him despair of his religion, and he is lost; and then he loses this world and the next.

125 (155). [There is nothing worse than poverty.][96]

126 (vs. 37). [The tree growing in a salt marsh,[94] eaten from every side, is (in a state) better than[95] the state of the poor man who is in want of human possessions.][96]

127 (vs. 39). Poverty is the source of every trial, and brings unto him who suffers it the hatred of men. And besides he is robbed of intelligence and valor, and is deprived of wisdom and refinement, and is subject to suspicion.[97]

128 (vs. 40). [For he upon whom poverty descends has no means of escape from][98] loss of shame.[98a] Whoever loses his shame loses his joy;[99] and [whoever loses his joy][100] is hated;[101]

---

one misreading of ال for لا, and omission of one من, of the text of deS and Kh, with OSp; merely expanded in J, JC, and BdB; much abbreviated in Gk; changed partly from lack of understanding, partly for religious reasons in NS; and, I believe, it underlies the much expanded ASu also. M. S.)

[94] NS adds, *and the interior of which is consumed by rottenness, and its fruit more bitter than aloes of Socotra.* (Cf. Pūrṇabhadra II, vs. 84, where the tree is described as worm-eaten).

[95] Ibn 'Abd Rabbihi with J (etc.), OSp, and NS; deS and Kh read, *is like.*

[96] These two sections supplied from passage quoted by Ibn 'Abd Rabbihi I. 313 (see Cheikho's note); section 126 also appearing in deS and Kh. The two sections are supported by J, JC, OSp, and NS. J, with JC, has here an insertion which, as Derenbourg points out, is taken from Job 12 17, 19, 20.

[97] OSp also, *suspicion;* deS, Kh, and Ibn 'Abd Rabbihi, *a mine of slander.* The last mentioned adds, *is become the gathering place of evils;* cf. J, *entasse les adversités* (JC, *aggregat tribulationes*). (OSp, slightly transposed, also adds, *e es suma de todas tribulaciones.* M. S.)

[98] Supplied from Kh, supported by J, JC, OSp, and OS.

[98a] I have translated Kh here. Ch attaches this passage to section 127 and reads, *and is deprived of shame.* (Thus OSp which, repeating the statement about 'shame', inserts it the first time before the addition quoted in note 97. M. S.)

[99] OSp, *nobleza de coraçón.*

[100] Supplied from Kh.

[101] Kh, *hates himself.*

whoever is hated is ruined; whoever is ruined suffers sorrow; whoever suffers sorrow is deprived of his unterstanding and loses his prudence and his intellectual grasp. And whoever is stricken in his intelligence and his prudence and his intellectual grasp—the most of his speech is (operative) to his disadvantage, not to his advantage.[102]

129. I found that when a man becomes poor—whoever used to trust him suspects him, and whoever used to think well of him thinks ill of him. And if someone other than he does wrong, (people) think of him in connection with it (i. e. suspect him), and he becomes a repository for suspicion and ill repute.

130. There is no quality which is a virtue in a rich man that is not a fault in a poor man. For if he is brave, he is called rash; if he is generous, he is called a trouble-maker;[103] if he is forbearing, he is called weak; if he is sedate, he is called a dunce; if he is eloquent, he is called a babbler; if he is reserved, he is called stupid.

131 (vs. 42). Death is better than poverty, which drives him who is subject to it to begging—more especially begging from the stingy and niggardly.

132 (vs. 41). For the noble man, even tho he should be compelled to insert his hand into the mouth of a dragon and extract poison and then swallow it, this would needs be easier for him than to beg of the stingy and niggardly.

133 (vs. 44). It is said that he who is afflicted with a disease of the body that will not quit him, or with separation from his friends and brothers, or with exile (in a land) where he knows no place to rest by night or rest by day, and from which he has no hope of returning, or with poverty that compels him to beg—surely life for him is death, and death is relief.

---

[102] OSp very close; Kh secondary; JC, 'Et quicumque vulneratus est vulnere paupertatis impossibile est quod non tollatur sibi mansuetudo et acquiratur promptitudo, et quicumque caret mansuetudine operum. caret nobilitate, (add from J, *et quicumque operum caret nobilitate peccabit, et quicumque*) peccabit praecipitabitur, et quicumque praecipitabitur contristatur, et quicumque contristatur perdit intellectum et obliviscitur sue intelligentie.' (Gk in abbreviated form, as is NS; ASu, much changed and expanded, also supports this section. M. S.)

[103] DeS, Kh, J (JC), OSp (add ASu. M. S.), *spendthrift.* (Gk, *ἄσωτός τε καὶ εὐδάπανος.* Ibn 'Abd Rabbihi supports Ch. M. S.)

134 (156). Often a man has an aversion to begging and (yet) has need, which brings him to stealing and robbing; and stealing and robbing are worse than (the misfortune) that he was avoiding. For it is said:

135 (vs. 43). Dumbness is better than eloquence in lying; fraud is better than violence and injury;[104] and poverty is better than ease and affluence (obtained) from the riches of (other) men.

136 (158). Now I had seen the guest when he took out my dinars and divided them with the ascetic. The ascetic put his share in a wallet (of leather) and placed it at his head for the night. I desired to get some of the dinars and return them to my hole, for I hoped that thru this some of my strength would return to me and some of my friends would come back to me.

137 (159). I crept up while the ascetic was asleep until I was at his head.

138 (160). I found the guest awake with a stick by him, and he struck me a painful blow on the head with it.

139 (161). And I hurried back to my hole.

140 (162). When my pain had subsided, greed and cupidity again gained control of me and overcame my discretion, and I went out moved by a desire similar to my former desire, until I was near, while the guest was watching me. Then he brought down the stick upon my head again with a blow that drew blood from it; and I rolled over upon my back and my belly until I reached my hole. And there I fell down in a faint. And there befell me so great a pain on account of wealth that I cannot to this day (bear to) hear mention of wealth; for terror seizes me thereat.[105]

---

[104] This second contrast, not found in the other Arabic texts or the offshoots thereof, seems incorrect. OS says, *besser ein Kastrat als ein Ehebrecher*; cf. the Sanskrit (Southern Pañcatantra II, vs. 38; and Pūrṇabhadra II, vs. 90), where the verse is: 'Better silence than speech that is false; better impotence than intercourse with another's wife; better death than delight in slander; better food from begging than ease thru the enjoyment of others' riches.'

[105] The first part of this sentence is very clumsy in Ch; the translation is by M. S. (literally, *And there befell me of pain a pain such as befell on account of wealth*). M. S. also quotes the variant of deS and Kh, supported by OSp, J, and Gk, *And there befell me such pain as to render money hateful to me, so that I cannot hear it mentioned, but that at the mention of money fear and trembling pervade me.*

141 (163). Then I recovered consciousness, and I found that the troubles of this world—only greed and cupidity bring them upon the people who suffer them.

142 (vs. 45). The man of the world never ceases falling into troubles and difficulties, for greed and cupidity never cease frequenting him.

143 (vs. 48). I saw that the difference between generosity and niggardliness is great.

144 (vs. 49). For I have found that it is easier for the greedy to encounter terrors and to endure distant journeys in search of wealth than it is for the generous to extend his hand to grasp wealth.[106]

145 (vs. 47). I have never seen anything equal to contentment.[107]

146 (vs. 46, ? 164). I have heard that wise men have said, 'There is no wisdom like deliberation, no piety [like restraint from doing what is forbidden, no lineage][108] like beauty of character, and no wealth like contentment. It is fitting to endure that which there is no means of altering.'[109]

147 (vs. 50). For it has been said: 'The most excellent of good works is mercy; the summit of love is confidence; the

---

[106] DeS, 'I found that it was easier for me (Kh adds, *to encounter terrors and*) to endure distant journeys in search of wealth than to extend the hand to him who is generous in the matter of wealth (Kh adds, *how much more so to him who is stingy in the matter of it*)'. The difference between deS and Kh here was pointed out to me by M. S.

[107] JC (J similar): 'Inveni enim, quomodo qui contentus est sua porcione bonorum nec appetit ultra quam datum fuerit sibi, dives est, et illud ei valet plus quam omnes divitie.' (Guidi's mss. F and M add after 'contentment', *and I have found satisfaction and contentment both are the true riches.* M. S.)

[108] Supplied from Kh (add Guidi's mss. F and M. M. S.), supported by OSp. (J and El similar to Ch, in whose text the accidental omission is merely a bit clearer. M. S.)

[109] Is it pure accident that BdB, which almost certainly represents here a different Hebrew than that preserved in the printed text or in JC, seems nearer than all others to Hertel's Tantrākhyāyika, vs. 78 (p. 79 of translation)? BdB says, 'Und hört die wysen vier ding sprechen: es sy kein vernunfft besser dann des, der sein eigen sach wol betracht, und niemans edel bei gūt sitten, und kein besser rychtum, dann da man sich benügen lasst, und der sy wyss, der sich davon thū, das jm nit werden mag'. M. S.

summit of intelligence is discrimination between what may be and what may not be, and peace of mind and beauty [of character][110] and abstinence from that which there is no means of accomplishing.

148 (165a). And my state became such that I was content and satisfied,[111] and I removed from the house of the ascetic into the desert. The mouse, the friend of the crow, said to the tortoise:[112] I had a friend among the doves, whose friendship for me antedated the friendship of the crow.[113] Then the crow informed me of that (friendship) which existed between you and him, and told me that he desired to come to you; and I was eager to come to you with him.

149. For I hate solitude. For truly there is no earthly joy that compares with the companionship of friends, and no sorrow equal to separation from friends.

150 (vs. 51). I have made trial, and I know that it is not fitting for an intelligent man to seek from the world more than the daily bread with which he fends off want and distress from himself; and that which easily fends off these from him is merely food and shelter, so long as (sufficient) expanse of land (for living) is provided, and nobility of soul.[114]

151 (vs. 52). Even if the world and what is in it were given

---

[110] Supplied from extract 46 in Guidi, *Studii sul Testo Arabo del Libro Calila e Dimna*, pp. 50 and xxvii. On the translation I have been assisted by M. S.

[111] Guidi's mss. supported by OSp, 'My affairs advanced unto satisfaction with my condition and contentment with what was at hand.' M. S.

[112] *The mouse . . . tortoise:* unoriginal passage, found only in Ch. (In the middle of this paragraph, after the mouse has told of his friendship with the dove and the crow and just as he is about to tell how the crow led him to the tortoise, Kh inserts, *and he turned to the tortoise and said.* M. S.)

[113] DeS and Kh, *thru his friendship the friendship of the crow was procured for me.* So also in sense J (JC, BdB), OSp, NS, ASu, and OS. (Gk supports Ch, as El seems to. Ch seems to be a simple misreading سبق for سيق, in Arabic a difference of a single point. This caused the insertion of قبل, without which the sentence with سبق could not be read. M. S.)

[114] The clause 'so long . . . soul' is not found in OSp, J, El, and Gk, and differs widely in the texts of Ch, deS (with Kh), Mosul (4th ed.), and NS, while OS seems not to have it. It appears to be most dubious, perhaps only a petty gloss varied according to pious fancy. M. S.

to a man, he could never profit by any of it except that little with which he could fend off want from himself. As for what is in excess of that, it is in a place which he cannot attain (i. e. where it is of no service to him).

152 (165b). It is in this frame of mind that I have come here with the crow, for I am a brother to you; and of this sort let my place also be in your heart.

153 (166). When the mouse finished his speech, the tortoise answered him in gentle, sweet words, saying: I have heard your speech; and, O what a delightful speech!—were it not that I see you do not take account of the rest of the things which are within you and of your exile among us.[115] It should not be thus.[116]

154 (vs. 54). Know that beauty of speech is not complete without [beauty of][117] deeds. The sick man who knows a remedy for his disease—if he does not treat himself with it, his knowledge is of no value to him, and he obtains no relief or ease.

155 (170). Make use of your knowledge and act according to your intelligence! Do not grieve over the paucity of your possessions!

156 (vs. 63). For the man of valor is honored (tho) without wealth, like a lion which is feared even when in repose; but the rich man who is without valor is despised even tho he has much wealth, like a dog, which is despised among men, even tho wearing a necklace and anklets [of gold.][118]

---

[115] Translation uncertain. M. S. suggests: 'You do not mention a remnant (a number) of matters, some of which were on your mind (or, in yourself) and nothing of your exile among us;' or, as a variant translation, reading لم as لِمَ: 'to what you mention there belong the rest of the things, of which and of your exile among us there was something on your mind'. My own idea is that the passage may mean: 'You look only on the dark side of your situation, and fail to be happy over the bright side, namely, your own good qualities and our good company'.

[116] Kh and Cheikho's Ms. C, *Drive this from your heart!*

[117] Supplied from deS and Kh, supported by J (JC), OSp, and NS. (Gk, El, and OS support Ch. M. S.)

[118] Supplied from Kh and Cheikho's Ms. B, supported by J (with JC). So in Sanskrit (Tantrākhyāyika II, vs. 99). (Gk also with Cheikho's Ms. B; but OSp, NS, and OS support Ch. M. S.)

157 (167, vs. 57). Be not distressed in your soul because of your exile!

158 (vs. 58). For the intelligent man is never in exile; for he never goes abroad but that he takes with him enough intelligence to suffice him,[119] like the lion which never wanders around without the strength with which he obtains his living wherever he turns his face.

159 (169). So turn your helpful suggestions to advantage for[120] yourself, since you deserve good. And if you do this, good will seek you out,

160 (vs. 59). just as water seeks the level, and water-birds the water.

161 (vs. 60). For distinction is obtained only by the perspicuous man, the resolute, who seeks (it).

162 (vs. 61). But as for the lazy, vacillating man, the irresolute, who trusts (to others)—distinction never befriends him, just as a young woman finds no profit in the company of an old man.[121]

163 (vs. 66). Let it not grieve you to say, 'I was wealthy and I have become needy.' For wealth and the rest of the goods of the world—their coming is quick when they come, and their departure is sudden when they depart, like a ball, which is swift in rising and quick in falling.

164 (vs. 67). It is said that there is no permanency or stability in certain things—in the shadow of the cloud, the friendship of the ignoble, the love of women, false praise, and great wealth.[122]

165 (vs. 70). Much wealth never brings elation to an intelligent man, nor does the scarcity of it dispirit him. But his wealth is his intelligence and those good deeds which he has previously performed; for he is assured that he will never

---

[119] In the translation of this part of section 158 I have received considerable help from M. S.

[120] DeS and Kh, *So take good care of* ... M. S.

[121] DeS with J (JC) says, *as to a young woman the company of a decrepit old man gives no pleasure.* Ch, apparently followed by OSp, misreads تطلب for تطيب. M. S.

[122] Gk reads *τὸ τοῦ νέου φρόνημα* instead of 'the shadow of the cloud'. ASu announces six things and inserts, as fourth, between 'love of women' and 'false praise', the word 'beauty'. M. S.

be despoiled of what he has done, nor will he ever be punished (in the next world) for anything he has not done.

166 (vs. 71). And it is fitting that he should not neglect the concerns of the other world, nor the making of provision for them. For death is always unexpected when it comes. There is no time that has been fixed upon between it and anyone.

167 (174). But you have no need of my admonitions, because you are well aware of what is good for you.[123] However, I thought to pay you your due of respect, for you are our brother and whatever we have is at your service.

168 (175). When the crow heard the tortoise's reply to the mouse, and her graciousness toward him, and the beauty of her speech to him—this pleased him, and delighted with it he said:

169 (176). You have pleased and gratified me, for you are justified in rejoicing over your heart just as I rejoice over it.[124]

170 (vs. 73). Now of the people of the world the chief in the matter of intensity of happiness and nobility of life and fairness of fame is he whose dwelling[125] does not cease to be well trodden on the part of his brothers and friends of good character, and with whom there never fails to be a throng of people whom he delights and who delight him, and whose necessities and concerns he supports (literally, he is behind).

171 (vs. 75). For when a noble man stumbles, he is not raised up by any but a noble man, just as when an elephant is mired, only elephants can extricate him.

172 (vs. 76). The intelligent man does not look at (take thought about) a kindness he performs, however great it may be. Even tho he risks his life or exposes it for (performing)

---

[123] Translation of the last clause by M. S.

[124] Translation of last clause partly by M. S.; cf. JC, *tu autem gaudere debes in animo tuo in eo quod deus perfecit te in omni bono.* So J; cf. OS, *aber auch du darfst dich füglich deiner Taten und deiner Rechtschaffenheit freuen.*

[125] Reading with Cheikho's Ms. B رحله instead of رجله ('his foot'). Cf. deS and Kh, *whose house never ceases to be inhabited by friends . . .*; OS is similar. J is like Ch: see JC, *pes non commoveatur a suis amicis.* (There is no doubt that J read رجل; he has it in the Hebrew; but he changed the verb to mûṭ 'slip' or 'stumble', and left out لا يزال; i. e., J simply misread, as did text of Ch, and then made the best he could out of a bad reading. M. S.)

some sort of kindness, he does not consider[126] this a fault. Rather he knows that he risks only the perishable for the eternal, and buys the great with the small.

173 (vs. 77). The most fortunate of men is he who most frequently causes to prosper (the suit) of one who seeks protection or begs.[127]

174 (vs. 74). But he who does not share his wealth is not considered rich.[128]

175 (177). While the crow was talking a gazelle approached them running.

176 (178). The crow was afraid of him, likewise the mouse and the tortoise.

177 (179—181). The tortoise jumped into the water; the mouse entered a hole; and the crow flew up and alighted upon a tree.

178 (182). The deer drew near the water and drank a little of it. Then he stood up in fear to look (around).

179 (183, 184). Then the crow hovered in the sky to see if he could observe anyone seeking the deer. He looked in every direction but saw nothing. Then he called to the tortoise to come out of the water, and said to the mouse: Come out, for there is nothing to fear here.

180 (185). The crow, the mouse, and the tortoise assembled at their place.

181 (186). On seeing the gazelle looking at the water and not drinking, the tortoise said to him: Drink if you are thirsty, and fear not; for there is nothing to frighten you.

182 (188). The gazelle drew near them, and the tortoise welcomed him and greeted him, and said to him: Whence have you come?

183 (189). He said: I have been[129] in these plains (literally, deserts) [a long time][130] and hunters (literally, mounted archers)

---

[126] Emending يرد to ير as in ms. Jos. Derenbourg.

[127] Translation of this section largely by M. S.

[128] Ms. Jos. Derenbourg, *And he is not accounted as living who is expelled from human society to solitude.* A similar clause is supported by J (JC, tho fragmentary) and ASu. OSp different, but still with a parallel clause. M. S.

[129] Kh and OSp, *have grazed.*

[130] Supplied from J (with JC, BdB), *longues années;* cf. OS, *schon lange Zeit.*

have never ceased pursuing me from place to place. To-day I saw an old man,[131] and I feared that he might be a hunter. So I came (here) in terror.

184 (190). The tortoise said: Fear not, for we have never seen any hunters here at all. We will grant you our love and our dwelling-place, and pasturage is near us.

185 (191). The gazelle desired their friendship and remained with them. They had a shelter of trees to which they used to come every day, and where they assembled and diverted themselves with stories and conversed.

186 (192). Now one day the crow, the mouse, and the tortoise were waiting at the shelter at their appointed time, but the gazelle was absent. They waited for him a while, [but he did not come].[132]

187 (193). When a long time had elapsed, they feared that harm had befallen him.

188 (194). They, [the mouse and the tortoise,][133] said to the crow: Fly up and see if you observe the gazelle in any of those (misfortunes) that distress us.

189 (195). The crow circled around and looked, and, behold, the gazelle was in a hunter's net.[134]

190 (198). He flew away swiftly to inform the mouse and the tortoise.

---

[131] Text شيخًا. DeS and Kh read شبحًا ('figure, phantom'); this is better; cf. OS, *etwas*. M. S.

[132] Supplied from deS and Kh, supported by J and OSp. (Add El. I am not sure that the fullest text, as represented by deS, OSp, and J, is the best. JC and BdB do not support J, but with NS come nearer to supporting Ch. El seems to omit in turn the initial phrase of 187. The two phrases, end of 186 and beginning of 187, really say the same thing in a slightly different way, and I am not at all sure that the fuller text is the better. M. S.)

[133] Supplied from deS and Kh, supported by J (JC) and OSp. (OS and ASu agree with Ch. NS, curiously, agrees with Tantrākhyāyika in having the tortoise alone make the request. M. S.)

[134] NS adds, 'And he descended to him, and said: Brother, who has caused you to fall into this net? The gazelle answered: Is it not the hour of death? But if you have some plan try it.' Curiously, NS is the only version of the K and D that in this place agrees with the Sanskrit texts (Sanskrit Reconstruction 196, 197). OSp and El have a lacuna here and put the speech of the mouse in Sanskrit 201 into the mouth of the crow, who in those versions, as in NS, flies down to the deer.

191 (199). The tortoise and the crow said to the mouse: This situation is hopeless except for you. Therefore help our brother!

192 (200—202). The mouse ran quickly until he reached the gazelle, and said: How did you fall into this misfortune? For you are one of the sharp-witted. The gazelle said:

193 (vs. 78). Is sharp wit of any avail against the predestined, the hidden,[135] which cannot be seen or avoided?

194 (223). And while they were (engaged) in conversation, the tortoise came to them.

195 (224, 225). The gazelle said to her: You have not done right in coming to us.[136]

196 (226, 227). For when the hunter comes and the mouse shall have finished cutting my bonds, I shall quickly outstrip him. The mouse has a roomy refuge among his holes,[137] and the crow can fly away. But you are slow and have no speed,[138] and I am fearful of the hunter on your account. The tortoise said:

197 (vs. 81). It is not considered living when one is separated from his friends.[139]

198 (vs. 83). For help toward the appeasing of cares and the consolation of the soul in misfortunes lies in the meeting

---

[135] Accepting Cheikho's emendation of المغيبة for المعيبة supported by OSp, *encubiertas.* JC says, *que desuper lata est* (J similar); NS, *which is from above.*

[136] Translation of final clause by M. S.

[137] Ch is inferior; deS and Kh, *the mouse has many holes;* J, *la souris trouvera assez de cachettes et de trous* (JC almost identical); OSp, *el mur a muechas cuevas que estan por aqui.*

[138] Text reads لا ستعابك. Cheikho suggests لا سَغَى لكِ which is the reading of deS and Kh and conforms in meaning with J and JC. Bolufer, editor of OSp, suggests the root عان which seems to be the source of the Spanish reading.

[139] J (literal translation by M. S.), *an intelligent (man) does not consider that he lives after the separation of the friends;* OSp, *he is not considered wise or living who separates himself from his friends;* OS, *Wer nicht mit seinen Freunden und Nächsten lebt und dennoch leben will, ist unvernünftig.* (This OS is gained only by emendation and appears to me uncertain, tho I have nothing better to offer — 'is without understanding' holds good; El, *a man is not accounted wise who is isolated by separating himself from his friends;* Gk, Ἀβίωτος ὁ μετὰ τὴν τῶν φίλων στέρησιν βίος. M. S.).

of a friend with a friend when each has revealed[140] to his companion his sorrow and his complaint.

199 (vs. 84). When separation occurs between a trusting friend and his confidant, he (the friend) is robbed of his heart and denied his happiness and deprived of his insight.

200 (228, 229). The tortoise had not yet finished her speech when the hunter came up, and at the same time as this the mouse finished (cutting) the snares. The gazelle escaped; the crow flew up; and the mouse entered the hole.[141]

201 (230, 231). When the hunter came to his snares and saw that they had been cut, he was astonished; and he began to look around him, but he saw nothing except the tortoise.[142]

202 (232). He took her and bound her with the cords.

203 (233). The gazelle, the crow, and the mouse assembled without delay, and they saw the hunter just as he was taking up the tortoise and binding her with the cords. At this their grief became oppressive, and the mouse said:

204 (vs. 85). It seems that we never pass the last stage of one misfortune without falling into another that is worse.

205 (vs. 86). He was right who said, 'A man does not cease walking firmly as long as he does not stumble; but if he stumbles once while walking on uneven ground, the stumbling continues with him, even tho he walks on even ground.'

206 (vs. 87, 234, ?235). Verily, the fate that was mine, which separated me from my family, my possessions, my home, and my country, was not to give me my fill until it should separate me from all that I was living with of the companionship of the tortoise,[143] the best of friends,

207 (vs. 88). whose love does not look for recompense nor seek a return, but whose love is a love of nobility and loyalty,

---

[140] Text اقضى. I accept Cheikho's emendation افضى which is the reading of ms. Jos. Derenbourg.

[141] DeS and Kh (M. S. adds ASu) add, *and only the tortoise remained;* JC similar. (But J, BdB, OSp, El, Gk, and OS like Ch. M. S.).

[142] DeS and Kh add, *crawling along;* cf. OS, *wie sie ihres Weges zog.*

[143] This translation is partly that of M. S. I emend من to ما as in de Sacy's ms. 1502 and ms. Jos. Derenbourg, which, as translated by M. S., say, *could not be satisfied until it should separate me from as much as I had of the friendship of the tortoise.* M. S. rejects this emendation, but emends صحبة to صحابة, and translates, ... *separate me from everyone with whom I lived of the companions of the tortoise.*

208 (vs. 89). a love that exceeds the affection of a parent for a child,

209 (vs. 90). a love which nothing brings to an end except death.

210 (vs. 92). Alas for this body, over which misfortune is the regent that never ceases to maintain sway and to cause change.

211 (vs. 93). Nothing is permanent for it (the body) or enduring with it, just as ascendancy is not permanent with stars in the ascendant, nor descendancy with (stars in) the descendant; but in their revolution the ascendant never fails to become the descendant, and the descendant the ascendant, and the rising the setting, and the setting the rising.

212 (vs. 94). This grief reminds me of my (former) griefs, like a wound that has healed upon which a blow falls; for (then) two pains come together upon him who has it—the pain of the blow and the pain of the breaking open[144] of the wound.[145]

213 (236). Just so is he who has assuaged his wounds in the company of his friends, and then has been bereft of them.

214 (237a). The crow and the gazelle said to the mouse: Our grief and your grief and your words,[146] tho eloquent, are of no avail whatever for the tortoise. Cease this, and concern yourself with finding (a means of) liberation for the tortoise. For it has been said:

215. 'Men of valor are known only in battle, [men of][147] probity in business, family and child in poverty, and friends in adversities.'

216 (237b). The mouse said: I consider it a good plan, that

---

[144] Text reads انهياص for which Cheikho proposes انهياض M. S. suggests with deS and Kh انتقاض 'which is said of wounds while انهياض is said only of bones.'

[145] J (JC), NS, and probably OSp (llaga) speak of an ulcer. In J etc. the ulcer is lanced by a surgeon and the patient suffers the double pain of the ulcer and the operation.

[146] DeS reads, ... *are one, but* ... This is probably correct; cf. OSp, *Nuestro dolor e el tuyo uno es, e maguer mucho se diga* ... M. S.

[147] Supplied on the basis of deS and Kh, supported by OSp, *lo fieles;* NS, *the upright man*; OS, *der Redliche* (emended from the Arabic, but emendation practically certain. J should be translated 'possessor of honesty', exactly equivalent to Arabic; ASu, *masters* (possessors) *of honesty;* El, *the trusted one;* Gk, ὁ δὲ πιστὸς. M. S.)

217 (238). you, o gazelle, shall run on until you are near the hunter's road, and shall lie down as tho wounded and dead.[148]

218 (239, 241a). And the crow shall alight upon you as tho he were about to eat you, the hunter following. Then be (keep) near him: And[149]

219 (240). I hope that if he observes you, he will put down the things he has with him — his bow and his arrows, and the tortoise[150] — and will hasten to you.

220 (242). When he draws near you, you must flee from him, limping, so that his lust for you will not be lessened. Offer him this opportunity several times, (remaining still) until he comes near you.[151] Then take him away thus as far as you can.[152]

221 (241b). I hope that the hunter will not return until I have finished cutting the cord with which the tortoise is bound, and we have left with the tortoise and reached our home.

222 (243). The gazelle and the crow did this, acting in concert and wearying[153] the hunter for a long while.[154] Then he turned back.

---

[148] Emending مثبت (disabled) to ميت, as suggested by Bolufer, supported by OSp. Other versions incomplete: deS and Kh, *as tho wounded*; NS, *as if you had received a severe wound*; J, *as tho near unto death*; JC, *quasi mortuum*. (Add BdB, *als ob er tod sy*; Gk, ὡς νεκρὸν; ASu, *as tho weary and wounded*; El omits. M. S.)

[149] Translation of last sentence by M. S. who remarks: Ch differs more or less from deS and Kh and the other versions, especially OSp, in which the mouse follows the hunter and it is the mouse, not the hunter, that observes in 219. In OS the mouse follows the hunter, but the hunter observes as in Ch.

[150] J (JC, BdB), *the net*; OSp, *the crossbow, the net and the tortoise*; OS, *the tortoise . . . with the bow and the net*. (Add Gk, *the bow and the quiver*; ASu, deS, and Kh, *the tortoise with the utensils*; NS, *the tortoise*. M. S.)

[151] DeS and Kh, *until he is far from us*. Offshoots of the Arabic omit or abbreviate.

[152] Translation of this sentence by M. S.

[153] Text اتعبا; perhaps better اتبع ('the hunter followed . . .'), as suggested by Bolufer. This is supported by Kh and OSp (add J, with JC and BdB, El, NS, and ASu. M. S.).

[154] DeS and Kh, 'The gazelle and the crow did what the mouse had told them, and the hunter came near them. The gazelle drew him on with pretended flight until he had led him far from the mouse and the tortoise.' J and JC similar but shorter.

223 (244). Meanwhile the mouse had cut the tortoise's cords, and they two saved themselves together.[155]

224 (246). When the hunter came, he found the cord cut; and he reflected on the matter of the gazelle that limped and the crow that seemed to be eating the gazelle and yet was not eating, and on the cutting of his snares[156] before this. He grew worried and said: This place is nothing else than a place of sorcerers or a place of jinns. Then he returned to the place from which he had come at first in search of something, without looking toward it.[157]

225 (247). The crow, the gazelle, the tortoise, and the mouse went away to their shelter safe and secure.[158]

226 (vs. 96). [If it happens that these creatures despite their smallness and weakness could effect their escape from the bonds of destruction time after time thru their love and loyalty and firmness of heart and the aid of one to the other; then men, who are endowed with understanding and intelligence and the instincts of good and evil and the gift of discrimination and knowledge, should much more readily unite and help one another.][159]

227 (Colophon). This is the illustration of the mutual aid of friends.

End of the Chapter of the Ringdove.

---

[155] DeS and Kh (connected with the preceding), 'while the mouse busied himself with cutting the thong until he had cut it and had escaped with the tortoise.' M. S. observes that the order of telling the events in Ch is perhaps nearer OS, while OSp also supports Ch.

[156] Text ولقربض الظبى. This is corrupt but perhaps represents a phrase meaning 'how the deer lay down.' However, I have substituted the reading of deS and Kh, وتقريض حبائله, which may be correct. Their sense is supported by OSp and J (JC, BdB).

[157] DeS and Kh, 'Then he returned to the place from which he had first come, not seeking (to take away) anything nor ever turning toward it.' OSp somewhat similar; JC, *et abiit in viam suam cum timore* (essentially like J and BdB). (El, *and he returned in fear and haste.* Ch must be emended from deS to be readable, by simply inserting لا before يلتمس and reading ولا for فلا. Then Ch means exactly the same thing as deS (Kh). Cf. Bolufer. M. S.).

[158] J (JC, BdB), OSp (M. S. adds NS, El, and the expanded ASu) insert here, *The king said to the philosopher.* The other versions, like the Sanskrit texts, omit this statement.

[159] This entire section, omitted in Ch, is supplied from deS and Kh. Parallels, less expanded, appear in other Arabic Mss. (see Cheikho's note) and in J (JC), OSp, NS, and OS.

THE MARATHA POET-SAINT DĀSOPANT DIGAMBAR

JUSTIN E. ABBOTT

SUMMIT, NEW JERSEY

Sources of information

TWENTY YEARS AGO Dāsopant Digambar was hardly more than a mere name in Western India. In 1902, however, that enthusiastic and devoted scholar, Vishvanāth Kashināth Rājwāḍe, in one of his journeys of research, discovered at Ambā Jogai (Mominabād) in the Haidarābād State, a branch of the descendants of Dāsopant, possessing many manuscripts of the voluminous works of this poet-saint, and in addition an account of his life, in manuscript, by an unknown author. Mr. Rājwāḍe published a short account of his discovery in the series known as Granthamālā.

In 1904, Mr. Vināyak Laxaman Bhāve, the well known scholar of Marathi literature (in 1919 the author of Mahārāshṭra Sārasvat, History of Marathi Literature) published in the series known as Mahārāshṭrakavi the Dāsopant Charitra (Life of Dāsopant) which had been discovered by Mr. Rājwāḍe. The manuscript of this work, and the only one known to exist, was given to Mr. Bhāve by one of Dāsopant's descendants at Ambā Jogai, Shridhar Avadhūta Deshpāṇḍe, the 12th in the line of discipleship-descent.

In 1905 Mr. V. L. Bhāve published in the Mahārāshṭrakavi two chapters of Dāsopant's great work, the Gītārṇava, a commentary on the Bhagavadgītā, the manuscript of which had been given him by Shridhar Avadhūta Deshpāṇḍe.

In 1912 Mr. Shankar Shri Kṛishṇa Dev, of Dhuliā, also an enthusiastic and devoted student of the Maratha Poet-Saints, published in the Journal of the Bhārat Itihās Saṅshodhak

Maṇḍal, Vol. 4, Part 1, page 10, a short note on Dāsopant and his Marathi and Sanskrit works.

In 1914 Mr. Dev published in the Proceedings of the Bhārat Itihās Saṅshodhak Maṇḍal the Grantharāj of Dāsopant. The preface contains such information regarding Dāsopant as Mr. Dev was able to collect.

In 1915 Mr. V. L. Bhāve published in the Journal of the Bhārat Itihās Saṅshodhak Maṇḍal, Vol. 12, page 106, a summary of Dāsopant's Santavijaya.[1]

In 1919 Mr. Bhāve published his History of Marathi Literature (Mahārāshṭra Sārasvat). See page 117 for his account of Dāsopant and his works. On page 145 a facsimile of what is believed to be Dāsopant's handwriting is given. Mr. Bhāve's chapter on Mahīpati and other historians (Mahīpati va itar Charitrakār), containing a reference to Dāsopant, is a reprint with slight changes of his article printed in the Journal of the Bhārat Itihās Saṅshodhak Maṇḍal, Vol. 12, page 108.

Early references to Dāsopant

Mahīpati (1715—1790) in his Bhaktavijaya, written in 1762, Chap. 57, 178, merely mentions his name in the list of Saints.

In the invocation to Bhaktalīlāmṛit (written in 1774), Chap. 1, Dāsopant is described as one who had received the blessing of atta *(Datta anugrahi).*

In Bhaktalīlāmṛit Chap. 22, 48 to 68, the meeting of Eknāth and Dāsopant in a forest is recorded. In chapter 22, 79 to 101, there is an account of a visit paid by Dāsopant to Eknāth at Paithan.

Moropant (1729—1794) in his Sanmaṇimālā, Jewel-necklace-of-Saints, says:

Dāsopantiṅ kelā Gītārṇava mānavā savā lākh
Grantha parama dustara to na tayachi jase na Vāsavālā kha.

Jayarāmasuta, a disciple of Rāmdās (1608—1681), mentions Dāsopant in his Santamālikā. See Kāvyetihāsasangraha, No. 24, Part 3, page 33.

Girdhar, a disciple of Rāmdās, in his Shri Samarthapratāpa 16, 34 mentions Gītārṇava as the work of Dāsopant.

---

[1] Mr. Bhāve thinks Mahīpati must have been acquainted with this work, see page 112.

The published works of Dāsopant

Grantharāj. This was printed in 1914 by Mr. S. S. Dev of Dhuliā from four MSS, two of which he obtained at Ambā Jogai, and two from Yekhehāl, found in the *Māth* of Atmārām, the author of Shri Dāsavishrāmadhāma. These MSS are designated by *Om, Shri, Ra,* and *Ma,* and their dates Mr. Dev gives as 1728, 1578, 1678, 1758 respectively. The Ms *Om* was used for printing, but the variations found in *Shri, Ra,* and *Ma* are indicated in foot notes. In printed form the Grantharāj covers 196 pages.[2]

The Grantharāj is a philosophical work in verse, consisting of eight chapters *(Prakaraṇ)* put in the form of a dialogue between *Guru* and Disciple. The Disciple asks questions regarding the true meaning of *Bandha* (Bondage of the Soul), *Moksha* (Deliverance) and *Jivanmukti* (Deliverance though still living). The answers of the *Guru* are in accord with the usual Vedantic formulae, and are corroborated by quotations from the Bṛihadāraṇyaka, Taittirīya and Chāndogya Upanishads.

Gītārṇava. The two first chapters of this work were published by Mr. V. L. Bhāve in 1905, in the Mahārāshṭrakavi series. The MS was given him by Shriḍhar Avadhūta Deshpāṇḍe of Ambā Jogai. The age of the MS is not indicated. The Gītārṇava is a commentary on the 18 chapters of the Bhagavadgītā. Every word of the original is commented upon, the whole making a voluminous work, said to consist of 125,000 verses. In the second chapter the author inserts at some length a story of human life and its sorrows, also an amusing story at considerable length, of a Brahman, who even under the greatest pressure refused to use Prākṛit for communication, employing only Sanskrit.

Dāsodigambarkṛit Santavijaya. Mr. Bhāve, in the Journal of the Bhārat Itihās Saṅshodhak Maṇḍal, 1915, vol. 12, page 106, gives a summary of the 34 chapters of the Santavijaya, with its long list of Maratha Saints, beginning with Dnyānadev.

List of published and unpublished Works

The following list of 52 works of Dāsopant in Marathi and Sanskrit is given by Mr. S. S. Dev. See preface to the Grantharāj, page 4.

[2] See Preface to Grantharāj, page 12.

Gītārṇava
Gītārthabodh
Avadhūtarāj
Grantharāj
Prabodhodaya Pūrvārdha
Prabodhodaya Uttarārdha
Sthūlagītā
Vākyavṛitti (in prose)
Panchīkaraṇ (written on cloth)
Padārṇava
Dattātreyamāhātmya
Gītābhāshya
Sārthagītā
Avadhūtagītā
Anugītā
Dattātreyasahasranāmastotra
Dattātreyadaśanāmastotra
Dattātreyadvādaśanāmastotra
Dattātreyashoḍaśanāmastotra
Dattātreyaśatanāmastotra
Siddhadattātreyāstotra
Shaḍguruyantra
Shoḍaśadalayantra
Atripanchakapradhānayantra
Śivastotra
Gurustotra
Shoḍaśastotra
Śītajvaranivāraṇastotra
Bhaktirājakavacha
Vajrapañjarakavacha
Sahasranāmaṭīkā
Dattātreyanāmāvali
Daśa, Dvādaśa, and Śata Nāmāvali
Mangalamūrtipūjā
Vāchakīpūjā
Mahāpūjā
Mānasikapūja
Vedoktapūjā
Vaidikapūjā
Yantrapūjā
Nāmāmṛitastotra
Gītāstotra
Prabandhastotra
Gītāprabandhastotra
Siddhamālāmantrastotra
Upakālastotra
Shoḍaśāvatārastotra
Shoḍaśāvatāraprādurbhāvastotra
Āgamanigama
Vedapādākhyastotra
Shoḍaśāvatāradhyānastotra
Daśopanishadbhāshya

Historical Notes

Dāsopant Digambar was born in A. D. 1551 and died in 1615.[3] He was thus the contemporary of the great Poet-Saint Eknāth (1548—1609) and tradition records their meeting together.[4] He lived during the reign of that tolerant Mohammedan Emperor Akbar, but under the immediate rule of the Mohammedan king at Bedar, Ali Barid Shah.[5] When Dāsopant died

[3] More exactly, in Indian chronology, he was born in Shaka 1473, Bhādrapada, Vadya 8 and died in Shaka 1537 Māgha, Vadya 6. This I give on the authority of Mr. Vishvanāth Kāshināth Rājwāḍe. See Granthamālā of 1902, also Mr. S. S. Dev in preface of Grantharāj page 2. Also Mr. V. L. Bhāve in Mahārāshṭra Sārasvat page 117. I am unaware of their authority, but presume the dates were obtained locally from Dāsopant's descendants at Ambā Jogai.

[4] Mahīpati in his Bhaktalīlāmṛit, Chap. 22, 48—68 and 81—101.

[5] The Barids were generals in the army of the Bāhmani kings at Bedar,

(1615), Tukārām at Dehu and Rāmdās at Jāmb were boys of seven years of age.

It is true of Dāsopant, as of the other Maratha Poet-Saints, that there is very little known of his life from a strictly historical point of view. The method that some of the biographers of the Maratha saints are adopting, of separating from the mass of tradition the miraculous, and calling that part legendary, and the balance historical, or probably historical, is misleading, and is to be rejected. With few exceptions, the plain fact is, that during the lifetime of these saints no eyewitness recorded the events of their lives. Stories were however handed down from generation to generation in the line of their family or discipleship. These traditions have in some instances been collected by some "lover of the Saints", and have been recorded, as in the case of Mahīpati in his Bhaktavijaya or Bhaktalīlāmṛit. These are not historical records in any sense. It is misleading to regard them as such. They may of course contain parts that are historical, but the only true course is to regard all as traditional, with the exception of what may in special instances be corroborated by outside evidence. I have therefore made two divisions—the historical, and the traditional.

The Historical Division

At Ambā Jogai, also known as Mominabād, in the Haidarābad State, there is the *Samādhi*, or tomb, of Dāsopant Digambar. There are also at the same place two families claiming descent from Dāsopant, the one called the major branch (*Thorleñ devghar*), the other the minor branch (*Dhākṭeñ devghar*). In the major branch the present representative in the line of discipleship is Shridhar Avadhūta Deshpāṇḍe. There is also a branch of the family at Bāvagi near Bedar, and still another at Chandrapūr near Nāgpūr.[6] All these branches are said to possess manuscript copies of Dāsopant's works.[7]

---

and in 1539 displaced the Bāhmani dynasty. Ali Barid Shah, under whom Dāsopant must have lived, died in 1582. See Kincaid's *History of the Maratha People*, The Bahmani Kingdom, pages 60 to 79 and 102.

[6] The family line is as follows: Digambar, Dāsopant, Dattājipant, Vishvabhār, Dāsobā, Dattāji, Devaji, Vishvāmbhar, Gurubovā, Avadhūta, Atrivarada, Vishvambhara. See Rājwāḍe in Granthamālā under Dāsopant, and Mahārāshṭra Sārasvat, page 119.

[7] Grantharāj, page 4 of preface. Also Mahārāshtrakavi, Part 2, page 39.

It is evident from the voluminous nature of Dāsopant's works, their contents, language, style, etc., that he was a man of learning and of piety, and given to untiring labor.

The question of his influence on his own and following times is not easy to answer. Copies of his works have been thus far found only with his descendants, and in the *Math* of Atmārām, the author of Shri Dāsavishrāmadhāma, at Yekhehal. His Gītārṇava was however known to Moropant (1729—1794), and Mahīpati (1715—1790) relates of Dāsopant's meeting Eknāth on two occasions. His works were probably known to Rāmdās. The evidence of this is twofold. (1) Girdhar, the disciple of Rāmdās, in his Samarthapratāpa,[8] conceives of a banquet given by Rāmdās to authors past and present, at which the viands were their respective literary works. Dāsopant is mentioned as guest, and the Gītārṇava as his special contribution to the banquet: *Dāso Digambara svayañpāki sovaḷe Gītārṇavarāśiṅ sampūrṇa jevile* (Shri Samarthapratāpa 16, 34). (2) There is a very noticeable similarity between some portions of Rāmdās' Dāsbodh and the Grantharāj and the Gītārṇava. Compare Rāmdās' picture of human life in Dāsbodh (Dashak 3, Samās 1—4) with Gītārṇava Chap. 2, 2115—2175, and Grantharāj Chap. 3, 55 and following

The Traditional Division

What is traditionally recorded of Dāsopant is found in the Dāsopantcharitra, the work of an unknown author, printed by Mr. V. L. Bhāve in the Mahārāshṭrakavi series. Mr. Bhāve states that he also came into possession of another Dāsopantcharitra, very modern and not thought worthy of printing.

Mahīpati in his Bhaktalīlāmṛit, Chap. 22, 48—68 and 79—101, relates the meeting of Eknāth with Dāsopant on two occasions.

Doubtless many local traditions regarding Dāsopant could be collected from his present descendants at Ambā Jogai and other places mentioned above.

The following is a translation of that portion of the Dāsopantcharitra that covers the eventful incident in Dāsopant's early life, when in his great distress God came in the form of

---

[8] Shri Samarthapratāpa by Girdhar, page 99; published by S. S. Dev at Dhuliā in the Rāmdās and Rāmdāsi series, 1912 (shaka 1834).

a humble servant to deliver him from the designs of the Mohammedan king. The remaining portion of the Dāsopantcharitra I shall give only in summary.

Shri Dāsopantcharitra

(1) Obeisance to Shri Gaṇesh! Obeisance to Shri Saraswatī! Obeisance to Shri Dattātreya, the First *Guru!* Om! Obeisance to Thee, O Digambar, the Good-Guru, Joy-Innate, Ocean-of-Happiness! Sun-that-drives-away-the-darkness-of-Ignorance, Gaṇesh-in-form! Obeisance to Thee! (2) One need merely call on Thee, Gaṇapati, and all the illusion of corporeal consciousness vanishes. Thou alone appearest in all existences, the Inner-Soul-of-all, Merciful One! (3) Victory, Victory to Thee, Primal Māyā, Mother-of-the-World! O Divine Moon in the forest of Joy! Thou who yearnest for thy worshipers! Thou-who-pervadest-the-Universe, Thou Joy-of-the-Universe! O Shāradā! (4) Now let me praise my caste Deity, who at the mere uttering of his name manifests himself in my lotus-heart, and shows his love without and within; (5) Whose praises Vyāsa and others sing, whom Brahma and the other Gods meditate upon, Mārtaṇḍa, my caste Deity. (6) When one meditates upon him in one's lotus-heart, its emotion is that of delight in his lotus-feet. And through it I shall certainly gain richness of expression. (7) Singing also with love the praises of my Mother and Father, who are in truth the abode of all the Deities, and receiving on my head their blessing, I have become the object of their love. (8) Now let me sing the praises of the good Saints who are the heavenly jewels in the ocean of Absence-of-Feeling. With their assurance of full success, the composing of this book will now proceed. (9) Dattātreya, the three-faced in form, the object of meditation for Brahma and the other gods, the inner sanctuary of the Upanishads, the inscrutable glory of the Vedas and other Scriptures, (10) He is my Good-Guru, His name is Shri Digambar, Giver-of-innate-Joy, the Inner-Soul-of-the-Animate-and-Inanimate, Lord-of-All. (11) Listen with joy to the story of his descent, that has taken place in varied forms from age to age, a story that is the happy quintessence of happiness. (12) He the Primal *Guru*, King of *Yoga*, the Original-Seed-of-the-Universe, descended voluntarily in the form of man to save the world. (13) Though

he truly appeared man, he was not man, but Lord-of-All. It is His story that I wish in substance to bring to my own mind. (14) But the inspiration of the mind, and the enlightenment of the intellect is truly the Good-Guru himself. Who can sing, and how can one sing His praises without His aid? (15) He entering into speech causes it to flow by His own power. Hence, kind listeners, give attention now with joyful heart.

(16) The Deshpāṇḍya of Nārāyaṇpeṭh, whose name was Digambarrāya, and whose wife's name was Pārvatī, stood first among those of good repute. (17) I know not how, in this or another life, they may have adored Shri Hari, but in their womb Avadhūta descended in the form of a son. (18) His name was Dāso Digambar, who truly was Lord also; from whose mouth there issued the voluminous "Commentary on the Gītā", consisting of 125,000 verses. (19) This Mahārāj Dāsopant, having the very form of Shri Datta, descended verily for the saving of the world into that household. (20) He whose face was full of smiles, long-eyed, straight-nosed, of fair complexion, his hands reaching to his knees, possessed of every noble quality, and beyond all comparison, descended into this world. (21) His Mother and Father, rich in their good fortune, joyfully spent their money and performed for him at the proper time the ceremonies of the sacred thread and of marriage. (22) Listen now with love to what happened to mother, father and son after the above events.

(23) Digambarrāya was the Deshasth of the five *Mahāls*, Nārāyaṇpeṭh and the other *peṭhs*. Being a very competent man he was the chief official of these *peṭhs*. (24) It was the rule that he should despatch the whole of the revenue of that district to the Government at Bedar. (25) It happened, however, in a year of failure of rain, that the Government money was not despatched, and he was called to Bedar. (26) The Bāhamani king had authority over the whole country, and lived at Bedar, hence Digambar was called there. (27) He was in default by 200,000 rupees. Now listen to the story in detail of what happened to him. (28) They thus questioned him: "As there is a debit balance against you of Government money, how can you expect to be released without making it good?" (29) He replied: "It is because of failure of rain that this balance of Government money stands against me. Have mercy

therefore. I ask your forgiveness. (30) If you give me your assurance, I will make the effort and raise the money." The king listened, and replied thus: (31) "I must have the money, if you are to be released. Obtain some security from the people here, or leave your son here, and go, and send back the money." (32) Listening to the demand of his Lord, the man thought to himself: "How can I leave my child here and go!" (33) When Digambar had been brought to Bedar, his son had come with him, the son who was an *Avatār*, Dāsopant Mahārāj. (34) As the king looked upon the boy he was greatly pleased with him, and said: "What a wonderful image God has made out of Beauty! (35) As I look at the child", he said to himself, "my craving is not satisfied by occasional glimpses. What a statue of Happiness! (36) If I had such a jewel in my house he would become the Lord of my realm. As I look over the whole animate and inanimate world I see no one equal to him. (37) Let all my wealth vanish, but this child I must have for my own." This idea came to his mind because he had no child of his own. (38) Still further he thought: "He looks like a Twice-born boy, but I see him stamped with a royal mark. (39) As I look at his moon-face, my *chakor*-eye gazes unsatisfied. If I can adopt him as my own son I shall place him on the royal throne." (40) Having determined on this plan he said to Digambar: "Leave your son here and go back to your home. (41) Make a promise of one month, and go from here quickly. As soon as I receive the money your son will be returned to you. (42) If however at the end of the month", the king continued, "the money does not arrive, your son will be initiated into my caste. Know this for a certainty." (43) In conformity with this, the king made him give a written agreement. The man, being helpless, gave such a writing. (44) Having given the document, Digambar left for his home, but with his heart full of anxiety. "Shall I ever see my son again?" he cried. (45) "How difficult of apprehension God is!" he thought. "How can I go and leave my son! He is not my son, but my very life. How can I leave him here?" (46) With mind full of anxiety, he thought however of Shri Avadhūta. Listen, O pious ones, to what he said to his son. (47) "O my son! my babe! How beautiful to me your body! To leave you but a moment seems to me like an age! (48) Burn, burn to ashes my life! Burn, burn to ashes my worldly affairs! You are my very life, how can I leave you and go!" (49) What did the noble son reply? "He, the King of the Yoga, dwelling in the heart, is concerned with his own honor. Why do you worry? (50) He is our caste Deity, He will preserve me. When He, the Soul-of-the-World, is with me, why fear? (51) At the mere thought of him worldly fears fly away. By the mere thought of him one is united with the Only-One. By the mere thought of him innate joy is aroused. What are these contemptible things of life to Him? (52) Do not hesitate, go home. He will provide the money, and we shall soon meet again." (53) The father listened to the words of his son, and immediately started. Keeping the image of Avadhūta in his heart, he arrived at his home. (54) Compassionate listeners, hearken with deep respect to what happened after he had returned to his home.

(55) Near Bedar was the shrine of Nṛisiṁha, called Nṛisiṁha Spring. The boy went there every day for his bath. (56) The King had granted him an allowance of a rupee a day, to meet the expense of his meals at this place, but what was food to him! (57) He would perform his bath, and give the rupee to the Brahmans, himself fasting, and meditating upon the image of Datta. (58) That meditation, which to him was drinking nectar, continuing every day, made the child appear glorious to all. (59) All the men and women of the place looked on the beautiful child with tender feelings, and made their many observations. (60) Some said: "He is possessed indeed with noble qualities." Others: "The Infatuation of the God-of-Love!" Still others: "Blessed is his mother, to have given birth to such a son!" (61) The Brahmans said: "He is not a mere child. His characteristics are not those of a mere child. He is a perpetual *Yogabhrashṭa.* We cannot understand him. (62) The money he receives for himself he gives to the Brahmans. We do not know whether he eats or remains fasting. (63) His father has gone and left him, but he is not troubled thereby. He is simply a mass of Glory! May Shri Hari protect him! (64) The Mohammedan King of this Province has no son, and desires to make him his son! But may the Husband of Umā, the Lord of Kailās, Shri Shankar, protect him from this." (65) Others remarked: "The Deity whom he worships will certainly protect him. Be assured that through

Him the boy will be freed." (66) Thus the various classes of people remarked to one another, but in the boy's heart there was not the least concern. (67) The King, however, was counting the days. "How many will complete the month? When shall I with joy place him on the throne?"

(68) Back in the home, however, the Mother and Father were in deep anxiety. Unable to raise the money by their efforts, they became much depressed. (69) Day by day rolled on, and the last day of the month arrived. The money had not come from the Father: but what did the child do? (70) He thought thus: "My birth took place with ease in the Brahman caste. I am, however, in supreme perplexity. (71) In the 8,400,000 births, attaining a human body is difficult, and attaining of birth in the Brahman caste still more difficult. (72) Now what is to be in reality my future condition? To whom shall I go for protection? Who will preserve my Brahmanhood? (73) The month is gradually coming to an end. Whence can the money be obtained? How can I be freed? Whom can I meet to deliver me?" (74) While he was thus anxious in mind the month came to its last day. At dawn the Mohammedan king said to the boy: (75) "I shall certainly wait until the evening. If the money comes by then, I shall truly send you back to your Father. (76) But if the money does not come to-day, I shall assuredly make you a Mohammedan." (77) As these words, like a lightning-bolt, fell on the boy's ears, they pierced through his heart. There was no deliverance now for him except through Datta. (78) His lotus-face wilted. Tears of pain flowed from his eyes. His heart was overcome with emotion. It was all incomprehensible. (79) He thought to himself: "Up to now I did have hope from my Father. Now I see no hope. I cannot discern the future. (80) I can see no one to ward off this calamity but the special Deity whom I worship, whom Brahma and other gods meditate upon." (81) With this feeling in his mind, he concentrated, and placed his meditation at the feet of Avadhūta, crying to Him for help. (82) "Victory, victory to Thee, Son-of-Atri, Home-of-Joy, Creator-of-Happiness, Thou whom multitudes worship. To whom can I now go for protection but to Thee, Shri King-of-Yoga? (83) Although Thou pervadest everything, Thou art without qualities, and unattached. Thy indivisible nature is

incomprehensible to Brahma and the other Gods. (84) Thy glory is incomprehensible. Wonderful are Thy acts, ever new! Thou All-witness, All-illuminate, Self-existent-in-form, Omnipresent! (85) Thou art Lord-of-All, therefore Thou art called Lord-of-the-World. One does not see at all in Thee the delusion of world-existence, so called. (86) Thou art Spotless, Changeless, taking form for the sake of Thy worshipers. Thou movest in the animate and inanimate world, O Thou-of-my-heart, Merciful-One! (87) There is no one as compassionate as Thou, no one so pitiful. Thou alone feelest for me tender compassion, O Thou Source-of-Soleness, Ocean-of-Pity! (88) Thou art the Non-Dual, Existence, Intelligence, Joy, Yearner-for-Thy-worshipers, Source-of-Innate-Joy! Thou claimest to be the Protector-of-Thy-worshipers, O Digambar! (89) If Thou art in truth the Protector of Thy worshipers, Thou wilt to-day prove it true. Thou art in truth one who yearns over the distressed, Giver-of-Joy, Inner-Soul, O Digambar! (90) My Father, from whose seed I was begotten, remains far away. Thou art the Father who art in my heart. Therefore I cry to Thee. (91) Thou art the Mother and Father of the Universe. Thou art He who cares for the Universe. Thou art the support of the Universe. The Pervader-of-the-Universe, O Soul-of-the-Universe, Lord-of-All! (92) This Tiger of a Mohammedan seeks to swallow me whole. But by the sword of Thy Mercy quickly kill him, and save me, O Merciful One! (93) This Ocean of a Mohammedan seeks to drown me, but Thou art my Saviour, O Holder-of-the-Helm! Deliver me, O compassionate One! (94) This Death-Serpent of a Mohammedan desires to bite me, and change me into one dead, but since Thou in Thy form of Pure-Intelligence art the Snake-Charmer, what fear have I? (95) This Hand-cuff of a Mohammedan with extreme haste seeks to manacle me, but Thou, Mighty Advocate, break the hand-cuff quickly, O Brother of the Distressed! (96) This Forest-fire of a Mohammedan seeks to force me into the fire, but Thou, Cloud of Compassion, rain and cool the fire, O Thou of Dark-form! (97) Who aside from Thee can protect me, a child? But Thou, O Protector-of-the-Distressed, run, run, O Shri Avadhūta! For what extremity art Thou waiting? (98) Whilst Thou art waiting for that extremity I shall certainly lose my life. So run, run quickly to my help and ward off the evil. (99) If a Mother should neglect her child, then who would care for it? Thou art truly my Mother dear, take me on Thy lap. (100) As the Sun goes to its setting tonight my Brahmanhood will suffer loss. This Thou knowest, O Thou who holdest the Rod, Ocean-of-Mercy, Compassionate One! (101) My pure pearl of Brahmanhood the King would sink in a Mohammedan hole. Protect me, O Preserver-of-the-Distressed, Punisher-of-the-Wicked! (102) Ward off, ward off this unbearable calamity, O! O! Digambara! Aside from Thee, O Digambara, I have no one!" (103) As he thus meditated in his heart, tears flowed from his eyes. His face turned to every quarter. He could not think what more to do.

(104) An hour only of the day now remained. The King could not contain himself for joy. He called the Mohammedan-ordained *Kājis*, and gave them his orders. (105) Calling together high and low, and many brahmans also, he put this question to them all. (106) "The father of the boy made an agreement of a month. The month is today completed. What shall we now do? (107) 'If I do not send the money within the month, you may make him a Mohammedan.' You know this is the agreement made by his father. (108) I am not responsible for the words of this agreement. You have of your own accord come together this night. Now what answer do you men and women, all here together, give to this?" (109) As they heard these harsh words, tears flowed from all eyes. All were choked with emotion, they could utter no words. (110) A great crowd of Brahmans was there, but no answer escaped their lips. With drooping faces they began to cry to God for His help. (111) "O God, Thou who hast a yearning for Thy worshipers! O God, Thou who carest for the Brahman caste, O God! Thou Great-Wave-of-Mercy, what a sight is this that Thou lookest upon! (112) This child is an ornament to the Brahman caste. This child is possessed of noble qualities. This child is the very life of our life. Protect him, protect him, Oh Compassionate-One!" (113) The child was now brought into the assembly. He was without bodily consciousness. The Soul that takes cognizance of the body had been summoned away in contemplation of the Only-One (114) His eyes remaining closed, he was imploring his Pro-

tector. This Protector was self-existent in his own heart. (115) He did not see men, but Janārdan in man. His feelings found their full joy in Janārdan, while in bodily unconsciousness. (116) Listen with joy to what the Good-Guru, Shri Digambar, the Protector-of-the-Distressed, now did.

(117) Becoming a *Mahār* (*paḍewār*), a staff in his hand, a blanket on his shoulder, and with cash and bills of exchange in hand, he suddenly appeared there in their midst. (118) He greeted them with "Salām! Salām!" Looking all around He saw extreme bewilderment. He was the Supreme Being in reality, but none of the dull of wit recognized him. (119) "Take, take these bills of exchange," cried, without doubt, the Protector-of-the-Distressed, but the cry was really this: "Preserve the Brahmanhood of the child." But no one recognized Him. (120) So again Shri Digambar exclaimed: "See here! I, a *Mahār*, have come here. Ask me why, Sirs, and I will tell you the reason." (121) An officer then said to him: "Well, where are you from? Who are you?" He replied: "I have come from Nārāyaṇpeṭh. See, I have come bringing these bills of exchange." (122) With these words in their ears the joy of all present was more than the heavens could contain. A flood of delight came flowing down the heart-streams of all. (123) Indeed what a flood of joy broke loose! What a rainfall of delight! What a well of happiness was discovered! It was joy everywhere. (124) As when a sinking ship reaches the shore; as when a dying man obtains the drink that gives immortality, there is joy, so all there present were filled with joy. (125) The total eclipse that the Moon-face of every one had suffered through sorrow, as Demon Ketu, now ended through their prayer to Avadhūta. (126) The assembly of Brahmans now exclaimed to the child: "Blessed, blessed is your fortune. He whose joy is non-duality, your Caste-Lord, being your helper, how can there be fear? (127) Now open your lotus-eyes. Your Father has sent the money. He (God) is before you in the form of a man." (128) The moment the boy heard this through the door of his ear, he opened his eyes and looked around, and there stood before him his Caste-Lord in human form. (129) Tears of love flowed from the boy's eyes. He fell prostrate in the presence of the assembly. His lips were unable to utter a word for joy. He began to

drown in the ocean of innate joy. (130) In describing that joy, the hungry are satisfied. How much more others! Who can fully describe that joy? (131) Just as the Moon, with its sixteen phases, arises on the night of full-moon, so now the Moon-face of the boy shone forth. (132) His lotus-face, that had been drooping in the night of sorrow, now filled out at the rising of the Sun Digambar. (133) The bees of Brahmans, taking their honey of happiness from his lotus-face, became Brahma-joy and sank in the ocean of Brahma-joy. (134) The King now questioned the man. "Hullo! Whence are you? Who are you? Who sent you?" (135) He replied: "I am the servant of Digambar. Regarding me as very faithful, he placed these bills of exchange in my hand and sent me here." (136) The King exclaimed: "You are a servant of how long standing? Tell me at once your name." 137) He replied: "My name is Dattāji. I am Digambar's servant from seven generations. You ask about my stipend? My food is all I ask of him. (138) He can never do without me a single moment. In waking hours, in deep sleep, or in dreams I am always at his side. (139) If he leaves me for a single moment it seems equal to an age. But because He has sent me here for this child I am here. (140) Here, see, are bills of exchange for the balance due you. These bills are absolutely good, payable at sight, and in cash. (141) If you do not trust these bills of exchange, I have the cash with me. I will pay you absolutely in full, receive it now." (142) Thus speaking he poured out a pile of money. All who saw it viewed it with wonder. (143) The man certainly stood there until the money had been counted. Was he man? He was Shri Avadhūta, My Lord, Shri Digambar. (144) Blessed are these fortunate people there assembled! Blessed the King of good repute! Blessed that Mahārāj Child, that *Avatār* into this world! (145) Men wear themselves out for him in Yoga, sacrifices, and the like; they spend a whole life going on pilgrimages to sacred waters. Very hard, very hard indeed for them! But can they get a revelation of Him like this? (146) Blessed is my Shri Digambar. Putting aside the Majesty of His Lordship, He took the form of a Mahār, and ran to the help of his worshipers. (147) He in whom there is no smallness or greatness, He whom the four Vedas have attempted in vain to describe, He whom the six shastras were unequal to, and the eighteen (Purāns) wholly fail in their attempt. (148) The majesty of whose Māyā is Creation and the other acts; even She cannot know his phases, such is He, King and Lord! (149) He to whom there is no coming or going, who fills the whole world to its absolute fulness, to call him a Mahār is strange indeed! (150) He is in Mahār and King alike. He fills all animate and inanimate things, but for his worshipers' sake he chooses from time to time to manifest such deeds. (151) Well, after the King had counted out the money he exclaimed: "Where is the Mahār? Give him a stamped receipt." (152) Who was the Mahār? Where was He? Where he manifested himself, there he vanished! But the King's heart was pierced at once. (153) He cried out: "Run, run, where is that Mahār? My eyes are bursting to see him again. He seems to me to be the light of the eye! (154) Let this heap of money burn to ashes! Burn to ashes! Because of it I failed to converse with him. I am a mass of sin, and yet he visited me. (155) Has he disappeared by casting a spell on this assembly? Where could he have gone, escaping the vision of all here? (156) I had intended to give him a rich gift that would overwhelm him, and to send back this child in his company. (157) Search! Search everywhere! Where, where has he gone? Bring him quickly before me! I am waiting for him." (158) His servants replied: "He was here a moment ago, but where he has now gone, escaping the vision of all, we do not know." (159) He whom Brahma and the other Gods are unable to see, how can he be found by human beings? He only can have a vision of him who is united at his Good-Guru's feet. (160) Still, because the King was good, and the people there also good, Shri Avadhūta had given a manifestation of himself in human form. (161) Blessed be that City of Vidur, called Bedar! Here for the help of his worshipers the Supreme manifested himself. (162) So also to help Dāmājipant the Yearner-for-his-worshipers, Shri Jagajjeṭṭhi joyfully and hastily ran from Paṇḍhari. (163) The King, in the midst of the Brahman assembly, gazing again and again at the child, exclaimed with joyful emotion: (164) "Blessed is His divine power! Blessed is this child! Blessed does his Caste appear! God has saved him from shame! (165) I must send this child back to his father. He is a mass of glory! I love him greatly." (166) The Brahmans from all sides now said to the King: "While meditating on God he used to fast. The money you allowed him he gave to the Brahmans. (167) That meditation was his food. By that meditation he has become free. By that meditation pity was aroused for him in your heart." (168) After listening to all the remarks, the King warmly embraced the child, and said: "I will richly clothe him and send him back." (169) He had a necklace made of the nine jewels brought, and bracelets and other ornaments, and many rich garments, and adorned the child. (170) He had a new comfortable litter brought, and in his joy said: "Be seated in it, in my presence." (171) With added pleasure he continued: "You are very dear to me. Leaving your Father at home, come every year to visit me." (172) Thus with hurried words, he gave joy to the lovely boy and sent him to his home.

(173) Now let us turn to what was happening there. Mother and Father were in distress night and day for their son, because they had not sent the money. (174) The Mother mourned: "Oh my little babe! My eyes are wasting away in not seeing you! When will they be filled with the sight of you? Will it be possible to see you again? (175) For twelve years I was not a moment without you. Who will now bring about a meeting with my child? To whom shall I go in supplication? (176) This separation has attacked my whole body. It is not separation, but wasting disease. What physician shall I supplicate? (177) This separation in the form of a horrible demon has completely possessed me. What exorciser shall I meet who will apply his supernatural powers to give me back my son? (178) For twelve years I nursed and cared for him! What a thing this King has done! How hard my fate to be separated from my babe! (179) How is it possible to have my son again! How is it possible to greet again that image of rest! Who will bring to my sight this very life of mine? (180) Let my life go, if need be, but let me meet again my Jewel-son." Thus speaking, her eyes were filled with tears, and she seemed about to die. (181) The women and men of the town and certain of her relations sought to comfort her in various ways, but she was unconsoled. (182) "I am a most unfortunate one! How can I expect to own so great a trea-

sure? Who has taken from me, a blind woman, my staff of a son? (183) What terrible sin have I committed? What failing has Hari-Hara seen in me? What have I failed in the recitation of their deeds, that I should receive this? (184) Or, have I insulted *Sādhus* or Saints? Or have I brought discord in the relationships of brotherhood or sonship, that I should have to suffer this sorrow?" (185) While she was thus bitterly mourning and loudly wailing, some people brought the welcome news: "Your son has come. (186) He is seated in a litter," they said. "He is accompanied by a large crowd. He is in the temple outside the city-gate. He will soon be here at his home." (187) The Mother replied: "Why this jesting, when you see me in grief?" While she was saying this, that joy of hers came and bowed before her. (188) When the Mother looked up, behold it was indeed her son standing before her, but in her confused mind she said: "Am I awake, or is it a dream?" (189) Separation from her son had caused her bodily unconsciousness, and in the reality of seeing her jewel of a son, she was drowning in the sea of joy.

(190) The Father now came running, and saw him making his prostrate obeisance, and standing with hands palm to palm in delight. (191) Streams of tears of love flowed from the eyes of both. They embraced with love, and kissed one another in their joy. (192) It seemed to them then, as when nectar is given to one about to die, or as when one about to drown is suddenly drawn out by some one. (193) The fulness of joy that the Mother and Father of Kṛishna had, when he came from Mathurā and Gokul, these had even more. (194) Both began to drown in the ocean of happiness. The joy of each the Heavens could not contain. Their happiness they could not contain within themselves, but through their organs of sense it became broadcast. (195) When they looked up to the ten directions they seemed all joy. The sorrow of separation totally disappeared as he saw the moon-face of his son. (196) Then all the relatives assembled, and with them many mendicants, and the father gratified them all by gifts and honors. (197) He invited the Brahmans and the men in authority, and gave a feast and presented gifts to Brahmans. It seemed (to the father) as though his son were just born again, (198) or as if he had just escaped from the jaws of a tiger,

or as if, carried off by a serpent, he had been dropped, or as if by good fortune he had drunk nectar, and come back again to life. (199) In his joy he forgot even to ask the son what had taken place, and how he had succeeded in returning. He was simply dazed. (200) Things continued thus for a few days. Then the Father questioned his son: "How did your escape take place? Tell me. (201) Or did you come away without taking leave? For if so, there will be trouble. Tell me, my boy, all in detail. (202) The King is wholly avaricious. How would he let you go without the money? How did you get free? It seems all wonderful to me! (203) He was watching for the opportunity to make you a Mohammedan. Who had mercy on you and freed you? How did you obtain the palanquin and these other pomps? (204) What generous, benevolent person, an Ocean-of-mercy, could you have met who would pay the debt, and free you, O son?"

(205) The son listened to the words of his Father, and replied with a confused air: "Why, you sent the money, and because of it I am come. (206) You made the agreement that as soon as you returned home you would send the money within the month. As the month came to its end, listen to what happened. (207) On the last day, as the last hour arrived, I was taken into the assembly where also Brahmans had been summoned, and the King then said: (208) "To-day the month is fulfilled. I am not responsible for the words of the agreement, that if the money is not sent by your father I may make you this night a Mohammedan." (209) The Brahmans listened to these harsh declarations, and could not think what to do or say. They stood silent, looking at one another, and not a word was able to escape their lips. (210) The faces of all drooped. They were choked with emotion, their eyes were filled with tears, they lost the power of speech. (211) How can I describe my condition? I had lost bodily consciousness in my fear of what might take place. (212) I had ceased entirely to hope that my eyes would again behold your feet, and so kept my mind on our Caste-Lord. (213) The Brahmans with one accord were praying to the Husband of Umā: 'Run, run, to our help, O Husband-of-Gaurī! Protect this child! (214) This child is absolutely without a protector, but Thou art one who yearns for Thy worshipers, O Protector of the weak! Run, run to

our help! O Lord of Kailās, O Merciful-One, O Shri Shankar!' (215) As the people were thus calling for help, what should happen? It will rejoice your soul to hear of it. (216) The Kājis were all ready in the assembly to initiate me into their beliefs, when most suddenly your messenger appeared. (217) He had his blanket on his shoulder, his complexion was that of a dark cloud, he looked again and again towards me, and exclaimed, smiling with joy: (218) 'I have come! I have come, a servant of Digambarrāya. I am his faithful servant; hence he has sent all the needed money by my hand. (219) I have bills of exchange. If you have not confidence in them, then I will pour out this pile of money, and you can at once count it. (220) Whatever is due you, take in full. I will give you however much money you may demand. (221) I am his messenger, and I have uncountable money. Take this at once and let his son go.' (222) As they heard these words of the messenger, their joy was more than the heavens could contain. It seemed to them as it would to a man who might obtain a life-giving potion when at the point of death. (223) All their lotus-faces that had drooped now blossomed out. The messenger was, as it were, in the form of the rising sun. (224) The anxiety of mind that filled me was also dissipated by the sun-messenger. His light spread without and within, and overflowed the ten directions. (225) The King's officer said to him: 'Who are you? Whence have you come?' He replied: 'I am from Nārāyaṇpeṭh; I have come with the money.' (226) Thus replying, he poured out a pile of money. All were astonished as they saw the money. (227) While the money was being counted he stood mutely by. When the avaricious King looked up the man was gone. (228) 'Search! Search for him!' cried the King, in great concern. When he was not found, the people said: 'He was here but a moment ago.' (229) In the King's heart arose a great desire to see him again. But no one could find him, though all looked for him. (230) Some said: 'Has he bewitched us and disappeared?' Thus the varied classes of men made their various remarks to one another. (231) Even I did not see him, but he was looking at me with great affection. (232) While the money was being counted he was standing looking at me, and was saying 'Send him back'. (233) He seemed infinitely near to me, and it seemed to me as though I should wave my offering about him. (234) He was my very life, or my Brahmanhood itself. Therefore He had come. Such was my joy! (235) How can I describe to you the emotions of this joy! He was not a messenger, but Joy itself, so it seemed to me. (236) The King then exclaimed: 'Blessed is your father, blessed his family line, true to his word, a noble jewel.' (237) Thus rejoicing, he honoured me, gave me jeweled ornaments, and sent me on my way. (238) He had a new easy palanquin brought, and had me seat myself in it in his presence. He spoke most kind words to me, and sent me to see you again. (239) And now, if I have your blessing I shall be happy for ever. Your feet are Joy itself." So saying, he worshiped his father.

(240) When the father heard these words of his son, his eyes were filled with the water of love, and to what he said hearken, ye pious folk. (241) "How could there have been money with me? Who could have sent that messenger? I cannot understand this! Whence could the man have come? Who could he have been? I do not know. (242) I am absolutely without money. Whence then could I have sent the full amount of money? I had given up all hope of you, and lived overwhelmed with anxiety. (243) But blessed is my Lord Shri Avadhūta, who is the Caste-deity of my Caste. It must surely be He who came and freed you, my son! (244) There are no limits to His kindness. He is my very own, my relation, my inner soul, the Merciful-One! (245) I am just a sinner above all sinners. There is no end to my transgressions. But He is the Yearner-after-His-Worshipers, the Saviour-of-the-World, the Giver-of-Joy-to-the-World. (246) In describing whom the Vedas had to be dumb, the Six Shastras failed in their attempt, and the eighteen (purāns) became dejected; how impossible then for others to describe Him! (247) At whose lotus-feet Indra and all the other Gods, becoming as bees, sip honey with delight; (248) He who is a Bee in the lotus-mind of the Yogi, Attributeless, Changeless, Unattached, Ever-happy, Pure, Indivisible, Indestructible, (249) for whom good deeds are done, for whom austerities are performed, for whom the Rājayogi wears himself out, and yet He is not discovered even by these. (250) Those who spend all their lives in visiting

sacred waters, even they do not attain Him. How is it that He became pleased with me, a lowly man, He who yearns for the lowly, the-Merciful-One! (251) He who longs for His worshipers, Wish-giving-Tree, All-Helper, Satisfier-of-Desires, Who-delights-the-Yogis-heart, Who-gives-rest-to-all-mankind! (252) Because His slave fell into distress He quickly ran to his aid. Such is the Yearner-for-His-Worshipers, the Lord-of-the-Earth. What can I do to repay Him? (253) The infant does not serve its Mother, but still she has compassion on it. So my Lord came quickly to my aid. (254) I knew not how to worship Him, I knew not how to sing His praises, I knew not at all how to call Him to my aid. (255) I am the lowest of the low, the greatest sinner of all sinners. My transgressions are truly immeasurable. I cannot understand how He should have mercy upon me. (256) He whom hundreds of thousands of worshipers ever place in the depth of their hearts, He does not visit even them. How then has He revealed Himself to me, one so lowly? (257) He who should be worshiped by the sixteen modes of worship, He who should be seated in the temple of the heart, He is my Lord, Digambar, the Protector of the lowly, Merciful-One! (258) Thou didst forget altogether the dignity of Thy Sovereignty and becamest a Mahār, and truly didst deliver Thy slave! (259) O my Digambar, Saviour of the Needy, O my Digambar, Compassionate One, O my Digambar, Remover-of-Sin, Ocean-of-Happiness, Dark-formed-One! (260) O my Digambar, King-of-the-Yoga, Giver-of-Blessing-to-Atri, Helper-of-Thine-Own, Thou didst leap down of Thine own free choice to help, O Dattātreya, Store-house-of-Mercy! (261) Extinguisher-of-the-fire-of-Destruction, Lover-of-Yogis, Willing-Nourisher-of-the-Universe, Womb-of-Intelligence, King-of-Accomplishers, Lover-of-Thine-own! Why hast Thou become (for me) an Ocean-of-Pity? (262) Ocean-of-Knowledge, Without-beginning-or-end, Nourisher-of-the-Universe, Avadhūta, Free-from-Māyā-yet-associated-with-Māyā, Ruler of Māyā, Primal-Guru! (263) Thou art truly in the form of Shiva, God-of-Gods, Yearner-after-the-lowly, O Digambar, Sovereign-of-the-World! (264) Dark-as-a-dark-cloud, Lotus-eyed, Remover-of-the-evil-of-the-Kaliyuga, Mine-of-Mercy, Beyond-cause-and-effect, Without-qualities, Spotless, Unassociated. (265) How is it that Thou for me in my need becamest a Mahār, O Shri Digambar? I am a transgressor! O forgive me this transgression, Ocean-of-Mercy!

(266) As he thus cried aloud, love-tears streamed from his eyes. His eight feelings flooded him within and without; he trembled and perspired. (267) He lost all bodily consciousness. "Is it I who am speaking to my son?" All thought of self absolutely vanished, and he was lost in happiness. (268) After a moment he said to his son in his joy: "Blessed, blessed are you, chief of true worshipers; the Brother-of-the-Needy has visited you. (269) I was indeed cruel and harsh. I, seduced by the love of my life, left you, my boy, in the care of that cruel one, and returned home. (270) What kind of a Mother or Father am I? What kind of a Protector am I? This appears evident to all. Your Father is our Caste Lord. (271) He, the-Mother-and-Father-of-the-universe, He, the Helper-of-His-Worshipers, the Protector-of-His-Worshipers, the Yearner-for-His-Worshipers, Giver-of-Joy-to-His-Worshipers, Deliverer-from-fear, Enemy-of-this-worldly-existence, (272) He it was who became a Mahār, and rushed to your aid as your Protector. There is no limit to your good fortune. You have seen that image! (273) One must also declare the King blessed. One must declare that country blessed, and blessed are its people, for they actually saw that image! (274) He whom Brahma and the other Gods find difficult of access, how came He to be easy of access? He the Helper-of-His-Worshipers, Lover-of-His-Worshipers! Wonderful are the deeds of the Lord! (275) I am simply outside of good fortune, I am simply filthy. How could I expect a sight of my Lord? (276) Blessed are you, Chief-Crown-Jewel-of-the-King-of-Worshipers! Blessed are you in the Three Worlds! Therefore you easily met Him Who-holds-the-rod-in-his-hand. (277) Through you I have become blessed. Your acquired merit of a previous birth is not a common one. Through you we shall be honored everywhere and always."

(278) Hearing his Father thus speaking, the boy thought to himself: "The Son-of-Atri must have revealed himself, for my lowly self, this Yearner-after-the-lowly, Merciful-One! (279) I had thought that my Mother and Father had felt anxious for me, and had sent their messenger to free their son! (280) I was evidently freed by that messenger. I see now that all

these (worldly things) are of no meaning to me. (281) Those who gave this body of mine birth bear heavy anxiety for me. Under their bringing up this body has grown. (282) To think thus seems to me infinite foolishness. Rather should I look to Him who freed me. (283) He is my Mother and Father. He is my Sister and Brother. He is my Protector. It is to Him that I must look. (284) He whom I had not meditated upon, nor sung His praises; He whose form I had not brought to mind, yet who felt concern for me, to that Lord I must continually look! (285) He who showed His power and preserved my Brahmanhood, He in truth is my *Swami.* To live without Him is to waste my life! (286) I have possessed this body for sixteen years without effort (on my part), but during it I have not seen the Lord-of-the-World, my Helper, my Sovereign King. (287) To forsake Him and live in worldly existence, how can it bring happiness? That *Swami* is my helper. Is it a laudable thing to live without him? (288) If for the future I live without him how can I expect happiness? My life will be spent quickly, and I may not again be born a man. (289) It is only after thousands of rebirths that I am possessed of this human body. I must make use of this happy possession. (290) Without the possession of a human body how can the seeing of Shri Datta take place? To see Shri Datta this human body seems to me necessary. (291) If I am born into a body other than human, there can be no knowledge of what my body is, then how can I at all possess the supreme knowledge? (292) The substance of that supreme knowledge is this; the inner meaning of all the Vedas is this—the possession of Shri Digambar. I must obtain it! (293) To remain here at home, and try to acquire Him will never be possible. Home, wife, and so on are but forms of sorrow. (294) In association with them come desires and hates, and the idea of Great-Difference will increase. How then can I acquire Sacchidānanda, my Swami Digambar? (295) In association with them, worldly existence will only increase, and I shall continually have to feel concern about happiness and pain. (296) Worldly existence is the jaw-of-death itself. Many have fallen into it. Even Brahma and the other Gods knew not their end! What indeed can it be? (297) Whence have we come, whither are we to go? Who am I? What is my condition? How am I to support wife and child and so on? (298) These form our snares, association with them is our snare, hard to avoid. To give them up is the easy way to escape from them. (299) Burn up, burn up association with them. Burn up, burn up all bodily consciousness. In association with them I shall never find rest. (300) Association with them is even worse than would be the state of a poor wretch who sought to make his bed on living coals! (301) If I say they are Mother and Father, and therefore I must now care for them, when their Mother and Father passed into the next world who cared for them there? (302) Janārdan is in this whole world. He is All in All. Who then is anyone's cherisher? Who then is anyone's supporter? (303) Whatever being comes to birth, it happens to him according to his Karma. He cannot find liberation until he reaps the result (of Karma). Such is the flow of birth and death. (304) Why should a seeing man leap into a fire plainly before him? It would bring him to hopelessness. What of happiness does he lack? (305) The door to the acquisition of happiness is this birth into a human body. Shall I reject this happiness and continually concern myself with bodily and household affairs? (306) No! No longer let this be my concern, but let it be how I may attain to Shri Avadhūta. I must devote myself to the certain attaining of him. (307) Through whom may come about the meeting with Digambara, at His feet I will make great haste and place my forehead." (308) After thinking thus, what did Dāsopant do, the royal image (of the Divine)? He who descended to this earth an avatar? He said to himself: (309) "If I inform my Mother and Father of this, and they refuse consent, and I remain with them, how will it be possible to meet Avadhūta?" (310) So what did this chief-jewel-of-worshipers plan and carry out? Be gracious to me, a lowly man. Oh listen and hear!

(311) He had heard the story that had come down from mouth to mouth, from father to son, that at Mātāpūr in the Sahyādri mountains Shri Digambar dwelt. (312) He said to himself: "Unless I go there I shall not meet with the Son-of-Atri. I will go at once without letting any one know." (313) Thus determining, and fixing his thought on the feet of Digambar, this chief-jewel-among-worshipers, Mahārāj Dāsopant, started on his way.

Summary of verses 314 to 778

With his mind absorbed in the contemplation of Dattātreya, Dāsopant continued on his way. He first came to the town of Hilālpur. The *kulkarṇi* of Hilālpur and Dokolgi, named Kṛishnājipant, was sitting in the shade of a tree when Dāsopant came by. To Kṛishnājipant he seemed the very image of Avadhūta, God himself. He fell at his feet and embraced him, urging him to come to his house. Dāsopant pleaded that duty called him onward, and continued his journey.

He next reached Premapur, and worshiped in the temple there. Further on he arrived at Nandigrām, also called Nāndeḍ, where the Gautami river flowed. Here he bathed and performed religious rites. For food he lived on whatever was given to him. His meat and drink were contemplation of Avadhūta. The people here were curious about him and asked him questions. "Where does your father live?" He replied: "Avadhūta is my mother and father, my protector. I have no one but him." Continuing on his way he now came to Gangāpur and began climbing the mountain to Mātāpūr, the original seat of Avadhūta. Full of joy and love he entered first the temple of Ambā, worshiping and praying that she would help him to meet Avadhūta. He remained here five days, and then ascended the higher spurs of the mountain, stopping by the way at the temple of Anasūyā. Finally he reached the shrine of Digambar, his caste Deity. People wondered at him, and asked about his parentage. He replied: "God is my Mother and Father, my Sister and Brother. I have no one but him." For twelve years he sojourned here. Avadhūta at last appeared to him in a dream and said: "Go down from here to Rākshasabhuvan, on the banks of the Gangā, where are my *pādukas*. There perform austerities and I will easily be seen by you." In obedience to this dream he journeyed down to Rākshasabhuvan, on the banks of the Godāvarī. Here, on the sands of the river by the *pādukas* of Digambar, he began his austerities. He continued these for twelve years, when finally Digambar manifested himself to him, and with his six arms embraced him, each addressing the other in words of love and praise.[9]

[9] The only known manuscript of this work ends abruptly here. Presumably the lost portion completes the narrative of Dāsopant's life.

The following is a translation of the two incidents in the life of Dāsopant told by Mahīpati in his Bhaktalīlāmrit.

Bhaktalīlāmṛit 22, 48—65

(48) As Eknāth journeyed on, his heart always full of joy, he unexpectedly met Dāsopant in his path. (49) From childhood Dāsopant had cherished the desire for a visible manifestation of Shri Dattātreya. He had therefore undertaken severe austerities in this loving desire. (50) You may ask how he performed them. Listen, ye fortunate hearers. He abandoned all his friends and went alone into the forest. (51) He lived on fallen leaves. He took not the least care of his body. He slept on the bare rock, enduring cold and heat. (52) If any human being unexpectedly appeared he would run away from him. Without ceasing he kept Shri Dattātreya in his mind. (53) From these austerities, lovingly carried on, he finally lost bodily consciousness, and because he lay on rocks his body was covered with sores. (54) For twenty years he carried on austerities in this way; then finally Dattātreya gave him a visible manifestation of himself. (55) As Dattātreya embraced him, his body became divine, and through the blessing bestowed upon him he became a prolific poet. (56) And through the grace of the *Sadguru*, and his good fortune, there came to him great wealth, and the respect of great men, as they recognized his great intelligence.

(57) Dāsopant had placed his abode in Ambā Jogai. He had heard of Shri Eknāth's good fame from everyone's lips. (58) As Eknāth was returning from the supreme pilgrimage (Benares), the two unexpectedly met. They embraced one another with great joy in their hearts. (59) They embraced one another's feet. They conversed together about their joy and happiness. Eknāth, full of joy, said to Dāsopant: "This is a fortunate meeting." (60) After much solicitation Dāsopant took Eknāth to his home. Waves of joy and happiness arose in his soul, and with pure reverence he paid him respect. (61) They dined on daintily cooked food. Then came the listening to the reading of the Bhāgavat, and at night Hari *Kirtans* took place, that deeply moved all as they listened.

(62) A month thus passed, and then Eknāth asked leave to go on. Dāsopant pleaded with him to accept horses and money

for the journey and its expenses. (63) Shri Eknāth, however, had a mind indifferent to worldly things, and would take none of Dāsopant's wealth. Nor would he even take a horse, "because," said he, "the way is difficult." (64) In leaving, Eknāth said to Dāsopant: "I am to celebrate at my home the festival of the birthday of Kṛishna. At that time come to the sacred city of Pratishṭhāna." (65) "I certainly will come," he replied. They made one another *namaskāra*. Shri Eknāth hastened on his journey, and arrived at the sacred city of Pratishṭhāna.

Bhaktalīlāmṛit 22, 79—101

(79) Two months passed in this way, and then came the festival of Kṛishna's birth. Uddhava, according to his custom, began to make all the necessary preparations. (80) He collected in the house an abundance of things needed to gratify the taste. He besmeared the walls within and without, and painted pictures upon them. (81) Suddenly, on the day of full moon, Dāsopant arrived for the festival. Eknāth had not heard that he had arrived, when unexpectedly he appeared at the main door. (82) A strange sight was now seen. Shri Datta, with his trident in his hands, stood watching at the entrance, as a doorkeeper. (83) Dāsopant saw him, and was supremely amazed. He leaped from his palanquin and made a *sāshṭānga namaskāra.* (84) He embraced Datta and exclaimed: "Why have you come here?" The Son of Anasūyā listened to the question, and replied: (85) "Eknāth is not a human *bhakta,* but a visible *avatār* of Shri Pāṇḍurang. For the salvation of the world he has become an *avatār* in this Kali Yuga. (86) Only if by good fortune there exists the richness of a *puṇya,* performed in a former birth, can one have the opportunity of serving him. Know this fact for a truth. (87) I hold this trident in my hand, and guard securely the door. I will go in and inform Eknāth of your presence. Until then, do not enter in." (88) As Avadhūta thus spoke Dāsopant was overcome with astonishment, and extolling Shri Nāth's glory said: "I did not recognize his extraordinary greatness." (89) Shri Datta informed Eknāth that Dāsopant had come to see him, and lovingly made him a *namaskāra.* (90) They fell at each other's feet, and embraced one another. Eknāth then took Dāsopant by the hand, and led him into the house.

(91) Uddhava made the proper arrangements for all the palanquins and carriages. He gave the men the materials and the necessities for cooking. Nothing was lacking. (92) Formerly in the time of Shri Kṛishna's avatarship Uddhava was greatly loved by the God. The desire of Uddhava to serve the God was not then fully satisfied, but that desire he was now having satisfied. (93) In the former birth there was the relationship of debtor, and so now the opportunity arrived for the unselfish service of Eknāth. (94) Dāsopant performed his bath, and finished his meal with Eknāth. All night he sat listening to the Hari *Kirtan*, until the sun began to rise. (95) He then perfumed the image of Pāṇḍurang, anointed him and worshiped him with the various ceremonies, experiencing the while loving joy. (96) Festal instruments were played at the door. Festal invocations were sung. The Brahmans recited aloud from the Vedas, and finally handfuls of flowers were offered. (97) The days were spent in giving gifts to Brahmans, the nights in Hari *Kirtans*. From the first day of the fortnight to the ninth, the festival was at its full. (98) On the tenth, the Gopālakāla was excellently dramatized. Dāsopant saw it all with joy in his heart, (99) and exclaimed: "I have seen with my own eyes the unprecedented, gracious voice of Shri Eknāth, his make-up, his dramatic power, and his mine of philosophic knowledge. (100) I thought myself to be a worshiper of Datta in visible form, but since seeing the glory of Eknāth with my own eyes, I have become one-who-recognizes-no-difference." (101) The great festival being ended, there was feasting on the twelfth day. Dāsopant then took his leave, and returned to his own home.

A PHARMACOLOGICAL NOTE ON PSALM 58 9

David I. Macht

Pharmacological Laboratory, Johns Hopkins University

While the first half of this verse presents some difficulty from the etymological and grammatical point of view, the rendering of the passage is almost uniformly the same on the part of all interpreters, rabbinical and modern. The poet prays that the wicked might dissolve like a snail dissolving in the slime; literally "which passes away into dissolution." A crawling snail or slug leaves a trail of slime, and this was popularly regarded as a gradual dissolution of its body. Snails, both of the so-called naked variety (e. g. *limax*) and of the shell variety (e. g. *helix*), were common in the Mediterranean regions. Of the older authorities, Rashi (1040—1105) translates *šablūl* as *limax* and regards the word as coming from the same root from which the noun *šibbolet* is formed, namely *šabal*, meaning "to flow." Altschul (1650) in his Meṣudot David speaks of the snail as "melting in the sun." Ibn Ezra (1042—1167) gives the same etymology as Rashi. Of the more modern Jewish commentators, Malbim remarks that the snail is stimulated to secrete slime when it is touched. S. R. Hirsch regards *šablūl* as related to *šebīl*, "a path", with reference to the slimy track left by the crawling mollusc. Alshech (1550), in his Romemot El, gives a similar rendition. Professor Haupt takes the word *šablūl* to come from *balal* (hence Aramaic *tiblālā*), "pour out" or "moisten". The word *temes* is explained by general consensus from the root *masas*, "melt" or "dissolve", and on the side of form, as a noun. All commentators are agreed that the psalmist is referring to the apparent dissolution of the snail during its progress. The present author wishes to suggest a new and somewhat interesting interpretation which equally well or even better fits into the context and also throws some light on obscure passages in rabbinical literature.

Bödecker and Troschel in 1854 (*Ber. Akad. Wiss.*, p. 468) discovered that the secretion of various snails contains a large amount of acid. These investigators examined in particular the species of snail, *Dolium Galea,* and found that it secreted sulphuric acid. These observations have been corroborated by other investigators, notably by Paola Pancheri ("Gli organi e la secrezione del Acido Solforico nei Gastropodi", Napoli, 1869. Mem. estr. dal Vol. 4 degli *Atti della reale academia delle scienze fisiche e matematiche*). Recently the whole subject of acid secretion by snails has been investigated very carefully, from both the anatomical and the physiological point of view, by K. Schönlein ("Über Säuresecretion bei Schnecken", *Zeit. f. Biol.*, 36, 1898, 523) and by F. N. Schulz ("Beiträge zur Kenntnis der Anatomie und Physiol. einiger Säureschnecken", *Zeit. f. allgemeine Physiol.* V, 1905, 206). Schulz, who has written the most important monograph on the subject, studied in particular the naked snail, *Pleurobranchaea Meckelii*, but also examined various other naked as well as shell-bearing varieties, namely, *Oscanius Membranaceus, Oscanius Tuberculatus, Cassidaria Echinofora,* a shell snail very much like the common garden variety *(Helix Pomatia), Dolium Galea, Murex Trunculus* and *Murex Brandaris.* All of these snails were found to secrete sulphuric acid. It was found that the very acid slime secreted by various snails is produced by special glands, tubular in structure. The amount of acid secreted is something extraordinary and serves to emphasize the old adage that microscopic and other small creatures are really more wonderful in their structure than large ones. It has been estimated that the amount of sulphuric acid secreted by Dolium Galea is at least 3% and sometimes more. Compare with this the acidity of gastric juice in higher animals. According to Pawlow, estimates of the maximum acidity in the human stomach range between 0.2—0.3% free hydrochloric acid, while the acidity of the gastric juice of the dog varies from 0.46 to 0.56%. The sulphur required to produce this amount of acid comes partly through a breaking down of the protoplasm itself and partly from salts ingested by the animal. The biological significance of this secretion is probably chiefly of a defensive but possibly also in part of an aggressive character.

In view of these remarkable pharmacological findings in

regard to the slimy secretions of snails, the scriptural passage under consideration admits of a new and very appropriate interpretation. The expression "dissolving snail" need not be rendered, as has been done by all interpreters, intransitively, referring to the apparent dissolution of the snail itself during its progress. The word *temes* may just as appropriately be rendered in the transitive sense, in which case the idea expressed is not figurative at all but an actual fact. The snail does actually dissolve or destroy marble, or limestone, or whatever other substratum it may crawl over by virtue of the highly acid content of its slimy secretion. The metaphor therefore may be taken to express the prayer of the Psalmist not only that the wicked may pass into dissolution as a snail appears to do, but that they may perish and dissolve themselves into nothingness because of the destruction that they spread along their path.

Such a translation certainly agrees better with the Targum. We read, *Hēḵ zāḥel tiḇlālā dĕ-mā'es orḥēh,* "Like the snail that crawleth and melteth (corrodes) its path." Furthermore, this transitive meaning of the word *temes* serves to explain an otherwise obscure passage in the Talmud. In Sabbath 77b we read that the Lord created the snail for the *katit* (*bara šablul le-katit*). The rabbinical commentators render the word *katit* as "scab". It is very plausible to assume that the snail's secretion may act favorably as a caustic in softening scabs and other thickenings of the skin. Acids are used by physicians for destroying granulations and other superfluous growths. In fact, an examination of the old pharmacopœias reveals that snails have been used for that purpose. In the *Thesaurus Pharmacologicus* of Johannes Schroeder, 1672, a *liquor limacum*, or snail juice, is mentioned, of which the following is stated:

> "Rubri limaces concisi misceantur cum pari pondere Sal. communis, conjicianturque in manicam Hipp. ut in cella defluant in liquorem, quo dolentes partes podagricae illinuntur, & verrucae scalpello prius abrasae facile averruncantur."

And again in the London *Dispensatory* of William Salmon, 1702, we read on page 260 of a *liquor cochlearum* that "it is good to anoint with in the gout, and it takes away corns and warts."

Zwelfer in his Pharmacopœia, 1572, gives directions for an

external application in skin conditions which contains the following ingredients:

Cerussae albae
Succi limionis
Limacum
Album ovarum
Camphore
Boracis
Myrrhae
Thuris
Mastichi

These older pharmacopœias, of course, for the most part copy their information from more ancient authorities, especially Pliny. Pliny mentions the medicinal uses of snails or *cochleae* repeatedly in his Natural History, especially in Book 30. Among other indications for the administration of snail preparations he speaks of podagra or gout (chapter 9, line 43) and "*contra maculas faciei*" or various blemishes of the face (chapter 4).

References to medicinal uses of snails we find even in the later English dispensatories. Thus James, in his *Dispensatory*, London 1747, page 517, states that "the liquor is used to anoint the parts affected with gout and to extirpate warts, being first scraped with a penknife. It also cures prolapsus or falling down of the anus". Even Cullen in his *Materia Medica*, 1789, speaks of the medicinal virtue of snails.

Perhaps the most interesting account of snails from a zoological as well as a medical point of view is found in the long treatise of the medieval writer on natural history, Ulysses Aldrovandus. In his great work on natural history, Bonn, 1606, volume 9, book 3, he gives a long dissertation *de testaceis*, in which he discusses various snails. Thus Book 3, chapter 29, contains 21 folio pages on the subject of snails. The etymology of the names in different languages, the morphological description, the geographical distribution, the embryology and reproduction, the literary allusions, the symbolism, and the uses of snails as foods and medicines are minutely described. In chapters 30 to 39 various species and varieties are distinguished and the book contains many very valuable and beautiful wood-cuts of which one is here reproduced. Aldrovandus describes numerous pathological conditions for which snails or snail extracts and secretion have been employed. Here again the application of snail juice for the removal of warts and callosities occupies a prominent place. Quoting from book 3, chapter 29, page 386, we read, "Adamus Lonicerus scribit de stillata e limacibus Maio vel Octobrio mense aqua, clavum refectu, si instilletur, sanare; manuumque verrucas purgare; et ferrum in ea extinctum chalybis induere duritiam tradi. Et Gualther Ryffius verrucas et clavos percidi primum jubet, quoad eius fieri commode potest, deinde linteum hoc liquore madidum imponi." (Adamus Lonicerus writes concerning water which is distilled from snails in the month of May or October, that it cures a tumor by refreshing it, if it is instilled, and that it purges warts of the hands, and that it is handed down in tradition that iron cooled in this puts on the hardness of steel. And Gualther Ryffius orders warts and tumors to be cut through first, as far as can be done properly, then that a linen cloth wet with this liquid be laid on.)

The pharmaceutical history of snails is thus but another illustration among many of the popular and empirical uses of various substances which have in the light of modern science at least a modicum of rational support.

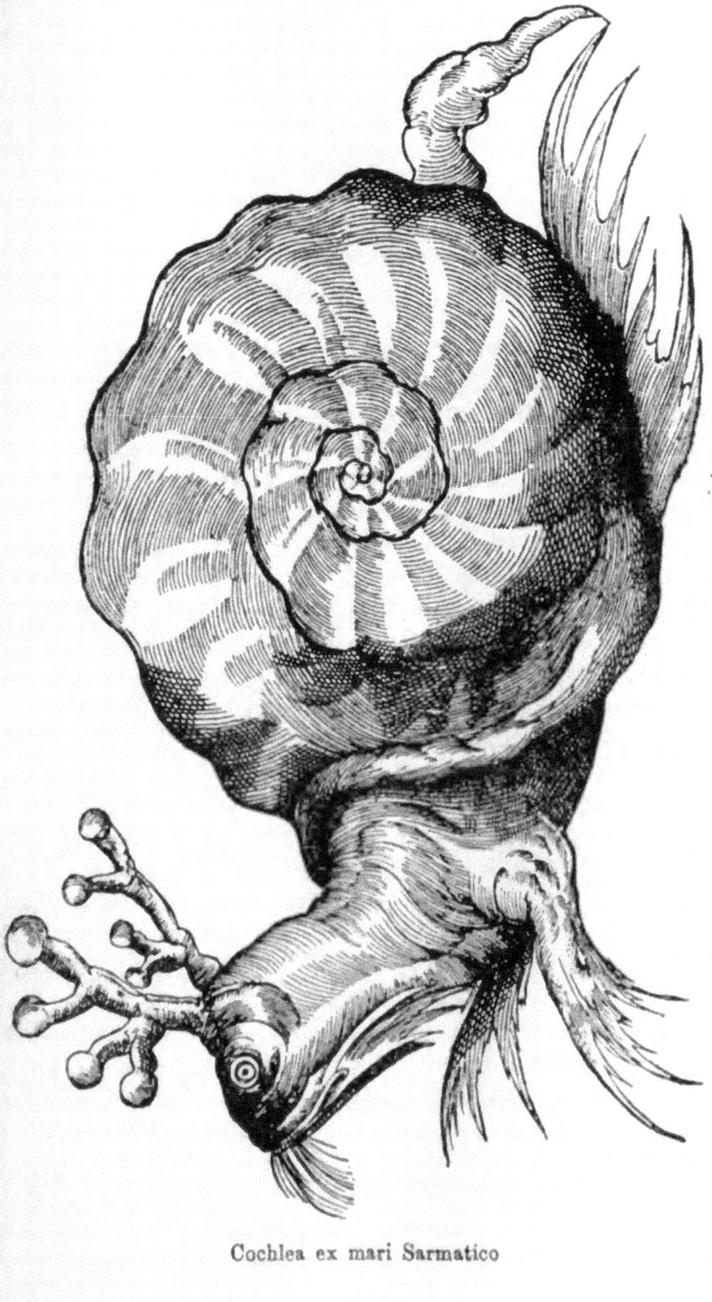

Cochlea ex mari Sarmatico

PRESTER JOHN AND JAPAN

Clarence Augustus Manning

Columbia University

The belief that a Christian Empire existed somewhere in Asia as a foil and balance to the Holy Roman Empire of the West was long current in Europe. It commenced in the twelfth century and continued in varying forms until the scientific exploration of Asia had rendered untenable any such theory. And why should this idea not have been held? It was hard to believe that Christianity had never taken firm root outside the range of classical culture. To the East there had been the great Nestorian Church with its centre at Edessa; and though heretical, it might have flourished and given effective aid to Christendom during the dark days when Islam was widening its boundaries and encroaching on the Western World.

In addition to this desire for material aid in the struggle against the unbeliever, Christians seemed to be influenced by the teaching of the Church. "From the East light; from the East the Saviour." This promise fulfilled in the spread of Christianity into Europe might indicate that somewhere to the East still remained a pure and holy pattern of the Faith.

This idea took fast hold in Russia and after the disorders of the seventeenth century, the Old Believers regarded the entire Russian Church as apostate and turned eagerly to the East to recover the lost hierarchy. For this purpose their agents travelled far and wide to see if they could not find some bishop who had maintained the Old Faith before the days of Nikon. How far deliberate fraud entered into the reports which were brought back we cannot determine but many of the agents returned with tidings of success. Others, more sincere, never returned, perishing in the wilderness and deserts of the heart of Asia. Still others tried to follow in the steps of those heroes, and to supply the demand there came into existence a series of guides to aid the pilgrims in their quest of the promised land.

The following description of this Eastern Paradise may be of interest. It is published in Melnikov, *Polnoye Sobraniye Sochinenii,* Vol. VII², p. 23. with the title, "The Wanderer or route to the Kingdom of Oponia, written by a returned traveller, the monk Marko of the Topozersky Monastery, who had been in the kingdom of Oponia. His route." Then comes the text. "The route or wanderer. From Moscow to Kazan, from Kazan to Ekaterinburg and to Tyumen, to Kamenogorsk, to the village Vybernum, to Izbensk, up the river Katunya to Krasnoyarsk, to the village Ustyuba, where one is to inquire for the hospitable Petr Kirillov. Near this place are many secret caves, and a little beyond are snow-capped mountains for three hundred versts, and the snow on these mountains never melts. Beyond these mountains is the village Ummenska (in another manuscript Ustmenska) and in it is a chapel; a monk, the anchorite Iosif. From this there is a route by the Chinese realm, requiring 44 days, across Guban (Gobi?), then to the kingdom of Oponia. There the inhabitants have a home in the confines of the ocean, called Byelovodiye.[1] There the people live on seventy islands, some of then 500 versts in length, and the small islands cannot be counted. The life of the people there is known to the devout members of the old rite of the Catholic and Apostolic Church. I assert this truly, for I was there, I the sinful and unworthy monk Marko with two other monks. We sought with great eagerness and zeal in the Eastern lands the old Rite of the Orthodox hierarchy, which is very necessary to salvation, with the help of God, and we found 179 churches of the Assyrian tongue; they have an Orthodox patriarch, of the line of Antioch, and four metropolitans. And as many as forty Russian churches there have also a metropolitan and bishops, of the Assyrian succession. From the persecutions of Roman heretics much people has come by boat through the Arctic Ocean and by land. God is filling this place. If any one doubts, I will call God to witness: the holy Sacrifice will be offered until the second coming

---

[1] White Waters.

of Christ. In this place they receive those who come from Russia in the first rank.[2] They baptize always with triple immersion those who wish to remain to the end of their lives. The two monks who were with me resolved to stay there forever; they received holy Baptism. And they say: 'You have all been polluted by great and diverse heresies of Antichrist, for it is written: Come from out of the midst of these dishonorable men and do not touch them, the serpent pursuing the woman; he cannot touch the woman who is hidden in the crevice of the earth.'[3] In these places there are no deeds of violence or robberies or other deeds contrary to the law. They have no secular government; the spiritual authorities govern the people and all men. There are trees equal in height to the highest trees. In winter there are unusual frosts with crevices in the earth. And there are thunders with no small shaking of the earth. And there are all the fruits of the earth; grapes and wheat grow there. And in the 'Swedish Pilgrim' it is said that there is no limit to their gold and silver, precious stones and very costly beads. And these people of Oponia admit no one into their land and they have war with no one; their country is isolated. In China there is a wonderful city, such as nowhere else on the whole earth. Their first capital is Kaban."

This seems to indicate a direct road to the East and has therefore a certain geographical basis. Another version (Anderson, *Staroobryadchestvo i Sektantstvo,* p. 174) is quite different. It commences in the same way but from Ekaterinburg the road passes to Tomsk, Barnaul, the River Katurnya and Krasny Yad. Then the pilgrim goes to the village of Aka and then to the village of Ustba, where there is the chapel of Petr Kirillov. He then goes to Alam (Elam?) from which point he can see the Snow Mountains which extend for three hundred versts. He then comes to Damascus where there is a chapel with the monk Ivan (or John). He then takes a forty day trip to the Kirzhissi (Kirghiz) and in four days more he comes to Tatania and then to Oponia in Byelovodiye. Here there are one hundred islands, dark forests and high mountains and

---

[2] As heretics who are to be rebaptized.

[3] Revelation XII.

there are no barbarians and "if all the Chinese were Christian, no one would ever perish."

It will at once be noted that this route is far less possible geographically. The pilgrim starts for the East and then in some mysterious way is back in Arabia and makes his way through the steppes of southern Asia to an island Oponia which is perhaps nearer to India or central Asia than it is to the Pacific Islands.

At different times during the nineteenth century, groups or sectarians set out in search of this happy land (cf. Melnikov, *op. cit.* p. 24 note). Impostors found a fruitful field of operations in pretending that they were clergy of the Oponian Church visiting in Russia. Among these we may mention "Bishop" Arkady of Byelovodiye, who appeared at the very end of the century with letters from the humble Melety, Patriarch of the Slavonic-Byelovodiye, Kambay, Japan, Indostan, India, Anglo-India, Ost-India (East India?) and Yust-India, and Fest-India (West India?) and Africa, and America, and the land of Khili (Chili?) and the lands of Magelan, and Brazil, and Abyssinia. Among other ecclesiastics who were connected with this see were the humble Vasily, Metropolitan of the City of New York, and Zakhary, Bishop of Ameyan (Amiens) a city in Galia (Gaul), and Simeon, Bishop of Altorf not far from the Mountain Gothard. (Khokhlov, *Journey of the Ural Cossacks to the Kingdom of Byelovodiye,* with introduction by V. G. Korolenko, p. 8f.) We need merely add that this modest man had apparently studied foreign names to good effect.

There seems to be little doubt that this mysterious Byelovodiye and Oponia with its countless islands, its mountain peaks, and its isolated character, is Japan. So most scholars have assumed and Conybeare (*Russian Dissenters,* p. 111) definitely regards the work of Mark or Marko as of the eighteenth century. This may be rather doubtful, since it would be questionable as to when the Russians first became acquainted with Japan. It is more interesting to ask exactly why and how the Russians came to assume that Japan was the home of Russian Old Believers.

Conybeare (*op. cit.*) assumes that we have here a reflection of the mission of St. Francis Xavier to Japan. He had gone there in 1549 and had established a native Church, but this was wiped out by persecution in 1640, although a considerable number of Christians remained and secretly handed down their faith by lay baptism. It would be interesting irony if this were correct. The idea that the Old Believers constantly attacking the Orthodox Church for making peace with the Western world were finding their ideal in a Western mission in the East would be most remarkable. Of course some tale of this mission might have penetrated the Archangel district where Marko lived, but this is unlikely. The mission of St. Francis Xavier had been officially and practically lost a century before and we should seek for some other explanation.

Korolenko (Khokhlov, *op. cit.* p. 6) suggests that Marko is simply a Russianized form of Marco Polo, the Italian traveller who visited China in the thirteenth century. The strange adventures of such a wanderer might again drift into Russia under an unrecognizable form but one which appealed to the people. In the wilds of northern Russia this meant a form available for the Old Believers and those sectarians who were seeking the true Faith somewhere in the East.

It may be objected that the reference to Roman persecutions would automatically exclude both of these hypotheses. Not so, for Nikon who was trying to bring the Orthodox Church into line with the usages of the Greeks was roundly denounced as a Romanizer by his foes and he might well have been the persecutor referred to. Despite this, however, there remains one source which was still more available for the sectarians.

Apparently the first Japanese to come to Russia was one Denbey, who was found on Kamchatka by explorers in 1697—8 and sent to Petersburg where he arrived about 1701. Peter the Great used him to open a school for the study of the Japanese language. He was however called an Indian. (N. N. Ogloblin, "The First Japanese in Russia", *Russkaya Starina*, Oct. 1891, p. 11).

India had long been known to the Russians as a Christian country. The *byliny* handed down for centuries by oral tradition in the swamps of the north and the Archangel and Perm provinces told how Dyuk Stepanovich came from India the Rich to vist Fair Sun Vladimir. He appears as a beautiful young *bogatyr* or hero of enormous wealth and enters into competition with all the richest members of Vladimir's court as Churilo Plenkovich the Fop. The home of Dyuk is sometimes Volynia and sometines India the Rich.

This special *bylina* is strongly influenced by the Tale of the Indian Kingdom, a prose letter written by the Tsar-Priest John to the Emperor Manuel of Constantinople (Porfirev, *Istoriya russkoy slovesnosti,* Vol. I, p. 232). This letter was widely spread among the Western nations of Europe and in a Latin version is printed by Zarncke ("Der Priester Johannes", in *Abhandlungen der sächsischen Gesellschaft der Wissenschaften, phil.-hist. Klasse,* Vol. VII, p. 872ff.).

We may be able to date with some degree of accuracy the appearance of this legend in Russia. The Ipatyevsky Chronicle tells that in 1165 the Tsarevich Andronikos, a foe of Manuel Comnenos of Constantinople, sought refuge at the court of Yaroslav Osmomysl of Galich. Manuel was at this time much interested in placing Stefan on the throne of Hungary, and the combination of Andronikos and Yaroslav threatened the success of this scheme. It is very likely that the Tale of the Indian Kingdom was introduced at this period by Andronikos in order to persuade the Russians that Manuel was not the most powerful ruler in the whole world, since the Priest-King of India far excelled him in wealth and power. Manuel failed in his intrigues and ultimately became reconciled to Andronikos, who returned to Constantinople, but the legend once introduced remained alive. (Keltuyala, *Kurs istorii russkoy literatury,* Vol. I, Part 1², p. 991.)

There are several details which show the striking similarity existing between the *bylina* and the tale. Thus Vladimir in answer to the boasts of Dyuk Stepanovich sends envoys to India the Rich to measure and list the wealth of the Asiatic ruler. As they enter the court, they greet several elaborately dressed women as the Queen but are informed each time that they are mistaken and that these are but servants dressed simply as compared with their mistress. After working for three years they decide that it will be necessary to sell Kiev in order to buy enough paper to finish their task. Similarly John writes to Manuel: "Tell your tsar Manuel: if you wish to know all my resources and the wonders of my realm of India, sell your entire Grecian realm and buy paper and come to my kingdom of India with your scribes and I will let you make an inventory of my land of India and you will not be able to make an inventory of my kingdom before your death" (Porfirev, *op. cit.* I, p. 89). Other similarities are in the golden stream of Dyuk which reminds us of the Tigris with its golden sands. Dyuk's palace has a golden and bejewelled roof, while the roof of the Indian palace is covered with self-lighting carbuncles. Wonderful columns adorned with figures of a tsar and tsaritsa in India are decorated like the costly buttons on the mantles of Dyuk.

This great wealth of India reappears in the riches of Oponia. A more striking similarity is the great piety and morality of its population. We have seen the great virtue of the Orthodox of Oponia. In India, "no one there lies or can lie; if any one attempts to lie, he immediately dies and his memory at the same time. We all walk in the steps of truth and love one another" (Keltuyala, *op. cit.* p. 348). The Latin version translates this: "Inter nos nullus mentitur, nec aliquis potest mentiri. Et si quis ibi mentiri coeperit, statim moritur, quasi mortuus inter nos reputatur, nec eius mentio fit apud nos nec honorem ulterius apud nos consequitur. Omnes sequimur veritatem et diligimus apud nos invicem" (§ 51—52. Zarncke, *op. cit.* p. 916).

Another point of similarity lies in the great number of high ecclesiastics who figure in the legend. Byelovodiye had a large number of them as we have seen, but in this it was not behind India. Prester John was surrounded by a large throng of kings, princes, armies, and officials. "In mensa nostra comedunt omni die iuxta latus nostrum in dextra parte archiepiscopi XII, in sinistra parte episcopi XX, praeter patriarcham sancti Thomae et protopapatem Sarmagantinum et archiprotopapatem de Susis" (§ 73, Zarncke, *op. cit.* p. 920).

The general outlines of the Church at Oponia and in India are so similar that we are led to assume some relationship. Melnikov says (*op. cit.* p. 25): The rumors about "the patriarch of the Assyrian tongue living in Japan, spreading more and more widely, finally spread throughout the entire Russian Old Faith, exactly as the rumor spread during the middle ages and was accepted as truth for several centuries of the existence somewhere in the East of Prester John. And in fact, the whole surroundings of the mediaeval Prester John are absolutely similar to the surroundings of the Raskolnik 'Assyrian Patriarch who is in the kingdom of Oponia'." It is strange that Melnikov did not mention the possibility of a new form of the old legend as the basis for Oponia. This relationship is the more likely when we remember that the home of Marko, the Topozersky Monastery, is in the Government of Archangel, almost in the region in which the *byliny* were preserved for so many centuries. The wandering minstrels and preachers who were telling about Oponia could hardly have failed to know of the wonders of the Christian land of India the Rich.

It remains now to explain the references to Antioch and Assyria in the story of Oponia. For some reason Antioch was always regarded with more favor than the other patriarchal sees by the Russian Old Believers. They could not bring themselves to believe that this see also agreed with the other Eastern patriarchates and they held that those Antioch ecclesiastics who in Russia associated with the Nikonian priests would be prevented by God from returning home. Similarly again and again the Old Believers asserted that their rites and traditions were not based on those of Constantinople but of Antioch and Syria, and apocryphal books were freely circulated under the name of various saints of Antioch. Of course Antioch was the most Eastern of all the sees, and its jurisdiction extended over Orthodox Christians to the East of the Empire when there were any in those regions.

Besides this, Syria and Assyria were closely associated in the minds of the Slavs. Another interesting example of this is the statement of the Monk Khrabar to the effect that the language which Adam and Eve spoke was Syrian and not Greek or Hebrew (cf. Novakovich, *Primeri Knjiznevosti i Jazika starago i staro-slovenskago*, p. 204). He then continues that after the dispersal of the languages God gave to the Assyrians the knowledge of magic and necromancy of different kinds. It was probably from such beliefs that the idea spread that the Syrian usages were the more ancient and therefore the more correct.

With such inconsistencies and conceptions well established it was easy for the see of Antioch to be confused and connected with India and Prester John. Otto von Freising declares that John was a Nestorian (Zarncke, *op. cit.* p. 848) but this is not emphasized by all the comtemporary narrators and is probably a mere surmise. As a matter of fact the Mongol leader Ku-Khan, who was probably not a Christian of any kind, seems to have been the conqueror known in the West as Prester John (Zarncke, *op. cit.* 863). Be that as it may, we are not here directly concerned with the development and growth of the legend in its better known phases.

Usually the legends of Prester John place his Christian country in the heart of Asia. Oponia is an island. It will however be noted that the anonymous account to which we owe the first information about the visit of the Patriarch John to Pope Calixtus (Zarncke, *op. cit.* p. 839) lays much stress on the fact that the shrine of St. Thomas is situated on a lofty mountain in the middle of a lake and is accessible only at the yearly ceremonies in honor of the saint. This detail may have had some effect upon the site of Byelovodiye.

There was also in northern China a small colony of Old Believers who had been transported in 1685 to a site near Pekin after their capture at Albazin. At times attempts were made to provide these people with priests, but this was not done regularly and it is said that part of this colony was converted to the Roman Catholic Faith by the Jesuits (Khokhlov, *op. cit.* p. 90). We can hardly assume that these scattered groups had any effect on the form of the story, although they may have had some influence on wanderers to the East.

We may sum up by saying that the account of Oponia contains no detailed description which will prove that the Old Believers had any substantial knowledge of Japan. An approximation to the name of the country and a story of mountainous islands are all that the story contains; but on this slight framework the Old Believers drew a charming picture of an ideal state. To supply the details they undoubtedly turned not to Marco Polo nor to stories of St. Francis Xavier but to their own oral tradition of India the Rich. Being ignorant of the details of geography they embellished this with striking results. In consequence Prester John, driven from Persia to China and to Abyssinia, seems to have found a last resting place in Japan where he furnished a refuge for the long-suffering Old Believers who sought to flee from Antichrist to a new land of promise and of peace, of piety and devotion, the Land of the Rising Sun.

NEU-PERSISCH YĀZDÄH

PAUL TEDESCO

VIENNA, AUSTRIA

MEHRERE ZAHLWÖRTER der 2. Dekade zeigen im Mittel- und Neu-Persischen ein auffallendes *ž*, bzw. *z*. Im Alt-Persischen, wo „12" und „13" vorkommen, sind sie unglücklicherweise nicht ausgeschrieben, sondern durch Zahlzeichen gegeben (Meillet *VP.* 37). Nur durch diesen Zufall konnte das *z* der späteren pers. Formen bisher überhaupt ein Problem bilden, denn mit der Erschließung der altpersischen Form ist es, wie sich zeigen wird, erklärt.

Die späteren persischen Dialekte haben:

mpT.[1] *yāzdaḥ(ôm), duvāzdah*[2]

mpM. u. mpB.[1] *y'čdḥ, dv'čdh* und *dvb∘, syčdh, čḥ(')rdḥ, pnčdḥ, ššdḥ* u. B. *š'č∘, ḥpdḥ* u. *ḥpt∘, ḥš∘* u. *ḥšt∘, nvč∘* u. *nḥvč∘* (vgl. mpM. *nvḥ*, B. *nḥv*).

np. *yāzdäh, duvāzdäh, sēzdäh, čahārdäh, pānzdäh, šānzdäh, haf(t)däh, haštdäh (hiždäh), nūzdäh (nuvāzdäh).*

Dagegen haben die Nord-Dialekte *z*-lose Formen:

aw. **aēvandasa, dvadasa, *ϑridasa, *čaϑrudasa, pančadasa* usw.[3]

nwT.[1] *'ēvandas, duvādês* u. *duvadas.*[4]

chr. soγd. *dvāṭas.*

---

[1] mpT. = mittelpersisch (im engeren Sinne) der Turfan-Handschriften; nwT. = nordwest-iranisch der T.-H.
mpM. u. B. = mittelpersisch der Münzen und Bücher.

[2] mpT. *duvāzah* neben *duvāzdah* vielleicht nicht „verschrieben" (so Salemann *Man. Stud.* 66), sondern jüngere Form. In den Pars-Dialekten wird *st>s, zd>z*, vgl. *nāzik, duzī* (Mann *Pers-D.* 14, 15).

[3] Die unbelegten Formen im Ordinale erhalten; vgl. Bartholomae, *Gr.* I_1, § 210).

[4] nwT. einmal *duvadas* (im selben Text *duvādēs* und *duvādês*) ist trotz ost-oss. *duvädäs* gegen west-osset. *duvadäs* wohl nur Defektiv-Schreibung, nicht altes Stammkompositum, wie die ost-oss. Form.

osset. o.-oss. *yuändäs*, *duvädäs* (aber west-oss. *duvadäs*), *ärtindäs* usw.

Eine Erklärung des *č(z)* versucht zuerst Darmesteter *Ét. Ir.* I, 147; auf ihr fußt Horn, *Gr.* I 2, 114 u. 72: *č* sei von *pančdah* aus übertragen, sei in ‚*yāčdah*', ‚*duvāčdah*' lautgesetzlich zu *z* geworden und von hier aus *z* auf *panǰdah* rückübertragen.

Solche Ausgleichs-Erscheinungen gibt es in der 2. Dekade nun allerdings: vgl. afγ. *diyār-las* ‚13', *spāṛas* ‚16' nach *cvār-las* ‚14'; osset. *ärtindäs* (d. i. **ϑrin-dasa*) nach *yuändäs; äχsärdäs* ‚16' nach *cippärdäs* ‚14' (also ‚16' nach ‚14' umgeformt genau wie im Afγanischen).

Dennoch erscheint die Verschleppung eines so schweren Wort-Elements wie des *č* von *pančdah*, das zudem in seinem Ausgangspunkte nichts für die 2. Dekade Charakteristisches war, sehr unwahrscheinlich; ebenso die Umgestaltung der jedenfalls häufigeren ‚11', ‚12', ‚13' nach ‚15'; meinem Sprachgefühl waren die Wörter ‚*duvāčdah*', ‚*sēčdah*' von jeher unmöglich.

Die Schwierigkeit der Hypothese wird noch größer, wenn man die Frage stellt: Wie sind die Vorformen von ‚*yāčdah*' usw. vor Übertragung des *č* zu denken? Wie man sich ap. ‚13' vorstellte, wissen wir: Hübschmann *P. St.* Nr. 763 gibt **ϑʳa-yadaϑa*, ebenso Brugmann *Gr.* 2, II, 24 **ϑʳayaʰdaϑa*. Das wäre eine ap. Neuzusammenrückung des einfachen Zahlworts (im Nomin.) mit **daϑa*. ‚11' und ‚12' wären analog als **aivaʰ-daϑa*, **duvādaϑa* anzusetzen, was mp. **ēvdah*, **duvādah*, **sēdah* ergeben hätte. Davon hätten die letzteren für ‚*duvāčdah*', ‚*sēčdah*', nicht aber das erstere für ‚*yāčdah*' die Basis gegeben.

Aber genug von diesen Unformen; schon die bloße Diskussion der Vorformen gibt die richtige Lösung: statt der obigen höchst sonderbaren Neu-Zusammenrückungen wie **ϑʳayaʰ-daϑa* haben wir doch naturgemäß alte Komposita vorauszusetzen; diese aber konnten nur vor-persisch

**aivazdaϑa*, **duvādaϑa*, **ϑrayazdaϑa*

lauten.

Davon ist **ϑrayazdaϑa* unmittelbar gleich np. *sēzdah* und verbindet sich weiter mit ai. *trayodaśa* und lat. *trēdecim* (aus **treịezdek̑m̥*).

**aivazdaϑa* und **duvādaϑa* wurden gewiß schon früh zu **aivāzdaϑa* und **duvāzdaϑa* ausgeglichen (wobei wohl älter, weil einfacher, die Übertragung der Länge in die ‚11'-Zahl; jünger, vielleicht erst nach-altpersisch, die das Wortbild stärker modifizierende des *z* in die ‚12‘-Zahl); das sind aber schon die unmittelbaren Vorformen von np. *yāzdah, duvāzdah.*[5]

Weiter ergibt sich, daß rein lautlich die ai.-Formen *ekādaśa, dvādaśa, trayodaśa* den np. *yāzdah, duvāzdah, sēzdah* direkt gleich (bzw. homolog) gesetzt werden können. Doch ist ai. *dvādaśa* kaum aus **dvāzdaśa* entstanden; eher schon *ekādaśa* aus **aikāzdaśa.*

ekādaśa wurde bisher erklärt 1. als Stamm-Kompositum **ekadaśa* mit *ā* nach *dvādaśa* und 2. als Zusammen-Rückung mit dem Nom. fem.

Ersteres ist aber schwierig, weil die übrigen Sprachen nominativische Zusammenrückungs-Komposita haben (so ἕνδεκα, *ūndecim* und selbst aw., wo in ‚12‘ und ‚13‘ Stamm-Kompositum, **aēvandasa*) und auch letzteres ist bei der relativen Seltenheit des Femininums nicht wahrscheinlich. Da scheint ein **aikāzdaśa* parallel vor-pers. **aivāzdasa* aus älterem **aikazdaśa* parallel **aivazdaśa* mindestens ebenso möglich. Das Eindringen des Langvokals in die ‚11‘-Zahl könnte dann schon indo-iran. gewesen sein, und es ist nicht ausgeschlossen, daß die Ersetzung von **aivaz- (*aikaz-) daśa* durch **aivāz- (*aikāz-) daśa* nicht nur durch *dvādaśa* verursacht wurde, sondern auch die pluralische Bedeutung des ganzen Kompositums und seine Verbindung mit dem Plural mitgespielt hat, d. h., daß **aivāz- (*aikāz) daśa* in gewissem Sinne Plural-Dvandva sind.[6]

Wir haben also folgende Kompositionsformen:

‚11‘: Durchwegs nominativisches Zusammenrückungs-Komp.; und zwar im Vorderglied entweder Nom. neutr.: aw. **aēvandasa* (fortgesetzt in nwT. *ʿēvandas*, ost-oss. *yuändäs*), griech. ἕνδεκα (und lat. *ūndecim*, wenn aus **oinomdekem*) —

oder Nom. mask., pers. und ind. wohl früh umgeformt in

---

[5] *yāzdah: *aivāzdaθa = yak: *aivaka-.* Zur Gestalt der Kompositions-Fuge vgl. Bartholomae *Gr.* I_1, § 304, IIa): jAw. *xvarᵊnaz-dā* (neben *xvarᵊnō. dā*), *aogazdastəma*; ap. *vahyazdāta-*; jAw. *māz-drājahīm.* Das Alt-iranische hat im Kompositum Wortinlauts-behandlung (**θrayazdaθa* wie *nazdišta-*); das Alt-indische Satzinlauts-behandlung (*trayodaśa* gegen *nediṣṭha-*).

[6] Herr Prof. Bartholomae (brieflich) lehnt das ab, weil *eka-* und *aiva-* pronominal flektieren; doch finden sich ja auch substantivische Formen (Whitney *Gr.* § 482, b) und bleibt als Hauptmoment der Einfluß von *dvādaśa.* — [The *ā* of *ekādaśa* might also be explained as ‘rhythmic lengthening’; Wackernagel, AIGr. II. 1. § 56. — F. E.]

Nom. Plural mask.: ai. *ekādaśa*, ap. **aivāzdaϑa* und Nachformen (; lat. *ūndecim*, falls aus **oinozdekem*).

‚12‘: Nominativisches Zusammenrückungs-Komp. in ai. *dvādaśa*, ap. **duvādaϑa;* gr. δυώδεκα, δώδεκα; lat. *duōdecim;*

aber Stamm-Komp. in aw. *dvadasa*, das wegen ost-osset. *duvädäs* nicht bloß graphisch (Defektiv-Schreibung) sein muß (auch ‚13‘ hat im Aw. entgegen dem Ind. und Pers. Stamm-Komp.); jedenfalls aber muß daneben auch in den nordiranischen Dialekten **duvādasa* bestanden haben, denn dies setzen nwT. *duvādês*, west-oss. *duvadäs* voraus.

‚13‘: Nominativisches Zusammenrückungs-Komp. in ai. *trayodaśa*, ap. **ϑʳagazdaϑa*, lat. *trēdecim;*

aber Stamm-Komp. in aw. **ϑridasa*, fortgesetzt durch ost-osset. *ärtindäs* (aus **ϑrindasa*, nach **aivandasa* umgeformtes **ϑridasa*).[7]

‚14‘: Aw. und ai. Stamm-Komp. (**čaϑrudaśa* und *caturdaśa*). Auffallenderweise geht also das Persische immer mit dem Indischen gegen das Awestische.

Das *z* ist also in ‚11‘ und ‚13‘ altererbt; in dem dazwischenliegenden ‚12‘ jedenfalls alte Analogiebildung; von diesen drei Zahlwörtern aus, wahrscheinlich den häufigsten der 2. Dekade, konnte es sich leicht ausbreiten, zumal da im Alt-persischen und Frühmittel-persischen das *z* gegenüber den entsprechenden Zahlen der ersten Dekade als für die zweite charakteristisch empfunden werden mußte (ap. **ϑʳagazdaϑa: *ϑʳayaʰ*, mp. *sēzdah: sē*).

Also np. *nōzdah* oder (nach *du: nuh* oder älter *dō: *nō = duvāzdah:* x) *nuvāzdah; z* statt des ursprünglichen Konsonanten in *pānzdah, šānzdah; čahārdah* durch mp. Neu-Komposition. [Für das Alt-persische wäre wohl nach Maßgabe des Altindischen **čaϑʳudaϑa* wie aw. **čaϑrudasa* anzusetzen, was mp. **tasdah* ergeben hätte, weshalb eben die Neu-Komposition eintrat.]

---

[7] [Auch aw. *ϑridasa* könnte (mit H. Prof. Bartholomae brieflich) Zusammenrückungs-Kompositum, mit dem Plural neutr. **ϑrī*, sein, vgl. aw. **aēvandasa*.]

Gegenüber gemeinind. *trayodaśa*, fortgesetzt in mi. usw. *terasa*, scheint sich das Nordwestindische mit Aśoka Šāhbāzgaṛhī *tidaśa* (vgl. Johansson *Šāhb.* II, 77) und heutigem Bašgalī *trits* < **tridaśa* (wo *ts* < *ś*, *d* gefallen, vgl. *dots* = *daśa*; Konow *JRAS.* 1911, 20) mit dem Nordiranischen (Awestischen) zu verbinden.

Das *n* dagegen in bal. (Lehnwort) *sēnzdah*, np. *šānzdah*, Kurd. (Kirmānjī) *yānzdah*, *dvānzdah*, (Amadia) *nunzdah* ist natürlich von *pānzdah* ausgegangen wie umgekehrt Mukrī-Kurd. *päzdä* nach *yäzdä*.

In diesen Zahlwörtern hat sich also eine indogermanische Kasus-Endung (der Nom. Pl. **-ās* der *a*-Stämme und **-ayas* der *i*-Stämme) bis heute rein erhalten. Da also die Zahlwörter der ersten und zweiten Dekade und im Pers. auch die Zehner auf den Nominativ zurückgehen,[8] ist es nicht auffallend, wenn auch das Substantiv in der Zahlwort-Verbindung den alten Nom. Plur. erhalten hat, während sonst der Obliquus durchgedrungen ist.[9] Es liegt in der Natur der Sache, daß die Zahlwortverbindung besonders oft außerhalb eines eigentlichen Satzzusammenhanges, d. h. im Nominativ steht.

Nur ein Punkt bleibt noch zu erklären: die Pählävī-Schreibung dieser Zahlwörter mit צ. Diese hat ja auch offenbar Darmesteter und Horn zu ihrer Erklärung veranlaßt. Nach dem Gesagten kann man צ hier zweifellos nur als Schreibung für *z* auffassen.

Nun wird allerdings die Gruppe *zd* im Pählävī sonst יז geschrieben; vgl. *öhrmazd, azd, nazdīk* usw.

duvāzdah, sēzdah usw. waren aber im Mp. offenbar sowohl phonetisch (durch stärkere Druckgrenze) als im Sprachbewußtsein, (indem das gemeinsame Hinterglied der zweiten Dekade *-dah* abstrahiert werden mußte), deutlich aus zwei Wörtern zusammengesetzte Komposita.

Sie fielen also nicht unter *nazdīk* usw. (noch weniger natürlich unter *-mazd, azd* mit tautosyllabischem *zd*), sondern das Vorderglied wurde als Einzelwort geschrieben. Dann fielen

---

[8] Hübschmann's Zurückführung von *sē* auf aw. Gen. Pl. *ϑrayąm* (S. 78) statt den Nom. Pl. *ϑrāyo* ist sprachgeschichtlich nicht möglich; der spätaltiran. Gen. Pl. kann nur **ϑrīnām* gelautet haben; und np. *du, čahār* lassen sich nur auf aw. *dva*, d. i. *duvā, čaϑwārō*, nicht auf *dvayå, čaturąm* (oder späteres **čaϑvārānām*) zurückführen.

Überhaupt ist aw. *ϑrayąm* nur falsche Transskription von *try'vm* gegenüber richtigem *ϑryąm*, d. i. *ϑriyōm* = gr. τριῶν. Andrerseits ist im aw. Nom. *ϑrāyō (tr'yv)* statt **ϑrayō ā* nur graphisch nach Andreas Wackernagel *GN*. 1911, S. 12, b). Yaγnōbī *tirāi* kann aw. *ϑrāyō* nicht stützen, sondern beruht auf Sonder-Entwicklung.

[9] Vgl. Verf. *Nom. Plur.* 6 ff. (*Anz. WAW*. 1921).

aber *yāz* und *duvāz* in die Gruppe *āz, rāz, varāz*, geschrieben *'č, r'č, vr'č, sēz* in die Gruppe *mēz-, (rist-) āχēz,* geschrieben *myč-, 'ḥyč*, und mußten daher *y'č-, dv'č-, syč-* geschrieben werden.

Überhaupt wird ja, um das nur einmal kurz klarzustellen, *z* intervokalisch (und nach *r*) im jüngeren Pählävī regelmäßig durch צ gegeben; vgl. außer obigen Beispielen *hazār* (צ) *āzardan* (צ), *frazānak* (צ), *virāz* (צ), *āzāδ* (צ, aber sehr bemerkenswerter Weise Hājīābād noch ז!); nur in wenigen Wörtern (*vāzišt, māzandar, uzīδan*) ז noch neben צ; nur in ganz wenigen (*frazand, nizār*) nur ז (vielleicht durch Kompos.-Anlaut).

Eine ausführliche Darstellung dieser Verhältnisse und ihrer sprach- und schriftgeschichtlichen ratio soll ein andermal gegeben werden.

Hier genügt es, zu erkennen, daß, um so mehr als awestisch gleichartige Formen, an die man sich in der Orthographie hätte anlehnen können, nicht vorlagen, *yāzdah* usw. im Pählävī nicht anders als mit צ geschrieben werden konnten.[10]

---

[10] Ein treffendes Analogon zur Schreibung verdanke ich der Freundlichkeit Herrn Prof. Barthelomae's: *'včdyḥ, 'včdyḥyk* neben *'vzdyḥyk* = aw. *uzdaḥyav-* (*Wb.* 412).

THE SUMERIAN AFFIXES *TAM* AND *KAM*

PAUL HAUPT
JOHNS HOPKINS UNIVERSITY

IN SUMERIAN we often find after numbers an affix *tam* (written TA-A-AN). It is used also in Assyrian, just as we write 1°, 2° (= It. *primo, secondo*) for *first* or *second occurrence*, respectively. We also use *No.* (= It. *numero*) for *number*. Similarly we retain the Latin preposition *per* in phrases like *per day, per hour*. In German you say *pro anno* for *per annum* (also *pro Stück*). We also use the French preposition *sans*. The *ta* of the cuneiform affix *ta-a-an* may be omitted (*NE* 49, n. 12; 136, n. 15; Lyon, *Sarg.* 16, n. 40).[1] This omission may be merely graphic: 1-*a-an* (*HW* 153[a]) was probably pronounced *aš-tân*. In iv R[2] 16, 7[a] (*cf.* 1, n. 25) Sum. *dingir* 1-*a-an* is rendered in the interlinear Assyrian version: *ilu ištânu*, the only god, written *iš-ta-a-nu*, which shows that the *a* was long. We say *quarto, octavo*, no matter whether we write 4to, 8vo or 4°, 8°.

This Sumerian numeral affix is preserved in Heb. *ʿaštê-ʿaśár*, eleven, *ʿaštê* (< *ʿaštên*) being the Ass. *eštên*, one, which is the Sum. *aš-tân*, the first syllable being the numeral, and *tân* the numeral affix. The final nasal is dropped also in the cuneiform texts: instead of *am* (*a-an*) we find also *â* (written A-A): *e. g.* Streck, *Assurb.* 577, l. 11; *cf.* SG § 198, c. For the apocope of the final nasal we may compare Talmud. *ammáį* < Ass. *ammêni*, wherefore. (*Mic.* 104; *JBL* 29. 104, n. 61; *JSOR* 1, 41). According to SG 61, n. 1 only the first syllable of Ass. * eštên*, one, is undoubtedly Sumerian. For the adverb *aš-e-eš* (*SG* § 78, b) = *ešteniš*, at one, in accord, in agreement, in the same way, see *MVAG* 26. 2, p. 43. Instead of *ša* (= 4) in *ASKT* 67. 3 *AV* 6360 has the figure 5; *cf.* also *JBL* 19. 68, n. 40.

---

[1] For the abbreviation see vol. 37 of this JOURNAL, p. 321; cf. *American Journal of Philology*, vol. 43, p. 238.

Am (written A-AN) is a common affix in Sumerian (Br. 11401; *SG* §§ 197–201). We have it also in *dam,* consort; *tam,* brother; *nam,* fate, which are contractions of *da* (or *ta*) + *am* = (at the) side being (*cf.* Hesychius' ἄπλευρος = ἡ μὴ ἔχουσα βοήθειαν) and *declaration being* (*SGl* v. 133. 156. 197). The abstract prefix *nam,* on the other hand, seems to be a contraction of *na,* verily (*SG* § 100) and *am,* anything (*SG* § 55, b) so that this *nam* would correspond to Heb. *lĕ-ḵól* (*GK*[28] § 143, e; *GB*[16] 372[a], c; *VS* 110).

Ta means in the litanic (*ZA* 31, 244) dialect: *what?* (*CV* xxxvii, *ad* n. 23) and this may denote *something* (cf. our *I'll tell you what*) or *portion,* amount (*cf.* a little *what*). Instead of *ta,* what? we find also *ta-am* (*SG* § 52, c). Also the common Chinese numerative *ko* may mean *something*: in the dialect of Shanghai *ku* (or *kau̯*) appears also as relative pronoun. There are more than 20 Chinese numeratives which are used only in special cases, *e. g.* in connection with circular things (rings, &c.) or globular things (pearls, &c.). Similar numeratives (or classifiers, numeral coefficients) are used in Siamese, Malay, &c. (*EB*[11] 6, 217[b]; 25, 9[b]; 17, 477[b]; Misteli, *Typen des Sprachbaues,* pp. 191. 219. 263). It has recently been suggested by Hüsing that there may be some affinity between Sumerian and Burmese. The Mongoloid people of the Far East must have come from the West; the cradle of mankind seems to have been in southwestern Europe (*cf.* Hrdlička, The Peopling of Asia, *PAPS* 60. 545).

For these numeratives we may compare our phrases *twenty head of deer* or *fifty sail of ships* (Maxwell, *Malay Manual*[4], pp. 70. 136). In the *lingua franca* of the Chinese ports and the Far East, known as Pidgin-English (*pidgin* being a Chinese corruption of *business*) we hear *one piecee man* or *three piecee dollar.* Similarly the driver of a Bavarian *Stellwagen* (stagecoach, omnibus) used to speak of *zehn Poststücke* (postal parcels) and *sechs Stück Fahrgäste* (passengers). Just as you say in Malay: *ampat bîji tĕlor* for *four eggs,* the word *bîji,* seed, being the numerative for globular things, so you can say in German: *vier Stück Eier* or *eine Meute von vierzig Stück Hunden,* or *er erlegte hundert Stück Wild* (cf. also *ein Laib Brot* and our *an orchestra of twenty pieces,* i. e. musicians). Ger. *vier Mann Soldaten* is different from Gr. ἄνδρες στρατιῶται and similar phrases where ἀνήρ corresponds to our *Mr.* in *Mr. President, Mr. Secretary, Mr. Ambassador.* For *your father* you say in French: *monsieur votre père,* Ger. *Ihr Herr Vater.*

The explanation given in *AJSL* 20. 231, No. 24 (cf. Muss-Arnolt's dict. p. 1176[a]) that the cuneiform affix TA-A-AN is to be read *ina ân,* in amount (*cf.* Syr. *dĕ-ḳâịlâ*) is untenable; in the first place, TA is used in Assyrian, as a rule, for *ištu,* from; moreover, we should expect *ina âni* or, rather, *anî*; the form *an* is the construct state of *anû,* just as the construct state of *šadû,* mountain, is *šad* (*AJSL* 22. 259[m]). This word (cf. *ZA* 10, 12, n. 3; *ZR* 64[a]) is derived from the stem of *unûtu* = *unaụtu,* pl. *unâti* = *unaụâti*; Arab. *inâ',* Heb. *ŏnî,* vessel. *Anû, an* does not mean *amount,* and *tam, tan* is found, not only in Assyrian, but also in Sumerian, e. g. *ASKT* 55. 37—42 and in the last line but one of the last Sumerian family-law (V R 25, 21). For *egir-bi-tam* in l. 7[c] cf. *JAOS* 38. 67; *SG* § 101, a[f].

Nor can we accept the view that 7-*ta-a-an* in an Assyrian text is to be read *sibîtan* or *šibîtan* (Streck, *Assurb.* 78. 577). Torczyner, *Die Entstehung des semitischen Sprachtypus* (Vienna, 1916) pp. 87—118 (*cf.* especially p. 115[i]) regards TA-A-AN and A-AN as Semitic endings, the *ta* being the Semitic fem. *t* (cf. *JAOS* 28. 115). According to Ungnad (who had prepared a paper on this question for the *Festschrift,* which was planned for the seventieth anniversary of Delitzsch, but could not be published) *a-an,* which afterwards became *â,* is a Semitic demonstrative pronoun which may be compared to the ending of the emphatic state in Aramaic; he thinks it possible that the original form of this *ân* or *â* was *ammâ* or *agâ* (*OLZ* 25. 8).

Muss-Arnolt's reading *ina ân* for TA-A-AN was based on *AL*[3] (1889) p. 36, No. 313: *ana ân,* in amount; *ana-ân,* however, on Bezold's pl. iii in *PSBA* 10. 418, is not the Assyrian preposition *ana,* but the Sumerian interrogative pronoun *ana,* what? (*SG* § 52, c). This *ta-am* (TA-A-AN) and *ana-am* (A-NA-A-AN) corresponds to the Heb. *mazzê GK*[28] § 136, c; *GB*[16] 193b[i]; *cf.* also *mî-hû-zê, JBL* 37. 217, v. 19 and *Nah.* 20[i]; *Mic.* 97[m]) or to Eth. *ment-nû.* The Assyrian equivalent may have been *minâ-ma* or *minâ-mi* (*BA* 2. 305; *AJSL* 28. 228. 239). For the affix *-mi* see *HW* 387[a]; for *annîtu-mî* and the vocative *ilâni annûti* (*KB* 6. 62, 28; 240, 165) *cf.* (ὦ) οὗτος. The *-mî* in Heb. *šimrû-mî ban-náʿr, bĕ-'Abšalôm*, look out for the boy, Absalom, may be miswriting for *lî* (so 𝔊𝔖𝔍𝔗 & 2 MSS). The explanation given in *GK*[28] § 137, c is unsatisfactory. For *-ma* in OT see the remarks on *bîšûʿatĕká-ma* (Ps. 21, 2) in *JBL* 37. 214.

According to AL[2] (1878) p. 10, No. 97, TA-A-AN was read *taian, tain* in Sumerian and meant *measure*, number (cf. *CG* 279; *SFG* 64. 4).

While the Sumerian numerative *tam, tan* may mean *something*, the affix after ordinal numbers, *kam*, is composed of the genitive particle *-ka* and *-am*: Sum. *aš-kam*, first, means lit. *one-of being*, being of one (*SG* § 88). Similarly Syriac uses for the ordinals the cardinal numbers with the prefixed exponent of the genitive e. g. *iáumâ da-tĕrên*, the day of two = the second day (Nöldeke, *Syr. Gr.*[2] § 239). In Malay the ordinal numbers have a prefixed *ka*: e. g. *tiga*, three; *ka-tiga*, third. Witzel in the first part of his *Keilinschriftliche Studien* (Leipsic, 1918) p. 89, n. 1 combines the ordinal affix *kan* with *gan*, totality, Ass. *kullatu*. He thinks the original meaning is *fulness*, so that the Sumerian ordinal affix would correspond to the Coptic ordinal prefix *meh* (= Eg. *meḥ*) which means orig. *filling out*, completing: the fifth of a series completes the number five. We find the same formation in Egyptian. But there is no evidence that Sum. *gan*, totality, means *fulness*. According to *SG* 84 the primary connotation of *gan*, totality, may be *union*, association. *Gan* denotes also *bolt*, bar (Ass. *sikkûru*) for fastening a door, and the original meaning may be *fastener*. A fastening binds and makes fast. In the cuneiform texts the ordinal affix *-kam* is generally added, not horizontally, but aslant (*cf. ASKT* 55. 35; iv R[2] 5. 14—25[a]) just as we write 4th for 4th = *fourth*, or as we use a slanting $_{and}$ in making out a check for Fourhundred$_{and}$twenty Dollars. Cf. *AJP* 43, 245.

NABONIDUS IN ARABIA

RAYMOND P. DOUGHERTY

GOUCHER COLLEGE

A CLAY TABLET[1] in the Goucher College Babylonian Collection, dated in the 5th year of Nabonidus (555—538 B. C.), directed the writer's attention to a study of the relations existing between Babylonia and Arabia in the 6th century B. C. The tablet in question is a temple record stating that fifty shekels of silver were given to a man for a donkey and some flour for the purpose of making a journey to *mât Te-ma-a*, i. e., the land of *Temâ*[2]. The document itself gives no clue as to where it was drawn up, but it belongs to a collection

---

[1] Text No. 294, *Archives from Erech, Time of Nebuchadrezzar and Nabonidus*, Vol. I of *Goucher College Cuneiform Inscriptions*.

[2] The transliteration and translation of the inscription are as follows: *50 šiqil kaspi a-na 1 imêri alakti (A-GUB-BA) ù a-na qîmi (ZÌD-DA)-šu a-na md Nabû-mušêtiq-urra apil md Ištar-na-din-aḫi ša a-na mât Te-ma-a šap-ra na-din araḫ Addaru ûmu 5 kam šattu 5 kam d Nabû-nâ'id šar Bâbili ki.* "Fifty shekels of silver for one road donkey and his flour are given to Nabû-mushêtiq-urra, the son of Ishtar-nâdin-aḫi, who is sent to the land of *Temâ*. The 5th day of Adar, the 5th year of Nabonidus, king of Babylon". The term *A-GUB-BA* = *alaktu* = "road" (see Brünnow 11494) evidently means that the donkey *(imêru)* was capable of making a long journey. It seems best to connect the pronominal suffix of the phrase *a-na qîmi (ZID-DA)-šu* with Nabû-mushêtiq-urra, as flour was generally supplied for the use of human beings. Cf. Strassmaier, *Nbn* 1065, 3. 6. 9. *Ibid.* 214, 7 and *Nbk* 282, 1. 2 show that it was possible to purchase a donkey and at least 5 kors of flour for 50 shekels of silver. According to *Nbn* 1065, 3. 1 *pi* of flour was dispensed as the food of 13 goldsmiths. If 1 *pi* of flour represents the rations of 13 men for one day, 5 kors of flour would last one man 325 days (1 kor = 5 *pi*). Thus 5 kors of flour would be a liberal allowance for a journey of about 500 miles from Erech to *Teimâ*, and return, even if more than 1 *pi* were used a day. It may be presumed that the main purpose of the donkey was to carry this large supply of food for the man on his long desert march. The primary meaning of *šapâru* indicates that the man was commissioned to deliver a message.

of nearly a thousand tablets coming mainly from Erech in southern Babylonia, and this practically determines its origin.

The inscriptions of Tiglathpileser IV (745—727 B. C.) give accurate information as to the geographical position of *Temâ*, for *âl Te-ma-a-a* is associated with *[âl] Ma-as-'-a-a-a* and *âl Sa-ba-'-a-a-a*[3]. The list of the sons of Ishmael in Genesis 25, 13—15 includes תֵּימָא and מַשָּׂא, and it is altogether likely that the expression *âl Sa-ba-'-a-a-a* is an Assyrian gentilic equivalent of שְׁבָא, Genesis 10, 7; 25, 3; and Job 1, 15. Thus the identification of *mât Te-ma-a* with Biblical תֵּימָא seems firmly established, and that the reference is to a district in Arabia is equally certain[4].

Teimâ, or *Teymâ* (تَيْمَاءُ), the well-known city of Arabia, has already been shown to be the same as Hebrew תֵּימָא and Assyrian *âl Te-ma-a*, which represents the name of the city, while *âl Te-ma-a-a* is equivalent to Arabic *Teimâny*, which means "A man of *Teimâ*"[5]. The district in which *âl Te-ma-a*, i. e., the city of *Teimâ*, was located was called *mât Te-ma-a* by the Babylonians. *Teimâ* was recognized as an important city in antiquity[6]. It is called Θαῖμα on Ptolemy's map of Arabia Felix. However, we are indebted to modern explorers and

---

[3] III Rawlinson, *The Cuneiform Inscriptions of Western Asia*, 10 No. 2, 38 ff. Cf. *Keilinschriftliche Bibliothek*, Band II, p. 20, line 53, Delitzsch, *Wo lag das Paradies?* p. 301 f.; Schrader *KAT*², p. 149; Meyer, *Die Israeliten und ihre Nachbarstämme*, pp. 318 f., 327, 346, 347, 462. For minor references to *Teimâ* consult Sprenger, *Die alte Geographie Arabiens*, §§ 28, 32, 148, 220, 332.

[4] Job 6, 19 associates תֵּימָא with שְׁבָא. In Isaiah 21, 13. 14, "The burden concerning Arabia" includes a reference to אֶרֶץ תֵּימָא = *mât Te-ma-a*. Jeremiah 25, 23, which mentions תֵּימָא, is followed by "and all the kings of Arabia, and all the kings of the mingled people that dwell in the wilderness".

[5] Cf. Delitzsch, *Wo lag das Paradies?* p. 303. See *ibid.* pp. 295 ff. for a discussion of all cuneiform references to Arabia. Note Text No. 175, 3, *Archives from Erech, Time of Nebuchadrezzar and Nabonidus*, for *ṣubât A-ra-bu* = "an Arabian garment". As to Arabic *Teimâny*, cp. תימניא, p. 385, Lidzbarski, *Handbuch der Nordsemitischen Epigraphik*, which has been related by some to "Temanite", Job 2, 11, etc. Note Gesenius, Buhl. 1921, p. 877. Others derive תֵּימָנִי from תֵּימָן.

[6] Consult Nicholson, *A Literary History of the Arabs*, p. 84, for a reference to a legend concerning Samaw'al, who lived in a castle at *Teimâ* and dug a well of sweet water. The Arabs have a tradition that *Teimâ* was built by Solomon. See El-Bekri in *Mara'sid*, IV, 23.

writers such as Wallin, Doughty and Hogarth[7] for detailed accounts concerning the city and its environs. Wallin's report of his visit to *Teimâ* in 1848 makes note of its favorable location, its mode of irrigation, and its excellent products[8]. Doughty, a generation later, reveals its attractive appearance[9], its prosperous condition[10], its good water supply[11], its flourish-

---

[7] Doughty, *Travels in Arabia Deserta*, 1921; Hogarth, *The Penetration of Arabia*, 1904.

[8] *Cyclopaedia of Biblical Literature,* Vol. X,p. 242f., "Teimâ stands on a mass of crystalline limestone. very slightly raised above the surrounding level. Patches of sand, which have encroached upon the rock, are the only spots which can be cultivated. The inhabitants, however, have considerable date plantations, which yield a great variety of fruit, of which one kind is esteemed the best flavored in all Arabia. Grain is cultivated, especially oats of a remarkably good quality, but the produce is never sufficient for the wants of the inhabitants. The greater portions of the gardens are watered from a copious well in the middle of the village. The hydraulic contrivance by which water is raised for distribution through channels among the plantations is the same as is used through Mesopotamia as well as in Nejd, viz., a bucket (Arabic *dullû* = Assyrian *dalû*) of camel skin hung to the end of a long lever moving upon an upright pole fixed in the ground".

[9] Doughty, *Travels in Arabia Deserta*, 1921, Vol. I, p. 285, "Delightful now was the green sight of *Teymâ*, the haven of our desert; we approached the tall island of palms, enclosed by long clay orchard-walls, fortified with high towers. *Teymâ* is a shallow, loamy, and very fertile old flood-bottom in these high open plains, which lie out from the west of Nejd". "We entered between grey orchard-walls, overlaid with blossoming boughs of plum trees; of how much amorous contentment to our eyes!"

[10] *Ibid.* p. 286, "Prosperous is this outlying settlement from Nejd, above any which I have seen in my Arabian travels"; p. 293f., "Their corn plots are ploughed, in the fall of the year, with the well-camels, and mucked from the camel-yards; a top-dressing is carried upon the land from loam pits digged in the field's sides. There is not so good tillage in the Syrian villages". Doughty enumerates the following products of *Teymâ*: wheat, barley, corn, millet, tobacco, plums, pomegranates, figs, citrons, lemons, grapes and dates.

[11] *Ibid.* p. 286; "If anyone here discover an antique well, without the walls, it is his own; and he encloses so much of the waste soil about as may suffice to the watering; after a plowing his new acre is fit for sowing and planting of palms, and fifteen years later every stem will be worth a camel". "Their wells are only the wells of the ancients, which finding again, they have digged them out for themselves".

ing groves and gardens[12], its valuable salt deposits[13], its height of 3400 ft. above sea level[14], its freedom from plagues and fevers[15], its manufacture of sleeping carpets[16], its trade with Damascus and Bagdad[17], its extensive ruins[18], its ancient inscriptions[19], and its old importance as the center of a large province[20]. Hogarth emphasizes the fact that *Teimâ* was "on the old route from the Gulf of Akabah to the Persian Gulf" and "a dividing point of roads from Petra to Gerra (on the Persian Gulf) in the east and Sheba in the south"[21]. It is in the Great Nafud, which furnishes plenty of food for horses and cattle and is the home of Bedouin tribesmen a large part of the year[22].

---

[12] *Ibid.* p. 293.

[13] *Ibid.* p. 296, "In the grounds below the last cultivated soil, are salt beds, the famous *memlahát Teymâ.* Thither resort the poorer Beduins, to dig it freely: and this is much, they say, 'sweeter' to their taste than the sea-salt from Wejh. *Teymâ* rock-salt is the daily sauce of the thousand nomad kettles in all these parts of Arabia". See *ibid.* p. 287, for a sketch of the oases, ruins, salt grounds, etc., of *Teimâ.*

[14] *Ibid.* p. 285.

[15] *Ibid.* pp. 286f.

[16] *Ibid.* p. 302.

[17] *Ibid.* p. 295.

[18] *Ibid.* p. 287, "Old *Teymâ* of the Jews, according to their tradition, had been (twice) destroyed by a flood. From these times there remain some great rude stone buildings; the work is dry-laid with balks and transoms of the same ironstone. Besides, there is a great circuit (I suppose almost three miles) of stone walling, which enclosed the ancient city"; p. 288, "But the great mosque, whither all the males resort for the Friday mid-day prayers, preaching and Koran reading, stands a little without the *sûks* to the eastward. It is perhaps the site of some ancient temple, for I found certain great rude pillars lying about it". Note also pp. 549 and 552.

[19] *Ibid.* pp. 291 and 296.

[20] *Teimâ* consists of three oases, *ibid.* p. 533, and originally included seven townships. Old *Teimâ* was the borough of the district. See *ibid.* p. 551. "Like other Arab tribes the children of *Temâ* had probably a nucleus at the town of *Teimâ*, while their pasture grounds extended westward to the borders of Edom and eastward to the Euphrates, just as those of the Beni Shummar do at the present time". *Cyclopaedia of Biblical Literature*, Vol. X, p. 243.

[21] Hogarth, *The Penetration of Arabia*, p. 280. P. 156, *ibid.*, notes the importance of the Shammar region in Arabian traffic with Babylonia.

[22] *Ibid.* p. 257f.

An exceedingly interesting indication of the ancient culture and central position of *Teimâ* is a monument known as the "Têma Stone", which may be compared with the Moabite Stone because of its valuable Semitic inscription, dealing with the introduction of the worship of a foreign deity[23]. The script is that of "the early part of the middle period of Aramaic writing". Cooke says, "Caravans (Job. 6, 19) on their way to Egypt or Assyria halted here (i. e., at *Teimâ*); and the influence of commerce with these two countries is evident in this stone: the name of the priest's father is Egyptian, the figures of the god and his minister are Assyrian"[24]. Another suggestion of Mesopotamian influence upon *Teimâ* is seen in certain words in the inscription supposed by some to have been borrowed from the Babylonians[25]. The name of one of the deities may also be compared with that of a Babylonian goddess[26]. It is thought that the "Têma Stone" belongs to the 5th century B. C. and that the city enjoyed a high degree of civilization at that time, with its religious life largely colored by Babylonian influence. If this is so, we can readily understand that a similar condition prevailed in the 6th century B. C., and possibly earlier, for, as has been noted, Tiglath-pileser IV refers to the people of *Teimâ* in the 8th century B. C.

Half-way between Mecca and Damascus and equidistant from Babylonia and Egypt, it is undoubtedly true that *Teimâ* occupied a strategic position in the trade routes of early times. Hence it is easy to perceive the importance of the Goucher tablet which indicates that a man was commissioned

---

[23] Cf. Cooke, *North Semitic Inscriptions*, pp. 195—199; *Revue d'Assyriologie*, Vol. I, pp. 41—45. Note references under *Temâ* in Hastings' *Dictionary of the Bible.*

[24] Cf. Cooke, *ibid.*, p. 197.

[25] Winckler suggests the following: צרקתא = *sattuku*, שימתא = *šîmtu*, and סותא = *asumitu*. See Winckler, *Altorientalische Forschungen*, I pp. 183 f. and II pp. 76 f. Professor Montgomery has called the writer's attention to the fact that the first two terms may be regarded as good Aramaic words, while סותא has been compared by Noeldeke to Arabic صُوَّة.

[26] Cf. Cooke, *ibid.* p. 198, where he discusses the deity שנגלא. He says, "The name has been compared (Corp.) with that of a Babylonian goddess שנגל, mentioned in the lexicon of Bar Bahul, and stated to be the Chaldaean equivalent of Aphrodite, Legarde, *Gesam. Abhandl.* 17. Another suggestion is that Singala *(Sin-gala)* is the moon-god, Neubauer, *St. Bibl. i* 224 *n*".

to make a journey from Babylonia to the land of *Teimâ* in the 6 th century B. C. That such a journey was not a hardship is shown by the line of oases within easy reach of one another stretching 500 miles from the Euphrates to the city of *Teimâ*[27]. The desert was not an impassable barrier, for Nebuchadrezzar, having pursued the Egyptians to the border of their land after the battle of Carchemish in 605 B. C., upon hearing the news of the death of his father Nabopolassar, hurried back across its sands to make sure of his throne in Babylonia[28].

The most interesting reference to *Teimâ* in cuneiform literature remains to be considered. In the Chronicle of Cyrus concerning the reign of Nabonidus and the fall of Babylon it is recorded that Nabonidus was in *âl Te-ma-a* in the 7th, 9th, 10th and 11th years of his reign, while the son of the king (i. e., Belshazzar), the princes and the soldiers were in *mât Akkadu*[29]. Pinches connects *âl Te-ma-a* with *Te-e ki ša ki-ir-ba Bâbili ki* and *Tu-ma ki*[30]. Aside from the difficulty of equating *âl Te-ma-a, Te-e ki* and *Tu-ma ki*, and thus proving that a section of the city of Babylon is meant, the statement in the Chronicle that Nabonidus was in *âl Te-ma-a* is almost immediately followed by the declaration that the king did not go to Babylon[31]. The conclusion is warranted that *âl Te-ma-a* was not in the city of Babylon. In fact, it is intimated that *âl Te-ma-a* was outside the country of Akkad, for the statement that Nabonidus was in *âl Te-ma-a* is opposed by the affirmation that Belshazzar, the princes and the soldiers were in *mât Akkadu*[32]. Thus it is apparent that *âl Te-ma-a* of the Chronicle

---

27 Cf. the excellent maps at the close of Hogarth, *The Penetration of Arabia. Ibid.* opp. p. 282, gives a good photograph of the "Têma Stone".

28 Cf. Winckler, *The History of Babylonia and Assyria,* p. 316. See Richter, *Berosi Chaldaeorum Historiae,* p. 66.

29 Cf. *Transactions of The Society of Biblical Archaeology,* 1882, Vol. VII, pp. 139—176; *Keilinschriftliche Bibliothek,* Band III, 2. Hälfte, pp. 130 f.; *Beiträge zur Assyriologie,* Vol. 2, pp. 214—225, 235—257.

30 Cf. *ibid.* p. 171, with illustration on page 152, showing plan of the city of Babylon, mentioning the district *Tu-ma ki.*

31 *Ibid.* pp. 156, 157, 160, 161.

32 Cf. King, *History of Sumer and Akkad,* p. 12, for reference to the fact that the Assyrians used the term Akkad loosely for the whole of Babylonia. The Neo-Babylonians evidently used the term in the same way. Cf. Halévy, *Mélanges de critique et d'histoire,* p. 2, note 2.

of Cyrus must be sought without the bounds not only of the city of Babylon but of Babylonia itself.

The fact that important religious ceremonies were not performed in the 7th, 9th, 10th and 11th years of the reign of Nabonidus may be adduced as corroborating evidence[33]. It is difficult to believe that the king failed to function at these exalted rites while within reach of his capital city. Furthermore, when the mother of Nabonidus died in the 9th year of his reign, one of the years when he was in *âl Te-ma-a*, he is not mentioned as taking part in the mourning which was observed in Akkad[34]. The only inference that can be drawn is that he was too far away to participate. Another link in the chain of evidence is a Yale tablet, dated in the 10th year of Nabonidus, when he was in *âl Te-ma-a*, indicating that food for the king was taken to *mât Te-ma-a*[35]. The Yale Babylonian Collection also contains two royal leases of land issued during the reign of Nabonidus. One, dated in the 1st year of his reign, was obtained from Nabonidus himself[36]. The other, dated in the 11th year of his reign, when he was in *âl Te-ma-a*, was obtained from Belshazzar who is mentioned by name[37]. Thus it may be claimed that there is sufficient documentary proof for the conclusion that Nabonidus spent at least portions of the 7th, 9th, 10th and 11th years of his reign outside of Babylonia proper at a city called *âl Te-ma-a*. That this *âl Te-ma-a* is the same Arabian city referred to by Tiglath-pileser IV can hardly be doubted. Its identification with Biblical תֵּימָא, Ptolemy's Θαῖμα and modern تيماء seems within the bounds of reason, if not inevitable.

---

[33] Cf. references given in note 31.

[34] Cf. *Transactions of the Society of Biblical Archaeology*, Vol. VII, p. 158 f.

[35] Text No. 134, *Records from Erech, Time of Nabonidus*, Vol. VI of *Yale Oriental Series, Babylonian Texts*. The food was brought back and sold by a slave, who was required to restore it at once to the temple in Erech. Cf. Text No. 131, 13, *ibid.*, dated in 10th year, and Text No. 155, 6, *ibid.*, dated in the 12th year.

[36] Text No. 11, *ibid.*

[37] Text No. 150, *ibid.* In this text Belshazzar is presented in the rôle of an exacting lord as compared with the more gracious attitude ascribed to Nabonidus in Text No. 11.

Various reasons may be suggested for the visits of Nabonidus to *âl Te-ma-a*, now known as *Teimâ*. In the first place, as a victim of the malarial climate of Babylonia he may have sought relief in the clear desert air and elevated atmosphere of *Teimâ*. Or, as an archaeological enthusiast and rebuilder of temples, he may have been attracted by the inscriptions and monumental structures at *Teimâ*. Goodspeed supposes that Nabonidus was forced into retirement in the 7th year of his reign and that Belshazzar then became the real ruler of the nation[38]. This view cannot be substantiated. In the 12th regnal year oaths were still sworn by the laws or decrees of "Nabonidus, king of Babylon, and Belshazzar, the son of the king"[39]. Crown prince Belshazzar, as the second ruler in the kingdom[40], had almost equal authority with his father, but he is not mentioned as king in a single instance on the numerous contract tablets covering all the years ascribed to Nabonidus[41]. Moreover, possession of full kingly authority

---

[38] Goodspeed, *A History of the Babylonians and Assyrians*, p. 372.

[39] Texts Nos. 225 and 232, *Records from Erech, Time of Nabonidus*, Vol. VI of *Yale Oriental Series, Babylonian Texts*. Cf. Text No. 39 and discussion on page 55 of *Miscellaneous Inscriptions in the Yale Babylonian Collection*, Vol. I of the same series, for a document dated in the 7th year of Nabonidus, recording two dreams which were interpreted as favorable to both Nabonidus and Belshazzar. See *Expository Times*, Vol. XXVI, pp. 297—299, for a corroborating text published by Pinches. These texts confirm the view that Nabonidus maintained his kingly authority with the help of Belshazzar. There is nothing to indicate that the latter revolted against his father.

[40] It was because of Belshazzar's position next to his father that Daniel was made the third ruler in the kingdom after he interpreted the handwriting on the wall. See Daniel 5, 29. Josephus refers to "Baltasar, who by the Babylonians was called Naboandelus", and states that Baltasar reigned 17 years, which corresponds to the number of years ascribed to Nabonidus. This confusion of Belshazzar with Nabonidus is not surprising under the circumstances.

[41] See Strassmaier, *Inschriften von Nabonidus*; Clay, *Legal and Commercial Transactions, dated in the Assyrian, Neo-Babylonian and Persian Periods, BE* Vol. VIII, Part I; Clay, *Babylonian Business Transactions of the First Millennium B. C.*, Part I of *Babylonian Records in the Library of J. P. Morgan*; Keiser, *Letters and Contracts from Erech*, Part I of *Babylonian Inscriptions in the Collection of J. B. Nies*; Dougherty,

by Belshazzar would have made unnecessary the non-performance of metropolitan rites and ceremonies during the absence of Nabonidus. Hence the theory that Nabonidus sought asylum at *Teimâ* as a deposed monarch is far from the truth.

Likewise, it is difficult to regard either ill health or archaeological zeal as a sufficient explanation for the extended stay of a Babylonian king in Arabia, 500 miles from the seat of his empire, over which he still maintained control, and within 150 miles of the Red Sea. If it must be admitted that Nabonidus spent much of his time at *Teimâ*, it is natural to suppose that the northern and central sections of Arabia were under his rule. As the inscriptions of Nabonidus deal mainly with his building operations very little is said in them concerning the bounds of his empire. The statement usually quoted belongs to his descriptions of the restoration of the temples in Harran and Sippar, in which he simply says that he caused his numerous troops to come from Gaza at the border of Egypt, from the upper sea (i. e., the Mediterranean), on the other side of the Euphrates, as far as the lower sea (i. e., the Persian)[42]. Such a brief geographical reference cannot be regarded as determining the true extent of his domain. In the 8th century B. C. the inhabitants of *Teimâ* along with other Arabian peoples were tributary to Tiglath-pileser IV[43]. It is unlikely that these Arabian districts became permanently independent during the rule of the powerful Assyrian monarchs that followed, viz., Shalmaneser, Sargon, Sennacherib,[43a] Esarhaddon and Asshurbanipal. So when Nineveh fell in 606 B. C. and Egypt lost to Nebuchadrezzar at Carchemish in 605 B. C., we may suppose that the new régime in Babylonia inherited the neighboring and more distant oases

---

Records from Erech, Time of Nabonidus, Vol. VI of *Yale Oriental Series, Babylonian Texts*; Nies and Keiser, *Historical, Religious and Economic Texts and Antiquities*, Part II of *Babylonian Inscriptions in the Collection of J. B. Nies*; and Dougherty, *Archives from Erech, Time of Nebuchadrezzar and Nabonidus*, Vol. I of *Goucher College Cuneiform Inscriptions.*

[42] Cf Langdon, *Die Neubabylonischen Königsinschriften*, pp. 220 f., Col. I, lines 38 f.

[43] See note 3.

[43a] Herodus, II. 141, calls Sennacherib "king of the Arabians and Assyrians".

of Arabia, if indeed it had not already absorbed them. The tradition preserved by Josephus that Nebuchadrezzar made Egypt a Babylonian province adds to the probability that the part of Arabia which was one of the highways of commerce and travel between the Mesopotamian and Nile valleys was similarly dominated[44].

Little light is thrown upon this problem by Greek, Latin and Arabic sources[45]. Ptolemy 6, 7, 17, mentions a people living on the Persian Gulf called Θαμοί or Θεμοί. Note also the بنو تيم, referred to by Jakut, *Moscht.*, pp. 310, 352, 413. Fleischer, *Hist. Anteislam*, p. 198, thinks that the *Beni Teim* may refer to the original inhabitants of *Teimâ* wandering in different parts of Arabia. Forster, *Geography of Arabia*, I, pp. 289 f., holds similarly that the *Beni Temim*, who dwelt mainly on the shores of the Persian Gulf, sprang from the city of *Teimâ*[46].

These indications that people of *Teimâ* had their abode in the region of the Persian Gulf are interesting. It must be remembered, however, that Cyrus in his Chronicle states definitely that Nabonidus was in *âl Te-ma-a*, i. e., the city of *Teimâ*. If he had meant to convey the impression that Nabonidus was simply in a district that was settled by people from *Teimâ*, he would have used the more general term *mât Te-ma-a*. Furthermore, the *âl Te-ma-a* cited by Cyrus was well-known or else he would have been more precise in his reference to the place.

Knowledge of only one important city, thus named, has come down to us, and there is no doubt that *Teimâ* in Arabia enjoyed a renown and prestige in the ancient Semitic world far beyond our present conjecture[47]. It is entirely within the range of historical possibility that *Teimâ* was the political center from which Nabonidus governed his Arabian province, while Belshazzar looked after affairs in Babylonia. Such a situation would corroborate and give added significance to the position occupied by Belshazzar as an energetic and masterful crown prince. The most interesting revelation, however, is

---

[44] Cf. King, *A History of Babylon*, p. 278.
[45] Cf. Weber, *Arabien vor dem Islam*, pp. 9f.
[46] Cf. note 20.
[47] See notes 18 and 20.

that Arabia seems to have been intimately connected with Babylonia in the 6th century B. C.[48]

---

[48] Cf. *JAOS* Vol. 41, p. 458 for a preliminary note on this subject. After the writer had come to his conclusions an interesting reference in Tiele, *Babylonisch-Assyrische Geschichte*, 1886, Part 1, pp. 470f., was found. Tiele arrived at the same view concerning the location of *âl Te-ma-a* without the bounds of Akkad, but specifically states that it cannot be the Arabian city mentioned by Tiglathpileser IV, although he suggests no proof for this latter inference beyond its apparent improbability. At the same time he recognizes the historical enigma presented by the absence of Nabonidus from Babylonia but finds no solution for it. Hagen in *Beiträge zur Assyriologie*, Vol. 2, 1894, pp. 236f. and note, also decides against the identification of *âl Te-ma-a* with *Teimâ* in Arabia. His theory is that *âl Te-ma-a* was the favorite residence of Nabonidus in Babylonia outside the capital city. He refers to the fact that it was customary for Babylonian kings to have such special living quarters from which they would depart for Babylon only at the time of the New Year's festival. However, it has already been shown that the direct intimation of the record is that *âl Te-ma-a* was not in Babylonia and that Nabonidus did not go to Babylon for the usual ceremonies at the beginning of the years he is mentioned as being at *âl Te-ma-a*. This can only be explained by the supposition that Nabonidus was at a considerable distance from the political center of his kingdom. Hagen also refers to the building operations which Nabonidus credits to himself at Sippar, Harran, etc., during the years when he spent at least part of his time at *âl Te-ma-a*. Hence he concludes that *âl Te-ma-a* must have been located in Babylonia, or the supervision of this work on the part of Nabonidus would have been impossible. It is true that the building inscriptions of Nabonidus, like those of his predecessors, are very detailed in their accounts of operations, but it is not necessary to suppose that everything was done under the royal eye. No doubt the work was supervised by special officers who made reports to the king when he could not be present. Nabonidus, even at *Teimâ* in Arabia, could have kept in touch with all the affairs of his domain in which he was interested, as an elaborate messenger service was maintained in ancient times. Cf. note 2. For instance, in the first month of the 7th year of his reign, when he was at *âl Te-ma-a*, he gave a command to Belshazzar to attend to a certain matter. Cf. Text No. 103, 1—3 of *Records from Erech, Time of Nabonidus*, Vol. VI of *Yale Oriental Series, Babylonian Texts*. Texts Nos. 71 and 72, *ibid.*, indicate that Nabonidus may also have been absent from Babylonia in the 6th year of his reign, as a very important question concerning the use of temple paraphernalia in Erech was referred to Belshazzar in that year. The records were investigated for the purpose of determining the precedents set by Nebuchadrezzar, Neriglissar and Nabonidus. A decision made by Nabonidus in the

first year of his reign was quoted. It must be presumed that a weighty matter was not decided without referring it to the absent king, unless a previous action on his part gave the needed authority. That Nabonidus seems to have been interested in the western part of his empire during the early years of his reign is indicated by the references to Hamath, Mt. Ammananu and the Sea of the Westland in the opening fragmentary lines of the Chronicle of Cyrus concerning Nabonidus. Cf. note 29.

NEW LIGHT ON MAGAN AND MELUḪA

W. F. Albright

American School in Jerusalem

The rapidity with which knowledge progresses in the ancient Oriental field is well illustrated by the flood of new material with reference to Magan and Meluḫa. In Schroeder's new volume, *Keilschrifttexte aus Assur verschiedenen Inhalts* (Leipzig, 1920) there is some very important evidence on the subject. Text No. 92 is a kind of geographical handbook, describing the extent and the mutual relation of the dominions of Sargon II of Assyria, but pedantically, and not always accurately, substituting names and terms from the age of Sargon of Akkad, wherever possible. Line 30 ff. reads: 120 double-hours *(bêrê)* of marching distance *(šiddu)* from the dam *(KUN = miḫru)* of the Euphrates to the border of Meluḫa and Mari *(MÀ(!)-RÍ-KI)* which Sargon (Šarrugina), king of the world, when he conquered the expanse of the heavens (sic, *siḫip šamê*) with might, traversed. Here we are informed that it was 240 marching hours from the fords of the Euphrates between Mari and Sumer, or Babylonia, as follows from line 29, to the boundary between Mari and Meluḫa.[1] But where could Mari, on the middle Euphrates, and Meluḫa in Africa have possibly met? Clay has long

---

[1] The 240 hours from the Euphrates to the Egyptian frontier imply, at three miles an hour, an actual marching distance of about 720 miles. The actual distance in a straight line from Thapsacus to Raphia, and thence to Pelusium is five hundred miles, but during the course of a month spent in walking over Palestine and Syria, the writer learned that it required eight marching hours to cover a distance of sixteen miles measured by the map, owing to the relatively large amount of climbing and detours which is necessary in this rough country. Accordingly, the 120 double-hours are precisely what we should expect. Similarly, the 30 double-hours from Aphek to Raphia, given is Esarhaddon's report, correspond to 130 miles in straight line.

maintained that Mari is really synonymous with *MAR-TU*, or Amurru, and refers to Syria, as well as to the middle Euphrates country, but few have accepted his view. Now, however, it is proved for the seventh century B. C. by the remarkable geographical vocabulary published by Schroeder, No. 183, line 11, where Mari is explained by *mât Ḫatti*, the Hittite country, which in late Assyrian texts is the regular expression for Syria, including Palestine.

In late Assyrian texts, from Sargon to Aššurbânapal, Meluḫa always refers to the Ethiopia *magna* of the Pianḫi dynasty, and is thus often extended to include Egypt, which formed a part of the Ethiopian Empire. Sargon II says, in his Triumphal Inscription, line 102 f., that Yamani of Ashdod fled *ana itî Muṣuri ša pâṭ mât Meluḫa*, "to the part (lit. border) of Egypt which is in the territory of Meluḫa". The king of Meluḫa in line 109 is the Ethiopian monarch. The same usage is found in the texts of Sennacherib. It explains the confusion in the mind of Esarhaddon's scribe when he says, describing Esarhaddon's famous desert march to Egypt, "From Magan I departed, to Meluḫa I approached", and then mentions the 30 double-hours from Aphek (Apqu = Fîq, east of the Sea of Galilee) in Samaria (Same[ri]na) to Raphia, which is just one-fourth the total distance from the Euphrates to the Egyptian frontier, in perfect agreement with the estimate given above. From Raphia, instead of taking the direct route by way of Pelusium, and attacking the strongly fortified frontier zone, Esarhaddon, gathering camels and supplies from "all" the tributary Arab sheikhs, made a terrible desert march by way, it would seem, of Suez, and outflanked the Egyptian army of defence. His description of the serpents met within the "Arabah" reads like an excerpt from the book of Numbers. In the Esarhaddon text Magan takes the place of the Mari of the geographical inscription, since under the Sargonids Egypt was included under the head of Meluḫa and there was thus no room in Africa for Magan. However, the old condition of affairs survives, as indicated by the alternation between Magan and Meluḫa in some texts and Muṣur and Meluḫa in others.

That Magan was not combined with Syria in the early period is shown by the Sumerian texts I have quoted in previous papers, and proved by a passage in the geographical text already cited, which in this case obviously derives its information from early Babylonian sources. Lines 41 ff. state: Anami,[2] Kaptara (Eg. *Kptr*, Bib. Caphtor), lands beyond *(BAL-RI)* the Upper Sea (Mediterranean), Tilmun, Magana, lands beyond the Lower Sea (Persian Gulf), and the lands from the rising of the sun to the setting of the sun, which Sargon, king of the world, up to his third (year?) conquered *(qâtsu ikšudu)*. So Magan is faithfully given, in accord with the old Sumerian tradition, as a land beyond the Persian Gulf by the sea route — and yet it is on the land route from the Euphrates to Meluḫa = Ethiopia!

Lest the problem should be cleared up too speedily, our new vocabulary furnishes an additional complication; line 13 has (b-d) *kúr Ma-gan-naki* = *mât Ṣi-id-di-ri* = *[mat M]i-iṣ-r[i]*. As Col. b contains only Old Babylonian names from the third millennium, we may consider *Ṣiddiri* as an early form of the same word which later appears in Babylonia as *Miṣri, Miṣir*, and in Assyria as *Muṣri, Muṣur*. The word has thus originally a *d* between the *ṣ* and the *r*, just as in the later Greek form, Μεσδ(τ)ραιμ, where the δ is, however, apparently a secondary parasitic element. The primary Egyptian name would then be approximately **ᵉmḏĕdrew*, heard by the Babylonians as **Čĕdere*, which would have to be written in cuneiform as *Ṣiddiri*, with accentual doubling of the *d*. Later we may suppose that the Western Semites corrupted the plural, **Miṣidrîm*, 'Egyptians', into the more compatible *Miṣrîm*, from which the various forms, Amarna *Miṣri*, Heb. dual *Miṣráyim*, singular *Maṣôr* (by popular etymology, following *maṣôr*, 'fortification') were derived by back-formation.

---

[2] The cuneiform text, as given by Schroeder, has *A-na-AZAG*, which is certainly a mistake, like *É-ZU* and *LIL-URU* for *MÀ-URU* = Mari elsewhere in our text. In a cramped Assyrian hand there is no noticeable difference between *AZAG* and *MI*. It is possible that Anami is the Anamim of Gen. 10 13, which may represent Cyrene, being followed by Lehabim, the Libyans of Marmarica. The Caphtorim of the next verse are naturally the people of Kaptara, or Crete. Cnossus in Crete is mentioned in a text of Esarhaddon found at Assur as Nusisi, if we may accept Peiser's identification (*OLZ* 14. 475; 15. 246). Cf. also the remarks in my paper to appear in *JPOS*, 'A Colony of Cretan Mercenaries on the Coast of the Negeb'.

The fact that Magan is in one passage termed a land of copper, so far from being against its identification with Egypt, is in favor of it. Hume, *Preliminary Report on the Geology of the Eastern Desert of Egypt*, 1907, pp. 56 f., says that copper ores are found in the eastern desert, and that there are old workings at Abskiel and Abu Hamamid, a statement confirmed by Mr. Thomas, *JEA* 7. 110. I have also been assured by a mining engineer, Mr. Walter Middleton, that there is an abundance of copper ore in the Nubian desert, in the region northwest of Port Sûdân, which to the Egyptians was the coast of Pûnt. This explains why the Egyptians and Sumerians brought malechite from *Pwnt* = Meluḫa.

Nor can there be any doubt now that the invasion of Egypt by a king of the Dynasty of Akkad was quite within the range of probability. Thanks to the remarkable discoveries of Forrer, Hrozný and others among the treasures of Boghazkeui, it is now certain that Sargon I extended his conquests far beyond Mari, or northeastern Syria, and Ibla, or northwestern Syria, into southwestern Cappadocia, where he captured the city of Buršaḫanda, Hittite Barsuḫanta, between Ḫubišna = Kybistra and Tuwanuwa = Tyana. Moreover, according to a text described by Forrer, *Die acht Sprachen der Boghazköi-Inschriften*, p. 1038 f., a king of Akkad, almost certainly Sargon, fought a coalition of the kings of Kanis, near Caesarea Mazaca, Ḫatte (Boghazkeui) and Kursaura, northwest of Tyana.

Despite recent assertions, it is absolutely certain that Yarimuta, as described in the Amarna tablets, lay to the south of Phoenicia. The indications of the letters sometimes point rather to the Delta than to the Plain of Sharon, but the non-Egyptian form of the name and the Semitic names of the two functionaries, Yanḫamu and Yapa-Addi, point rather to Palestine. Moreover, Amarna, No. 296, can only mean (which does not appear to have been observed) that Gaza and Joppa, both Egyptian garrison towns, were in the district controlled directly by Yanḫamu, that is, in Yarimuta. In *JEA* 7. 80, the writer was unable to check Professor Sayce's identification of Yarimuta with 'classical Armuthia', but since this paper was written the necessary books have been acquired. There is no classical Armuthia at all! The source of it is Tompkins, *TSBA* 9. 242, *ad* 218 (of the Tuthmosis list): 'Maũti. Perhaps the Yari-mūta of the Tel el-Amarna tablets, now (I think) Armūthia, south of Killis.' 'Armūthia' is only a bad orthography for Armûdja, a small village some three miles south of Killis, and thirty north of Aleppo, not on the coast at all, but in the heart of Syria. Moreover, instead of the Nos. 298—301 of the Tuthmosis list, quoted by Professor Sayce as Arsha, Mari, Ibl, and Qarmatia, we really have Nos. 298—299, *Ỉ3-r3-š3-[ ]*, *M3-ry-[ ]*, and 306—307(!) *Ỉy-b-r3*, *K3-r3-my-ty*. The first two identifications, as well as the fourth, are impossible, though the third is probably right. In this connection it should be observed that Professor Sayce's effort to do away with Ethiopians in the Amarna texts by creating a north-Syrian Kus (*JRAS* 1921, 54) is useless. He quotes an Assyrian letter which locates the cities of Arpad, Kullania, and Dana in the land of the *Ku-sa-a* (pronounced *Kûšâ'a*), but the latter is simply the gentilic corresponding to the well-known Bît-Gûsi, or Beth Gosh. Arpad was the capital of Bît-Gûsi, and Kullania is generally located in it by Assyriologists, while there is no geographical objection to placing Dana there as well.

Since the conquests of Narâm-Šin extended further toward the southwest than those of Sargon, there is no place for Magan but Egypt, unless one insists on identifying it with Winckler's ill-fated Arabian Muṣri in Midian. Hall's observation (*JEA* 7. 40) that Manium is undeniably a common Semitic name is very strange; the writer would very much like to have it pointed out in other inscriptions. The ending *ium* is found also affixed by the Akkadians to non-Semitic names, as *Gutium*; it is exactly parallel to Lat. *Arminius* for *Herrmann*, &c.

It is quite premature to say that the chronological situation forbids our synchronism. Langdon's date for Narâm-Šin, given in his lecture on 'The Early Chronology of Sumer and Egypt' (cf. *Near East*, May 5, 1921, p. 530 b) as 2795(3?)—2739 is a *terminus ad quem*. For the reasons previously outlined, it seems to me necessary to allow fully 125 years between the expulsion of the Guti and the accession of Ur-Nammu (formerly called Ur-Engur) B. C. 2475, which will bring the accession of Narâm-Šin to at least 2875[3]. The new 'short chronology'

---

[3] Thanks to the kindness of Professor Clay, I have been able to read

for Babylonia, which would reduce the date for Ur-Nammu to about 2300, has been disposed of in an article to appear in the *Revue d'Assyriologie.* Egyptian chronology naturally offers a more complicated problem, but the writer fails to see any particular difficulty in the scheme which reduces the period between the Sixth and the Twelfth Dynasty to 160 years, and allows an average of eighteen years each to the kings of the first two dynasties. Since it is steadily becoming clearer that the history of Egyptian civilization, especially in the Delta, reaches far back into the predynastic age, before 4000 B. C., why should an Egyptologist assume that the crude beginnings of Babylonian monumental art, in the days of Mesilim and Ur-Nina, must fall later than Menes? Our theory places them only two to three centuries earlier. Even with our rectification of the chronology, Egyptian art remains superior to contemporary Babylonian art, as will be easy to see on comparing, for example, the Tanite art of the Thinite period, as found by Capart in the group of 'Nile gods' in Cairo, and the Ludovisi statue at Rome, with the art of the Akkadian epoch in Babylonia.

---

the translation of the new dynastic fragment found in the Philadelphia Museum by Legrain. It offers very useful confirmation of the view outlined that there was an interval of some length between Utu-ĝegal and Ur-Nammu. The ninth column of the tablet contained the dynasty of Utu-ĝegal and the dynasty of Ur; it begins with the regnal years of the last monarch of Guti, and closes with the name of the third king of Isin, Idin-Dagân, thus containing the names of eight kings, and the record of three dynastic changes. While only the first seven lines of the column are preserved, we may estimate the number of names lost by comparing the situation in the seventh and eighth columns, where we are on firm historical ground. Col. VII contained the names of all the twelve kings of Akkad, and the five kings of Erech, with the record of two dynastic changes, and the partial account of another. Col. VIII contained the names of all twenty-one monarchs of Guti. Accordingly, Col. IX gave a least six, and probably seven names of the dynasty of Utu-ĝegal — less, naturally, if there were two dynasties here instead of one, which is hardly probable, despite Lugal-anna-mundu of Adab.

THE INDIAN GOD DHANVANTARI

Louis H. Gray
University of Nebraska

Although Dhanvantari is a deity of minor rank and importance, he merits somewhat detailed consideration since he is the only real Indian god of healing. The earliest known allusion to him appears to be *Kauśika Sūtra* 74. 6, which prescribes that a portion of the daily offering (*baliharaṇa*) be placed "in the water-holder for Dhanvantari, [? Cloud-] Ocean, Herbs, Trees, Sky, and Earth" (*udadhāne dhanvantaraye samudrāyauṣadhivanaspatibhyo dyāvāpṛthivībhyām*). In this connexion it should be observed that healing properties are very widely ascribed to water and herbs.

Sacrifice to Dhanvantari is frequently mentioned. "At evening and in the morning one should make offering of dressed *ghee* to the Agnihotṛ-gods, to Soma, to Vanaspati, to Agni-Soma, to Indra-Agni, to Heaven-Earth, to Dhanvantari, to Indra, to the All-Gods, to Brahmā, saying, '*svāhā*'" (*Āśvalāyana Gṛhya-Sūtra* 1. 2. 1—2),[1] and Dhanvantari receives a "Dhanvantari-leaf" (*dhanvantaritaparṇa*, *Mānava Gṛhya-Sutra* 2. 12. 19). At the *pākayajña*, a Brāhman must officiate at the "Dhanvantari-sacrifice", as he must at the similar rite in the *caityayajña* (*Ā. G-S.* 1. 3. 6; 1. 12. 5).[2] One year after the *nāmakaraṇa*, a goat and a sheep must be offered to Agni and Dhanvantari

---

[1] In *M. G-S.* 2. 12. 2—3, the order is Agni-Soma, Dhanvantari, All-Gods, Prajāpati, Agni Sviṣṭakṛt; in *Gautama Dharma-Śāstra* 5. 10, Agni, Dhanvantari, All-Gods, Prajāpati Sviṣṭakṛt; in Manu 3. 84—86, Agni, Soma, Agni-Soma, All-Gods, Dhanvantari, Kuhū, Anumati, Prajāpati, Heaven-Earth, Sviṣṭakṛt.

[2] For the *baliharaṇa*, *pākayajña*, and *caityayajña* see Hillebrandt, *Ritual-Litteratur*, pp. 74; 20, 71, 72—73; 86—87.

(*M. G-S.* 1. 18. 8). According to the *Mārkaṇḍeya Purāṇa* (29. 17), the oblation to Dhanvantari must be placed to the north-east, the quarter in which he dwells (cf. also *Viṣṇu Purāṇa*, tr. Wilson, 3. 118; *Mahābhārata* 13. 97. 12).

In the *Mahābhārata* (3. 3. 25; 13. 17. 104) Dhanvantari is one of the 108 names of the Sun and one of the 1008 names of Śiva; but it is doubtful whether these facts are of real significance in view of the Indian tendency to identify deities of divergent character by syncretism. The epic also recounts the legend most generally known concerning him, telling how, after the Ocean of Milk had been churned for a thousand years, he arose, the very Āyur-Veda, bearing a staff and a white bowl containing *amṛta* (*dhanvantaris tato devo vapuṣmān udatiṣṭhata, śvetaṃ kamaṇḍaluṃ bibhrad amṛtaṃ yatra tiṣṭhati*, *Mahābhārata* 1. 18. 38; *atha varṣasahasreṇa āyurvedamayaḥ pumān, udatiṣṭhat sudharmātmā sadaṇḍaḥ sakamaṇḍaluḥ, atha dhanvantarir nāma*, *Rāmāyaṇa* 1. 45. 31—32; cf. *Viṣṇu Purāṇa*, tr. Wilson, 1. 144). According to the *Bhāgavata Purāṇa* (1. 13. 17), he was the twelfth avatar of Viṣṇu, from whom he, "beholding the Āyur-Veda" (*āyurvedadṛg*), "was manifestly risen, limb for limb" (*sa vai bhagavataḥ sākṣād viṣṇor aṃśāṃśasambhavaḥ dhanvantarir*; ib. 8. 8. 34).

Besides this incarnation, Dhanvantari had a second avatar. The *Viṣṇu Purāṇa* (tr. Wilson, 4. 32—33) makes him a King of Kāśi (Benares), the great-great-great-great-great grandson of the famous Purūravas. He was free from human infirmities and possessed universal knowledge in every incarnation. In the life just previous to his avatar as Dhanvantari, Viṣṇu had conferred upon him the boon of being born a Kṣatriya and of becoming the author of medical science, besides being entitled to a share of the oblations offered to the gods. Similarly the *Trikāṇḍaśeṣa* (2. 7. 21) identifies him with "Divodāsa, King of Kāśi, nectar-born" (*dhanvantarir divodāsaḥ kāśirājaḥ sudhodbhavaḥ*). The *Bhāgavata Purāṇa* (2. 7. 21) also knows of this, speaking of "the glorious Dhanvantari, the very mention of whose name straightway slays the diseases of men oppressed with many diseases; . . . and, incarnate in the world, he teaches the Āyur-Veda" (*dhanvantariś ca bhagavān svayam eva kīrtir nāmnaḥ nṛṇām pururujāṃ ruja āśu hanti . . . āyuś ca vedam anuśāsty avatīrya loke*). This same Purāṇa gives (9. 17. 4—5) the genealogy Kāśya, Kāśi, Rāṣṭra, Dīrghatamas, Dhanvantari, Ketumant, and Bhīmaratha; while the *Harivaṃśa* (29.10.26—28; 32. 21—22) makes the line Kāśa (or Kāśika), Dīrghatapas, Dhanvantari, Ketumant, Bhīmaratha. In the latter poem (29. 9—28) we have a somewhat detailed account which may briefly be summarised. In reward for the penances of the aged King Dīrghatapas, Dhanvantari again arose from the ocean and for a second time became incarnate on earth. In his former birth he had meditated upon Viṣṇu as soon as he perceived the mighty god; and Hari had named him Abja ("Water-Born"). He had besought Viṣṇu, whose son he considered himself, for a share in sacrificial offerings and for a position upon earth; but the former had already been portioned, and only the latter remained available. Nevertheless, in his second avatar he would enjoy the dignity of a god, and would be worshipped by the twice-born with *caru* (oblations of boiled rice or barley; cf. the *pākayajña* of the Sūtras), *mantras*, vows, and *japas* (muttered prayers); while he would also promulgate the Āyur-Veda, which he already knew. The second incarnation, as Viṣṇu promised, took place in the second Dvāpara Yuga, when Dīrghatapas besought Abja for a son. Thus Dhanvantari was born in the King's house and in due time became ruler of Kāśi, whereupon, having acquired knowledge of the Āyur-Veda from Bharadvāja, he divided the duties of physicians into eight classes and conferred his lore upon his disciples.

According to medical tradition, as given in the *Suśruta-saṃhitā* (1. 2, 12, 16), the divine physician Dhanvantari, incarnate as Divodāsa, King of Kāśi, received the Āyur-Veda from Brahmā through the successive mediation of Prajāpati (or Dakṣa), the Aśvins, and Indra, and then taught it to Suśruta and the latter's six colleagues. To Dhanvantari are likewise ascribed the *Dhanvantarinighaṇṭu*, the oldest Indian medical glossary (though not of very ancient date), and a number of minor treatises.[3]

Later still, Dhanvantari, together with Kṣapaṇaka, Amarasiṃha, Śaṅku, Vetālabhaṭṭa, Ghaṭakarpara, Kālidāsa, Varāhamihira, and Vararuci, constituted the "nine gems" at the court

---

[3] Jolly, *Medicin*, pp. 12—14; Aufrecht, *Catalogus Catalogorum*, 1. 267, 3. 38; cf. Lassen, *Indische Alterthumskunde*, 2nd ed., 2. 518—519.

of Vikrama (Haeberlin, *Kāvya-Saṅgraha*, p. 1). It became a proverb that even the physician Dhanvantari could not help the dead (*api dhanvantarir vaidyaḥ kiṃ karoti gatāyuṣi*, *Hitopadeśa* 3. 141 = 4. 62); tradition told that, although he was "a goodly leech, a poet and a prince, and (an incarnation of both) Viṣṇu and Śiva, his gain was only the killing of a cow, since in the house of a fool neither profit, weal, nor wealth is received" (*sadvaidye kavibhūpatau harihare lābhaḥ paraṃ govadhaḥ*, Böhtlingk, *Indische Sprüche*, 2nd ed., no. 6486); and he, too, died, though, like Vetaraṇi and Bhoja, he had been able to cure serpents' bites (*dhammantarī vetaraṇī ca bhojo | visāni hantvāna bhujaṅgamānaṁ | sūyanti te kālakatā tath' eva*, *Jātaka* 510, *Visatinipāta* 340).[4]

Dhanvantari's name is still known in India. One tradition of the origin of the caste of Camārs (the curriers, tanners, and daylaborers found throughout Upper India)

> "makes them out to be the descendants of Nona or Lona Chamârin, who is a deified witch much dreaded in the eastern part of the Province. Her legend tells how Dhanwantari, the physician of the gods, was bitten by Takshaka, the king of the snakes, and knowing that death approached he ordered his sons to cook and eat his body after his death, so that they might thereby inherit his skill in medicine. They accordingly cooked his body in a cauldron, and were about to eat it, when Takshaka appeared to them in the form of a Brâhman, and warned them against this act of cannibalism. So they let the cauldron float down the Ganges, and as it floated down, Lona, the Chamârin, who was washing on the bank of the river, not knowing that the vessel contained human flesh, took it out and partook of the ghastly food. She at once obtained power to cure diseases, and especially snake-bite" (Crooke, *The Tribes and Castes of the North-Western Provinces and Oudh*, 2. 170—171; cf. also his *Popular Religion and Folk-Lore of Northern India*, 2nd ed., 2. 285).

Dhanvantari is likewise an important figure in the Panjābī legend of Princess Niwal Daī. According to this tale, Rājā Pārag (the Parikṣit of the *Mahābhārata*) was King of Safīdoṅ (a town in the Jind District of the Panjāb) and a disciple (*chelā*) of "Dhanvantari the Physician" (*Dhanhantar* [or *Dhāntar*, *Dhanantar*, *Dhănthar*] *Baid*); and in his capital were three

[4] A chapter in the fourth book of the *Brahmavaivarta Purāṇa* is entitled *Dhanvantaridarpabhaṅga;* but the text is not accessible to me at present.

wells, one of which contained *amṛta* (Temple, *The Legends of the Panjâb,* 1. 415, 440, 441, 451, 492, 494, 501). Against her father's will, he married Niwal Daī, daughter of the Nāga monarch Bāsak (Vāsuki); wherefore Bāsak sent the Nāg Chhīmbā, who bit Pārag and killed him. A charm recited by Niwal Daī restored him to life, but Bāsak sent two other Nāgs, Sūtak and Pātak, who again slew Pārag, to be revived once more by his wife.[5] A Nāg named Jīwan now caused his death for a third time, and Niwal Daī was unable to bring him back. She therefore summoned Dhanthar, who dwelt in the Ābū forest; and though Pārag had already been cremated, he revivified the ashes by touching them with *sejūn* (*Euphorbia antiquorum*, or milk-hedge).[6] Nevertheless, the Nāg Tatīg succeeded in biting Pārag, who thus met his fourth death. This time Dhanthar was not only unable to bring him back to life, but was himself fatally bitten (ib. pp. 490—492, 494, 497, 499—505, 512). As he lay dying, he bade his disciples to "cook and eat me; cut up all my flesh, and you will all become as Dhānthar the Leech" (*mujhe sab pakāke khā lenā, jī; merā mās sab kāṭ lo, jī; tum sab dhānthar baid ho jāo, jī*); but Tatīg induced the farmers to stone the *chelās*, and birds of prey carried off the flesh (ib. pp. 504—506). The development of the story is shown by the fact that in the standard Sanskrit version (*Mahābhārata* 1. 40—44) Parikṣit (Pārag)—here King of Hāstinapura—dies when bitten by the serpent Takṣaka, and no mention is made of any attempt to restore him to life.

Shrines in honor of Dhanvantari are rare. Nevertheless, about two miles east of Naoli, near the boundary of Bhainsror and Bhanpura, in Udaipur, is a Takaji-ka-kūnd ("Fountain of the Snake-King").

"The road, through a jungle, over the flat highland, or Pat'har, presents no indication of the fountain, until you suddenly find yourself

---

[5] The repeated deaths of Pārag preserve the tradition that Parikṣit was killed before birth by Aśvatthāman, but revived by Kṛṣṇa (*Mahābhārata* 10. 16. 1—16; 14. 64. 8; 70. 12).

[6] In Bengal the related *Euphorbia ligularia* is sacred to the serpent-goddess Mūṃsa, and its root, mixed with black pepper, is used both internally and externally for the cure of snake-bite (Roxburgh, *Flora Indica*, Calcutta, 1874, p. 392).

on the brink of a precipice nearly 200 feet in depth, crowded with noble trees, on which the knotted korū is conspicuous. The descent to this glen is over masses of rock; and about half-way down a small platform, are two shrines, one containing the statue of Takshac, the snake-king, the other of Dhanwantari, the physician who was produced at the churning of the ocean. The coond or fountain is at the southern extremity of the abyss" (Balfour, *Cyclopædia of India*, 3rd ed., 1. 932—933).

The meaning of the name Dhanvantari is not wholly certain. The Major Petrograd Dictionary (3. 863) explains it as "he who passes through [*tari*] in the bow [*dhánvan*]"; but there is no allusion whatever to the deity's association with a bow. There is, however, a homonymous, though etymologically unrelated, word *dhánvan*, "arid land, desert", and its cognate, *dhánu*, denotes "sandbank, island" (especially "island in the cloud-ocean", i. e. "cloud"; ib. coll. 863, 858).[7] The word *dhánu* has been examined with great care by Persson (*Beiträge zur indogermanischen Wortforschung*, pp. 39—44), who connects it with Lithuanian *dẽnis*, "deck (of a boat)", Irish *don*, "terra, ground, place",[8] Old High German *tenni*, "area", Anglo-Saxon *denu*, "valley, dale" (Scottish *den*, *dean*), as well as with Greek θέναρ "palm of the hand, sole of the foot, hollow of the sea and in the altar", Old High German *tenar*, *tenra*, "hollow of the hand". It would appear, then, that the name means "whose boat is the [cloud-]island" (for *tari* in the sense of "boat" see Major Petrograd Dictionary, 3. 269).

A study of Dhanvantari's birth from the churning of the cosmic Ocean of Milk (the later surrogate of the Vedic sky-ocean) and of his association in the Sūtras with the celestial deities Soma (as the moon), Indra, Agni (in his heavenly aspect), and Brahmā suggests that he also was a celestial divinity; more especially, it would seem, a cloud-god. On the other hand, the clouds play curiously little part in Vedic

---

7 Cf. also Macdonell and Keith, *Vedic Index of Names and Subjects*, 1. 388, 389—390. The view of Pischel (*Vedische Studien*, 2. 69—70) that *dhánu* means "water, fluids, Soma", and is connected with *dhan(v)*, "to run, flow", is quite improbable. The word *dhanú*, "bow", is oxytone.

8 Pedersen (*Vergleichende Grammatik der keltischen Sprachen*, 1. 89) connects *don* rather with Greek χθών, etc.

religion;[9] and, accordingly, a cloud-deity would tend to be dropped from the company of the great gods, though still receiving honor in actual cult among the people. Thus it was only natural that Dhanvantari should not be named in the Vedas, but should be worshipped in the Sūtras and should figure in the epics and Purāṇas, as well as in folk-stories of the present day. It may well have been that he was absorbed, in the Vedas, by the rain-god Parjanya.[10]

If this argumentation is correct, it is not difficult to see why Dhanvantari was conceived as a deity of healing. From the ocean of the sky the clouds pour down fertilising rain, water which gives life to plants and trees, which revives parched and suffering vegetation, which heals the distress of man and beast. From this special healing it was but a natural step to healing from all suffering and from disease. Then, when the art of medicine and surgery was developed, it was felt that gods, like men, must have their physician, and that so vital a science must have a divine head. Thus it was, perchance, that Dhanvantari regained the status which he had lost, though transferred, so to speak, from the old Cloud-Bureau, absorbed in the Rain-Ministry, to the newly created Department for Medicine. Later still, he again suffered demotion, and an attempt was made to euhemerise him; so that, from being an independent god, he became an avatar of Viṣṇu, then, aided by the development of a medical school at Kāśi which needed a divine patron, an earthly king, and at last a leech who was mortal. Our outline, if rightly sketched, is an interesting history of the vicissitudes of an Indian god!

Cloud-deities are none too common outside India. In Greece Νεφέλη appears as the wife of Athamas, by whom she was the mother of Phrixus and Helle; and another Nephele was mother of the Centaurs by Ixion.[11] In an Irish poem by Gilla Coemain († 1072), Nél ("Cloud"), who married Scote, a daughter of Pharaoh, is the father of Gaedel the Blue:

---

[9] Bergaigne, *La Religion védique*, 1. 5, 252; 2. 377, 398, 504; 3. 27—28; Hillebrandt, *Vedische Mythologie*, 1. 313; 3. 185; Macdonell, *Vedic Mythology*, pp. 60, 78, 83.

[10] Cf. Bergaigne, 3. 27—28; Macdonell, p. 83.

[11] Gruppe, *Griechische Mythologie und Religionsgeschichte*, pp. 79, 565, 921; 465, 830.

Gaidel glas o-tát Gaedil,	"Gaedel the Blue, whence the Gaidels,
Mac síde Níuil nert-máinig;	Was son of the Síd[12] Nél, rich in strength;
Robo thrén tíar acus tair	Mighty was he in the west and the east,
Nél, mac Foeniusa Farsaid.	Nél, son of Feinius Farsaid."[13]

In Teutonic mythology, E. H. Meyer has sought to interpret Frigg and Freyja as cloud-goddesses, but in this he is quite wrong.[14] Similarly, the Slavic Vily have been explained as originally cloud-maidens; but although some of them actually live in the clouds, where they build fantastic castles, they are, more probably, spirits of the dead, their name being possibly connected with Lithuanian *vẽlė*, "ghost".[15]

The Babylonians, Jastrow suggests (*Die Religion Babyloniens und Assyriens*, 1. 60), may have had a cloud-goddess in Gatum-dug, whom magic texts term the mother of Ea, the divinity of the watery deep. It is also possible that the pagan Aramaeans worshipped a cloud-deity if the מענן of an inscription from Têma (*CIS* 2. 114; cf. Cooke, *Text-Book of North-Semitic Inscriptions*, p. 199) is an abbreviation of a theophorous name, and if it is an *m*-formation from the group represented by Hebrew עָנָן, Syriac ܥܢܢܐ, Arabic عَنَانٌ, "cloud", from عَنَّ, "to appear" (cf. also عَنَنٌ, "appearance of an object before one"—corresponding exactly in form to עָנָן—عَانٌ, "phenomenon, cloud"; Cooke compares, further, the Nabataean and Palmyrene proper names מענא and מעני, "Μανναῖος"). If, for example, מענן is a Pa'el participle, corresponding to a Syriac ܡܥܢܢ, the name may answer precisely, in meaning, to the Homeric Νεφεληγερέτα.

[12] Concering the Síd see MacCulloch, *The Religion of the Ancient Celts*, pp. 63—65; *Celtic Mythology* (in *Mythology of All Races*, 3), pp. 49—53.

[13] *Book of Leinster*, p. 3, col. 2; cf. D'Arbois de Jubainville, *Introduction à l'étude de la littérature celtique*, pp. 291—292; *Le Cercle mythologique irlandais*, pp. 39—40, 88—89.

[14] *Germanische Mythologie*, pp. 202, 266—293 (for his cloud-theories generally see ib. pp. 81, 87—91, 97, 108—109, 112, 123—124, 156—157, 189); cf. against this interpretation Mogk, *Germanische Mythologie*, 2nd ed., pp. 140—144. The name Frigg is connected with Sanskrit *priyā*, "wife", and Freyja with Old High German *frouwa*, "lady", Greek πρῶτος <*προ-ϝο-τος, etc.

[15] Krek, *Einleitung in die slavische Literaturgeschichte*, 2nd ed., p. 799; but see Leger, *La Mythologie slave*, pp. 166—177; Máchal, *Slavic Mythology* (in *Mythology of All Races*, 3), pp. 256—260. Cf. also Hanusch, *Wissenschaft des slawischen Mythus*, pp. 305—308.

Cooke further notes that מענן may lie behind the Edessan deity Μόνιμος, associated with the sun-god (Julian, *Orationes*, 4. 150, ed. Spanheim) and identified by Iamblichus (*apud* Julian, *loc. cit.*), who terms him ἡλίου πάρεδρος, with Hermes (cf. Baethgen, *Beiträge zur semitischen Religionsgeschichte*, p. 76). It must be emphasised, however, that the etymology here suggested is the reverse of certain and that it is advanced merely as a possibility.

Among the Polynesians, on the other hand, true cloud-gods seem to have been known. Here belong a series of sister deities of the volcano of Kirauea in Hawaii, recorded by Ellis (*Polynesian Researches*, 4. 248): Hiata-wawahi-lani ("Heaven-rending Cloud-holder"), Hiata-noho-lani ("Heaven-dwelling Cloud-holder"), Hiata-taarava-mata ("quick-glancing-eyed Cloud-holder"), Hiata-hoi-te-pori-a-Pele ("Cloud-holder embracing the bosom of Pele"), Hiata-ta-bu-enaena ("Red-hot Cloud-holding Mountain"), Hiata-tareiia ("Garland-encircled Cloud-holder"), and Hiata-opio ("Young Cloud-holder"). In Tonga, Tui sua Bulotu, to whom appeal was made in household misfortunes, was perhaps a god of cloud and fog (Waitz-Gerland, *Anthropologie der Naturvölker*, 6. 289); and so possibly was the Maori Tawhaki (ib. p. 274).

As regards the American Indians, I am indebted to my colleague, Professor H. B. Alexander, for the following note:

> "The Pueblo and Navaho Indians of the arid south-west of North America have a highly developed cloud-symbolism in their art and ritual associated with a variety of mythic beings which are, or have been, virtual cloud-deities. Hump-backed sky-daemons—the hump being a cloud-pack—occur frequently in myth and not infrequently in art; the Navaho Ganaskidi serves as a type. The Zuñi Uwannami, the shadow-people who rise from earth as vapour, floating on feather-plumes, are apparently associated with the worship of ancestors as well as with the cult of the sky: cirrus clouds tell that the Uwannami are floating about for pleasure; cumulus and nimbus clouds reveal that the earth is to be watered. But undoubtedly the most striking of the nephelomorphic deities of the New World is the Plumed Serpent, in art invariably represented with cloud-symbols, and in myth clearly an embodiment of the rain-cloud as a source of fertility; while, in some mythic elements, he is interestingly extended to the cloudy star-path, the Milky Way. The very ancient Pueblo *triskelion*, the Awanyu, is an early precursor of this deity, who is, with little doubt, identical with the Aztec and Maya 'Green Feather-Snake' (Quetzalcoatl, Kukulcan, Gucumatz) and with the Maya Itzamna ('House [or 'Lap'] of the Dews'), whose idol at Izamal,

according to Lizana, gave his worshippers the ritual phrase, *ytzen caan, ytzen muyal* ('I am the dew, the substance of the sky and of the clouds'). In the Andean region, Bochica and Viracocha seem certainly to belong to the Plumed-Serpent cycle, though Viracocha had apparently developed into an embodiment of the whole vault of the sky; yet that he was no 'Shining Sky', but rather a giver of rain, is evidenced by the streams of tears flowing from his eyes in glyptic representations. The Sisiutl, or horned serpent, of the American North-West Coast appears to be an entirely analogous embodiment of the clouds that form above the ocean."

Excursus I—Divodāsa.

The monarch Divodāsa, ruler of Kāśi, in whom, according to some traditions, Dhanvantari became incarnate, is himself a legendary figure. The name was borne by more than one other famous personage in Vedic and post-Vedic times;[16] but the Divodāsa whom we are here considering was a Bharata, so that the later Divodāsa, King of Kāśi, naturally appears in the *Mahābhārata*, which is, indeed, our principal source of knowledge concerning him. In this connexion the most important passage of the epic is 13. 30. 10—57. In Kāśi reigned King Haryaśva, who was slain in battle with the sons of Haihaya Vītahavya, the same fate befalling Haryaśva's son and successor, Sudeva. The latter's son, Divodāsa, followed him on the throne and, at Indra's command, rebuilt and fortified Kāśi, ruling over a great and prosperous realm until he, in his turn, was defeated by the hereditary foe. He fled to the hermitage of Bharadvāja, whose sacrifice in the King's behalf was so potent that the monarch begat a son, Pratardana, whom his father set upon the throne and who slew the sons of Haihaya, who himself sought refuge in Bhṛgu's hermitage. The story of the birth of Pratardana is told in 5. 117. 1—21; and in 12. 96. 21, we learn that Divodāsa forfeited the fruits of his conquests because, after subduing his foes, he deprived them of their sacrificial fires, their *ghee*, and their food.[17]

---

[16] Major Petrograd Dictionary, 3. 624. For the Vedic Divodāsa see Bergaigne, 2. 341—345; Macdonell and Keith, 1. 363—364.

[17] For references in the *Harivaṃśa* and the Purāṇas see Viṣṇu Purāṇa, tr. Wilson, 4. 33—36; for an attempt to reconstruct these events as history see Pargiter, in *Journal of the Royal Asiatic Society*, 1910, pp. 38—40.

It is not evident at first sight why Dhanvantari should be regarded as incarnate in this King, but study of the earlier literature reveals what is at least a plausible reason. The Vedic Divodāsa is associated with the bardic family of the Bharadvājas (Rig-Veda 1. 116. 18; 6. 16. 5, 19; 31. 4). According to the *Pañcaviṃśa Brāhmaṇa* (15. 3. 7), Bharadvāja was the household priest (*purohita*) of Divodāsa; the *Kāṭhaka-Saṃhitā* (31. 10) states that he gave a kingdom to Pratardana; and the *Kauṣītaki Upaniṣad* (3. 1) speaks of "Divodāsian Pratardana" (*pratardano daivodāsir*; cf. Macdonell and Keith, 1. 363—364, 2. 29—30, 97—98).

But if Bharadvāja is thus associated with Divodāsa, he is also brought into connexion, in at least one passage (*Śāṅkhāyana Gṛhya-Sūtra* 2. 14. 4), with Dhanvantari, who is there termed "Bharadvāja Dhanvantari" when worshipped in the Vaiśvadeva ("All-God") sacrifice. Possibly we may thus proceed a step farther. The Bharadvājas formed one of the two chief branches of the Āṅgirasas (Ludwig, *Der Rigveda*, 3. 128), and the *Bṛhaddevatā* expressly states (5. 102—103) that "Bharadvāja, who was a preceptor among the Maruts, was a grandson of Aṅgiras" (*bharadvājo . . . marutsv āsīd gurur yaś ca sa evā 'ṅgiraso napāt*). The Āṅgirasas were pre-eminently priests of magic (Bloomfield, *The Atharvaveda*, p. 9); while their art (*āṅgirasa*) was "fearful" (*ghora*) and was essentially witchcraft, sorcery, spells, evil magic (ib. pp. 8, 9, 22). Their name is etymologically connected with Old Persian ἄγγαρος (ἐργάτης, ὑπηρέτης, ἀχθοφόρος. ἡ λέξις δὲ Περσική. σημαίνει δὲ καὶ τοὺς ἐκ διαδοχῆς βασιλικοὺς γραμματηφόρους, Hesychius), and Greek ἄγγελος, "messenger".[18] Thus the Āṅgirasas were originally messengers

[18] See Excursus II. The word *aṅgiras* has hesitatingly been connected by Hopkins (*The Religions of India*, p. 167) with Sanskrit *áṅgāra*, "coal"; by L. Meyer (*Handbuch der griechischen Etymologie*, 1. 210) with Sanskrit *áṅga*, "member of the body"; by Bugge (in *Bezzenbergers Beiträge*, 14. 62) with Latin *ambulo*, "to go back and forth, journey"; and by Prellwitz (*Etymologisches Wörterbuch der griechischen Sprache*, 2nd ed., p. 3) with Lithuanian *algis*, "angelus summorum deorum." None of these etymologies is convincing. For various views concerning the Āṅgirasas see Bergaigne, 1. 47—48; 2. 307—321; Oldenberg, *Religion des Veda*, pp. 127—128; Macdonell, pp. 142—143; Hillebrandt, *Vedische Mythologie*, 2. 156—169. It is suggested by G. W. Brown, in this Journal (41. 159—160), that

between gods and men, very possibly shamanists. Their ancestor was derived, according to the *Gopatha Brāhmaṇa* (1. 7), successively from the saline ocean, from Varuṇa, and from Mṛtyu ("Death"), thus establishing his dread, though celestial, nature.

It was in this manner, we may conjecture, that, since both Dhanvantari and Divodāsa were associated with Bharadvāja, the cloud-deity was believed to have been incarnate in the king. Furthermore, since the Bharadvājas were probably in origin chanters of magic songs, as is shown by their connexion with the Āṅgirasas and by the attribution to them of the sixth book of the Rig-Veda, it was, very possibly, they who intoned the spells which constrained the clouds to pour down blessings on vegetation, animals, and men, healing all their distress and curing all their ills. In course of time, on earth the sorcerer disappeared, and the pious bard lived on; in heaven the cloud-deity vanished, and the healing god remained.

Excursus II—Aṅgiras and Ἄγγαρος.

The Hesychian gloss ἄγγαρος, quoted in the preceding Excursus, has commonly been treated as one word (e. g. by Lagarde, *Gesammelte Abhandlungen*, p. 184), thus leading to considerable confusion. It seems preferable to see in the gloss two etymologically unrelated homonyms: (1) ἄγγαρος· ὁ ἐκ διαδοχῆς βασιλικὸς γραμματηφόρος; (2) ἄγγαρος· ἐργάτης, ὑπηρέτης, ἀχθοφόρος. The statements of Suidas add nothing new; but the author of the *Etymologicum Magnum* attempts to make a semantic connexion between the two words: ἔλεγον δὲ καὶ τοὺς σταθμοὺς ἄγγαρα, καὶ τοὺς ἐπὶ τῷ καθοδηγεῖν παραλαμβανομένους ἄκοντας . . . ὅθεν καὶ τὸ εἰς βασιλικὰς ἀπάγειν τὶ χρείας ἀγγαρεύειν λέγεται· καὶ ἀγγαρεία, δουλεία· καὶ ἀγγάριος, δοῦλος (*s. vv.* ἀγγαρεύω, ἀγγάρους). This seems rather strained; forced labor in the delicate duties of the Royal Post would scarcely be satisfactory.

Aṅgiras is mentioned in a charm published by J. A. Montgomery (*Incantation Texts from Nippur*, p. 196), where "in the name of אנגרוס" occurs between similar invocations of איבול בר פלג and מלילא. It seems somewhat more probable, however, that the allusion is to ἄγγαρος, particularly as the other names in the text to which Brown appeals—Hindu and Hinduîthâ—are Persian rather than Indian in form.

The first ἄγγαρος is doubtless connected with Greek ἄγγελος. It occasionally appears in Greek as a Persian term, e. g. Herodotus 8. 98 (τοῦτο τὸ δράμημα τῶν ἵππων καλέουσι Πέρσαι ἀγγαρήιον; cf. 3. 126), Josephus (*Antiquitates*, 11. 2), and Plato Comicus (frag. 220, ed. Kock, *Fragmenta comicorum Graecorum*, 1. 161; cf. also Aristophanes of Byzantium, *Fragmenta*, ed. Nauck, p. 172); and may even be found, as we have seen (note 18), in an Aramaic charm. Whether, on the other hand, the ἄγγαρος of Aeschylus (*Agamemnon* 269: φρυκτὸς δὲ φρυκτὸν δεῦρ' ἀπ' ἀγγάρου πυρὸς ἔπεμπεν) is the Persian word, as is usually supposed (e. g. Schrader, *Reallexikon der indogermanischen Altertumskunde*, p. 636; L. Meyer, 1. 209—210), seems doubtful. Like Latin *angarius*, "messenger" (e. g. Lucilius, 200; also regarded by Walde, *Lateinisches etymologisches Wörterbuch*, 2nd ed., p. 41, as borrowed), it is quite explicable from the pre-form **aŋgr̥ʳo-*, which is likewise the basis of Sanskrit *áṅgiras* and Old Persian ἄγγαρος (cf. Brugmann, *Grundriß der vergleichenden Grammatik der indogermanischen Sprachen*, 2nd ed., 1. 452, 456, 460, 464, 467; Wackernagel, *Altindische Grammatik*, 1. 24, 141). This view of the independent origin of the Greek and Latin words receives support from Spanish *ángaro*, "signal smoke", and Modern Greek ἄγγαρα, "(couriers') stations". From the Greek ἄγγαρος are derived the verb ἀγγαρεύω, "to dispatch as a post-messenger", and the noun ἀγγαρεῖα, "slow, heavy, ox-drawn public vehicle" (Van Herwerden, *Lexicon Graecum suppletorium et dialecticum*, pp. 8—9; cf. also Latin *angaria*, "clabularis currus vel iumentum", e. g. *Digesta*, 50. 4. 18. 21).

Another formation from the same base appears in Greek ἀγγέριος· ἄγγελος (Hesychius) from *ἄγγερος i. e. a *-ro*-suffix where Greek ἄγγελος shows a suffix in *-lo-*;[19] and this possibly survives in Old Spanish *anguera*, *enguera*, *engera*, "compensation for unauthorised use of an animal", Portuguese *angueira*, "hire of an animal for riding or burden".[20]

---

[19] It is quite incorrect to consider ἄγγελος as a Hellenised form of ἄγγαρος, as does Keller (*Lateinische Volksetymologie und Verwandtes*, pp. 328—329).

[20] For the Romance words see Körting, *Lateinisch-Romanisches Wörterbuch*, 2nd ed., no. 643, where—as is too often the case—words from different bases are jumbled together in a single article.

Plainly this group is unconnected with Pahlavi and New Persian *angārdan*, "to estimate, think, recount", as Horn (*Grundriß der neupersischen Etymologie*, p. 28) maintains against Lagarde *(loc. cit.)*. Nor is it wholly clear that it is to be found in Hebrew אִגֶּרֶת, Aramaic אִגְּרָא, Syriac ܐܶܓܰܪܬܳܐ, "letter", as Andreas (in Marti, *Kurzgefaßte Grammatik der biblisch-aramäischen Sprache*, p. 51*) holds, for these are more probably borrowed from Assyrian *egirtu* (*Oxford Hebrew Dictionary*, pp. 8, 1078).

The second ἄγγαρος has in Greek the derivatives ἀγγαρεία· δουλεία (Hesychius), ἀγγαρεύω, "to compel" (e. g. Matthew 5. 41, where the Vulgate has *angario* and the Gothic, *ananauþjan*; Hesychius also cites the meaning "to pledge"—ἐγγυᾶται), ἀγγαροφορέω, "to suffer distress" (examples in Van Herwerden, p. 9). In Latin, *angaria*, "villanage"—whence Italian *angheria*, "extortion", and obsolete English *angariate*—is found; and through the Osmanli Turkish borrowed word come Bulgarian *angaríya, garíya*, "compulsory service", Albanian *angarí* "oppression, compulsion" (Berneker, *Slavisches etymologisches Wörterbuch*, 1, 29; G. Meyer, *Etymologisches Wörterbuch der albanesischen Sprache*, p. 12), and Modern Greek ἀγγαρεία, "extortion, ungrateful toil", ἀγγαρεύω, "to overtax, vex." Here, too, perhaps belongs Judaeo-Persian *angūryā*, "distress" (אנגוריא של דסת ופאי; Bacher, *Ein hebräisch-persisches Wörterbuch aus dem vierzehnten Jahrhundert*, Hebrew part, p. 46), as is certainly the case with Talmudic אַנְגַּרְיָא, "forced labor, *corvée*", אַנְגְּרְוָטָא, "commissioner of forced public labor" (Jastrow, *Dictionary of the Targumim*, p. 81).

The group is derived by Jensen (in Horn, pp. 28 [note 3], 254) from Assyrian *agru*, "hireling" (cf. Arabic أَجَرَ, "to recompense, give wages to", Syriac ܐܓܰܪ, "to hire", Hebrew אֲגוֹרָה, "payment", Palmyrene באגוריא = τῇ μισθώσει [Cooke, p. 333]), the development postulated being *agru* > **aggaru* > **angaru*, and the other Semitic cognates being borrowed from the Assyrian.

Without pretending definitely to determine the problem of the origin of this ἄγγαρος, one may at least suggest the possibility that it is a *-ro-* formation to a base **onog-*, which appears in Old Irish *ong*, "tribulation, chastisement, groan" (*ong i. fochaid ocus cosc, i. uch; Cormac's Glossary*, p. 34), Old Danish *ank*, "grief, distress", Middle Dutch *anken*, "to sigh, groan" (Lidén, *Studien zur altindischen und vergleichenden Sprach-*

geschichte, p. 71; cf., further, Walde, p. 850; Berneker, 1. 268—269; Boisacq, *Dictionnaire étymologique de la langue grecque*, p. 683; Falk and Torp, *Norwegisch-dänisches etymologisches Wörterbuch*, pp. 30, 1432).

The group of Old Church Slavic *ędza*, "disease", Anglo-Saxon *inca*, "doubt, grievance", Lithuanian *énkti*, "to torment, oppress", *ìngis* "sluggard", sometimes connected with the group of *ong*, scarcely belongs to it. Gegish Albanian *angóy*, "to sigh, groan, weep, lament, comfort," might seem to be cognate, but is connected by G. Meyer (p. 304) directly with its Toskish equivalent *ñekóñ*. Neither does Greek ἀγανακτέω, "to be vexed", or Lithuanian *ùngau*, "whimper like a dog", form part of this group, despite Bezzenberger (in *Bezzenbergers Beiträge*, 27. 144; see Boisacq, p. 5), though they may possibly be compared with Afghān *angolā* (انگولا), "howl of a wild animal".

To summarise the etymologies here proposed, the first Old Persian ἄγγαρος (connected with Sanskrit *áṅgiras*, Greek ἄγγαρος, ἀγγέριος—and ultimately with ἄγγελος—Latin *angarius*) means "messenger"; the second ἄγγαρος (connected with Greek ἀγγαρεία, Latin *angaria*, Old Irish *ong*, Old Danish *ank*) is derived from a base meaning "to oppress, afflict".

THE ARCHAIC INSCRIPTION IN DÉCOUVERTES EN CHALDÉE, PLATE 1 bis

GEORGE A. BARTON

BRYN MAWR COLLEGE

NO TRANSLATION of this very archaic and difficult inscription has, so far as I know, ever been published. Four or five years ago I worked out a translation of it, but the only portion of it which has been published was five lines which I quoted in the article 'Poles and Posts' in Hastings' *Encyclopaedia of Religion and Ethics,* Vol. 9, p. 91. Since that time I have given the text further study and herewith present the results.

Face.

i, 1. *nêr eš nunuz*[1]*-gál*[2]*-ti*[3]	i, 1. 630 strong, living saplings,
2. *giš-nu-rú nu-gi-rú en-nam-àg*	2. wood unworked, reeds unworked, Ennamag,
3. *išib*[4] *te*[5]*-ti*[6]*-gĕ*[7] *gin*	3. the priest suitable for a dwelling brought.
4. *nu-ġup sag-pa nu-ġup en-nam-àg*	4. Uninjured was the chief officer, uninjured was Ennamag.

[1] The sign *nunuz,* which primarily means 'necklace' means also 'shoot', 'offspring'; see Barton, *Babylonian Writing* (hereafter cited as OBW) no. 348, 2 and 6. It is either equivalent to the Akkadian *lîpu* (Brünnow, 8177; hereafter cited as B.) or to *pir'u,* (B. 8179). The next line implies that the material designated by this sign was large enough to be 'worked'; it must, therefore, have been a young growth of some size. I have accordingly rendered it 'sapling'.

[2] See OBW, 87 5. [3] See OBW, 76 5. [4] See OBW, 478 27. [5] OBW, 330 33.

[6] Cf. OBW, 76 2 which gives the verb *ašâbu.* A sign which stands for an act usually also stands for the corresponding noun.

[7] *gĕ* (OBW, 439 6) stands for the numeral 'one'. Here it is used in the sense of the indefinite article 'a', or, better, as a substitute for *ge,* the post-position, (OBW, 269 1).

5. *àg-nam-en*[8] *šag-sam gub gār*[9] *urù*[10]*-maš rú*	5. Ennamag in the vegetation placed bricks; the princely dwelling made.
6. *igi-da-šù sam-gid sam-šù gú*[11] *gub*	6. At the front side was tall vegetation; by the vegetation he placed the wall.
7. *igi urù tu*[12] *en-nam-ag*	7. At the front of the dwelling entered Ennamag.
8. *šag sam gà(?)*[13] *en-nam-àg*	8. In the vegetation Ennamag established (it).

Reverse.

i, 1. *nu n[am]-lal*[14] *šu*[15] *engar*[16]	i, 1. No peasant raised a curse.
2. *me-me*[17] *zag*[18]*-ka*	2. It was the command of the oracle;
3. *nin-gir-su išib zag*	3. Ningirsu was priest of the oracle.
4. *en-ši igi-gà gál*	4. The seeing lord guards before the house;
5. *[nin]-su-gir išib.*	5. Ningirsu is priest.
ii, 1. *bara lil ner-v ba-gál*	ii, 1. The sanctuary the spirits, the five igigi[19], protect;
2. ^{d}*nin(?) gál*	2. the divine lady protects.
3. *eš*	3. Thirty . . . .
4.	4. . . . .
iii, 1. *en-nam-àg*	iii, 1. Ennamag,
2. *ud tu gà nin-[gir-su] išib-lal*[20] *ba-ge*[21]*-ti*	2. when he entered the house, Ningirsu, the high priest, received (him).

---

[8] This is an example of the fact that in early Sumerian writing of proper names the order of the syllables frequently varies. So long as all the elements were written, they seem to have been careless of the order.

[9] This is an unusual form of *gār*, but is, I believe, rightly identified with that sign. Cf. OBW, 509.

[10] OBW, 57_{15}. [11] OBW, 120_{2}. [12] OBW, 57_{4}.

[13] OBW, 230_{21}. [14] OBW, 440_{2}. [15] OBW, 311_{1}.

[16] OBW, 55_{5}. [17] OBW, 478_{22}. [18] OBW, 491_{36}.

[19] For the use of this ideogram to designate *igigi*, see OBW, 442_{2}.

[20] For this meaning of *lal* see OBW, 440_{52}. It seems to be used here instead of *maġ*.

[21] This use of *ge* as a verb infix is most unusual. I take it to be an

3. *ba-an-gál*	3. There guarded it *(a-gál)*
4. *dka[l]*	4. the god Kal.
iv, 1. *tab gizi*[22] *é-ǵu me nirba ú*	iv, 1. (There were) two posts, a bird-house where was grain for food.
2. *nin-gir-su gizi*[23]*-dingir-dim*[24] *te(?)*	2. Ningirsu propitiated the great plant god(?).
3. *nig-gan da-še*	3. The possession of a field bearing grain
4. *nin é-dim*	4. was the lady's of the great house.
v, 1. *nin-gir-su dingir*	v, 1. Ningirsu is a god;
2. *gir-su išib*	2. (at) Girsu he is priest.
3. *nirba ú ǵu me tab-é*	3. Grain is the food of birds; they are companions of the house.
4. *nin-gir-su [nir]ba . . . .*	4. Ningirsu the grain.....
5. *gan šar nig-uri*[25]	5. A field, a garden, a possession of palm-tree land,
vi, 1. *gan iv bur zal-ter*	vi, 1. a field of 4 *bur*, abounding in trees;
2. *xxxvic bur šar-uri*	2. 3600 bur, a garden of palm-tree land;
3. *l ǵu išib-šù*	3. 50 birds for divining;
4. *xxx suǵur*[26]*-a*	4. 30 goat-fish(?);
5. *xviiic bur zal dŭ*	5. 1800 *bur* abounding in dwellings;
6. *i uzu*	6. 1 diviner.

It cannot be too strongly emphasized that any translation of an inscription of this nature is, in the present state of our knowledge, purely tentative. Nevertheless the way in which, according to the interpretation reached, the parts of the text fit together lends a good degree of probability that the rendering is on the right track. The text describes the building

---

example of that carelessness as to the order of the signs which appears in the early writing. In other words it is for *ge-ba-ti*, the *ge* being for *ǵe* = 'verily'.

[22] OBW, 327 16. [23] OBW, 327 21, 26-28. [24] OBW, 60 7.

[25] OBW, 316 3, 5, 6. [26] OBW, 363 1.

of a primitive sanctuary, the establishment of a god in it, the equipment of the temple with a flock of sacred birds, for divining, and the endowment of the temple with lands for its support.

The name of the builder of the temple, Ennamag, means 'lord of building' and might be translated 'architect'. One is at some loss to know whether so to translate it, or to regard it as a proper name. After much hesitation it was decided to regard it as a proper name. At the front of the structure two posts were erected. These remind one of the Asheras erected in connection with Semitic sanctuaries. The face of the tablet pictures a man, probably Ennamag, in the act of grasping one of these posts.

The statement that 'no peasant raised a curse' shows that Ennamag had taken care to satisfy the land-owners and cultivators of the vicinity, so as to prevent their invoking the ill-will of any supernatural powers against the building. This was, from the ancient point of view, very important. Manishtusu, as we learn from his obelisk inscription, took great pains to do the same for a new settlement that he undertook, as did Sargon king of Assyria, centuries afterwards.[27] The appearance of the name 'Ningirsu' in the various parts of the tablet is interesting and somewhat puzzling. In i, 3 of the reverse of the tablet Ningirsu, written without determinative for deity, is said to be *išib zag*, 'priest of the high-place' or 'oracle'. Again in i, 5 Ningirsu, again without determinative for deity, is said to be *išib*, 'priest'. Again in iii, 2 it is said that, when Ennamag entered the house, Ningirsu, still written with no determinative for deity—Ningirsu, described as *išib-lal*, 'exalted priest' or 'high priest', received him. It is natural to assume in all these cases that Ningirsu is the name of a human being who is acting as a priest. But in v, 1 and 2 it is stated, that Ningirsu, again without a determinative, 'is a god, at Girsu, a priest'. Does this mean that Ningirsu was, at the time this text was written, a man on the point of being deified? That is a tempting theory. In that case the famous god of Lagash, who is so prominent in the texts from that city from those of Ur-nina to those of Gudea, originated in the deification of a human being.

---

[27] See *KB* ii. 46. 47.

There is, however, another possibility. Ningirsu may be the name of a deity wherever it occurs in our text, and this deity may have been regarded as a kind of priest among the gods.

The god 'Kal', mentioned in iii, 4 of the reverse, is designated by the sign which afterward designated *lamassu* or *šêdu*, the guardian deities which guarded the portals of temples and palaces. We might render the two lines referring to him, 'He (Ennamag) set up the god Kal'. If Ningirsu were the deity within the sanctuary, then Kal was the spirit which guarded the doors.

Finally, the sign *uri*, which I have translated 'palm-tree land', is the sign later employed as the ideogram for Akkad. Professor Clay has shown that *uri* or *uru* is another spelling of Amurru. This might, therefore, be translated 'a possession of Amurru', a 'garden of Amurru'. True, the sign has in the text no determinative for place, but neither is the name Girsu followed by such a determinative. Indeed, it seems probable that the text comes from a time before the use of determinatives had fully developed.

THE POLLINATION OF THE DATE PALM

Paul Popenoe

Coachella, California

One of the outstanding characteristics of the date palm, *Phoenix dactylifera* Linn., is its dioecious nature, the pollen-bearing and fruit-bearing, or male and female, flowers being borne on separate trees. Among wild palms reproducing from seed, the two sexes are produced in approximately equal numbers, and this abundance of males furnishes a large supply of pollen which, carried by the wind, suffices to pollinate at least enough of the female blossoms to perpetuate the species.

An understanding of this fact was of importance to the first systematic cultivators of the date palm, for by hand-pollination, instead of wind-pollination, they could dispense with all males except three or four for each hundred females, and thus economize on space and labor, while ensuring a better crop.

On the other hand, the separation of the sexes appealed to the religiously-tinged imagination of the primitive mind, and was doubtless one of the factors leading to the veneration with which the palm was regarded by the early dwellers in the Tigris-Euphrates region.

While, therefore, the artificial pollination of the palm has an interest to the student from several points of view, it has often been misunderstood by Occidentals,[1] to whom date-growing is foreign. European dictionaries give but a confused idea of

[1] The first Occidental account I have seen is that of Herodotus, *History*, Bk. I, ch. 193, who describes what he saw in Babylonia but confuses it with the caprification of the fig tree. Theophrastus, *Historia Plantarum*, ed. Wimmer, II, p. 6, corrects him, and gives a fair account. Pliny, *Historia Naturalis*, Bk. XIII, ch. 7, seems hazy as to the principles involved.

the rich Arabic vocabulary connected with this subject. The following brief notes will, it is hoped, give an accurate picture of the manner in which the date palm has been pollinated in Muslim countries, so far back as records exist; and will organize in a preliminary way some of the commoner Arabic terms connected with the procedure.[2]

I. The male palm is called (1) *ḏakr* in Egypt and the Maghrib: this word is not only classical but is recognizable in some of the earliest cuneiform references. The root ذكر applies to a male of any kind, and not merely a palm. In Algeria the only form[3] of the singular I ever heard is *ḏokkār*, although G. Schweinfurth[4] records *ḏakr* at Biskra. (2) *faḥl*, in the Orient generally. The root meaning is "to be masculine", and this word also has a wide range of applications, as to a vigorous man, or a strong camel. (3) *ʿabr*, which is said originally to mean a needle, — the penis being likened to that instrument; or it may be merely a dialectal variant of *ʿafr* = to dust, hence, to pollinate. (4) *bʿal*, a primitive meaning of which is sexual intercourse.[5] (5) *ǵilf*, from a root meaning "to take off the bark"; because, I suppose, the spathe is removed from the male flower before it is used for pollination. (6) *rāʿil*, originally meaning pendent, cf. *rʿilah* = prepuce; the root also means "to pierce"; its connection on both accounts with the

---

[2] I am much indebted to Père Anastase-Marie de St. Elie, of the Mission des Carmes, Baghdād, for suggestions concerning many of the Arabic terms mentioned.

[3] In general, I have not thought it worth while to enumerate the differences in vocalization, and the like, which are on record. The interested reader can get them from such sources as the *Kitāb-al-naḫl* of al-Aṣmaʿī, ed. by Aug. Haffner and pub. at Bayrūt, 1907; from the similarly named and better-organized compilation of Ibn Sīdah in the *Kitāb al-Muḫaṣṣaṣ*; or in Lane's Dict.

[4] *Arabische Pflanzennamen aus Ägypten, Algerien u. Jemen*, von G. Schweinfurth, Berlin, 1912. All of my information regarding the modern Egyptian vocabulary is, unless otherwise noted, derived from this source.

[5] Another meaning of *bʿal* is a palm which is not irrigated. The connection between these two meanings is not apparent to me, unless it be an example of antiphrasis. *Bʿal* as a god of unirrigated land is a well-known figure. Cf. *ball* = to moisten. This question has been discussed in detail by G. A. Barton, *A Sketch of Semitic Origins*, New York, 1902.

idea of maleness is obvious. (7) *kušš*, ordinarily pronounced *goš*, is the word generally heard around the Persian Gulf, e. g., in ʿOmān; in Sindh, however, the male palm is called *mū*. *Kušš* or *ǵušš* is said to be from Pers. *kušš* or *ḫušhšh*, an angle, as e. g. made by the saw in a board; the insertion of branchlets of the male inflorescence into the female flower being likened to this. In Multan, according to E. Bonavia, the whole bunch of dates is called *goša*. All of the foregoing terms are classical.

II. When they first appear in the spring, the flowers of the female palm (*naḫl*) are enclosed in a hard envelope or spathe, which is called (1) *kafūr*, because it *conceals* the flowers. This is probably the most elegant of all the names for the spathe. A dial. var. is *qafūr*. (2) *kimm*, the root meaning of which is "to cover". A parallel is *akamm* or *aqamm*, to impregnate a female camel. A palm with spathes appearing is described as *makmūm*. In the Sahara, according to E. L. Bertherand, the name of the spathe is *quemamine* — which sounds like a plural from this root. (3) *kaṯar*, because, as I suppose, the increase or multiplication, كثر, of the palm comes from the flowers. (4) *qīqāʾh*, comparing the spathe to an egg-shell; the word is defined succinctly by Ibn Sīdah as *qišr al-ṭalʿah*. (5) *ǵuff*, comparable in meaning to (3) above, جفّ = "to increase". *ǵubb*[6] may be a dial. var. of this; but cf. also XII, 6, for another correct derivation. (6) *walīʿ*, although Abū Ḥanīfah says this properly refers not to the spathe itself, but to the flowers within the spathe. ولع = violent love. (7) *ǵurbah*, = a sac. In Assiūt *gerāb*, according to Dr. Schweinfurth. *ḥarabah* is apparently a var. of this, although plausibly connected with *ḥarbah* = a lance. (8) *ǵalāfah*, reported by Dr. Schweinfurth from El-Qorēn, Egypt, has the same meaning as the preceding.[7] He also reports *kūss ǵilāf* or simply *kūss*, which is perhaps Pers. *kušš*, *vide* I, 7. (9) *ṭalʿ*, or some var. of it, as in Egypt.

---

[6] A proverb says جِبَابٌ فَلَا تَعَنَّ أَبْرًا: "They are merely *spathes* [and not flowers]; therefore don't waste time pollinating them [for you won't get anything out of them]" — applied to a man who is, as one might say, a "gold brick".

[7] Brown, T. W., "The Date Palm in Egypt", *Agric. Journal of Egypt*, 5 (1916), p. 75, gives "*relaf* or *gerab*" as the current names for the female spathe.

ṭalḥ, is sometimes applied to the spathe, but incorrectly, as it properly designates the flowers within the spathe, V, 1, *infra.* This use goes back at least as far as the compilation of the 'Ain, however. (10) *tašo* I have heard only at El Kantara in Algeria; it is evidently from *ṭašā'* = sexual intercourse; cf. *ṭašš* = rain, and see also V. 13. (11) *tara,* a name used around the Persian Gulf, appears to be from Pers. *tar* = humid, because of the fresh viscosity of the flowers inside the spathe, and the tender texture of the spathe itself, while still young. Tara water is a well known perfume in the region mentioned. (12) *girif,* a Baṣrah expression, and *qurrāfah,* the usual term in the Ḥadhramaut,[8] are doubtless to be connected with *qārif* = sexual intercourse. (13) *dāmiġah,* = a skull wound disclosing the brain, evidently derives its significance from the somewhat gruesome but not inapt comparison of the splitting spathe revealing the densely crowded mass of flowers inside. (14) *ḥabb,* if not a dial. var. of (5), is easily attached to خبّ = conceal.

III. Prior to the opening of the spathe or envelope mentioned in the preceding paragraph, the flowers concealed within it are called (1) *haḍīm,* because they are crowded together, هضم. (2) *fāliq,* erroneously given sometimes as *qāliq,* from *falaq* = to split open in the middle.

IV. A few days after its protrusion from between the leaf-bases of the palm, the spathe splits open, at which time it is called (1) *ḍaḥk,* as if it were smiling ضحك. (2) *dāmiġah,* see II. 13. (3) *baġwah* = admirable to behold — but cf. بغى = a prostitute, as "exceeding" (sc., that which is proper). (4) *naǵm,* = appearing or breaking forth. (5) *ġaḍīḍ,* explained by the lexicographers as from غضّ = fresh or tender, and sometimes written *faḍīḍ* or *faḍīṣ*; but the original form may have been فضيض = deflowered (applied to a woman), and the other forms variants of this.

V. When the spathe has split open, the flowers within are finally exposed to view. These flowers, taken collectively as an inflorescence or raceme, technically known as a spadix, are

---

[8] Landberg, C., *Études sur les Dialectes de l'Arabie Meridionale,* vol. i, Leyden, 1901.

called (1) *ṭal'*, because they *ascend*; this is probably the most widely current term, both classical and modern, and has variants such as the grossly ignorant *ṭalḥ* (Egypt) and *tālah* (Persia). (2) *Ḫaṣbah*, = abundance; sometimes spelt with ض, and Lane says the latter is the correct form; if so, it is, I suppose, because the flowers, at first white, quickly become *tinted* on exposure to the air. Abū 'Ubayd supports this by remarking that when the *ṭal'* has become greenish, one says خَضَبَ النخل. (3) *iġrīḍ* expresses the fact of their whiteness, while (4) *ḥaṣal* applies after they have slightly yellowed. (5) The Pers. *kardō* is perhaps connected with *kard* = a cut branch. (6) *hin'a*, = agreeable or favorable, applies to a bunch of ripe dates as well as to the young flowers. (7) *'ilib* is said by F. E. Crow[9] to be the prevailing term at al-Baṣrah: if so, I did not happen to hear it there. It would presumably be connected with *'alib* = hard to the touch. (8) *walī'*, see II. 6. (9) *farūḥ*, in Egypt and the Ḥadhramaut, is likewise unknown to me, but might be linked with *farḥ* = happiness. (10) *subāṭah* is, as the Taǵ al-'Arūs correctly observes, an Egyptian dial. name for a bunch of dates, but Dr. Schweinfurth gives it as the current Egyptian name for "weiblicher Blütenstand", and ascribes it also to Biskra, where, however, I never heard it and believe it is not generally accepted. The picture of "flowing hair" called up by the root *sbṭ* is easily transferred to the many-branched cluster of flowers. Silas C. Mason (*Bull.* 223, U. S. Dept. of Agriculture, p. 22), who gives "sobata" as the name for the stem alone of the spadix, was evidently misinformed. (11) *'urǵūn*, the most widely-used name in modern Arabic, means "ascending". It is, however, applied to the stem of the inflorescence (VI. 8, *infra*) as well as to the cluster of flowers as a whole. (12) *qanā* or *qunw*, modern Egyptian *ginū*, = "possession". (13) *ṭuš*, at Baghdād, is doubtless from *ṭušš* (II. 10); it was explained to me as meaning "the young spadix when it turns from white to greenish", after exposure to the air; and also "dates when first formed", i. e. a few weeks after the flowers are pollinated. (14) *šaml* is a purely classical name which refers to the inflorescence as *enveloped* by the spathe.

[9] In *Kew Bull.* No. 7 (1908), p. 286.

VI. The stem of the spadix or raceme[10] is called (1) *matyaḥah*, = a stick or staff.[11] (2) *'ūd*, = wood. (3) *ǵāriḥah*, = leg, etc. (4) At Biskra, *gunt* (from *qnw?* see V. 12). (5) At al-Baṣrah and in 'Omān the classical *'asqah* is used, from عسق = to attach itself. (6) At Assiūt and Luxor *ǵurbah*, a word unknown to me. (7) *ǵidl*, on the authority of the Qamūs; the word usually applies to the trunk of a tree. (8) *kināz* is given in Richardson's Dictionary as a Persian name for the stem of the cluster. In Arabic, words from this root refer naturally to the idea of storage, e. g., *kanīz* = stored dates. (9) *'urǵūn* is a Protean word, which means either (and nowadays most properly) the entire spadix; or else the stem thereof; or in Egypt (*fide* Taǵ al-'Arūs) the individual branches or "threads" of the cluster; but the last-named usage must be regarded as "bad language". Muhammad employs the word in the second sense, when in the Yā Sīn chapter (36. 39) he describes the moon, waning until it becomes like the old stem of a date spadix,[12] عاد كالعرجون القديم. Despite this authority, the word nowadays probably belongs more to the raceme or bunch as a whole, and *qua* dates, not *qua* flowers. I shall not here

---

[10] Classically, a palm bearing long-stemmed racemes is (1) *bā'inah* <*būn*, = an interval or distance between two things; or (2) *ṭarūḥ*, from *ṭrḥ* = to push away. If the stems are short, the palm is (1) *ḥāḍinah*, a pretty simile likening the palm to a woman bearing a child on her breast; or (2) *kābis*, which presents the picture of the bunch *pressing* on or *invading* the palm; or (3) *ǵaṯm*, from جثم = to lie on one's chest; although Abū Ḥanīfah says the last-mentioned term is not applied until the bunch has attained some size.—The length of stems is mainly a question of variety of palm.

[11] See Damīrī's Ḥayat al-Ḥayawān, tr. Jayakar, 2, p. 764.

[12] At harvest time the ground around a plantation is strewn with these stems, from one to three feet in length and often bright yellow or red in color. The resemblance to the waning moon is obvious enough. The English translators (Sale, Rodwell, Palmer) of the Koran have, however, rendered *'urjūn* in this verse as a "palm branch", entirely missing the idea. Moreover, the palm has no branches, but consists merely of a trunk with a crown of leaves at the top. It may be added that the common expression "palm tree" is likewise inexact: the palm is a palm, *tout simplement*. Arabic usage in designating it merely as the date palm, *al-naḫl*, is therefore in accord with good botanical usage; although for purposes of definition a lexicographer may explain that it is the tree which bears dates, *šaǵarah al-tamr*.

go into the extensive synonymy of the bunch of dates, since it surpasses the field of pollination. Finally, *'urǵūn* is often applied nowadays to the entire male inflorescence. (10) *ihān*, a classical word which I have never heard colloquially; presumably <*hān* = to be despised, etc. — the stem being, after the dates are picked, of little value as compared with leaves, fibre, and other parts of the palm used in home industries.

VII. The base of this stem is more or less farinaceous, and it is sometimes cut, while still young and soft, and eaten. It is called (1) *ǵummār*, pronounced *ǵunbar* at Biskra; but this word more correctly applies to the terminal bud[13] of the palm, which is also eaten if for any reason a palm has to be cut down, and *ǵummāz*, a variant of the foregoing. (2) In South-Arabia, *kūrzān*, = cheese, according to Th. Bent. (3) *pānir-i-ḫurmā* (Pers. date cheese). C. Doughty mentions that at Khaybār the terminal bud (*ǵummār, sensu stricto*) was eaten under the name of "Khaybār cheese". (4) *ṭarīdah*, a dictionary word apparently referring to its *distance* from the cluster.

VIII. Following along the stem of the cluster, one finds that it gives rise to a large number (sometimes 50 or more) branches, "strands", "threads", or "spikes", to which the flowers (which later become the dates) are attached,[14] ranged one after another. These strands are called (1) *šimrāḫ*, a word of Aramaic origin, meaning pendent; and the most general and correct name. (2) *'iṯkāl*, from عثكل = to hang down; though this name is also applied, as at al-Baṣrah, to the entire cluster. The first letter is sometimes ا instead of ع; and Abū Ḥanīfah endeavors to make the distinction that a strand bearing *flowers* is an *'uṯkūl*, whereas if it bears dates it is an *'iṯkāl*. (3) *bint al-'urǵūn*, "daughter of the spadix". (4) *'urǵūn*, see VI. 9, *supra*. (5) *miṭw*, = companion, <مطا = to join a friend; because

[13] The root meaning of "assembled" or "united" is easily seen in the terminal bud, where the bases of the leaves are joined in a circle. The use of *ǵummār* to mean terminal bud is well-nigh universal, both in classical and modern Arabic: only in 'Omān have I heard anything else. There the name is *qimmah*, which regularly means the top of the head, the summit of a mountain, etc.

[14] After the *šimrāḫ* has been stripped of its flowers, or dates, it is called a *ṭarīk*, abandoned.

of the large number of similar threads together. (6) *kināb*, <كنب = to contain something. (7) *'ās*, <عس = to become hard or tough. The three names last mentioned are, so far as my experience goes, purely lexicological. (8) *habbah* — or something which sounded like that — in 'Omān: I neglected to get it spelled. I suspect that it may be connected with *ḥabb* = a grain, etc. (9) *shoa shoa*, in Egypt, and more especially in Nubia, according to T. W. Brown: I cannot even make a guess at this. If it is Arabic it must have been corrupted by Nubians.

IX. Ranged along the strands, *šamārīḫ*, are the individual flowers, called (1) *ǵummah*, from the root *ǵamm* = to become abundant. Variants of this are *ǵumbah*, *ǵunbah*, and possibly *ǵūm*, although the last-named is also explained as Pers. = a vessel. (2) *zirr*, = a bud, etc. (3) *qaḥf*, = skull, because of the shape and general appearance, to a slightly imaginative eye. (4) At Biskra, *qiṭmīrah;* but this is an incorrect usage, the word applying rather to the calyx of a flower and, most correctly, to the membrane which surrounds the seed of a mature date, which is a proverbial simile for a valueless thing.[15]

X. So far, only the inflorescence of the female or fruit-bearing palm has been considered. The inflorescence of the male or pollen-bearing palm is similar in general outlines. When it is still enclosed in its spathe, it is called (1) *saff*, = much interlaced, because the flowers are compressed so tightly together. (2) *šir'af*, from شرع with suffix ف, = to extend; (3) *kušš*, Pers., *vide supra.* (4) *anbār-i-naḫl*, Pers., granary of the palm. (5) *'urǵūn, vide supra.* (6) in Egypt, *kūz*, = a pot.

XI. The branches, threads, or strands of the male inflorescence are (1) *'aṭīl*, that which increases the size of a body: this is the classical term. (2) *ǵuṣnah*, a branch, from *ǵuṣn* = to pull off. (3) At al-Baṣrah *ligaḥ* (<لقح), according to Major Crow.

XII. The flowers of the male palm are cut and dried indoors

---

[15] Cf. Koran 35. 14, where the heathen gods are depreciated by this figure of speech. *Qiṭmīr* has been used for at least three different things: (1) the membrane around the seed; (2) the ventral channel of the seed, *naqīr*, in modern Egypt *nuqṭah*; (3) the germ-pore of the seed, *fūfah.*— Dr. Schweinfurth notes that in Egypt the name "*gullāfa*" (see II. 8, above) is also given to this membrane.

for a day or longer. When the female inflorescence splits open, it is pollinated. This operation is called (1) *laqqaḥ* or *talqīḥ*, from *lqḥ* = to become pregnant. Count Landberg notes that in the Ḥadhramaut this word is used of the camel, and of the camel only, among animals. A *hadīṯ* cited by al-Suyūṭī comments on the likeness of the date palm to the human species, in that it is (allegedly) the only plant which copulates لقح. (2) *aḥṯar*, presumably connected with حثر = seeds. (3) *nawwaq*, originally = to separate the fat from the meat; thence, to do anything neatly. (4) *'affar*, to throw dust, see I. 2. (5) *tawbīr*, the root meaning of which relates to wool or hair, whence is derived the idea of making anything grow or increase like abundant hair. (6) *ǵabāb*, from a root which means to extirpate anything, especially the testicles. (7) *abbar*, see I. 2; or perhaps a dial. form of وبر, see (5) above. (8) *tadkīr*, see I. 1; this is the current name in the Hijāz (according to R. F. Burton) and in Egypt. (9) *taṭlīq*, from طلق = to release. A derived meaning of the root applies to parturition in women. Lane indicates that *ṭlq* applies particularly to the pollination of a *tall* palm. (10) *faḥḥaṭ*, a corruption of *faḥḥad* = sexual intercourse. The Ḥadhramaut name; C. Landberg says that *qḥṭ*, given by dictionaries as synonymous, is merely a misprint of this. (11) *sammad*, which may be related to *samād*, fertilizer; it is also given as شمد, which must be either a misprint of copyists, or a dialectal variant; and سمد which, if not another dialectal variant, can be referred to *samīd*, white flour, to which the pollen is comparable. (12) *anbār dāden*, *conferre plenitudinem*, on the Persian side of the Gulf, *teste* Kaempffer. (13) *ṭa'm*, which may be interpreted as "to satisfy the hunger" for food, or sexual intercourse, etc.

XIII. The season of pollination, February to May, depending on climate and variety of palm, is known as the (1) *waqt al-faḥṭah*, (2) *zamān al-ǵabāb*, (3) *tarīḥ al-ṭa'm* and so on.

XIV. The man who performs the operation is called (1) *laqqaḥ*, or *mulaqqaḥ*; this is the classical designation. (2) *naḥwālī*, a vulgar word for the classical *naḥḥāl;* or by the proper nominal form of one of the other names applied to pollination.

XV. The process of pollination[16] is, in outline, as follows.

---

[16] At al-Koton in the Ḥadhramaut, Th. Bent heard the pollinator

First, if the female spathe has not yet split open, but looks as if it were about ready to do so, the operator cuts it open; (1) *qaṣṣ*, onomatopoeic, cf. French *casser*. (2) *maqq*, = to open vertically.

XVI. Then he shakes over the female flowers a piece or branch (*ġuṣnah*) of the male inflorescence, often tying it among them.[17] Thus it continues to liberate pollen for several days. This pollen, cream-colored and finer than dust, is called (1) *ṭaḥīn* or *ṭiḥn*, = flour, milled. (2) *daqīq*, = very fine or small. (3) *ġubār*, = dust. The three foregoing are post-classical. (4) *ḥurq*, = milled; but apparently of Aramaic origin <*ḥraq* = to enter by small cracks. (5) *kušš*, Pers., *vide supra*. (6) *ātā*, a word used in Sindh and said to = flour or fine dust; perhaps a corruption of *'aṭa* = a benefit. (7) *laqḥ*, referring to the fecundating property of the pollen. (8) *wazīm*, from وزم = to tie up in parcels, or to add a little to a little.

XVII. If the operation has been skilfully performed, and other conditions (e. g., absence of rain or frost) are favorable, the palm remains fecundated; (1) *ḥaṯir;* (2) *munawwaq;* (3) *iltaqqaḥ;* and so on.

XVIII. But the pollen may have been applied too soon: (1) *basr*, originally meaning, to do anything rapidly; before the female flowers were open to receive the pollen.

XIX. Or for some other reason, e. g., rainy weather, or sterility of the pollen used,[18] the palm remains unfecundated: (1) *ḥāl*, also said of a camel which has been unsuccessfully served by the male; the root means to change or alter. It

---

exclaim, "May Allah make you grow and be fruitful", as he pollinated the inflorescence. I have read of something of the kind in Morocco, but in general this operation is carried out nowadays without even a bismillah.

[17] Count Landberg, whose account of pollination is the most accurate of any I have seen in philological writings, says that in the Ḥadhramaut the pollinator *rubs* the male flower over the females (يمشّط به). I have not known this to be done elsewhere, and suspect that, as the Arab verb implies, the rubbing amounts to no more than "combing" the branchlets lightly.

[18] In Egypt, a male which produces little pollen, or pollen of no value, is said by Mr. Brown to be called "*dakar ḫunta*", from خنث = effeminate, impotent; or "*dakar farat*", which may be referred to فرت = soft, weak.

likewise applies to a palm which bears fruit only in alternate years; and this use probably explains the derivation of the meaning first-mentioned. (2) *d̲ayyaḥ*, = masculine? (3) *šīš*, see next paragraph. (4) *miǵlaḥ*, = sterile, from *ǵlḥ* = to become bald. (5) *ǵildah*, = patient. The last two on the authority of Abū Ḥanīfah.

XX. If the female flowers are not pollinated, or not pollinated successfully, they continue to develop, nevertheless, and produce three imperfect, seedless dates on one stem, in place of the usual single, well-formed and seeded berry.[19] Such a worthless date is called (1) in some parts of Egypt *faṣṣ*, the root meaning of which is to separate. (2) *šīš*, the most usual word,[20] and found in a variety of spellings which ring all the changes on س, ش and ص. Arabic lexicologists ascribe this to a Pers. word *kīkā*; Lane notes that Fraenkel attributed it to Aramaic. (3) *barūk*, at Assiut. This derivation of *brk* is not clear to me. A possible parallel is mentioned by the Qamūs: *barūk* = a woman who marries, having a big son. (4) *ḫaṣī*, = a eunuch: in the Tūāt oases *ḫesyān*, which is, or ought to be, the plural of the foregoing. It is there explained, however, as from *ḫas* = to be unsalable. (5) *balaḥ*, at Biskra: but incorrectly, for this classical word properly designates a normal date, but one not wholly ripe. In modern Egypt and Syria it signifies any ripe date, being the equivalent of the classical *tamr*. (6) *mīḥ*, on the authority of the Qamūs; but of unknown origin. (7) *salang* (Pers.?) at Baḥrain, *teste* Th. Bent. (8) *suḫḫalah*, at al-Madīnah, according to the lexicographers, from a root meaning weak or inferior. (9) *munmiq*, from *nimq* = to strike the eye, the seedless cavity[21] apparently being likened to an eye that has been "poked out". (10) *fāḫir*, which from its root (= splendid, etc.) would seem to be the contribution of some one with more of a sense of humor than the ordinary Arab lexicographer.

XXI. But if pollination is successful, the fruit "sets" and

---

[19] In the normal process of development of a pollinated flower, two of its three carpels are aborted, leaving one to attain to maturity.

[20] But not confined to dates alone, for 'Abd al-Rizzāq al-Ǵazairī, in his *Revelation of Enigmas*, speaks of a seedless colocynth as *ṣīṣ*.

[21] More exactly, the cavity contains a thin, soft, undeveloped seed. The seeds of these *šīṣ* dates are described as معجوز مفوق, etc.

the dates develop to maturity, which involves a copious vocabulary, as is evident to one who opens an Arabic dictionary at random.

XXII. On the other hand, if the female palm bears no flowers at all, one says (1) *istafḥal*, i. e., it is like a male.

XXIII. As the fruit-cluster develops, the remains of its natal spathe or envelope (*kafūr*) become dry, but hang indefinitely on the palm and are called (1) *ṣawaḥ*, from a root meaning to dry out; or in Algeria (2) *tergiša*, < *rqš?* = spotted with black and white.

CAMPHOR

WILFRED H. SCHOFF

PHILADELPHIA COMMERCIAL MUSEUM

THE GUM CAMPHOR of modern commerce is not the same product as the camphor which was one of the costliest items of earlier sea-trade, worth more than its weight in gold, and so scarce that it was hardly to be found outside of royal treasure houses. Modern camphor is obtained by passing steam over the leaves, wood and bark of the tree laurel (*Laurus camphora*) of Southern China and Formosa. It is also prepared synthetically from coal-tar. Its uses are prosaïc and utilitarian. The original camphor was a natural accumulation in the light and fibrous wood of the camphor tree of Sumatra and Borneo (*Dryobalanops camphora*), a vegetable giant, until the discovery of the sequoia of California, probably the mightiest tree known in the world.[1] It was regarded by Sumatran man as an earthly copy of the heavenly Tree of Fate. Mula Gadi the father-god dwelt by that tree with his two wives, the Writer and the Weigher. Under the tree every earth-bound soul must pass, to receive one of its leaves, whereon was a writing of that soul's earthly destiny—riches or poverty, power or weakness, sickness or health.[2] And although camphor crystals are in fact the product of a natural process resembling gout or arterio-sclerosis, they were supposed to be the very life and essence of the heavenly tree, the possessor of which had power to unravel "the Master-knot of human fate."

---

[1] Engler and Prantl, *Natürliche Pflanzenfamilien*, III. 6. 254—259. Cf. Yule's note to Marco Polo III, xi, on the Kingdoms of Lambri and Fansur; Cordier's edition, 2. 300—4.

[2] Warneck, *Die Religion der Batak*, 4—5; 49, 115, 125.

This heavenly tree figures most largely in the belief of the Bataks, a tribe of the hill country of northern Sumatra. Of this people much has been written [3]—of their primitive animism, which anthropologists accept as typical; of their cannibal ceremonies and head-hunting which loom large among the "Marvels of the East" of the Arab writers. The magic tree of the island of Wāḳwāḳ, bearing as fruit human heads which shout in chorus, is frequently described in Arabic literature.[4] Such legends usually have a foundation in fact. This one may be an echo of the Batak custom of hanging up on a pole or tree before the house door the skull of a slain enemy filled with camphor, which they consult upon questions of daily life. The taker of the head is supposed to possess the soul which the camphor enables him to keep alive and control.

But it is with the burial ceremonies of the Bataks that we are now concerned. The burial of the poor takes place without ceremony soon after death, but when the local chief dies, there is much ceremony, and when the great chief dies, a messenger goes forth with the jawbone of a buffalo, and all the local chiefs come to the funeral with live buffaloes which are slaughtered together. A catafalque is built upon which rests a coffin of heavy *durio* wood. Within the coffin is the body clothed with full regalia and covered flush with camphor crystals. There it lies for many months, at the end of which it is uncovered for a last look at the sun, and then lowered into the grave. The horns and jawbones of the slaughtered buffaloes are hung up on a wooden framework before the grave.[5] Similar customs are noted among head-hunting tribes of Bali, Borneo and the Philippines.

Camphor was used, then, at the burial of kings and potentates that they might have the spirit gift of power in the next world, and something of the life of Mula Gadi the father-god.

---

[3] Kruijt, *Animism in the Indian Archipelago*; Warneck, *Ancestor and Spirit Worship*; Low, "An Account of the Batta Race in Sumatra", *JRAS* 2. 43 ff.

[4] E. g. Al-Maḳdisī, cf. Ferrand, *Textes Arabes relatifs à l'Extrême-Orient*, 117; Kazwīnī, Ferrand 300; Ibn Sa'īd, Ferrand 334; Dimaškī, Ferrand 375; Digest of Marvels, Ferrand 157.

[5] Breuner, *Besuch bei den Kannibalen Sumatras*; Junghuhn, *Die Battaländer Sumatras*, 296.

Chemically, of course, camphor is contained in many volatile oils, from which it can be separated. It is a solid residue in the oil similar to the tallow in animal fats. Some chemists would prefer to use for it the word stearoptene, literally, "like tallow." Menthol is a camphor obtained from the oil of peppermint; thymol from the oil of thyme; and many other oils will yield a similar residue, the oil of camphor in far the greatest volume.[6] But the distillation of volatile oils is a comparatively recent process. The "fragrant ointments" and "anointing oils" of antiquity were neutral oils like olive and sesame, or animal fats, flavored or scented by steeping with flowers, gum, bark, leaves, grasses or chips of wood. Mohammedan Arabs and Persians were probably the first to work out the distillation of volatile oils, and the separation of the camphors was not studied in Europe before the 17th century. Royalty before that time had to be content with the scanty supply of crystals from the Indian Archipelago, or the imitation which the crafty Chinese learned how to produce by boiling in open kettles the wood of their own tree laurel, or certain fragrant herbaceous plants,[7] catching the solid residue by stretching straws or wool across the top of the kettle.[8] The Chinese still counterfeit the Sumatra camphor and sell it at large gain to trusting Sumatrans,

---

[6] Gildemeister, *Volatile Oils*, 370; cf. Herodotus 2, 85; Dioscorides I; Pliny XV—XVI; Theophrastus IX.

[7] *Blumea balsamifera* is the plant used by the Chinese for this imitation camphor, which they call *ngai* (cf. Flückiger and Hanbury, *Pharmacographia*, 518—519). The market price of the Sumatra camphor is about ten times that of the *ngai* camphor, and fifty times that of the tree-laurel camphor. In the South of France and other Mediterranean lands another herbaceous plant, *Camphorosma monspeliaca*, is used. (Cf. Baillon, Dict. de Botanique *sub verbo*). Ibn al Baiṭar mentions a "Jewish camphor" which was a herbaceous plant of Khorassan, probably the *Camphorosma* (Ferrand 274—5). For Chinese counterfeiting, cf. Abū'l Fazl, Ferrand 544—5. So also I am informed by C. O. Spamer, American Consul at Medan, Sumatra, who has kindly supplied me specimens of the true Dryobalanops camphor and camphor oil, and of the counterfeit Chinese production. Some of the writers confuse camphor with aloe. Ibn Serapion and Ibn al Baiṭar (Ferrand 112, 289) say that in its natural state it is bright red, and becomes white through sublimation. Abū'l Fazl (Ferrand 544) corrects this statement, saying that he himself has taken it white from the tree.

[8] Gildemeister, *op. cit.* and references.

and to a much larger market in India. To the rest of the world it was introduced, probably, by seafaring Arabs who knew how to make the most of its alleged virtues in assuring the immortality of kings, and who studied its more immediate uses in medicine and ointments, and in the preparation of cooling drinks in palaces and homes of wealth. The supply was limited. The tree grows only on the lower hills near the coast and is found here and there in the forests, never thickly. Not every tree yields camphor. Many are felled and cut up to no purpose.[9] The most generous yield may be 10 to 15 pounds of crystals to be had from a tree perhaps 200 feet high and 15 feet in diameter. The natives believe that the yield is greater in times of supernatural activity, exemplified by earthquakes and volcanic eruptions,[10] and that it is increased by the sacrifice of rice, buffaloes or men before the tree. Human sacrifice is supposed to result in a larger find of crystals, so that the Bataks are not to be blamed for setting a high price upon it. Gathering is done by the tribe at seasons advised by their *datu* or priest as propitious, and the tree is selected with similar precautions. A space is cleared for sacrifice. The camphor spirit is summoned by flute-playing and appears to the tribe in dreams, pointing out the tree. On no account is the object of the expedition to be named, lest the ubiquitous *begu* or malignant spirit cause the crystals to disappear into the wood. An artificial language is spoken. It is forbidden to pronounce the names of tree or crystal, which are utterly taboo.[11] The tapper of the tree, when selected by the *datu*, climbs well up the trunk, fastens a jar and pierces the bark, from which the sap is allowed to flow. Face and hands are carefully protected, for a drop touching the skin, being the flowing blood of divinity, would blast a mere mortal.[12] The tree is then tapped lower down, and a whitish gum sometimes appears. Still lower a pocket may be found in the trunk filled with the precious crystals. If the prospect seems favorable, the tree is felled and the tribe sets to work with primitive tools to dissect it, being careful

---

9 Breuner, *op. cit.* 354.

10 Mas'ūdī, Ferrand 97—8; Abū'l Fazl, cf. Ferrand 544.

11 Frazer, *Taboo and the Perils of the Soul,* 405—7; 36; 45—6; 65; 116; Warneck, *op. cit.*, 20; Breuner, 354.

12 Dimaškī; cf. Ferrand, 368—9.

first to shroud the top to prevent the spirit from escaping. That it can escape, let the doubter prove by exposing a crystal to the rays of the sun. The vanishing of the white solid into invisible vapor is thus explained. To prevent this the crystals must be preserved in jars of a certain form, mixed with certain grains or seed, and wrapped securely from the warmth of the body.[13] The vanishing of the camphor, so Dr. Abbott tells me, gives a very definite illustration in modern Indian ceremonial of the disappearance of the human soul from the earth.

The present question is how and when camphor became an article of regular commerce, and whence the word is derived. To the Greeks and Romans it was unknown. No description of it can be found in Theophrastus, Dioscorides or Pliny. It appears in the writings of Symeon Seth, Aetius, Paulus Aegineta and Leo Medicus, Hellenistic medical writers of the 4th to 6th centuries of our era, and a remark of Aetius in one of his prescriptions: "if you have a supply of camphor," indicates the difficulty with which it was obtained. It appears also in the Syrian Book of Medicine recently published by Budge. This is a work of uncertain date, embodying medical data collected at Alexandria and elsewhere, and may be ascribed to the Greek medical school at Edessa, which is known to have been fostered by the Sassanian kings between the 3rd and 5th centuries of our era. It appears also in the Āyur-Veda of Suśruta, a Sanskrit medical work, which Professor Edgerton tells me is believed to be at least as old as the fourth century A. D., although it is thought to contain, also, interpolations from a later time. In the Syriac the form of the word is *kāpūr*; in the Greek two forms appear, *kaphoura* and *kamphora*; in Sanskrit *karpūra*, but in all Indian vernaculars *kāpūr* or *kăppūr*.

The ceremonial use of camphor must have become general in Sassanian times. Dr. Yohannan tells me that Shiite Muslims in Persia to this day rub camphor into the nostrils of the dead to drive away evil spirits and to assist in the resurrection. An Arab prince, Imru-l-Qais, writing before the time of Mohammed, mentions camphor, and Weil, in his History of the Caliphs, relates that when the Arabs pillaged the palace

---

[13] Abū'l Faḍl Ja'far; Ferrand, *op. cit.*, 604; Ibn Khordādhbeh, De Goeje's ed., p. 45.

of the last Sassanian Khusrau in 636 A. D., they took musk, amber, sandalwood and other Eastern aromatics, and "much camphor".[14]

The earliest literary reference of the first rank is in the Koran. In such passages as Sura 37 it is explained how the unrighteous when they reach hell are given boiling water to drink. By contrast Sura 76 tells of the joys of Paradise, where the righteous receive at the hands of the black-eyed maidens cooling drinks, camphor from "a fountain from which the servants of Allah shall drink," and ginger from "a fountain which is named Salsabil" (the softly-flowing). Camphor and ginger are both refrigerants widely used as ingredients in cooling drinks in both tropical and temperate lands; camphor in India especially, where it is often so alluded to in Sanskrit literature. While one's first inclination is to regard them in these passages of the Koran as material delights of the blest in contradistinction to the torments of the damned, some Muslims interpret them as symbolic of the ascent of the soul toward perfection. In Maulvi Mohammed Ali's version of the Koran, it is explained that *kāfūr*, the Arabic form of the word, is from a stem *kfr*, meaning to cover, or hide, and so means "suppression," the extinction of worldly desires on the part of those who have drunk of the cup of Allah; and *zanjbil*, the word for ginger, is derived from *zana'a* and *jabal*, and means "ascent of the mountain"—that is, the steep and difficult heights to attain which spiritual strength must be gained.[15] This etymology is not here defended.

Mohammed himself was very fond of perfumes, and an early tradition quotes Ayesha as saying that he indulged in "men's scents", musk and ambergris, and that he burned camphor on fragrant wood and enjoyed the pleasant odor. Anas, his servant, said, "We always knew when Mohammed had come out of his chamber by the sweet perfume that filled the air."[16]

---

[14] *Geschichte der Chalifen*, 75. Cosmas Indicopleustes, who visited Ceylon in the 6th century and wrote at length of its trade, makes no mention of camphor.

[15] The Holy Qur'ān with English Translation and Commentary, London, *Islamic Review*, 1917, p. 1143, note 2626.

[16] Muir, *Life of Moḥammad*, 330—1.

This high authority was sufficient to fix the form *kāfūr* throughout the world of Islam, and in such estimation is the word held that, so Dr. Sprengling informs me, among dark-skinned African Muslims to this day *Kāfūr* is a favorite given name.

The commercial interest of the Arabs in camphor is shown in the second voyage of Sindbad the Sailor to the island of Riha, which may be identified with Sumatra, in which a clear account is given of the tree and the search for its crystals.[17]

In the 89th Sura of the Koran is a reference to Iram Ḏāt Al-'Imād (Iram with the Pillars), supposed by some Muslim writers to have been a town built in the highlands of Yemen as an imitation of Paradise. Its stones were gold and silver, and its walls studded with jewels. Mas'udi relates with some reserve a story about a certain camel-driver who chanced upon the buried town, from the ruins of which he brought musk, camphor and pearls to the Caliph Mu'awiya.[18] The name is South Arabian, and it appears also in Hamdani; but the idea of an apocalyptic Heavenly City was very general in Semitic lands.

Arabian writers about voyages to the East speak of a similar white city, al-Barraqa, the brilliant, built of shining white stone with white domes, in which cries and songs were heard, but no inhabitants seen.[19] Sailors landed there to take water and found it clear and sweet with an odor of camphor, but the houses receded as fast as approached, and finally faded from view.[20]

There were certain affinities in the word *kāfūr* which no doubt appealed to the Arabic mind. The stem is the same in form and meaning as our word "cover". It suggests Hebrew *kopher*, bitumen or pitch, with which Noah's Ark and Moses'

---

[17] *Thousand and One Nights*, Payne edition, V, 167—8.

[18] *Encyclopaedia of Islam*, No. 26, pp. 519—520.

[19] The word *barraqa* is the same as *bareqeth*, one of the stones of the high priest's breast-plate in Exod. 30, said by Talmudic writers to have been caught up into heaven by an angel when the Babylonians destroyed the Temple at Jerusalem; and this is the same as *smaragdos*, one of the foundations of the Heavenly City of the Apocalypse (Rev. 18). In terms of gem-stones this was the rock-crystal rather than the beryl. Both are hexahedral and appear in many hues.

[20] Digest of Marvels; Ferrand, op. cit. 145.

ark of bulrushes are said to have been covered, and also a whole series of ideas connected with atonement, offerings, and sacrifice. *Yom Kippur*, the Day of Atonement, is from the same stem; also *kapporeth*, the mercy seat above the Ark of the Covenant. The same word *kopher* means henna,[21] from the original meaning to cover over or smear, thence to hide or conceal, or even to suppress—all these meanings naturally follow.[22] Closely related is Arabic *qubūr*, "grave". But the form *kāfūr* is irregular in Arabic and suggests a foreign origin or influence, even though the Arabs apply the same word to the covered spathe of their own date-palm. India lies half-way between Arabia and Sumatra, and we might infer some borrowing from Indic vernaculars; but this would not help us much, for Professor Jackson and Professor Edgerton seem to think that the Indic and Persian words have no indigenous flavor. Dr. Laufer has traced the forms of the word from India through Tibet to Mongolia, and thinks that the differences between Sanskrit and the vernaculars are dialectic variants.[23] It is possible, of course, that the Sanskrit form *karpūra* is the result of "back-writing" from a vernacular *kāpūr*, or *kappūr*. Dr. Laufer seems to be of the opinion, however, that the word is not Indic, and traces it to an early form, *giadbura*, or *giadbula*. This is not difficult to carry back to a Malay original, which indeed is probable because of the known Sumatran origin of the substance. The word can probably be identified with the name of the Heavenly Tree of the Bataks, *gābū*, or *gāmbū*, and their ceremonial meal, *gāmbūr*.

While probably derived from a common Malayo-Indonesian stock, the Bataks have held themselves aloof from all modern Malays, whom they regard as foreigners and distinguish from Europeans only by the color of their teeth.[24] The name of the heavenly tree in the Batak language is *Gambū-barus*. *Baru* is spirit. *Gambu*, with a root form *gābū*, means "to scatter", "to

---

[21] But the Arabs call it *al-hinnā*, the leaf, whence our henna, and Malay *inei*.

[22] Cf. Haupt, *Biblische Liebeslieder*, 127—129; also *Journal of Biblical Literature*, 35. 282.

[23] *Sino-Iranica*, 585—591.

[24] Cf. Warneck, *Tobataksch-Deutsches Wörterbuch*, 246; Anderson, *Mission to the East Coast of Sumatra in 1823*, p. 147.

hand out", or "to distribute". A derivative form *gambūr*, with variants, *hambūr*, *hampūr*, *kampūr*, is "that which is handed out" or distributed—rice at a tribal ceremony, human fate at the hands of the father-god. Literally the name of the tree may be rendered "spirit-gift". The *m* is a Malay infix, implying manner, internal movement, happening, duration, or repetition. The final *r* is a derivative form and may be a transposed infix. Among these variant Malay forms is *kāpūr*, which may mean the white crystals found in the camphor tree, or a similar substance found in a variety of bamboo, or chalk, or the lime used in betel chewing. The initial guttural varies in intensity, for in modern Malay we have *abur*, "to lavish", "to waste", or "to be prodigal in expenditure", with derivatives *ambur* and *hambur*, "strewing", "dropping down", or "scattering". Also *kapar*, "scattered about", with which *kapur* would seem to be connected. The word may have, therefore, a dual significance; material, as relating to the crystals found scattered through the trunk of the tree, and ceremonial, as connected with the heavenly Tree of Fate. All modern Malay dialects apply the word to chalk, in connection with the whitening of shoes or bleaching of fabrics, and to lime, whether for betel chewing or for whitewashing and construction. But these applications of the word seem to be relatively late and are probably due to similarity of appearance.[25] *Kāfūrī* in modern Persian and Hindustani means "white", obviously derived through Arabic from these Malay forms.[26]

The Greek forms *kaphoura* and *kamphora*, the Sanskrit *karpūra*, the later Indic *kapūr* and *kappūra*, the Syriac *kāpūr* and the Arabic *kāfūr*, are apparently all traceable to Malay variations. Infixed *m* and *r* and suffixed *r* have already been noted. In a Malay dictionary I note three variations of a single word in as many dialects—Malacca *kārsiq*, Sunda *kāsiq*, and Macassar *kăsiq*. The name of the water buffalo, which the Spaniards spell *carabao*, is a Malay word *karbau*, and its

---

[25] Cf. Winstedt, *Malay Grammar*; Joustra, *Karo-Bataksch Woordenboek*, 34, 60; Shellabear, *A Malay-English Vocabulary*, 53, 37, 114; Van der Tuuk, *Bataksch Nederduitsch Woordenboek* 88, 189; Skeat, *Etymological Dictionary of the English Language*, *sub verbo* camphor.

[26] As to which Prof. Haupt cites Meyer's *Grofses Konversations-Lexikon*, 6th ed., 10, 524—a.

original form is *kabau*, as seen in the name of another primitive Sumatran tribe, the *Menang-kabau*.

The Chinese, who found camphor at about the same time as the Arabs and placed a very high value upon it, paid no attention to its names in Malay or Arabic and called it "dragon's brains", *lung-nau*.[27] This seems to be a fanciful name due to the appearance of the crystals. Various forms of this name are still found in Indonesian dialects, notably in the Philippines; and to the Japanese it is "brain-matter", *sho-no*.[28] The land of Chryse, the meeting point between commercial Chinese and Arabic, is the line between "brain-matter" and "hidden-matter" as commercial names for camphor.

In Arabic the word becomes *kāfūr* with a significance of "hidden" or "covered up", instead of "scattered about" or "distributed" which it seems to have in Malay. Again the meaning is so apt as to explain the ready passage of the word between the two languages. The substance does not appear in commerce until after the time of Ptolemy, who had reports from Greek, Indian and Arabian sources of voyages to Chryse and beyond. There is no reason why the Arabs should not have found it locally used and perceived its commercial value based on its mysterious divine virtues, of which they could make much with the credulous peoples with whom they dealt.

Whether its origin be Malay or Semitic, the word *kāpūr* or *kāfūr* is an unusual form in either,[29] and its persistence as a trade name may be due to its manifold and appropriate affinities. Is it unreasonable to suppose that the Bataks of Sumatra adopted a foreign form of the name for their Heavenly Tree which could be spoken without breaking the taboo? The Kayans of Borneo when hunting camphor, say merely "the thing that smells".[30] Did the Bataks of Sumatra refrain from

---

27 Cf. Cordier's *Yule's Marco Polo*, II. 303; Adams, *Comment. Paulus Aegineta*, 3; 427—9.

28 Yuhodo, *Japanese-English Pocket Dictionary*, 635. I-tsing, the Chinese Buddhist pilgrim writing in the 7th century, mentions Baros camphor; *Records of the Buddhist Religion*, Oxford 1896, Chap. 27.

29 Two long vowels are unusual in a Semitic noun, but not impossible, for we have Hebrew *qīṭōr*, smoke; and the form is probably South-Arabian, not classical.

30 Frazer, *op. cit.*, 406; cf. also Beccari, *Wanderings in the Great Forests of Borneo*, 272—5.

saying "spirit gift" and prefer "the thing that is hidden", borrowing from the seafaring traders who paid them such a fabulous price for it? Were they not, in fact, safeguarded by so doing, because their *begu* could not be supposed to understand Arabic? It is possible at least that the elaborate ceremonies connected with the gathering of camphor were not worked out until a foreign demand appeared for it which taxed the productive capacity of their forests. Similar customs are noted in the mining for tin among Malay tribes in Banka and Billiton, all being essentially propitiatory rites to obtain the benevolence of good spirits or to deceive evil spirits and thus enhance the fortunes of the tribe.[31] It is by no means impossible that the Arabic word was carried over into Batak as the spoken name of their Tree of Fate, and its real name successfully concealed.

The Sanskrit and Prakrit forms may have been derived from the Malacca Peninsula rather than Sumatra, direct from the Malay without Arabic influence. A northern origin for the Bataks is suggested by their own legend. The name of their port on the west coast of Sumatra, Baros, is the word for spirit, and recalls the name Langabalus, or Langabaros, an old name for the Nicobar islands—traces possibly of the southward migration of a tribal god.[32]

Only the Bataks could solve for us the original form from which the word camphor is derived. It is taboo, and so they would not if they could; but as their *Singamangaraja* (Malay for Sinha Maharajah, that is, lion-great-ruler) claims descent from one of the three sons of Alexander the Great, named Sri Iskander, they probably could not if they would.[33]

It is a fact that the Arabs, finding a world market for

---

[31] Frazer, *op. cit.* 407.

[32] Cf. Ferrand, *op. cit.* 25, 181; *Batakspiegel*, pub. by the Batak Institute, The Hague, *Lijst van de voornaamste aardrijkskunde namen in den Nederlandsch Indischen Archipel*, Batavia, 1906. Sulaiman, writing in 851, says "these people do not understand Arabic, nor any of the languages spoken by the merchants." (Ferrand 39.) Dimaškī confuses Balus with Langabalus, which he says is the place where the camphor tree grows. (Ferrand 382—3.)

[33] Junghuhn, *op. cit.* Mas'ūdī, writing in 955, observes of these islands "all their kings bear the title of Maharajah." (Ferrand 99.)

frankincense greater than the supply available at the ports of the Gulf of Aden, found a nearly related tree in Sumatra which they called *luban jāwī*; that is, frankincense of Jāwa, which was the early name for Sumatra. Frankincense was another very holy tree, and the fumes from the burning of its gum brought human benefits valued at a high price, which Arab merchants found it profitable to secure. The virtues of the *luban jāwī* were asserted to be identical with those of the incense of the land of Punt sought out by the fleets of the Pharaohs. This name we, following the Portuguese, have corrupted into *benzoin*,[34] and Marsden, a century ago, into *benjamin*. But this tree was first found in the Batak territory of Sumatra and the Bataks still call that tree *aloban*.[35] Surely that is pure Arabic; and it is not unreasonable to suppose that Arab merchants seeking a more generous supply of the sacred frankincense found at the same time a tree held similarly sacred by the Bataks of Sumatra, and that they commercialized the divine virtues of its crystals just as they did the virtues of the frankincense. The market was rather different. Frankincense was treasured especially in Egypt, Palestine, Mesopotamia and the Mediterranean world; camphor in India and the East; yet the Arabs succeeded in convincing the Chinese of the virtues of frankincense, and the Persians of the virtues of camphor.

The rapid spread of Islam over the Indian Archipelago followed lines of trade established by Arab shipping long before the time of Mohammed.[36]

POSTSCRIPT

After this paper was presented to the Society, additional details were received through Consul Spamer at Medan,

---

[34] Cf. Laufer, *op. cit.*; Marsden, *History of Sumatra*; Anderson, *op. cit.* 204.

[35] Anderson, op. cit. 204. Schreiber, *Die Battas in ihrem Verhältnis zu den Malaien von Sumatra.*

[36] Cf. Van den Berg, *Le Hadramaut et les Colonies Arabes dans l'Archipel Indien*, Batavia, 1886; also various notes to Alberuni's India, Sachau's edition.

including an unpublished Batak legend, which it seems worth while to append.

According to Assistant Resident Schroeder of Tartutung, Tapanuli, Sumatra, the native stories about the influence of earthquakes and insects upon camphor are founded upon fact. Camphor is found only in holes or cracks in the wood. This wood is rather firm, but splits easily, especially in a radial direction, and this in fact results from severe earthquakes. In order to transform the camphor oil into borneol crystals, an oxidation process is necessary, and the possibility for this is furnished by the presence of wood-boring insects. According to several accounts the camphor seekers can tell by a rustling sound within the tree when camphor is present, and for this sound the gnawing of the larvae is said to be responsible. The tree is felled in order to obtain the product, and the camphor veins usually run in spirals around the heart of the tree.

The consul has also obtained from Bona haju (chief of camphor expeditions) Pa Tambok of Pardomuan (Barus) an account of the legendary origin of camphor as told by the Bataks. A beautiful girl of supernatural origin named Nan Tar Tar Nan Tor Tor was married to a mortal named Si Pagedag Si Pagedog, under an agreement that the husband would never allow her to dance; but a dissolute neighbor, enamored of her beauties, beguiled the husband in an unguarded moment into sending his wife a message asking her to dance. She obeyed; but hardly had she begun when with a shriek she vanished upwards, Begu Sombaon, the evil spirit, having thus been given power over the spirit of her unborn child. She flew to a *langkukung* bush and took on the properties of camphor, but the bush was too small and was nibbled at by the cattle, and she moved to a *johar* tree. Not finding this tree an ideal abode, she then moved to a *suja* tree, the present camphor tree, where she lives to the present day. Her husband, stricken by grief and remorse, hunted her everywhere, and in a dream it was revealed to him that she lived inside the *suja* tree. He tried to find her by beating against each tree with a stick, but not finding her, he made an end of his life. His soul still torments camphor-seekers, who hear his cries and the striking of his stick against the trees. If his spirit hovers near a tree, then Nan Tar Tar Nan Tor Tor disappears and no camphor is found. To this day the chief of the camphor seekers does not place his hut near a tree from which the cries of Si Pagedag Si Pagedog can be heard, since he knows that Nan Tar Tar Nan Tor Tor has already fled. Batak wives still wear leaves of the camphor tree in their hair to protect them from Begu Sombaon, the kidnapper of Nan Tar Tar Nan Tor Tor.

According to the Acting Controller of Barus, camphor seeking is usually undertaken by a ruler or village head, who engages a camphor seeker or Bona haju, who is a diviner. During the search this man uses opium excessively and lives strictly secluded in abnormal mental condition, living wholly in the thought of finding camphor. When the necessary funds have been advanced by the village head the Bona haju and his helpers go into the forests and build a hut in some section where camphor trees abound. Places where knocking sounds are heard in the trees are avoided because no camphor will be found there. The Bona haju then lays on the ground a leaf picked from the *pandajangan* tree, the point toward himself and the stem toward the camphor trees. On the outside of the leaf he places a complete chew of betel, to gain the favor of Nan Tar Tar Nan Tor Tor, and as many cubes of ginger root cooked with salt as there are partakers in the expedition. Three, five, seven or even twelve persons may take part. The Bona haju sits before the leaf until ants appear. The direction from which they come shows where the hunt is to take place. The color of the ants approaching the salted ginger indicates the color of the animal to be sacrificed; a red ant calls for a white buffalo, and a black ant for a black one. Each piece of ginger root laid on the leaf is named for one of the expedition, and he whose cube is first attacked by the ants becomes the leader of the chipping expedition. According as the ginger root is eaten at either end or in the middle, it tells whether camphor is to be found in the valley, on the slope or at the top of the hill. The Bona haju then returns to his hut and by the use of opium induces a dream in which there appears to him a woman who offers him rice. Her rank and the quantity of rice give further instruction as to the kind of tree to be tapped and whether it will pay. The seekers distinguish between three kinds of camphor trees having bark of different shades. The color of the face of the dream-woman determines what trees are to be tapped. The length of her hair indicates whether or not trees having long aerial roots should be tapped. If she wears a short jacket then the trees with smooth trunks are to be tapped. If she offers much rice, the tree tapped will have much camphor. After her appearance in the dream, a white, brown and black chicken is killed in honor of Begu Sombaon, the evil spirit, upon whom the Bona haju then calls beseeching the grant of finding camphor, without which he declares he must kill himself. He then goes to the village head to inform him as to the color of the carabao to be sacrificed. Sometimes other sacrifices are called for. The spirit of the child of a ruler may be asked. In that case the child is kidnapped from some neighboring village and left alone in the woods, a prey in their belief for Begu Sombaon, the evil spirit, but in reality for the tigers. It is thought to be a good sign when a tiger, which is the riding animal of Begu Sombaon, comes to a native hut. This is a sure sign of a rich harvest of camphor, and it is only necessary to follow the beast and observe the trees on which he makes a mark with his claws. This is a proof of the favorable inclination of Begu Sombaon, the tiger acting as his messenger. Another good sign is the presence in a tree of the nest of a snake, *Celar ratarata.* This snake is said to have been appointed by Begu Sombaon as the keeper of Nan Tar Tar Nan Tor Tor, and where he is much camphor is found.

When the instructions of the Bona haju are wrong and no camphor is found, this is attributed to failure to observe the ceremonial taboos. In such cases the arts of divination begin anew, larger sacrifices are called for, and if the village head refuses to furnish them, the Bona haju as priest and mediator must give his own life as security to Begu Sombaon for fulfillment of his pledges. However, to avert this evil from himself, he may appoint one of his helpers as substitute. Since the extension of the jurisdiction of the Dutch Government over the Bataks, Sombaon, like all other spirits, is said to care less for human offerings and people are less apt to disappear.

When there has been a rich harvest of camphor, the whole neighborhood turns out with great joy and the happy return is celebrated with drums and dancing.

According to the custom of the Bataks, a Bona haju cannot

be prosecuted for debt and he is exempt from taxation, but it is his lot to die poor.

The old men disapprove modern neglect of ancient custom and claim that this has its effect in the chopping down of empty trees. "They incense the spirit Sombaon; fools they are, in company with Si Pagedag Si Pagedog."

BRIEF NOTES

Regencies in Babylon

Professor Dougherty's note on Ancient Teima and Babylon (*JAOS* 41. 458—459) throws new light upon an interesting political situation. The later Assyrian and Neo-Babylonian dynasties pursued a policy of aggression in all possible directions. Tribute lists indicate that they were more successful toward the West and South than toward the North and East. Most of Arabia paid tribute, and control was maintained by garrisons at points which commanded the trade-routes. These were always few in number and fixed by the water-supply. Both dynasties succumbed to combinations of Eastern enemies with discontented elements within their own boundaries. This condition is reflected in certain passages in the Hebrew prophets, Isaiah and Ezekiel, which appear to be incitements to rebellion against the oppressive central government, mentioned under names not its own, which were chosen for reasons of political safety. Isaiah had no special grievance against Babylon, but a very real one against Nineveh because of the aggression of Sennacherib; yet (chapters 13 and 14) he avoids the open prediction of retribution upon Nineveh, and predicts it upon Babylon. As Nineveh was then engaged upon the reduction of Babylon, the prophecy of destruction would pass for subserviency rather than sedition; yet those who had ears might hear. Perhaps also the command in Exod. 22 27, "revile not God, nor curse a ruler among thy people," caused the curse to be expressed indirectly. Ezekiel had no grievance against Tyre, but a very real one against Babylon because of the aggression of Nebuchadrezzar II; yet (chapters 27 and 28) he avoids the open prediction of retribution upon Babylon and predicts it of Tyre, upon the reduction of which Babylon was then engaged. But his real meaning appears in his statement (17 3-4, 12) that Canaan (i. e., Tyre) = Babylon, and that the "land of traffic" and its merchants centered there. And the precious substances for the possession of which "Tyre" is condemned are precisely those of which Nebuchadrezzar II had plundered the temple and palace at Jerusalem. The *haram* had been violated and the prophets applied the *lex talionis.*

The employment of Phoenician shipbuilders and sailors by Sennacherib in his naval campaign against Elam is well known. The fruits of such assistance are indicated in a passage in Isaiah (22 13) for which the Jewish Revision offers a new and striking version:

> "Behold, the land of the Chaldeans—this is the people that was not, when Asshur founded it for shipmen."

Subsequent activities of these seafarers in the Persian Gulf and at Gerrha and other ports controlling the Central Arabian caravan routes are also well known. We may infer that the Neo-Babylonian kings would have been glad to curtail the favors extended to them by their Assyrian predecessors.

The tablets described by Professor Dougherty tell of a regency of the Crown Prince in Babylon while the ruling monarch was absent during long intervals on affairs of state, to be understood as military. The same condition is shown in Ezekiel where (chapter 28) a doom is pronounced jointly upon the Prince and King of "Tyre" (the Prince receiving the most attention), because of their possession of the Jerusalem plunder. The tablets refer to Nabonidus and Belshazzar. Ezekiel refers probably to Nebuchadrezzar II and Amil-Marduk. The King may have been absent on some military enterprise, or he may have been temporarily incapacitated, as we read in the book of Daniel (4 30).

Further light in this direction may be confidently expected as other tablets of the period are published.

WILFRED H. SCHOFF

Philadelphia Commercial Museum

Heb. kôhên *and* qahâl

In *AJSL* 32. 64 (cf. *JBL* 38. 151, n. 15)[1] I showed that Heb. *komr*, idol-priest, was identical with Ass. *ramku*, priest, prop.

[1] For the abbreviations see above, p. 301, n. 1.

lustrator. My explanation has been adopted in n. 31 to the new (1921) edition of Delitzsch's *Babel und Bibel.* Both *kamar* and *ramak* are transposed doublets of *makar,* to water, a denominative stem derived from *makâru,* well < *kâru,* to dig. (*JBL* 36. 254; 34. 55; 37. 227; 40, 171. 172). *JBL* 36. 89 I pointed out that the original meaning of Heb. *rô'ê* and *ḥôzê,* seer, as well as *mĕ'ônên,* diviner, was *scryer.* Even the elaborate system of hepatoscopy which we find in the cuneiform omen tablets was originally, it may be supposed, merely gazing on the smooth, shiny surface of a liver. The tribes of the Northwest-Indian frontier use the liver of an animal for scrying (*EB*[11] 7, 567[a8]). David Ḳimḥi states in his remarks on Ez. 21, 26, where the king of Babylon stands at the fork of the road to practice divination, polishing arrows, consulting teraphim, gazing on a liver, that diviners gaze not only on a polished arrow-head, or thumb-nail, or sword-blade, or mirror, but also on a liver, because it possesses gloss, *i. e.* a reflective surface (*JBL* 36, 38). For consulting the teraphim see my paper *Was David an Aryan?* (*OC* 33, 44) and for the proper pronunciation *târâpîm* (i. e. *providers*) cf. *JBL* 38, 84[i].

The German terms for *scrying* or *crystal-gazing* (cf. CD, Supplement *s. v.* and *EB*[11] 22, 544[b4]) are *Kristallschauen, Kristallomantie, Beryllomantie* (*MK*[6] 11, 718) or *Katoptromantie* (*MK*[6] 10, 754) or *Hydromantie* (*MK*[6] 9, 695). Scrying is a form of autohypnotization. A *scryer* is called in German also *Engelseher*: in an article on *Alt-Gotha* by Marie v. Bunsen, published in the German weekly *Daheim,* Sept. 6, 1919, p. 10[a], the author says that Duke John Frederick, who induced his father to found the university of Jena in 1558, *traute* (1566) *einem Engelseher, der das Kommende in einer Kristallkugel erkannte* (cf. *EB*[11] 12, 639[b], l. 7; 15, 459[a]). We may also compare the *peep-stone* or *gazing-crystal* of the founder of Mormonism (*EB*[11] 18, 842[b]; *RE*[3] 13, 466, l. 29; 469, l. 59). *Cf.* also Karl Kiesewetter, *Faust in der Geschichte und Tradition* (Leipsic, 1893).

Heb. *kôhên,* priest, is identical with Arab. *kâhin,* diviner. The original meaning is not *preparing, serving,* as König states in his Hebrew dictionary, but *soothsayer* which means originally *telling the truth.* Ger. *Wahrsager* has the same meaning, while *Weissager,* prophet, is connected with *wissen,* to know = Lat.

videre, Eng. *wit* > *witch, wizard*, &c. AS *witga* means *seer*, prophet, soothsayer, magician; *wizard* denoted orig. *wise man*, sage, and *wise woman* signified *fortune-teller*; cf. Heb. *i̯iddĕ'ônî*, Ass. *mûdû*, Arab. *šâ'ir* (*JHUC* 316. 24; *JAOS* 40. 218, a).

Our *sooth*, which is connected with Skt. *sat* and Gr. ἐτεός, true, means *truth* and *true*. Sir Walter Scott says: *Announced by prophet sooth and true.* The prophetic old man of the sea, Proteus, who knew all things, past, present, and future, has the epithet νημερτής, infallible, reliable, veracious, true, a compound of νη and ἁμαρτάνειν. In Greek, Heb. *kôhén* appears as κοίης which according to Hesychius (κοίης· ἱερεὺς Καβείρων ὁ καθαίρων φονέα) denotes a priest in the Samothracian mysteries in connection with the cult of the Cabiri. Also γόης, magician, may be derived from it; the *g* represents a partial assimilation of the *k* to the *n* (*JBL* 36. 141, n. 3; *PAPS* 58. 243[a]). Similarly we have in Ethiopic: *gŭĕhán* or *gu̯ĕhĕn*, mystery, instead of *kŭhn*. There is, of course, a close interrelation between magic and priesthood (*EB*[11] 22. 317[a.a]).

The stem of Heb. *kôhén* is a modification of *kûn* from which we have in Assyrian: *kêttu* = *kêntu*, truth, fem. of *kênu*. We have in Gen. 42, 11: *kênîm ănáḥnû*, we are true (*i. e.* honest) *men*, and in Eccl. 8, 10: *ăšér kên 'aśû*, who did right. Heb. *kên*, true, right, appears also in *lak̲ên*, all right (*JBL* 29. 105[a]) and in *ak̲ên*, verily, where the initial vowel is a remnant of the preposition *ina*, as it is also in *ät̲môl* and *ämš*, yesterday, *az* = *azái̯*, then, &c. (*JBL* 36. 148). For the adversative use of *ak̲ên* (lit. *in sooth*, in truth, indeed) *cf.* Lat. *verum, vero.* The *e* in *kên* is long; *cf.* the spellings of *kênâ* in Syriac (Nöldeke, *Syr. Gr.*[2] § 98, B) and cuneiform *ki-e-nu* (*HW* 322[b]). Heb. *kên*, *mêt* = *kau̯în, mau̯ît.*

Ass. *muškînu* (> Heb. *miskén*) is not derived from *kûn*, but from *kîn*, Arab. *kâna-i̯akînu* = *xáḏa'a* (*AJSL* 23. 226[i]; *JBL* 33. 295[a]). Arab. *istakâna* belongs to the same stem. Ass. *muškînu* denotes *free-born*, and *mâr amîli*: full-born; see my paper *The Son of Man* in *Monist* 29, 125 (cf. *JAOS* 37. 14[i]; *JBL* 40. 183). The synonym of *mâr-amîli*, son of a man, *mâr-bânî*, son of a father (*HW* 178[b]; *AL*[5] 19, 148) corresponds to the Roman *patrician*; Lat. *patricius* means *fathered*, i. e. a man with a family and genealogy (*EB*[11] 20, 931[b.i]).

Just as *sooth* is connected with Lat. *esse*, to be; *sunt*, they are, so *kûn* is the common verb for *to be* in Arabic and Phenician (Lidzbarski, *Epigraphik* 294). For the original meaning of Heb. *haiâ*, to be, cf. *JBL* 38. 163[i]. A medial *h* is often secondary: we have in Aramaic e. g. *běhêṯ*, to be ashamed; *rěhêṭ*, to run; *kěhêl*, to be able, for Heb. *bôš*, *rûç*, *kûl* = *iaḵól*, and *núhrâ*, light, for Arab. *nûr* (*AJSL* 20. 171; 22, 250[i]; *Nah.* 46[m]). In the same way the stem of Heb. *qahál* or *qěhillâ*, congregation, is a modification of *qûl*, to call; the original meaning is *convocation*. In Arabic, *qâla* is the common word for *to say*. The same root is preserved in Arab. *naql*, tale, and *náqal*, ready repartee; cf. Arab. *nazf* < *nafz* and Eth. *zafána* < *nafáza*, also Arab. *náfara* which is a N of *fárra*: the diminutive *nufáir* corresponds in some respects to Heb. *pělêṭâ* (*AJP* 43, 241).

Of course, many priests and prophets were unrighteous (Jer. 23, 11) and there were many false prophets who deceived many (Matt. 24, 11) but they pretended to be soothsayers telling the truth, just as Sennacherib's father, who on the death of Shalmaneser IV during the siege of Samaria in 722 seized the crown, called himself *Šarru-kênu*, the true king, a name like the Heb. *malkî-çädq*, legitimate king (*JBL* 37. 209[i]; *JPOS* 1. 69, n. 2).

Paul Haupt

Johns Hopkins University

Heb. qîṭôr *a doublet of* ʿašán.

Dimorphism is much more common in Semitic than is generally supposed. I have discussed transposed doublets in a number of passages (e. g. *JBL* 34. 61[a]. 63[a]; 35. 158[m]. 322[i]; 36. 140[i]; 37. 229[i]; 38. 47[a]. 152[i]; 39. 163[i]. 168[a]; *AJSL* 26. 234[a]; 33. 45[m]). Doublets are often very dissimilar: both *cattle* and *chattel* are doublets of *capital*, principal, stock; *grotto* is a doublet of *crypt*, and *zero* a doublet of *cypher* > Ass. *šipru*, message (*Kings* 198, 47). In the same way Heb. *qîṭôr*, smoke, is a doublet of *ʿašán*. The stem of *qîṭôr* is identical with Syr. *ʿěṭár*, to rise up as vapor, steam, or smoke. The *ṭ* is due to partial assimilation of *t* to *q* as in Heb. *qaṭál* = Arab. *qátala* (*SFG* 73[i]; *VG* 154, h). The *t* is preserved in Ass. *qutru*, smoke, and *qutrênu*, sacrifice (*HW* 600; *JBL* 37. 219). In Arabic we have *qutâr*, fragrant steam of roasted meat, with *t*, but *miqṭar*, censer, and *qúṭur*, aloes (*i. e.* eaglewood which yields a fragrant odor when burnt) with *ṭ*. Both Arab. *quṭâr* and *'áṭar* are Aramaic loanwords: the genuine Arabic form is *'áṯan*, smoke, and the corresponding Hebrew word is *'ašán*. For Aram. *ṭ* = Arab. *ṯ* cf. Aram. *qaṭṭáiiâ*, cucumbers = Arab. *qiṯṯâ'* (*JBL* 39. 162). For *n* = *r* cf. Aram. *madnĕḥâ* = Heb. *mizráḥ*, sunrise, and for *q* = ': Aram. *árqâ*, earth = *ár'â*, also Heb. *qarâ* = Aram. *'ărá'* (or *'ărâ'*) to meet (Aram. *lĕ-'ur'êh* = Heb. *liqrâṯô*) = Arab. *'áraḍa*, to appear, to happen > *'arḍ-al-ǧáiš*, military review, parade = Heb. *'ăçérṯ*, festal assembly, which has passed into Aramaic as *'ăçártâ*, Pentecost > Arab. *'ánçarah*. For the final *â* in Heb. *qarâ* cf. Syr. *mĕḥâ*, to strike < *mĕḥá'* = Ass. *maxâçu*, Arab. *máxaḍa*. Heb. *maḥáq* in Jud. 5, 26 can hardly be a dialectic form of this stem (*WF* 222).

The primary connotation of Heb. *'ašán*, smoke = Arab. *'áṯan* is *ascending* (cf. Arab. *'áṯana*, or *'áfana*, *fî-'l-ǧábali*, to ascend a mountain). For Arab. *'áfina*, to stink, we may compare our *reek* (= Ger. *rauchen*) which meant orig. *to smoke*, steam, exhale, while it now denotes *to stink*. The noun *reek* was formerly used for *incense*. Another doublet of this stem is Arab. *'árifa*, to know (orig. *to scent*) = Ass. *erêšu* (*JBL* 34. 72; *JHUC* 316. 24). Hoffmann's combination of Arab. *'áṯan* with Syr. *tĕnânâ* is impossible: *tĕnânâ* is transposition of *nĕtânâ* = Arab. *natânah*, stench (*ZDMG* 69. 564). For the meaning of Eth. *astantána* cf. Arab. *u̯âtana* < *u̯atan* (Phen. *i̯atan*) = Heb. *natán* (*NBSS* 200). Heb. *êṯán*, unceasing, is derived from the same stem. We should expect *ôṯán*; cf. Heb. *ôçár*, treasure (< *u̯açar* = *naçar*) and Aram. *ôǧár*, heap of stones = *i̯ĕǧár* (*PAPS* 58. 241). On the other hand, we find in Syriac: *au̯bíš*, to dry, instead of *ai̯bíš*, and *au̯dá'*, to make known, instead of *ai̯dá'*, although the *i̯* of these verbs does not represent an original *u̯* (*SFG* 22. 1; *JBL* 34. 72). The root *tn* appears in Arab. *ṯádina*, to stink, with partial assimilation of *t* to *n*, as in Ass. *nadânu*, to give (*SFG* 43. 2). For the prefixed *ṯ* see *JBL* 35. 321[4]. We have it also in Heb. *tannîm*, jackals; the wild jackals emit a highly offensive odor. Similarly goats are called *'izzîm*, strong, *i. e.* ill-smelling. The goats are therefore symbols of evil (*JBL* 39. 154, l. 9). The *n* in Ass. *enzu* (Sum. *uzu*, *us*) is secondary (*JAOS* 41. 177[4]).

Nor can Syr. *tĕnânâ* be connected with *attônâ*, oven < Sum. *udun* (*MLN* 33. 433) or with Ass. *tumru* (cf. Heb. *zärm* = Eth. *zĕnâm* = Ass. *zunnu* = Arab. *múznah*). Ass. *tumru*, smoke (*JAOS* 38. 336, l. 8) and Heb. *tamár*, palm (= Arab. *tamr*, dates) are derived from the secondary reflexive stem *tamar* < *amar,* to be high > Heb. *amîr,* top of a tree, and Arab. *amîr,* prince (*ZDMG* 63. 518, l. 37). The verb *amar,* to command, is denominative (*cf.* our *to lord*). From the same stem we must derive also Heb. *tîmôrâ* (< *tômôrâ*; cf. *AJSL* 22. 256, *; *JBL* 39. 160) column of smoke (*Khull.* 112^a = *BT* 8, 1163, l. 1).

Paul Haupt

Johns Hopkins University

NOTES OF THE SOCIETY

The Executive Committee has by unanimous vote elected the following to membership in the Society:

Dr. N. Adriani
Mrs. Robert A. Bailey Jr.
Mr. Alfred M. Campbell
Mr. Morris G. Cohen
Mr. Nariman M. Dhalla
Pres. D. C. Gilmore
Mr. Ernest P. Horrwitz
Mr. Elmer D. Merrill
Prof. Luther Parker
Mr. Antonio M. Paterno
Dr. Otto Scheerer
Mr. Victor Sharenkoff
Rev. James Watt
Prof. Harry Clinton York

NOTES OF OTHER SOCIETIES, ETC.

On July 10—13, 1922, a meeting was held in Paris to celebrate the double centenary of the foundation of the Société Asiatique and of the discovery of Champollion. The delegates from this Society appointed by the Directors, upon invitation from the Société Asiatique, were the following: The President, Professor Hopkins; Dr. Abbott, Prof. Bloomfield, Prof. Breasted, Prof. Gottheil, Prof. Jackson, Prof. Jewett, Prof. Lanman, Mr. Newell, Dr. Nies, Prof. Prince, and Prof. Woods. Of these, Dr. Abbott, and Professors Breasted, Gottheil, Jackson, Jewett, and Lanman were present.

The centenary of Champollion's discovery was also celebrated at a later meeting held in Grenoble, October 7 and 8, 1922, at which this Society was represented by Professor Breasted.

The K. R. Cama Oriental Institute (172, Sukhadwala Building, Hornby Road, Fort, Bombay) invites competitive essays for the Sarosh K. R. Cama Prize, of the value of 225 Rupees, on the following subject: "A lucid and thoroughly intelligible translation in English of the 32nd, 33rd, and 34th chapters of the Yasna (the last three chapters of the Ahnuvaiti Gatha), in due accordance with grammar and philology, with notes and comments wherever necessary, and with the substance of the whole at the end." The instructions state that "the essay should be designated by a motto and should be accompanied by a sealed cover containing the name of the competitor and his Post Office adress, and should reach the Honorary Secretaries of the Institute [address as above] on or before 5th July 1923. The competition is open to all."

PERSONALIA

Professor Theophile J. Meek has been appointed Professor of Semitic Languages in Bryn Mawr College.

Professor Julian Morgenstern has been appointed President of Hebrew Union College, Cincinnati, Ohio.

The Rev. Geo. S. Kukhi has had his name changed by legislative enactment to George S. Cooke. He has accepted the pastorate of the First Church, Houlton, Maine.

SPECIAL NOTICE

To authors and publishers of books on oriental subjects

The Directors of the American Oriental Society have instructed the editors to enlarge the JOURNAL and to devote approximately one-fourth of its space to reviews of important works on oriental subjects. It is intended to begin publication of such reviews with the next volume, to appear in the year 1923. The editors will be glad to receive for review copies of new publications within the fields which the JOURNAL covers. They reserve the right to decide in the case of each book whether a review of it would be suitable for the JOURNAL. All books for review should be sent to one of the editors (Max L. Margolis, 152 West Hortter St., Philadelphia, Pa., or Franklin Edgerton, 107 Bryn Mawr Avenue, Lansdowne, Pa.), and should be accompanied by a statement to the effect that they are intended for review in the JOURNAL. It is requested that books on Indo-Iranian and other Indo-European subjects be addrest to Mr. Edgerton, and those on Semitic and allied fields to Mr. Margolis.

PROCEEDINGS

OF THE

AMERICAN ORIENTAL SOCIETY

AT THE MEETING IN CHICAGO, ILLINOIS, 1922

The annual sessions of the Society, forming its one hundred and thirty-fourth meeting, were held in Chicago, Illinois, at the University of Chicago, on Tuesday, Wednesday and Thursday of Easter Week, April 18, 19, 20, 1922: this was a joint meeting with the Middle West Branch of the Society.

The following members were present at one or more sessions:

Abbott	Jackson, A. V. W.	Schaeffer
Allen	Jackson, Mrs.	Schmidt
Barret	Judson	Schoff
Breasted	Kelly	Scott, J. A.
Buck	Keyfitz	Smith, J. M. P.
Bull	Laufer	Snyder
Buttenwieser	Leavitt	Sprengling
Clark	Luckenbill	Turner
Cohon	Maynard	Waterman
Dorf	Mercer	Wicker, Miss
Edgerton, W. F.	Montgomery	Willett
Efros	Morgenstern	Williams, Mrs. C. R.
Eiselen	Nykl	Wolfenson
Fuller	Ogden, C. J.	Yohannan
Grant	Olmstead	*[Total: 48]*
Haupt	Price	
Hewes	Robinson, G. L.	

THE FIRST SESSION

At 2:23 P. M., after the business session of the Middle West Branch (see page 401 f.), the first session of the Society was called to order by Vice-president Nathaniel Schmidt. The reading of the Proceedings at Baltimore in 1921 was dispensed with, as they had already been printed in the JOURNAL

(41.161—187): there were no corrections and they were approved as printed.

Professor Breasted, as Chairman of the Committee on Arrangements, presented its report in the form of a printed program. The succeeding sessions were appointed for Tuesday evening at 8:00 P. M., to be a meeting of public character, Wednesday morning at 9:30 A. M., Thursday morning at 9:30 A. M., and Thursday afternoon at 2:30 P. M. It was announced that arrangements had been made for the members to go in a body on Wednesday afternoon to the Field Museum, and thence to the Art Institute: and that the members were invited to a dinner at the Art Institute at 7 P. M., as guests of the University of Chicago, the Field Museum of Natural History, and the Art Institute of Chicago.

REPORT OF THE CORRESPONDING SECRETARY

The Corresponding Secretary, Doctor Charles J. Ogden, presented the following report:

The past year has been one of growth for the Society both extensively, in its membership, and intensively, in its activities. At the last annual meeting 124 corporate members were added, and since that date 43 others have been elected by the Executive Committee, by far the largest number of accessions in any one year since the organization of the Society. Despite the inevitable losses, we have now a membership of all classes amounting to 603, which is an increase of over fifty per cent in two years. Not merely these numbers but their geographical distribution as well indicate the widening influence of the Society. We are already a national organization, a fact shown by the establishment of the Middle West Branch five years ago, and now happily attested by the presence of the Society as a whole in its corporate personality at this joint meeting in the center of the country; soon, with the ripening of plans already formed, we may reasonably assert our international scope.

While the work of the Society has been chiefly carried on thru its officers and committees, there have been some acts of a more public nature which may be referred to here in anticipation of fuller reports by the participants. At the inauguration of President Angell of Yale University last June the Society was officially represented by Professor Lanman. Upon the invitation of the American Academy of Arts and Sciences, the President of the Society and a number of its prominent members attended the meeting held in Boston on October 5, 6, and 7 in honor of the visiting representatives of the Royal Asiatic Society and the Société Asiatique. An occasion of different character but even greater obligation was the memorial meeting for the late Professor Jastrow, held in Philadelphia on November 22 last, at which this Society, thru Dr. Nies, its President, and Professors Edgerton, R. G. Kent, Olmstead, Schmidt, and Talcott Williams, joined with many other organizations in the last tribute to its distinguished and devoted member. The international correspondence of the Society has not been great during the past year, but it is a pleasure to inform the members that a foreign organization working in a related field, the Gypsy Lore Society, is resuming its activities, interrupted during and after the war, with the publication of the first volume of the Third Series of its Journal.

There remains the mention of those whom death has taken from our number, a list not embracing many names, only ten in all, yet of peculiar and melancholy interest.

Professor Berthold Delbrück, one of our oldest honorary members, was professor of Sanskrit and comparative philology at the University of Jena from 1870 until his retirement in 1913. In his chosen domain, that of the comparative syntax of the Indo-European languages, he was incontestably the leading scholar of his generation, and he has left an enduring monument of his comprehensive learning in the three volumes of his *Vergleichende Syntax der indogermanischen Sprachen* (1893—1900). For Orientalists, however, there is a special significance in his earlier researches concerning the ancient tongue of India, such as those contained in his *Syntaktische Forschungen* (5 vols., 1871—1888) and *Das altindische Verbum* (1874). Elected in 1878. Died January 3, 1922.

Professor Ignaz Goldziher, since 1894 at the University of Budapest, was likewise an honorary member of the Society, a distinction well merited by his illuminating investigations into Muhammadan theology and tradition, concerning which he was an unsurpassed authority. Among his numerous works, his *Muhammedanische Studien* (1889—1890) and *Vorlesungen über den Islam* (1910) may be particularly mentioned, the latter being a development of a series of lectures originally planned to be given in America. Elected in 1906. Died November 13, 1921. (See the Journal, 42. 189 ff.)

Mrs. Camilla Clarke Abbott, wife of Rev. Dr. Justin E. Abbott, of Summit, N. J., had shared his residence in India and had cooperated in his labors thru her many deeds of charity, so that it was not unfitting that she should find her final resting-place in that country while revisiting it last year. When in America, she was a frequent attendant at the meetings of the Society, where her gracious personality will be sorely missed. Elected in 1912. Died June 26, 1921.

Rev. Dr. David Stuart Dodge, of New York City, one of our oldest members, was a worthy representative of a family distinguished for its services to religion, philanthropy, and education. For many years he was President of the Presbyterian Board of Home Missions, and even to the date of his death he retained the presidency of the Syrian Protestant College (now the American University) at Beirut. Elected in 1867. Died December 17, 1921.

Rev. Walter Drum, S.J., had been since 1908 professor of Scripture and Semitics at Woodstock College, Maryland. A profound and accurate scholar, whose training had included a period of study in Syria and in

Europe, he combined unswerving fidelity to the standards of his Church with an active interest in modern Biblical exegesis. He was a supporter of organizations devoted to Palestinian research and contributed many articles on Scriptural subjects to periodicals and encyclopedias. Elected in 1915. Died December 10, 1921.

Mr. J. Walter Freiberg, of Cincinnati, was nationally known as having been, since 1911, the President of the Union of American Hebrew Congregations. He took a leading part in both the business and the civic affairs of his city and was widely interested in philanthropic endeavors, besides being a member of the Board of Governors of the Hebrew Union College. Elected in 1921. Died June 9, 1921.

Professor Morris Jastrow, Jr., of the University of Pennsylvania, scarcely needs commemoration here, when the impress of his personality is still fresh in all our minds, and his scholarship has been worthily appraised in the recent pages of our Journal, the value of which has so often been enhanced by his contributions. Yet it may be permitted to recall especially his services in the administration of the Society's affairs, as Secretary of the Section for the Historical Study of Religions from 1897 to 1911, as President for the year 1914—15, and at other times as a Director, a position that he held at the date of his death, together with that of Chairman of the Publication Committee. Fertile in suggestion and prompt in execution, his organizing mind will be greatly missed in our deliberations. Elected in 1886. Died June 22, 1921.

Rev. Dr. John Punnett Peters, from 1885 to 1893 professor of Hebrew at the University of Pennsylvania and at the Protestant Episcopal Divinity School in Philadelphia, rector of St. Michael's Church, New York City, from 1893 to 1919, and since the latter date professor of New Testament Language and Interpretation at the University of the South, united in a rare degree the qualities of the scholar, the pastor, and the champion of civic righteousness. The members of this Society will remember him most of all as the excavator of Nippur (*Nippur*, 2 vols., 1897) and the student of Hebrew religion (*The Old Testament and the New Scholarship*, 1901; *The Religion of the Hebrews*, 1914). Besides his independent publications, he enriched our Journal with many articles from his trenchant pen, and our meetings are the poorer without the charm of his spoken word. Elected in 1882. Died November 10, 1921.

Mr. Arshag K. Schmavonian, of the Department of State in Washington, had been for the last twenty years the legal adviser and first dragoman of the American Embassy at Constantinople. He was a specialist in Muhammadan law and was greatly interested in all matters touching the Orient. Elected in 1921. Died January 3, 1922.

Miss Cornelia Warren, of Waltham, Mass., was the sister of the late Henry Clarke Warren, Treasurer of this Society from 1892 to 1899 and joint founder of the *Harvard Oriental Series*. She had maintained her membership for many years in faithful memory of her distinguished brother. Elected in 1894. Died June 4, 1921.

In concluding this report, the Corresponding Secretary would express his hearty appreciation of the cooperation of the members in general and more particularly of the officers of the Society in responding to his numerous and sometimes burdensome requests for information. Especial thanks are due to the officers of the Middle West Branch for their help with many details of the program of this joint meeting.

Upon motion the report of the Corresponding Secretary was accepted.

The following resolutions were adopted:

In the death of Professor MORRIS JASTROW, JR., on the 22d of June, 1921, the American Oriental Society has suffered a severe loss. A member of the Society since 1886, he took a very active part in its work during thirty-five years. Numerous articles from his pen have appeared in the JOURNAL, all of them notable contributions to science. For many years he was one of the Directors of the Society, a position he held at his death. In this capacity he rendered valuable services by his conscientiousness and wise counsel. He was elected a Vice-President for the year 1912—13, and was President of the Society in 1914—15. As an Orientalist, Professor Jastrow devoted himself particularly to Assyriology and Hebrew lore, but had an extensive familiarity with other sections of the field of Semitic studies. His *opus magnum* is *Die Religion Babyloniens und Assyriens* (1905—1912). This publication, whose importance is universally recognized, reveals his extraordinary capacity for work, the comprehensiveness of his research, and the soundness of his judgment. A comparison of this German edition in three volumes with his earlier book in English, *The Religion of Babylonia and Assyria* (1898), shows not only the constant growth of scientific study in this field but also his own steadily increasing mastery of the vast material. His intense occupation with the subject of religion, which has long been one branch of our Society's special interests, prepared him in a peculiar manner to deal with this phase of the life of the ancient Babylonians and Assyrians. In several books and a large number of articles he discussed various aspects of Sumerian, Akkadian, and Assyrian religion. One of his last publications (in conjunction with A. T. Clay) was *An Old Babylonian Version of the Gilgamesh Epic* (1921). Results of his lifelong study of the Hebrew scriptures were embodied in numerous articles in the leading encyclopedias, and particularly in his commentaries: *A Gentle Cynic* (1919), an interpretation of Ecclesiastes, *The Book of Job* (1920), and *The Song of Songs* (posthumous, 1921). In 1916 he was President of the Society of Biblical Literature and Exegesis, and he was a constant contributor to its *Journal*. His interests, as a citizen of the republic and of the world, in the great problems confronting mankind at the present time found expression in a series of volumes, succeeding one another in rapid succession: *The War and the Bagdad Railway* (1917); *The War and the Coming Peace* (1918); *Zionism and the Future of Palestine* (1919); and *The Eastern Question and its Solution* (1920). Professor Jastrow was a worthy representative of American scholarship at many international congresses of Orientalists and students of the history of religion and had many friends in academic circles both in Europe and America who will deeply regret his departure in the maturity of his powers and at a time when, humanly speaking, the ripest fruits of his extraordinary industry and great and varied erudition might have been expected.

Whereas, by the death of Dr. John P. Peters the American Oriental Society has lost one of its most honored and esteemed members, one who during forty years rendered to it conspicuous service as active member, officer, frequent contributor to its Journal, and participant in all its affairs;

Resolved: That the Society herewith expresses its high appreciation of the record of achievement made by its deceased member and of the spirit in which his work was done, in each of the many fields of his busy and fruitful life; as scholar and teacher in Oriental and Biblical fields of science, author of many important works, explorer and excavator in Eastern lands, pastor of a metropolitan church, active participant in the work of social reform in New York City;

Resolved: That the American Oriental Society expresses its sympathy with the relatives and friends of its deceased member, and with all of the many who have been wont to look to him for instruction, counsel, and assistance;

Resolved: That these resolutions be entered in the records of the Society and published in the minutes of this meeting, and that a copy of the resolutions be sent to the family of Dr. Peters.

REPORT OF THE TREASURER

The Corresponding Secretary presented the report of the Treasurer, Professor A. T. Clay, and that of the Auditing Committee:

Receipts and Expenditures for the Year ending December 31, 1921

Receipts

Jan. 1, 1921 Balance		$5,023.24
Annual Dues		2,639.22
Life Memberships		300.00
Interest on Bonds		
Minn. Gen. Elec.	$50.00	
U. S. Liberty Loan	127.50	
Lackawanna Steel	100.00	
Virginian Ry.	50.00	
		327.50
Dividend:		
Chicago R. I. & Pacific		120.00
Interest on Deposit-Yale University		196.52
Repayment Author's corrections		75.20
Sale Offprints		4.25
Sales		913.34
Repayment Protested check		33.94
		$9,633.21

Expenditures

Purchase $4000 U. S. 3rd Liberty Loan Bonds		$3,608.60
Purchased interest		65.88
Contribution to American Council of Learned Societies		25.00
C. Snouk Hurgronje, Islam Dictionary		50.25
W. Drugulin		14.18
Editors' Expense		24.51
Guttman, Stern & Guttman, Expense books from Holland		8.75
Express, on Proceedings to Yale University Press		24.41
J. C. Winston Co.-Matrices		98.00
Mailing Journal		31.83
Printing Journal Vol. 40, No. 4 Balance	$360.87	
40, No. 5	443.85	
41, No. 1	589.75	
41, No. 2	560.72	
41, No. 3	497.39	
41, No. 4	513.51	
		2,966.09
Protested check		33.94
J. B. Nies 20,000 Marks Publication		109.00
Dr. E. M. Grice, Honorarium		100.00
J. A. Montgomery, "		100.00
F. Edgerton, "		100.00
Corresponding Secretary's Expense	$28.00	
Printing	119.59	
Postage	39.76	
Clerical	11.62	
		198.97
Middle West Branch Expense		54.50
Membership Committee, Printing	$59.86	
Miscellaneous	5.00	
		64.86
Treasurer's Expense		
Printing	$25.27	
Postage	3.57	
Miscellaneous	1.80	
		30.64
Library, Clerical	$52.78	
Miscellaneous	4.51	
		57.29
Jan. 1, 1922 Balance (including $300.00 for Life Membership Fund)		1,866.51
		$9,633.21

The following funds are held by the Society:

Charles W. Bradley Fund	$3,000.00
Alexander I. Cotheal Fund	1,500.00
William Dwight Whitney Fund	1,000.00
Life Membership Fund	2,750.00
Publication Fund	78.50

The foregoing funds, the interest on which is used for publication of the Journal, are represented in the assets of the Society held by Yale University for the Treasurer, which on January 1, 1922, were as follows:

Cash, Balance	$1,866.51
Bonds:	
$4,000 Third U. S. Liberty Bonds	3,608.60
2,000 Lackawanna Steel Co. 5's 1923 (present value)	1,875.00
1,000 Virginian Railway Co. 5's 1962 (present value)	805.00
1,000 Minneapolis General Electric Co. 5's 1934 (present value)	860.00
Stocks:	
20 shares Chicago, Rock Island and Pacific Railway pfd. (present value)	1,120.00
(Received in the reorganization of the road in exchange for $2,000 5 % bonds of 1932).	10,135.11

REPORT OF THE AUDITING COMMITTEE

We hereby certify that we have examined the account of the Treasurer of the Society, and have found the same correct, and that the foregoing account is in conformity therewith. We have also compared the entries with the vouchers and the account book as held for the Society by the Treasurer of Yale University, and have found all correct.

Charles C. Torrey
F. W. Williams
Auditors

Upon motion the reports of the Treasurer and the Auditing Committee were accepted.

REPORT OF THE LIBRARIAN

The Corresponding Secretary presented the report of the Librarian, Professor A. T. Clay, and upon motion it was accepted:

The accessions to the Library have been regularly catalogued, and placed upon the shelves. As previously reported, the cataloguing of the Library, made possible by donations on the part of several members, is so nearly completed that the work of printing the catalogue which has been so long promised the members could be started with comparatively little additional work. For this purpose the late Mrs. Nies gave a hundred dollars. The Librarian trusts that it will be made possible to consummate this undertaking in the near future, so that the Library may be made more available to those far removed from it. Following is a list of accessions for the year:

Accessions to the Library, year 1921/22

Abdallâh Muhammad bin 'Omar al-Makki, al-Âsafi, Ulughkhani. An Arabic history of Gujarat. v. 2, 1921.

Die Bhagavadgîtâ aus dem Sanskrit übersetzt, von R. Garbe. 1921.

Briggs, G. W. The Chamārs. 1920.

Buch, M. A. Zoroastrian ethics.
Buddhaghosa's Commentary on the four Nikayas of the Sutta-Pitaka. 12 v. 1921.
Brandstetter, R. Wir Menschen der indonesischen Erde. 1921.
Catalogue raisonné of the Bûhâr library, Calcutta. 1921.
Journal of the Department of Letters, Calcutta University. 3 v. 1920.
Postgraduate teaching in the University of Calcutta. 1919—1920.
Ezerman, J. L. J. F. Beschrijving van den Koan Iem-tempel „Tia-Kak-Sie" te Cheribon. 1919.
Gadd, C. J. The early dynasties of Sumer and Akkad. 1921.
Grierson, G. A. Ishkashmi, Zebaki, and Yazghulami, an account of three Eranian dialects. 1920.
Halper, B. Post-Biblical Hebrew literature. 1921.
Hume, R. E. The thirteen principal Upanishads. 1921.
Jhabvala, S. H. A brief history of Persia. 1920.
Jhabvala, S. H. Sir Jamshedji Jeejeebhoy. 1920.
Jordan, L. H. Comparative religion. 1920.
The Kalpaka. v. 16, nos. 7, 9. 1921.
Keay, F. E. A history of Hindī literature. 1920.
Kincaid, C. A. Tales of the saints of Pandharpur. 1919.
Kingsbury, F. Hymns of the Tamil Śaivite saints. 1921.
Krishna Sastri, H. South Indian inscriptions. Volume III. 1920.
Krom, N. J. and T. van Erp. Beschrijving van Barabuḍur. 1920.
Liebich, B. Zur Einführung in die indische einheimische Sprachwissenschaft. 1919—20.
Mann, J. The Jews in Egypt and in Palestine under the Fātimid Caliphs. 1920.
Michelson, T. The owl sacred pack of the Fox Indians. 1921.
Milne, Mrs. L. An elementary Palaung grammar. 1921.
Morse, H. B. The trade and administration of China. 3d ed. 1921.
Mythic society. The Quarterly journal of the Mythic society. v. 11, v. 12, nos. 1—2. 1921—22.
Nariman, G. K. Literary history of Sanskrit Buddhism. 1920.
The Nighantu and the Nirukta, by Lakshman Sarup. 1920.
Obermann, J. Der philosophische und religiöse Subjektivismus Ghazalis. 1921.
Collected Sanskrit writings of the Parsees. Pt. V. 1920.
Proceedings and transactions of the first Oriental conference at Poona. 1920.
Pieris, P. E. Ceylon and the Portuguese. 1920.
Pithawalla, M. Sacred sparks. 1920.
Reitzenstein, R. Das iranische Erlösungsmysterium. 1921.
Rescher, O. Algerisch-tunesische Briefe. 1917—1919.
Revue d'assyriologie et d'archéologie orientale. 1920—21.
Russell, C. Sonnets, poems, and translations. 1920.
Salmon, W. H. An account of the Ottoman conquest of Egypt.
The first campaign of Sennacherib . . . Ed. by Sidney Smith. 1921.
Stevenson, Mrs. S. The rites of the twice-born. 1920.
Vogel, J. Ph. Tile-mosaics of the Lahore fort. 1920.

REPORT OF THE EDITORS OF THE JOURNAL

Professor J. A. Montgomery, Senior Editor of the JOURNAL, presented the report of the Editors, and upon motion it was accepted:

With the approval of the Executive Committee Volume 41 was dedicated to the memory of Professor Morris Jastrow, Jr. The last Part of the Volume contained appreciations of the honored scholar and his Bibliography. This and an accumulation of other material served to swell Part 5 so that the Volume attained the extent of 496 pages, the largest for an annual issue in the history of the JOURNAL. On the recommendation of the Executive Committee it was decided to print the JOURNAL hereafter in Germany; the contract has been given to Mr. W. Drugulin of Leipzig, and copy for the next volume is now in press. In consequence of slow postal transportation the JOURNAL will for the present appear semi-annually, but it is hoped to reestablish more frequent appearance as soon as possible. The German rates for printing purport to be very much lower than American rates, and the Editors trust that the money so saved to the Society can be applied to the enlargement and enrichment of the JOURNAL. An Index to Volumes 21—40 is now in preparation by Prof. R. K. Yerkes and will soon appear in print.

JAMES A. MONTGOMERY
FRANKLIN EDGERTON
Editors.

REPORT OF THE EXECUTIVE COMMITTEE

The Corresponding Secretary presented the report of the Executive Committee, as printed in the JOURNAL (41. 238, 320, 472—3), and also reported that the Executive Committee had subsequently elected the following persons to membership in the Society:

Rev. R. D. Cornuelle
Dr. William Cowen
Mr. Morris M. Feuerlicht
Mr. Ely Jacques Kahn
Mr. John Ellerton Lodge
Rev. Dr. Theodore H. Robinson

Upon motion the report of the Executive Committee was accepted.

ELECTION OF MEMBERS

The following persons, recommended by the Directors, were duly elected corporate members of the Society; the list includes one elected at a later session:

Mr. Moses Bailey
Pres. Guy Potter Benton
Dr. William J. Chapman
Rev. Douglas Hilary Corley
Prof. Charles Duroiselle
Mr. Wallace Cranston Fairweather

Mr. Sol. Baruch Finesinger
Mr. Maynard Dauchy Follin
Prof. A. Eustace Haydon
Mr. E. B. Hewes
Mrs. Morris Jastrow, Jr.
Mr. Taw Sein Ko
Rev. W. H. McClellan, S. J.
Miss Eleanor McDougall
Mr. J. Arthur MacLean
Dr. A. R. Nykl
Mr. George N. Roerich
Mr. Alexander Scott
Rev. J. K. Shryock
Mr. Don C. Shumaker
Rev. H. Framer Smith
Mr. J. W. Stanley
Mr. Yung-Tung Tang
Mr. James B. Weaver
Rev. Adolf Louis Wismar
Rabbi Louis Wolsey

[Total: 26]

ELECTION OF OFFICERS

Professor A. V. W. Jackson, for the Committee on the Nomination of Officers for 1922, reported nominations for the several offices as follows:

President—Professor E. Washburn Hopkins of Yale University.

Vice-presidents—Professor James A. Montgomery of the University of Pennsylvania, Professor Leroy Waterman of the University of Michigan, and Professor F. G. C. Eiselen of Garrett Biblical Institute.

Corresponding Secretary—Doctor Charles J. Ogden of New York City.

Recording Secretary—Professor LeRoy C. Barret of Trinity College (Hartford).

Treasurer—Professor Albert T. Clay of Yale University.

Librarian—Professor Albert T. Clay of Yale University.

Editors of the Journal—Professor Franklin Edgerton of the University of Pennsylvania, and Professor Max L. Margolis of Dropsie College.

Directors, term expiring in 1925 — Professor Maurice Bloomfield of Johns Hopkins University, Professor A. T. Olmstead of the University of Illinois, Doctor Frank K. Sanders of New York.

The officers thus nominated were duly elected.

It was voted: that the Corresponding Secretary send to Doctor J. B. Nies, the retiring president, the greetings of the Society, its regrets at his absence, and its wishes for success in the undertaking in which he is engaged.

The reading of papers was begun:

Professor Ira M. Price, of the University of Chicago: The Geography of the Gudea Inscriptions.

Professor A. V. Williams Jackson, of Columbia University: Poet-Kings in the history of Sanskrit Literature. Remarks by Professor Buttenwieser.

This paper, which has a special bearing on the subject of the Indian king Harṣadeva (seventh century A. D.) as author and literary patron, draws attention first to a number of royal authors in other literatures. It then presents a list, collected from various Sanskrit sources, of kings known for their literary activity in that language from early times down almost to the Mughal period. Evidence is adduced in confirmation of the view that King Harṣa was the actual author of the Sanskrit dramas which bear his name.

Dr. Israel Efros, of the Baltimore Hebrew College: Some Glosses to the Hebrew Bible.

Exod. 32 2 r. לחטת (= לחטאת) for להטת; Deut. 32 35 עת דת 'the time of the decree' for עתדת; Isai. 1 18 נְכוּחָה (comp. 57 2 Amos 3 10) for ונוכחה; *ibid.* 28 וְשָׁבוּ for ושבר; 2 12 וְעָפֶל (comp. Hab. 2 4) for ושפל; 5 7 משפר (= מספר) for משפח; 10 13 בחבור (comp. 2 Kings 17 6 18 11) for כאביר, or possibly read כְּבָר (comp. Ezek. 1 3); Hosea 11 4 ודם (= דודים) for אדם; Eccl. 1 5 זורח for וזרח; *ibid.* 8 לא יְכַל ('ceaseth not') for לא יוכל; 2 1 for אנסכה (the א is certainly due to dittography) r. וּסְכָה 'and look' (comp. משכית, שכיה, possibly יסכה; common in later Hebrew, e. g. Megilla 14 a); 5 5 לחטיא את בשרך refers to the self-torture imposed by the Nazirite vow; 9 12 r. כה מיוקשים for כהם יוקשים; 12 5 הַגַּב ('the back') for החגב.

Dr. A. R. Nykl, of Northwestern University: Love Theories of Ibn Ḥazm and Early Provençal Poetry. Remarks by Professor Sprengling, Dr. Efros, and Professor Barret.

Professor Ira M. Price, of the University of Chicago: An Inscribed Eye from a Babylonian Statue.

The session adjourned at 4:47 p. m.

THE SECOND SESSION

The second session was held on Tuesday evening. After President Judson of the University of Chicago had extended to the Society a cordial welcome, Vice-President Schmidt delivered an address on 'Eighty Years' Progress in Oriental Studies', and Professor Olmstead, President of the Middle West Branch, delivered an address on 'The Assyrian Wolf.' A congratulatory resolution was adopted in honor of the centenary of the founding of the Société Asiatique. Professor Breasted then gave an illustrated account of Champollion's decipherment of Egyptian hieroglyphic.

This session was of a public character, and was arranged to commemorate the eightieth anniversary of the Society, likewise the centenary of the Société Asiatique and of Champollion's discovery.

The address to the Société Asiatique which was adopted was as follows:

TO THE ASIATIC SOCIETY OF FRANCE

Founded in 1822

FROM THE AMERICAN ORIENTAL SOCIETY
Chicago, April 18, 1922

Gentlemen:

To you, who will soon assemble at Paris to celebrate the hundredth anniversary of the founding of your Society, we, members of the American Oriental Society, convened at Chicago for our annual session, send over the seas our warmest greetings, — and with them, our congratulations upon the completion of a century of honorable public service, and our best hopes for your future.

Ernest Renan calls the early decades of your history the golden age of oriental studies. It is a wonderful testimony to the indomitable spirit of France, that, in spite of all the uncertainties of the year 1822, your founders, the Count de Lasteyrie, Messrs. Rémusat, Saint-Martin, de Sacy, and their colleagues, did in fact have the vision and the faith and the courage to realize ideals so remote as are the goals of oriental study.

Courage was theirs. For in the first half of the nineteenth century the orientalist faced the gravest difficulties: political upheavals past or impending, and with them the natural indifference of the people at large to undertakings which seemed to be of no practical import. And to these were added minor, but no less real, obstacles: a journey of months before one could reach China or India or even Mesopotamia; the wide dispersion of the manuscripts needed for text-editions, before the great collections of Paris, London, Oxford, Berlin, and Poona had come into being; the lack of grammars and dictionaries to help in understanding and translating the texts, and the expense and trouble of printing the texts when once understood and edited; and the fewness of the positions in which a man could earn his support while devoting his whole life to oriental study.

Vision too was theirs. For they beheld the time approaching when West and East must have ever more and more to do each with the other, and when our treatment of each other must be inspired by unfeigned respect, — for which, in turn, on our part, a real knowledge of Eastern history and achievement in politics, literature, art, philosophy, religion, and morals, is the inexorable condition.

And faith was theirs. For they believed that their labors as investigators and as teachers would be part of a force — subtle and impalpable, but none the less potent — in determining the mutual reactions of East and West, and so of directing the whole current of human destiny.

This courage, this vision, this faith, — how has it been confirmed, justified, rewarded! The relations of Europe and America to the Far East have at last become one of the two or three most weighty factors in making or marring the peace and happiness of the entire world. And we have seen the conduct of public affairs in China and Japan, and of international relations with the West, entrusted to Oriental statesmen who have been profoundly influenced by education in the Occident. And the rewards — are they not in a measure the fruit of the splendid achievements in which your Society has borne so great a part, and which you may now call to mind with so just a pride?

Thus — to mention only those who have long been dead, and even these only by way of example — was it not your Jean François Champollion who made the ancient records of Egypt, silent for centuries, to speak aloud once more? And how do those two honored names, Silvestre de Sacy and Eugène Burnouf, still challenge our admiration? de Sacy, one of your founders, your first president, indefatigable administrator, to whose fecundity as a scholar his monumental works upon Arabic grammar and literature (to mention no others) bear so ample witness! and Burnouf, whose labors as a pioneer in the field of Buddhism and its sacred language, the Pali, and upon the religion and books of Zoroaster, are the amazing outcome of a life which, heedless of wealth and fame, was given to scientific discovery with a veritable passion! It is moreover a high distinction for your Society that these two great scholars were also great teachers, men who charmed and inspired their pupils — not only Frenchmen but foreigners — who then in turn passed onward the sacred flame to pupils and pupils' pupils, thus forming here and there a "line of teachers" (a vaṅśa or guru-paramparā, as the Hindus so proudly call it), which, even here in distant America, already extends to the seventh generation!

And what timelier service of your Society can we today call to mind than this, that she has shown us that the East has lessons for the West? Whether Stanislas Julien translates for us the work of Buddha's immortal contemporary, Lao-tse, or describes to us the ancient Chinese ways of breeding silkworms and making porcelain, or opens to us the simple and touching records of the journeys of the Chinese pilgrims to the "Far West," to bring back home from India the books of Buddha's teachings—through it all runs the admonition that we maintain the teachable habit of mind. That was the dominating spirit of those pilgrims, the illustrious Fa-hien and his confrères. If we moderns would emulate that spirit, how boundless the possibilities of good will and happiness among the nations!

But splendid as these examples of your achievements are, and great as the sum total of them is, — we rejoice in them, and we are persuaded that you rejoice in them, not chiefly because they are yours, but because they constitute a substantial and practical service to a world that sorely needs this service. And as we consider the superb vigor with which the Society, even in recent times, has maintained its fruitful activities, both at home and also in the Far East and India and Central Asia, our rejoicing is coupled with confident and abounding hope for your future. In this sense, we bid you Hail and God-speed.

THE THIRD SESSION

The third session was called to order by Vice-President Schmidt at 9:33 o' clock on Wednesday morning. The reading of papers was immediately begun:

Mr. Ludlow S. Bull, of the University of Chicago: An Unpublished Middle Kingdom Coffin. Remarks by Professor Breasted.

Professor LeRoy C. Barret, of Trinity College: The Kashmirian Atharva-Veda, Book Nine. Remarks by Dr. Ogden.

Rev. Dr. John A. Maynard, of the University of Chicago: New Building Inscriptions of Nabonidus.

Professor Paul Haupt, of Johns Hopkins University: (a) Numeratives in Sumerian and Chinese; (b) The Original Meaning of *kôhên*, 'priest.' (c) The Hebrew Names for Silver and Gold; (d) Oriental Philology and Archeology. Remarks by Professors Buttenwieser, Breasted, Luckenbill, Dr. Ogden, and the author.

(a) The Sumerian affix after numbers, *tam*, written *ta-a-an*, which is preserved in Heb. *'aštê*, one = Ass. *ištên* = Sum. *aštân*, is a compound of *ta* (what? then *something*, amount; *cf.* our *a little what*) and *am* (*SG* § 199, b). We may compare the Chinese numerative *ko* (*EB*[11] 6, 217^b; 25, 9^b; 17, 477^b). The explanation given in AL[3] 36, 313; *AJSL* 20, 231, 24 is untenable; *ta-a-an* on pl. iii in *PSBA* 10,418 corresponds to Ass. *minâ-ma*, Eth. *ment-nû*. 1-*a-an* instead of 1*š-ta-a-an* is an abbreviation like our 4°, 8° for 4to, 8vo (contrast *OLZ* 25, 8). For the ordinal affix *kam*, e. g. *aš-kam*, first, lit. *being of one* (*SG* § 88) *cf.* Nöldeke, *Syr. Gr.* § 239. In Malay the ordinal numbers have a prefixed *ka*. For the slanting position of the ordinal affix *kam* in cuneiform texts *cf.* our superior th in 4th.

(b) The stem of Heb. *kĕmarîm*, idol-priests, is a transposition of Ass. *ramâku*, to lustrate = *makâru* < *kûr*, whereas the primary connotation of Heb. *rô'ê*, *ḥôzê*, and *mĕ'ônên* is *scryer* (*JBL* 36, 89.254; 37,227; 38,151, n. 15). Heb. *kôhên*, priest, is identical with Arab. *kâhin*, soothsayer, *i. e.* one who tells the truth (Ass. *kêttu* = *kêntu* < *kûn*). Just as *kahan* = *kûn* (*JBL* 26, 46) so the stem of *qahál*, congregation (prop. *convocation*) = *qûl*, to call >Heb. *qôl*, voice (Syr. and Eth. *qâl* = *qâųal*) and Arab. *qáųl*, word; *qâla*, he said (cf. also *naql*, tale, and *náqal*, ready repartee).

(c) Heb. *käsf*, silver, must be combined with Arab. *sákaba* = *sábaka*, to smelt, syn. *aḏâba* (cf. *sabîkah* and Ass. *çarpu*, silver < *çurrupu*, to smelt; Arab. *çarîf*, pure silver; modern Arab. *rûbâç*, and *muráųbaç*, refined). *Záhab*, gold, is connected with *zûb*, to run = Arab. *ḏâba*, to melt. *Zêb*, wolf, means *tawny* (cf. *canis aureus*). The primary connotation of *ḥarûç*, gold (>Gr. *chrysós*) is *dug out*; the meaning of Syr. *ḥarrû'â*, yellow (cf. Arab. *xáḍir*, green; also Eth. *ųarq*, gold) is secondary. *Kätm* means prop. *subduable* (*HW* 362^b) = non-refractory (*JSOR* 1, 8). For *paz* cf. *fázza*, to run. *Bäçr* is prop. *zahâb baḥûn*, tried gold (cf. Arab. *istábçara* = *istabâna*; Syr. *bĕráç*, also Eth. *tabâráça*, to shine, and *bĕrûr*, silver). Michaelis' *aurum spectatissimum* was correct.

(d) Archeology is just as important as Philology, but an orientalist can be an archeologist without conducting excavations. Excavations should be conducted by an engineer, or architect, or by men familiar with the country. Some of the most successful excavators were not able to read any of the inscriptions they discovered. At any rate, a scholar devoted to research cannot be expected to raise funds for archeological expeditions (cf. *AJSL* 35, 196).

Professor Walter E. Clark, of the University of Chicago: The Study of Sanskrit in India. Remarks by Professors Jackson and Haupt, and Dr. Abbott.

This paper gives the results of the speaker's personal observation of the present-day study of Sanskrit in India when on a visit to that country during the past year.

Professor James A. Montgomery, of the University of Pennsylvania: The Problem of Theodotion's Translation of the Hebrew Bible. Remarks by Professors Olmstead, Schmidt, and Buttenwieser.

Rev. Dr. Abraham Yohannan, of Columbia University, and Mr. J. F. Springer, of New York City: A New Branch of Textual Criticism.

Nucleus of an organon which seeks to utilize the facts of the constitution and construction of old rolls and codices in explaining many textual derangements, particularly misplacements, as non-purposive phenomena. Illustrated by examples from 2 Samuel (5.6-25, 21.1-14), Hosea (1.1-3.5), Matthew (10.17-23, 26.6-13), Mark (1.1-6, 13, 11.11-26), Luke (4.5-12), John (12.36b-50). The explanation of the two Markan sections as regions of accidental misplacements of a mechanical character paves the way for a reconciliation between Matthew and Mark, in respect to the historical progression of events. The new methods are supplementary to and in contrast with the ordinary processes of textual criticism.

Rev. Dr. Abraham Yohannan, of Columbia University: A Reference to Zoroaster's Life and Doctrine in the Syriac Treatise of Theodore bar Khoni.

Mr. Wilfred H. Schoff, of the Commercial Museum, Philadelphia: Camphor, and Early Trade in the Indian Ocean. Remarks by Professor Haupt, and Dr. Efros.

This paper presents some considerations concerning early trade in the Indian Ocean, suggested by varying forms of the name 'camphor.'

Professor Martin Sprengling, of the University of Chicago: A Syrian Edition of Ibn al Habbârîya's Kalîla wa Dimna. Remarks by Professors Haupt, Jackson, Breasted, Dr. Ogden, and the author.

Houtsma on a Bombay Edition of 1900. Orientalische Studien—Nöldeke . . . gewidmet, Vol. I, 91—96. Cheikho, Mashriq. 1901, p. 980: Bombay ed. of 1886. Not noticed in Occident: Edition of El Khûrî Ni'mat Allâh al-Asmar in Ba'abdâ near Beirut in 1900 from a good Syrian manuscript. Text pretty carefully edited. Additions of editor, carefully distinguished from text. Value of Ibn al Habbârîya; of the Syrian edition.

The session adjourned at 12:50 P. M.

THE FOURTH SESSION

The fourth session was called to order by Vice-President Schmidt at 9:43 o'clock on Thursday morning.

The Corresponding Secretary reported that the Directors had voted to meet at Princeton in Easter Week, April 3—5, 1923.

The Corresponding Secretary reported that the Directors had formally accepted the invitation of the Société Asiatique to be represented at their centenary celebration to be held in Paris July 10—13, 1922.

An informal report was made concerning a meeting in Boston October 5—7, 1921, at which were present members of our Society and a number of distinguished Orientalists from England and France.

Dr. Ogden presented a report of the Society's delegates, Professor Clay and Dr. Ogden, to the American Council of Learned Societies. The report was accepted.

The Corresponding Secretary presented a report from Dr. Frank K. Sanders, Chairman of the Committee on the Enlargement of Membership and Resources.

It was voted: that the report be accepted with thanks and appreciation of the Committee's activities.

It was voted: that the questions arising out of this report be referred to the Directors.

Mr. Schoff made an informal report on the activities of the American Schools of Oriental Research, a full report being already in print. In this connection Professors Breasted and Montgomery made informal report of what is being accomplished in coordinating archaeological research work.

A resolution by Professor Wolfenson concerning an effort to stimulate interest in oriental studies in the schools of this country was referred to the Directors.

Upon recommendation of the Directors Professor Friedrich Hirth and Don Leone Caetani were elected honorary members of the Society.

Upon recommendation of the Directors the following persons were elected honorary associates of the Society: President Warren G. Harding, Secretary Charles E. Hughes, Major-General Leonard Wood, Hon. Oscar Straus, President Harry

Pratt Judson, Field Marshal Viscount Allenby, Minister S. K. Alfred Sze.

Vice President Schmidt announced the appointment of the following committees:

On Nominations for 1923—Professors Haupt and Clark and Miss Hussey.

Auditors for 1923—Professors Torrey and F. W. Williams.

On Arrangements for 1923—Professors Bender, Allis, Davis, Butler, Eno, Marquand, and the Corresponding Secretary *ex officio*.

The reading of papers was begun:

Dr. T. George Allen, of the University of Chicago: The Archives of the Oriental Institute. Remarks by Professors Haupt, Montgomery, Maynard, Mercer, and Wolfenson.

Dr. Charles J. Ogden, of New York City: The Site of Ancient Kauśāmbī. Remarks by Dr. Yohannan and Mr. Schoff.

> Kauśāmbī was one of the great cities of India during the Buddhist period but later sank into obscurity. Cunningham in 1861 identified it with the extensive ruins at Kosam on the Jumna above Allahabad, but this identification was challenged by Vincent Smith (*JRAS* 1898, pp. 503—519) and by Vost (*ib.* 1904, pp. 249—267), as being irreconcilable with the data of Hiuen Tsang. The present paper reviews the testimony of history, epigraphy, and Sanskrit literature, and finds that it strongly favors Kosam as the site. Some explanations of Hiuen Tsang's itinerary are suggested.

Rev. J. Edward Snyder, of Fargo, N. Dak.: Edom's Doom in Malachi. Remarks by Prof. Haupt.

> The prediction of Edom's doom in Malachi was originally attached to the preceding Maccabean poems in Deutero-Zechariah. The two genuine poems in Malachi were composed about 460, but Mal. 1, 1—5.11.14^b originated about the beginning of the reign of John Hyrcanus (135—104). For the reason why some Jews at that time doubted that Jhvh loved them, see Joseph. *Ant.* 13, 8, 2.3. The Edomites were judaized in 128. The fortifications of their capital had been destroyed by Judas Maccabaeus in 164 (1 Mac. 5, 65). The title prefixed to the Book of Malachi was originally: Utterance of Jhvh through His messenger; *dabar* is a gloss to *maśśā*, and *Iahuê* a gloss to *El Isra'ēl* (Ps. 68, 36). The messenger in Mal. 3, 1 is Ezra (*JBL* 38, 143, n. 4).

Professor Daniel D. Luckenbill, of the University of Chicago: The Progress of the New Assyrian Dictionary. Remarks by Professors Breasted and Haupt.

Professor Moses Buttenwieser, of the Hebrew Union College: The Emphatic and Conditional Particles in Hebrew and Aramaic. Remarks by Professor Wolfenson.

The prevailing view that the use of *hēn* in Hebrew as conditional particle is due to Aramaic influence, and that emphatic *hēn* is unknown in Aramaic, has no basis in fact. As in the Indo-European languages, so throughout the Semitic languages the emphatic and conditional particles prove to be in reality not two different particles, but two different functions of the same particle, the emphatic being the primary, and the conditional the secondary function.

Professor Louis B. Wolfenson, of the University of Wisconsin: *Lāhēn*, "therefore," in Hebrew. Remarks by Professors Haupt and Wolfenson.

The purpose of this paper is to show that often the thought-connective "therefore" is not actually expressed, but is inferred from the context; and that *lāhēn*, the word so rendered, actually had another meaning.

Professor George L. Robinson, of McCormick Theological Seminary: A Visit to the Cave of Machpelah in 1914. Remarks by Prof. Sprengling.

The following resolution was unanimously voted:

In accepting the resignation of Professor James A. Montgomery as an Editor of the Journal, the Society desires to express its profound regret that he has found it necessary to relinquish this work, its sense of indebtedness to him for the long service which he has given to the Journal, and likewise its deep appreciation of the devotion, literary skill, learning, and efficiency which have characterized that service, and which have contributed essentially to the high quality of our Journal.

The session adjourned at 12:43 P. M.

THE FIFTH SESSION

The fifth session was called to order by Vice President Schmidt at 2:40 o'clock on Thursday afternoon.

The following resolution was unanimously voted:

The American Oriental Society, at fourscore years of age, has renewed its youth by going West. It desires to acknowledge the delightful courtesies received from the institutions and citizens of Chicago and to express the happy memories it will bear away of its first visit to the great interior metropolis of our country, inspiring the hope that it may return in the future.

The warm thanks of the Society are due to the University of Chicago which has given it the freedom of the University; to the Field Museum of Natural History and the Art Institute of Chicago for the display of their notable exhibits, as well as for the hospitality in which they participated with the University; and to the Quadrangle Club for their courteous entertainment.

The reading of papers was begun:

Rev. Dr. Justin E. Abbott, of Summit, N. J.: The Maratha Poet-Saint Dāsopant Digambar.

Dāsopant was born in 1551 and died in 1615. He is the most voluminous of Maratha poets. Scholars have estimated that it would require ten to fifteen thousand pages to print the manuscripts ascribed to him that are found at Amba Jogai in the Hyderabad State, where his tomb is, and where his descendants of the twelfth generation live. Three only of his works have been printed. He wrote in Sanskrit as well as Marathi. His Commentary in Marathi on the Bhagavadgītā consists of 125,000 verses. Each word of the original is commented upon. His works are philosophical and devotional, but interspersed with moral precepts.

Professor Leroy Waterman, of the University of Michigan: The Date of the Deluge. Remarks by Professor Olmstead.

This paper discusses the early chronological data concerning the Deluge and recent attempts to reformulate them.

Professor John A. Scott, of Northwestern University: An Unpublished Chapter in the Life of Schliemann. Remarks by Miss Wicker.

Professor Samuel A. B. Mercer, of the Western Theological Seminary, Chicago: Some Liturgical Elements in the Pyramid Texts. Remarks by Professors Waterman, Buttenwieser, Morgenstern and Haupt.

Professor J. M. Powis Smith, of the University of Chicago: Traces of Emperor Worship in the Old Testament. Remarks by Professors Morgenstern, Olmstead, Mercer, Buttenwieser, and Haupt.

Emperor worship was common all through the ancient Oriental world. It is natural, then, to expect evidences of its presence among the Hebrews. Such evidences are found in the custom of anointing the king, and in Samuel's kissing Saul. The facts of the history of the monarchy, together with the development of monotheism, killed this conception among the Hebrews. The 82d Psalm is a reflection of the attitude of the later Jews toward this matter.

Professor Julian Morgenstern, of the Hebrew Union College: The Gates of Righteousness.

The "Golden Gate," the eastern gate in the Temple Area at Jerusalem, is walled up. Moslem tradition tells that this was done after the Moslem conquest of the city. But earlier pilgrim records show that this gate was walled up long before this. The worship of the sun, according to Ezek. 8, 16, took place at this eastern gate. According to the *Mishna* this ceremony was part of the ancient Succoth-New Year's Day festival. In ancient Israel the New Year's Day was celebrated at the autumnal equinox. The ceremony of Ezek. 8, 16 was an equinoctial rite. The first rays of the rising sun on the two equinoctial days shone through the eastern gate, into the Temple and the Holy of Holies. This same ceremony underlies the idea of the entrance into the Temple of the Deity in the form of the "Glory of Yahwe" in Ezek. 43, 1 ff. and Ps. 24, 7—10. Ezek. 44, 1 ff. commands that this eastern gate be thenceforth kept closed forever.

Professor Henry Schaeffer, of the Evangelical Lutheran Seminary, Chicago: Hebrew Tribal Economy and the Year of Jubilee as illustrated in Semitic and Indo-European Village Communities.

The communalistic features of Israelitish economy, as set forth in the year of jubilee, presuppose a tribal background, and may best be explained as the logical development of the old tribal system, which was on the ascendant in pre-monarchical days. The writer's investigation, which is soon to appear in book form, disproves the Wellhausen theory regarding the origin of the year of jubilee.

Mr. Darwin A. Leavitt, of the University of Chicago: The Old Testament Attitude towards Labor.

Mr. E. B. Hewes, of the University of Illinois: The Indian National Congress.

The following papers were presented by title:

Professor James A. Montgomery, of the University of Pennsylvania: Nephtoah and Similar Place-names in the Hebrew; Issachar.

Dr. William Rosenau, of Johns Hopkins University: Some Prayers in the Book of Tobit.

Dr. Frank R. Blake, of Johns Hopkins University: (a) Long-distance Collection of Philippine Linguistic Material; (b) The Expression *man hû elâh dî* . . . in Daniel 3:15.

(a) In order to secure a large number of examples of certain constructions in the Philippine languages through the aid of persons in contact with the languages themselves, the writer sent to one of his Philippine correspondents, who had offered to supervise the collection of such material, a number of copies of a circular containing a list of coordinated words in English for translation into the native dialects with some explanatory remarks. Complete sets of these constructions have thus been secured for four of the most important languages of the archipelago, and it is hoped by this means to secure material also from the less known languages.

(b) This expression means 'who is the god that . . .' The predicate of a sentence introduced by the personal interrogative should be definite, hence *elâh* is perhaps haplography for *elâhâh*=*elâhâ*'. In the passages which can be cited in Hebrew and Arabic to support the indefinite character of such a predicate, *mî* and *man*, in spite of the statements of the grammarians to the contrary, are probably adjectival, modifying the indefinite noun in the sense of 'which,' 'what'.

Professor Albert T. Clay, of Yale University: The Early Amorite King Humbaba.

Professor Raymond P. Dougherty, of Goucher College: The Comparative Value of Metals in Babylonia.

Several interesting tablets in the Yale Babylonian Collection, dated in the reign of Nabonidus, enable us to compute the comparative value of metals in Babylonia in the 6th century B. C. Gold was worth from 8½ to 13 times as much as silver, and silver was worth

90 times as much as lead, 180 times as much as copper, and from 240 to 360 times as much as iron. This means that lead was worth twice as much as copper and from $2\frac{2}{3}$ to 4 times as much as iron. Copper was worth from $1\frac{1}{3}$ to 2 times as much as iron.

Professor LOUIS H. GRAY, of the University of Nebraska: The Indian God Dhanvantari.

Dr. DAVID I. MACHT, of Johns Hopkins University: A Pharmacological Appreciation of Psalm 58:9.

Dr. CLARENCE A. MANNING, of Columbia University: Prester John and Japan.

Certain Russian sects have developed a tradition that Japan is the home of the pure Orthodox Faith which disappeared from Russia at the time of Nikon. This seems to be closely connected with the medieval legends of Prester John, which were known in Russia as well as in Western Europe and Constantinople. In all probability the Patriarch of Opunia or Byelovodiye is none other than Prester John under a new form.

Mr. PAUL POPENOE, of Coachella, Cal. The Pollination of the Date Palm.

Dr. GEORGE C. O. HAAS, of New York City: A Medieval French Parallel to the Buddhist Tale of the Luck-child Ghosaka.

A remarkable parallel to the story of Ghosaka *(Dhammapada Commentary*, 2. 1. 2) is found in the 13th-century French tale, *Li Contes dou roi Coustant l'empereur*, and its verse counterpart, *Li Dis de l'empereour Coustant*. The correspondence extends even to minor details of the plot.

The Society adjourned at 5:15 P.M. to meet at Princeton in 1923.

PROCEEDINGS

OF THE

MIDDLE WEST BRANCH

OF THE

AMERICAN ORIENTAL SOCIETY

AT ITS SIXTH MEETING AT CHICAGO, APRIL 18—20, 1922

The business meeting of the Middle West Branch convened April 18, 1922, at 2:15 P. M., in Ida Noyes Hall at the University of Chicago. President Olmstead called the meeting to order and told briefly how the Branch had grown until it now includes more than one fourth of the Society's members.

The report of the Secretary-Treasurer, Dr. Allen, followed. It was very brief, since a full account of the 1921 meeting of the Branch at Madison, written by the previous Secretary, Professor Olmstead, had been published in the JOURNAL, vol. 41, pp. 188—194. As to the treasury, expenses paid or payable amounted to $ 14.55 out of $ 40.00 which had been provided, leaving a balance of $ 25.45 still available.

A committee to nominate officers for the ensuing year was then chosen by nominations from the floor. Its members, Professors Wolfenson, Eiselen, and J. M. P. Smith, reported as follows:

For President, Professor Eiselen;
For Vice-president, Professor Price;
For Secretary-Treasurer, Dr. Allen;
For additional members of the Executive Committee, Professors Olmstead and Clark.

The secretary was instructed to cast a unanimous ballot in favor of these nominees; this was done and they were duly elected.

It was voted to leave to the incoming Executive Committee the choice of time and place for the next meeting of the Branch.

The other sessions of the meeting were held jointly with the general Society, and are fully reported in its Proceedings as printed above.

Adjourned.

T. George Allen,
Secretary-Treasurer.

LIST OF MEMBERS

The number placed after the address indicates the year of election.
† designates members deceased during the past year.

HONORARY MEMBERS

Prof. Theodor Nöldeke, Ettlingerstr. 53, Karlsruhe, Germany. 1878.

Sir Ramkrishna Gopal Bhandarkar, K.C.I.E., Deccan College, Poona, India. 1887.

Prof. Eduard Sachau, University of Berlin, Germany. (Wormserstr. 12, W.) 1887.

†Prof. Friedrich Delitzsch, Südstr. 47^{II}, Leipzig, Germany. 1893.

Prof. Ignazio Guidi, University of Rome, Italy. (Via Botteghe Oscure 24.) 1893.

Prof. Archibald H. Sayce, University of Oxford, England. 1893.

Prof. Richard v. Garbe, University of Tübingen, Germany. (Biesinger Str. 14.) 1902.

Prof. Adolf Erman, University of Berlin, Germany. (Peter Lennéstr. 36, Berlin-Dahlem.) 1903.

Prof. Karl F. Geldner, University of Marburg, Germany. 1905.

Sir George A. Grierson, K.C.I.E., Rathfarnham, Camberley, Surrey, England. Corporate Member, 1899; Honorary, 1905.

†Prof. T. W. Rhys Davids, Cotterstock, Chipstead, Surrey, England. 1907.

Prof. Eduard Meyer, University of Berlin, Germany. (Mommsenstr. 7, Gross-Lichterfelde-West.) 1908.

Emile Senart, Membre de l'Institut de France, 18 Rue François Ier, Paris, France. 1908.

Prof. Charles Clermont-Ganneau, Collège de France, Paris, France. (1 Avenue de l'Alma.) 1909.

Prof. Hermann Jacobi, University of Bonn, Germany. (Niebuhrstrasse 59.) 1909.

Prof. C. Snouck Hurgronje, University of Leiden, Netherlands. (Rapenberg 61.) 1914.

Prof. Sylvain Lévi, Collège de France, Paris, France. (9 Rue Guy-de-la-Brosse, Paris, V^{e}.) 1917.

Prof. Arthur Anthony Macdonell, University of Oxford, England. 1918.

François Thureau-Dangin, Musée du Louvre, Paris, France. 1918.

Sir ARTHUR EVANS, Ashmolean Museum, Oxford, England. 1919.

Prof. V. SCHEIL, Membre de l'Institut de France, 4bis Rue du Cherche-Midi, Paris, France. 1920.

Dr. F. W. THOMAS, The Library, India Office, London S. W. 1, England. 1920.

Rév. Père M.-J. LAGRANGE, Ecole française archéologique de Palestine, Jerusalem, Palestine. 1921.

Don LEONE CAETANI, DUCA DI SERMONETA, Palazzo Sermoneta, 30 Via Monte Savello, Rome, Italy. 1922.

Prof. FRIEDRICH HIRTH, Haimhauserstr. 19, München, Germany. Corporate Member, 1903; Honorary, 1922. [Total: 23]

HONORARY ASSOCIATES

Hon. WARREN G. HARDING, President of the United States, The White House, Washington, D. C. 1922.

Field Marshal Viscount ALLENBY, G. C. B., G. C. M. G., Naval and Military Club, London, England. 1922.

Hon. CHARLES R. CRANE, 31 West 12th St., New York, N. Y. 1921.

Rev. Dr. OTIS A. GLAZEBROOK, American Consul, Nice, France. 1921.

Pres. FRANK J. GOODNOW, The Johns Hopkins University, Baltimore, Md. 1921.

Hon. CHARLES EVANS HUGHES, Secretary of State, Washington, D. C. 1922.

Pres. HARRY PRATT JUDSON, The University of Chicago, Chicago, Ill. 1922.

Hon. HENRY MORGENTHAU, 30 West 72d St., New York, N. Y. 1921.

Dr. PAUL S. REINSCH, 204 Southern Building, Washington, D. C. 1921.

Hon. OSCAR S. STRAUS, 5 West 76th St., New York, N. Y. 1922.

Hon. SAO-KE ALFRED SZE, Chinese Minister to the United States, Chinese Legation, Washington, D. C. 1922.

Hon. WILLIAM HOWARD TAFT, Chief Justice, The Supreme Court of the United States, Washington, D. C. 1921.

Major General LEONARD WOOD, Governor-General of the Philippine Islands, Manila, P. I. 1922. [Total: 13]

CORPORATE MEMBERS

Names marked with * are those of life members.

MARCUS AARON, 402 Winebiddle Ave., Pittsburgh, Pa. 1921.

Rev. Dr. JUSTIN EDWARDS ABBOTT, 120 Hobart Ave., Summit, N. J. 1900.

Pres. CYRUS ADLER (Dropsie College), 2041 North Broad St., Philadelphia, Pa. 1884.

Dr. N. ADRIANI, Posso, Central Celebes, Dutch East Indies. 1922.

Prof. S. KRISHNASWAMI AIYANGAR (Univ. of Madras), Sri Venkatesa Vilas, Nadu St., Mylapore, Madras, India. 1921.

Dr. WILLIAM FOXWELL ALBRIGHT, Director, American School of Oriental Research, P. O. Box 333, Jerusalem, Palestine. 1915.

Prof. HERBERT C. ALLEMAN, Lutheran Theological Seminary, Gettysburg, Pa. 1921.

Dr. T. GEORGE ALLEN (Univ. of Chicago), 5743 Maryland Ave., Chicago, Ill. 1917.

Dr. OSWALD T. ALLIS, 26 Alexander Hall, Princeton Theological Seminary, Princeton, N. J. 1916.

Prof. SHIGERU ARAKI, The Peeress' School, Aoyama, Tokyo, Japan. 1915.

Prof. J. C. ARCHER (Yale Univ.), 84 Linden St., New Haven, Conn. 1916.

Prof. KAN-ICHI ASAKAWA, Yale University Library, New Haven, Conn. 1904.

L. A. AULT, P. O. Drawer 880, Cincinnati, Ohio. 1921.

Dean WILLIAM FREDERIC BADÈ (Pacific School of Religion), 2616 College Ave., Berkeley, Cal. 1920.

Rev. MOSES BAILEY, M. A., 6 Norfolk Terrace, Wellesley, Mass. 1922.

Mrs. ROBERT A. (Emily Tyler) BAILEY, JR., Harlicourt Apts., Cliff Road, Birmingham, Ala. 1922.

CHARLES CHANEY BAKER, Box 296, Lancaster, Cal. 1916.

Hon. SIMEON E. BALDWIN, LL.D., 44 Wall St., New Haven, Conn. 1898.

*Dr. HUBERT BANNING, 17 East 128th St., New York, N. Y. 1915.

*PHILIP LEMONT BARBOUR, care of Mercantile Trust Co., San Francisco, Cal. 1917.

Rabbi HENRY BARNSTON, Ph.D., 3515 Main St, Houston, Texas, 1921.

Prof. LEROY CARR BARRET, Trinity College, Hartford, Conn. 1903.

Prof. GEORGE A. BARTON (Univ. of Pennsylvania), 3725 Chestnut St., Philadelphia, Pa. 1888.

Mrs. FRANCES CROSBY BARTTER, Box 655, Manila, P. I. 1921.

Mrs. DANIEL M. BATES, 51 Brattle St., Cambridge, Mass. 1912.

Prof. LORING W. BATTEN (General Theol. Seminary), 6 Chelsea Square, New York, N. Y. 1894.

Prof. HARLAN P. BEACH (Yale Univ.), 346 Willow St., New Haven, Conn. 1898.

Miss ETHEL BEERS, 3414 South Paulina St., Chicago, Ill. 1915.

*Prof. SHRIPAD K. BELVALKAR (Deccan College), Bilvakunja Bhamburda, Poona, India. 1914.

Prof. HAROLD H. BENDER, Princeton University, Princeton, N. J. 1906.

Pres. GUY POTTER BENTON, University of the Philippines, Manila, P. I. 1922.

†E. BEN YEHUDA, care of Zionist Commission, Jerusalem, Palestine. 1916.

Prof. C. THEODORE BENZE, D. D. (Mt. Airy Theol. Seminary), 7304 Boyer St., Mt. Airy, Pa. 1916.

OSCAR BERMAN, Third, Plum and McFarland Sts., Cincinnati, Ohio. 1920.

PIERRE A. BERNARD, Rossiter House, Braeburn Club, Nyack, N. Y. 1914.

ISAAC W. BERNHEIM, Inter-Southern Building, Louisville, Ky. 1920.

Prof. GEORGE R. BERRY, Colgate University, Hamilton, N. Y. 1907.

Prof. JULIUS A. BEWER, Union Theological Seminary, Broadway and 120th St., New York, N. Y. 1907.

Prof. D. R. BHANDARKAR (Univ. of Calcutta), 16 Lansdowne Road, Calcutta, India. 1921.

Prof. A. E. BIGELOW, Jaro Industrial School, Iloilo, P. I. 1922.

WILLIAM STURGIS BIGELOW, M. D., 60 Beacon St., Boston, Mass. 1894.

Prof. FREDERICK L. BIRD, Occidental College, Los Angeles, Cal. 1917.

Carl W. Bishop, Smithsonian Institution, Washington, D.C. 1917.

Dr. Frank Ringgold Blake (Johns Hopkins Univ.), 923 W. North Ave., Baltimore, Md. 1900.

Dr. Frederick J. Bliss, 1155 Yale Station, New Haven, Conn. 1898.

Dr. Joshua Bloch (New York Univ.), 346 East 173d St., New York, N.Y. 1921.

Prof. Carl August Blomgren (Augustana College and Theol. Seminary), 825 35th St., Rock Island, Ill. 1900.

Prof. Maurice Bloomfield, The Johns Hopkins University, Baltimore, Md. 1881.

Rev. Paul F. Bloomhardt, Ph. D., 1080 Main St., Buffalo, N.Y. 1916.

Emanuel Boasberg, 1296 Delaware Ave., Buffalo, N.Y. 1921.

Dr. Alfred Boissier, Le Rivage près Chambéry, Genève, Switzerland. 1897.

Rev. August M. Bolduc, S.T.B., The Marist College, Brookland, Washington, D.C. 1921.

Prof. George M. Bolling (Ohio State Univ.), 777 Franklin Ave., Columbus, Ohio. 1896.

Prof. Campbell Bonner, University of Michigan, Ann Arbor, Mich. 1920.

Dean Edward I. Bosworth (Oberlin Graduate School of Theology), 78 South Professor St., Oberlin, Ohio. 1920.

Prof. James Henry Breasted, University of Chicago, Chicago, Ill. 1891.

Miss Emilie Grace Briggs, 124 Third St., Lakewood, N.J. 1920.

Prof. C. A. Brodie Brockwell, McGill University, Montreal, P. Q., Canada. 1920 (1906).

Rev. Charles D. Brokenshire, Lock Box 56, Alma, Mich. 1917.

Mrs. Beatrice Allard Brooks, Ph.D., Summit Road, Wellesley, Mass. 1919.

Milton Brooks, 3 Clive Row, Calcutta, India. 1918.

David A. Brown, 60 Boston Boulevard, Detroit, Mich. 1921.

G. M. L. Brown, care of "Orientalia", 32 West 58th St., New York, N.Y. 1921.

Rev. Dr. George William Brown, College of Missions, Indianapolis, Ind. 1909.

Leo M. Brown, P. O. Box 953, Mobile, Ala. 1920.

Dr. W. Norman Brown, Care Thos. Cook and Son, Hornby Road, Bombay, India. 1916.

Prof. Carl Darling Buck, University of Chicago, Chicago, Ill. 1892.

Ludlow S. Bull, Assistant Curator, Metropolitan Museum of Art, New York, N.Y. 1917.

Alexander H. Bullock, State Mutual Building, Worcester, Mass. 1910.

†*Prof. John M. Burnam (Univ. of Cincinnati), 3413 Whitfield Ave., Cincinnati, Ohio. 1920.

Charles Dana Burrage, 85 Ames Building, Boston, Mass. 1909.

Prof. Romanus Butin, Catholic University of America, Washington, D.C. 1915.

†Prof. Howard Crosby Butler, Princeton University, Princeton, N.J. 1908.

Prof. Moses Buttenwieser (Hebrew Union College), 252 Loraine Ave., Cincinnati, Ohio. 1917.

Prof. EUGENE H. BYRNE (Univ. of Wisconsin), 240 Lake Lawn Place, Madison, Wis. 1917.

Prof. HENRY J. CADBURY (Andover Theol. Seminary), 1075 Massachusetts Ave., Cambridge, Mass. 1914.

ALFRED M. CAMPBELL, 204 East Wishart St., Philadelphia, Pa. 1922.

Rev. JOHN CAMPBELL, Ph. D., 3055 Kingsbridge Ave., New York, N. Y. 1896.

Rev. ISAAC CANNADAY, M. A., Ranchi, Bihar, India. 1920.

Prof. ALBERT J. CARNOY (Univ. of Louvain), Sparrenhof, Corbeek-Loo, Belgium. 1916.

Dr. I. M. CASANOWICZ, U. S. National Museum, Washington, D. C. 1893.

HENRY HARMON CHAMBERLIN, 22 May St., Worcester, Mass. 1921.

Rev. JOHN S. CHANDLER, Sunnyside, Rayapettah, Madras, India. 1899.

Prof. RAMAPRASAD CHANDRA, University of Calcutta, Calcutta, India. 1921.

Dr. WILLIAM J. CHAPMAN (Hartford Theol. Seminary), 1507 Broad St., Hartford, Conn. 1922.

Dr. F. D. CHESTER, The Bristol, Boston, Mass. 1891.

Dr. EDWARD CHIERA (Univ. of Pennsylvania), 1538 South Broad St., Philadelphia, Pa. 1915.

EMERSON B. CHRISTIE (Department of State), 3220 McKinley St., N. W., Washington, D. C. 1921.

Prof. WALTER E. CLARK, Box 222, University of Chicago, Chicago, Ill. 1906.

Prof. ALBERT T. CLAY (Yale Univ.), 401 Humphrey St., New Haven, Conn. 1907.

*ALEXANDER SMITH COCHRAN, 820 Fifth Ave., New York, N. Y. 1908.

CHARLES P. COFFIN, 1744-208 South LaSalle St., Chicago, Ill. 1921.

ALFRED M. COHEN, 9 West 4th St., Cincinnati, Ohio. 1920.

Dr. GEORGE H. COHEN, 120 Capitol Ave., Hartford, Conn. 1920.

Rabbi HENRY COHEN, D. D., 1920 Broadway, Galveston, Texas. 1920.

MORRIS GABRIEL COHEN, 946 St. Marks Ave., Brooklyn, N. Y. 1923.

Rabbi SAMUEL S. COHON, 6634 Newgard St., Chicago, Ill. 1917.

Prof. KENNETH COLEGROVE (Northwestern Univ.), 105 Harris Hall, Evanston, Ill. 1920.

Prof. HERMANN COLLITZ (Johns Hopkins Univ.), 1027 Calvert St., Baltimore, Md. 1887.

Prof. C. EVERETT CONANT, Carleton College, Northfield, Minn. 1905.

Dr. MAUDE GAECKLER (Mrs. H. M.) COOK, Belton, Texas. 1915.

Rev. Dr. GEORGE S. COOKE, Houlton, Maine. 1917.

Dr. ANANDA K. COOMARASWAMY, Museum of Fine Arts, Boston, Mass. 1917.

*Rev. DOUGLAS HILARY CORLEY, Box 145, Fisk University, Nashville, Tenn. 1922.

Rev. RALPH D. CORNUELLE, American Presbyterian Mission, Jhansi, U. P., India. 1922.

Dr. WILLIAN COWEN, 35 East 60th St., New York, N. Y. 1922.

Rev. WILLIAM MERRIAM CRANE, Richmond, Mass. 1902.

CECIL M. P. CROSS, care of Consular Bureau, Washington, D. C. 1921.

Prof. GEORGE DAHL (Yale Univ.), 93 Linden St., New Haven, Conn. 1918.

Prof. GEORGE H. DANTON, Tsing Hua College, Peking, China. 1921.

Prof. ISRAEL DAVIDSON (Jewish Theol. Seminary), 92 Morningside Ave, New York, N. Y. 1921.

Prof. JOHN D. DAVIS, Princeton Theological Seminary, Princeton, N. J. 1888.

Prof. FRANK LEIGHTON DAY, Randolph-Macon College, Ashland, Va. 1920.

Prof. IRWIN HOCH DELONG (Theol. Seminary of the Reformed Church), 523 West James St., Lancaster, Pa. 1916.

Prof. ROBERT E. DENGLER (Pennsylvania State College), 706 West College Ave., State College, Pa. 1920.

NARIMAN M. DHALLA, Hartley Hall, Columbia University, New York, N. Y. 1922.

Pro-Vice-Chancellor A. B. DHRUVA, The Benares Hindu University, Benares, India. 1921.

Mrs. FRANCIS W. DICKINS, 2015 Columbia Road, Washington, D. C. 1911.

LEON DOMINIAN, care of American Consulate-General, Rome, Italy. 1916.

Rev. A. T. DORF, 1635 North Washtenaw Ave., Chicago, Ill. 1916.

Prof. RAYMOND P. DOUGHERTY, Goucher College, Baltimore, Md. 1918.

Rev. WILLIAM HASKELL DUBOSE, University of the South, Sewanee, Tenn. 1912.

Prof. FREDERIC C. DUNCALF, University of Texas, Austin, Texas. 1919.

Prof. GEORGE S. DUNCAN (American Univ., Y. M. C. A. School of Religion), 2900 Seventh St., N. E., Washington, D. C. 1917.

Rev. EDWARD SLATER DUNLAP, 2629 Garfield St., N. W., Washington, D. C. 1921.

Prof. CHARLES DUROISELLE, M. A. (Rangoon Univ.), "C" Road, Mandalay, Burma. 1922.

Prof. FRANKLIN EDGERTON (Univ. of Pennsylvania), 107 Bryn Mawr Ave., Lansdowne, Pa. 1910.

Dr. WILLIAM F. EDGERTON (Univ. of Chicago), 1401 East 53d St., Chicago, Ill. 1917.

Mrs. ARTHUR C. EDWARDS, 309 West 91st St., New York, N. Y. 1915.

Prof. GRANVILLE D. EDWARDS (Missouri Bible College), 811 College Ave., Columbia, Mo. 1917.

Rev. JAMES F. EDWARDS, Gordon Hall House, New Nogpada Road, Bombay, India. 1921.

Dr. ISRAEL EFROS (Baltimore Hebrew College), 2040 East Baltimore St., Baltimore, Md. 1918.

Dean FREDERICK C. EISELEN, Garrett Biblical Institute, Evanston, Ill. 1901.

Rabbi ISRAEL ELFENBEIN, D.H.L., 128 West 95th St., New York, N. Y. 1920.

ABRAM I. ELKUS, 111 Broadway, New York, N. Y. 1921.

ALBERT W. ELLIS, 40 Central St., Boston, Mass. 1917.

Prof. AARON EMBER, The Johns Hopkins University, Baltimore, Md. 1902.

Rabbi H. G. ENELOW, D. D., Temple Emanu-El, 521 Fifth Ave., New York, N. Y. 1921.

Prof. HENRY LANE ENO, Princeton University, Princeton, N. J. 1916.

Rabbi HARRY W. ETTELSON, Ph.D., 1505 Diamond St., Philadelphia, Pa. 1918.

Pres. MILTON G. EVANS, Crozer Theological Seminary, Chester, Pa. 1921.

Prof. Charles P. Fagnani (Union Theol. Seminary), 606 West 122d St., New York, N. Y. 1901.

Benjamin Fain, 1269 President St., Brooklyn, N. Y. 1921.

Wallace Cranston Fairweather, 62 Saint Vincent St., Glasgow, Scotland. 1922.

Rabbi Abraham J. Feldman, Temple Keneseth Israel, Broad St. above Columbia Ave., Philadelphia, Pa. 1920.

Rev. Dr. John F. Fenlon, Catholic University of America, Washington, D. C. 1915.

Dr. John C. Ferguson, Peking, China. 1900.

Morris M. Feuerlicht, 3034 Washington Boulevard, Indianapolis, Ind. 1922.

Sol. Baruch Finesinger, The Johns Hopkins University, Baltimore, Md. 1922.

Rabbi Joseph L. Fink, 540 South 6th St., Terre Haute, Ind. 1920.

Dr. Louis Finkelstein, Jewish Theological Seminary, 531 West 123d St., New York, N. Y. 1921.

Clarence S. Fisher, University of Pennsylvania Museum, Philadelphia, Pa. 1914.

*Maynard Dauchy Follin, P. O. Box 118, Detroit, Mich. 1922.

Dean Hughell E. W. Fosbroke, General Theological Seminary, Chelsea Square, New York, N. Y. 1917.

Rabbi Solomon Foster, 90 Treacy Ave., Newark, N. J. 1921.

Prof. James Everett Frame, Union Theological Seminary, Broadway and 120th St., New York, N. Y. 1892.

W. B. Frankenstein, 110 South Dearborn St., Chicago, Ill. 1921.

Rabbi Leo M. Franklin, M.A., 10 Edison Ave., Detroit, Mich. 1920.

Rabbi Solomon B. Freehof, D.D., 3426 Burnet Ave., Cincinnati, Ohio. 1918.

Maurice J. Freiberg, 701 First National Bank Building, Cincinnati, Ohio. 1920.

Sigmund Frey, 632 Irvington Ave., Huntington Park, Cal. 1920.

Harry Friedenwald, M.D., 1029 Madison Ave., Baltimore, Md. 1921.

Prof. Leslie Elmer Fuller, Garrett Biblical Institute, Evanston, Ill. 1916.

Prof. Kemper Fullerton, Oberlin Theological Seminary, Oberlin, Ohio. 1916.

*Prof. A. B. Gajendragadkar, Elphinstone College, Bombay, India. 1921.

Alexander B. Galt, 2219 California St., Washington, D. C. 1917.

Mrs. H. P. Gamboe, Kulpahar, U. P., India. 1921.

Mrs. William Tudor Gardiner, 29 Brimmer St., Boston, Mass. 1915.

Rev. Frank Gavin, Nashotah House, Nashotah, Wis. 1917.

Dr. Henry Snyder Gehman, 5720 North 6th St., Philadelphia, Pa. 1916.

Eugene A. Gellot, 290 Broadway, N. Y., 1911.

Rev. Phares B. Gibble, 112 West Conway St., Baltimore, Md. 1921.

Prof. Basil Lanneau Gildersleeve (Johns Hopkins Univ.), 1002 North Calvert St., Baltimore, Md. 1858.

Pres. D. C. Gilmore, D. D., Judson College, Rangoon, Burma. 1922.

Rabbi S. H. Goldenson, Ph.D., 4905 Fifth Ave., Pittsburgh, Pa. 1920.

Rabbi SOLOMON GOLDMAN, 55th and Scoville Sts., Cleveland, Ohio. 1920.
Prof. ALEXANDER R. GORDON, Presbyterian College, Montreal, P. Q., Canada. 1912.
Prof. RICHARD J. H. GOTTHEIL, Columbia University, New York, N. Y. 1886.
KINGDON GOULD, 165 Broadway, New York, N. Y. 1914.
Prof. HERBERT HENRY GOWEN, D.D. (Univ. of Washington), 5005 22d Ave., N. E., Seattle, Wash. 1920.
Prof. WILLIAM CREIGHTON GRAHAM (Wesleyan Theol. College), 756 University St., Montreal, P. Q., Canada. 1921.
Prof. ELIHU GRANT, Haverford College, Haverford, Pa. 1907.
Prof. LOUIS H. GRAY, University of Nebraska, Lincoln, Neb. 1897.
Mrs. LOUIS H. GRAY, care of University of Nebraska, Lincoln, Neb. 1907.
Prof. EVARTS B. GREENE (Univ. of Illinois), 315 Lincoln Hall, Urbana, Ill. 1921.
Dr. LILY DEXTER GREENE, care Methodist Episcopal Mission, Delhi, India. 1921.
M. E. GREENEBAUM, 4504 Drexel Boulevard, Chicago, Ill. 1920.
Dr. ETTALENE M. GRICE, care of Babylonian Collection, Yale University, New Haven, Conn. 1915.
Miss LUCIA C. G. GRIEVE, 211 Wardwell Ave., Westerleigh, S. I., N. Y. 1894.
Rev. Dr. HERVEY D. GRISWOLD, "The Abbey," Lahore, Panjab, India. 1920.
Prof. LOUIS GROSSMANN (Hebrew Union College), 2212 Park Ave., Cincinnati, Ohio. 1890.
Prof. LÉON GRY (Université libre d'Angers), 10 Rue La Fontaine, Angers, M.-et-L., France. 1921.
Babu SHIVA PRASAD GUPTA, Seva-Upavana, Hindu University, Benares, India. 1921.
Pres. WILLIAM W. GUTH, Ph.D., Goucher College, Baltimore, Md. 1920.
*Dr. GEORGE C. O. HAAS, 323 West 22d St., New York, N. Y. 1903.
Miss LUISE HAESSLER, 100 Morningside Drive, New York, N. Y. 1909.
Rev. ALEXANDER D. HAIL (Osaka Theol. Training School), 946 of 3. Tezukayama, Sumiyoshi Mura, Setsu, Japan. 1921.
Dr. GEORGE ELLERY HALE, Director, Mt. Wilson Observatory, Pasadena, Cal. 1920.
Dr. B. HALPER, Dropsie College, Philadelphia, Pa. 1919.
Rev. EDWARD R. HAMME, 1511 Hanover St., Baltimore, Md. 1921.
Prof. MAX S. HANDMAN, University of Texas, Austin, Texas. 1919.
Prof. PAUL HAUPT (Johns Hopkins Univ.), 215 Longwood Road, Roland Park, Baltimore, Md. 1883.
Prof. A. EUSTACE HAYDON, University of Chicago, Chicago, Ill. 1922.
DANIEL P. HAYS, 115 Broadway, New York, N. Y. 1920.
Rabbi JAMES G. HELLER, 3634 Reading Road, Cincinnati, Ohio. 1920.
Prof. MAXIMILIAN HELLER (Tulane Univ.), 1828 Marengo St., New Orleans, La. 1920.
PHILIP S. HENRY, Zealandia, Asheville, N. C. 1914.
Rev. CHARLES W. HEPNER, 5305 Oshigatsuji, Osaka, Japan. 1921.
EDWIN B. HEWES, 307 South Lincoln St., Urbana, Ill. 1922.

Prof. William Bancroft Hill, Vassar College, Poughkeepsie, N. Y. 1921.
Prof. Herman V. Hilprecht, 1830 South Rittenhouse Square, Philadelphia, Pa. 1887.
Prof. William J. Hinke (Auburn Theol. Seminary), 156 North St., Auburn, N. Y. 1907.
†Prof. Emil G. Hirsch (Univ. of Chicago), 4608 Drexel Boulevard, Chicago, Ill. 1917.
Bernard Hirshberg, 260 Tod Lane, Youngstown, Ohio. 1920.
Prof. Philip K. Hitti, American University, Beirut, Syria. 1915.
Rev. Dr. Charles T. Hock (Bloomfield Theol. Seminary), 222 Liberty St., Bloomfield, N. J. 1921 (1903).
Rev. Dr. Lewis Hodous (Hartford Seminary Foundation), 9 Sumner St., Hartford, Conn. 1919.
G. F. Hoff, 403 Union Building, San Diego, Cal. 1920.
Miss Alice M. Holmes, Southern Pines, N. C. 1920.
*Prof. E. Washburn Hopkins (Yale Univ.), 299 Lawrence St., New Haven, Conn. 1881.
Samuel Horchow, 1307 Fourth St., Portsmouth, Ohio. 1920.
Ernest P. Horrwitz, 560 West 171st St., New York, N. Y. 1923.
Prof. Jacob Hoschander (Dropsie College), 3220 Monument Ave., Philadelphia, Pa. 1914.
Henry R. Howland, Buffalo Society of Natural Sciences, Buffalo, N. Y. 1907.
Dr. Edward H. Hume, The Hunan-Yale College of Medicine, Changsha, Hunan, China. 1909.
Prof. Robert Ernest Hume (Union Theol. Seminary), 606 West 122d St., New York, N. Y. 1914.
*Dr. Archer M. Huntington, 15 West 81st St., New York, N. Y. 1912.
Prof. Isaac Husik, College Hall, University of Pennsylvania, Philadelphia, Pa. 1916.
Prof. Mary Inda Hussey, Mt. Holyoke College, South Hadley, Mass. 1901.
Rev. Dr. Moses Hyamson (Jewish Theol. Seminary), 1335 Madison Ave., New York, N. Y. 1921.
*James Hazen Hyde, 67 Boulevard Lannes, Paris, France. 1909.
Prof. Walter Woodburn Hyde, College Hall, University of Pennsylvania, Philadelphia, Pa. 1920.
Prof. Henry Hyvernat (Catholic Univ. of America), 3405 Twelfth St., N. E. (Brookland), Washington, D. C. 1889.
Harald Ingholt, Graduate College, Princeton University, Princeton, N. J. 1921.
Rabbi Edward L. Israel, 1404 Upper First St., Evansville, Ind. 1920.
Prof. A. V. Williams Jackson, Columbia University, New York, N. Y. 1885.
Mrs. A. V. Williams Jackson, care of Columbia University, New York, N. Y. 1912.
Prof. Frederick J. Foakes Jackson, D.D. (Union Theol. Seminary), Dana Place, Englewood, N. J. 1920.
Rev. Ernest P. Janvier, Ewing Christian College, Allahabad, India. 1919.

Mrs. Morris Jastrow, Jr., 248 South 23d St., Philadelphia, Pa. 1922.
Prof. James Richard Jewett, Harvard University, Cambridge, Mass. 1887.
Frank Edward Johnson, 31 General Lee St., Marianao, Cuba. 1916.
Franklin Plotinos Johnson, Osceola, Mo. 1921.
Dr. Helen M. Johnson, Osceola, Mo. 1921.
Nelson Trusler Johnson, Department of State, Washington, D. C. 1921.
Charles Johnston, 80 Washington Square, New York, N. Y. 1921.
Reginald F. Johnston, The Forbidden City, Peking, China. 1919.
Florin Howard Jones, Saunders Cottage, N. Broadway, Upper Nyack, N. Y. 1918.
Mrs. Russell K. (Alice Judson) Jones, Metropolitan Museum of Art, New York, N. Y. 1920.
Ely Jacques Kahn, 56 West 45th St., New York, N. Y. 1922.
Julius Kahn, 429 Wick Ave., Youngstown, Ohio. 1920.
Rabbi Jacob H. Kaplan, 780 East Ridgeway Ave., Cincinnati, Ohio. 1918.
Rabbi C. E. Hillel Kauvar, Ph.D., 1607 Gilpin St., Denver, Colo. 1921.
Prof. Elmer Louis Kayser (George Washington Univ.), 3129 O St., N. W., Washington, D. C. 1921.
Rev. Dr. C. E. Keiser, Lyon Station, Pa. 1913.
Prof. Maximilian L. Kellner, Episcopal Theological School, Cambridge, Mass. 1886.
Prof. Frederick T. Kelly (Univ. of Wisconsin), 2019 Monroe St., Madison, Wis. 1917.
Pres. James A. Kelso, Western Theological Seminary, Pittsburgh, Pa. 1915.
Rev. James L. Kelso, 501 North Walnut St., Bloomington, Ind. 1921.
Prof. Eliza H. Kendrick, Wellesley College, Wellesley, Mass. 1896.
Prof. Charles Foster Kent, Yale University, New Haven, Conn. 1890.
Prof. Roland G. Kent, University of Pennsylvania, Philadelphia, Pa. 1910
Leeds C. Kerr, Royal Oak, Md. 1916.
Isadore Keyfitz, 5037 Evanston Ave., Chicago, Ill. 1920.
Prof. Anis E. Khuri, American University, Beirut, Syria. 1921.
Prof. Taiken Kimura, Tokyo Imperial University, Tokyo, Japan. 1921.
Prof. George L. Kittredge (Harvard Univ.), 8 Hilliard St., Cambridge, Mass. 1899.
Eugene Klein, 44 North 50th St., Philadelphia, Pa. 1920.
Taw Sein Ko, C. I. E., Peking Lodge, Mandalay, Burma. 1922.
Rabbi Samuel Koch, M.A., 916 Twentieth Ave., Seattle, Wash. 1921.
Pres. Kaufmann Kohler (Hebrew Union College), 3016 Stanton Ave., Cincinnati, Ohio. 1917.
Rev. Emil G. H. Kraeling, Ph.D. (Union Theol. Seminary), 132 Henry St., Brooklyn, N. Y. 1920.
Rev. Dr. Melvin G. Kyle, 1132 Arrott St., Frankford, Philadelphia, Pa. 1909.
Harold Albert Lamb, 7 West 92d St., New York, N. Y. 1920.
Miss M. Antonia Lamb, 212 South 46th St., Philadelphia, Pa. 1921.
Prof. Gotthard Landstrom, Box 12, Zap, Mercer Co., N. Dak. 1917.
*Prof. Charles Rockwell Lanman (Harvard Univ.), 9 Farrar St., Cambridge, Mass. 1876.

AMBROSE LANSING, Metropolitan Museum of Art, New York, N. Y. 1921.

Prof. KENNETH S. LATOURETTE, Yale University, New Haven, Conn. 1917.

Dr. BERTHOLD LAUFER, Field Museum of Natural History, Chicago, Ill. 1900.

Prof. JACOB Z. LAUTERBACH, Hebrew Union College, Cincinnati, Ohio. 1918.

SIMON LAZARUS, High and Town Sts., Columbus, Ohio. 1921.

Prof. DARWIN A. LEAVITT (Meadville Theol. School), Divinity Hall, Meadville, Pa. 1920.

Rabbi DAVID LEFKOWITZ, 2415 South Boulevard, Dallas, Texas. 1921.

Rev. Dr. LÉON LEGRAIN, Univ. of Penna. Museum, Philadelphia, Pa. 1921.

Rabbi GERSON B. LEVI, Ph.D., 5000 Grand Boulevard, Chicago, Ill. 1917.

Rabbi SAMUEL J. LEVINSON, 522 East 8th St., Brooklyn, N. Y. 1920.

Rev. Dr. FELIX A. LEVY, 707 Melrose St., Chicago, Ill. 1917.

Dr. H. S. LINFIELD, Bureau of Jewish Social Research, 114 Fifth Ave., New York, N. Y. 1912.

JOHN ELLERTON LODGE, Museum of Fine Arts, Boston, Mass. 1922.

Mrs. LEE LOEB, 53 Gibbes St., Charleston, S. C. 1920.

Prof. LINDSAY B. LONGACRE, 2272 South Fillmore St., Denver, Colo. 1918.

Rev. ARNOLD E. LOOK, 614 North Frazier St., Philadelphia, Pa. 1920.

Dr. STEPHEN B. LUCE, JR., 267 Clarendon St., Boston, Mass. 1916.

Prof. DANIEL D. LUCKENBILL, University of Chicago, Chicago, Ill. 1912.

Prof. HENRY F. LUTZ, University of California, Berkeley, Cal. 1916.

Prof. ALBERT HOWE LYBYER, (Univ. of Illinois), 1009 West California St., Urbana, Ill. 1917 (1909).

Prof. DAVID GORDON LYON, Harvard University Semitic Museum, Cambridge, Mass. 1882.

ALBERT MORTON LYTHGOE, Curator, Metropolitan Museum of Art, New York, N. Y. 1899.

Rev. WILLIAM H. MCCLELLAN, S. J., Woodstock College, Woodstock, Md. 1922.

Prof. CHESTER CHARLTON MCCOWN, D.D. (Pacific School of Religion), 2223 Atherton St., Berkeley, Cal. 1920.

Prof. DUNCAN B. MACDONALD, Hartford Theological Seminary, Hartford, Conn. 1893.

Miss ELEANOR MCDOUGALL, M.A., Principal, The Women's Christian College, Madras, India. 1922.

DAVID ISRAEL MACHT, M.D., The Johns Hopkins University Medical School, Monument and Washington Sts., Baltimore, Md. 1918.

RALPH W. MACK, 3836 Reading Road, Cincinnati, Ohio. 1920.

J. ARTHUR MACLEAN, Assistant Director, The Art Institute, Chicago, Ill. 1922.

Dr. ROBERT CECIL MACMAHON, 78 West 55th St., New York, N. Y. 1921.

Dr. JUDAH L. MAGNES, 114 Fifth Ave., New York, N. Y. 1921.

Rabbi EDGAR F. MAGNIN, 2187 West 16th St., Los Angeles, Cal. 1920.

Prof. HERBERT W. MAGOUN, Hillcrest Road, Belmont, Cambridge, Mass. 1887.

WALTER ARTHUR MAIER, 6438 Eggleston Ave., Chicago, Ill. 1917.

Prof. HENRY MALTER (Dropsie College), 1531 Diamond St., Philadelphia, Pa. 1920.

Prof. JACOB MANN, Hebrew Union College, Cincinnati, Ohio. 1921.
Rabbi LOUIS L. MANN, 92 Linden St., New Haven, Conn. 1917.
Dr. CLARENCE A. MANNING (Columbia Univ.), 144 East 74th St., New York, N. Y. 1921.
*Rev. JAMES CAMPBELL MANRY, 36, The Quadrangle, Iowa City, Iowa. 1921.
Rabbi JACOB R. MARCUS, bei Eschelbacher, Oranienburgerstr. 68, Berlin, Germany. 1920.
RALPH MARCUS, 531 West 124th St., New York, N. Y. 1920.
ARTHUR WILLIAM MARGET, 157 Homestead St., Roxbury, Mass. 1920.
HARRY S. MARGOLIS, Hebrew Union College, Cincinnati, Ohio. 1920.
Prof. MAX L. MARGOLIS (Dropsie College), 152 West Hortter St., Philadelphia, Pa. 1890.
Prof. ALLAN MARQUAND, Princeton University, Princeton, N. J. 1888.
JAMES P. MARSH, M.D., 1828 Fifth Ave., Troy, N. Y. 1919.
Pres. H. I. MARSHALL, Karen Theol. Seminary, Insein, Burma, India. 1920.
JOHN MARTIN, North Adams, Mass. 1917.
Prof. D. ROY MATHEWS, 307 South Oak Park Ave., Oak Park, Ill. 1920.
Prof. ISAAC G. MATTHEWS, Crozer Theological Seminary, Chester, Pa. 1921 (1906).
Rabbi HARRY H. MAYER, 3512 Kenwood Ave., Kansas City, Mo. 1921.
Rev. Dr. JOHN A. MAYNARD (Univ. of Chicago), 2132 West 110th Place, Chicago, Ill. 1917.
Prof. THEOPHILE J. MEEK, Bryn Mawr College, Bryn Mawr, Pa. 1917.
HENRY MEIS, 806 Walnut St., Cincinnati, Ohio. 1920.
Rabbi RAPHAEL H. MELAMED, Ph.D., 1295 Central Ave., Far Rockaway, N. Y. 1921.
Dean SAMUEL A. B. MERCER, Bexley Hall, Gambier, Ohio. 1912.
ELMER D. MERRILL, Director, Bureau of Science, Manila, P. I. 1922.
R. D. MESSAYEH, 49 East 127th St., New York, N. Y. 1919.
Mrs. EUGENE MEYER, Seven Springs Farm, Mt. Kisco, N. Y. 1916.
Rev. Dr. MARTIN A. MEYER, 3108 Jackson St., San Francisco, Cal. 1906.
Rabbi MYRON M. MEYEROVITZ, Alexandria, La. 1920.
Dr. TRUMAN MICHELSON, Bureau of American Ethnology, Washington, D. C. 1899.
MERTON L. MILLER, care of International Banking Corporation, Cebu, P.I. 1921.
Rabbi LOUIS A. MISCHKIND, M.A., Tremont Temple, Grand Concourse and Burnside Ave., New York, N. Y. 1920.
Rev. JOHN MONCURE, Maryland College for Women, Lutherville, Md. 1921.
Dr. ROBET LUDWIG MOND, 7 Cavendish Mansions, Langham St., London W. 1, England. 1921.
Prof. J. A. MONTGOMERY (Univ. of Pennsylvania), 6806 Greene St., Germantown, Philadelphia, Pa. 1903.
FREDERICK MOORE, Japanese Embassy, Washington, D. C. 1921.
*Mrs. MARY H. MOORE, 3 Divinity Ave., Cambridge, Mass. 1902.
Rev. HUGH A. MORAN, 221 Eddy St., Ithaca, N. Y. 1920.
Pres. JULIAN MORGENSTERN (Hebrew Union College), 3988 Parker Place, Cincinnati, Ohio. 1915.
*EFFINGHAM B. MORRIS, "Tyn-y-Coed," Ardmore, Pa. 1920.

Hon. ROLAND S. MORRIS, 1617 Land Title Building, Philadelphia, Pa. 1921.
Prof. EDWARD S. MORSE, Peabody Museum, Salem, Mass. 1894.
Rev. OMER HILLMAN MOTT, O.S.B., Belmont Abbey, Belmont, N. C. 1921.
Rev. Dr. PHILIP STAFFORD MOXOM (International Y. M. C. A. College), 90 High St., Springfield, Mass. 1921 (1898).
DHAN GOPAL MUKERJI, 2 Jane St., New York, N. Y. 1922.
Mrs. ALBERT H. MUNSELL, 203 Radnor Hall, Cambridge, Mass. 1908.
Dr. WILLIAM MUSS-ARNOLT, 245 East Tremont Ave., New York, N. Y. 1887.
Prof. THOMAS KINLOCH NELSON, Virginia Theological Seminary, Alexandria, Va. 1920.
Rev. Dr. WILLIAM M. NESBIT, Hotel St. George, 51 Clark St., Brooklyn, N. Y. 1916.
Professor WILLIAM ROMAINE NEWBOLD, University of Pennsylvania, Philadelphia, Pa. 1918.
EDWARD THEODORE NEWELL, American Numismatic Society, 156th St. and Broadway, New York, N. Y. 1914.
† Rev. Dr. JAMES B. NIES, 12 Schermerhorn St., Brooklyn, N. Y. 1906.
Ven. Archdeacon WILLIAM E. NIES, care of Union Bank, Geneva, Switzerland. 1908.
Mrs. CHARLES F. NORTON, Transylvania College, Lexington, Ky. 1919.
Dr. WILLIAM FREDERICK NOTZ, 5402 39th St., N. W., Washington, D. C. 1915.
Dr. ALOIS RICHARD NYKL, Northwestern University, Evanston, Ill. 1922.
ADOLPH S. OCHS, The New York Times, New York, N. Y. 1921.
Rt. Rev. DENIS J. O'CONNELL, 800 Cathedral Place, Richmond, Va. 1903.
Dr. FELIX, Freiherr von OEFELE, 326 East 58th St. New York, N. Y. 1913.
HERBERT C. OETTINGER, Eighth and Walnut Sts., Cincinnati, Ohio. 1920.
NAOYOSHI OGAWA, Bureau of Education, Government of Formosa, Taihoku, Formosa. 1921.
Dr. CHARLES J. OGDEN, 628 West 114th St., New York, N. Y. 1906.
Dr. ELLEN S. OGDEN, Bishop Hopkins Hall, Burlington, Vt. 1898.
Prof. SAMUEL G. OLIPHANT, Grove City College, Grove City, Pa. 1906.
Prof. ALBERT TENEYCK OLMSTEAD (Univ. of Illinois), 706 South Goodwin St., Urbana, Ill. 1909.
Prof. CHARLES A. OWEN, Assiut College, Assiut, Egypt. 1921.
Prof. LUTHER PARKER, Cabanatuan, P. I. 1922.
ANTONIO M. PATERNO, 605 East Daniel St., Champaign, Ill. 1922.
Prof. LEWIS B. PATON, Hartford Theological Seminary, Hartford, Conn. 1894.
ROBERT LEET PATTERSON, Shields, Allegheny Co., Pa. 1920.
Pres. CHARLES T. PAUL, College of Missions, Indianapolis, Ind. 1921.
JAL Dastur CURSETJI PAVRY, Furnald Hall, Columbia University, New York, N. Y. 1921.
Dr. CHARLES PEABODY (Harvard Univ.), 197 Brattle St., Cambridge, Mass. 1892.
Prof. GEORGE A. PECKHAM, Hiram College, Hiram, Ohio. 1912.
HAROLD PEIRCE, 222 Drexel Building, Philadelphia, Pa. 1920.

Prof. Ismar J. Peritz, Syracuse University, Syracuse, N. Y. 1894.
Dr. Joseph Louis Perrier (Columbia Univ.), 352 West 115th St., New York, N. Y. 1920.
Prof. Marshall Livingston Perrin, Boston University, 688 Boylston St,, Boston, Mass. 1921.
Prof. Edward Delavan Perry (Columbia Univ.), 542 West 114th St., New York, N. Y. 1879.
Dr. Arnold Peskind, 2414 East 55th St., Cleveland, Ohio 1920.
Prof. Walter Petersen, Westminster College, New Wilmington, Pa. 1909.
Robert Henry Pfeiffer, 39 Winthrop St., Cambridge, Mass. 1920.
Rev. Dr. David Philipson, 3947 Beechwood Ave., Cincinnati, Ohio. 1889.
Hon. William Phillips, Department of State, Washington, D. C. 1917.
Rev. Dr. Z. T. Phillips, 3723 Chestnut St., Philadelphia, Pa. 1922.
Julian A. Pollak, 927 Redway Ave., Cincinnati, Ohio. 1920.
Paul Popenoe, Box 13, Coachella, Cal. 1914.
Prof. William Popper, University of California, Berkeley, Cal. 1897.
Rev. Dr. Thomas J. Porter (Presbyterian Theol. Seminary), 3 Rua Padre Vieira, Campinos, São Paulo, Brazil. 1921.
Prof. D. V. Potdar (New Poona College), 180 Shanvar Peth, Poona, India. 1921.
Rev. Dr. Sartell Prentice, 127 South Broadway, Nyack, N. Y. 1921.
Prof. Ira M. Price, University of Chicago, Chicago, Ill. 1887.
Prof. John Dyneley Prince (Columbia Univ.), American Legation, Copenhagen, Denmark. 1888.
Carl E. Pritz, 101 Union Trust Building, Cincinnati, Ohio. 1920.
Rev. Dr. A. H. Pruessner, Gang Sakotah 10, Kramat, Weltevreden, Java, Dutch East Indies. 1921.
Prof. Alexander C. Purdy, Hartford Theological Seminary, Hartford, Conn. 1921.
Prof. Herbert R. Purinton, Bates College, Lewiston, Maine. 1921.
Rev. Francis J. Purtell, S.T.L., Overbrook Seminary, Philadelphia, Pa. 1916.
Prof. Charles Lynn Pyatt, The College of the Bible, Lexington, Ky. 1921 (1917).
Dr. G. Payn Quackenbos, Northrup Ave., Tuckahoe, N. Y. 1904.
Rev. Dr. Max Raisin, Barnett Memorial Temple, Paterson, N. J. 1920.
Dr. V. V. Ramana-Sâstrin, Vedaraniam, Tanjore District, India. 1921.
Prof. Horace M. Ramsey, Seabury Divinity School, Faribault, Minn. 1920.
Marcus Rauh, 951 Penn Ave., Pittsburgh, Pa. 1920.
Prof. John H. Raven (New Brunswick Theol. Seminary), 9 Union St., New Brunswick, N. J. 1920.
Prof. Harry B. Reed (Northwestern Lutheran Theol. Seminary), 1852 Polk St., N. E., Minneapolis, Minn. 1921.
Dr. Joseph Reider, Dropsie College, Philadelphia, Pa. 1913.
John Reilly, Jr., American Numismatic Society, 156th St. and Broadway, New York, N. Y. 1918.
Prof. August Karl Reischauer, Meiji Gakuin, Shirokane Shiba, Tokyo, Japan. 1920.

Prof. George Andrew Reisner (Harvard Univ.), Museum of Fine Arts, Boston, Mass. 1891.

Rt. Rev. Philip M. Rhinelander, 251 South 22d St., Philadelphia, Pa. 1908.

Prof. Robert Thomas Riddle, St. Charles Seminary, Overbrook, Pa. 1920.

Prof. Edward Robertson, University College of North Wales, Bangor, Wales. 1921.

Rev. Charles Wellington Robinson, Christ Church, Bronxville, N. Y. 1916.

Prof. David M. Robinson, The Johns Hopkins University, Baltimore, Md. 1921.

Prof. George Livingston Robinson (McCormick Theol. Seminary), 2312 North Halsted St., Chicago, Ill. 1892.

Rev. Dr. Theodore H. Robinson, University College, Cardiff, Wales. 1922.

George N. Roerich, 1678 Massachusetts Ave., Cambridge, Mass. 1922.

Prof. James Hardy Ropes (Harvard Univ.), 13 Follen St., Cambridge, Mass. 1893.

Harry L. Rosen, 1720 N. 51st St., Philadelphia, Pa. 1919.

Dr. William Rosenau, The Johns Hopkins University, Baltimore, Md. 1897.

*Julius Rosenwald, care of Sears, Roebuck and Co., Chicago, Ill. 1920.

Samuel Rothenberg, M.D., 22 West 7th St., Cincinnati, Ohio. 1921.

Miss Adelaide Rudolph, Columbia University, College of Pharmacy, 115 West 68th St., New York, N. Y. 1894.

Dr. Elbert Russell, Woolman House, Swarthmore, Pa. 1916.

Dr. Najeeb M. Saleeby, P. O. Box 226, Manila, P. I. 1922.

Rabbi Marcus Salzman, Ph.D., 94 West Ross St., Wilkes-Barre, Pa. 1920.

Rev. Frank K. Sanders, Ph.D., 25 Madison Ave., New York, N. Y. 1897.

Mrs. A. H. Saunders, 552 Riverside Drive, New York, N. Y. 1915.

Prof. Henry Schaeffer (Lutheran Theol. Seminary), 1606 South 11th Ave., Maywood, Chicago, Ill. 1916.

Gottlieb Schaenzlin, 2618 Oswego Ave., Baltimore, Md. 1921.

Dr. Israel Schapiro, Library of Congress, Washington, D. C. 1914.

Dr. Otto Scheerer (Univ. of the Philippines), P. O. Box 659, Manila, P. I. 1922.

Dr. Johann F. Scheltema, care of Kerkhoven and Co., 115 Heerengracht, Amsterdam, Netherlands. 1906.

John F. Schlichting, 1430 Woodhaven Boulevard, Woodhaven, N. Y. 1920.

Prof. Nathaniel Schmidt, Cornell University, Ithaca, N. Y. 1894.

Adolph Schoenfeld, 321 East 84th St., New York, N. Y. 1921.

Wilfred H. Schoff, The Commercial Museum, Philadelphia, Pa. 1912.

William Bacon Scofield, Worcester Club, Worcester, Mass. 1919.

Prof. Gilbert Campbell Scoggin, University of Michigan, Ann Arbor, Mich. 1906.

Alexander Scott, 222 Central Park South, New York, N. Y. 1922.

Prof. John A. Scott, Northwestern University, Evanston, Ill. 1920.

*Mrs. Samuel Bryan Scott (*née* Morris), 2106 Spruce St., Philadelphia, Pa. 1903.

Prof. Helen M. Searles, Mt. Holyoke College, South Hadley, Mass. 1921.

Dr. Moses Seidel (Rabbi Isaac Elchanan Theol. Seminary), 9—11 Montgomery St., New York, N. Y. 1917.
H. A. Seinsheimer, Fourth and Pike Sts., Cincinnati, Ohio. 1921.
Rev. Dr. William G. Seiple, Tsuchidoi, Sendai, Miyagi Ken, Japan. 1902.
Samuel Seligman, 2739 Augusta St., Chicago, Ill. 1922.
Dr. Ovid R. Sellers (McCormick Theol. Seminary), 10 Chalmers Place, Chicago, Ill. 1917.
Max Senior, 21 Mitchell Building, Cincinnati, Ohio. 1920.
Victor Sharenkoff, 241 Princeton Ave., Jersey City, N. J. 1922.
G. Howland Shaw, Department of State, Washington, D. C. 1921.
Rev. Dr. William G. Shellabear, 43 Madison Ave., Madison, N. J. 1919.
Prof. William A. Shelton, Emory University, Atlanta, Ga. 1921.
Prof. Charles N. Shepard (General Theol. Seminary), 9 Chelsea Square, New York, N. Y. 1907.
Andrew R. Sheriff, The Chicago Club, 404 South Michigan Ave., Chicago, Ill. 1921.
Charles C. Sherman, 447 Webster Ave,, New Rochelle, N. Y. 1904.
Gyokshu Shibata, 330 East 57th St., New York, N. Y. 1920.
Rev. John Knight Shryock, Anking, China. 1922.
Don Cameron Shumaker, 347 Madison Ave., Room 1007, New York, N. Y. 1922.
Rabbi Abba Hillel Silver, The Temple, East 55th St. and Central Ave., Cleveland, Ohio. 1920.
Rev. Hiram Hill Sipes, Bhimavaram, Kistna District, India. 1920.
Jack H. Skirball, Hebrew Union College, Cincinnati, Ohio. 1920.
Prof. S. B. Slack, Arts Building, McGill University, Montreal, P. Q., Canada. 1921.
*John R. Slattery, 14 rue Montaigne, Paris, France. 1903.
Rev. H. Framer Smith, 324 West Duval St., Philadelphia, Pa. 1922.
Prof. Henry Preserved Smith, Union Theological Seminary, Broadway and 120th St., New York, N. Y. 1877.
Prof. J. M. Powis Smith, University of Chicago, Chicago, Ill. 1906.
Dr. Louise P. Smith, Wellesley College, Wellesley, Mass. 1918.
Rev. Wilbur Moorehead Smith, Ocean City, Md. 1921.
Rev. Joseph Edward Snyder, Box 796, Fargo, N. Dak. 1916.
Rev. Dr. Elias L. Solomon, 1326 Madison Ave., New York, N. Y. 1921.
Alexander N. Spanakidis. 1920.
Dr. David B. Spooner, Assistant Director General of Archaeology in India, "Benmore," Simla, Panjab, India. 1918.
Prof. Martin Sprengling, University of Chicago, Chicago, Ill. 1912.
John Franklin Springer, 618 West 136th St., New York, N. Y. 1921.
J. W. Stanley, 19 South LaSalle St., Suite 1500, Chicago, Ill. 1922.
Dr. W. Stede, Osterdeich 195, Bremen, Germany. 1920.
Rev. Dr. James D. Steele, 232 Mountain Way, Rutherford, N. J. 1892.
Herman Steinberg, 103 Park Ave., New York, N. Y. 1921.
Max Steinberg, 103 Park Ave., New York, N. Y. 1921.
Rev. Dr. Thomas Stenhouse, Mickley Vicarage, Stocksfield-on-Tyne, England. 1921.

M. T. Sterelny, P. O. Box 7, Vladivostok, East Siberia. 1919.
Horace Stern, 1524 North 16th St., Philadelphia, Pa. 1921.
†Mrs. W. Yorke Stevenson, 251 South 18th St., Philadelphia, Pa. 1919.
Rev. Dr. Anson Phelps Stokes, West Stockbridge, Mass. 1900.
Rev. Dr. Joseph Stolz, 4714 Grand Boulevard, Chicago, Ill. 1917.
Prof. Frederick Annes Stuff (Univ. of Nebraska), Station A 1263, Lincoln, Neb. 1921.
Dr. Vishnu S. Sukthankar, 22 Carnac Road, Kalbadevi P. O., Bombay, India. 1921.
Hon. Mayer Sulzberger, 1303 Girard Ave., Philadelphia, Pa. 1888.
A. J. Sunstein, Farmers Bank Building, Pittsburgh, Pa. 1920.
Prof. Leo Suppan (St. Louis College of Pharmacy), 2109a Russell Ave., St. Louis, Mo. 1920.
Prof. George Sverdrup, Jr., Augsburg Seminary, Minneapolis, Minn. 1907.
Prof. Yung-Tung Tang, Southeastern University, Nanking, China. 1922.
Prof. Frederick J. Teggart, University of California, Berkeley, Cal. 1919.
Eben Francis Thompson, 311 Main St., Worcester, Mass. 1906.
Rev. William Gordon Thompson, 126 Manhattan Ave., New York, N. Y. 1921.
Prof. Henry A. Todd (Columbia Univ.), 824 West End Ave., New York, N. Y. 1885.
Baron Dr. Gyoyu Tokiwai (Imperial Univ. of Kyoto), Isshinden, Province of Ise, Japan. 1921.
Dean Herbert Cushing Tolman, Vanderbilt University, Nashville, Tenn. 1917.
*Prof. Charles C. Torrey, Yale University, New Haven, Conn. 1891.
I. Newton Trager, 944 Marion Ave., Avondale, Cincinnati, Ohio. 1920.
Rev. Archibald Tremayne, 4138 Brooklyn Ave., Seattle, Wash. 1918.
Pandit Ram Prasad Tripathi, M.A., University of Allahabad, Allahabad, India. 1921.
Prof. Harold H. Tryon, Union Theological Seminary, 3041 Broadway, New York, N. Y. 1921.
Rabbi Jacob Turner, 4167 Ogden Ave., Hawthorne Station, Chicago, Ill., 1921.
Rev. Dudley Tyng, 721 Douglas Ave., Providence, R. I. 1922.
*Rev. Dr. Lemon Leander Uhl, College Bungalow, Arundelpet, Guntur, Madras Presidency, India. 1921.
Rev. Sydney N. Ussher, 44 East 76th St., New York, N. Y. 1909.
Rev. Frederick Augustus Vanderburgh, Ph.D. (Columbia Univ.), 55 Washington Square, New York, N. Y. 1908.
Rev. John Van Ess, Basra, Mesopotamia. 1921.
†Addison Van Name (Yale Univ.), 121 High St., New Haven, Conn. 1863.
Rev. M. Vanoverbergh, Bangar Catholic School, Bangar La Union, P. I. 1921.
Mrs. John King Van Rensselaer, 157 East 37th St., New York, N. Y. 1920.
Prof. Arthur A. Vaschalde, Catholic University of America, Washington, D. C. 1915.

Prof. J. Ph. Vogel (Univ. of Leiden), Noordeindsplein 4a, Leiden, Netherlands. 1921.

Ludwig Vogelstein, 61 Broadway, New York, N. Y. 1920.

Prof. Jacob Wackernagel (Univ. of Basle), Gartenstr. 93, Basle, Switzerland. 1921.

*Felix M. Warburg, 52 William St., New York, N. Y. 1921.

Prof. William F. Warren (Boston Univ.), 131 Davis Ave., Brookline, Mass. 1877.

Prof. Leroy Waterman, University of Michigan, Ann Arbor, Mich. 1912.

Rev. James Watt, Graduate College, Princeton University, Princeton, N. J. 1923.

James B. Weaver, 412 Iowa National Bank Building, Des Moines, Iowa. 1922.

*Prof. Hutton Webster (Univ. of Nebraska), Station A, Lincoln, Neb. 1921.

Miss Isabel C. Wells, 1609 Connecticut Ave., Washington, D. C. 1921.

Rev. O. V. Werner, Jeypore, Vizagapatam District, India. 1921.

Prof. J. E. Werren, 1667 Cambridge St., Cambridge, Mass. 1894.

Arthur J. Westermayr, 12—16 John St., New York, N. Y. 1912.

Morris F. Westheimer, Traction Building, Cincinnati, Ohio. 1920.

Rev. Milton C. J. Westphal, Union Baptist Church, 19th and Carson Sts., Pittsburgh, Pa. 1920.

Richard B. Wetherill, M.D., 525 Columbia St., Lafayette, Ind. 1921.

Pres. Benjamin Ide Wheeler, University of California, Berkeley, Cal. 1885.

†Frederick B. Wheeler, R. F. D. No. 1, Seymour, Conn. 1921.

John G. White, Williamson Building, Cleveland, Ohio. 1912.

Pres. Wilbert W. White, D.D., Bible Teachers Training School, 541 Lexington Ave., New York, N. Y. 1921.

Miss Ethel E. Whitney, Hotel Hemenway, Boston, Mass. 1921.

*Miss Margaret Dwight Whitney, 227 Church St., New Haven, Conn. 1908.

Miss Carolyn M. Wicker, 520 West 114th St., New York, N. Y. 1921.

Peter Wiernik, 220 Henry St., New York, N. Y. 1920.

Herman Wile, Ellicott and Carroll Sts., Buffalo, N. Y. 1920.

Prof. Herbert L. Willett (Univ. of Chicago), 6119 Woodlawn Ave., Chicago, Ill. 1917.

Mrs. Caroline Ransom Williams, The Chesbrough Dwellings, Toledo, Ohio. 1912.

Prof. Clarence Russell Williams, 418 Magnolia St., New Brunswick, N. J. 1920.

Hon. E. T. Williams (Univ. of California), 1410 Scenic Ave., Berkeley, Cal. 1901.

Prof. Frederick Wells Williams (Yale Univ.), 155 Whitney Ave., New Haven, Conn. 1895.

Mrs. Frederick Wells Williams, 155 Whitney Ave., New Haven, Conn. 1918.

Prof. Talcott Williams, Columbia University, New York, N. Y. 1884.

Prof. Curt Paul Wimmer, Columbia University, College of Pharmacy, 115 West 68th St., New York, N. Y. 1920.

Major HERBERT E. WINLOCK, Metropolitan Museum of Art, New York, N. Y. 1919.

Rev. Dr. WILLIAM COPLEY WINSLOW, 525 Beacon St., Boston, Mass. 1885.

Rabbi JONAH B. WISE, 715 Chamber of Commerce, Portland, Ore. 1921.

Rev. Dr. STEPHEN S. WISE, 23 West 90th St., New York, N. Y. 1894.

Prof. JOHN E. WISHART (Xenia Theol. Seminary), 6834 Washington Ave., St. Louis, Mo. 1911.

Rev. ADOLF LOUIS WISMAR, 419 West 145th St., New York, N. Y. 1922.

HENRY B. WITTON, 290 Hess St., South, Hamilton, Ont., Canada. 1885.

Dr. UNRAI WOGIHARA, 20 Tajimacho, Asakusa, Tokyo, Japan. 1921.

Prof. LOUIS B. WOLFENSON (Hebrew Union College), C—18 Landon Ct., Burnet Ave., Cincinnati, Ohio. 1904.

Prof. HARRY A. WOLFSON (Harvard Univ.), 35 Divinity Hall, Cambridge, Mass. 1917.

Rabbi LOUIS WOLSEY, 8206 Euclid Ave., Cleveland, Ohio. 1922.

HOWLAND WOOD, Curator, American Numismatic Society, 156th St. and Broadway, New York, N. Y. 1919.

Prof. IRVING F. WOOD, Smith College, Northampton, Mass. 1905.

Prof. WILLIAM H. WOOD (Dartmouth College), 23 North Main St., Hanover, N. H. 1917.

Prof. JAMES H. WOODS (Harvard Univ.), 16 Prescott Hall, Cambridge, Mass. 1900.

Prof. ALFRED COOPER WOOLNER, M. A., University of the Panjab, 11 Racecourse Road, Lahore, India. 1921.

Prof. JESSE ERWIN WRENCH (Univ. of Missouri), 1104 Hudson Ave., Columbia, Mo. 1917.

Rev. HORACE K. WRIGHT, Vengurla, Bombay Presidency, India. 1921.

JOHN MAX WULFING, 3448 Longfellow Boulevard, St. Louis, Mo. 1921.

Miss ELEANOR F. F. YEAWORTH, 6237 Bellona Ave., Baltimore, Md. 1921.

Rev. Dr. ROYDEN KEITH YERKES (Philadelphia Divinity School), Box 247, Merion, Pa. 1916.

Rev. S. C. YLVISAKER, Ph.D., 1317 Dayton Ave., St. Paul, Minn. 1913.

Rev. ABRAHAM YOHANNAN, Ph.D., Columbia University, New York, N. Y. 1894.

Prof. HARRY CLINTON YORK, Hood College, Frederick, Md. 1922.

LOUIS GABRIEL ZELSON, 427 Titan St., Philadelphia, Pa. 1920.

Rev. ROBERT ZIMMERMAN, S. J., St. Xavier's College, Cruickshank Road, Bombay, India. 1911.

JOSEPH SOLOMON ZUCKERBAUM (Mizrachi Teachers' Institute), 2 West 111th St., New York, N. Y. 1920.

Rev. Dr. SAMUEL M. ZWEMER, care of Nile Mission Press, Cairo, Egypt. 1920.

(Total: 577)

Lightning Source UK Ltd.
Milton Keynes UK
UKHW040639270820
368917UK00001B/156

9 789354 048807